The Essential Writings of Origen

of Origen

Translated by Rev. Frederick Crombie

Animus Classics edition
First published 2021
Animus Publishing
ISBN-13: 9798536066140

CONTENTS

EDITOR'S PREFACE

THIS Animus Classics edition compiles the essential writings of the early Christian scholar Origen (A.D. 185–253). It includes, complete and unabridged: *De Principiis* (*On First Principles*), a letter to Origen from Africanus, a letter from Origen to Africanus, a letter from Origen to Gregory, and *Against Celsus*. The translation is by Rev. Frederick Crombie (1827–89), as published in the *Ante-Nicene Fathers* series of books. In *De Principiis*, the translation of portions of the text which are extant in the original Greek have been placed after their equivalent passage translated from the Latin version of Rufinus (in which the bulk of the text is exclusively preserved). In each text, Greek words have been transliterated.

PROLOGUE OF RUFINUS

I KNOW that very many of the brethren, induced by their thirst for a knowledge of the Scriptures, have requested some distinguished men, well versed in Greek learning, to translate Origen into Latin, and so make him accessible to Roman readers. Among these, when our brother and colleague had, at the earnest entreaty of Bishop Damasus, translated two of the Homilies on the Song of Songs out of Greek into Latin, he prefixed so elegant and noble a preface to that work, as to inspire every one with a most eager desire to read and study Origen, saying that the expression, "The King hath brought me into his chamber," was appropriate to his feelings, and declaring that while Origen in his other works surpassed all writers, he in the Song of Songs surpassed even himself. He promises, indeed, in that very preface, that he will present the books on the Song of Songs, and numerous others of the works of Origen, in a Latin translation, to Roman readers. But he, finding greater pleasure in compositions of his own, pursues an end that is attended with greater fame, viz., in being the author rather than the translator of works. Accordingly we enter upon the undertaking, which was thus begun and approved of by him, although we cannot compose in a style of elegance equal to that of a man of such distinguished eloquence; and therefore I am afraid lest, through my fault, the result should follow, that that man, whom he deservedly esteems as the second teacher of knowledge and wisdom in the Church after the apostles, should, through the poverty of my language, appear far inferior to what he is. And this consideration, which frequently recurred to my mind, kept me silent, and prevented me from yielding to the numerous entreaties of my brethren, until your influence, my very faithful brother Macarius, which is so great, rendered it impossible for my unskilfulness any longer to offer resistance. And therefore, that I might not find you too grievous an exactor, I gave way, even contrary to my resolution; on the condition and arrangement, however, that in my translation I should follow as far as possible the rule observed by my predecessors, and especially by that distinguished man whom I have mentioned above, who, after translating into Latin more than seventy of those treatises of Origen which are styled *Homilies* and a considerable number also of his writings on the apostles, in which a good many "stumbling-blocks" are found in the original Greek, so smoothed and corrected them in his translation, that a Latin reader would meet with nothing which could appear discordant with our belief. His example, therefore, we follow, to the best of our ability; if not with equal power of eloquence, yet at least with the same strictness of rule, taking care not to reproduce those expressions occurring in the works of Origen which are inconsistent with and opposed to each other. The cause of these variations we have explained more freely in the *Apologeticus*, which Pamphilus wrote in defence of the works of Origen, where we added a brief tract, in which we showed, I think, by unmistakeable proofs, that his books had been corrupted in numerous places by heretics and malevolent persons, and especially those books of which you now require me to undertake the translation, i.e., the books which may be entitled *De Principiis* or *De Principatibus*, and which are indeed in other respects full of obscurities and difficulties. For he there discusses those subjects with respect to which philosophers, after spending all their lives upon them, have been unable to discover anything. But here our author strove, as much as in him lay, to turn to the service of religion the belief in a Creator, and the rational nature of created beings, which the latter had degraded to purposes of wickedness. If, therefore, we have found anywhere in his writings, any statement opposed to that view, which elsewhere in his works he had himself piously laid down regarding the Trinity, we have either omitted it, as being corrupt, and not the composition of Origen, or we have brought it forward agreeably to the rule which we frequently find affirmed by himself. If, indeed, in his desire to pass rapidly on, he has, as speaking to persons of skill and knowledge, sometimes expressed himself obscurely, we have, in order that the passage might be clearer, added what we had read more fully stated on the same subject in his other works, keeping explanation in view, but adding nothing of our own, but simply restoring to him what was his, although occurring in other portions of his writings.

These remarks, therefore, by way of admonition, I have made in the preface, lest slanderous individuals perhaps should think that they had a second time discovered matter of accusation. But let perverse and disputatious men have a care what they are about. For we have in the meantime undertaken this heavy labour, if God should aid your prayers, not to shut the mouths of slanderers (which is impossible, although God perhaps will do it), but to afford material to those who desire to advance in the knowledge of these things. And, verily, in the presence of God the Father, and of the Son, and of the Holy Spirit, I adjure and beseech every one, who may either transcribe or read these books, by his belief in the kingdom to come, by the mystery of the resurrection from the dead, and by that everlasting fire prepared for the devil and his angels, that, as he would not possess for an eternal inheritance that place where there is weeping and gnashing of teeth, and where their fire is not quenched and their worm dieth not, he add nothing to Scripture, and take nothing away from it, and make no insertion or alteration, but that he compare his transcript with the copies from which he made it, and make the emendations and distinctions according to the letter, and not have his manuscript incorrect or indistinct, lest the difficulty of ascertaining the sense, from the indistinctness of the copy, should cause greater difficulties to the readers.

PREFACE

1. ALL who believe and are assured that grace and truth were obtained through Jesus Christ, and who know Christ to be the truth, agreeably to His own declaration, "I am the truth," derive the knowledge which incites men to a good and happy life from no other source than from the very words and teaching of Christ. And by the words of Christ we do not mean those only which He spake when He became man and tabernacled in the flesh; for before that time, Christ, the Word of God, was in Moses and the prophets. For without the Word of God, how could they have been able to prophesy of Christ? And were it not our purpose to confine the present treatise within the limits of all attainable brevity, it would not be difficult to show, in proof of this statement, out of the Holy Scriptures, how Moses or the prophets both spake and performed all they did through being filled with the Spirit of Christ. And therefore I think it sufficient to quote this one testimony of Paul from the Epistle to the Hebrews, in which he says: "By faith Moses, when he was come to years, refused to be called the son of Pharaoh's daughter; choosing rather to suffer affliction with the people of God, than to enjoy the pleasures of sin for a season; esteeming the reproach of Christ greater riches than the treasures of the Egyptians." Moreover, that after His ascension into heaven He spake in His apostles, is shown by Paul in these words: "Or do you seek a proof of Christ who speaketh in me?"

2. Since many, however, of those who profess to believe in Christ differ from each other, not only in small and trifling matters, but also on subjects of the highest importance, as, e.g., regarding God, or the Lord Jesus Christ, or the Holy Spirit; and not only regarding these, but also regarding others which are created existences, viz., the powers and the holy virtues; it seems on that account necessary first of all to fix a definite limit and to lay down an unmistakable rule regarding each one of these, and then to pass to the investigation of other points. For as we ceased to seek for truth (notwithstanding the professions of many among Greeks and Barbarians to make it known) among all who claimed it for erroneous opinions, after we had come to believe that Christ was the Son of God, and were persuaded that we must learn it from Himself; so, seeing there are many who think they hold the opinions of Christ, and yet some of these think differently from their predecessors, yet as the teaching of the Church, transmitted in orderly succession from the apostles, and remaining in the Churches to the present day, is still preserved, that alone is to be accepted as truth which

differs in no respect from ecclesiastical and apostolical tradition.

3. Now it ought to be known that the holy apostles, in preaching the faith of Christ, delivered themselves with the utmost clearness on certain points which they believed to be necessary to every one, even to those who seemed somewhat dull in the investigation of divine knowledge; leaving, however, the grounds of their statements to be examined into by those who should deserve the excellent gifts of the Spirit, and who, especially by means of the Holy Spirit Himself, should obtain the gift of language, of wisdom, and of knowledge: while on other subjects they merely stated the fact that things were so, keeping silence as to the manner or origin of their existence; clearly in order that the more zealous of their successors, who should be lovers of wisdom, might have a subject of exercise on which to display the fruit of their talents,—those persons, I mean, who should prepare themselves to be fit and worthy receivers of wisdom.

4. The particular points clearly delivered in the teaching of the apostles are as follow:—

First, That there is one God, who created and arranged all things, and who, when nothing existed, called all things into being—God from the first creation and foundation of the world—the God of all just men, of Adam, Abel, Seth, Enos, Enoch, Noe, Sere, Abraham, Isaac, Jacob, the twelve patriarchs, Moses, and the prophets; and that this God in the last days, as He had announced beforehand by His prophets, sent our Lord Jesus Christ to call in the first place Israel to Himself, and in the second place the Gentiles, after the unfaithfulness of the people of Israel. This just and good God, the Father of our Lord Jesus Christ, Himself gave the law and the prophets, and the Gospels, being also the God of the apostles and of the Old and New Testaments.

Secondly, That Jesus Christ Himself, who came (into the world), was born of the Father before all creatures; that, after He had been the servant of the Father in the creation of all things—"For by Him were all things made"—He in the last times, divesting Himself (of His glory), became a man, and was incarnate although God, and while made a man remained the God which He was; that He assumed a body like to our own, differing in this respect only, that it was born of a virgin and of the Holy Spirit: that this Jesus Christ was truly born, and did truly suffer, and did not endure this death common (to man) in appearance only, but did truly die; that He did truly rise from the dead; and that after His resurrection He conversed with His disciples, and was taken up (into heaven).

Then, *Thirdly*, the apostles related that the Holy Spirit was associated in honour and dignity with the Father and the Son. But in His case it is

9

not clearly distinguished whether He is to be regarded as born or innate, or also as a Son of God or not: for these are points which have to be inquired into out of sacred Scripture according to the best of our ability, and which demand careful investigation. And that this Spirit inspired each one of the saints, whether prophets or apostles; and that there was not one Spirit in the men of the old dispensation, and another in those who were inspired at the advent of Christ, is most clearly taught throughout the Churches.

5. After these points, also, the apostolic teaching is that the soul, having a substance and life of its own, shall, after its departure from the world, be rewarded according to its deserts, being destined to obtain either an inheritance of eternal life and blessedness, if its actions shall have procured this for it, or to be delivered up to eternal fire and punishments, if the guilt of its crimes shall have brought it down to this: and also, that there is to be a time of resurrection from the dead, when this body, which now "is sown in corruption, shall rise in incorruption," and that which "is sown in dishonour will rise in glory." This also is clearly defined in the teaching of the Church, that every rational soul is possessed of free-will and volition; that it has a struggle to maintain with the devil and his angels, and opposing influences, because they strive to burden it with sins; but if we live rightly and wisely, we should endeavour to shake ourselves free of a burden of that kind. From which it follows, also, that we understand ourselves not to be subject to necessity, so as to be compelled by all means, even against our will, to do either good or evil. For if we are our own masters, some influences perhaps may impel us to sin, and others help us to salvation; we are not forced, however, by any necessity either to act rightly or wrongly, which those persons think is the case who say that the courses and movements of the stars are the cause of human actions, not only of those which take place beyond the influence of the freedom of the will, but also of those which are placed within our own power. But with respect to the soul, whether it is derived from the seed by a process of traducianism, so that the reason or substance of it may be considered as placed in the seminal particles of the body themselves, or whether it has any other beginning; and this beginning, itself, whether it be by birth or not, or whether bestowed upon the body from without or no, is not distinguished with sufficient clearness in the teaching of the Church.

6. Regarding the devil and his angels, and the opposing influences, the teaching of the Church has laid down that these beings exist indeed; but what they are, or how they exist, it has not explained with sufficient clearness. This opinion, however, is held by most, that the devil was an

angel, and that, having become an apostate, he induced as many of the angels as possible to fall away with himself, and these up to the present time are called his angels.

7. This also is a part of the Church's teaching, that the world was made and took its beginning at a certain time, and is to be destroyed on account of its wickedness. But what existed before this world, or what will exist after it, has not become certainly known to the many, for there is no clear statement regarding it in the teaching of the Church.

8. Then, finally, that the Scriptures were written by the Spirit of God, and have a meaning, not such only as is apparent at first sight, but also another, which escapes the notice of most. For those (words) which are written are the forms of certain mysteries, and the images of divine things. Respecting which there is one opinion throughout the whole Church, that the whole law is indeed spiritual; but that the spiritual meaning which the law conveys is not known to all, but to those only on whom the grace of the Holy Spirit is bestowed in the word of wisdom and knowledge.

The term *asomaton*, i.e., incorporeal, is disused and unknown, not only in many other writings, but also in our own Scriptures. And if any one should quote it to us out of the little treatise entitled *The Doctrine of Peter*, in which the Saviour seems to say to His disciples, "I am not an incorporeal demon," I have to reply, in the first place, that that work is not included among ecclesiastical books; for we can show that it was not composed either by Peter or by any other person inspired by the Spirit of God. But even if the point were to be conceded, the word asomaton there does not convey the same meaning as is intended by Greek and Gentile authors when incorporeal nature is discussed by philosophers. For in the little treatise referred to he used the phrase "incorporeal demon" to denote that that form or outline of demoniacal body, whatever it is, does not resemble this gross and visible body of ours; but, agreeably to the intention of the author of the treatise, it must be understood to mean that He had not such a body as demons have, which is naturally fine, and thin as if formed of air (and for this reason is either considered or called by many incorporeal), but that He had a solid and palpable body. Now, according to human custom, everything which is not of that nature is called by the simple or ignorant incorporeal; as if one were to say that the air which we breathe was incorporeal, because it is not a body of such a nature as can be grasped and held, or can offer resistance to pressure.

9. We shall inquire, however, whether the thing which Greek philosophers call *asomaton*, or "incorporeal," is found in holy Scripture under another name. For it is also to be a subject of investigation how

11

God himself is to be understood,—whether as corporeal, and formed according to some shape, or of a different nature from bodies,—a point which is not clearly indicated in our teaching. And the same inquiries have to be made regarding Christ and the Holy Spirit, as well as respecting every soul, and everything possessed of a rational nature.

10. This also is a part of the teaching of the Church, that there are certain angels of God, and certain good influences, which are His servants in accomplishing the salvation of men. When these, however, were created, or of what nature they are, or how they exist, is not clearly stated. Regarding the sun, moon, and stars, whether they are living beings or without life, there is no distinct deliverance.

Every one, therefore, must make use of elements and foundations of this sort, according to the precept, "Enlighten yourselves with the light of knowledge," if he would desire to form a connected series and body of truths agreeably to the reason of all these things, that by clear and necessary statements he may ascertain the truth regarding each individual topic, and form, as we have said, one body of doctrine, by means of illustrations and arguments,—either those which he has discovered in holy Scripture, or which he has deduced by closely tracing out the consequences and following a correct method.

BOOK I

CHAPTER I—ON GOD

1. I KNOW that some will attempt to say that, even according to the declarations of our own Scriptures, God is a body, because in the writings of Moses they find it said, that "our God is a consuming fire;" and in the Gospel according to John, that "God is a Spirit, and they who worship Him must worship Him in spirit and in truth." Fire and spirit, according to them, are to be regarded as nothing else than a body. Now, I should like to ask these persons what they have to say respecting that passage where it is declared that God is light; as John writes in his Epistle, "God is light, and in Him there is no darkness at all." Truly He is that light which illuminates the whole understanding of those who are capable of receiving truth, as is said in the thirty-sixth Psalm, "In Thy light we shall see light." For what other light of God can be named, "in which any one sees light," save an influence of God, by which a man, being enlightened, either thoroughly sees the truth of all things, or comes to know God Himself, who is called the truth? Such is the meaning of the expression, "In Thy light we shall see light;" i.e., in Thy word and wisdom which is Thy Son, in Himself we shall see Thee the Father. Because He is called light, shall He be supposed to have any resemblance to the light of the sun? Or how should there be the slightest ground for imagining, that from that corporeal light any one could derive the cause of knowledge, and come to the understanding of the truth?

2. If, then, they acquiesce in our assertion, which reason itself has demonstrated, regarding the nature of light, and acknowledge that God cannot be understood to be a body in the sense that light is, similar reasoning will hold true of the expression "a consuming fire." For what will God consume in respect of His being fire? Shall He be thought to consume material substance, as wood, or hay, or stubble? And what in this view can be called worthy of the glory of God, if He be a fire, consuming materials of that kind? But let us reflect that God does indeed consume and utterly destroy; that He consumes evil thoughts, wicked actions, and sinful desires, when they find their way into the minds of believers; and that, inhabiting along with His Son those souls which are rendered capable of receiving His word and wisdom, according to His own declaration, "I and the Father shall come, and We shall make our abode with him?" He makes them, after all their vices and passions have been consumed, a holy temple, worthy of

Himself. Those, moreover, who, on account of the expression "God is a Spirit," think that He is a body, are to be answered, I think, in the following manner. It is the custom of sacred Scripture, when it wishes to designate anything opposed to this gross and solid body, to call it spirit, as in the expression, "The letter killeth, but the spirit giveth life," where there can be no doubt that by "letter" are meant bodily things, and by "spirit" intellectual things, which we also term "spiritual." The apostle, moreover, says, "Even unto this day, when Moses is read, the veil is upon their heart: nevertheless, when it shall turn to the Lord, the veil shall be taken away: and where the Spirit of the Lord is, there is liberty." For so long as any one is not converted to a spiritual understanding, a veil is placed over his heart, with which veil, i.e., a gross understanding, Scripture itself is said or thought to be covered: and this is the meaning of the statement that a veil was placed over the countenance of Moses when he spoke to the people, i.e., when the law was publicly read aloud. But if we turn to the Lord, where also is the word of God, and where the Holy Spirit reveals spiritual knowledge, then the veil is taken away, and with unveiled face we shall behold the glory of the Lord in the holy Scriptures.

3. And since many saints participate in the Holy Spirit, He cannot therefore be understood to be a body, which being divided into corporeal parts, is partaken of by each one of the saints; but He is manifestly a sanctifying power, in which all are said to have a share who have deserved to be sanctified by His grace. And in order that what we say may be more easily understood, let us take an illustration from things very dissimilar. There are many persons who take a part in the science or art of medicine: are we therefore to suppose that those who do so take to themselves the particles of some body called medicine, which is placed before them, and in this way participate in the same? Or must we not rather understand that all who with quick and trained minds come to understand the art and discipline itself, may be said to be partakers of the art of healing? But these are not to be deemed altogether parallel instances in a comparison of medicine to the Holy Spirit, as they have been adduced only to establish that that is not necessarily to be considered a body, a share in which is possessed by many individuals. For the Holy Spirit differs widely from the method or science of medicine, in respect that the Holy Spirit is an intellectual existence and subsists and exists in a peculiar manner, whereas medicine is not at all of that nature.

4. But we must pass on to the language of the Gospel itself, in which it is declared that "God is a Spirit," and where we have to show how that is to be understood agreeably to what we have stated. For let us

inquire on what occasion these words were spoken by the Saviour, before whom He uttered them, and what was the subject of investigation. We find, without any doubt, that He spoke these words to the Samaritan woman, saying to her, who thought, agreeably to the Samaritan view, that God ought to be worshipped on Mount Gerizim, that "God is a Spirit." For the Samaritan woman, believing Him to be a Jew, was inquiring of Him whether God ought to be worshipped in Jerusalem or on this mountain; and her words were, "All our fathers worshipped on this mountain, and ye say that in Jerusalem is the place where we ought to worship." To this opinion of the Samaritan woman, therefore, who imagined that God was less rightly or duly worshipped, according to the privileges of the different localities, either by the Jews in Jerusalem or by the Samaritans on Mount Gerizim, the Saviour answered that he who would follow the Lord must lay aside all preference for particular places, and thus expressed Himself: "The hour is coming when neither in Jerusalem nor on this mountain shall the true worshippers worship the Father. God is a Spirit, and they who worship Him must worship Him in spirit and in truth." And observe how logically He has joined together the spirit and the truth: He called God a Spirit, that He might distinguish Him from bodies; and He named Him the truth, to distinguish Him from a shadow or an image. For they who worshipped in Jerusalem worshipped God neither in truth nor in spirit, being in subjection to the shadow or image of heavenly things; and such also was the case with those who worshipped on Mount Gerizim.

5. Having refuted, then, as well as we could, every notion which might suggest that we were to think of God as in any degree corporeal, we go on to say that, according to strict truth, God is incomprehensible, and incapable of being measured. For whatever be the knowledge which we are able to obtain of God, either by perception or reflection, we must of necessity believe that He is by many degrees far better than what we perceive Him to be. For, as if we were to see any one unable to bear a spark of light, or the flame of a very small lamp, and were desirous to acquaint such a one, whose vision could not admit a greater degree of light than what we have stated, with the brightness and splendour of the sun, would it not be necessary to tell him that the splendour of the sun was unspeakably and incalculably better and more glorious than all this light which he saw? So our understanding, when shut in by the fetters of flesh and blood, and rendered, on account of its participation in such material substances, duller and more obtuse, although, in comparison with our bodily nature, it is esteemed to be far superior, yet, in its efforts to examine and behold incorporeal things,

scarcely holds the place of a spark or lamp. But among all intelligent, that is, incorporeal beings, what is so superior to all others—so unspeakably and incalculably superior—as God, whose nature cannot be grasped or seen by the power of any human understanding, even the purest and brightest?

6. But it will not appear absurd if we employ another similitude to make the matter clearer. Our eyes frequently cannot look upon the nature of the light itself—that is, upon the substance of the sun; but when we behold his splendour or his rays pouring in, perhaps, through windows or some small openings to admit the light, we can reflect how great is the supply and source of the light of the body. So, in like manner. the works of Divine Providence and the plan of this whole world are a sort of rays, as it were, of the nature of God, in comparison with His real substance and being. As, therefore, our understanding is unable of itself to behold God Himself as He is, it knows the Father of the world from the beauty of His works and the comeliness of His creatures. God, therefore, is not to be thought of as being either a body or as existing in a body, but as an uncompounded intellectual nature, admitting within Himself no addition of any kind; so that He cannot be believed to have within him a greater and a less, but is such that He is in all parts *Monas*, and, so to speak, *Enas*, and is the mind and source from which all intellectual nature or mind takes its beginning. But mind, for its movements or operations, needs no physical space, nor sensible magnitude, nor bodily shape, nor colour, nor any other of those adjuncts which are the properties of body or matter. Wherefore that simple and wholly intellectual nature can admit of no delay or hesitation in its movements or operations, lest the simplicity of the divine nature should appear to be circumscribed or in some degree hampered by such adjuncts, and lest that which is the beginning of all things should be found composite and differing, and that which ought to be free from all bodily intermixture, in virtue of being the one sole species of Deity, so to speak, should prove, instead of being one, to consist of many things. That mind, moreover, does not require space in order to carry on its movements agreeably to its nature, is certain from observation of our own mind. For if the mind abide within its own limits, and sustain no injury from any cause, it will never, from diversity of situation, be retarded in the discharge of its functions; nor, on the other hand, does it gain any addition or increase of mobility from the nature of particular places. And here, if any one were to object, for example, that among those who are at sea, and tossed by its waves the mind is considerably less vigorous than it is wont to be on land, we are to believe that it is in this state, not from diversity of situation, but from

the commotion or disturbance of the body to which the mind is joined or attached. For it seems to be contrary to nature, as it were, for a human body to live at sea; and for that reason it appears, by a sort of inequality of its own, to enter upon its mental operations in a slovenly and irregular manner, and to perform the acts of the intellect with a duller sense, in as great degree as those who on land are prostrated with fever; with respect to whom it is certain, that if the mind do not discharge its functions as well as before, in consequence of the attack of disease, the blame is to be laid not upon the place, but upon the bodily malady, by which the body, being disturbed and disordered, renders to the mind its customary services under by no means the well-known and natural conditions: for we human beings are animals composed of a union of body and soul, and in this way (only) was it possible for us to live upon the earth. But God, who is the beginning of all things, is not to be regarded as a composite being, lest perchance there should be found to exist elements prior to the beginning itself, out of which everything is composed, whatever that be which is called composite. Neither does the mind require bodily magnitude in order to perform any act or movement; as when the eye by gazing upon bodies of larger size is dilated, but is compressed and contracted in order to see smaller objects. The mind, indeed, requires magnitude of an intellectual kind, because it grows, not after the fashion of a body, but after that of intelligence. For the mind is not enlarged, together with the body, by means of corporal additions, up to the twentieth or thirtieth year of life; but the intellect is sharpened by exercises of learning, and the powers implanted within it for intelligent purposes are called forth; and it is rendered capable of greater intellectual efforts, not being increased by bodily additions, but carefully polished by learned exercises. But these it cannot receive immediately from boyhood, or from birth, because the framework of limbs which the mind employs as organs for exercising itself is weak and feeble; and it is unable to bear the weight of its own operations, or to exhibit a capacity for receiving training.

7. If there are any now who think that the mind itself and the soul is a body, I wish they would tell me by way of answer how it receives reasons and assertions on subjects of such importance—of such difficulty and such subtlety? Whence does it derive the power of memory? and whence comes the contemplation of invisible things? How does the body possess the faculty of understanding incorporeal existences? How does a bodily nature investigate the processes of the various arts, and contemplate the reasons of things? How, also, is it able to perceive and understand divine truths, which are manifestly

incorporeal? Unless, indeed, some should happen to be of opinion, that as the very bodily shape and form of the ears or eyes contributes something to hearing and to sight, and as the individual members, formed by God, have some adaptation, even from the very quality of their form, to the end for which they were naturally appointed; so also he may think that the shape of the soul or mind is to be understood as if created purposely and designedly for perceiving and understanding individual things, and for being set in motion by vital movements. I do not perceive, however, who shall be able to describe or state what is the colour of the mind, in respect of its being mind, and acting as an intelligent existence. Moreover, in confirmation and explanation of what we have already advanced regarding the mind or soul—to the effect that it is better than the whole bodily nature—the following remarks may be added. There underlies every bodily sense a certain peculiar sensible substance, on which the bodily sense exerts itself. For example, colours, form, size, underlie vision; voices and sound, the sense of hearing; odours, good or bad, that of smell; savours, that of taste; heat or cold, hardness or softness, roughness or smoothness, that of touch. Now, of those senses enumerated above, it is manifest to all that the sense of mind is much the best. How, then, should it not appear absurd, that under those senses which are inferior, substances should have been placed on which to exert their powers, but that under this power, which is far better than any other, i.e., the sense of mind, nothing at all of the nature of a substance should be placed, but that a power of an intellectual nature should be an accident, or consequent upon bodies? Those who assert this, doubtless do so to the disparagement of that better substance which is within them; nay, by so doing, they even do wrong to God Himself, when they imagine He may be understood by means of a bodily nature, so that according to their view He is a body, and that which may be understood or perceived by means of a body; and they are unwilling to have it understood that the mind bears a certain relationship to God, of whom the mind itself is an intellectual image, and that by means of this it may come to some knowledge of the nature of divinity, especially if it be purified and separated from bodily matter.

8. But perhaps these declarations may seem to have less weight with those who wish to be instructed in divine things out of the holy Scriptures, and who seek to have it proved to them from that source how the nature of God surpasses the nature of bodies. See, therefore, if the apostle does not say the same thing, when, speaking of Christ, he declares, that "He is the image of the invisible God, the first-born of every creature." Not, as some suppose, that the nature of God is visible

to some and invisible to others: for the apostle does not say "the image of God invisible" to men or "invisible" to sinners, but with unvarying constancy pronounces on the nature of God in these words: "the image of the invisible God." Moreover, John, in his Gospel, when asserting that "no one hath seen God at any time," manifestly declares to all who are capable of understanding, that there is no nature to which God is visible: not as if, He were a being who was visible by nature, and merely escaped or baffled the view of a frailer creature, but because by the *nature* of His being it is impossible for Him to be seen. And if you should ask of me what is my opinion regarding the Only-begotten Himself, whether the nature of God, which is naturally invisible, be not visible even to Him, let not such a question appear to you at once to be either absurd or impious, because we shall give you a logical reason. It is one thing to see, and another to know: to see and to be seen is a property of bodies; to know and to be known, an attribute of intellectual being. Whatever, therefore, is a property of bodies, cannot be predicated either of the Father or of the Son; but what belongs to the nature of deity is common to the Father and the Son. Finally, even He Himself, in the Gospel, did not say that no one has *seen* the Father, save the Son, nor any one the Son, save the Father; but His words are: "No one *knoweth* the Son, save the Father; nor any one the Father, save the Son." By which it is clearly shown, that whatever among bodily natures is called seeing and being seen, is termed, between the Father and the Son, a knowing and being known, by means of the power of knowledge, not by the frailness of the sense of sight. Because, then, neither seeing nor being seen can be properly applied to an incorporeal and invisible nature, neither is the Father, in the Gospel, said to be seen by the Son, nor the Son by the Father, but the one is said to be known by the other.

9. Here, if any one lay before us the passage where it is said, "Blessed are the pure in heart, for they shall see God," from that very passage, in my opinion, will our position derive additional strength; for what else is seeing God in heart, but, according to our exposition as above, understanding and knowing Him with the mind? For the names of the organs of sense are frequently applied to the soul, so that it may be said to see with the eyes of the heart, i.e., to perform an intellectual act by means of the power of intelligence. So also it is said to hear with the ears when it perceives the deeper meaning of a statement. So also we say that it makes use of teeth, when it chews and eats the bread of life which cometh down from heaven. In like manner, also, it is said to employ the services of other members, which are transferred from their bodily appellations, and applied to the powers of the soul, according to

the words of Solomon, "You will find a divine sense." For he knew that there were within us two kinds of senses: the one mortal, corruptible, human; the other immortal and intellectual, which he now termed divine. By this divine sense, therefore, not of the eyes, but of a pure heart, which is the mind, God may be seen by those who are worthy. For you will certainly find in all the Scriptures, both old and new, the term "heart" repeatedly used instead of "mind," i.e., intellectual power. In this manner, therefore, although far below the dignity of the subject, have we spoken of the nature of God, as those who understand it under the limitation of the human understanding. In the next place, let us see what is meant by the name of Christ.

CHAPTER II—ON CHRIST

1. In the first place, we must note that the nature of that deity which is in Christ in respect of His being the only-begotten Son of God is one thing, and that human nature which He assumed in these last times for the purposes of the dispensation (of grace) is another. And therefore we have first to ascertain what the only-begotten Son of God is, seeing He is called by many different names, according to the circumstances and views of individuals. For He is termed Wisdom, according to the expression of Solomon: "The Lord created me—the beginning of His ways, and among His works, before He made any other thing; He founded me before the ages. In the beginning, before He formed the earth, before He brought forth the fountains of waters, before the mountains were made strong, before all the hills, He brought me forth." He is also styled First-born, as the apostle has declared: "who is the first-born of every creature." The first-born, however, is not by nature a different person from the Wisdom, but one and the same. Finally, the Apostle Paul says that "Christ (is) the power of God and the wisdom of God."

2. Let no one, however, imagine that we mean anything impersonal when we call Him the wisdom of God; or suppose, for example, that we understand Him to be, not a living being endowed with wisdom, but something which makes men wise, giving itself to, and implanting itself in, the minds of those who are made capable of receiving His virtues and intelligence. If, then, it is once rightly understood that the only-begotten Son of God is His wisdom hypostatically existing, I know not whether our curiosity ought to advance beyond this, or entertain any suspicion that that *hupostasis* or *substantia* contains anything of a bodily nature, since everything that is corporeal is distinguished either by form, or colour, or magnitude. And who in his

sound senses ever sought for form, or colour, or size, in wisdom, in respect of its being wisdom? And who that is capable of entertaining reverential thoughts or feelings regarding God, can suppose or believe that God the Father ever existed, even for a moment of time, without having generated this Wisdom? For in that case he must say either that God was unable to generate Wisdom before He produced her, so that He afterwards called into being her who formerly did not exist, or that He possessed the power indeed, but—what cannot be said of God without impiety—was unwilling to use it; both of which suppositions, it is patent to all, are alike absurd and impious: for they amount to this, either that God advanced from a condition of inability to one of ability, or that, although possessed of the power, He concealed it, and delayed the generation of Wisdom. Wherefore we have always held that God is the Father of His only-begotten Son, who was born indeed of Him, and derives from Him what He is, but without any beginning, not only such as may be measured by any divisions of time, but even that which the mind alone can contemplate within itself, or behold, so to speak, with the naked powers of the understanding. And therefore we must believe that Wisdom was generated before any beginning that can be either comprehended or expressed. And since all the creative power of the coming creation was included in this very existence of Wisdom (whether of those things which have an original or of those which have a derived existence), having been formed beforehand and arranged by the power of foreknowledge; on account of these very creatures which had been described, as it were, and prefigured in Wisdom herself, does Wisdom say, in the words of Solomon, that she was created the beginning of the ways of God, inasmuch as she contained within herself either the beginnings, or forms, or species of all creation.

3. Now, in the same way in which we have understood that Wisdom was the beginning of the ways of God, and is said to be created, forming beforehand and containing within herself the species and beginnings of all creatures, must we understand her to be the Word of God, because of her disclosing to all other beings, i.e., to universal creation, the nature of the mysteries and secrets which are contained within the divine wisdom; and on this account she is called the Word, because she is, as it were, the interpreter of the secrets of the mind. And therefore that language which is found in the *Acts of Paul*, where it is said that "here is the Word a living being," appears to me to be rightly used. John, however, with more sublimity and propriety, says in the beginning of his Gospel, when defining God by a special definition to be the Word, "And God was the Word, and this was in the beginning with God." Let him, then, who assigns a beginning to the Word or

Wisdom of God, take care that he be not guilty of impiety against the unbegotten Father Himself, seeing he denies that He had always been a Father, and had generated the Word, and had possessed wisdom in all preceding periods, whether they be called times or ages, or anything else that can be so entitled.

4. This Son, accordingly, is also the truth and life of all things which exist. And with reason. For how could those things which were created live, unless they derived their being from life? or how could those things which are, truly exist, unless they came down from the truth? or how could rational beings exist, unless the Word or reason had previously existed? or how could they be wise, unless there were wisdom? But since it was to come to pass that some also should fall away from life, and bring death upon themselves by their declension—for death is nothing else than a departure from life—and as it was not to follow that those beings which had once been created by God for the enjoyment of life should utterly perish, it was necessary that, before death, there should be in existence such a power as would destroy the coming death, and that there should be a resurrection, the type of which was in our Lord and Saviour, and that this resurrection should have its ground in the wisdom and word and life of God. And then, in the next place, since some of those who were created were not to be always willing to remain unchangeable and unalterable in the calm and moderate enjoyment of the blessings which they possessed, but, in consequence of the good which was in them being theirs not by nature or essence, but by accident, were to be perverted and changed, and to fall away from their position, therefore was the Word and Wisdom of God made the Way. And it was so termed because it leads to the Father those who walk along it.

Whatever, therefore, we have predicated of the wisdom of God, will be appropriately applied and understood of the Son of God, in virtue of His being the Life, and the Word, and the Truth and the Resurrection: for all these titles are derived from His power and operations, and in none of them is there the slightest ground for understanding anything of a corporeal nature which might seem to denote either size, or form, or colour; for those children of men which appear among us, or those descendants of other living beings, correspond to the seed of those by whom they were begotten, or derive from those mothers, in whose wombs they are formed and nourished, whatever that is, which they bring into this life, and carry with them when they are born. But it is monstrous and unlawful to compare God the Father, in the generation of His only-begotten Son, and in the substance of the same, to any man or other living thing engaged in such an act; for we must of necessity hold that there is something exceptional and worthy of God which does not admit of any comparison at all, not merely in things, but which cannot even be conceived by thought or discovered by perception, so that a human mind should be able to apprehend how the unbegotten God is made the Father of the only-begotten Son. Because His generation is as eternal and everlasting as the brilliancy which is produced from the sun. For it is not by receiving the breath of life that He is made a Son, by *any outward act*, but by His own nature.

5. Let us now ascertain how those statements which we have advanced are supported by the authority of holy Scripture. The Apostle Paul says, that the only-begotten Son is the "image of the invisible God," and "the first-born of every creature." And when writing to the Hebrews, he says of Him that He is "the brightness of His glory, and the express image of His person." Now, we find in the treatise called the Wisdom of Solomon the following description of the wisdom of God: "For she is the breath of the power of God, and the purest efflux of the glory of the Almighty." Nothing that is polluted can therefore come upon her. For she is the splendour of the eternal light, and the stainless mirror of God's working, and the image of His goodness. Now we say, as before, that Wisdom has her existence nowhere else save in Him who is the beginning of all things: from whom also is derived everything that is wise, because He Himself is the only one who is by nature a Son, and is therefore termed the Only-begotten.

6. Let us now see how we are to understand the expression "invisible image," that we may in this way perceive how God is rightly called the Father of His Son; and let us, in the first place, draw our conclusions from what are customarily called images among men. That is sometimes called an image which is painted or sculptured on some material substance, such as wood or stone; and sometimes a child is called the image of his parent, when the features of the child in no respect belie their resemblance to the father. I think, therefore, that that man who was formed after the image and likeness of God may be fittingly compared to the first illustration. Respecting him, however, we shall see more precisely, God willing, when we come to expound the passage in Genesis. But the image of the Son of God, of whom we are now speaking, may be compared to the second of the above examples, even in respect of this, that He is the invisible image of the invisible God, in the same manner as we say, according to the sacred history, that the image of Adam is his son Seth. The words are, "And Adam begat Seth in his own likeness, and after his own image." Now this image contains the unity of nature and substance belonging to Father

and Son. For if the Son do, in like manner, all those things which the Father doth, then, in virtue of the Son doing all things like the Father, is the image of the Father formed in the Son, who is born of Him, like an act of His will proceeding from the mind. And I am therefore of opinion that the will of the Father ought alone to be sufficient for the existence of that which He wishes to exist. For in the exercise of His will He employs no other way than that which is made known by the counsel of His will. And thus also the existence of the Son is generated by Him. For this point must above all others be maintained by those who allow nothing to be unbegotten, i.e., unborn, save God the Father only. And we must be careful not to fall into the absurdities of those who picture to themselves certain emanations, so as to divide the divine nature into parts, and who divide God the Father as far as they can, since even to entertain the remotest suspicion of such a thing regarding an incorporeal being is not only the height of impiety, but a mark of the greatest folly, it being most remote from any intelligent conception that there should be any physical division of any incorporeal nature. Rather, therefore, as an act of the will proceeds from the understanding, and neither cuts off any part nor is separated or divided from it, so after some such fashion is the Father to be supposed as having begotten the Son, His own image; namely, so that, as He is Himself invisible by nature, He also begat an image that was invisible. For the Son is the Word, and therefore we are not to understand that anything in Him is cognisable by the senses. He is wisdom, and in wisdom there can be no suspicion of anything corporeal. He is the true light, which enlightens every man that cometh into this world; but He has nothing in common with the light of this sun. Our Saviour, therefore, is the image of the invisible God, inasmuch as compared with the Father Himself He is the truth: and as compared with us, to whom He reveals the Father, He is the image by which we come to the knowledge of the Father, whom no one knows save the Son, and he to whom the Son is pleased to reveal Him. And the method of revealing Him is through the understanding. For He by whom the Son Himself is understood, understands, as a consequence, the Father also, according to His own words: "He that hath seen Me, hath seen the Father also."

7. But since we quoted the language of Paul regarding Christ, where He says of Him that He is "the brightness of the glory of God, and the express figure of His person," let us see what idea we are to form of this. According to John, "God is light." The only-begotten Son, therefore, is the glory of this light, proceeding inseparably from (God) Himself, as brightness does from light, and illuminating the whole of

creation. For, agreeably to what we have already explained as to the manner in which He is the Way, and conducts to the Father; and in which He is the Word, interpreting the secrets of wisdom, and the mysteries of knowledge, making them known to the rational creation; and is also the Truth, and the Life, and the Resurrection,—in the same way ought we to understand also the meaning of His being the brightness: for it is by its splendour that we understand and feel what light itself is. And this splendour, presenting itself gently and softly to the frail and weak eyes of mortals, and gradually training, as it were, and accustoming them to bear the brightness of the light, when it has put away from them every hindrance and obstruction to vision, according to the Lord's own precept, "Cast forth the beam out of thine eye," renders them capable of enduring the splendour of the light, being made in this respect also a sort of mediator between men and the light.

8. But since He is called by the apostle not only the brightness of His glory, but also the express figure of His person or *subsistence*, it does not seem idle to inquire how there can be said to be another figure of that person besides the person of God Himself, whatever be the meaning of person and subsistence. Consider, then, whether the Son of God, seeing He is His Word and Wisdom, and alone knows the Father, and reveals Him to whom He will (i.e., to those who are capable of receiving His word and wisdom), may not, in regard of this very point of making God to be understood and acknowledged, be called the figure of His person and subsistence; that is, when that Wisdom, which desires to make known to others the means by which God is acknowledged and understood by them, describes Himself first of all, it may by so doing be called the express figure of the person of God. In order, however, to arrive at a fuller understanding of the manner in which the Saviour is the figure of the person or subsistence of God, let us take an instance, which, although it does not describe the subject of which we are treating either fully or appropriately, may nevertheless be seen to be employed for this purpose only, to show that the Son of God, who was in the form of God, divesting Himself (of His glory), makes it His object, by this very divesting of Himself, to demonstrate to us the fulness of His deity. For instance, suppose that there were a statue of so enormous a size as to fill the whole world, and which on that account could be seen by no one; and that another statue were formed altogether resembling it in the shape of the limbs, and in the features of the countenance, and in form and material, but without the same immensity of size, so that those who were unable to behold the one of enormous proportions, should, on seeing the latter, acknowledge that they had seen the former, because it preserved all the

features of its limbs and countenance, and even the very form and material, so closely, as to be altogether undistinguishable from it; by some such similitude, the Son of God, divesting Himself of His equality with the Father, and showing to us the way to the knowledge of Him, is made the express image of His person: so that we, who were unable to look upon the glory of that marvellous light when placed in the greatness of His Godhead, may, by His being made to us brightness, obtain the means of beholding the divine light by looking upon the brightness. This comparison, of course, of statues, as belonging to material things, is employed for no other purpose than to show that the Son of God, though placed in the very insignificant form of a human body, in consequence of the resemblance of His works and power to the Father, showed that there was in Him an immense and invisible greatness, inasmuch as He said to His disciples, "He who sees Me, sees the Father also;" and, "I and the Father are one." And to these belong also the similar expression, "The Father is in Me, and I in the Father."

9. Let us see now what is the meaning of the expression which is found in the Wisdom of Solomon, where it is said of Wisdom that "it is a kind of breath of the power of God, and the purest efflux of the glory of the Omnipotent, and the splendour of eternal light, and the spotless mirror of the working or power of God, and the image of His goodness." These, then, are the definitions which he gives of God, pointing out by each one of them certain attributes which belong to the Wisdom of God, calling wisdom the power, and the glory, and the everlasting light, and the working, and the goodness of God. He does not say, however, that wisdom is the breath of the glory of the Almighty, nor of the everlasting light, nor of the working of the Father, nor of His goodness, for it was not appropriate that breath should be ascribed to any one of these; but, with all propriety, he says that wisdom is the breath of the power of God. Now, by the power of God is to be understood that by which He is strong; by which He appoints, restrains, and governs all things visible and invisible; which is sufficient for all those things which He rules over in His providence; among all which He is present, as if one individual. And although the breath of all this mighty and immeasurable power, and the vigour itself produced, so to speak, by its own existence, proceed from the power itself, as the will does from the mind, yet even this will of God is nevertheless made to become the power of God.

Another power accordingly is produced, which exists with properties of its own,—a kind of breath, as Scripture says, of the primal and unbegotten power of God, deriving from Him its being, and never at any time non-existent. For if any one were to assert that it did not formerly exist, but came afterwards into existence, let him explain the reason why the Father, who gave it being, did not do so before. And if he shall grant that there was once a beginning, when that breath proceeded from the power of God, we shall ask him again, why not even before the beginning, which he has allowed; and in this way, ever demanding an earlier date, and going upwards with our interrogations, we shall arrive at this conclusion, that as God was always possessed of power and will, there never was any reason of propriety or otherwise, why He may not have always possessed that blessing which He desired. By which it is shown that that breath of God's power always existed, having no beginning save God Himself. Nor was it fitting that there should be any other beginning save God Himself, from whom it derives its birth. And according to the expression of the apostle, that Christ "is the power of God," it ought to be termed not only the breath of the power of God, but power out of power.

10. Let us now examine the expression, "Wisdom is the purest efflux of the glory of the Almighty;" and let us first consider what the glory of the omnipotent God is, and then we shall also understand what is its efflux. As no one can be a father without having a son, nor a master without possessing a servant, so even God cannot be called omnipotent unless there exist those over whom He may exercise His power; and therefore, that God may be shown to be almighty, it is necessary that all things should exist. For if any one would have some ages or portions of time, or whatever else he likes to call them, to have passed away, while those things which were afterwards made did not yet exist, he would undoubtedly show that during those ages or periods God was not omnipotent, but became so afterwards, viz., from the time that He began to have persons over whom to exercise power; and in this way He will appear to have received a certain increase, and to have risen from a lower to a higher condition; since there can be no doubt that it is better for Him to be omnipotent than not to be so. And now how can it appear otherwise than absurd, that when God possessed none of those things which it was befitting for Him to possess, He should afterwards, by a kind of progress, come into the possession of them? But if there never was a time when He was not omnipotent, of necessity those things by which He receives that title must also exist; and He must always have had those over whom He exercised power, and which were governed by Him either as king or prince, of which we shall speak more fully in the proper place, when we come to discuss the subject of the creatures. But even now I think it necessary to drop a word, although cursorily, of warning, since the question before us is, how wisdom is the purest efflux of the glory of the Almighty, lest any one

should think that the title of Omnipotent was anterior in God to the birth of Wisdom, through whom He is called Father, seeing that Wisdom, which is the Son of God, is the purest efflux of the glory of the Almighty. Let him who is inclined to entertain this suspicion hear the undoubted declaration of Scripture pronouncing, "In wisdom hast Thou made them all," and the teaching of the Gospel, that "by Him were all things made, and without Him nothing was made;" and let him understand from this that the title of Omnipotent in God cannot be older than that of Father; for it is through the Son that the Father is almighty. But from the expression "glory of the Almighty," of which glory Wisdom is the efflux, this is to be understood, that Wisdom, through which God is called omnipotent, has a share in the glory of the Almighty. For through Wisdom, which is Christ, God has power over all things, not only by the authority of a ruler, but also by the voluntary obedience of subjects. And that you may understand that the omnipotence of Father and Son is one and the same, as God and the Lord are one and the same with the Father, listen to the manner in which John speaks in the Apocalypse: "Thus saith the Lord God, which is, and which was, and which is to come, the Almighty." For who else was "He which is to come" than Christ? And as no one ought to be offended, seeing God is the Father, that the Saviour is also God; so also, since the Father is called omnipotent, no one ought to be offended that the Son of God is also called omnipotent. For in this way will that saying be true which He utters to the Father, "All Mine are Thine, and Thine are Mine, and I am glorified in them." Now, if all things which are the Father's are also Christ's, certainly among those things which exist is the omnipotence of the Father; and doubtless the only-begotten Son ought to be omnipotent, that the Son also may have all things which the Father possesses. "And I am glorified in them," He declares. For "at the name of Jesus every knee shall bow, of things in heaven, and things in earth, and things under the earth; and every tongue shall confess that the Lord Jesus is in the glory of God the Father." Therefore He is the efflux of the glory of God in this respect, that He is omnipotent—the pure and limpid Wisdom herself—glorified as the efflux of omnipotence or of glory. And that it may be more clearly understood what the glory of omnipotence is, we shall add the following. God the Father is omnipotent, because He has power over all things, i.e., over heaven and earth, sun, moon, and stars, and all things in them. And He exercises His power over them by means of His Word, because at the name of Jesus every knee shall bow, both of things in heaven, and things on earth, and things under the earth. And if every knee is bent to Jesus, then, without doubt, it is Jesus to whom all things are subject, and He it is who exercises power over all things, and through whom all things are subject to the Father; for through wisdom, i.e., by word and reason, not by force and necessity, are all things subject. And therefore His glory consists in this very thing, that He possesses all things, and this is the purest and most limpid glory of omnipotence, that by reason and wisdom, not by force and necessity, all things are subject. Now the purest and most limpid glory of wisdom is a convenient expression to distinguish it from that glory which cannot be called pure and sincere. But every nature which is convertible and changeable, although glorified in the works of righteousness or wisdom, yet by the fact that righteousness or wisdom are accidental qualities, and because that which is accidental may also fall away, its glory cannot be called sincere and pure. But the Wisdom of God, which is His only-begotten Son, being in all respects incapable of change or alteration, and every good quality in Him being essential, and such as cannot be changed and converted, His glory is therefore declared to be pure and sincere.

11. In the third place, wisdom is called the splendour of eternal light. The force of this expression we have explained in the preceding pages, when we introduced the similitude of the sun and the splendour of its rays, and showed to the best of our power how this should be understood. To what we then said we shall add only the following remark. That is properly termed everlasting or eternal which neither had a beginning of existence, nor can ever cease to be what it is. And this is the idea conveyed by John when he says that "God is light." Now His wisdom is the splendour of that light, not only in respect of its being light, but also of being everlasting light, so that His wisdom is eternal and everlasting splendour. If this be fully understood, it clearly shows that the existence of the Son is derived from the Father but not in time, nor from any other beginning, except, as we have said, from God Himself.

12. But wisdom is also called the stainless mirror of the *energeia* or working of God. We must first understand, then, what the working of the power of God is. It is a sort of vigour, so to speak, by which God operates either in creation, or in providence, or in judgment, or in the disposal and arrangement of individual things, each in its season. For as the image formed in a mirror unerringly reflects all the acts and movements of him who gazes on it, so would Wisdom have herself to be understood when she is called the stainless mirror of the power and working of the Father: as the Lord Jesus Christ also, who is the Wisdom of God, declares of Himself when He says, "The works which the Father doeth, these also doeth the Son likewise." And again He says,

that the Son cannot do anything of Himself, save what He sees the Father do. As therefore the Son in no respect differs from the Father in the power of His works, and the work of the Son is not a different thing from that of the Father, but one and the same movement, so to speak, is in all things, He therefore named Him a stainless mirror, that by such an expression it might be understood that them is no dissimilarity whatever between the Son and the Father. How, indeed, can those things which are said by some to be done after the manner in which a disciple resembles or imitates his master, or according to the view that those things are made by the Son in bodily material which were first formed by the Father in their spiritual essence, agree with the declarations of Scripture, seeing in the Gospel the Son is said to do not similar things, but the *same* things in a similar manner?

13. It remains that we inquire what is the "image of His goodness;" and here, I think, we must understand the same thing which we expressed a little ago, in speaking of the image formed by the mirror. For He is the primal goodness, doubtless, out of which the Son is born, who, being in all respects the image of the Father, may certainly also be called with propriety the image of His goodness. For there is no other second goodness existing in the Son, save that which is in the Father. And therefore also the Saviour Himself rightly says in the Gospel, "There is none good save one only, God the Father," that by such an expression it may be understood that the Son is not of a different goodness, but of that only which exists in the Father, of whom He is rightly termed the image, because He proceeds from no other source but from that primal goodness, lest there might appear to be in the Son a different goodness from that which is in the Father. Nor is there any dissimilarity or difference of goodness in the Son. And therefore it is not to be imagined that there is a kind of blasphemy, as it were, in the words, "There is none good save one only, God the Father," as if thereby it may be supposed to be denied that either Christ or the Holy Spirit was good. But, as we have already said, the primal goodness is to be understood as residing in God the Father, from whom both the Son is born and the Holy Spirit proceeds, retaining within them, without any doubt, the nature of that goodness which is in the source whence they are derived. And if there be any other things which in Scripture are called good, whether angel, or man, or servant, or treasure, or a good heart, or a good tree, all these are so termed catachrestically, having in them an accidental, not an essential goodness. But it would require both much time and labour to collect together all the titles of the Son of God, such, e.g., as the true light, or the door, or the righteousness, or the sanctification, or the redemption, and countless

others; and to show for what reasons each one of them is so given. Satisfied, therefore, with what we have already advanced, we go on with our inquiries into those other matters which follow.

CHAPTER III—ON THE HOLY SPIRIT

1. The next point is to investigate as briefly as possible the subject of the Holy Spirit. All who perceive, in whatever manner, the existence of Providence, confess that God, who created and disposed all things, is unbegotten, and recognise Him as the parent of the universe. Now, that to Him belongs a Son, is a statement not made by us only; although it may seem a sufficiently marvellous and incredible assertion to those who have a reputation as philosophers among Greeks and Barbarians, by some of whom, however, an idea of His existence seems to have been entertained, in their acknowledging that all things were created by the word or reason of God. We, however, in conformity with our belief in that doctrine, which we assuredly hold to be divinely inspired, believe that it is possible in no other way to explain and bring within the reach of human knowledge this higher and diviner reason as the Son of God, than by means of those Scriptures alone which were inspired by the Holy Spirit, i.e., the Gospels and Epistles, and the law and the prophets, according to the declaration of Christ Himself. Of the existence of the Holy Spirit no one indeed could entertain any suspicion, save those who were familiar with the law and the prophets, or those who profess a belief in Christ. For although no one is able to speak with certainty of God the Father, it is nevertheless possible for some knowledge of Him to be gained by means of the visible creation and the natural feelings of the human mind; and it is possible, moreover, for such knowledge to be confined from the sacred Scriptures. But with respect to the Son of God, although no one knoweth the Son save the Father, yet it is from sacred Scripture also that the human mind is taught how to think of the Son; and that not only from the New, but also from the Old Testament, by means of those things which, although done by the saints, are figuratively referred to Christ, and from which both His divine nature, and that human nature which was assumed by Him, may be discovered.

2. Now, what the Holy Spirit is, we are taught in many passages of Scripture, as by David in the fifty-first Psalm, when he says, "And take not Thy Holy Spirit from me;" and by Daniel, where it is said, "The Holy Spirit which is in thee." And in the New Testament we have abundant testimonies, as when the Holy Spirit is described as having descended upon Christ, and when the Lord breathed upon His apostles

after His resurrection, saying, "Receive the Holy Spirit;" and the saying of the angel to Mary, "The Holy Spirit will come upon thee;" the declaration by Paul, that no one can call Jesus Lord, save by the Holy Spirit. In the Acts of the Apostles, the Holy Spirit was given by the imposition of the apostles' hands in baptism. From all which we learn that the person of the Holy Spirit was of such authority and dignity, that saving baptism was not complete except by the authority of the most excellent Trinity of them all, i.e., by the naming of Father, Son, and Holy Spirit, and by joining to the unbegotten God the Father, and to His only-begotten Son, the name also of the Holy Spirit. Who, then, is not amazed at the exceeding majesty of the Holy Spirit, when he hears that he who speaks a word against the Son of man may hope for forgiveness; but that he who is guilty of blasphemy against the Holy Spirit has not forgiveness, either in the present world or in that which is to come!

3. That all things were created by God, and that there is no creature which exists but has derived from Him its being, is established from many declarations of Scripture; those assertions being refuted and rejected which are falsely alleged by some respecting the existence either of a matter co-eternal with God, or of unbegotten souls, in which they would have it that God implanted not so much the power of existence, as equality and order. For even in that little treatise called *The Pastor or Angel of Repentance*, composed by Hermas, we have the following: "First of all, believe that there is one God who created and arranged all things; who, when nothing formerly existed, caused all things to be; who Himself contains all things, but Himself is contained by none." And in the book of Enoch also we have similar descriptions. But up to the present time we have been able to find no statement in holy Scripture in which the Holy Spirit could be said to be made or created, not even in the way in which we have shown above that the divine wisdom is spoken of by Solomon, or in which those expressions which we have discussed are to be understood of the life, or the word, or the other appellations of the Son of God. The Spirit of God, therefore, which was borne upon the waters, as is written in the beginning of the creation of the world, is, I am of opinion, no other than the Holy Spirit, so far as I can understand; as indeed we have shown in our exposition of the passages themselves, not according to the historical, but according to the spiritual method of interpretation.

4. Some indeed of our predecessors have observed, that in the New Testament, whenever the Spirit is named without that adjunct which denotes quality, the Holy Spirit is to be understood; as e.g., in the expression, "Now the fruit of the Spirit is love, joy, and peace;" and,

"Seeing ye began in the Spirit, are ye now made perfect in the flesh?"
We are of opinion that this distinction may be observed in the Old
Testament also, as when it is said, "He that giveth His Spirit to the
people who are upon the earth, and Spirit to them who walk thereon."
For, without doubt, every one who walks upon the earth (i.e., earthly
and corporeal beings) is a partaker also of the Holy Spirit, receiving it
from God. My Hebrew master also used to say that those two seraphim
in Isaiah, which are described as having each six wings, and calling to
one another, and saying, "Holy, holy, holy, is the Lord God of hosts,"
were to be understood of the only-begotten Son of God and of the
Holy Spirit. And we think that that expression also which occurs in the
hymn of Habakkuk, "In the midst either of the two living things, or of
the two lives, Thou wilt be known," ought to be understood of Christ
and of the Holy Spirit. For all knowledge of the Father is obtained by
revelation of the Son through the Holy Spirit, so that both of these
beings which, according to the prophet, are called either "living things"
or "lives," exist as the ground of the knowledge of God the Father. For
as it is said of the Son, that "no one knoweth the Father but the Son,
and he to whom the Son will reveal Him," the same also is said by the
apostle of the Holy Spirit, when He declares, "God hath revealed them
to us by His Holy Spirit; for the Spirit searcheth all things, even the
deep things of God;" and again in the Gospel, when the Saviour,
speaking of the divine and profounder parts of His teaching, which His
disciples were not yet able to receive, thus addresses them: "I have yet
many things to say unto you, but ye cannot bear them now; but when
the Holy Spirit, the Comforter, is come, He will teach you all things,
and will bring all things to your remembrance, whatsoever I have said
unto you." We must understand, therefore, that as the Son, who alone
knows the Father, reveals Him to whom He will, so the Holy Spirit,
who alone searches the deep things of God, reveals God to whom He
will: "For the Spirit bloweth where He listeth." We are not, however,
to suppose that the Spirit derives His knowledge through revelation
from the Son. For if the Holy Spirit knows the Father through the Son's
revelation, He passes from a state of ignorance into one of knowledge;
but it is alike impious and foolish to confess the Holy Spirit, and yet to
ascribe to Him ignorance. For even although something else existed
before the Holy Spirit, it was not by progressive advancement that He
came to be the Holy Spirit; as if any one should venture to say, that at
the time when He was not yet the Holy Spirit He was ignorant of the
Father, but that after He had received knowledge He was made the
Holy Spirit. For if this were the case, the Holy Spirit would never be
reckoned in the Unity of the Trinity, i.e., along with the unchangeable

Father and His Son, unless He had always been the Holy Spirit. When we use, indeed, such terms as "always" or "was," or any other designation of time, they are not to be taken absolutely, but with due allowance; for while the significations of these words relate to time, and those subjects of which we speak are spoken of by a stretch of language as existing in time, they nevertheless surpass in their real nature all conception of the finite understanding.

5. Nevertheless it seems proper to inquire what is the reason why he who is regenerated by God unto salvation has to do both with Father and Son and Holy Spirit, and does not obtain salvation unless with the co-operation of the entire Trinity; and why it is impossible to become partaker of the Father or the Son without the Holy Spirit. And in discussing these subjects, it will undoubtedly be necessary to describe the special working of the Holy Spirit, and of the Father and the Son. I am of opinion, then, that the working of the Father and of the Son takes place as well in saints as in sinners, in rational beings and in dumb animals; nay, even in those things which are without life, and in all things universally which exist; but that the operation of the Holy Spirit does not take place at all in those things which are without life, or in those which, although living, are yet dumb; nay, is not found even in those who are endued indeed with reason, but are engaged in evil courses, and not at all converted to a better life. In those persons alone do I think that the operation of the Holy Spirit takes place, who are already turning to a better life, and walking along the way which leads to Jesus Christ, i.e., who are engaged in the performance of good actions, and who abide in God.

6. That the working of the Father and the Son operates both in saints and in sinners, is manifest from this, that all who are rational beings are partakers of the word, i.e., of reason, and by this means bear certain seeds, implanted within them, of wisdom and justice, which is Christ. Now, in Him who truly exists, and who said by Moses, "I Am Who I Am," all things, whatever they are, participate; which participation in God the Father is shared both by just men and sinners, by rational and irrational beings, and by all things universally which exist. The Apostle Paul also shows truly that all have a share in Christ, when he says, "Say not in thine heart, Who shall ascend into heaven? (i.e., to bring Christ down from above;) or who shall descend into the deep? (that is, to bring up Christ again from the dead.) But what saith the Scripture? The word is nigh thee, even in thy mouth, and in thy heart." By which he means that Christ is in the heart of all, in respect of His being the word or reason, by participating in which they are rational beings. That declaration also in the Gospel, "If I had not come

34

and spoken unto them, they had not had sin; but now they have no excuse for their sin," renders it manifest and patent to all who have a rational knowledge of how long a time man is without sin, and from what period he is liable to it, how, by participating in the word or reason, men are said to have sinned, viz., from the time they are made capable of understanding and knowledge, when the reason implanted within has suggested to them the difference between good and evil; and after they have already begun to know what evil is, they are made liable to sin, if they commit it. And this is the meaning of the expression, that "men have no excuse for their sin," viz., that, from the time the divine word or reason has begun to show them internally the difference between good and evil, they ought to avoid and guard against that which is wicked: "For to him who knoweth to do good, and doeth it not, to him it is sin." Moreover, that all men are not without communion with God, is taught in the Gospel thus, by the Saviour's words: "The kingdom of God cometh not with observation; neither shall they say, Lo here! or, lo there! but the kingdom of God is within you." But here we must see whether this does not bear the same meaning with the expression in Genesis: "And He breathed into his face the breath of life, and man became a living soul." For if this be understood as applying generally to all men, then all men have a share in God.

7. But if this is to be understood as spoken of the Spirit of God, since Adam also is found to have prophesied of some things, it may be taken not as of general application, but as confined to those who are saints. Finally, also, at the time of the flood, when all flesh had corrupted their way before God, it is recorded that God spoke thus, as of undeserving men and sinners: "My Spirit shall not abide with those men for ever, because they are flesh." By which, it is clearly shown that the Spirit of God is taken away from all who are unworthy. In the Psalms also it is written: "Thou wilt take away their spirit, and they will die, and return to their earth. Thou wilt send forth Thy Spirit, and they shall be created, and Thou wilt renew the face of the earth;" which is manifestly intended of the Holy Spirit, who, after sinners and unworthy persons have been taken away and destroyed, creates for Himself a new people, and renews the face of the earth, when, laying aside, through the grace of the Spirit, the old man with his deeds, they begin to walk in newness of life. And therefore the expression is competently applied to the Holy Spirit, because He will take up His dwelling, not in all men, nor in those who are flesh, but in those whose land has been renewed. Lastly, for this reason was the grace and revelation of the Holy Spirit bestowed by the imposition of the apostles' hands after baptism. Our

Saviour also, after the resurrection, when old things had already passed away, and all things had become new, Himself a new man, and the first-born from the dead, His apostles also being renewed by faith in His resurrection, says, "Receive the Holy Spirit." This is doubtless what the Lord the Saviour meant to convey in the Gospel, when He said that new wine cannot be put into old bottles, but commanded that the bottles should be made new, i.e., that men should walk in newness of life, that they might receive the new wine, i.e., the newness of grace of the Holy Spirit. In this manner, then, is the working of the power of God the Father and of the Son extended without distinction to every creature; but a share in the Holy Spirit we find possessed only by the saints. And therefore it is said, "No man can say that Jesus is Lord, but by the Holy Ghost." And on one occasion, scarcely even the apostles themselves are deemed worthy to hear the words, "Ye shall receive the power of the Holy Ghost coming upon you." For this reason, also, I think it follows that he who has committed a sin against the Son of man is deserving of forgiveness; because if he who is a participator of the word or reason of God cease to live agreeably to reason, he seems to have fallen into a state of ignorance or folly, and therefore to deserve forgiveness; whereas he who has been deemed worthy to have a portion of the Holy Spirit, and who has relapsed, is, by this very act and work, said to be guilty of blasphemy against the Holy Spirit. Let no one indeed suppose that we, from having said that the Holy Spirit is conferred upon the saints alone, but that the benefits or operations of the Father and of the Son extend to good and bad, to just and unjust, by so doing give a preference to the Holy Spirit over the Father and the Son, or assert that His dignity is greater, which certainly would be a very illogical conclusion. For it is the peculiarity of His grace and operations that we have been describing. Moreover, nothing in the Trinity can be called greater or less, since the fountain of divinity alone contains all things by His word and reason, and by the Spirit of His mouth sanctifies all things which are worthy of sanctification, as it is written in the Psalm: "By the word of the Lord were the heavens strengthened, and all their power by the Spirit of His mouth." There is also a special working of God the Father, besides that by which He bestowed upon all things the gift of natural life. There is also a special ministry of the Lord Jesus Christ to those upon whom he confers by nature the gift of reason, by means of which they are enabled to be rightly what they are. There is also another grace of the Holy Spirit, which is bestowed upon the deserving, through the ministry of Christ and the working of the Father, in proportion to the merits of those who are rendered capable of receiving it. This is most clearly pointed out by the Apostle Paul, when demonstrating that the power of the Trinity is one and the same, in the words, "There are diversities of gifts, but the same Spirit; there are diversities of administrations, but the same Lord; and there are diversities of operations, but it is the same God who worketh all in all. But the manifestation of the Spirit is given to every man to profit withal." From which it most clearly follows that there is no difference in the Trinity, but that which is called the gift of the Spirit is made known through the Son, and operated by God the Father. "But all these worketh that one and the self-same Spirit, dividing to every one severally as He will."

8. Having made these declarations regarding the Unity of the Father, and of the Son, and of the Holy Spirit, let us return to the order in which we began the discussion. God the Father bestows upon all, existence; and participation in Christ, in respect of His being the word of reason, renders them rational beings. From which it follows that they are deserving either of praise or blame, because capable of virtue and vice. On this account, therefore, is the grace of the Holy Ghost present, that those beings which are not holy in their essence may be rendered holy by participating in it. Seeing, then, that firstly, they derive their existence from God the Father; secondly, their rational nature from the Word; thirdly, their holiness from the Holy Spirit,—those who have been previously sanctified by the Holy Spirit are again made capable of receiving Christ, in respect that He is the righteousness of God; and those who have earned advancement to this grade by the sanctification of the Holy Spirit, will nevertheless obtain the gift of wisdom according to the power and working of the Spirit of God. And this I consider is Paul's meaning, when he says that to "some is given the word of wisdom, to others the word of knowledge, according to the same Spirit." And while pointing out the individual distinction of gifts, he refers the whole of them to the source of all things, in the words, "There are diversities of operations, but one God who worketh all in all." Whence also the working of the Father, which confers existence upon all things, is found to be more glorious and magnificent, while each one, by participation in Christ, as being wisdom, and knowledge, and sanctification, makes progress, and advances to higher degrees of perfection; and seeing it is by partaking of the Holy Spirit that any one is made purer and holier, he obtains, when he is made worthy, the grace of wisdom and knowledge, in order that, after all stains of pollution and ignorance are cleansed and taken away, he may make so great an advance in holiness and purity, that the nature which he received from God may become such as is worthy of Him who gave it to be pure and perfect, so that the being which exists may be as worthy as He who

called it into existence. For, in this way, he who is such as his Creator wished him to be, will receive from God power always to exist, and to abide for ever. That this may be the case, and that those whom He has created may be unceasingly and inseparably present with HIM, WHO IS, it is the business of wisdom to instruct and train them, and to bring them to perfection by confirmation of His Holy Spirit and unceasing sanctification, by which alone are they capable of receiving God. In this way, then, by the renewal of the ceaseless working of Father, Son, and Holy Spirit in us, in its various stages of progress, shall we be able at some future time perhaps, although with difficulty, to behold the holy and the blessed life, in which (as it is only after many struggles that we are able to reach it) we ought so to continue, that no satiety of that blessedness should ever seize us; but the more we perceive its blessedness, the more should be increased and intensified within us the longing for the same, while we ever more eagerly and freely receive and hold fast the Father, and the Son, and the Holy Spirit. But if satiety should ever take hold of any one of those who stand on the highest and perfect summit of attainment, I do not think that such an one would suddenly be deposed from his position and fall away, but that he must decline gradually and little by little, so that it may sometimes happen that if a brief lapsus take place, and the individual quickly repent and return to himself, he may not utterly fall away, but may retrace his steps, and return to his former place, and again make good that which had been lost by his negligence.

CHAPTER IV—ON DEFECTION, OR FALLING AWAY

1. To exhibit the nature of defection or falling away, on the part of those who conduct themselves carelessly, it will not appear out of place to employ a similitude by way of illustration. Suppose, then, the case of one who had become gradually acquainted with the art or science, say of geometry or medicine, until he had reached perfection, having trained himself for a lengthened time in its principles and practice, so as to attain a complete mastery over the art: to such an one it could never happen, that, when he lay down to sleep in the possession of his skill, he should awake in a state of ignorance. It is not our purpose to adduce or to notice here those accidents which are occasioned by any injury or weakness, for they do not apply to our present illustration. According to our point of view, then, so long as that geometer or physician continues to exercise himself in the study of his art and in the practice of its principles, the knowledge of his profession abides with

him; but if he withdraw from its practice, and lay aside his habits of industry, then, by his neglect, at first a few things will gradually escape him, then by and by more and more, until in course of time everything will be forgotten, and be completely effaced from the memory. It is possible, indeed, that when he has first begun to fall away, and to yield to the corrupting influence of a negligence which is small as yet, he may, if he be aroused and return speedily to his senses, repair those losses which up to that time are only recent, and recover that knowledge which hitherto had been only slightly obliterated from his mind. Let us apply this now to the case of those who have devoted themselves to the knowledge and wisdom of God, whose learning and diligence incomparably surpass all other training; and let us contemplate, according to the form of the similitude employed, what is the acquisition of knowledge, or what is its disappearance, especially when we hear from the apostle what is said of those who are perfect, that they shall behold face to face the glory of the Lord in the revelation of His mysteries.

2. But in our desire to show the divine benefits bestowed upon us by Father, Son, and Holy Spirit, which Trinity is the fountain of all holiness, we have fallen, in what we have said, into a digression, having considered that the subject of the soul, which accidentally came before us, should be touched on, although cursorily, seeing we were discussing a cognate topic relating to our rational nature. We shall, however, with the permission of God through Jesus Christ and the Holy Spirit, more conveniently consider in the proper place the subject of all rational beings, which are distinguished into three genera and species.

CHAPTER V—ON RATIONAL NATURES

1. After the dissertation, which we have briefly conducted to the best of our ability, regarding the Father, Son, and Holy Spirit, it follows that we offer a few remarks upon the subject of rational natures, and on their species and orders, or on the offices as well of holy as of malignant powers, and also on those which occupy an intermediate position between these good and evil powers, and as yet are placed in a state of struggle and trial. For we find in holy Scripture numerous names of certain orders and offices, not only of holy beings, but also of those of an opposite description, which we shall bring before us, in the first place; and the meaning of which we shall endeavour, in the second place, to the best of our ability, to ascertain. There are certain holy angels of God whom Paul terms "ministering spirits, sent forth to minister for them who shall be heirs of salvation." In the writings also

of St. Paul himself we find him designating them, from some unknown source, as thrones, and dominions, and principalities, and powers; and after this enumeration, as if knowing that there were still other rational offices and orders besides those which he had named, he says of the Saviour: "Who is above all principality, and power, and might, and dominion, and every name that is named, not only in this world, but also in that which is to come." From which he shows that there were certain beings besides those which he had mentioned, which may be named indeed in this world, but were not now enumerated by him, and perhaps were not known by any other individual; and that there were others which may not be named in this world, but will be named in the world to come.

2. Then, in the next place, we must know that every being which is endowed with reason, and transgresses its statutes and limitations, is undoubtedly involved in sin by swerving from rectitude and justice. Every rational creature, therefore, is capable of earning praise and censure: of praise, if, in conformity to that reason which he possesses, he advance to better things; of censure, if he fall away from the plan and course of rectitude, for which reason he is justly liable to pains and penalties. And this also is to be held as applying to the devil himself, and those who are with him, and are called his angels. Now the titles of these beings have to be explained, that we may know what they are of whom we have to speak. The name, then, of Devil, and Satan, and Wicked One, who is also described as Enemy of God, is mentioned in many passages of Scripture. Moreover, certain angels of the devil are mentioned, and also a prince of this world, who, whether the devil himself or some one else, is not yet clearly manifest. There are also certain princes of this world spoken of as possessing a kind of wisdom which will come to nought; but whether these are those princes who are also the principalities with whom we have to wrestle, or other beings, seems to me a point on which it is not easy for any one to pronounce. After the principalities, certain powers also are named with whom we have to wrestle, and carry on a struggle even against the princes of this world and the rulers of this darkness. Certain spiritual powers of wickedness also, in heavenly places, are spoken of by Paul himself. What, moreover, are we to say of those wicked and unclean spirits mentioned in the Gospel? Then we have certain heavenly beings called by a similar name, but which are said to bend the knee, or to be about to bend the knee, at the name of Jesus; nay, even things on earth and things under the earth, which Paul enumerates in order. And certainly, in a place where we have been discussing the subject of rational natures, it is not proper to be silent regarding ourselves, who

are human beings, and are called rational animals; nay, even this point is not to be idly passed over, that even of us human beings certain different orders are mentioned in the words, "The portion of the Lord is His people Jacob; Israel is the cord of His inheritance." Other nations, moreover, are called a part of the angels; since "when the Most High divided the nations, and dispersed the sons of Adam, He fixed the boundaries of the nations according to the number of the angels of God." And therefore, with other rational natures, we must also thoroughly examine the reason of the human soul.

3. After the enumeration, then, of so many and so important names of orders and offices, underlying which it is certain that there are personal existences, let us inquire whether God, the creator and founder of all things, created certain of them holy and happy, so that they could admit no element at all of an opposite kind, and certain others so that they were made capable both of virtue and vice; or whether we are to suppose that He created some so as to be altogether incapable of virtue, and others again altogether incapable of wickedness, but with the power of abiding only in a state of happiness, and others again such as to be capable of either condition. In order, now, that our first inquiry may begin with the names themselves, let us consider whether the holy angels, from the period of their first existence, have always been holy, and are holy still, and will be holy, and have never either admitted or had the power to admit any occasion of sin. Then in the next place, let us consider whether those who are called holy principalities began from the moment of their creation by God to exercise power over some who were made subject to them, and whether these latter were created of such a nature, and formed for the very purpose of being subject and subordinate. In like manner, also, whether those which are called powers were created of such a nature and for the express purpose of exercising power, or whether their arriving at that power and dignity is a reward and desert of their virtue. Moreover, also, whether those which are called thrones or seats gained that stability of happiness at the same time with their coming forth into being, so as to have that possession from the will of the Creator alone; or whether those which are called dominions had their dominion conferred on them, not as a reward for their proficiency, but as the peculiar privilege of their creation, so that it is something which is in a certain degree inseparable from them, and natural. Now, if we adopt the view that the holy angels, and the holy powers, and the blessed seats, and the glorious virtues, and the magnificent dominions, are to be regarded as possessing those powers and dignities and glories in virtue of their nature, it will doubtless appear to follow that those

beings which have been mentioned as holding offices of an opposite kind must be regarded in the same manner; so that those principalities with whom we have to struggle are to be viewed, not as having received that spirit of opposition and resistance to all good at a later period, or as falling away from good through the freedom of the will, but as having had it in themselves as the essence of their being from the beginning of their existence. In like manner also will it be the case with the powers and virtues, in none of which was wickedness subsequent or posterior to their first existence. Those also whom the apostle termed rulers and princes of the darkness of this world, are said, with respect to their rule and occupation of darkness, to fall not from perversity of intention, but from the necessity of their creation. Logical reasoning will compel us to take the same view with regard to wicked and malignant spirits and unclean demons. But if to entertain this view regarding malignant and opposing powers seem to be absurd, as it is certainly absurd that the cause of their wickedness should be removed from the purpose of their own will, and ascribed of necessity to their Creator, why should we not also be obliged to make a similar confession regarding the good and holy powers, that, viz., the good which is in them is not theirs by essential being, which we have manifestly shown to be the case with Christ and the Holy Spirit alone, as undoubtedly with the Father also? For it was proved that there was nothing compound in the nature of the Trinity, so that these qualities might seem to belong to it as accidental consequences. From which it follows, that in the case of every creature it is a result of his own works and movements, that those powers which appear either to hold sway over others or to exercise power or dominion, have been preferred to and placed over those whom they are said to govern or exercise power over, and not in consequence of a peculiar privilege inherent in their constitutions, but on account of merit.

4. But that we may not appear to build our assertions on subjects of such importance and difficulty on the ground of inference alone, or to require the assent of our hearers to what is only conjectural, let us see whether we can obtain any declarations from holy Scripture, by the authority of which these positions may be more credibly maintained. And, firstly, we shall adduce what holy Scripture contains regarding wicked powers; we shall next continue our investigation with regard to the others, as the Lord shall be pleased to enlighten us, that in matters of such difficulty we may ascertain what is nearest to the truth, or what ought to be our opinions agreeably to the standard of religion. Now we find in the prophet Ezekiel two prophecies written to the prince of Tyre, the former of which might appear to any one, before he heard

the second also, to be spoken of some man who was prince of the Tyrians. In the meantime, therefore, we shall take nothing from that first prophecy; but as the second is manifestly of such a kind as cannot be at all understood of a man, but of some superior power which had fallen away from a higher position, and had been reduced to a lower and worse condition, we shall from it take an illustration, by which it may be demonstrated with the utmost clearness, that those opposing and malignant powers were not formed or created so by nature, but fell from a better to a worse position, and were converted into wicked beings; that those blessed powers also were not of such a nature as to be unable to admit what was opposed to them if they were so inclined and became negligent, and did not guard most carefully the blessedness of their condition. For if it is related that he who is called the prince of Tyre was amongst the saints, and was without stain, and was placed in the paradise of God, and adorned also with a crown of comeliness and beauty, is it to be supposed that such an one could be in any degree inferior to any of the saints? For he is described as having been adorned with a crown of comeliness and beauty, and as having walked stainless in the paradise of God: and how can any one suppose that such a being was not one of those holy and blessed powers which, as being placed in a state of happiness, we must believe to be endowed with no other honour than this? But let us see what we are taught by the words of the prophecy themselves. "The word of the LORD," says the prophet, "came to me, saying, Son of man, take up a lamentation over the prince of Tyre, and say to him, Thus saith the Lord God, Thou hast been the seal of a similitude, and a crown of comeliness among the delights of paradise; thou wert adorned with every good stone or gem, and wert clothed with sardonyx, and topaz, and emerald, and carbuncle, and sapphire, and jasper, set in gold and silver, and with agate, amethyst, and chrysolite, and beryl, and onyx: with gold also didst thou fill thy treasures, and thy storehouses within thee. From the day when thou wert created along with the cherubim, I placed thee in the holy mount of God. Thou wert in the midst of the fiery stones: thou wert stainless in thy days, from the day when thou wert created, until iniquities were found in thee: from the greatness of thy trade, thou didst fill thy storehouses with iniquity, and didst sin, and wert wounded from the mount of God. And a cherub drove thee forth from the midst of the burning stones; and thy heart was elated because of thy comeliness, thy discipline was corrupted along with thy beauty: on account of the multitude of thy sins, I cast thee forth to the earth before kings; I gave thee for a show and a mockery on account of the multitude of thy sins, and of thine iniquities: because of thy trade thou hast polluted thy holy

43

places. And I shall bring forth fire from the midst of thee, and it shall devour thee, and I shall give thee for ashes and cinders on the earth in the sight of all who see thee: and all who know thee among the nations shall mourn over thee. Thou hast been made destruction, and thou shalt exist no longer for ever." Seeing, then, that such are the words of the prophet, who is there that on hearing, "Thou wert a seal of a similitude, and a crown of comeliness among the delights of paradise," or that "From the day when thou wert created with the cherubim, I placed thee in the holy mount of God," can so enfeeble the meaning as to suppose that this language is used of some man or saint, not to say the prince of Tyre? Or what fiery stones can he imagine in the midst of which any man could live? Or who could be supposed to be stainless from the very day of his creation, and wickedness being afterwards discovered in him, it be said of him then that he was cast forth upon the earth? For the meaning of this is, that He who was not yet on the earth is said to be cast forth upon it: whose holy places also are said to be polluted. We have shown, then, that what we have quoted regarding the prince of Tyre from the prophet Ezekiel refers to an adverse power, and by it it is most clearly proved that that power was formerly holy and happy; from which state of happiness it fell from the time that iniquity was found in it, and was hurled to the earth, and was not such by nature and creation. We are of opinion, therefore, that these words are spoken of a certain angel who had received the office of governing the nation of the Tyrians, and to whom also their souls had been entrusted to be taken care of. But what Tyre, or what souls of Tyrians, we ought to understand, whether that Tyre which is situated within the boundaries of the province of Phoenicia, or some other of which, this one which we know on earth is the model; and the souls of the Tyrians, whether they are those of the former or those which belong to that Tyre which is spiritually understood, does not seem to be a matter requiting examination in this place; lest perhaps we should appear to investigate subjects of so much mystery and importance in a cursory manner, whereas they demand a labour and work of their own.

5. Again, we are taught as follows by the prophet Isaiah regarding another opposing power. The prophet says, "How is Lucifer, who used to arise in the morning, fallen from heaven! He who assailed all nations is broken and beaten to the ground. Thou indeed saidst in thy heart, I shall ascend into heaven; above the stars of heaven shall I place my throne; I shall sit upon a lofty mountain, above the lofty mountains which are towards the north; I shall ascend above the clouds; I shall be like the Most High. Now shalt thou be brought down to the lower world, and to the foundations of the earth. They who see thee shall be

44

amazed at thee, and shall say, This is the man who harassed the whole earth, who moved kings, who made the whole world a desert, who destroyed cities, and did not unloose those who were in chains. All the kings of the nations have slept in honour, every one in his own house; but thou shalt be cast forth on the mountains, accursed with the many dead who have been pierced through with swords, and have descended to the lower world. As a garment cloned with blood, and stained, will not be clean; neither shalt thou be clean, because thou hast destroyed my land and slain my people: thou shalt not remain for ever, most wicked seed. Prepare thy sons for death on account of the sins of thy father, lest they rise again and inherit the earth, and fill the earth with wars. And I shall rise against them, saith the LORD of hosts, and I shall cause their name to perish, and their remains, and their seed." Most evidently by these words is he shown to have fallen from heaven, who formerly was Lucifer, and who used to arise in the morning. For if, as some think, he was a nature of darkness, how is Lucifer said to have existed before? Or how could he arise in the morning, who had in himself nothing of the light? Nay, even the Saviour Himself teaches us, saying of the devil, "Behold, I see Satan fallen from heaven like lightning." For at one time he was light. Moreover our Lord, who is the truth, compared the power of His own glorious advent to lightning, in the words, "For as the lightning shineth from the height of heaven even to its height again, so will the coming of the Son of man be." And notwithstanding He compares him to lightning, and says that he fell from heaven, that He might show by this that he had been at one time in heaven, and had had a place among the saints, and had enjoyed a share in that light in which all the saints participate, by which they are made angels of light, and by which the apostles are termed by the Lord the light of the world. In this manner, then, did that being once exist as light before he went astray, and fell to this place, and had his glory turned into dust, which is peculiarly the mark of the wicked, as the prophet also says; whence, too, he was called the prince of this world, i.e., of an earthly habitation: for he exercised power over those who were obedient to his wickedness, since "the whole of this world"—for I term this place of earth, world—"lieth in the wicked one," and in this apostate. That he is an apostate, i.e., a fugitive, even the Lord in the book of Job says, "Thou wilt take with a hook the apostate dragon," i.e., a fugitive. Now it is certain that by the dragon is understood the devil himself. If then they are called opposing powers, and are said to have been once without stain, while spotless purity exists in the essential being of none save the Father, Son, and Holy Spirit, but is an accidental quality in every created thing; and since that which is accidental may also fall away, and since those opposite powers once were spotless, and were once among those which still remain unstained, it is evident from all this that no one is pure either by essence or nature, and that no one was by nature polluted. And the consequence of this is, that it lies within ourselves and in our own actions to possess either happiness or holiness; or by sloth and negligence to fall from happiness into wickedness and ruin, to such a degree that, through too great proficiency, so to speak, in wickedness (if a man be guilty of so great neglect), he may descend even to that state in which he will be changed into what is called an "opposing power."

CHAPTER VI—ON THE END OR CONSUMMATION

1. An end or consummation would seem to be an indication of the perfection and completion of things. And this reminds us here, that if there be any one imbued with a desire of reading and understanding subjects of such difficulty and importance, he ought to bring to the effort a perfect and instructed understanding, lest perhaps, if he has had no experience in questions of this kind, they may appear to him as vain and superfluous; or if his mind be full of preconceptions and prejudices on other points, he may judge these to be heretical and opposed to the faith of the Church, yielding in so doing not so much to the convictions of reason as to the dogmatism of prejudice. These subjects, indeed, are treated by us with great solicitude and caution, in the manner rather of an investigation and discussion, than in that of fixed and certain decision. For we have pointed out in the preceding pages those questions which must be set forth in clear dogmatic propositions, as I think has been done to the best of my ability when speaking of the Trinity. But on the present occasion our exercise is to be conducted, as we best may, in the style of a disputation rather than of strict definition.

The end of the world, then, and the final consummation, will take place when every one shall be subjected to punishment for his sins; a time which God alone knows, when He will bestow on each one what he deserves. We think, indeed, that the goodness of God, through His Christ, may recall all His creatures to one end, even His enemies being conquered and subdued. For thus says holy Scripture, "The LORD said to My Lord, Sit Thou at My right hand, until I make Thine enemies Thy footstool." And if the meaning of the prophet's language here be less clear, we may ascertain it from the Apostle Paul, who speaks more openly, thus: "For Christ must reign until He has put all enemies under His feet." But if even that unreserved declaration of the apostle do not sufficiently inform us what is meant by "enemies being placed under His feet," listen to what he says in the following words, "For all things must be put under Him." What, then, is this "putting under" by which all things must be made subject to Christ? I am of opinion that it is this very subjection by which we also wish to be subject to Him, by which the apostles also were subject, and all the saints who have been followers of Christ. For the name "subjection," by which we are subject to Christ, indicates that the salvation which proceeds from Him belongs to His subjects, agreeably to the declaration of David, "Shall not my soul be subject unto God? From Him cometh my salvation."

2. Seeing, then, that such is the end, when all enemies will be subdued to Christ, when death—the last enemy—shall be destroyed, and when the kingdom shall be delivered up by Christ (to whom all things are subject) to God the Father; let us, I say, from such an end as this, contemplate the beginnings of things. For the end is always like the beginning: and, therefore, as there is one end to all things, so ought we to understand that there was one beginning; and as there is one end to many things, so there spring from one beginning many differences and varieties, which again, through the goodness of God, and by subjection to Christ, and through the unity of the Holy Spirit, are recalled to one end, which is like unto the beginning: all those, viz., who, bending the knee at the name of Jesus, make known by so doing their subjection to Him: and these are they who are in heaven, on earth, and under the earth: by which three classes the whole universe of things is pointed out, those, viz., who from that one beginning were arranged, each according to the diversity of his conduct, among the different orders, in accordance with their desert; for there was no goodness in them by essential being, as in God and His Christ, and in the Holy Spirit. For in the Trinity alone, which is the author of all things, does goodness exist in virtue of essential being; while others possess it as an accidental and perishable quality, and only then enjoy blessedness, when they participate in holiness and wisdom, and in divinity itself. But if they neglect and despise such participation, then is each one, by fault of his own slothfulness, made, one more rapidly, another more slowly, one in a greater, another in a less degree, the cause of his own downfall. And since, as we have remarked, the lapse by which an individual falls away from his position is characterized by great diversity, according to the movements of the mind and will, one man falling with greater ease, another with more difficulty, into a lower condition; in this is to be seen the just judgment of the providence of God, that it should happen to every one according to the diversity of his conduct, in proportion to the desert of his declension and defection. Certain of those, indeed,

who remained in that beginning which we have described as resembling the end which is to come, obtained, in the ordering and arrangement of the world, the rank of angels; others that of influences, others of principalities, others of powers, that they may exercise power over those who need to have power upon their head. Others, again, received the rank of thrones, having the office of judging or ruling those who require this; others dominion, doubtless, over slaves; all of which are conferred by Divine Providence in just and impartial judgment according to their merits, and to the progress which they had made in the participation and imitation of God. But those who have been removed from their primal state of blessedness have not been removed irrecoverably, but have been placed under the rule of those holy and blessed orders which we have described; and by availing themselves of the aid of these, and being remoulded by salutary principles and discipline, they may recover themselves, and be restored to their condition of happiness. From all which I am of opinion, so far as I can see, that this order of the human race has been appointed in order that in the future world, or in ages to come, when there shall be the new heavens and new earth, spoken of by Isaiah, it may be restored to that unity promised by the Lord Jesus in His prayer to God the Father on behalf of His disciples: "I do not pray for these alone, but for all who shall believe on Me through their word: that they all may be one, as Thou, Father, art in Me, and I in Thee, that they also may be one in Us;" and again, when He says: "That they may be one, even as We are one; I in them, and Thou in Me, that they may be made perfect in one." And this is further confirmed by the language of the Apostle Paul: "Until we all come in the unity of the faith to a perfect man, to the measure of the stature of the fulness of Christ." And in keeping with this is the declaration of the same apostle, when he exhorts us, who even in the present life are placed in the Church, in which is the form of that kingdom which is to come, to this same similitude of unity: "That ye all speak the same thing, and that there be no divisions among you; but that ye be perfectly joined together in the same mind and in the same judgment."

3. It is to be borne in mind, however, that certain beings who fell away from that one beginning of which we have spoken, have sunk to such a depth of unworthiness and wickedness as to be deemed altogether undeserving of that training and instruction by which the human race, while in the flesh, are trained and instructed with the assistance of the heavenly powers; and continue, on the contrary, in a state of enmity and opposition to those who are receiving this instruction and teaching. And hence it is that the whole of this mortal

life is full of struggles and trials, caused by the opposition and enmity of those who fell from a better condition without at all looking back, and who are called the devil and his angels, and the other orders of evil, which the apostle classed among the opposing powers. But whether any of these orders who act under the government of the devil, and obey his wicked commands, will in a future world be converted to righteousness because of their possessing the faculty of freedom of will, or whether persistent and inveterate wickedness may be changed by the power of habit into nature, is a result which you yourself, reader, may approve of, if neither in these present worlds which are seen and temporal, nor in those which are unseen and are eternal, that portion is to differ wholly from the final unity and fitness of things. But in the meantime, both in those temporal worlds which are seen, as well as in those eternal worlds which are invisible, all those beings are arranged, according to a regular plan, in the order and degree of their merits; so that some of them in the first, others in the second, some even in the last times, after having undergone heavier and severer punishments, endured for a lengthened period, and for many ages, so to speak, improved by this stern method of training, and restored at first by the instruction of the angels, and subsequently by the powers of a higher grade, and thus advancing through each stage to a better condition, reach even to that which is invisible and eternal, having travelled through, by a kind of training, every single office of the heavenly powers. From which, I think, this will appear to follow as an inference, that every rational nature may, in passing from one order to another, go through each to all, and advance from all to each, while made the subject of various degrees of proficiency and failure according to its own actions and endeavours, put forth in the enjoyment of its power of freedom of will.

4. But since Paul says that certain things are visible and temporal, and others besides these invisible and eternal, we proceed to inquire how those things which are seen are temporal—whether because there will be nothing at all after them in all those periods of the coming world, in which that dispersion and separation from the one beginning is undergoing a process of restoration to one and the same end and likeness; or because, while the form of those things which are seen passes away, their essential nature is subject to no corruption. And Paul seems to confirm the latter view, when he says, "For the fashion of this world passeth away." David also appears to assert the same in the words, "The heavens shall perish, but Thou shalt endure; and they all shall wax old as a garment, and Thou shalt change them like a vesture, and like a vestment they shall be changed." For if the heavens are to be

changed, assuredly that which is changed does not perish, and if the fashion of the world passes away, it is by no means an annihilation or destruction of their material substance that is shown to take place, but a kind of change of quality and transformation of appearance. Isaiah also, in declaring prophetically that there will be a new heaven and a new earth, undoubtedly suggests a similar view. For this renewal of heaven and earth, and this transmutation of the form of the present world, and this changing of the heavens will undoubtedly be prepared for those who are walking along that way which we have pointed out above, and are tending to that goal of happiness to which, it is said, even enemies themselves are to be subjected, and in which God is said to be "all and in all." And if any one imagine that at the end material, i.e., bodily, nature will be entirely destroyed, he cannot in any respect meet my view, how beings so numerous and powerful are able to live and to exist without bodies, since it is an attribute of the divine nature alone—i.e., of the Father, Son, and Holy Spirit—to exist without any material substance, and without partaking in any degree of a bodily adjunct. Another, perhaps, may say that in the end every bodily substance will be so pure and refined as to be like the aether, and of a celestial purity and clearness. How things will be, however, is known with certainty to God alone, and to those who are His friends through Christ and the Holy Spirit.

CHAPTER VII—ON INCORPOREAL AND CORPOREAL BEINGS

1. The subjects considered in the previous chapter have been spoken of in general language, the nature of rational beings being discussed more by way of intelligent inference than strict dogmatic definition, with the exception of the place where we treated, to the best of our ability, of the persons of Father, Son, and Holy Spirit. We have now to ascertain what those matters are which it is proper to treat in the following pages according to our dogmatic belief, i.e., in agreement with the creed of the Church. All souls and all rational natures, whether holy or wicked, were formed or created, and all these, according to their proper nature, are incorporeal; but although incorporeal, they were nevertheless created, because all things were made by God through Christ, as John teaches in a general way in his Gospel, saying, "In the beginning was the Word, and the Word was with God, and the Word was God. The same was in the beginning with God. All things were made by Him, and without Him was nothing made." The Apostle Paul, moreover, describing created things by species and numbers and

orders, speaks as follows, when showing that all things were made through Christ: "And in Him were all things created, that are in heaven, and that are in earth, visible and invisible, whether they be thrones, or dominions, or principalities, or powers: all things were created by Him, and in Him: and He is before all, and He is the head." He therefore manifestly declares that in Christ and through Christ were all things made and created, whether things visible, which are corporeal, or things invisible, which I regard as none other than incorporeal and spiritual powers. But of those things which he had termed generally corporeal or incorporeal, he seems to me, in the words that follow, to enumerate the various kinds, viz., thrones, dominions, principalities, powers, influences.

These matters now have been previously mentioned by us, as we are desirous to come in an orderly manner to the investigation of the sun, and moon, and stars by way of logical inference, and to ascertain whether they also ought properly to be reckoned among the principalities on account of their being said to be created in *Archas*, i.e., for the government of day and night; or whether they are to be regarded as having only that government of day and night which they discharge by performing the office of illuminating them, and are not in reality chief of that order of principalities.

2. Now, when it is said that all things were made by Him, and that in Him were all things created, both things in heaven and things on earth, there can be no doubt that also those things which are in the firmament, which is called heaven, and in which those luminaries are said to be placed, are included amongst the number of heavenly things. And secondly, seeing that the course of the discussion has manifestly discovered that all things were made or created, and that amongst created things there is nothing which may not admit of good and evil, and be capable of either, what are we to think of the following opinion which certain of our friends entertain regarding sun, moon, and stars, viz., that they are unchangeable, and incapable of becoming the opposite of what they are? Not a few have held that view even regarding the holy angels, and certain heretics also regarding souls, which they call spiritual natures.

In the first place, then, let us see what reason itself can discover respecting sun, moon, and stars,—whether the opinion, entertained by some, of their unchangeableness be correct,—and let the declarations of holy Scripture, as far as possible, be first adduced. For Job appears to assert that not only may the stars be subject to sin, but even that they are actually not clean from the contagion of it. The following are his words: "The stars also are not clean in Thy sight." Nor is this to be understood of the splendour of their physical substance, as if one were to say, for example, of a garment, that it is not clean; for if such were the meaning, then the accusation of a want of cleanness in the splendour of their bodily substance would imply an injurious reflection upon their Creator. For if they are unable, through their own diligent efforts, either to acquire for themselves a body of greater brightness, or through their sloth to make the one they have less pure, how should they incur censure for being stars that are not clean, if they receive no praise because they are so?

3. But to arrive at a clearer understanding on these matters, we ought first to inquire after this point, whether it is allowable to suppose that they are living and rational beings; then, in the next place, whether their souls came into existence at the same time with their bodies, or seem to be anterior to them; and also whether, after the end of the world, we are to understand that they are to be released from their bodies; and whether, as we cease to live, so they also will cease from illuminating the world. Although this inquiry may seem to be somewhat bold, yet, as we are incited by the desire of ascertaining the truth as far as possible, there seems no absurdity in attempting an investigation of the subject agreeably to the grace of the Holy Spirit.

We think, then, that they may be designated as living beings, for this reason, that they are said to receive commandments from God, which is ordinarily the case only with rational beings. "I have given a commandment to all the stars," says the Lord. What, now, are these commandments? Those, namely, that each star, in its order and course, should bestow upon the world the amount of splendour which has been entrusted to it. For those which are called "planets" move in orbits of one kind, and those which are termed aplaneis are different. Now it manifestly follows from this, that neither can the movement of that body take place without a soul, nor can living things be at any time without motion. And seeing that the stars move with such order and regularity, that their movements never appear to be at any time subject to derangement, would it not be the height of folly to say that so orderly an observance of method and plan could be carried out or accomplished by irrational beings? In the writings of Jeremiah, indeed, the moon is called the queen of heaven. Yet if the stars are living and rational beings, there will undoubtedly appear among them both an advance and a falling back. For the language of Job, "the stars are not clean in His sight," seems to me to convey some such idea.

4. And now we have to ascertain whether those beings which in the course of the discussion we have discovered to possess life and reason, were endowed with a soul along with their bodies at the time

mentioned in Scripture, when "God made two great lights, the greater light to rule the day, and the lesser light to rule the night, and the stars also," or whether their spirit was implanted in them, not at the creation of their bodies, but from without, after they had been already made. I, for my part, suspect that the spirit was implanted in them from without; but it will be worth while to prove this from Scripture: for it will seem an easy matter to make the assertion on conjectural grounds, while it is more difficult to establish it by the testimony of Scripture. Now it may be established conjecturally as follows. If the soul of a man, which is certainly inferior while it remains the soul of a man, was not formed along with his body, but is proved to have been implanted strictly from without, much more must this be the case with those living beings which are called heavenly. For, as regards man, how could the soul of him, viz., Jacob, who supplanted his brother in the womb, appear to be formed along with his body? Or how could his soul, or its images, be formed along with his body, who, while lying in his mother's womb, was filled with the Holy Ghost? I refer to John leaping in his mother's womb, and exulting because the voice of the salutation of Mary had come to the ears of his mother Elisabeth. How could his soul and its images be formed along with his body, who, before he was created in the womb, is said to be known to God, and was sanctified by Him before his birth? Some, perhaps, may think that God fills individuals with His Holy Spirit, and bestows upon them sanctification, not on grounds of justice and according to their deserts; but undeservedly. And how shall we escape that declaration: "Is there unrighteousness with God? God forbid!" or this: "Is there respect of persons with God?" For such is the defence of those who maintain that souls come into existence with bodies. So far, then, as we can form an opinion from a comparison with the condition of man, I think it follows that we must hold the same to hold good with heavenly beings, which reason itself and scriptural authority show us to be the case with men.

5. But let us see whether we can find in holy Scripture any indications properly applicable to these heavenly existences. The following is the statement of the Apostle Paul: "The creature was made subject to vanity, not willingly, but by reason of Him who subjected the same in hope, because the creature itself also shall be delivered from the bondage of corruption into the glorious liberty of the children of God." To what vanity, pray, was the creature made subject, or what creature is referred to, or how is it said "not willingly," or "in hope of what?" And in what way is the creature itself to be delivered from the bondage of corruption? Elsewhere, also, the same apostle says: "For the expectation of the creature waiteth for the manifestation of the sons

of God." And again in another passage, "And not only we, but the creation itself groaneth together, and is in pain until now." And hence we have to inquire what are the groanings, and what are the pains. Let us see then, in the first place, what is the vanity to which the creature is subject. I apprehend that it is nothing else than the body; for although the body of the stars is ethereal, it is nevertheless material. Whence also Solomon appears to characterize the whole of corporeal nature as a kind of burden which enfeebles the vigour of the soul in the following language: "Vanity of vanities, saith the Preacher; all is vanity. I have looked, and seen all the works that are done under the sun; and, behold, all is vanity." To this vanity, then, is the creature subject, that creature especially which, being assuredly the greatest in this world, holds also a distinguished principality of labour, i.e., the sun, and moon, and stars, are said to be subject to vanity, because they are clothed with bodies, and set apart to the office of giving light to the human race. "And this creature," he remarks, "was subjected to vanity not willingly." For it did not undertake a voluntary service to vanity, but because it was the will of Him who made it subject, and because of the promise of the Subjector to those who were reduced to this unwilling obedience, that when the ministry of their great work was performed, they were to be freed from this bondage of corruption and vanity when the time of the glorious redemption of God's children should have arrived. And the whole of creation, receiving this hope, and looking for the fulfilment of this promise now, in the meantime, as having an affection for those whom it serves, groans along with them, and patiently suffers with them, hoping for the fulfilment of the promises. See also whether the following words of Paul can apply to those who, although not willingly, yet in accordance with the will of Him who subjected them, and in hope of the promises, were made subject to vanity, when he says, "For I could wish to be dissolved," or "to return and be with Christ, which is far better." For I think that the sun might say in like manner, "I would desire to be dissolved," or "to return and be with Christ, which is far better." Paul indeed adds, "Nevertheless, to abide in the flesh is more needful for you;" while the sun may say, "To abide in this bright and heavenly body is more necessary, on account of the manifestation of the sons of God." The same views are to be believed and expressed regarding the moon and stars.

Let us see now what is the freedom of the creature, or the termination of its bondage. When Christ shall have delivered up the kingdom to God even the Father, then also those living things, when they shall have first been made the kingdom of Christ, shall be delivered, along with the whole of that kingdom, to the rule of the

54

Father, that when God shall be all in all, they also, since they are a part of all things, may have God in themselves, as He is in all things.

CHAPTER VIII—ON THE ANGELS

1. A similar method must be followed in treating of the angels; nor are we to suppose that it is the result of accident that a particular office is assigned to a particular angel: as to Raphael, e.g., the work of curing and healing; to Gabriel, the conduct of wars; to Michael, the duty of attending to the prayers and supplications of mortals. For we are not to imagine that they obtained these offices otherwise than by their own merits, and by the zeal and excellent qualities which they severally displayed before this world was formed; so that afterwards in the order of archangels, this or that office was assigned to each one, while others deserved to be enrolled in the order of angels, and to act under this or that archangel, or that leader or head of an order. All of which things were disposed, as I have said, not indiscriminately and fortuitously, but by a most appropriate and just decision of God, who arranged them according to deserts, in accordance with His own approval and judgment: so that to one angel the Church of the Ephesians was to be entrusted; to another, that of the Smyrnaeans; one angel was to be Peter's, another Paul's; and so on through every one of the little ones that are in the Church, for such and such angels as even daily behold the face of God must be assigned to each one of them; and there must also be some angel that encampeth round about them that fear God. All of which things, assuredly, it is to be believed, are not performed by accident or chance, or because they (the angels) were so created, lest on that view the Creator should be accused of partiality; but it is to be believed that they were conferred by God, the just and impartial Ruler of all things, agreeably to the merits and good qualities and mental vigour of each individual spirit.

2. And now let us say something regarding those who maintain the existence of a diversity of spiritual natures, that we may avoid falling into the silly and impious fables of such as pretend that there is a diversity of spiritual natures both among heavenly existences and human souls, and for that reason allege that they were called into being by different creators; for while it seems, and is really, absurd that to one and the same Creator should be ascribed the creation of different natures of rational beings, they are nevertheless ignorant of the cause of that diversity. For they say that it seems inconsistent for one and the same Creator, without any existing ground of merit, to confer upon some beings the power of dominion, and to subject others again to

authority; to bestow a principality upon some, and to render others subordinate to rulers. Which opinions indeed, in my judgment, are completely rejected by following out the reasoning explained above, and by which it was shown that the cause of the diversity and variety among these beings is due to their conduct, which has been marked either with greater earnestness or indifference, according to the goodness or badness of their nature, and not to any partiality on the part of the Disposer. But that this may more easily be shown to be the case with heavenly beings, let us borrow an illustration from what either has been done or is done among men, in order that from visible things we may, by way of consequence, behold also things invisible.

Paul and Peter are undoubtedly proved to have been men of a spiritual nature. When, therefore, Paul is found to have acted contrary to religion, in having persecuted the Church of God, and Peter to have committed so grave a sin as, when questioned by the maid-servant, to have asserted with an oath that he did not know who Christ was, how is it possible that these—who, according to those persons of whom we speak, were spiritual beings—should fall into sins of such a nature, especially as they are frequently in the habit of saying that a good tree cannot bring forth evil fruits? And if a good tree cannot produce evil fruit, and as, according to them, Peter and Paul were sprung from the root of a good tree, how should they be deemed to have brought forth fruits so wicked? And if they should return the answer which is generally invented, that it was not Paul who persecuted, but some other person, I know not whom, who was in Paul; and that it was not Peter who uttered the denial, but some other individual in him; how should Paul say, if he had not sinned, that "I am not worthy to be called an apostle, because I persecuted the Church of God?" Or why did Peter weep most bitterly, if it were another than he who sinned? From which all their silly assertions will be proved to be baseless.

3. According to our view, there is no rational creature which is not capable both of good and evil. But it does not follow, that because we say there is no nature which may not admit evil, we therefore maintain that every nature has admitted evil, i.e., has become wicked. As we may say that the nature of every man admits of his being a sailor, but it does not follow from that, that every man will become so; or, again, it is possible for every one to learn grammar or medicine, but it is not therefore proved that every man is either a physician or a grammarian; so, if we say that there is no nature which may not admit evil, it is not necessarily indicated that it has done so. For, in our view, not even the devil himself was incapable of good; but although capable of admitting good, he did not therefore also desire it, or make any effort after virtue.

For, as we are taught by those quotations which we adduced from the prophets, there was once a time when he was good, when he walked in the paradise of God between the cherubim. As he, then, possessed the power either of receiving good or evil, but fell away from a virtuous course, and turned to evil with all the powers of his mind, so also other creatures, as having a capacity for either condition, in the exercise of the freedom of their will, flee from evil, and cleave to good. There is no nature, then, which may not admit of good or evil, except the nature of God—the fountain of all good things—and of Christ; for it is wisdom, and wisdom assuredly cannot admit folly; and it is righteousness, and righteousness will never certainly admit of unrighteousness; and it is the Word, or Reason, which certainly cannot be made irrational; nay, it is also the light, and it is certain that the darkness does not receive the light. In like manner, also, the nature of the Holy Spirit, being holy, does not admit of pollution; for it is holy by nature, or essential being. If there is any other nature which is holy, it possesses this property of being made holy by the reception or inspiration of the Holy Spirit, not having it by nature, but as an accidental quality, for which reason it may be lost, in consequence of being accidental. So also a man may possess an accidental righteousness, from which it is possible for him to fall away. Even the wisdom which a man has is still accidental, although it be within our own power to become wise, if we devote ourselves to wisdom with the zeal and effort of our life; and if we always pursue the study of it, we may always be participators of wisdom: and that result will follow either in a greater or less degree, according to the desert of our life or the amount of our zeal. For the goodness of God, as is worthy of Him, incites and attracts all to that blissful end, where all pain, and sadness, and sorrow fall away and disappear.

4. I am of opinion, then, so far as appears to me, that the preceding discussion has sufficiently proved that it is neither from want of discrimination, nor from any accidental cause, either that the "principalities" hold their dominion, or the other orders of spirits have obtained their respective offices; but that they have received the steps of their rank on account of their merits, although it is not our privilege to know or inquire what those acts of theirs were, by which they earned a place in any particular order. It is sufficient only to know this much, in order to demonstrate the impartiality and righteousness of God, that, conformably with the declaration of the Apostle Paul, "there is no acceptance of persons with Him," who rather disposes everything according to the deserts and moral progress of each individual. So, then, the angelic office does not exist except as a consequence of their

desert; nor do "powers" exercise power except in virtue of their moral progress; nor do those which are called "seats," i.e., the powers of judging and ruling, administer their powers unless by merit; nor do "dominions" rule undeservedly, for that great and distinguished order of rational creatures among celestial existences is arranged in a glorious variety of offices. And the same view is to be entertained of those opposing influences which have given themselves up to such places and offices, that they derive the property by which they are made "principalities," or "powers," or rulers of the darkness of the world, or spirits of wickedness, or malignant spirits, or unclean demons, not from their essential nature, nor from their being so created, but have obtained these degrees in evil in proportion to their conduct, and the progress which they made in wickedness. And that is a second order of rational creatures, who have devoted themselves to wickedness in so headlong a course, that they are unwilling rather than unable to recall themselves; the thirst for evil being already a passion, and imparting to them pleasure. But the third order of rational creatures is that of those who are judged fit by God to replenish the human race, i.e., the souls of men, assumed in consequence of their moral progress into the order of angels; of whom we see some assumed into the number: those, viz., who have been made the sons of God, or the children of the resurrection, or who have abandoned the darkness, and have loved the light, and have been made children of the light; or those who, proving victorious in every struggle, and being made men of peace, have been the sons of peace, and the sons of God; or those who, mortifying their members on the earth, and, rising above not only their corporeal nature, but even the uncertain and fragile movements of the soul itself, have united themselves to the Lord, being made altogether spiritual, that they may be for ever one spirit with Him, discerning along with Him each individual thing, until they arrive at a condition of perfect spirituality, and discern all things by their perfect illumination in all holiness through the word and wisdom of God, and are themselves altogether undistinguishable by any one.

We think that those views are by no means to be admitted, which some are wont unnecessarily to advance and maintain, viz., that souls descend to such a pitch of abasement that they forget their rational nature and dignity, and sink into the condition of irrational animals, either large or small; and in support of these assertions they generally quote some pretended statements of Scripture, such as, that a beast, to which a woman has unnaturally prostituted herself, shall be deemed equally guilty with the woman, and shall be ordered to be stoned; or that a bull which strikes with its horn, shall be put to death in the same way; or even the speaking of Balaam's ass, when God opened its mouth, and the dumb beast of burden, answering with human voice, reproved the madness of the prophet. All of which assertions we not only do not receive, but, as being contrary to our belief, we refute and reject. After the refutation and rejection of such perverse opinions, we shall show, at the proper time and place, how those passages which they quote from the sacred Scriptures ought to be understood.

FRAGMENT FROM THE FIRST BOOK OF THE DE PRINCIPIIS.
Translated by Jerome in His Epistle to Avitus.

"It is an evidence of great negligence and sloth, that each one should fall down to such (a pitch of degradation), and be so emptied, as that, in coming to evil, he may be fastened to the gross body of irrational beasts of burden."

ANOTHER FRAGMENT FROM THE SAME.
Translated in the Same Epistle to Avitus.

"At the end and consummation of the world, when souls and rational creatures shall have been sent forth as from bolts and barriers, some of them walk slowly on account of their slothful habits, others fly with rapid flight on account of their diligence. And since all are possessed of free-will, and may of their own accord admit either of good or evil, the former will be in a worse condition than they are at present, while the latter will advance to a better state of things; because different conduct and varying wills will admit of a different condition in either direction, i.e., angels may become men or demons, and again from the latter they may rise to be men or angels."

BOOK II

CHAPTER I—ON THE WORLD

1. ALTHOUGH all the discussions in the preceding book have had reference to the world and its arrangements, it now seems to follow that we should specially re-discuss a few points respecting the world itself, i.e., its beginning and end, or those dispensations of Divine Providence which have taken place between the beginning and the end, or those events which are supposed to have occurred before the creation of the world, or are to take place after the end.

In this investigation, the first point which clearly appears is, that the world in all its diversified and varying conditions is composed not only of rational and diviner natures, and of a diversity of bodies, but of dumb animals, wild and tame beasts, of birds, and of all things which live in the waters; then, secondly, of places, i.e., of the heaven or heavens, and of the earth or water, as well as of the air, which is intermediate, and which they term aether, and of everything which proceeds from the earth or is born in it. Seeing, then, there is so great a variety in the world, and so great a diversity among rational beings themselves, on account of which every other variety and diversity also is supposed to have come into existence, what other cause than this ought to be assigned for the existence of the world, especially if we have regard to that end by means of which it was shown in the preceding book that all things are to be restored to their original condition? And if this should seem to be logically stated, what other cause, as we have already said, are we to imagine for so great a diversity in the world, save the diversity and variety in the movements and declensions of those who fell from that primeval unity and harmony in which they were at first created by God, and who, being driven from that state of goodness, and drawn in various directions by the harassing influence of different motives and desires, have changed, according to their different tendencies, the single and undivided goodness of their nature into minds of various sorts?

2. But God, by the ineffable skill of His wisdom, transforming and restoring all things, in whatever manner they are made, to some useful aim, and to the common advantage of all, recalls those very creatures which differed so much from each other in mental conformation to one agreement of labour and purpose; so that, although they are under the influence of different motives, they nevertheless complete the fulness and perfection of one world, and the very variety of minds tends

to one end of perfection. For it is one power which grasps and holds together all the diversity of the world, and leads the different movements towards one work, lest so immense an undertaking as that of the world should be dissolved by the dissensions of souls. And for this reason we think that God, the Father of all things, in order to ensure the salvation of all His creatures through the ineffable plan of His word and wisdom, so arranged each of these, that every spirit, whether soul or rational existence, however called, should not be compelled by force, against the liberty of his own will, to any other course than that to which the motives of his own mind led him (lest by so doing the power of exercising free-will should seem to be taken away, which certainly would produce a change in the nature of the being itself); and that the varying purposes of these would be suitably and usefully adapted to the harmony of one world, by some of them requiring help, and others being able to give it, and others again being the cause of struggle and contest to those who are making progress, amongst whom their diligence would be deemed more worthy of approval, and the place of rank obtained after victory be held with greater certainty, which should be established by the difficulties of the contest.

3. Although the whole world is arranged into offices of different kinds, its condition, nevertheless, is not to be supposed as one of internal discrepancies and discordances; but as our one body is provided with many members, and is held together by one soul, so I am of opinion that the whole world also ought to be regarded as some huge and immense animal, which is kept together by the power and reason of God as by one soul. This also, I think, is indicated in sacred Scripture by the declaration of the prophet, "Do not I fill heaven and earth? saith the Lord;" and again, "The heaven is My throne, and the earth is My footstool;" and by the Saviour's words, when He says that we are to swear "neither by heaven, for it is God's throne; nor by the earth, for it is His footstool." To the same effect also are the words of Paul, in his address to the Athenians, when he says, "In Him we live, and move, and have our being." For how do we live, and move, and have our being in God, except by His comprehending and holding together the whole world by His power? And how is heaven the throne of God, and the earth His footstool, as the Saviour Himself declares, save by His power filling all things both in heaven and earth, according to the Lord's own words? And that God, the Father of all things, fills and holds together the world with the fulness of His power, according to those passages which we have quoted, no one, I think, will have any difficulty in admitting. And now, since the course of the preceding

discussion has shown that the different movements of rational beings, and their varying opinions, have brought about the diversity that is in the world, we must see whether it may not be appropriate that this world should have a termination like its beginning. For there is no doubt that its end must be sought amid much diversity and variety; which variety, being found to exist in the termination of the world, will again furnish ground and occasion for the diversities of the other world which is to succeed the present.

4. If now, in the course of our discussion, it has been ascertained that these things are so, it seems to follow that we next consider the nature of corporeal being, seeing the diversity in the world cannot exist without bodies. It is evident from the nature of things themselves, that bodily nature admits of diversity and variety of change, so that it is capable of undergoing all possible transformations, as, e.g., the conversion of wood into fire, of fire into smoke, of smoke into air, of oil into fire. Does not food itself, whether of man or of animals, exhibit the same ground of change? For whatever we take as food, is converted into the substance of our body. But how water is changed into earth or into air, and air again into fire, or fire into air, or air into water, although not difficult to explain, yet on the present occasion it is enough merely to mention them, as our object is to discuss the nature of bodily matter. By matter, therefore, we understand that which is placed under bodies, viz., that by which, through the bestowing and implanting of qualities, bodies exist; and we mention four qualities—heat, cold, dryness, humidity. These four qualities being implanted in the *hule*, or matter (for matter is found to exist in its own nature without those qualities before mentioned), produce the different kinds of bodies. Although this matter is, as we have said above, according to its own proper nature without qualities, it is never found to exist without a quality. And I cannot understand how so many distinguished men have been of opinion that this matter, which is so great, and possesses such properties as to enable it to be sufficient for all the bodies in the world which God willed to exist, and to be the attendant and slave of the Creator for whatever forms and species He wished in all things, receiving into itself whatever qualities He desired to bestow upon it, was uncreated, i.e., not formed by God Himself, who is the Creator of all things, but that its nature and power were the result of chance. And I am astonished that they should find fault with those who deny either God's creative power or His providential administration of the world, and accuse them of impiety for thinking that so great a work as the world could exist without an architect or overseer; while they themselves incur a similar charge of impiety in saying that matter is

uncreated, and co-eternal with the uncreated God. According to this view, then, if we suppose for the sake of argument that matter did not exist, as these maintain, saying that God could not create anything when nothing existed, without doubt He would have been idle, not having matter on which to operate, which matter they say was furnished Him not by His own arrangement, but by accident; and they think that this, which was discovered by chance, was able to suffice Him for an undertaking of so vast an extent, and for the manifestation of the power of His might, and by admitting the plan of all His wisdom, might be distinguished and formed into a world. Now this appears to me to be very absurd, and to be the opinion of those men who are altogether ignorant of the power and intelligence of uncreated nature. But that we may see the nature of things a little more clearly, let it be granted that for a little time matter did not exist, and that God, when nothing formerly existed, caused those things to come into existence which He desired, why are we to suppose that God would create matter either better or greater, or of another kind, than that which He did produce from His own power and wisdom, in order that that might exist which formerly did not? Would He create a worse and inferior matter, or one the same as that which they call uncreated? Now I think it will very easily appear to any one, that neither a better nor inferior matter could have assumed the forms and species of the world, if it had not been such as that which actually did assume them. And does it not then seem impious to call that uncreated, which, if believed to be formed by God, would doubtless be found to be such as that which they call uncreated?

5. But that we may believe on the authority of holy Scripture that such is the case, hear how in the book of Maccabees, where the mother of seven martyrs exhorts her son to endure torture, this truth is confirmed; for she says, "I ask of thee, my son, to look at the heaven and the earth, and at all things which are in them, and beholding these, to know that God made all these things when they did not exist." In the book of the Shepherd also, in the first commandment, he speaks as follows: "First of all believe that there is one God who created and arranged all things, and made all things to come into existence, and out of a state of nothingness." Perhaps also the expression in the Psalms has reference to this: "He spake, and they were made; He commanded, and they were created." For the words, "He spake, and they were made," appear to show that the substance of those things which exist is meant; while the others, "He commanded, and they were created," seem spoken of the qualities by which the substance itself has been moulded.

CHAPTER II—ON THE PERPETUITY OF BODILY NATURE

1. On this topic some are wont to inquire whether, as the Father generates an uncreated Son, and brings forth a Holy Spirit, not as if He had no previous existence, but because the Father is the origin and source of the Son or Holy Spirit, and no anteriority or posteriority can be understood as existing in them; so also a similar kind of union or relationship can be understood as subsisting between rational natures and bodily matter. And that this point may be more fully and thoroughly examined, the commencement of the discussion is generally directed to the inquiry whether this very bodily nature, which bears the lives and contains the movements of spiritual and rational minds, will be equally eternal with them, or will altogether perish and be destroyed. And that the question may be determined with greater precision, we have, in the first place, to inquire if it is possible for rational natures to remain altogether incorporeal after they have reached the summit of holiness and happiness (which seems to me a most difficult and almost impossible attainment), or whether they must always of necessity be united to bodies. If, then, any one could show a reason why it was possible for them to dispense wholly with bodies, it will appear to follow, that as a bodily nature, created out of nothing after intervals of time, was produced when it did not exist, so also it must cease to be when the purposes which it served had no longer an existence.

2. If, however, it is impossible for this point to be at all maintained, viz., that any other nature than the Father, Son, and Holy Spirit can live without a body, the necessity of logical reasoning compels us to understand that rational natures were indeed created at the beginning, but that material substance was separated from them only in thought and understanding, and appears to have been formed for them, or after them, and that they never have lived nor do live without it; for an incorporeal life will rightly be considered a prerogative of the Trinity alone. As we have remarked above, therefore, that material substance of this world, possessing a nature admitting of all possible transformations, is, when dragged down to beings of a lower order, moulded into the crasser and more solid condition of a body, so as to distinguish those visible and varying forms of the world; but when it becomes the servant of more perfect and more blessed beings, it shines in the splendour of celestial bodies, and adorns either the angels of God or the sons of the resurrection with the clothing of a spiritual body, out of all which will be filled up the diverse and varying state of the one world. But if any one should desire to discuss these matters more fully,

it will be necessary, with all reverence and fear of God, to examine the sacred Scriptures with greater attention and diligence, to ascertain whether the secret and hidden sense within them may perhaps reveal anything regarding these matters; and something may be discovered in their abstruse and mysterious language, through the demonstration of the Holy Spirit to those who are worthy, after many testimonies have been collected on this very point.

CHAPTER III—ON THE BEGINNING OF THE WORLD, AND ITS CAUSES

1. The next subject of inquiry is, whether there was any other world before the one which now exists; and if so, whether it was such as the present, or somewhat different, or inferior; or whether there was no world at all, but something like that which we understand will be after the end of all things, when the kingdom shall be delivered up to God, even the Father; which nevertheless may have been the end of another world,—of that, namely, after which this world took its beginning; and whether the various lapses of intellectual natures provoked God to produce this diverse and varying condition of the world. This point also, I think, must be investigated in a similar way, viz., whether after this world there will be any (system of) preservation and amendment, severe indeed, and attended with much pain to those who were unwilling to obey the word of God, but a process through which, by means of instruction and rational training, those may arrive at a fuller understanding of the truth who have devoted themselves in the present life to these pursuits, and who, after having had their minds purified, have advanced onwards so as to become capable of attaining divine wisdom; and after this the end of all things will immediately follow, and there will be again, for the correction and improvement of those who stand in need of it, another world, either resembling that which now exists, or better than it, or greatly inferior; and how long that world, whatever it be that is to come after this, shall continue; and if there will be a time when no world shall anywhere exist, or if there has been a time when there was no world at all; or if there have been, or will be several; or if it shall ever come to pass that there will be one resembling another, like it in every respect, and indistinguishable from it.

2. That it may appear more clearly, then, whether bodily matter can exist during intervals of time, and whether, as it did not exist before it was made, so it may again be resolved into non-existence, let us see, first of all, whether it is possible for any one to live without a body. For if one person can live without a body, all things also may dispense with

them; seeing our former treatise has shown that all things tend towards one end. Now, if all things may exist without bodies, there will undoubtedly be no bodily substance, seeing there will be no use for it. But how shall we understand the words of the apostle in those passages, in which, discussing the resurrection of the dead, he says, "This corruptible must put on incorruption, and this mortal must put on immortality. When this corruptible shall have put on incorruption, and this mortal shall have put on immortality, then shall be brought to pass the saying which is written, Death is swallowed up in victory! Where, O death, is thy victory? O death, thy sting has been swallowed up: the sting of death is sin, and the strength of sin is the law." Some such meaning, then, as this, seems to be suggested by the apostle. For can the expression which he employs, "this corruptible," and "this mortal," with the gesture, as it were, of one who touches or points out, apply to anything else than to bodily matter? This matter of the body, then, which is now corruptible shall put on incorruption when a perfect soul, and one furnished with the marks of incorruption, shall have begun to inhabit it. And do not be surprised if we speak of a perfect soul as the clothing of the body (which, on account of the Word of God and His wisdom, is now named incorruption), when Jesus Christ Himself, who is the Lord and Creator of the soul, is said to be the clothing of the saints, according to the language of the apostle, "Put ye on the Lord Jesus Christ." As Christ, then, is the clothing of the soul, so for a kind of reason sufficiently intelligible is the soul said to be the clothing of the body, seeing it is an ornament to it, covering and concealing its mortal nature. The expression, then, "This corruptible must put on incorruption," is as if the apostle had said, "This corruptible nature of the body must receive the clothing of incorruption—a soul possessing in itself incorruptibility," because it has been clothed with Christ, who is the Wisdom and Word of God. But when this body, which at some future period we shall possess in a more glorious state, shall have become a partaker of life, it will then, in addition to being immortal, become also incorruptible. For whatever is mortal is necessarily also corruptible; but whatever is corruptible cannot also be said to be mortal. We say of a stone or a piece of wood that it is corruptible, but we do not say that it follows that it is also mortal. But as the body partakes of life, then because life may be, and is, separated from it, we consequently name it mortal, and according to another sense also we speak of it as corruptible. The holy apostle therefore, with remarkable insight, referring to the general first cause of bodily matter, of which (matter), whatever be the qualities with which it is endowed (now indeed carnal, but by and by more refined and pure, which are termed

66

spiritual), the soul makes constant use, says, "This corruptible must put on incorruption." And in the second place, looking to the special cause of the body, he says, "This mortal must put on immortality." Now, what else will incorruption and immortality be, save the wisdom, and the word, and the righteousness of God, which mould, and clothe, and adorn the soul? And hence it happens that it is said, "The corruptible will put on incorruption, and the mortal immortality." For although we may now make great proficiency, yet as we only know in part, and prophesy in part, and see through a glass, darkly, those very things which we seem to understand, this corruptible does not yet put on incorruption, nor is this mortal yet clothed with immorality; and as this training of ours in the body is protracted doubtless to a longer period, up to the time, viz., when those very bodies of ours with which we are enveloped may, on account of the word of God, and His wisdom and perfect righteousness, earn incorruptibility and immortality, therefore is it said, "This corruptible must put on incorruption, and this mortal must put on immortality."

3. But, nevertheless, those who think that rational creatures can at any time lead an existence out of the body, may here raise such questions as the following. If it is true that this corruptible shall put on incorruption, and this mortal put on immortality, and that death is swallowed up at the end; this shows that nothing else than a material nature is to be destroyed, on which death could operate, while the mental acumen of those who are in the body seems to be blunted by the nature of corporeal matter. If, however, they are out of the body, then they will altogether escape the annoyance arising from a disturbance of that kind. But as they will not be able immediately to escape all bodily clothing, they are just to be considered as inhabiting more refined and purer bodies, which possess the property of being no longer overcome by death, or of being wounded by its sting; so that at last, by the gradual disappearance of the material nature, death is both swallowed up, and even at the end exterminated, and all its sting completely blunted by the divine grace which the soul has been rendered capable of receiving, and has thus deserved to obtain incorruptibility and immortality. And then it will be deservedly said by all, "O death, where is thy victory? O death, where is thy sting? The sting of death is sin." If these conclusions, then, seem to hold good, it follows that we must believe our condition at some future time to be incorporeal; and if this is admitted, and all are said to be subjected to Christ, this (incorporeity) also must necessarily be bestowed on all to whom the subjection to Christ extends; since all who are subject to Christ will be in the end subject to God the Father, to whom Christ is

said to deliver up the kingdom; and thus it appears that then also the need of bodies will cease. And if it ceases, bodily matter returns to nothing, as formerly also it did not exist.

Now let us see what can be said in answer to those who make these assertions. For it will appear to be a necessary consequence that, if bodily nature be annihilated, it must be again restored and created; since it seems a possible thing that rational natures, from whom the faculty of free-will is never taken away, may be again subjected to movements of some kind, through the special act of the Lord Himself, lest perhaps, if they were always to occupy a condition that was unchangeable, they should be ignorant that it is by the grace of God and not by their own merit that they have been placed in that final state of happiness; and these movements will undoubtedly again be attended by variety and diversity of bodies, by which the world is always adorned; nor will it ever be composed (of anything) save of variety and diversity,—an effect which cannot be produced without a bodily matter.

4. And now I do not understand by what proofs they can maintain their position, who assert that worlds sometimes come into existence which are not dissimilar to each other, but in all respects equal. For if there is said to be a world similar in all respects (to the present), then it will come to pass that Adam and Eve will do the same things which they did before: there will be a second time the same deluge, and the same Moses will again lead a nation numbering nearly six hundred thousand out of Egypt; Judas will also a second time betray the Lord; Paul will a second time keep the garments of those who stoned Stephen; and everything which has been done in this life will be said to be repeated,—a state of things which I think cannot be established by any reasoning, if souls are actuated by freedom of will, and maintain either their advance or retrogression according to the power of their will. For souls are not driven on in a cycle which returns after many ages to the same round, so as either to do or desire this or that; but at whatever point the freedom of their own will aims, thither do they direct the course of their actions. For what these persons say is much the same as if one were to assert that if a medimnus of grain were to be poured out on the ground, the fall of the grain would be on the second occasion identically the same as on the first, so that every individual grain would lie for the second time close beside that grain where it had been thrown before, and so the medimnus would be scattered in the same order, and with the same marks as formerly; which certainly is an impossible result with the countless grains of a medimnus, even if they were to be poured out without ceasing for many ages. So therefore it seems to me impossible for a world to be restored for the second time,

with the same order and with the same amount of births, and deaths, and actions; but that a diversity of worlds may exist with changes of no unimportant kind, so that the state of another world may be for some unmistakeable reasons better (than this), and for others worse, and for others again intermediate. But what may be the number or measure of this I confess myself ignorant, although, if any one can tell it, I would gladly learn.

5. But this world, which is itself called an age, is said to be the conclusion of many ages. Now the holy apostle teaches that in that age which preceded this, Christ did not suffer, nor even in the age which preceded that again; and I know not that I am able to enumerate the number of anterior ages in which He did not suffer. I will show, however, from what statements of Paul I have arrived at this understanding. He says, "But now once in the consummation of ages, He was manifested to take away sin by the sacrifice of Himself." For He says that He was once made a victim, and in the consummation of ages was manifested to take away sin. Now that after this age, which is said to be formed for the consummation of other ages, there will be other ages again to follow, we have clearly learned from Paul himself, who says, "That in the ages to come He might show the exceeding riches of His grace in His kindness towards us." He has not said, "in the age to come," nor "in the two ages to come," whence I infer that by his language many ages are indicated. Now if there is something greater than ages, so that among created beings certain ages may be understood, but among other beings which exceed and surpass visible creatures, (ages still greater) (which perhaps will be the case at the restitution of all things, when the whole universe will come to a perfect termination), perhaps that period in which the consummation of all things will take place is to be understood as something more than an age. But here the authority of holy Scripture moves me, which says, "For an age and more." Now this word "more" undoubtedly means something greater than an age; and see if that expression of the Saviour, "I will that where I am, these also may be with Me; and as I and Thou are one, these also may be one in Us," may not seem to convey something more than an age and ages, perhaps even more than ages of ages,—that period, viz., when all things are now no longer in an age, but when God is in all.

6. Having discussed these points regarding the nature of the world to the best of our ability, it does not seem out of place to inquire what is the meaning of the term world, which in holy Scripture is shown frequently to have different significations. For what we call in Latin *mundus*, is termed in Greek *kosmos*, and *kosmos* signifies not only a world,

but also an ornament. Finally, in Isaiah, where the language of reproof is directed to the chief daughters of Sion, and where he says, "Instead of an ornament of a golden head, thou wilt have baldness on account of thy works," he employs the same term to denote ornament as to denote the world, viz., *kosmos*. For the plan of the world is said to be contained in the clothing of the high priest, as we find in the Wisdom of Solomon, where he says, "For in the long garment was the whole world." That earth of ours, with its inhabitants, is also termed the world, as when Scripture says, "The whole world lieth in wickedness." Clement indeed, a disciple of the apostles, makes mention of those whom the Greeks called *Antichthones*, and other parts of the earth, to which no one of our people can approach, nor can any one of those who are there cross over to us, which he also termed worlds, saying, "The ocean is impassable to men; and those are worlds which are on the other side of it, which are governed by these same arrangements of the ruling God." That universe which is bounded by heaven and earth is also called a world, as Paul declares: "For the fashion of this world will pass away." Our Lord and Saviour also points out a certain other world besides this visible one, which it would indeed be difficult to describe and make known. He says, "I am not of this world." For, as if He were of a certain other world, He says, "I am not of this world." Now, of this world we have said beforehand, that the explanation was difficult; and for this reason, that there might not be afforded to any an occasion of entertaining the supposition that we maintain the existence of certain images which the Greeks call "ideas:" for it is certainly alien to our (writers) to speak of an incorporeal world existing in the imagination alone, or in the fleeting world of thoughts; and how they can assert either that the Saviour comes from thence, or that the saints will go thither, I do not see. There is no doubt, however, that something more illustrious and excellent than this present world is pointed out by the Saviour, at which He incites and encourages believers to aim. But whether that world to which He desires to allude be far separated and divided from this either by situation, or nature, or glory; or whether it be superior in glory and quality, but confined within the limits of this world (which seems to me more probable), is nevertheless uncertain, and in my opinion an unsuitable subject for human thought. But from what Clement seems to indicate when he says, "The ocean is impassable to men, and those worlds which are behind it," speaking in the plural number of the worlds which are behind it, which he intimates are administered and governed by the same providence of the Most High God, he appears to throw out to us some germs of that view by which the whole universe of existing things, celestial and super-celestial, earthly and infernal, is generally called one perfect world, within which, or by which, other worlds, if any there are, must be supposed to be contained. For which reason he wished the globe of the sun or moon, and of the other bodies called planets, to be each termed worlds. Nay, even that pre-eminent globe itself which they call the non-wandering (*aplane*), they nevertheless desire to have properly called world. Finally, they summon the book of Baruch the prophet to bear witness to this assertion, because in it the seven worlds or heavens are more clearly pointed out. Nevertheless, above that sphere which they call non-wandering (*aplane*), they will have another sphere to exist, which they say, exactly as our heaven contains all things which are under it, comprehends by its immense size and indescribable extent the spaces of all the spheres together within its more magnificent circumference; so that all things are within it, as this earth of ours is under heaven. And this also is believed to be called in the holy Scriptures the good land, and the land of the living, having its own heaven, which is higher, and in which the names of the saints are said to be written, or to have been written, by the Saviour; by which heaven that earth is confined and shut in, which the Saviour in the Gospel promises to the meek and merciful. For they would have this earth of ours, which formerly was named "Dry," to have derived its appellation from the name of that earth, as this heaven also was named firmament from the title of that heaven. But we have treated at greater length of such opinions in the place where we had to inquire into the meaning of the declaration, that in the beginning "God made the heavens and the earth." For another heaven and another earth are shown to exist besides that "firmament" which is said to have been made after the second day, or that "dry land" which was afterwards called "earth." Certainly, what some say of this world, that it is corruptible because it was made, and yet is not corrupted, because the will of God, who made it and holds it together lest corruption should rule over it, is stronger and more powerful than corruption, may more correctly be supposed of that world which we have called above a "non-wandering" sphere, since by the will of God it is not at all subject to corruption, for the reason that it has not admitted any causes of corruption, seeing it is the world of the saints and of the thoroughly purified, and not of the wicked, like that world of ours. We must see, moreover, lest perhaps it is with reference to this that the apostle says, "While we look not at the things which are seen, but at the things which are not seen; for the things which are seen are temporal, but the things which are unseen are eternal. For we know that if our earthly house of this tabernacle were dissolved, we have a building of God, an house not made with hands,

71

eternal in the heavens." And when he says elsewhere, "Because I shall see the heavens, the works of Thy fingers," and when God said, regarding all things visible, by the mouth of His prophet, "My hand has formed all these things," He declares that that eternal house in the heavens which He promises to His saints was not made with hands, pointing out, doubtless, the difference of creation in things which are seen and in those which are not seen. For the same thing is not to be understood by the expressions, "those things which are not seen," and "those things which are invisible." For those things which are invisible are not only not seen, but do not even possess the property of visibility, being what the Greeks call *asomata*, i.e., incorporeal; whereas those of which Paul says, "They are not seen," possess indeed the property of being seen, but, as he explains, are not yet beheld by those to whom they are promised.

7. Having sketched, then, so far as we could understand, these three opinions regarding the end of all things, and the supreme blessedness, let each one of our readers determine for himself, with care and diligence, whether any one of them can be approved and adopted. For it has been said that we must suppose either that an incorporeal existence is possible, after all things have become subject to Christ, and through Christ to God the Father, when God will be all and in all; or that when, notwithstanding all things have been made subject to Christ, and through Christ to God (with whom they formed also one spirit, in respect of spirits being rational natures), then the bodily substance itself also being united to most pure and excellent spirits, and being changed into an ethereal condition in proportion to the quality or merits of those who assume it (according to the apostle's words, "We also shall be changed"), will shine forth in splendour; or at least that when the fashion of those things which are seen passes away, and all corruption has been shaken off and cleansed away, and when the whole of the space occupied by this world, in which the spheres of the planets are said to be, has been left behind and beneath, then is reached the fixed abode of the pious and the good situated above that sphere, which is called non-wandering (*aplanes*), as in a good land, in a land of the living, which will be inherited by the meek and gentle; to which land belongs that heaven (which, with its more magnificent extent, surrounds and contains that land itself) which is called truly and chiefly heaven, in which heaven and earth, the end and perfection of all things, may be safely and most confidently placed,—where, viz., these, after their apprehension and their chastisement for the offences which they have undergone by way of purgation, may, after having fulfilled and discharged every obligation, deserve a habitation in that land; while

those who have been obedient to the word of God, and have henceforth by their obedience shown themselves capable of wisdom, are said to deserve the kingdom of that heaven or heavens; and thus the prediction is more worthily fulfilled, "Blessed are the meek, for they shall inherit the earth;" and, "Blessed are the poor in spirit, for they shall inherit the kingdom of heaven;" and the declaration in the Psalm, "He shall exalt thee, and thou shalt inherit the land." For it is called a descent to this earth, but an exaltation to that which is on high. In this way, therefore, does a sort of road seem to be opened up by the departure of the saints from that earth to those heavens; so that they do not so much appear to abide in that land, as to inhabit it with an intention, viz., to pass on to the inheritance of the kingdom of heaven, when they have reached that degree of perfection also.

CHAPTER IV—THE GOD OF THE LAW AND THE PROPHETS, AND THE FATHER OF OUR LORD JESUS CHRIST, IS THE SAME GOD

1. Having now briefly arranged these points in order as we best could, it follows that, agreeably to our intention from the first, we refute those who think that the Father of our Lord Jesus Christ is a different God from Him who gave the answers of the law to Moses, or commissioned the prophets, who is the God of our fathers, Abraham, Isaac, and Jacob. For in this article of faith, first of all, we must be firmly grounded. We have to consider, then, the expression of frequent recurrence in the Gospels, and subjoined to all the acts of our Lord and Saviour, "that it might be fulfilled which was spoken by this or that prophet," it being manifest that the prophets are the prophets of that God who made the world. From this therefore we draw the conclusion, that He who sent the prophets, Himself predicted what was to be foretold of Christ. And there is no doubt that the Father Himself, and not another different from Him, uttered these predictions. The practice, moreover, of the Saviour or His apostles, frequently quoting illustrations from the Old Testament, shows that they attribute authority to the ancients. The injunction also of the Saviour, when exhorting His disciples to the exercise of kindness, "Be ye perfect, even as your Father who is in heaven is perfect; for He commands His sun to rise upon the evil and the good, and sendeth rain on the just and on the unjust," most evidently suggests even to a person of feeble understanding, that He is proposing to the imitation of His disciples no other God than the maker of heaven and the bestower of the rain. Again, what else does the expression, which ought to be used by those

who pray, "Our Father who art in heaven," appear to indicate, save that God is to be sought in the better parts of the world, i.e., of His creation? Further, do not those admirable principles which He lays down respecting oaths, saying that we ought not to "swear either by heaven, because it is the throne of God; nor by the earth, because it is His footstool," harmonize most clearly with the words of the prophet, "Heaven is My throne, and the earth is My footstool?" And also when casting out of the temple those who sold sheep, and oxen, and doves, and pouring out the tables of the money-changers, and saying, "Take these things, hence, and do not make My Father's house a house of merchandise," He undoubtedly called Him His Father, to whose name Solomon had raised a magnificent temple. The words, moreover, "Have you not read what was spoken by God to Moses: I am the God of Abraham, and the God of Isaac, and the God of Jacob; He is not a God of the dead, but of the living," most clearly teach us, that He called the God of the patriarchs (because they were holy, and were alive) the God of the living, the same, viz., who had said in the prophets, "I am God, and besides Me there is no God." For if the Saviour, knowing that He who is written in the law is the God of Abraham, and that it is the same who says, "I am God, and besides Me there is no God," acknowledges that very one to be His Father who is ignorant of the existence of any other God above Himself, as the heretics suppose, He absurdly declares Him to be His Father who does not know of a greater God. But if it is not from ignorance, but from deceit, that He says there is no other God than Himself, then it is a much greater absurdity to confess that His Father is guilty of falsehood. From all which this conclusion is arrived at, that He knows of no other Father than God, the Founder and Creator of all things.

2. It would be tedious to collect out of all the passages in the Gospels the proofs by which the God of the law and of the Gospels is shown to be one and the same. Let us touch briefly upon the Acts of the Apostles, where Stephen and the other apostles address their prayers to that God who made heaven and earth, and who spoke by the mouth of His holy prophets, calling Him the "God of Abraham, of Isaac, and of Jacob;" the God who "brought forth His people out of the land of Egypt." Which expressions undoubtedly clearly direct our understandings to faith in the Creator, and implant an affection for Him in those who have learned piously and faithfully thus to think of Him; according to the words of the Saviour Himself, who, when He was asked which was the greatest commandment in the law, replied, "Thou shalt love the Lord thy God with all thy heart, and with all thy soul, and with all thy mind. And the second is like unto it, Thou shalt

love thy neighbour as thyself." And to these He added: "On these two commandments hang all the law and the prophets." How is it, then, that He commends to him whom He was instructing, and was leading to enter on the office of a disciple, this commandment above all others, by which undoubtedly love was to be kindled in him towards the God of that law, inasmuch as such had been declared by the law in these very words? But let it be granted, notwithstanding all these most evident proofs, that it is of some other unknown God that the Saviour says, "Thou shalt love the Lord thy God with all thy heart," etc., etc. How, in that case, if the law and the prophets are, as they say, from the Creator, i.e., from another God than He whom He calls good, shall that appear to be logically said which He subjoins, viz., that "on these two commandments hang the law and the prophets?" For how shall that which is strange and foreign to God depend upon Him? And when Paul says, "I thank my God, whom I serve in my spirit from my forefathers with pure conscience," he clearly shows that he came not to some new God, but to Christ. For what other forefathers of Paul can be intended, except those of whom he says, "Are they Hebrews? so am I: are they Israelites? so am I." Nay, will not the very preface of his Epistle to the Romans clearly show the same thing to those who know how to understand the letters of Paul, viz., what God he preaches? For his words are: "Paul, the servant of Jesus Christ, called to be an apostle, set apart to the Gospel of God, which He had promised afore by His prophets in the holy Scriptures concerning His Son, who was made of the seed of David according to the flesh, and who was declared to be the Son of God with power, according to the spirit of holiness, by the resurrection from the dead of Christ Jesus our Lord," etc. Moreover, also the following, "Thou shalt not muzzle the mouth of the ox that treadeth out the corn. Doth God take care for oxen? or saith he it altogether for our sakes? For our sakes, no doubt, this is written, that he that plougheth should plough in hope, and he that thresheth in hope of partaking of the fruits." By which he manifestly shows that God, who gave the law on our account, i.e., on account of the apostles, says, "Thou shalt not muzzle the mouth of the ox that treadeth out the corn;" whose care was not for oxen, but for the apostles, who were preaching the Gospel of Christ. In other passages also, Paul, embracing the promises of the law, says, "Honour thy father and thy mother, which is the first commandment with promise; that it may be well with thee, and that thy days may be long upon the land, the good land, which the Lord thy God will give thee." By which he undoubtedly makes known that the law, and the God of the law, and His promises, are pleasing to him.

3. But as those who uphold this heresy are sometimes accustomed to mislead the hearts of the simple by certain deceptive sophisms, I do not consider it improper to bring forward the assertions which they are in the habit of making, and to refute their deceit and falsehood. The following, then, are their declarations. It is written, that "no man hath seen God at any time." But that God whom Moses preaches was both seen by Moses himself, and by his fathers before him; whereas He who is announced by the Saviour has never been seen at all by any one. Let us therefore ask them and ourselves whether they maintain that He whom they acknowledge to be God, and allege to be a different God from the Creator, is visible or invisible. And if they shall say that He is visible, besides being proved to go against the declaration of Scripture, which says of the Saviour, "He is the image of the invisible God, the first-born of every creature," they will fall also into the absurdity of asserting that God is corporeal. For nothing can be seen except by help of form, and size, and colour, which are special properties of bodies. And if God is declared to be a body, then He will also be found to be material, since every body is composed of matter. But if He be composed of matter, and matter is undoubtedly corruptible, then, according to them, God is liable to corruption! We shall put to them a second question. Is matter made, or is it uncreated, i.e., not made? And if they shall answer that it is not made, i.e., uncreated, we shall ask them if one portion of matter is God, and the other part the world? But if they shall say of matter that it is made, it will undoubtedly follow that they confess Him whom they declare to be God to have been made!— a result which certainly neither their reason nor ours can admit. But they will say, God is invisible. And what will you do? If you say that He is invisible by nature, then neither ought He to be visible to the Saviour. Whereas, on the contrary, God, the Father of Christ, is said to be seen, because "he who sees the Son," he says, "sees also the Father." This certainly would press us very hard, were the expression not understood by us more correctly of understanding, and not of seeing. For he who has understood the Son will understand the Father also. In this way, then, Moses too must be supposed to have seen God, not beholding Him with the bodily eye, but understanding Him with the vision of the heart and the perception of the mind, and that only in some degree. For it is manifest that He, viz., who gave answers to Moses, said, "You shall not see My face, but My hinder parts." These words are, of course, to be understood in that mystical sense which is befitting divine words, those old wives' fables being rejected and despised which are invented by ignorant persons respecting the anterior and posterior parts of God. Let no one indeed suppose that we have indulged any feeling of impiety

in saying that even to the Saviour the Father is not visible. Let him consider the distinction which we employ in dealing with heretics. For we have explained that it is one thing to see and to be seen, and another to know and to be known, or to understand and to be understood. To see, then, and to be seen, is a property of bodies, which certainly will not be appropriately applied either to the Father, or to the Son, or to the Holy Spirit, in their mutual relations with one another. For the nature of the Trinity surpasses the measure of vision, granting to those who are in the body, i.e., to all other creatures, the property of vision in reference to one another. But to a nature that is incorporeal and for the most part intellectual, no other attribute is appropriate save that of knowing or being known, as the Saviour Himself declares when He says, "No man knoweth the Son, save the Father; nor does any one know the Father, save the Son, and he to whom the Son will reveal Him." It is clear, then, that He has not said, "No one has seen the Father, save the Son;" but, "No one knoweth the Father, save the Son."

4. And now, if, on account of those expressions which occur in the Old Testament, as when God is said to be angry or to repent, or when any other human affection or passion is described, (our opponents) think that they are furnished with grounds for refuting us, who maintain that God is altogether impassible, and is to be regarded as wholly free from all affections of that kind, we have to show them that similar statements are found even in the parables of the Gospel; as when it is said, that he who planted a vineyard, and let it out to husbandmen, who slew the servants that were sent to them, and at last put to death even the son, is said in anger to have taken away the vineyard from them, and to have delivered over the wicked husbandmen to destruction, and to have handed over the vineyard to others, who would yield him the fruit in its season. And so also with regard to those citizens who, when the head of the household had set out to receive for himself a kingdom, sent messengers after him, saying, "We will not have this man to reign over us;" for the head of the household having obtained the kingdom, returned, and in anger commanded them to be put to death before him, and burned their city with fire. But when we read either in the Old Testament or in the New of the anger of God, we do not take such expressions literally, but seek in them a spiritual meaning, that we may think of God as He deserves to be thought of. And on these points, when expounding the verse in the second Psalm, "Then shall He speak to them in His anger, and trouble them in His fury," we showed, to the best of our poor ability, how such an expression ought to be understood.

CHAPTER V—ON JUSTICE AND GOODNESS

1. Now, since this consideration has weight with some, that the leaders of that heresy (of which we have been speaking) think they have established a kind of division, according to which they have declared that justice is one thing and goodness another, and have applied this division even to divine things, maintaining that the Father of our Lord Jesus Christ is indeed a good God, but not a just one, whereas the God of the law and the prophets is just, but not good; I think it necessary to return, with as much brevity as possible, an answer to these statements. These persons, then, consider goodness to be some such affection as would have benefits conferred on all, although the recipient of them be unworthy and undeserving of any kindness; but here, in my opinion, they have not rightly applied their definition, inasmuch as they think that no benefit is conferred on him who is visited with any suffering or calamity. Justice, on the other hand, they view as that quality which rewards every one according to his deserts. But here, again, they do not rightly interpret the meaning of their own definition. For they think that it is just to send evils upon the wicked and benefits upon the good; i.e., so that, according to their view, the just God does not appear to wish well to the bad, but to be animated by a kind of hatred against them. And they gather together instances of this, wherever they find a history in the Scriptures of the Old Testament, relating, e.g., the punishment of the deluge, or the fate of those who are described as perishing in it, or the, destruction of Sodom and Gomorrah by a shower of fire and brimstone, or the falling of all the people in the wilderness on account of their sins, so that none of those who had left Egypt were found to have entered the promised land, with the exception of Joshua and Caleb. Whereas from the New Testament they gather together words of compassion and piety, through which the disciples are trained by the Saviour, and by which it seems to be declared that no one is good save God the Father only; and by this means they have ventured to style the Father of the Saviour Jesus Christ a good God, but to say that the God of the world is a different one, whom they are pleased to term just, but not also good.

2. Now I think they must, in the first place, be required to show, if they can, agreeably to their own definition, that the Creator is just in punishing according to their deserts, either those who perished at the time of the deluge, or the inhabitants of Sodom, or those who had quitted Egypt, seeing we sometimes behold committed crimes more wicked and detestable than those for which the above-mentioned persons were destroyed, while we do not yet see every sinner paying

the penalty of his misdeeds. Will they say that He who at one time was just has been made good? Or will they rather be of opinion that He is even now just, but is patiently enduring human offences, while that then He was not even just, inasmuch as He exterminated innocent and sucking children along with cruel and ungodly giants? Now, such are their opinions, because they know not how to understand anything beyond the letter; otherwise they would show how it is literal justice for sins to be visited upon the heads of children to the third and fourth generation, and on children's children after them. By us, however, such things are not understood literally; but, as Ezekiel taught when relating the parable, we inquire what is the inner meaning contained in the parable itself. Moreover, they ought to explain this also, how He is just, and rewards every one according to his merits, who punishes earthly-minded persons and the devil, seeing they have done nothing worthy of punishment. For they could not do any good if, according to them, they were of a wicked and ruined nature. For as they style Him a judge, He appears to be a judge not so much of actions as of natures; and if a bad nature cannot do good, neither can a good nature do evil. Then, in the next place, if He whom they call good is good to all, He is undoubtedly good also to those who are destined to perish. And why does He not save them? If He does not desire to do so, He will be no longer good; if He does desire it, and cannot effect it, He will not be omnipotent. Why do they not rather hear the Father of our Lord Jesus Christ in the Gospels, preparing fire for the devil and his angels? And how shall that proceeding, as penal as it is sad, appear to be, according to their view, the work of the good God? Even the Saviour Himself, the Son of the good God, protests in the Gospels, and declares that "if signs and wonders had been done in Tyre and Sidon, they would have repented long ago, sitting in sackcloth and ashes." And when He had come near to those very cities, and had entered their territory, why, pray, does He avoid entering those cities, and exhibiting to them abundance of signs and wonders, if it were certain that they would have repented, after they had been performed, in sackcloth and ashes? But as He does not do this, He undoubtedly abandons to destruction those whom the language of the Gospel shows not to have been of a wicked or ruined nature, inasmuch as it declares they were capable of repentance. Again, in a certain parable of the Gospel, where the king enters in to see the guests reclining at the banquet, he beheld a certain individual not clothed with wedding raiment, and said to him, "Friend, how camest thou in hither, not having a wedding garment?" and then ordered his servants, "Bind him hand and foot, and cast him into outer darkness; there will be weeping and gnashing of teeth." Let them tell us who is that king who entered in to see the guests, and finding one amongst them with unclean garments, commanded him to be bound by his servants, and thrust out into outer darkness. Is he the same whom they call just? How then had he commanded good and bad alike to be invited, without directing their merits to be inquired into by his servants? By such procedure would be indicated, not the character of a just God who rewards according to men's deserts, as they assert, but of one who displays undiscriminating goodness towards all. Now, if this must necessarily be understood of the good God, i.e., either of Christ or of the Father of Christ, what other objection can they bring against the justice of God's judgment? Nay, what else is there so unjust charged by them against the God of the law as to order him who had been invited by His servants, whom He had sent to call good and bad alike, to be bound hand and foot, and to be thrown into outer darkness, because he had on unclean garments?

3. And now, what we have drawn from the authority of Scripture ought to be sufficient to refute the arguments of the heretics. It will not, however, appear improper if we discuss the matter with them shortly, on the grounds of reason itself. We ask them, then, if they know what is regarded among men as the ground of virtue and wickedness, and if it appears to follow that we can speak of virtues in God, or, as they think, in these two Gods. Let them give an answer also to the question, whether they consider goodness to be a virtue; and as they will undoubtedly admit it to be so, what will they say of injustice? They will never certainly, in my opinion, be so foolish as to deny that justice is a virtue. Accordingly, if virtue is a blessing, and justice is a virtue, then without doubt justice is goodness. But if they say that justice is not a blessing, it must either be an evil or an indifferent thing. Now I think it folly to return any answer to those who say that justice is an evil, for I shall have the appearance of replying either to senseless words, or to men out of their minds. How can that appear an evil which is able to reward the good with blessings, as they themselves also admit? But if they say that it is a thing of indifference, it follows that since justice is so, sobriety also, and prudence, and all the other virtues, are things of indifference. And what answer shall we make to Paul, when he says, "If there be any virtue, and, if there be any praise, think on these things, which ye have learned, and received, and heard, and seen in me?" Let them learn, therefore, by searching the holy Scriptures, what are the individual virtues, and not deceive themselves by saying that that God who rewards every one according to his merits, does, through hatred of evil, recompense the wicked with evil, and not because those who have sinned need to be treated with severer

80

remedies, and because He applies to them those measures which, with the prospect of improvement, seem nevertheless, for the present, to produce a feeling of pain. They do not read what is written respecting the hope of those who were destroyed in the deluge; of which hope Peter himself thus speaks in his first Epistle: "That Christ, indeed, was put to death in the flesh, but quickened by the Spirit, by which He went and preached to the spirits who were kept in prison, who once were unbelievers, when they awaited the long-suffering of God in the days of Noah, when the ark was preparing, in which a few, i.e., eight souls, were saved by water. Whereunto also baptism by a like figure now saves you." And with regard to Sodom and Gomorrah, let them tell us whether they believe the prophetic words to be those of the Creator God—of Him, viz., who is related to have rained upon them a shower of fire and brimstone. What does Ezekiel the prophet say of them? "Sodom," he says, "shall be restored to her former condition." But why, in afflicting those who are deserving of punishment, does He not afflict them for their good?—who also says to Chaldea, "Thou hast coals of fire, sit upon them; they will be a help to thee." And of those also who fell in the desert, let them hear what is related in the seventy-eighth Psalm, which bears the superscription of Asaph; for he says, "When He slew them, then they sought Him." He does not say that some sought Him after others had been slain, but he says that the destruction of those who were killed was of such a nature that, when put to death, they sought God. By all which it is established, that the God of the law and the Gospels is one and the same, a just and good God, and that He confers benefits justly, and punishes with kindness; since neither goodness without justice, nor justice without goodness, can display the (real) dignity of the divine nature.

We shall add the following remarks, to which we are driven by their subtleties. If justice is a different thing from goodness, then, since evil is the opposite of good, and injustice of justice, injustice will doubtless be something else than an evil; and as, in your opinion, the just man is not good, so neither will the unjust man be wicked; and again, as the good man is not just, so the wicked man also will not be unjust. But who does not see the absurdity, that to a good God one should be opposed that is evil; while to a just God, whom they allege to be inferior to the good, no one should be opposed! For there is none who can be called unjust, as there is a Satan who is called wicked. What, then, are we to do? Let us give up the position which we defend, for they will not be able to maintain that a bad man is not also unjust, and an unjust man wicked. And if these qualities be indissolubly inherent in these opposites, viz., injustice in wickedness, or wickedness in injustice, then unquestionably the good man will be inseparable from the just man, and the just from the good; so that, as we speak of one and the same wickedness in malice and injustice, we may also hold the virtue of goodness and justice to be one and the same.

4. They again recall us, however, to the words of Scripture, by bringing forward that celebrated question of theirs, affirming that it is written, "A bad tree cannot produce good fruits; for a tree is known by its fruit." What, then, is their position? What sort of tree the law is, is shown by its fruits, i.e., by the language of its precepts. For if the law be found to be good, then undoubtedly He who gave it is believed to be a good God. But if it be just rather than good, then God also will be considered a just legislator. The Apostle Paul makes use of no circumlocution, when he says, "The law is good; and the commandment is holy, and just, and good." From which it is clear that Paul had not learned the language of those who separate justice from goodness, but had been instructed by that God, and illuminated by His Spirit, who is at the same time both holy, and good, and just; and speaking by whose Spirit he declared that the commandment of the law was holy, and just, and good. And that he might show more clearly that goodness was in the commandment to a greater degree than justice and holiness, repeating his words, he used, instead of these three epithets, that of goodness alone, saying, "Was then that which is good made death unto me? God forbid." As he knew that goodness was the *genus* of the virtues, and that justice and holiness were *species* belonging to the *genus*, and having in the former verses named *genus* and *species* together, he fell back, when repeating his words, on the *genus* alone. But in those which follow he says, "Sin wrought death in me by that which is good," where he sums up generically what he had beforehand explained specifically. And in this way also is to be understood the declaration, "A good man, out of the good treasure of his heart, bringeth forth good things; and an evil man, out of the evil treasure, bringeth forth evil things." For here also he assumed that there was a *genus* in good or evil, pointing out unquestionably that in a good man there were both justice, and temperance, and prudence, and piety, and everything that can be either called or understood to be good. In like manner also he said that a man was wicked who should without any doubt be unjust, and impure, and unholy, and everything which singly makes a bad man. For as no one considers a man to be wicked without these marks of wickedness (nor indeed can he be so), so also it is certain that without these virtues no one will be deemed to be good. There still remains to them, however, that saying of the Lord in the Gospel, which they think is given them in a special manner as a shield, viz., "There is none good

but one, God the Father." This word they declare is peculiar to the Father of Christ, who, however, is different from the God who is Creator of all things, to which Creator he gave no appellation of goodness. Let us see now if, in the Old Testament, the God of the prophets and the Creator and Legislator of the word is not called good. What are the expressions which occur in the Psalms? "How good is God to Israel, to the upright in heart!" and, "Let Israel now say that He is good, that His mercy endureth for ever;" the language in the Lamentations of Jeremiah, "The Lord is good to them that wait for Him, to the soul that seeketh Him." As therefore God is frequently called good in the Old Testament, so also the Father of our Lord Jesus Christ is styled just in the Gospels. Finally, in the Gospel according to John, our Lord Himself, when praying to the Father, says, "O just Father, the world hath not known Thee." And lest perhaps they should say that it was owing to His having assumed human flesh that He called the Creator of the world "Father," and styled Him "Just," they are excluded from such a refuge by the words that immediately follow, "The world hath not known Thee." But, according to them, the world is ignorant of the good God alone. For the world unquestionably recognises its Creator, the Lord Himself saying that the world loveth what is its own. Clearly, then, He whom they consider to be the good God, is called just in the Gospels. Any one may at leisure gather together a greater number of proofs, consisting of those passages, where in the New Testament the Father of our Lord Jesus Christ is called just, and in the Old also, where the Creator of heaven and earth is called good; so that the heretics, being convicted by numerous testimonies, may perhaps some time be put to the blush.

CHAPTER VI—ON THE INCARNATION OF CHRIST

1. It is now time, after this cursory notice of these points, to resume our investigation of the incarnation of our Lord and Saviour, viz., how or why He became man. Having therefore, to the best of our feeble ability, considered His divine nature from the contemplation of His own works rather than from our own feelings, and having nevertheless beheld (with the eye) His visible creation while the invisible creation is seen by faith, because human frailty can neither see all things with the bodily eye nor comprehend them by reason, seeing we men are weaker and frailer than any other rational beings (for those which are in heaven, or are supposed to exist above the heaven, are superior), it remains that we seek a being intermediate between all created things and God, i.e., a Mediator, whom the Apostle Paul styles the "first-born of every

creature." Seeing, moreover, those declarations regarding His majesty which are contained in holy Scripture, that He is called the "image of the invisible God, and the first-born of every creature," and that "in Him were all things created, visible and invisible, whether they be thrones, or dominions, or principalities, or powers, all things were created by Him, and in Him: and He is before all things, and by Him all things consist," who is the head of all things, alone having as head God the Father; for it is written, "The head of Christ is God;" seeing clearly also that it is written, "No one knoweth the Father, save the Son, nor doth any one know the Son, save the Father" (for who can know what wisdom is, save He who called it into being? or, who can understand clearly what truth is, save the Father of truth? who can investigate with certainty the universal nature of His Word, and of God Himself, which nature proceeds from God, except God alone, with whom the Word was), we ought to regard it as certain that this Word, or Reason (if it is to be so termed), this Wisdom, this Truth, is known to no other than the Father only; and of Him it is written, that "I do not think that the world itself could contain the books which might be written," regarding, viz., the glory and majesty of the Son of God. For it is impossible to commit to writing (all) those particulars which belong to the glory of the Saviour. After the consideration of questions of such importance concerning the being of the Son of God, we are lost in the deepest amazement that such a nature, pre-eminent above all others, should have divested itself of its condition of majesty and become man, and tabernacled amongst men, as the grace that was poured upon His lips testifies, and as His heavenly Father bore Him witness, and as is confessed by the various signs and wonders and miracles that were performed by Him; who also, before that appearance of His which He manifested in the body, sent the prophets as His forerunners, and the messengers of His advent; and after His ascension into heaven, made His holy apostles, men ignorant and unlearned, taken from the ranks of tax-gatherers or fishermen, but who were filled with the power of His divinity, to itinerate throughout the world, that they might gather together out of every race and every nation a multitude of devout believers in Himself.

2. But of all the marvellous and mighty acts related of Him, this altogether surpasses human admiration, and is beyond the power of mortal frailness to understand or feel, how that mighty power of divine majesty, that very Word of the Father, and that very wisdom of God, in which were created all things, visible and invisible, can be believed to have existed within the limits of that man who appeared in Judea; nay, that the Wisdom of God can have entered the womb of a woman,

84

and have been born an infant, and have uttered wailings like the cries of little children! And that afterwards it should be related that He was greatly troubled in death, saying, as He Himself declared, "My soul is sorrowful even unto death;" and that at the last He was brought to that death which is accounted the most shameful among men, although He rose again on the third day. Since, then, we see in Him some things so human that they appear to differ in no respect from the common frailty of mortals, and some things so divine that they can appropriately belong to nothing else than to the primal and ineffable nature of Deity, the narrowness of human understanding can find no outlet; but, overcome with the amazement of a mighty admiration, knows not whither to withdraw, or what to take hold of, or whither to turn. If it think of a God, it sees a mortal; if it think of a man, it beholds Him returning from the grave, after overthrowing the empire of death, laden with its spoils. And therefore the spectacle is to be contemplated with all fear and reverence, that the truth of both natures may be clearly shown to exist in one and the same Being; so that nothing unworthy or unbecoming may be perceived in that divine and ineffable substance, nor yet those things which were done be supposed to be the illusions of imaginary appearances. To utter these things in human ears, and to explain them in words, far surpasses the powers either of our rank, or of our intellect and language. I think that it surpasses the power even of the holy apostles; nay, the explanation of that mystery may perhaps be beyond the grasp of the entire creation of celestial powers. Regarding Him, then, we shall state, in the fewest possible words, the contents of our creed rather than the assertions which human reason is wont to advance; and this from no spirit of rashness, but as called for by the nature of our arrangement, laying before you rather (what may be termed) our suspicions than any clear affirmations.

3. The Only-begotten of God, therefore, through whom, as the previous course of the discussion has shown, all things were made, visible and invisible, according to the view of Scripture, both made all things, and loves what He made. For since He is Himself the invisible image of the invisible God, He conveyed invisibly a share in Himself to all His rational creatures, so that each one obtained a part of Him exactly proportioned to the amount of affection with which he regarded Him. But since, agreeably to the faculty of free-will, variety and diversity characterized the individual souls, so that one was attached with a warmer love to the Author of its being, and another with a feebler and weaker regard, that soul (*anima*) regarding which Jesus said, "No one shall take my life (*animam*) from me," inhering, from the beginning of the creation, and afterwards, inseparably and

indissolubly in Him, as being the Wisdom and Word of God, and the Truth and the true Light, and receiving Him wholly, and passing into His light and splendour, was made with Him in a pre-eminent degree one spirit, according to the promise of the apostle to those who ought to imitate it, that "he who is joined in the Lord is one spirit." This substance of a soul, then, being intermediate between God and the flesh—it being impossible for the nature of God to intermingle with a body without an intermediate instrument—the God-man is born, as we have said, that substance being the intermediary to whose nature it was not contrary to assume a body. But neither, on the other hand, was it opposed to the nature of that soul, as a rational existence, to receive God, into whom, as stated above, as into the Word, and the Wisdom, and the Truth, it had already wholly entered. And therefore deservedly is it also called, along with the flesh which it had assumed, the Son of God, and the Power of God, the Christ, and the Wisdom of God, either because it was wholly in the Son of God, or because it received the Son of God wholly into itself. And again, the Son of God, through whom all things were created, is named Jesus Christ and the Son of man. For the Son of God also is said to have died—in reference, viz., to that nature which could admit of death; and He is called the Son of man, who is announced as about to come in the glory of God the Father, with the holy angels. And for this reason, throughout the whole of Scripture, not only is the divine nature spoken of in human words, but the human nature is adorned by appellations of divine dignity. More truly indeed of this than of any other can the statement be affirmed, "They shall both be in one flesh, and are no longer two, but one flesh." For the Word of God is to be considered as being more in one flesh with the soul than a man with his wife. But to whom is it more becoming to be also one spirit with God, than to this soul which has so joined itself to God by love as that it may justly be said to be one spirit with Him?

4. That the perfection of his love and the sincerity of his deserved affection formed for it this inseparable union with God, so that the assumption of that soul was not accidental, or the result of a personal preference, but was conferred as the reward of its virtues, listen to the prophet addressing it thus: "Thou hast loved righteousness, and hated wickedness: therefore God, thy God, hath anointed thee with the oil of gladness above thy fellows." As a reward for its love, then, it is anointed with the oil of gladness; i.e., the soul of Christ along with the Word of God is made Christ. Because to be anointed with the oil of gladness means nothing else than to be filled with the Holy Spirit. And when it is said "above thy fellows," it is meant that the grace of the Spirit was

not given to it as to the prophets, but that the essential fulness of the Word of God Himself was in it, according to the saying of the apostle, "In whom dwelt all the fulness of the Godhead bodily." Finally, on this account he has not only said, "Thou hast loved righteousness;" but he adds, "and Thou hast hated wickedness." For to have hated wickedness is what the Scripture says of Him, that "He did no sin, neither was any guile found in His mouth," and that "He was tempted in all things like as we are, without sin." Nay, the Lord Himself also said, "Which of you will convince Me of sin?" And again He says with reference to Himself, "Behold, the prince of this world cometh, and findeth nothing in Me." All which (passages) show that in Him there was no sense of sin; and that the prophet might show more clearly that no sense of sin had ever entered into Him, he says, "Before the boy could have knowledge to call upon father or mother, He turned away from wickedness."

5. Now, if our having shown above that Christ possessed a rational soul should cause a difficulty to any one, seeing we have frequently proved throughout all our discussions that the nature of souls is capable both of good and evil, the difficulty will be explained in the following way. That the nature, indeed, of His soul was the same as that of all others cannot be doubted, otherwise it could not be called a soul were it not truly one. But since the power of choosing good and evil is within the reach of all, this soul which belonged to Christ elected to love righteousness, so that in proportion to the immensity of its love it clung to it unchangeably and inseparably, so that firmness of purpose, and immensity of affection, and an inextinguishable warmth of love, destroyed all susceptibility (*sensum*) for alteration and change; and that which formerly depended upon the will was changed by the power of long custom into nature; and so we must believe that there existed in Christ a human and rational soul, without supposing that it had any feeling or possibility of sin.

6. To explain the matter more fully, it will not appear absurd to make use of an illustration, although on a subject of so much difficulty it is not easy to obtain suitable illustrations. However, if we may speak without offence, the metal iron is capable of cold and heat. If, then, a mass of iron be kept constantly in the fire, receiving the heat through all its pores and veins, and the fire being continuous and the iron never removed from it, it become wholly converted into the latter; could we at all say of this, which is by nature a mass of iron, that when placed in the fire, and incessantly burning, it was at any time capable of admitting cold? On the contrary, because it is more consistent with truth, do we not rather say, what we often see happening in furnaces, that it has become wholly fire, seeing nothing but fire is visible in it? And if any

one were to attempt to touch or handle it, he would experience the action not of iron, but of fire. In this way, then, that soul which, like an iron in the fire, has been perpetually placed in the Word, and perpetually in the Wisdom, and perpetually in God, is God in all that it does, feels, and understands, and therefore can be called neither convertible nor mutable, inasmuch as, being incessantly heated, it possessed immutability from its union with the Word of God. To all the saints, finally, some warmth from the Word of God must be supposed to have passed; and in this soul the divine fire itself must be believed to have rested, from which some warmth may have passed to others. Lastly, the expression, "God, thy God, anointed thee with the oil of gladness above thy fellows," shows that that soul is anointed in one way with the oil of gladness, i.e., with the word of God and wisdom; and his fellows, i.e., the holy prophets and apostles, in another. For they are said to have "run in the odour of his ointments;" and that soul was the vessel which contained that very ointment of whose fragrance all the worthy prophets and apostles were made partakers. As, then, the substance of an ointment is one thing and its odour another, so also Christ is one thing and His fellows another. And as the vessel itself, which contains the substance of the ointment, can by no means admit any foul smell; whereas it is possible that those who enjoy its odour may, if they remove a little way from its fragrance, receive any foul odour which comes upon them: so, in the same way, was it impossible that Christ, being as it were the vessel itself, in which was the substance of the ointment, should receive an odour of an opposite kind, while they who are His "fellows" will be partakers and receivers of His odour, in proportion to their nearness to the vessel.

7. I think, indeed, that Jeremiah the prophet, also, understanding what was the nature of the wisdom of God in him, which was the same also which he had assumed for the salvation of the world, said, "The breath of our countenance is Christ the Lord, to whom we said, that under His shadow we shall live among the nations." And inasmuch as the shadow of our body is inseparable from the body, and unavoidably performs and repeats its movements and gestures, I think that he, wishing to point out the work of Christ's soul, and the movements inseparably belonging to it, and which accomplished everything according to His movements and will, called this the shadow of Christ the Lord, under which shadow we were to live among the nations. For in the mystery of this assumption the nations live, who, imitating it through faith, come to salvation. David also, when saying, "Be mindful of my reproach, O Lord, with which they reproached me in exchange for Thy Christ," seems to me to indicate the same. And what else does

Paul mean when he says, "Your life is hid with Christ in God;" and again in another passage, "Do you seek a proof of Christ, who speaketh in me?" And now he says that Christ was hid in God. The meaning of which expression, unless it be shown to be something such as we have pointed out above as intended by the prophet in the words "shadow of Christ," exceeds, perhaps, the apprehension of the human mind. But we see also very many other statements in holy Scripture respecting the meaning of the word "shadow," as that well-known one in the Gospel according to Luke, where Gabriel says to Mary, "The Spirit of the Lord shall come upon thee, and the power of the Highest shall overshadow thee." And the apostle says with reference to the law, that they who have circumcision in the flesh, "serve for the similitude and shadow of heavenly things." And elsewhere, "Is not our life upon the earth a shadow?" If, then, not only the law which is upon the earth is a shadow, but also all our life which is upon the earth is the same, and we live among the nations under the shadow of Christ, we must see whether the truth of all these shadows may not come to be known in that revelation, when no longer through a glass, and darkly, but face to face, all the saints shall deserve to behold the glory of God, and the causes and truth of things. And the pledge of this truth being already received through the Holy Spirit, the apostle said, "Yea, though we have known Christ after the flesh, yet now henceforth know we Him no more."

The above, meanwhile, are the thoughts which have occurred to us, when treating of subjects of such difficulty as the incarnation and deity of Christ. If there be any one, indeed, who can discover something better, and who can establish his assertions by clearer proofs from holy Scriptures, let his opinion be received in preference to mine.

CHAPTER VII—ON THE HOLY SPIRIT

1. As, then, after those first discussions which, according to the requirements of the case, we held at the beginning regarding the Father, Son, and Holy Spirit, it seemed right that we should retrace our steps, and show that the same God was the creator and founder of the world, and the Father of our Lord Jesus Christ, i.e., that the God of the law and of the prophets and of the Gospel was one and the same; and that, in the next place, it ought to be shown, with respect to Christ, in what manner He who had formerly been demonstrated to be the Word and Wisdom of God became man; it remains that we now return with all possible brevity to the subject of the Holy Spirit.

It is time, then, that we say a few words to the best of our ability regarding the Holy Spirit, whom our Lord and Saviour in the Gospel according to John has named the Paraclete. For as it is the same God Himself, and the same Christ, so also is it the same Holy Spirit who was in the prophets and apostles, i.e., either in those who believed in God before the advent of Christ, or in those who by means of Christ have sought refuge in God. We have heard, indeed, that certain heretics have dared to say that there are two Gods and two Christs, but we have never known of the doctrine of two Holy Spirits being preached by any one. For how could they maintain this out of Scripture, or what distinction could they lay down between Holy Spirit and Holy Spirit, if indeed any definition or description of Holy Spirit can be discovered? For although we should concede to Marcion or to Valentinus that it is possible to draw distinctions in the question of Deity, and to describe the nature of the good God as one, and that of the just God as another, what will he devise, or what will he discover, to enable him to introduce a distinction in the Holy Spirit? I consider, then, that they are able to discover nothing which may indicate a distinction of any kind whatever.

2. Now we are of opinion that every rational creature, without any distinction, receives a share of Him in the same way as of the Wisdom and of the Word of God. I observe, however, that the chief advent of the Holy Spirit is declared to men, after the ascension of Christ to heaven, rather than before His coming into the world. For, before that, it was upon the prophets alone, and upon a few individuals—if there happened to be any among the people deserving of it—that the gift of the Holy Spirit was conferred; but after the advent of the Saviour, it is written that the prediction of the prophet Joel was fulfilled, "In the last days it shall come to pass, and I will pour out my Spirit upon all flesh, and they shall prophesy," which is similar to the well-known statement, "All nations shall serve Him." By the grace, then, of the Holy Spirit, along with numerous other results, this most glorious consequence is clearly demonstrated, that with regard to those things which were written in the prophets or in the law of Moses, it was only a few persons at that time, viz., the prophets themselves, and scarcely another individual out of the whole nation, who were able to look beyond the mere corporeal meaning and discover something greater, i.e., something spiritual, in the law or in the prophets; but now there are countless multitudes of believers who, although unable to unfold methodically and clearly the results of their spiritual understanding, are nevertheless most firmly persuaded that neither ought circumcision to be understood literally, nor the rest of the Sabbath, nor the pouring out of the blood of an animal, nor that answers were given by God to Moses on these points. And this method of apprehension is undoubtedly suggested to the minds of all by the power of the Holy

Spirit.

3. And as there are many ways of apprehending Christ, who, although He is wisdom, does not act the part or possess the power of wisdom in all men, but only in those who give themselves to the study of wisdom in Him; and who, although called a physician, does not act as one towards all, but only towards those who understand their feeble and sickly condition, and flee to His compassion that they may obtain health; so also I think is it with the Holy Spirit, in whom is contained every kind of gifts. For on some is bestowed by the Spirit the word of wisdom, on others the word of knowledge, on others faith; and so to each individual of those who are capable of receiving Him, is the Spirit Himself made to be that quality, or understood to be that which is needed by the individual who has deserved to participate. These divisions and differences not being perceived by those who hear Him called Paraclete in the Gospel, and not duly considering in consequence of what work or act He is named the Paraclete, they have compared Him to some common spirits or other, and by this means have tried to disturb the Churches of Christ, and so excite dissensions of no small extent among brethren; whereas the Gospel shows Him to be of such power and majesty, that it says the apostles could not yet receive those things which the Saviour wished to teach them until the advent of the Holy Spirit, who, pouring Himself into their souls, might enlighten them regarding the nature and faith of the Trinity. But these persons, because of the ignorance of their understandings, are not only unable themselves logically to state the truth, but cannot even give their attention to what is advanced by us; and entertaining unworthy ideas of His divinity, have delivered themselves over to errors and deceits, being depraved by a spirit of error, rather than instructed by the teaching of the Holy Spirit, according to the declaration of the apostle, "Following the doctrine of devils, forbidding to marry, to the destruction and ruin of many, and to abstain from meats, that by an ostentatious exhibition of stricter observance they may seduce the souls of the innocent."

4. We must therefore know that the Paraclete is the Holy Spirit, who teaches truths which cannot be uttered in words, and which are, so to speak, unutterable, and "which it is not lawful for a man to utter," i.e., which cannot be indicated by human language. The phrase "it is not lawful" is, we think, used by the apostle instead of "it is not possible;" as also is the case in the passage where he says, "All things are lawful for me, but all things are not expedient: all things are lawful for me; but all things edify not." For those things which are in our power because we may have them, he says are lawful for us. But the Paraclete, who is

called the Holy Spirit, is so called from His work of consolation, *paraclesis* being termed in Latin *consolatio*. For if any one has deserved to participate in the Holy Spirit by the knowledge of His ineffable mysteries, he undoubtedly obtains comfort and joy of heart. For since he comes by the teaching of the Spirit to the knowledge of the reasons of all things which happen—how or why they occur—his soul can in no respect be troubled, or admit any feeling of sorrow; nor is he alarmed by anything, since, clinging to the Word of God and His wisdom, he through the Holy Spirit calls Jesus Lord. And since we have made mention of the Paraclete, and have explained as we were able what sentiments ought to be entertained regarding Him; and since our Saviour also is called the Paraclete in the Epistle of John, when he says, "If any of us sin, we have a Paraclete with the Father, Jesus Christ the righteous, and He is the propitiation for our sins;" let us consider whether this term Paraclete should happen to have one meaning when applied to the Saviour, and another when applied to the Holy Spirit. Now Paraclete, when spoken of the Saviour, seems to mean intercessor. For in Greek, Paraclete has both significations—that of intercessor and comforter. On account, then, of the phrase which follows, when he says, "And He is the propitiation for our sins," the name Paraclete seems to be understood in the case of our Saviour as meaning intercessor; for He is said to intercede with the Father because of our sins. In the case of the Holy Spirit, the Paraclete must be understood in the sense of comforter, inasmuch as He bestows consolation upon the souls to whom He openly reveals the apprehension of spiritual knowledge.

CHAPTER VIII—ON THE SOUL (ANIMA)

1. The order of our arrangement now requires us, after the discussion of the preceding subjects, to institute a general inquiry regarding the soul; and, beginning with points of inferior importance, to ascend to those that are of greater. Now, that there are souls in all living things, even in those which live in the waters, is, I suppose, doubted by no one. For the general opinion of all men maintains this; and confirmation from the authority of holy Scripture is added, when it is said that "God made great whales, and every living creature that moveth which the waters brought forth after their kind." It is confirmed also from the common intelligence of reason, by those who lay down in certain words a definition of soul. For soul is defined as follows: a substance *phantastike* and *hormetike*, which may be rendered into Latin, although not so appropriately, *sensibilis et mobilis*. This

certainly may be said appropriately of all living beings, even of those which abide in the waters; and of winged creatures too, this same definition of *anima* may be shown to hold good. Scripture also has added its authority to a second opinion, when it says, "Ye shall not eat the blood, because the life of all flesh is its blood; and ye shall not eat the life with the flesh;" in which it intimates most clearly that the blood of every animal is its life. And if any one now were to ask how it can be said with respect to bees, wasps, and ants, and those other things which are in the waters, oysters and cockles, and all others which are without blood, and are most clearly shown to be living things, that the "life of all flesh is the blood," we must answer, that in living things of that sort the force which is exerted in other animals by the power of red blood is exerted in them by that liquid which is within them, although it be of a different colour; for colour is a thing of no importance, provided the substance be endowed with life. That beasts of burden or cattle of smaller size are endowed with souls, there is, by general assent, no doubt whatever. The opinion of holy Scripture, however, is manifest, when God says, "Let the earth bring forth the living creature after its kind, four-footed beasts, and creeping things, and beasts of the earth after their kind." And now with respect to man, although no one entertains any doubt, or needs to inquire, yet holy Scripture declares that "God breathed into his countenance the breath of life, and man became a living soul." It remains that we inquire respecting the angelic order whether they also have souls, or are souls; and also respecting the other divine and celestial powers, as well as those of an opposite kind. We nowhere, indeed, find any authority in holy Scripture for asserting that either the angels, or any other divine spirits that are ministers of God, either possess souls or are called souls, and yet they are felt by very many persons to be endowed with life. But with regard to God, we find it written as follows: "And I will put My soul upon that soul which has eaten blood, and I will root him out from among his people;" and also in another passage, "Your new moons, and sabbaths, and great days, I will not accept; your fasts, and holidays, and festal days, My soul hateth." And in the twenty-second Psalm, regarding Christ—for it is certain, as the Gospel bears witness, that this Psalm is spoken of Him—the following words occur: "O LORD, be not far from helping me; look to my defence: O God, deliver my soul from the sword, and my beloved one from the hand of the dog;" although there are also many other testimonies respecting the soul of Christ when He tabernacled in the flesh.

2. But the nature of the incarnation will render unnecessary any inquiry into the soul of Christ. For as He truly possessed flesh, so also

He truly possessed a soul. It is difficult indeed both to feel and to state how that which is called in Scripture the soul of God is to be understood; for we acknowledge that nature to be simple, and without any intermixture or addition. In whatever way, however, it is to be understood, it seems, meanwhile, to be named the soul of God; whereas regarding Christ there is no doubt. And therefore there seems to me no absurdity in either understanding or asserting some such thing regarding the holy angels and the other heavenly powers, since that definition of soul appears applicable also to them. For who can rationally deny that they are "sensible and moveable?" But if that definition appear to be correct, according to which a soul is said to be a substance rationally "sensible and moveable," the same definition would seem also to apply to angels. For what else is in them than rational feeling and motion? Now those beings who are comprehended under the same definition have undoubtedly the same substance. Paul indeed intimates that there is a kind of animal-man who, he says, cannot receive the things of the Spirit of God, but declares that the doctrine of the Holy Spirit seems to him foolish, and that he cannot understand what is to be spiritually discerned. In another passage he says it is sown an animal body, and arises a spiritual body, pointing out that in the resurrection of the just there will be nothing of an animal nature. And therefore we inquire whether there happen to be any substance which, in respect of its being *anima*, is imperfect. But whether it be imperfect because it falls away from perfection, or because it was so created by God, will form the subject of inquiry when each individual topic shall begin to be discussed in order. For if the animal man receive not the things of the Spirit of God, and because he is animal, is unable to admit the understanding of a better, i.e., of a divine nature, it is for this reason perhaps that Paul, wishing to teach us more plainly what that is by means of which we are able to comprehend those things which are of the Spirit, i.e., spiritual things, conjoins and associates with the Holy Spirit an understanding rather than a soul. For this, I think, he indicates when he says, "I will pray with the spirit, I will pray with the understanding also; I will sing with the spirit, I will sing with the understanding also." And he does not say that "I will pray with the soul," but with the spirit and the understanding. Nor does he say, "I will sing with the soul," but with the spirit and the understanding.

3. But perhaps this question is asked, If it be the understanding which prays and sings with the spirit, and if it be the same which receives both perfection and salvation, how is it that Peter says, "Receiving the end of your faith, even the salvation of your souls?" If the soul neither prays nor sings with the spirit, how shall it hope for

94

salvation? or when it attains to blessedness, shall it be no longer called a soul? Let us see if perhaps an answer may be given in this way, that as the Saviour came to save what was lost, that which formerly was said to be lost is not lost when it is saved; so also, perhaps, this which is saved is called a soul, and when it has been placed in a state of salvation will receive a name from the Word that denotes its more perfect condition. But it appears to some that this also may be added, that as the thing which was lost undoubtedly existed before it was lost, at which time it was something else than destroyed, so also will be the case when it is no longer in a ruined condition. In like manner also, the soul which is said to have perished will appear to have been something at one time, when as yet it had not perished, and on that account would be termed soul, and being again freed from destruction, it may become a second time what it was before it perished, and be called a soul. But from the very signification of the name soul which the Greek word conveys, it has appeared to a few curious inquirers that a meaning of no small importance may be suggested. For in sacred language God is called a fire, as when Scripture says," Our God is a consuming fire." Respecting the substance of the angels also it speaks as follows: "Who maketh His angels spirits, and His ministers a burning fire;" and in another place, "The angel of the LORD appeared in a flame of fire in the bush." We have, moreover, received a commandment to be "fervent in spirit;" by which expression undoubtedly the Word of God is shown to be hot and fiery. The prophet Jeremiah also hears from Him, who gave him his answers, "Behold, I have given My words into thy mouth a fire." As God, then, is a fire, and the angels a flame of fire, and all the saints are fervent in spirit, so, on the contrary, those who have fallen away from the love of God are undoubtedly said to have cooled in their affection for Him, and to have become cold. For the Lord also says, that, "because iniquity has abounded, the love of many will grow cold." Nay, all things, whatever they are, which in holy Scripture are compared with the hostile power, the devil is said to be perpetually finding cold; and what is found to be colder than he? In the sea also the dragon is said to reign. For the prophet intimates that the serpent and dragon, which certainly is referred to one of the wicked spirits, is also in the sea. And elsewhere the prophet says, "I will draw out my holy sword upon the dragon the flying serpent, upon the dragon the crooked serpent, and will slay him." And again he says: "Even though they hide from my eyes, and descend into the depths of the sea, there will I command the serpent, and it shall bite them." In the book of Job also, he is said to be the king of all things in the waters. The prophet threatens that evils will be kindled by the north wind upon all who inhabit the earth. Now the north wind is described in holy Scripture as cold, according to the statement in the book of Wisdom, "That cold north wind;" which same thing also must undoubtedly be understood of the devil. If, then, those things which are holy are named fire, and light, and fervent, while those which are of an opposite nature are said to be cold; and if the love of many is said to wax cold; we have to inquire whether perhaps the name soul, which in Greek is termed *psuche*, be so termed from growing cold out of a better and more divine condition, and be thence derived, because it seems to have cooled from that natural and divine warmth, and therefore has been placed in its present position, and called by its present name. Finally, see if you can easily find a place in holy Scripture where the soul is properly mentioned in terms of praise: it frequently occurs, on the contrary, accompanied with expressions of censure, as in the passage, "An evil soul ruins him who possesses it;" and, "The soul which sinneth, it shall die." For after it has been said, "All souls are Mine; as the soul of the father, so also the soul of the son is Mine," it seemed to follow that He would say, "The soul that doeth righteousness, it shall be saved," and "The soul which sinneth, it shall die." But now we see that He has associated with the soul what is censurable, and has been silent as to that which was deserving of praise. We have therefore to see if, perchance, as we have said is declared by the name itself, it was called *psuche*, i.e., *anima*, because it has waxed cold from the fervour of just things, and from participation in the divine fire, and yet has not lost the power of restoring itself to that condition of fervour in which it was at the beginning. Whence the prophet also appears to point out some such state of things by the words, "Return, O my soul, unto thy rest." From all which this appears to be made out, that the understanding, falling away from its status and dignity, was made or named soul; and that, if repaired and corrected, it returns to the condition of the understanding.

4. Now, if this be the case, it seems to me that this very decay and falling away of the understanding is not the same in all, but that this conversion into a soul is carried to a greater or less degree in different instances, and that certain understandings retain something even of their former vigour, and others again either nothing or a very small amount. Whence some are found from the very commencement of their lives to be of more active intellect, others again of a slower habit of mind, and some are born wholly obtuse, and altogether incapable of instruction. Our statement, however, that the understanding is converted into a soul, or whatever else seems to have such a meaning, the reader must carefully consider and settle for himself, as these views

are not be regarded as advanced by us in a dogmatic manner, but simply as opinions, treated in the style of investigation and discussion. Let the reader take this also into consideration, that it is observed with regard to the soul of the Saviour, that of those things which are written in the Gospel, some are ascribed to it under the name of soul, and others under that of spirit. For when it wishes to indicate any suffering or perturbation affecting Him, it indicates it under the name of soul; as when it says, "Now is My soul troubled;" and, "My soul is sorrowful, even unto death;" and, "No man taketh My soul from Me, but I lay it down of Myself." Into the hands of His Father He commends not His soul, but His spirit; and when He says that the flesh is weak, He does not say that the soul is willing, but the spirit: whence it appears that the soul is something intermediate between the weak flesh and the willing spirit.

5. But perhaps some one may meet us with one of those objections which we have ourselves warned you of in our statements, and say, "How then is there said to be also a soul of God?" To which we answer as follows: That as with respect to everything corporeal which is spoken of God, such as fingers, or hands, or arms, or eyes, or feet, or mouth, we say that these are not to be understood as human members, but that certain of His powers are indicated by these names of members of the body; so also we are to suppose that it is something else which is pointed out by this title—soul of God. And if it is allowable for us to venture to say anything more on such a subject, the soul of God may perhaps be understood to mean the only-begotten Son of God. For as the soul, when implanted in the body, moves all things in it, and exerts its force over everything on which it operates; so also the only-begotten Son of God, who is His Word and Wisdom, stretches and extends to every power of God, being implanted in it; and perhaps to indicate this mystery is God either called or described in Scripture as a body. We must, indeed, take into consideration whether it is not perhaps on this account that the soul of God may be understood to mean His only-begotten Son, because He Himself came into this world of affliction, and descended into this valley of tears, and into this place of our humiliation; as He says in the Psalm, "Because Thou hast humiliated us in the place of affliction." Finally, I am aware that certain critics, in explaining the words used in the Gospel by the Saviour, "My soul is sorrowful, even unto death," have interpreted them of the apostles, whom He termed His soul, as being better than the rest of His body. For as the multitude of believers is called His body, they say that the apostles, as being better than the rest of the body, ought to be understood to mean His soul.

We have brought forward as we best could these points regarding the rational soul, as topics of discussion for our readers, rather than as dogmatic and well-defined propositions. And with respect to the souls of animals and other dumb creatures, let that suffice which we have stated above in general terms.

CHAPTER IX—ON THE WORLD AND THE MOVEMENTS OF RATIONAL CREATURES, WHETHER GOOD OR BAD; AND ON THE CAUSES OF THEM

1. But let us now return to the order of our proposed discussion, and behold the commencement of creation, so far as the understanding can behold the beginning of the creation of God. In that commencement, then, we are to suppose that God created so great a number of rational or intellectual creatures (or by whatever name they are to be called), which we have formerly termed understandings, as He foresaw would be sufficient. It is certain that He made them according to some definite number, predetermined by Himself: for it is not to be imagined, as some would have it, that creatures have not a limit, because where there is no limit there can neither be any comprehension nor any limitation. Now if this were the case, then certainly created things could neither be restrained nor administered by God. For, naturally, whatever is infinite will also be incomprehensible. Moreover, as Scripture says, "God has arranged all things in number and measure;" and therefore number will be correctly applied to rational creatures or understandings, that they may be so numerous as to admit of being arranged, governed, and controlled by God. But measure will be appropriately applied to a material body; and this measure, we are to believe, was created by God such as He knew would be sufficient for the adorning of the world. These, then, are the things which we are to believe were created by God in the beginning, i.e., before all things. And this, we think, is indicated even in that beginning which Moses has introduced in terms somewhat ambiguous, when he says, "In the beginning God made the heaven and the earth." For it is certain that the firmament is not spoken of, nor the dry land, but that heaven and earth from which this present heaven and earth which we now see afterwards borrowed their names.

2. But since those rational natures, which we have said above were made in the beginning, were created when they did not previously exist, in consequence of this very fact of their nonexistence and

98

commencement of being, are they necessarily changeable and mutable; since whatever power was in their substance was not in it by nature, but was the result of the goodness of their Maker. What they are, therefore, is neither their own nor endures for ever, but is bestowed by God. For it did not always exist; and everything which is a gift may also be taken away, and disappear. And a reason for removal will consist in the movements of souls not being conducted according to right and propriety. For the Creator gave, as an indulgence to the understandings created by Him, the power of free and voluntary action, by which the good that was in them might become their own, being preserved by the exertion of their own will; but slothfulness, and a dislike of labour in preserving what is good, and an aversion to and a neglect of better things, furnished the beginning of a departure from goodness. But to depart from good is nothing else than to be made bad. For it is certain that to want goodness is to be wicked. Whence it happens that, in proportion as one falls away from goodness, in the same proportion does he become involved in wickedness. In which condition, according to its actions, each understanding, neglecting goodness either to a greater or more limited extent, was dragged into the opposite of good, which undoubtedly is evil. From which it appears that the Creator of all things admitted certain seeds and causes of variety and diversity, that He might create variety and diversity in proportion to the diversity of understandings, i.e., of rational creatures, which diversity they must be supposed to have conceived from that cause which we have mentioned above. And what we mean by variety and diversity is what we now wish to explain.

3. Now we term world everything which is above the heavens, or in the heavens, or upon the earth, or in those places which are called the lower regions, or all places whatever that anywhere exist, together with their inhabitants. This whole, then, is called world. In which world certain beings are said to be super-celestial, i.e., placed in happier abodes, and clothed with heavenly and resplendent bodies; and among these many distinctions are shown to exist, the apostle, e.g., saying, "That one is the glory of the sun, another the glory of the moon, another the glory of the stars; for one star differeth from another star in glory." Certain beings are called earthly, and among them, i.e., among men, there is no small difference; for some of them are Barbarians, others Greeks; and of the Barbarians some are savage and fierce, and others of a milder disposition. And certain of them live under laws that have been thoroughly approved; others, again, under laws of a more common or severe kind; while some, again, possess customs of an inhuman and savage character, rather than laws. And certain of them,

from the hour of their birth, are reduced to humiliation and subjection, and brought up as slaves, being placed under the dominion either of masters, or princes, or tyrants. Others, again, are brought up in a manner more consonant with freedom and reason: some with sound bodies, some with bodies diseased from their early years; some defective in vision, others in hearing and speech; some born in that condition, others deprived of the use of their senses immediately after birth, or at least undergoing such misfortune on reaching manhood. And why should I repeat and enumerate all the horrors of human misery, from which some have been free, and in which others have been involved, when each one can weigh and consider them for himself? There are also certain invisible powers to which earthly things have been entrusted for administration; and amongst them no small difference must be believed to exist, as is also found to be the case among men. The Apostle Paul indeed intimates that there are certain lower powers, and that among them, in like manner, must undoubtedly be sought a ground of diversity. Regarding dumb animals, and birds, and those creatures which live in the waters, it seems superfluous to require; since it is certain that these ought to be regarded not as of primary, but of subordinate rank.

4. Seeing, then, that all things which have been created are said to have been made through Christ, and in Christ, as the Apostle Paul most clearly indicates, when he says, "For in Him and by Him were all things created, whether things in heaven or things on earth, visible and invisible, whether they be thrones, or powers, or principalities, or dominions; all things were created by Him, and in Him;" and as in his Gospel John indicates the same thing, saying, "In the beginning was the Word, and the Word was with God, and the Word was God: the same was in the beginning with God: all things were made by Him; and without Him was not anything made;" and as in the Psalm also it is written, "In wisdom hast Thou made them all;"—seeing, then, Christ is, as it were, the Word and Wisdom, and so also the Righteousness, it will undoubtedly follow that those things which were created in the Word and Wisdom are said to be created also in that righteousness which is Christ; that in created things there may appear to be nothing unrighteous or accidental, but that all things may be shown to be in conformity with the law of equity and righteousness. How, then, so great a variety of things, and so great a diversity, can be understood to be altogether just and righteous, I am sure no human power or language can explain, unless as prostrate suppliants we pray to the Word, and Wisdom, and Righteousness Himself, who is the only-begotten Son of God, and who, pouring Himself by His graces into our senses, may

deign to illuminate what is dark, to lay open what is concealed, and to reveal what is secret; if, indeed, we should be found either to seek, or ask, or knock so worthily as to deserve to receive when we ask, or to find when we seek, or to have it opened to us when we knock. Not relying, then, on our own powers, but on the help of that Wisdom which made all things, and of that Righteousness which we believe to be in all His creatures, although we are in the meantime unable to declare it, yet, trusting in His mercy, we shall endeavour to examine and inquire how that great variety and diversity in the world may appear to be consistent with all righteousness and reason. I mean, of course, merely reason in general; for it would be a mark of ignorance either to seek, or of folly to give, a special reason for each individual case.

5. Now, when we say that this world was established in the variety in which we have above explained that it was created by God, and when we say that this God is good, and righteous, and most just, there are numerous individuals, especially those who, coming from the school of Marcion, and Valentinus, and Basilides, have heard that there are souls of different natures, who object to us, that it cannot consist with the justice of God in creating the world to assign to some of His creatures an abode in the heavens, and not only to give such a better habitation, but also to grant them a higher and more honourable position; to favour others with the grant of principalities; to bestow powers upon some, dominions on others; to confer upon some the most honourable seats in the celestial tribunals; to enable some to shine with more resplendent glory, and to glitter with a starry splendour; to give to some the glory of the sun, to others the glory of the moon, to others the glory of the stars; to cause one star to differ from another star in glory. And, to speak once for all, and briefly, if the Creator God wants neither the will to undertake nor the power to complete a good and perfect work, what reason can there be that, in the creation of rational natures, i.e., of beings of whose existence He Himself is the cause, He should make some of higher rank, and others of second, or third, or of many lower and inferior degrees? In the next place, they object to us, with regard to terrestrial beings, that a happier lot by birth is the case with some rather than with others; as one man, e.g., is begotten of Abraham, and born of the promise; another, too, of Isaac and Rebekah, and who, while still in the womb, supplants his brother, and is said to be loved by God before he is born. Nay, this very circumstance,—especially that one man is born among the Hebrews, with whom he finds instruction in the divine law; another among the Greeks, themselves also wise, and men of no small learning; and then another amongst the Ethiopians, who are accustomed to feed on human flesh; or amongst the Scythians,

with whom parricide is an act sanctioned by law; or amongst the people of Taurus, where strangers are offered in sacrifice,—is a ground of strong objection. Their argument accordingly is this: If there be this great diversity of circumstances, and this diverse and varying condition by birth, in which the faculty of free-will has no scope (for no one chooses for himself either where, or with whom, or in what condition he is born); if, then, this is not caused by the difference in the nature of souls, i.e., that a soul of an evil nature is destined for a wicked nation, and a good soul for a righteous nation, what other conclusion remains than that these things must be supposed to be regulated by accident and chance? And if that be admitted, then it will be no longer believed that the world was made by God, or administered by His providence; and as a consequence, a judgment of God upon the deeds of each individual will appear a thing not to be looked for. In which matter, indeed, what is clearly the truth of things is the privilege of Him alone to know who searches all things, even the deep things of God.

6. We, however, although but men, not to nourish the insolence of the heretics by our silence, will return to their objections such answers as occur to us, so far as our abilities enable us. We have frequently shown, by those declarations which we were able to produce from the holy Scriptures, that God, the Creator of all things, is good, and just, and all-powerful. When He in the beginning created those beings which He desired to create, i.e., rational natures, He had no other reason for creating them than on account of Himself, i.e., His own goodness. As He Himself, then, was the cause of the existence of those things which were to be created, in whom there was neither any variation nor change, nor want of power, He created all whom He made equal and alike, because there was in Himself no reason for producing variety and diversity. But since those rational creatures themselves, as we have frequently shown, and will yet show in the proper place, were endowed with the power of free-will, this freedom of will incited each one either to progress by imitation of God, or reduced him to failure through negligence. And this, as we have already stated, is the cause of the diversity among rational creatures, deriving its origin not from the will or judgment of the Creator, but from the freedom of the individual will. Now God, who deemed it just to arrange His creatures according to their merit, brought down these different understandings into the harmony of one world, that He might adorn, as it were, one dwelling, in which there ought to be not only vessels of gold and silver, but also of wood and clay (and some indeed to honour, and others to dishonour), with those different vessels, or souls, or understandings. And these are the causes, in my opinion, why that world presents the

aspect of diversity, while Divine Providence continues to regulate each individual according to the variety of his movements, or of his feelings and purpose. On which account the Creator will neither appear to be unjust in distributing (for the causes already mentioned) to every one according to his merits; nor will the happiness or unhappiness of each one's birth, or whatever be the condition that falls to his lot, be deemed accidental; nor will different creators, or souls of different natures, be believed to exist.

7. But even holy Scripture does not appear to me to be altogether silent on the nature of this secret, as when the Apostle Paul, in discussing the case of Jacob and Esau, says: "For the children being not yet born, neither having done any good or evil, that the purpose of God according to election might stand, not of works, but of Him who calleth, it was said, The elder shall serve the younger, as it is written, Jacob have I loved, but Esau have I hated." And after that, he answers himself, and says, "What shall we say then? Is there unrighteousness with God?" And that he might furnish us with an opportunity of inquiring into these matters, and of ascertaining how these things do not happen without a reason, he answers himself, and says, "God forbid." For the same question, as it seems to me, which is raised concerning Jacob and Esau, may be raised regarding all celestial and terrestrial creatures, and even those of the lower world as well. And in like manner it seems to me, that as he there says, "The children being not yet born, neither having done any good or evil," so it might also be said of all other things, "When they were not yet" created, "neither had yet done any good or evil, that the decree of God according to election may stand," that (as certain think) some things on the one hand were created heavenly, some on the other earthly, and others, again, beneath the earth, "not of works" (as they think), "but of Him who calleth," what shall we say then, if these things are so? "Is there unrighteousness with God? God forbid." As, therefore, when the Scriptures are carefully examined regarding Jacob and Esau, it is not found to be unrighteousness with God that it should be said, before they were born, or had done anything in this life, "the elder shall serve the younger;" and as it is found not to be unrighteousness that even in the womb Jacob supplanted his brother, if we feel that he was worthily beloved by God, according to the deserts of his previous life, so as to deserve to be preferred before his brother; so also is it with regard to heavenly creatures, if we notice that diversity was not the original condition of the creature, but that, owing to causes that have previously existed, a different office is prepared by the Creator for each one in proportion to the degree of his merit, on this ground, indeed, that each one, in

103

respect of having been created by God an understanding, or a rational spirit, has, according to the movements of his mind and the feelings of his soul, gained for himself a greater or less amount of merit, and has become either an object of love to God, or else one of dislike to Him; while, nevertheless, some of those who are possessed of greater merit are ordained to suffer with others for the adorning of the state of the world, and for the discharge of duty to creatures of a lower grade, in order that by this means they themselves may be participators in the endurance of the Creator, according to the words of the apostle: "For the creature was made subject to vanity, not willingly, but by reason of him who hath subjected the same in hope." Keeping in view, then, the sentiment expressed by the apostle, when, speaking of the birth of Esau and Jacob, he says, "Is there unrighteousness with God? God forbid," I think it right that this same sentiment should be carefully applied to the case of all other creatures, because, as we formerly remarked, the righteousness of the Creator ought to appear in everything. And this, it appears to me, will be seen more clearly at last, if each one, whether of celestial or terrestrial or infernal beings, be said to have the causes of his diversity in himself, and antecedent to his bodily birth. For all things were created by the Word of God, and by His Wisdom, and were set in order by His Justice. And by the grace of His compassion He provides for all men, and encourages all to the use of whatever remedies may lead to their cure, and incites them to salvation.

8. As, then, there is no doubt that at the day of judgment the good will be separated from the bad, and the just from the unjust, and all by the sentence of God will be distributed according to their deserts throughout those places of which they are worthy, so I am of opinion some such state of things was formerly the case, as, God willing, we shall show in what follows. For God must be believed to do and order all things and at all times according to His judgment. For the words which the apostle uses when he says, "In a great house there are not only vessels of gold and silver, but also of wood and of earth, and some to honour and some to dishonour;" and those which he adds, saying, "If a man purge himself, he will be a vessel unto honour, sanctified and meet for the Master's use, unto every good work," undoubtedly point out this, that he who shall purge himself when he is in this life, will be prepared for every good work in that which is to come; while he who does not purge himself will be, according to the amount of his impurity, a vessel unto dishonour, i.e., unworthy. It is therefore possible to understand that there have been also formerly rational vessels, whether purged or not, i.e., which either purged themselves or did not do so, and that consequently every vessel, according to the measure of its

purity or impurity, received a place, or region, or condition by birth, or an office to discharge, in this world. All of which, down to the humblest, God providing for and distinguishing by the power of His wisdom, arranges all things by His controlling judgment, according to a most impartial retribution, so far as each one ought to be assisted or cared for in conformity with his deserts. In which certainly every principle of equity is shown, while the inequality of circumstances preserves the justice of a retribution according to merit. But the grounds of the merits in each individual case are only recognised truly and clearly by God Himself, along with His only-begotten Word, and His Wisdom, and the Holy Spirit.

CHAPTER X—ON THE RESURRECTION, AND THE JUDGMENT, THE FIRE OF HELL, AND PUNISHMENTS

1. But since the discourse has reminded us of the subjects of a future judgment and of retribution, and of the punishments of sinners, according to the threatenings of holy Scripture and the contents of the Church's teaching—viz., that when the time of judgment comes, everlasting fire, and outer darkness, and a prison, and a furnace, and other punishments of like nature, have been prepared for sinners—let us see what our opinions on these points ought to be. But that these subjects may be arrived at in proper order, it seems to me that we ought first to consider the nature of the resurrection, that we may know what that (body) is which shall come either to punishment, or to rest, or to happiness; which question in other treatises which we have composed regarding the resurrection we have discussed at greater length, and have shown what our opinions were regarding it. But now, also, for the sake of logical order in our treatise, there will be no absurdity in restating a few points from such works, especially since some take offence at the creed of the Church, as if our belief in the resurrection were foolish, and altogether devoid of sense; and these are principally heretics, who, I think, are to be answered in the following manner. If they also admit that there is a resurrection of the dead, let them answer us this, What is that which died? Was it not a body? It is of the body, then, that there will be a resurrection. Let them next tell us if they think that we are to make use of bodies or not. I think that when the Apostle Paul says, that "it is sown a natural body, it will arise a spiritual body," they cannot deny that it is a body which arises, or that in the resurrection we are to make use of bodies. What then? If it is certain that we are to make use of bodies, and if the bodies which have fallen are declared to rise again

(for only that which before has fallen can be properly said to rise again), it can be a matter of doubt to no one that they rise again, in order that we may be clothed with them a second time at the resurrection. The one thing is closely connected with the other. For if bodies rise again, they undoubtedly rise to be coverings for us; and if it is necessary for us to be invested with bodies, as it is certainly necessary, we ought to be invested with no other than our own. But if it is true that these rise again, and that they arise "spiritual" bodies, there can be no doubt that they are said to rise from the dead, after casting away corruption and laying aside mortality; otherwise it will appear vain and superfluous for any one to arise from the dead in order to die a second time. And this, finally, may be more distinctly comprehended thus, if one carefully consider what are the qualities of an animal body, which, when sown into the earth, recovers the qualities of a spiritual body. For it is out of the animal body that the very power and grace of the resurrection educe the spiritual body, when it transmutes it from a condition of indignity to one of glory.

2. Since the heretics, however, think themselves persons of great learning and wisdom, we shall ask them if every body has a form of some kind, i.e., is fashioned according to some shape. And if they shall say that a body is that which is fashioned according to no shape, they will show themselves to be the most ignorant and foolish of mankind. For no one will deny this, save him who is altogether without any learning. But if, as a matter of course, they say that every body is certainly fashioned according to some definite shape, we shall ask them if they can point out and describe to us the shape of a spiritual body; a thing which they can by no means do. We shall ask them, moreover, about the differences of those who rise again. How will they show that statement to be true, that there is "one flesh of birds, another of fishes; bodies celestial, and bodies terrestrial; that the glory of the celestial is one, and the glory of the terrestrial another; that one is the glory of the sun, another the glory of the moon, another the glory of the stars; that one star differeth from another star in glory; and that so is the resurrection of the dead?" According to that gradation, then, which exists among heavenly bodies, let them show to us the differences in the glory of those who rise again; and if they have endeavoured by any means to devise a principle that may be in accordance with the differences in heavenly bodies, we shall ask them to assign the differences in the resurrection by a comparison of earthly bodies. Our understanding of the passage indeed is, that the apostle, wishing to describe the great difference among those who rise again in glory, i.e., of the saints, borrowed a comparison from the heavenly bodies, saying,

"One is the glory of the sun, another the glory of the moon, another the glory of the stars." And wishing again to teach us the differences among those who shall come to the resurrection, without having purged themselves in this life, i.e., sinners, he borrowed an illustration from earthly things, saying, "There is one flesh of birds, another of fishes." For heavenly things are worthily compared to the saints, and earthly things to sinners. These statements are made in reply to those who deny the resurrection of the dead, i.e., the resurrection of bodies.

3. We now turn our attention to some of our own (believers), who, either from feebleness of intellect or want of proper instruction, adopt a very low and abject view of the resurrection of the body. We ask these persons in what manner they understand that an animal body is to be changed by the grace of the resurrection, and to become a spiritual one; and how that which is sown in weakness will arise in power; how that which is planted in dishonour will arise in glory; and that which was sown in corruption, will be changed to a state of incorruption. Because if they believe the apostle, that a body which arises in glory, and power, and incorruptibility, has already become spiritual, it appears absurd and contrary to his meaning to say that it can again be entangled with the passions of flesh and blood, seeing the apostle manifestly declares that "flesh and blood shall not inherit the kingdom of God, nor shall corruption inherit incorruption." But how do they understand the declaration of the apostle, "We shall all be changed?" This transformation certainly is to be looked for, according to the order which we have taught above; and in it, undoubtedly, it becomes us to hope for something worthy of divine grace; and this we believe will take place in the order in which the apostle describes the sowing in the ground of a "bare grain of corn, or of any other fruit," to which "God gives a body as it pleases Him," as soon as the grain of corn is dead. For in the same way also our bodies are to be supposed to fall into the earth like a grain; and (that germ being implanted in them which contains the bodily substance) although the bodies die, and become corrupted, and are scattered abroad, yet by the word of God, that very germ which is always safe in the substance of the body, raises them from the earth, and restores and repairs them, as the power which is in the grain of wheat, after its corruption and death, repairs and restores the grain into a body having stalk and ear. And so also to those who shall deserve to obtain an inheritance in the kingdom of heaven, that germ of the body's restoration, which we have before mentioned, by God's command restores out of the earthly and animal body a spiritual one, capable of inhabiting the heavens; while to each one of those who may be of inferior merit, or of more abject condition, or even the

lowest in the scale, and altogether thrust aside, there is yet given, in proportion to the dignity of his life and soul, a glory and dignity of body,—nevertheless in such a way, that even the body which rises again of those who are to be destined to everlasting fire or to severe punishments, is by the very change of the resurrection so incorruptible, that it cannot be corrupted and dissolved even by severe punishments. If, then, such be the qualities of that body which will arise from the dead, let us now see what is the meaning of the threatening of eternal fire.

4. We find in the prophet Isaiah, that the fire with which each one is punished is described as his own; for he says, "Walk in the light of your own fire, and in the flame which ye have kindled." By these words it seems to be indicated that every sinner kindles for himself the flame of his own fire, and is not plunged into some fire which has been already kindled by another, or was in existence before himself. Of this fire the fuel and food are our sins, which are called by the Apostle Paul "wood, and hay, and stubble." And I think that, as abundance of food, and provisions of a contrary kind and amount, breed fevers in the body, and fevers, too, of different sorts and duration, according to the proportion in which the collected poison supplies material and fuel for disease (the quality of this material, gathered together from different poisons, proving the causes either of a more acute or more lingering disease); so, when the soul has gathered together a multitude of evil works, and an abundance of sins against itself, at a suitable time all that assembly of evils boils up to punishment, and is set on fire to chastisements; when the mind itself, or conscience, receiving by divine power into the memory all those things of which it had stamped on itself certain signs and forms at the moment of sinning, will see a kind of history, as it were, of all the foul, and shameful, and unholy deeds which it has done, exposed before its eyes: then is the conscience itself harassed, and, pierced by its own goads, becomes an accuser and a witness against itself. And this, I think, was the opinion of the Apostle Paul himself, when he said, "Their thoughts mutually accusing or excusing them in the day when God will judge the secrets of men by Jesus Christ, according to my Gospel." From which it is understood that around the substance of the soul certain tortures are produced by the hurtful affections of sins themselves.

5. And that the understanding of this matter may not appear very difficult, we may draw some considerations from the evil effects of those passions which are wont to befall some souls, as when a soul is consumed by the fire of love, or wasted away by zeal or envy, or when the passion of anger is kindled, or one is consumed by the greatness of

his madness or his sorrow; on which occasions some, finding the excess of these evils unbearable, have deemed it more tolerable to submit to death than to endure perpetually torture of such a kind. You will ask indeed whether, in the case of those who have been entangled in the evils arising from those vices above enumerated, and who, while existing in this life, have been unable to procure any amelioration for themselves, and have in this condition departed from the world, it be sufficient in the way of punishment that they be tortured by the remaining in them of these hurtful affections, i.e., of the anger, or of the fury, or of the madness, or of the sorrow, whose fatal poison was in this life lessened by no healing medicine; or whether, these affections being changed, they will be subjected to the pains of a general punishment. Now I am of opinion that another species of punishment may be understood to exist; because, as we feel that when the limbs of the body are loosened and torn away from their mutual supports, there is produced pain of a most excruciating kind, so, when the soul shall be found to be beyond the order, and connection, and harmony in which it was created by God for the purposes of good and useful action and observation, and not to harmonize with itself in the connection of its rational movements, it must be deemed to bear the chastisement and torture of its own dissension, and to feel the punishments of its own disordered condition. And when this dissolution and rending asunder of soul shall have been tested by the application of fire, a solidification undoubtedly into a firmer structure will take place, and a restoration be effected.

6. There are also many other things which escape our notice, and are known to Him alone who is the physician of our souls. For if, on account of those bad effects which we bring upon ourselves by eating and drinking, we deem it necessary for the health of the body to make use of some unpleasant and painful drug, sometimes even, if the nature of the disease demand, requiring the severe process of the amputating knife; and if the virulence of the disease shall transcend even these remedies, the evil has at last to be burned out by fire; how much more is it to be understood that God our Physician, desiring to remove the defects of our souls, which they had contracted from their different sins and crimes, should employ penal measures of this sort, and should apply even, in addition, the punishment of fire to those who have lost their soundness of mind! Pictures of this method of procedure are found also in the holy Scriptures. In the book of Deuteronomy, the divine word threatens sinners with the punishments of fevers, and colds, and jaundice, and with the pains of feebleness of vision, and alienation of mind and paralysis, and blindness, and weakness of the

reins. If any one, then, at his leisure gather together out of the whole of Scripture all the enumerations of diseases which in the threatenings addressed to sinners are called by the names of bodily maladies, he will find that either the vices of souls, or their punishments, are figuratively indicated by them. To understand now, that in the same way in which physicians apply remedies to the sick, in order that by careful treatment they may recover their health, God so deals towards those who have lapsed and fallen into sin, is proved by this, that the cup of God's fury is ordered, through the agency of the prophet Jeremiah, to be offered to all nations, that they may drink it, and be in a state of madness, and vomit it forth. In doing which, He threatens them, saying, That if any one refuse to drink, he shall not be cleansed. By which certainly it is understood that the fury of God's vengeance is profitable for the purgation of souls. That the punishment, also, which is said to be applied by fire, is understood to be applied with the object of healing, is taught by Isaiah, who speaks thus of Israel: "The Lord will wash away the filth of the sons or daughters of Zion, and shall purge away the blood from the midst of them by the spirit of judgment, and the spirit of burning." Of the Chaldeans he thus speaks: "Thou hast the coals of fire; sit upon them: they will be to thee a help." And in other passages he says, "The Lord will sanctify in a burning fire" and in the prophecies of Malachi he says, "The Lord sitting will blow, and purify, and will pour forth the cleansed sons of Judah."

7. But that fate also which is mentioned in the Gospels as overtaking unfaithful stewards who, it is said, are to be divided, and a portion of them placed along with unbelievers, as if that portion which is not their own were to be sent elsewhere, undoubtedly indicates some kind of punishment on those whose spirit, as it seems to me, is shown to be separated from the soul. For if this Spirit is of divine nature, i.e., is understood to be a Holy Spirit, we shall understand this to be said of the gift of the Holy Spirit: that when, whether by baptism, or by the grace of the Spirit, the word of wisdom, or the word of knowledge, or of any other gift, has been bestowed upon a man, and not rightly administered, i.e., either buried in the earth or tied up in a napkin, the gift of the Spirit will certainly be withdrawn from his soul, and the other portion which remains, that is, the substance of the soul, will be assigned its place with unbelievers, being divided and separated from that Spirit with whom, by joining itself to the Lord, it ought to have been one spirit. Now, if this is not to be understood of the Spirit of God, but of the nature of the soul itself, that will be called its better part which was made in the image and likeness of God; whereas the other part, that which afterwards, through its fall by the exercise of free-

will, was assumed contrary to the nature of its original condition of purity,—this part, as being the friend and beloved of matter, is punished with the fate of unbelievers. There is also a third sense in which that separation may be understood, this viz., that as each believer, although the humblest in the Church, is said to be attended by an angel, who is declared by the Saviour always to behold the face of God the Father, and as this angel was certainly one with the object of his guardianship; so, if the latter is rendered unworthy by his want of obedience, the angel of God is said to be taken from him, and then that part of him—the part, viz., which belongs to his human nature—being rent away from the divine part, is assigned a place along with unbelievers, because it has not faithfully observed the admonitions of the angel allotted it by God.

8. But the outer darkness, in my judgment, is to be understood not so much of some dark atmosphere without any light, as of those persons who, being plunged in the darkness of profound ignorance, have been placed beyond the reach of any light of the understanding. We must see, also, lest this perhaps should be the meaning of the expression, that as the saints will receive those bodies in which they have lived in holiness and purity in the habitations of this life, bright and glorious after the resurrection, so the wicked also, who in this life have loved the darkness of error and the night of ignorance, may be clothed with dark and black bodies after the resurrection, that the very mist of ignorance which had in this life taken possession of their minds within them, may appear in the future as the external covering of the body. Similar is the view to be entertained regarding the prison. Let these remarks, which have been made as brief as possible, that the order of our discourse in the meantime might be preserved, suffice for the present occasion.

CHAPTER XI—ON COUNTER PROMISES

1. Let us now briefly see what views we are to form regarding promises. It is certain that there is no living thing which can be altogether inactive and immoveable, but delights in motion of every kind, and in perpetual activity and volition; and this nature, I think it evident, is in all living things. Much more, then, must a rational animal, i.e., the nature of man, be in perpetual movement and activity. If, indeed, he is forgetful of himself, and ignorant of what becomes him, all his efforts are directed to serve the uses of the body, and in all his movements he is occupied with his own pleasures and bodily lusts; but if he be one who studies to care or provide for the general good, then,

either by consulting for the benefit of the state or by obeying the magistrates, he exerts himself for that, whatever it is, which may seem certainly to promote the public advantage. And if now any one be of such a nature as to understand that there is something better than those things which seem to be corporeal, and so bestow his labour upon wisdom and science, then he will undoubtedly direct all his attention towards pursuits of that kind, that he may, by inquiring into the truth, ascertain the causes and reason of things. As therefore, in this life, one man deems it the highest good to enjoy bodily pleasures, another to consult for the benefit of the community, a third to devote attention to study and learning; so let us inquire whether in that life which is the true one (which is said to be hidden with Christ in God, i.e., in that eternal life), there will be for us some such order and condition of existence.

2. Certain persons, then, refusing the labour of thinking, and adopting a superficial view of the letter of the law, and yielding rather in some measure to the indulgence of their own desires and lusts, being disciples of the letter alone, are of opinion that the fulfilment of the promises of the future are to be looked for in bodily pleasure and luxury; and therefore they especially desire to have again, after the resurrection, such bodily structures as may never be without the power of eating, and drinking, and performing all the functions of flesh and blood, not following the opinion of the Apostle Paul regarding the resurrection of a spiritual body. And consequently they say, that after the resurrection there will be marriages, and the begetting of children, imagining to themselves that the earthly city of Jerusalem is to be rebuilt, its foundations laid in precious stones, and its walls constructed of jasper, and its battlements of crystal; that it is to have a wall composed of many precious stones, as jasper, and sapphire, and chalcedony, and emerald, and sardonyx, and onyx, and chrysolite, and chrysoprase, and jacinth, and amethyst. Moreover, they think that the natives of other countries are to be given them as the ministers of their pleasures, whom they are to employ either as tillers of the field or builders of walls, and by whom their ruined and fallen city is again to be raised up; and they think that they are to receive the wealth of the nations to live on, and that they will have control over their riches; that even the camels of Midian and Kedar will come, and bring to them gold, and incense, and precious stones. And these views they think to establish on the authority of the prophets by those promises which are written regarding Jerusalem; and by those passages also where it is said, that they who serve the Lord shall eat and drink, but that sinners shall hunger and thirst; that the righteous shall be joyful, but that sorrow

shall possess the wicked. And from the New Testament also they quote the saying of the Saviour, in which He makes a promise to His disciples concerning the joy of wine, saying, "Henceforth I shall not drink of this cup, until I drink it with you new in My Father's kingdom." They add, moreover, that declaration, in which the Saviour calls those blessed who now hunger and thirst, promising them that they shall be satisfied; and many other scriptural illustrations are adduced by them, the meaning of which they do not perceive is to be taken figuratively. Then, again, agreeably to the form of things in this life, and according to the gradations of the dignities or ranks in this world, or the greatness of their powers, they think they are to be kings and princes, like those earthly monarchs who now exist; chiefly, as it appears, on account of that expression in the Gospel: "Have thou power over five cities." And to speak shortly, according to the manner of things in this life in all similar matters, do they desire the fulfilment of all things looked for in the promises, viz., that what now is should exist again. Such are the views of those who, while believing in Christ, understand the divine Scriptures in a sort of Jewish sense, drawing from them nothing worthy of the divine promises.

3. Those, however, who receive the representations of Scripture according to the understanding of the apostles, entertain the hope that the saints will eat indeed, but that it will be the bread of life, which may nourish the soul with the food of truth and wisdom, and enlighten the mind, and cause it to drink from the cup of divine wisdom, according to the declaration of holy Scripture: "Wisdom has prepared her table, she has killed her beasts, she has mingled her wine in her cup, and she cries with a loud voice, Come to me, eat the bread which I have prepared for you, and drink the wine which I have mingled." By this food of wisdom, the understanding, being nourished to an entire and perfect condition like that in which man was made at the beginning, is restored to the image and likeness of God; so that, although an individual may depart from this life less perfectly instructed, but who has done works that are approved of, he will be capable of receiving instruction in that Jerusalem, the city of the saints, i.e., he will be educated and moulded, and made a living stone, a stone elect and precious, because he has undergone with firmness and constancy the struggles of life and the trials of piety; and will there come to a truer and clearer knowledge of that which here has been already predicted, viz., that "man shall not live by bread alone, but by every word which proceedeth from the mouth of God." And they also are to be understood to be the princes and rulers who both govern those of lower rank, and instruct them, and teach them, and train them to divine

things.

4. But if these views should not appear to fill the minds of those who hope for such results with a becoming desire, let us go back a little, and, irrespective of the natural and innate longing of the mind for the thing itself, let us make inquiry so that we may be able at last to describe, as it were, the very forms of the bread of life, and the quality of that wine, and the peculiar nature of the principalities, all in conformity with the spiritual view of things. Now, as in those arts which are usually performed by means of manual labour, the reason why a thing is done, or why it is of a special quality, or for a special purpose, is an object of investigation to the mind, while the actual work itself is unfolded to view by the agency of the hands; so, in those works of God which were created by Him, it is to be observed that the reason and understanding of those things which we see done by Him remains undisclosed. And as, when our eye beholds the products of an artist's labour, the mind, immediately on perceiving anything of unusual artistic excellence, burns to know of what nature it is, or how it was formed, or to what purposes it was fashioned; so, in a much greater degree, and in one that is beyond all comparison, does the mind burn with an inexpressible desire to know the reason of those things which we see done by God. This desire, this longing, we believe to be unquestionably implanted within us by God; and as the eye naturally seeks the light and vision, and our body naturally desires food and drink, so our mind is possessed with a becoming and natural desire to become acquainted with the truth of God and the causes of things. Now we have received this desire from God, not in order that it should never be gratified or be *capable* of gratification; otherwise the love of truth would appear to have been implanted by God into our minds to no purpose, if it were never to have an opportunity of satisfaction. Whence also, even in this life, those who devote themselves with great labour to the pursuits of piety and religion, although obtaining only some small fragments from the numerous and immense treasures of divine knowledge, yet, by the very circumstance that their mind and soul is engaged in these pursuits, and that in the eagerness of their desire they outstrip themselves, do they derive much advantage; and, because their minds are directed to the study and love of the investigation of truth, are they made fitter for receiving the instruction that is to come; as if, when one would paint an image, he were first with a light pencil to trace out the outlines of the coming picture, and prepare marks for the reception of the features that are to be afterwards added, this preliminary sketch in outline is found to prepare the way for the laying on of the true colours of the painting; so, in a measure, an outline and sketch may be traced on the

tablets of our heart by the pencil of our Lord Jesus Christ. And therefore perhaps is it said, "Unto every one that hath shall be given, and be added." By which it is established, that to those who possess in this life a kind of outline of truth and knowledge, shall be added the beauty of a perfect image in the future.

5. Some such desire, I apprehend, was indicated by him who said, "I am in a strait betwixt two, having a desire to depart, and to be with Christ, which is far better;" knowing that when he should have returned to Christ he would then know more clearly the reasons of all things which are done on earth, either respecting man, or the soul of man, or the mind; or regarding any other subject, such as, for instance, what is the Spirit that operates, what also is the vital spirit, or what is the grace of the Holy Spirit that is given to believers. Then also will he understand what Israel appears to be, or what is meant by the diversity of nations; what the twelve tribes of Israel mean, and what the individual people of each tribe. Then, too, will he understand the reason of the priests and Levites, and of the different priestly orders, the type of which was in Moses, and also what is the true meaning of the jubilees, and of the weeks of years with God. He will see also the reasons for the festival days, and holy days, and for all the sacrifices and purifications. He will perceive also the reason of the purgation from leprosy, and what the different kinds of leprosy are, and the reason of the purgation of those who lose their seed. He will come to know, moreover, what are the good influences, and their greatness, and their qualities; and those too which are of a contrary kind, and what the affection of the former, and what the strife-causing emulation of the latter is towards men. He will behold also the nature of the soul, and the diversity of animals (whether of those which live in the water, or of birds, or of wild beasts), and why each of the genera is subdivided into so many species; and what intention of the Creator, or what purpose of His wisdom, is concealed in each individual thing. He will become acquainted, too, with the reason why certain properties are found associated with certain roots or herbs, and why, on the other hand, evil effects are averted by other herbs and roots. He will know, moreover, the nature of the apostate angels, and the reason why they have power to flatter in some things those who do not despise them with the whole power of faith, and why they exist for the purpose of deceiving and leading men astray. He will learn, too, the judgment of Divine Providence on each individual thing; and that, of those events which happen to men, none occur by accident or chance, but in accordance with a plan so carefully considered, and so stupendous, that it does not overlook even the number of the hairs of the heads, not merely of the

saints, but perhaps of all human beings, and the plan of which providential government extends even to caring for the sale of two sparrows for a denarius, whether sparrows there be understood figuratively or literally. Now indeed this providential government is still a subject of investigation, but then it will be fully manifested. From all which we are to suppose, that meanwhile not a little time may pass by until the reason of those things only which are upon the earth be pointed out to the worthy and deserving after their departure from life, that by the knowledge of all these things, and by the grace of full knowledge, they may enjoy an unspeakable joy. Then, if that atmosphere which is between heaven and earth is not devoid of inhabitants, and those of a rational kind, as the apostle says, "Wherein in times past ye walked according to the course of this world, according to the prince of the power of the air, the spirit who now worketh in the children of disobedience." And again he says, "We shall be caught up in the clouds to meet Christ in the air, and so shall we ever be with the Lord."

6. We are therefore to suppose that the saints will remain there until they recognise the twofold mode of government in those things which are performed in the air. And when I say "twofold mode," I mean this: When we were upon earth, we saw either animals or trees, and beheld the differences among them, and also the very great diversity among men; but although we saw these things, we did not understand the reason of them; and this only was suggested to us from the visible diversity, that we should examine and inquire upon what principle these things were either created or diversely arranged. And a zeal or desire for knowledge of this kind being conceived by us on earth, the full understanding and comprehension of it will be granted after death, if indeed the result should follow according to our expectations. When, therefore, we shall have fully comprehended its nature, we shall understand in a twofold manner what we saw on earth. Some such view, then, must we hold regarding this abode in the air. I think, therefore, that all the saints who depart from this life will remain in some place situated on the earth, which holy Scripture calls paradise, as in some place of instruction, and, so to speak, class-room or school of souls, in which they are to be instructed regarding all the things which they had seen on earth, and are to receive also some information respecting things that are to follow in the future, as even when in this life they had obtained in some degree indications of future events, although "through a glass darkly," all of which are revealed more clearly and distinctly to the saints in their proper time and place. If any one indeed be pure in heart, and holy in mind, and more practised in

perception, he will, by making more rapid progress, quickly ascend to a place in the air, and reach the kingdom of heaven, through those mansions, so to speak, in the various places which the Greeks have termed spheres, i.e., globes, but which holy Scripture has called heavens; in each of which he will first see clearly what is done there, and in the second place, will discover the reason why things are so done: and thus he will in order pass through all gradations, following Him who hath passed into the heavens, Jesus the Son of God, who said, "I will that where I am, these may be also." And of this diversity of places He speaks, when He says, "In My Father's house are many mansions." He Himself is everywhere, and passes swiftly through all things; nor are we any longer to understand Him as existing in those narrow limits in which He was once confined for our sakes, i.e., not in that circumscribed body which He occupied on earth, when dwelling among men, according to which He might be considered as enclosed in some one place.

7. When, then, the saints shall have reached the celestial abodes, they will clearly see the nature of the stars one by one, and will understand whether they are endued with life, or their condition, whatever it is. And they will comprehend also the other reasons for the works of God, which He Himself will reveal to them. For He will show to them, as to children, the causes of things and the power of His creation, and will explain why that star was placed in that particular quarter of the sky, and why it was separated from another by so great an intervening space; what, e.g., would have been the consequence if it had been nearer or more remote; or if that star had been larger than this, how the totality of things would not have remained the same, but all would have been transformed into a different condition of being. And so, when they have finished all those matters which are connected with the stars, and with the heavenly revolutions, they will come to those which are not seen, or to those whose names only we have heard, and to things which are invisible, which the Apostle Paul has informed us are numerous, although what they are, or what difference may exist among them, we cannot even conjecture by our feeble intellect. And thus the rational nature, growing by each individual step, not as it grew in this life in flesh, and body, and soul, but enlarged in understanding and in power of perception, is raised as a mind already perfect to perfect knowledge, no longer at all impeded by those carnal senses, but increased in intellectual growth; and ever gazing purely, and, so to speak, face to face, on the causes of things, it attains perfection, firstly, viz., that by which it ascends to (the truth), and secondly, that by which it abides in it, having problems and the understanding of things, and the causes of

events, as the food on which it may feast. For as in this life our bodies grow physically to what they are, through a sufficiency of food in early life supplying the means of increase, but after the due height has been attained we use food no longer to grow, but to live, and to be preserved in life by it; so also I think that the mind, when it has attained perfection, eats and avails itself of suitable and appropriate food in such a degree, that nothing ought to be either deficient or superfluous. And in all things this food is to be understood as the contemplation and understanding of God, which is of a measure appropriate and suitable to this nature, which was made and created; and this measure it is proper should be observed by every one of those who are beginning to see God, i.e., to understand Him through purity of heart.

BOOK III

PREFACE OF RUFINUS

READER, remember me in your prayers, that we too may deserve to be made emulators of the spirit. The two former books on *The Principles* I translated not only at your instance, but even under pressure from you during the days of Lent; but as you, my devout brother Macarius, were not only living near me during that time, but had more leisure at your command than now, so I also worked the harder; whereas I have been longer in explaining these two latter books, seeing you came less frequently from a distant extremity of the city to urge on my labour. Now if you remember what I warned you of in my former preface,— that certain persons would be indignant, if they did not hear that we spoke some evil of Origen,—that, I imagine, you have forthwith experienced, has come to pass. But if those demons who excite the tongues of men to slander were so infuriated by that work, in which he had not as yet fully unveiled their secret proceedings, what, think you, will be the case in this, in which he will expose all those dark and hidden ways, by which they creep into the hearts of men, and deceive weak and unstable souls? You will immediately see all things thrown into confusion, seditions stirred up, clamours raised throughout the whole city, and that individual summoned to receive sentence of condemnation who endeavoured to dispel the diabolical darkness of ignorance by means of the light of the Gospel lamp. Let such things, however, be lightly esteemed by him who is desirous of being trained in divine learning, while retaining in its integrity the rule of the Catholic faith. I think it necessary, however, to remind you that the principle observed in the former books has been observed also in these, viz., not to translate what appeared contrary to Origen's other opinions, and to our own belief, but to pass by such passages as being interpolated and forged by others. But if he has appeared to give expression to any novelties regarding rational creatures (on which subject the essence of our faith does not depend), for the sake of discussion and of adding to our knowledge, when perhaps it was necessary for us to answer in such an order some heretical opinions, I have not omitted to mention these either in the present or preceding books, unless when he wished to repeat in the following books what he had already stated in the previous ones, when I have thought it convenient, for the sake of brevity, to curtail some of these repetitions. Should any one, however, peruse these passages from a desire to enlarge his knowledge, and not to raise captious objections, he will do better to have them expounded by persons of skill. For it is an absurdity to have the fictions of poetry and the ridiculous plays of comedy interpreted by grammarians, and to suppose that without a master and an interpreter any one is able to learn those things which are spoken either of God or of the heavenly virtues, and of the whole universe of things, in which some deplorable error either of pagan philosophers or of heretics is confuted; and the result of which is, that men would rather rashly and ignorantly condemn things that are difficult and obscure, than ascertain their meaning by diligence and study.

CHAPTER I [FROM THE LATIN OF RUFINUS]—ON THE FREEDOM OF THE WILL

1. Some such opinions, we believe, ought to be entertained regarding the divine promises, when we direct our understanding to the contemplation of that eternal and infinite world, and gaze on its ineffable joy and blessedness. But as the preaching of the Church includes a belief in a future and just judgment of God, which belief incites and persuades men to a good and virtuous life, and to an avoidance of sin by all possible means; and as by this it is undoubtedly indicated that it is within our own power to devote ourselves either to a life that is worthy of praise, or to one that is worthy of censure, I therefore deem it necessary to say a few words regarding the freedom of the will, seeing that this topic has been treated by very many writers in no mean style. And that we may ascertain more easily what is the freedom of the will, let us inquire into the nature of will and of desire.

2. Of all things which move, some have the cause of their motion within themselves, others receive it from without: and all those things only are moved from without which are without life, as stones, and pieces of wood, and whatever things are of such a nature as to be held together by the constitution of their matter alone, or of their bodily substance. That view must indeed be dismissed which would regard the dissolution of bodies by corruption as motion, for it has no bearing upon our present purpose. Others, again, have the cause of motion in themselves, as animals, or trees, and all things which are held together by natural life or soul; among which some think ought to be classed the veins of metals. Fire, also, is supposed to be the cause of its own motion, and perhaps also springs of water. And of those things which have the causes of their motion in themselves, some are said to be moved out of themselves, others by themselves. And they so distinguish them, because those things are moved out of themselves

which are alive indeed, but have no soul; whereas those things which have a soul are moved by themselves, when a phantasy, i.e., a desire or incitement, is presented to them, which excites them to move towards something. Finally, in certain things endowed with a soul, there is such a phantasy, i.e., a will or feeling, as by a kind of natural instinct calls them forth, and arouses them to orderly and regular motion; as we see to be the case with spiders, which are stirred up in a most orderly manner by a phantasy, i.e., a sort of wish and desire for weaving, to undertake the production of a web, some natural movement undoubtedly calling forth the effort to work of this kind. Nor is this very insect found to possess any other feeling than the natural desire of weaving; as in like manner bees also exhibit a desire to form honeycombs, and to collect, as they say, aerial honey.

3. But since a rational animal not only has within itself these natural movements, but has moreover, to a greater extent than other animals, the power of reason, by which it can judge and determine regarding natural movements, and disapprove and reject some, while approving and adopting others, so by the judgment of this reason may the movements of men be governed and directed towards a commendable life. And from this it follows that, since the nature of this reason which is in man has within itself the power of distinguishing between good and evil, and while distinguishing possesses the faculty of selecting what it has approved, it may justly be deemed worthy of praise in choosing what is good, and deserving of censure in following that which is base or wicked. This indeed must by no means escape our notice, that in some dumb animals there is found a more regular movement than in others, as in hunting-dogs or war-horses, so that they may appear to some to be moved by a kind of rational sense. But we must believe this to be the result not so much of reason as of some natural instinct, largely bestowed for purposes of that kind. Now, as we had begun to remark, seeing that such is the nature of a rational animal, some things may happen to us human beings from without; and these, coming in contact with our sense of sight, or hearing, or any other of our senses, may incite and arouse us to good movements, or the contrary; and seeing they come to us from an external source, it is not within our own power to prevent their coming. But to determine and approve what use we ought to make of those things which thus happen, is the duty of no other than of that reason within us, i.e., of our own judgment; by the decision of which reason we use the incitement, which comes to us from without for that purpose, which reason approves, our natural movements being determined by its authority either to good actions or the reverse.

4. If any one now were to say that those things which happen to us from an external cause, and call forth our movements, are of such a nature that it is impossible to resist them, whether they incite us to good or evil, let the holder of this opinion turn his attention for a little upon himself, and carefully inspect the movements of his own mind, unless he has discovered already, that when an enticement to any desire arises, nothing is accomplished until the assent of the soul is gained, and the authority of the mind has granted indulgence to the wicked suggestion; so that a claim might seem to be made by two parties on certain probable grounds as to a judge residing within the tribunals of our heart, in order that, after the statement of reasons, the decree of execution may proceed from the judgment of reason. For, to take an illustration: if, to a man who has determined to live continently and chastely, and to keep himself free from all pollution with women, a woman should happen to present herself, inciting and alluring him to act contrary to his purpose, that woman is not a complete and absolute cause or necessity of his transgressing, since it is in his power, by remembering his resolution, to bridle the incitements to lust, and by the stern admonitions of virtue to restrain the pleasure of the allurement that solicits him; so that, all feeling of indulgence being driven away, his determination may remain firm and enduring. Finally, if to any men of learning, strengthened by divine training, allurements of that kind present themselves, remembering forthwith what they are, and calling to mind what has long been the subject of their meditation and instruction, and fortifying themselves by the support of a holier doctrine, they reject and repel all incitement to pleasure, and drive away opposing lusts by the interposition of the reason implanted within them.

5. Seeing, then, that these positions are thus established by a sort of natural evidence, is it not superfluous to throw back the causes of our actions on those things which happen to us from without, and thus transfer the blame from ourselves, on whom it wholly lies? For this is to say that we are like pieces of wood, or stones, which have no motion in themselves, but receive the causes of their motion from without. Now such an assertion is neither true nor becoming, and is invented only that the freedom of the will may be denied; unless, indeed, we are to suppose that the freedom of the will consists in this, that nothing which happens to us from without can incite us to good or evil. And if any one were to refer the causes of our faults to the natural disorder of the body, such a theory is proved to be contrary to the reason of all teaching. For, as we see in very many individuals, that after living unchastely and intemperately, and after being the captives of luxury and

lust, if they should happen to be aroused by the word of teaching and instruction to enter upon a better course of life, there takes place so great a change, that from being luxurious and wicked men, they are converted into those who are sober, and most chaste and gentle; so, again, we see in the case of those who are quiet and honest, that after associating with restless and shameless individuals, their good morals are corrupted by evil conversation, and they become like those whose wickedness is complete. And this is the case sometimes with men of mature age, so that such have lived more chastely in youth than when more advanced years have enabled them to indulge in a freer mode of life. The result of our reasoning, therefore, is to show that those things which happen to us from without are not in our own power; but that to make a good or bad use of those things which do so happen, by help of that reason which is within us, and which distinguishes and determines how these things ought to be used, *is* within our power.

6. And now, to confirm the deductions of reason by the authority of Scripture—viz., that it is our own doing whether we live rightly or not, and that we are not compelled, either by those causes which come to us from without, or, as some think, by the presence of fate—we adduce the testimony of the prophet Micah, in these words: "If it has been announced to thee, O man, what is good, or what the LORD requires of thee, except that thou shouldst do justice, and love mercy, and be ready to walk with the Lord thy God." Moses also speaks as follows: "I have placed before thy face the way of life and the way of death: choose what is good, and walk in it." Isaiah, moreover, makes this declaration: "If you are willing, and hear me, ye shall eat the good of the land. But if you be unwilling, and will not hear me, the sword shall consume you; for the mouth of the LORD has spoken this." In the Psalm, too, it is written: "If My people had heard Me, if Israel had walked in My ways, I would have humbled her enemies to nothing;" by which he shows that it was in the power of the people to hear, and to walk in the ways of God. The Saviour also saying, "I say unto you, Resist not evil;" and, "Whoever shall be angry with his brother, shall be in danger of the judgment;" and, "Whosoever shall look upon a woman to lust after her, hath already committed adultery with her in his heart;" and in issuing certain other commands,—conveys no other meaning than this, that it is in our own power to observe what is commanded. And therefore we are rightly rendered liable to condemnation if we transgress those commandments which we are able to keep. And hence He Himself also declares: "Every one who hears my words, and doeth them, I will show to whom he is like: he is like a wise man who built his house upon a rock," etc. So also the

declaration: "Whoso heareth these things, and doeth them not, is like a foolish man, who built his house upon the sand," etc. Even the words addressed to those who are on His right hand, "Come unto Me, all ye blessed of My Father," etc.; "for I was an hungered, and ye gave Me to eat; I was thirsty, and ye gave Me drink," manifestly show that it depended upon themselves, that either these should be deserving of praise for doing what was commanded and receiving what was promised, or those deserving of censure who either heard or received the contrary, and to whom it was said, "Depart, ye cursed, into everlasting fire." Let us observe also, that the Apostle Paul addresses us as having power over our own will, and as possessing in ourselves the causes either of our salvation or of our ruin: "Dost thou despise the riches of His goodness, and of His patience, and of His long-suffering, not knowing that the goodness of God leadeth thee to repentance? But, according to thy hardness and impenitent heart, thou art treasuring up for thyself wrath on the day of judgment and of the revelation of the just judgment of God, who will render to every one according to his work: to those who by patient continuance in well-doing seek for glory and immortality, eternal life; while to those who are contentious, and believe not the truth, but who believe iniquity, anger, indignation, tribulation, and distress, on every soul of man that worketh evil, on the Jew first, and (afterwards) on the Greek; but glory, and honour, and peace to every one that doeth good, to the Jew first, and (afterwards) to the Greek." You will find also innumerable other passages in holy Scripture, which manifestly show that we possess freedom of will. Otherwise there would be a contrariety in commandments being given us, by observing which we may be saved, or by transgressing which we may be condemned, if the power of keeping them were not implanted in us.

7. But, seeing there are found in the sacred Scriptures themselves certain expressions occurring in such a connection, that the opposite of this may appear capable of being understood from them, let us bring them forth before us, and, discussing them according to the rule of piety, let us furnish an explanation of them, in order that from those few passages which we now expound, the solution of those others which resemble them, and by which any power over the will seems to be excluded, may become clear. Those expressions, accordingly, make an impression on very many, which are used by God in speaking of Pharaoh, as when He frequently says, "I will harden Pharaoh's heart." For if he is hardened by God, and commits sin in consequence of being so hardened, the cause of his sin is not himself. And if so, it will appear that Pharaoh does not possess freedom of will; and it will be

maintained, as a consequence, that, agreeably to this illustration, neither do others who perish owe the cause of their destruction to the freedom of their own will. That expression, also, in Ezekiel, when he says, "I will take away their stony hearts, and will give them hearts of flesh, that they may walk in My precepts, and keep My ways," may impress some, inasmuch as it seems to be a gift of God, either to walk in His ways or to keep His precepts, if He take away that stony heart which is an obstacle to the keeping of His commandments, and bestow and implant a better and more impressible heart, which is called now a heart of flesh. Consider also the nature of the answer given in the Gospel by our Lord and Saviour to those who inquired of Him why He spoke to the multitude in parables. His words are: "That seeing they may not see; and hearing they may hear, and not understand; lest they should be converted, and their sins be forgiven them." The words, moreover, used by the Apostle Paul, that "it is not of him that willeth, nor of him that runneth, but of God that showeth mercy;" in another passage also, "that to will and to do are of God:" and again, elsewhere, "Therefore hath He mercy upon whom He will, and whom He will He hardeneth. Thou wilt say then unto me, Why doth He yet find fault? For who shall resist His will? O man, who art thou that repliest against God? Shall the thing formed say to him who hath formed it, Why hast thou made me thus? Hath not the potter power over the clay, of the same lump to make one vessel unto honour, and another to dishonour?"—these and similar declarations seem to have no small influence in preventing very many from believing that every one is to be considered as having freedom over his own will, and in making it appear to be a consequence of the will of God whether a man is either saved or lost.

8. Let us begin, then, with those words which were spoken to Pharaoh, who is said to have been hardened by God, in order that he might not let the people go; and, along with his case, the language of the apostle also will be considered, where he says, "Therefore He hath mercy on whom He will, and whom He will He hardeneth." For it is on these passages chiefly that the heretics rely, asserting that salvation is not in our own power, but that souls are of such a nature as must by all means be either lost or saved; and that in no way can a soul which is of an evil nature become good, or one which is of a virtuous nature be made bad. And hence they maintain that Pharaoh, too, being of a ruined nature, was on that account hardened by God, who hardens those that are of an earthly nature, but has compassion on those who are of a spiritual nature. Let us see, then, what is the meaning of their assertion; and let us, in the first place, request them to tell us whether they maintain that the soul of Pharaoh was of an earthly nature, such

as they term lost. They will undoubtedly answer that it was of an earthly nature. If so, then to believe God, or to obey Him, when his nature opposed his so doing, was an impossibility. And if this were his condition by nature, what further need was there for his heart to be hardened, and this not once, but several times, unless indeed because it was possible for him to yield to persuasion? Nor could any one be said to be hardened by another, save him who of himself was not obdurate. And if he were not obdurate of himself, it follows that neither was he of an earthly nature, but such an one as might give way when overpowered by signs and wonders. But he was necessary for God's purpose, in order that, for the saving of the multitude, He might manifest in him His power by his offering resistance to numerous miracles, and struggling against the will of God, and his heart being by this means said to be hardened. Such are our answers, in the first place, to these persons; and by these their assertion may be overturned, according to which they think that Pharaoh was destroyed in consequence of his evil nature. And with regard to the language of the Apostle Paul, we must answer them in a similar way. For who are they whom God hardens, according to your view? Those, namely, whom you term of a ruined nature, and who, I am to suppose, would have done something else had they not been hardened. If, indeed, they come to destruction in consequence of being hardened, they no longer perish naturally, but in virtue of what befalls them. Then, in the next place, upon whom does God show mercy? On those, namely, who are to be saved. And in what respect do those persons stand in need of a second compassion, who are to be saved once by their nature, and so come naturally to blessedness, except that it is shown even from their case, that, because it was possible for them to perish, they therefore obtain mercy, that so they may not perish, but come to salvation, and possess the kingdom of the good. And let this be our answer to those who devise and invent the fable of good or bad natures, i.e., of earthly or spiritual souls, in consequence of which, as they say, each one is either saved or lost.

9. And now we must return an answer also to those who would have the God of the law to be just only, and not also good; and let us ask such in what manner they consider the heart of Pharaoh to have been hardened by God—by what acts or by what prospective arrangements. For we must observe the conception of a God who in our opinion is both just and good, but according to them only just. And let them show us how a God whom they also acknowledge to be just, can with justice cause the heart of a man to be hardened, that, in consequence of that very hardening, he may sin and be ruined. And how shall the justice of

God be defended, if He Himself is the cause of the destruction of those whom, owing to their unbelief (through their being hardened), He has afterwards condemned by the authority of a judge? For why does He blame him, saying, "But since thou wilt not let My people go, lo, I will smite all the first-born in Egypt, even thy first-born," and whatever else was spoken through Moses by God to Pharaoh? For it behoves every one who maintains the truth of what is recorded in Scripture, and who desires to show that the God of the law and the prophets is just, to render a reason for all these things, and to show how there is in them nothing at all derogatory to the justice of God, since, although they deny His goodness, they admit that He is a just judge, and creator of the world. Different, however, is the method of our reply to those who assert that the creator of this world is a malignant being, i.e., a devil.

10. But since we acknowledge the God who spoke by Moses to be not only just, but also good, let us carefully inquire how it is in keeping with the character of a just and good Deity to have hardened the heart of Pharaoh. And let us see whether, following the example of the Apostle Paul, we are able to solve the difficulty by help of some parallel instances: if we can show, e.g., that by one and the same act God has pity upon one individual, but hardens another; not purposing or desiring that he who is hardened should be so, but because, in the manifestation of His goodness and patience, the heart of those who treat His kindness and forbearance with contempt and insolence is hardened by the punishment of their crimes being delayed; while those, on the other hand, who make His goodness and patience the occasion of their repentance and reformation, obtain compassion. To show more clearly, however, what we mean, let us take the illustration employed by the Apostle Paul in the Epistle to the Hebrews, where he says, "For the earth, which drinketh in the rain that cometh oft upon it, and bringeth forth herbs meet for them by whom it is dressed, will receive blessing from God; but that which beareth thorns and briers is rejected, and is nigh unto cursing, whose end is to be burned." Now from those words of Paul which we have quoted, it is clearly shown that by one and the same act on the part of God—that, viz., by which He sends rain upon the earth—one portion of the ground, when carefully cultivated, brings forth good fruits; while another, neglected and uncared for, produces thorns and thistles. And if one, speaking as it were in the person of the rain, were to say, "It is I, the rain, that have made the good fruits, and it is I that have caused the thorns and thistles to grow," however hard the statement might appear, it would nevertheless be true; for unless the rain had fallen, neither fruits, nor thorns, nor thistles would have sprung up, whereas by the coming of

the rain the earth gave birth to both. Now, although it is due to the beneficial action of the rain that the earth has produced herbs of both kinds, it is not to the rain that the diversity of the herbs is properly to be ascribed; but on those will justly rest the blame for the bad seed, who, although they might have turned up the ground by frequent ploughing, and have broken the clods by repeated harrowing, and have extirpated all useless and noxious weeds, and have cleared and prepared the fields for the coming showers by all the labour and toil which cultivation demands, have nevertheless neglected to do this, and who will accordingly reap briers and thorns, the most appropriate fruit of their sloth. And the consequence therefore is, that while the rain falls in kindness and impartiality equally upon the whole earth, yet, by one and the same operation of the rain, that soil which is cultivated yields with a blessing useful fruits to the diligent and careful cultivators, while that which has become hardened through the neglect of the husbandman brings forth only thorns and thistles. Let us therefore view those signs and miracles which were done by God, as the showers furnished by Him from above; and the purpose and desires of men, as the cultivated and uncultivated soil, which is of one and the same nature indeed, as is every soil compared with another, but not in one and the same state of cultivation. From which it follows that every one's will, if untrained, and fierce, and barbarous, is either hardened by the miracles and wonders of God, growing more savage and thorny than ever, or it becomes more pliant, and yields itself up with the whole mind to obedience, if it be cleared from vice and subjected to training.

11. But, to establish the point more clearly, it will not be superfluous to employ another illustration, as if, e.g., one were to say that it is the sun which hardens and liquefies, although liquefying and hardening are things of an opposite nature. Now it is not incorrect to say that the sun, by one and the same power of its heat, melts wax indeed, but dries up and hardens mud: not that its power operates one way upon mud, and in another way upon wax; but that the qualities of mud and wax are different, although according to nature they are one thing, both being from the earth. In this way, then, one and the same working upon the part of God, which was administered by Moses in signs and wonders, made manifest the hardness of Pharaoh, which he had conceived in the intensity of his wickedness but exhibited the obedience of those other Egyptians who were intermingled with the Israelites, and who are recorded to have quitted Egypt at the same time with the Hebrews. With respect to the statement that the heart of Pharaoh was subdued by degrees, so that on one occasion he said, "Go not far away; ye shall go a three days' journey, but leave your wives, and your children, and

your cattle," and as regards any other statements, according to which he appears to yield gradually to the signs and wonders, what else is shown, save that the power of the signs and miracles was making some impression on him, but not so much as it ought to have done? For if the hardening were of such a nature as many take it to be, he would not indeed have given way even in a few instances. But I think there is no absurdity in explaining the tropical or figurative nature of that language employed in speaking of "hardening," according to common usage. For those masters who are remarkable for kindness to their slaves, are frequently accustomed to say to the latter, when, through much patience and indulgence on their part, they have become insolent and worthless: "It is I that have made you what you are; I have spoiled you; it is my endurance that has made you good for nothing: I am to blame for your perverse and wicked habits, because I do not have you immediately punished for every delinquency according to your deserts." For we must first attend to the tropical or figurative meaning of the language, and so come to see the force of the expression, and not find fault with the word, whose inner meaning we do not ascertain. Finally, the Apostle Paul, evidently treating of such, says to him who remained in his sins: "Despisest thou the riches of His goodness, and forbearance, and long-suffering; not knowing that the goodness of God leadeth thee to repentance? but, after thy hardness and impenitent heart, treasurest up unto thyself wrath on the day of wrath and revelation of the righteous judgment of God." Such are the words of the apostle to him who is in his sins. Let us apply these very expressions to Pharaoh, and see if they also are not spoken of him with propriety, since, according to his hardness and impenitent heart, he treasured and stored up for himself wrath on the day of wrath, inasmuch as his hardness could never have been declared and manifested, unless signs and wonders of such number and magnificence had been performed.

12. But if the proofs which we have adduced do not appear full enough, and the similitude of the apostle seem wanting in applicability, let us add the voice of prophetic authority, and see what the prophets declare regarding those who at first, indeed, leading a righteous life, have deserved to receive numerous proofs of the goodness of God, but afterwards, as being human beings, have fallen astray, with whom the prophet, making himself also one, says: "Why, O LORD, hast Thou made us to err from Thy way? and hardened our heart, that we should not fear Thy name? Return, for Thy servants' sake, for the tribes of Thine inheritance, that we also for a little may obtain some inheritance from Thy holy hill." Jeremiah also employs similar language: "O LORD, Thou hast deceived us, and we were deceived; Thou hast held (us), and

Thou hast prevailed." The expression, then, "Why, O Lord, hast Thou hardened our heart, that we should not fear Thy name?" used by those who prayed for mercy, is to be taken in a figurative, moral acceptation, as if one were to say, "Why hast Thou spared us so long, and didst not requite us when we sinned, but didst abandon us, that so our wickedness might increase, and our liberty of sinning be extended when punishment ceased?" In like manner, unless a horse continually feel the spur of his rider, and have his mouth abraded by a bit, he becomes hardened. And a boy also, unless constantly disciplined by chastisement, will grow up to be an insolent youth, and one ready to fall headlong into vice. God accordingly abandons and neglects those whom He has judged undeserving of chastisement: "For whom the Lord loveth He chasteneth, and scourgeth every son whom He receiveth." From which we are to suppose that those are to be received into the rank and affection of sons, who have deserved to be scourged and chastened by the Lord, in order that they also, through endurance of trials and tribulations, may be able to say, "Who shall separate us from the love of God which is in Christ Jesus? shall tribulation, or anguish, or famine, or nakedness, or peril, or sword?" For by all these is each one's resolution manifested and displayed, and the firmness of his perseverance made known, not so much to God, who knows all things before they happen, as to the rational and heavenly virtues, who have obtained a part in the work of procuring human salvation, as being a sort of assistants and ministers to God. Those, on the other hand, who do not yet offer themselves to God with such constancy and affection, and are not ready to come into His service, and to prepare their souls for trial, are said to be abandoned by God, i.e., not to be instructed, inasmuch as they are not prepared for instruction, their training or care being undoubtedly postponed to a later time. These certainly do not know what they will obtain from God, unless they first entertain the desire of being benefited; and this finally will be the case, if a man come first to a knowledge of himself, and feel what are his defects, and understand from whom he either ought or can seek the supply of his deficiencies. For he who does not know beforehand of his weakness or his sickness, cannot seek a physician; or at least, after recovering his health, that man will not be grateful to his physician who did not first recognise the dangerous nature of his ailment. And so, unless a man has first ascertained the defects of his life, and the evil nature of his sins, and made this known by confession from his own lips, he cannot be cleansed or acquitted, lest he should be ignorant that what he possesses has been bestowed on him by favour, but should consider as his own property what flows from the divine liberality, which idea undoubtedly generates arrogance of mind and pride, and finally becomes the cause of the individual's ruin. And this, we must believe, was the case with the devil, who viewed as his own, and not as given him by God, the primacy which he held at the time when he was unstained; and thus was fulfilled in him the declaration, that "every one who exalteth himself shall be abased." From which it appears to me that the divine mysteries were concealed from the wise and prudent, according to the statement of Scripture, that "no flesh should glory before God," and revealed to children—to those, namely, who, after they have become infants and little children, i.e., have returned to the humility and simplicity of children, then make progress; and on arriving at perfection, remember that they have obtained their state of happiness, not by their own merits, but by the grace and compassion of God.

13. It is therefore by the sentence of God that he is abandoned who deserves to be so, while over some sinners God exercises forbearance; not, however, without a definite principle of action. Nay, the very fact that He is long-suffering conduces to the advantage of those very persons, since the soul over which He exercises this providential care is immortal; and, as being immortal and everlasting, it is not, although not immediately cared for, excluded from salvation, which is postponed to a more convenient time. For perhaps it is expedient for those who have been more deeply imbued with the poison of wickedness to obtain this salvation at a later period. For as medical men sometimes, although they could quickly cover over the scars of wounds, keep back and delay the cure for the present, in the expectation of a better and more perfect recovery, knowing that it is more salutary to retard the treatment in the cases of swellings caused by wounds, and to allow the malignant humours to flow off for a while, rather than to hasten a superficial cure, by shutting up in the veins the poison of a morbid humour, which, excluded from its customary outlets, will undoubtedly creep into the inner parts of the limbs, and penetrate to the very vitals of the viscera, producing no longer mere disease in the body, but causing destruction to life; so, in like manner, God also, who knows the secret things of the heart, and foreknows the future, in much forbearance allows certain events to happen, which, coming from without upon men, cause to come forth into the light the passions and vices which are concealed within, that by their means those may be cleansed and cured who, through great negligence and carelessness, have admitted within themselves the roots and seeds of sins, so that, when driven outwards and brought to the surface, they may in a certain degree be cast forth and dispersed. And thus, although a man may appear to be afflicted

with evils of a serious kind, suffering convulsions in all his limbs, he may nevertheless, at some future time, obtain relief and a cessation from his trouble; and, after enduring his afflictions to satiety, may, after many sufferings, be restored again to his (proper) condition. For God deals with souls not merely with a view to the short space of our present life, included within sixty years or more, but with reference to a perpetual and never-ending period, exercising His providential care over souls that are immortal, even as He Himself is eternal and immortal. For He made the rational nature, which He formed in His own image and likeness, incorruptible; and therefore the soul, which is immortal, is not excluded by the shortness of the present life from the divine remedies and cures.

14. But let us take from the Gospels also the similitudes of those things which we have mentioned, in which is described a certain rock, having on it a little superficial earth, on which, when a seed falls, it is said quickly to spring up; but when sprung up, it withers as the sun ascends in the heavens, and dies away, because it did not cast its root deeply into the ground. Now this rock undoubtedly represents the human soul, hardened on account of its own negligence, and converted into stone because of its wickedness. For God gave no one a stony heart by a creative act; but each individual's heart is said to become stony through his own wickedness and disobedience. As, therefore, if one were to blame a husbandman for not casting his seed more quickly upon rocky ground, because seed cast upon other rocky soil was seen to spring up speedily, the husbandman would certainly say in reply: "I sow this soil more slowly, for this reason, that it may retain the seed which it has received; for it suits this ground to be sown somewhat slowly, lest perhaps the crop, having sprouted too rapidly, and coming forth from the mere surface of a shallow soil, should be unable to withstand the rays of the sun." Would not he who formerly found fault acquiesce in the reasons and superior knowledge of the husbandman, and approve as done on rational grounds what formerly appeared to him as founded on no reason? And in the same way, God, the thoroughly skilled husbandman of all His creation, undoubtedly conceals and delays to another time those things which we think ought to have obtained health sooner, in order that not the outside of things, rather than the inside, may be cured. But if any one now were to object to us that certain seeds do even fall upon rocky ground, i.e., on a hard and stony heart, we should answer that even this does not happen without the arrangement of Divine Providence; inasmuch as, but for this, it would not be known what condemnation was incurred by rashness in hearing and indifference in investigation, nor, certainly,

what benefit was derived from being trained in an orderly manner. And hence it happens that the soul comes to know its defects, and to cast the blame upon itself, and, consistently with this, to reserve and submit itself to training, i.e., in order that it may see that its faults must first be removed, and that then it must come to receive the instruction of wisdom. As, therefore, souls are innumerable, so also are their manners, and purposes, and movements, and appetencies, and incitements different, the variety of which can by no means be grasped by the human mind; and therefore to God alone must be left the art, and the knowledge, and the power of an arrangement of this kind, as He alone can know both the remedies for each individual soul, and measure out the time of its cure. It is He alone then who, as we said, recognises the ways of individual men, and determines by what way He ought to lead Pharaoh, that through him His name might be named in all the earth, having previously chastised him by many blows, and finally drowning him in the sea. By this drowning, however, it is not to be supposed that God's providence as regards Pharaoh was terminated; for we must not imagine, because he was drowned, that therefore he had forthwith completely perished: "for in the hand of God are both we and our words; all wisdom, also, and knowledge of workmanship," as Scripture declares. But these points we have discussed according to our ability, treating of that chapter of Scripture in which it is said that God hardened the heart of Pharaoh, and agreeably to the statement, "He hath mercy on whom He will have mercy, and whom He will He hardeneth."

15. Let us now look at those passages of Ezekiel where he says, "I will take away from them their stony heart, and I will put in them a heart of flesh, that they may walk in My statutes, and keep Mine ordinances. For if God, when He pleases, takes away a heart of stone and bestows a heart of flesh, that His ordinances may be observed and His commandments may be obeyed, it will then appear that it is not in our power to put away wickedness. For the taking away of a stony heart seems to be nothing else than the removal of the wickedness by which one is hardened, from whomsoever God pleases to remove it. Nor is the bestowal of a heart of flesh, that the precepts of God may be observed and His commandments obeyed, any other thing than a man becoming obedient, and no longer resisting the truth, but performing works of virtue. If, then, God promises to do this, and if, before He takes away the stony heart, we are unable to remove it from ourselves, it follows that it is not in our power, but in God's only, to cast away wickedness. And again, if it is not our doing to form within us a heart of flesh, but the work of God alone, it will not be in our power to live

133

virtuously, but it will in everything appear to be a work of divine grace. Such are the assertions of those who wish to prove from the authority of Holy Scripture that nothing lies in our own power. Now to these we answer, that these passages are not to be so understood, but in the following manner. Take the case of one who was ignorant and untaught, and who, feeling the disgrace of his ignorance, should, driven either by an exhortation from some person, or incited by a desire to emulate other wise men, hand himself over to one by whom he is assured that he will be carefully trained and competently instructed. If he, then, who had formerly hardened himself in ignorance, yield himself, as we have said, with full purpose of mind to a master, and promise to obey him in all things, the master, on seeing clearly the resolute nature of his determination, will appropriately promise to take away all ignorance, and to implant knowledge within his mind; not that he undertakes to do this if the disciple refuse or resist his efforts, but only on his offering and binding himself to obedience in all things. So also the Word of God promises to those who draw near to Him, that He will take away their stony heart, not indeed from those who do not listen to His word, but from those who receive the precepts of His teaching; as in the Gospels we find the sick approaching the Saviour, asking to receive health, and thus at last be cured. And in order that the blind might be healed and regain their sight, their part consisted in making supplication to the Saviour, and in believing that their cure could be effected by Him; while His part, on the other hand, lay in restoring to them the power of vision. And in this way also does the Word of God promise to bestow instruction by taking away the stony heart, i.e., by the removal of wickedness, that so men may be able to walk in the divine precepts, and observe the commandments of the law.

16. There is next brought before us that declaration uttered by the Saviour in the Gospel: "That seeing they may see, and not perceive; and hearing they may hear, and not understand; lest they should happen to be converted, and their sins be forgiven them." On which our opponent will remark: "If those who shall hear more distinctly are by all means to be corrected and converted, and converted in such a manner as to be worthy of receiving the remission of sins, and if it be not in their own power to hear the word distinctly, but if it depend on the Instructor to teach more openly and distinctly, while he declares that he does not proclaim to them the word with clearness, lest they should perhaps hear and understand, and be converted, and be saved, it will follow, certainly, that their salvation is not dependent upon themselves. And if this be so, then we have no free-will either as regards salvation or destruction." Now were it not for the words that are added,

134

"Lest perhaps they should be converted, and their sins be forgiven them," we might be more inclined to return the answer, that the Saviour was unwilling that those individuals whom He foresaw would not become good, should understand the mysteries of the kingdom of heaven, and that therefore He spoke to them in parables; but as that addition follows, "Lest perhaps they should be converted, and their sins be forgiven them," the explanation is rendered more difficult. And, in the first place, we have to notice what defence this passage furnishes against those heretics who are accustomed to hunt out of the Old Testament any expressions which seem, according to their view, to predicate severity and cruelty of God the Creator, as when He is described as being affected with the feeling of vengeance or punishment, or by any of those emotions, however named, from which they deny the existence of goodness in the Creator; for they do not judge of the Gospels with the same mind and feelings, and do not observe whether any such statements are found in them as they condemn and censure in the Old Testament. For manifestly, in the passage referred to, the Saviour is shown, as they themselves admit, not to speak distinctly, for this very reason, that men may not be converted, and when converted, receive the remission of sins. Now, if the words be understood according to the letter merely, nothing less, certainly, will be contained in them than in those passages which they find fault with in the Old Testament. And if they are of opinion that any expressions occurring in such a connection in the New Testament stand in need of explanation, it will necessarily follow that those also occurring in the Old Testament, which are the subject of censure, may be freed from aspersion by an explanation of a similar kind, so that by such means the passages found in both Testaments may be shown to proceed from one and the same God. But let us return, as we best may, to the question proposed.

17. We said formerly, when discussing the case of Pharaoh, that sometimes it does not lead to good results for a man to be cured too quickly, especially if the disease, being shut up within the inner parts of the body, rage with greater fierceness. Whence God, who is acquainted with secret things, and knows all things before they happen, in His great goodness delays the cure of such, and postpones their recovery to a remoter period, and, so to speak, cures them by not curing them, lest a too favourable state of health should render them incurable. It is therefore possible that, in the case of those to whom, as being "without," the words of our Lord and Saviour were addressed, He, seeing from His scrutiny of the hearts and reins that they were not yet able to receive teaching of a clearer type, veiled by the covering of

language the meaning of the profounder mysteries, lest perhaps, being rapidly converted and healed, i.e., having quickly obtained the remission of their sins, they should again easily slide back into the same disease which they had found could be healed without any difficulty. For if this be the case, no one can doubt that the punishment is doubled, and the amount of wickedness increased; since not only are the sins which had appeared to be forgiven repeated, but the court of virtue also is desecrated when trodden by deceitful and polluted beings, filled within with hidden wickedness. And what remedy can there ever be for those who, after eating the impure and filthy food of wickedness, have tasted the pleasantness of virtue, and received its sweetness into their mouths, and yet have again betaken themselves to the deadly and poisonous provision of sin? And who doubts that it is better for delay and a temporary abandonment to occur, in order that if, at some future time, they should happen to be satiated with wickedness, and the filth with which they are now delighted should become loathsome, the word of God may at last be appropriately made clear to them, and that which is holy be not given to the dogs, nor pearls be cast before swine, which will trample them under foot, and turn, moreover, and rend and assault those who have proclaimed to them the word of God? These, then, are they who are said to be "without," undoubtedly by way of contrast with those who are said to be "within," and to hear the word of God with greater clearness. And yet those who are "without" do hear the word, although it is covered by parables, and overshadowed by proverbs. There are others, also, besides those who are without, who are called Tyrians, and who do not hear at all, respecting whom the Saviour knew that they would have repented long ago, sitting in sackcloth and ashes, if the miracles performed among others had been done amongst them, and yet these do not hear those things which are heard even by those who are "without:" and I believe, for this reason, that the rank of such in wickedness was far lower and worse than that of those who are said to be "without," i.e., who are not far from those who are within, and who have deserved to hear the word, although in parables; and because, perhaps, their cure was delayed to that time when it will be more tolerable for them on the day of judgment, than for those before whom those miracles which are recorded were performed, that so at last, being then relieved from the weight of their sins, they may enter with more ease and power of endurance upon the way of safety. And this is a point which I wish impressed upon those who peruse these pages, that with respect to topics of such difficulty and obscurity we use our utmost endeavour, not so much to ascertain clearly the solutions of the questions (for every one will do this as the Spirit gives him utterance), as to maintain the rule of faith in the most unmistakeable manner, by striving to show that the providence of God, which equitably administers all things, governs also immortal souls on the justest principles, (conferring rewards) according to the merits and motives of each individual; the present economy of things not being confined within the life of this world, but the pre-existing state of merit always furnishing the ground for the state that is to follow, and thus by an eternal and immutable law of equity, and by the controlling influence of Divine Providence, the immortal soul is brought to the summit of perfection. If one, however, were to object to our statement, that the word of preaching was purposely put aside by certain men of wicked and worthless character, and (were to inquire) why the word was preached to those over whom the Tyrians, who were certainly despised, are preferred in comparison (by which proceeding, certainly, their wickedness was increased, and their condemnation rendered more severe, that they should hear the word who were not to believe it), they must be answered in the following manner: God, who is the Creator of the minds of all men, foreseeing complaints against His providence, especially on the part of those who say, "How could we believe when we neither beheld those things which others saw, nor heard those words which were preached to others? in so far is the blame removed from us, since they to whom the word was announced, and the signs manifested, made no delay whatever, but became believers, overpowered by the very force of the miracles;" wishing to destroy the grounds for complaints of this kind, and to show that it was no concealment of Divine Providence, but the determination of the human mind which was the cause of their ruin, bestowed the grace of His benefits even upon the unworthy and the unbelieving, that every mouth might indeed be shut, and that the mind of man might know that all the deficiency was on its own part, and none on that of God; and that it may, at the same time, be understood and recognised that he receives a heavier sentence of condemnation who has despised the divine benefits conferred upon him than he who has not deserved to obtain or hear them, and that it is a peculiarity of divine compassion, and a mark of the extreme justice of its administration, that it sometimes conceals from certain individuals the opportunity of either seeing or hearing the mysteries of divine power, lest, after beholding the power of the miracles, and recognising and hearing the mysteries of its wisdom, they should, on treating them with contempt and indifference, be punished with greater severity for their impiety.

18. Let us now look to the expression, "It is not of him that willeth, nor of him that runneth, but of God that showeth mercy." For our

opponents assert, that if it does not depend upon him that willeth, nor on him that runneth, but on God that showeth mercy, that a man be saved, our salvation is not in our own power. For our nature is such as to admit of our either being saved or not, or else our salvation rests solely on the will of Him who, if He wills it, shows mercy, and confers salvation. Now let us inquire, in the first place, of such persons, whether to desire blessings be a good or evil act; and whether to hasten after good as a final aim be worthy of praise. If they were to answer that such a procedure was deserving of censure, they would evidently be mad; for all holy men both desire blessings and run after them, and certainly are not blameworthy. How, then, is it that he who is not saved, if he be of an evil nature, desires blessing, and runs after them, but does not find them? For they say that a bad tree does not bring forth good fruits, whereas it is a good fruit to desire blessings. And how is the fruit of a bad tree good? And if they assert that to desire blessings, and to run after them, is an act of indifference, i.e., neither good nor bad, we shall reply, that if it be an indifferent act to desire blessings, and to run after them, then the opposite of that will also be an indifferent act, viz., to desire evils, and to run after them; whereas it is certain that it is not an indifferent act to desire evils, and to run after them, but one that is manifestly wicked. It is established, then, that to desire and follow after blessings is not an indifferent, but a virtuous proceeding.

Having now repelled these objections by the answer which we have given, let us hasten on to the discussion of the subject itself, in which it is said, "It is not of him that willeth, nor of him that runneth, but of God that showeth mercy." In the book of Psalms—in the Songs of Degrees, which are ascribed to Solomon—the following statement occurs: "Except the LORD build the house, they labour in vain that build it; except the LORD keep the city, the watchman waketh but in vain." By which words he does not indeed indicate that we should cease from building or watching over the safe keeping of that city which is within us; but what he points out is this, that whatever is built without God, and whatever is guarded without him, is built in vain, and guarded to no purpose. For in all things that are well built and well protected, the Lord is held to be the cause either of the building or of its protection. As if, e.g., we were to behold some magnificent structure and mass of splendid building reared with beauteous architectural skill, would we not justly and deservedly say that such was built not by human power, but by divine help and might? And yet from such a statement it will not be meant that the labour and industry of human effort were inactive, and effected nothing at all. Or again, if we were to see some city surrounded by a severe blockade of the enemy, in which threatening engines were brought against the walls, and the place hard pressed by a vallum, and weapons, and fire, and all the instruments of war, by which destruction is prepared, would we not rightly and deservedly say, if the enemy were repelled and put to flight, that the deliverance had been wrought for the liberated city by God? And yet we would not mean, by so speaking, that either the vigilance of the sentinels, or the alertness of the young men, or the protection of the guards, had been wanting. And the apostle also must be understood in a similar manner, because the human will alone is not sufficient to obtain salvation; nor is any mortal running able to win the heavenly (rewards), and to obtain the prize of our high calling of God in Christ Jesus, unless this very good will of ours, and ready purpose, and whatever that diligence within us may be, be aided or furnished with divine help. And therefore most logically did the apostle say, that "it is not of him that willeth, nor of him that runneth, but of God that showeth mercy;" in the same manner as if we were to say of agriculture what is actually written: "I planted, Apollos watered; but God gave the increase. So then neither is he that planteth anything, neither he that watereth; but God that giveth the increase." As, therefore, when a field has brought good and rich crops to perfect maturity, no one would piously and logically assert that the husbandman had made those fruits, but would acknowledge that they had been produced by God; so also is our own perfection brought about, not indeed by our remaining inactive and idle, (but by some activity on our part): and yet the consummation of it will not be ascribed to us, but to God, who is the first and chief cause of the work. So, when a ship has overcome the dangers of the sea, although the result be accomplished by great labour on the part of the sailors, and by the aid of all the art of navigation, and by the zeal and carefulness of the pilot, and by the favouring influence of the breezes, and the careful observation of the signs of the stars, no one in his sound senses would ascribe the safety of the vessel, when, after being tossed by the waves, and wearied by the billows, it has at last reached the harbour in safety, to anything else than to the mercy of God. Not even the sailors or pilot venture to say, "I have saved the ship," but they refer all to the mercy of God; not that they feel that they have contributed no skill or labour to save the ship, but because they know that while they contributed the labour, the safety of the vessel was ensured by God. So also in the race of our life we ourselves must expend labour, and bring diligence and zeal to bear; but it is from God that salvation is to be hoped for as the fruit of our labour. Otherwise, if God demand none of our labour, His commandments will appear to be superfluous. In vain, also, does Paul blame some for having fallen from the truth, and praise others for abiding in the faith; and to no purpose does he deliver certain precepts and institutions to the Churches: in vain, also, do we ourselves either desire or run after what is good. But it is certain that these things are not done in vain; and it is certain that neither do the apostles give instructions in vain, nor the Lord enact laws without a reason. It follows, therefore, that we declare it to be in vain, rather, for the heretics to speak evil of these good declarations.

19. After this there followed this point, that "to will and to do are of God." Our opponents maintain that if to will be of God, and if to do be of Him, or if, whether we act or desire well or ill, it be of God, then in that case we are not possessed of free-will. Now to this we have to answer, that the words of the apostle do not say that to will evil is of God, or that to will good is of Him; nor that to do good or evil is of God; but his statement is a general one, that to will and to do are of God. For as we have from God this very quality, that we are men, that we breathe, that we move; so also we have from God (the faculty) by which we will, as if we were to say that our power of motion is from God, or that the performing of these duties by the individual members, and their movements, are from God. From which, certainly, I do not understand this, that because the hand moves, e.g., to punish unjustly, or to commit an act of theft, the act is of God, but only that the power of motion is from God; while it is our duty to turn those movements, the power of executing which we have from God, either to purposes of good or evil. And so what the apostle says is, that we receive indeed the power of volition, but that we misuse the will either to good or evil desires. In a similar way, also, we must judge of results.

20. But with respect to the declaration of the apostle, "Therefore hath He mercy on whom He will have mercy, and whom He will He hardeneth. Thou wilt say then unto me, Why doth He yet find fault? For who hath resisted His will? Nay but, O man, who art thou that repliest against God? Shall the thing formed say to him that formed it, Why hast thou made me thus? Hath not the potter power over the clay, of the same lump to make one vessel unto honour, and another unto dishonour?" Some one will perhaps say, that as the potter out of the same lump makes some vessels to honour, and others to dishonour, so God creates some men for perdition, and others for salvation; and that it is not therefore in our own power either to be saved or to perish; by which reasoning we appear not to be possessed of free-will. We must answer those who are of this opinion with the question, Whether it is possible for the apostle to contradict himself? And if this cannot be imagined of an apostle, how shall he appear, according to them, to be

140

just in blaming those who committed fornication in Corinth, or those who sinned, and did not repent of their unchastity, and fornication, and uncleanness, which they had committed? How, also, does he greatly praise those who acted rightly, like the house of Onesiphorus, saying, "The Lord give mercy to the house of Onesiphorus; for he oft refreshed me, and was not ashamed of my chain: but, when he had come to Rome, he sought me out very diligently, and found me. The Lord grant unto him that he may find mercy of the Lord in that day." Now it is not consistent with apostolic gravity to blame him who is worthy of blame, i.e., who has sinned, and greatly to praise him who is deserving of praise for his good works; and again, as if it were in no one's power to do any good or evil, to say that it was the Creator's doing that every one should act virtuously or wickedly, seeing He makes one vessel to honour, and another to dishonour. And how can he add that statement, "We must all stand before the judgment-seat of Christ, that every one of us may receive in his body, according to what he hath done, whether it be good or bad?" For what reward of good will be conferred on him who could not commit evil, being formed by the Creator to that very end? or what punishment will deservedly be inflicted on him who was unable to do good in consequence of the creative act of his Maker? Then, again, how is not this opposed to that other declaration elsewhere, that "in a great house there are not only vessels of gold and silver, but also of wood and of earth, and some to honour, and some to dishonour. If a man therefore purge himself from these, he shall be a vessel unto honour, sanctified, and meet for the Master's use, prepared unto every good work." He, accordingly, who purges himself, is made a vessel unto honour, while he who has disdained to cleanse himself from his impurity is made a vessel unto dishonour. From such declarations, in my opinion, the cause of our actions can in no degree be referred to the Creator. For God the Creator makes a certain vessel unto honour, and other vessels to dishonour; but that vessel which has cleansed itself from all impurity He makes a vessel unto honour, while that which has stained itself with the filth of vice He makes a vessel unto dishonour. The conclusion from which, accordingly, is this, that the cause of each one's actions is a pre-existing one; and then every one, according to his deserts, is made by God either a vessel unto honour or dishonour. Therefore every individual vessel has furnished to its Creator out of itself the causes and occasions of its being formed by Him to be either a vessel unto honour or one unto dishonour. And if the assertion appear correct, as it certainly is, and in harmony with all piety, that it is due to previous causes that every vessel be prepared by God either to honour or to dishonour, it does not appear absurd that, in discussing remoter causes in the same order, and in the same method, we should come to the same conclusion respecting the nature of souls, and (believe) that this was the reason why Jacob was beloved before he was born into this world, and Esau hated, while he still was contained in the womb of his mother.

21. Nay, that very declaration, that from the same lump a vessel is formed both to honour and to dishonour, will not push us hard; for we assert that the nature of all rational souls is the same, as one lump of clay is described as being under the treatment of the potter. Seeing, then, the nature of rational creatures is one, God, according to the previous grounds of merit, created and formed out of it, as the potter out of the one lump, some persons to honour and others to dishonour. Now, as regards the language of the apostle, which he utters as if in a tone of censure, "Nay but, O man, who art thou that repliest against God?" he means, I think, to point out that such a censure does not refer to any believer who lives rightly and justly, and who has confidence in God, i.e., to such an one as Moses was, of whom Scripture says that "Moses spake, and God answered him by a voice;" and as God answered Moses, so also does every saint answer God. But he who is an unbeliever, and loses confidence in answering before God owing to the unworthiness of his life and conversation, and who, in relation to these matters, does not seek to learn and make progress, but to oppose and resist, and who, to speak more plainly, is such an one as to be able to say those words which the apostle indicates, when he says, "Why, then, does He yet find fault? for who will resist His will?"—to such an one may the censure of the apostle rightly be directed, "Nay but, O man, who art thou that repliest against God?" This censure accordingly applies not to believers and saints, but to unbelievers and wicked men.

Now, to those who introduce souls of different natures, and who turn this declaration of the apostle to the support of their own opinion, we have to reply as follows: If even they are agreed as to what the apostle says, that out of the one lump are formed both those who are made to honour and those who are made to dishonour, whom they term of a nature that is to be saved and destroyed, there will then be no longer souls of different natures, but one nature for all. And if they admit that one and the same potter may undoubtedly denote one Creator, there will not be different creators either of those who are saved, or of those who perish. Now, truly, let them choose whether they will have a good Creator to be intended who creates bad and ruined men, or one who is not good, who creates good men and those who are prepared to honour. For the necessity of returning an answer will extort from them one of these two alternatives. But according to our declaration, whereby we say that it is owing to preceding causes that God makes vessels either to honour or to dishonour, the approval of God's justice is in no respect limited. For it is possible that this vessel, which owing to previous causes was made in this world to honour, may, if it behave negligently, be converted in another world, according to the deserts of its conduct, into a vessel unto dishonour: as again, if any one, owing to preceding causes, was formed by his Creator in this life a vessel unto dishonour, and shall mend his ways and cleanse himself from all filth and vice, he may, in the new world, be made a vessel to honour, sanctified and useful, and prepared unto every good work. Finally, those who were formed by God in this world to be Israelites, and who have lived a life unworthy of the nobility of their race, and have fallen away from the grandeur of their descent, will, in the world to come, in a certain degree be converted, on account of their unbelief, from vessels of honour into vessels of dishonour; while, on the other hand, many who in this life were reckoned among Egyptian or Idumean vessels, having adopted the faith and practice of Israelites, when they shall have done the works of Israelites, and shall have entered the Church of the Lord, will exist as vessels of honour in the revelation of the sons of God. From which it is more agreeable to the rule of piety to believe that every rational being, according to his purpose and manner of life, is converted, sometimes from bad to good, and falls away sometimes from good to bad: that some abide in good, and others advance to a better condition, and always ascend to higher things, until they reach the highest grade of all; while others, again, remain in evil, or, if the wickedness within them begin to spread itself further, they descend to a worse condition, and sink into the lowest depth of wickedness. Whence also we must suppose that it is possible there may be some who began at first indeed with small offences, but who have poured out wickedness to such a degree, and attained such proficiency in evil, that in the measure of their wickedness they are equal even to the opposing powers: and again, if, by means of many severe administrations of punishment, they are able at some future time to recover their senses, and gradually attempt to find healing for their wounds, they may, on ceasing from their wickedness, be restored to a state of goodness. Whence we are of opinion that, seeing the soul, as we have frequently said, is immortal and eternal, it is possible that, in the many and endless periods of duration in the immeasurable and different worlds, it may descend from the highest good to the lowest evil, or be restored from the lowest evil to the highest good.

22. But since the words of the apostle, in what he says regarding vessels of honour or dishonour, that "if a man therefore purge himself, he will be a vessel unto honour, sanctified and meet for the Master's service, and prepared unto every good work," appear to place nothing in the power of God, but all in ourselves; while in those in which he declares that "the potter hath power over the clay, to make of the same lump one vessel to honour, another to dishonour," he seems to refer the whole to God,—it is not to be understood that those statements are contradictory, but the two meanings are to be reduced to agreement, and one signification must be drawn from both, viz., that we are not to suppose either that those things which are in our own power can be done without the help of God, or that those which are in God's hand can be brought to completion without the intervention of our acts, and desires, and intention; because we have it not in our own power so to will or do anything, as not to know that this very faculty, by which we are able to will or to do, was bestowed on us by God, according to the distinction which we indicated above. Or again, when God forms vessels, some to honour and others to dishonour, we are to suppose that He does not regard either our wills, or our purposes, or our deserts, to be the causes of the honour or dishonour, as if they were a sort of matter from which He may form the vessel of each one of us either to honour or to dishonour; whereas the very movement of the soul itself, or the purpose of the understanding, may of itself suggest to him, who is not unaware of his heart and the thoughts of his mind, whether his vessel ought to be formed to honour or to dishonour. But let these points suffice, which we have discussed as we best could, regarding the questions connected with the freedom of the will.

CHAPTER I [FROM THE GREEK]—ON THE FREEDOM OF THE WILL, WITH AN EXPLANATION AND INTERPRETATION OF THOSE STATEMENTS OF SCRIPTURE WHICH APPEAR TO NULLIFY IT

1. Since in the preaching of the Church there is included the doctrine respecting a just judgment of God, which, when believed to be true, incites those who hear it to live virtuously, and to shun sin by all means, inasmuch as they manifestly acknowledge that things worthy of praise and blame are within our own power, come and let us discuss by themselves a few points regarding the freedom of the will—a question of all others most necessary. And that we may understand what the

freedom of the will is, it is necessary to unfold the conception of it, that this being declared with precision, the subject may be placed before us.

2. Of things that move, some have the cause of their motion within themselves; others, again, are moved only from without. Now only portable things are moved from without, such as pieces of wood, and stones, and all matter that is held together by their constitution alone. And let that view be removed from consideration which calls the flux of bodies motion, since it is not needed for our present purpose. But animals and plants have the cause of their motion within themselves, and in general whatever is held together by nature and a soul, to which class of things they say that metals also belong. And besides these, fire too is self-moved, and perhaps also fountains of water. Now, of those things which have the cause of their movement within themselves, some, they say, are moved out of themselves, others from themselves: things without life, out of themselves; animate things, from themselves. For animate things are moved from themselves, a phantasy springing up in them which incites to effort. And again, in certain animals phantasies are formed which call forth an effort, the nature of the phantasy stirring up the effort in an orderly manner, as in the spider is formed the phantasy of weaving; and the attempt to weave follows, the nature of its phantasy inciting the insect in an orderly manner to this alone. And besides its phantasial nature, nothing else is believed to belong to the insect. And in the bee there is formed the phantasy to produce wax.

3. The rational animal, however, has, in addition to its phantasial nature, also reason, which judges the phantasies, and disapproves of some and accepts others, in order that the animal may be led according to them. Therefore, since there are in the nature of reason aids towards the contemplation of virtue and vice, by following which, after beholding good and evil, we select the one and avoid the other, we are deserving of praise when we give ourselves to the practice of virtue, and censurable when we do the reverse. We must not, however, be ignorant that the greater part of the nature assigned to all things is a varying quantity among animals, both in a greater and a less degree; so that the instinct in hunting-dogs and in war-horses approaches somehow, so to speak, to the faculty of reason. Now, to fall under some one of those external causes which stir up within us this phantasy or that, is confessedly not one of those things that are dependent upon ourselves; but to determine that we shall use the occurrence in this way or differently, is the prerogative of nothing else than of the reason within us, which, as occasion offers, arouses us towards efforts inciting to what is virtuous and becoming, or turns us aside to what is the

reverse.

4. But if any one maintain that this very external cause is of such a nature that it is impossible to resist it when it comes in such a way, let him turn his attention to his own feelings and movements, (and see) whether there is not an approval, and assent, and inclination of the controlling principle towards some object on account of some specious arguments. For, to take an instance, a woman who has appeared before a man that has determined to be chaste, and to refrain from carnal intercourse, and who has incited him to act contrary to his purpose, is not a perfect cause of annulling his determination. For, being altogether pleased with the luxury and allurement of the pleasure, and not wishing to resist it, or to keep his purpose, he commits an act of licentiousness. Another man, again (when the same things have happened to him who has received more instruction, and has disciplined himself), encounters, indeed, allurements and enticements; but his reason, as being strengthened to a higher point, and carefully trained, and confirmed in its views towards a virtuous course, or being near to confirmation, repels the incitement, and extinguishes the desire.

5. Such being the case, to say that we are moved from without, and to put away the blame from ourselves, by declaring that we are like to pieces of wood and stones, which are dragged about by those causes that act upon them from without, is neither true nor in conformity with reason, but is the statement of him who wishes to destroy the conception of free-will. For if we were to ask such an one what was free-will, he would say that it consisted in this, that when purposing to do some thing, no external cause came inciting to the reverse. But to blame, on the other hand, the mere constitution of the body, is absurd; for the disciplinary reason, taking hold of those who are most intemperate and savage (if they will follow her exhortation), effects a transformation, so that the alteration and change for the better is most extensive,—the most licentious men frequently becoming better than those who formerly did not seem to be such by nature; and the most savage men passing into such a state of mildness, that those persons who never at any time were so savage as they were, appear savage in comparison, so great a degree of gentleness having been produced within them. And we see other men, most steady and respectable, driven from their state of respectability and steadiness by intercourse with evil customs, so as to fall into habits of licentiousness, often beginning their wickedness in middle age, and plunging into disorder after the period of youth has passed, which, so far as its nature is concerned, is unstable. Reason, therefore, demonstrates that external events do not depend on us, but that it is our own business to use them

in this way or the opposite, having received reason as a judge and an investigator of the manner in which we ought to meet those events that come from without.

6. Now, that it is our business to live virtuously, and that God asks this of us, as not being dependent on Him nor on any other, nor, as some think, upon fate, but as being our own doing, the prophet Micah will prove when he says: "If it has been announced to thee, O man, what is good, or what does the LORD require of thee, except to do justice and to love mercy?" Moses also: "I have placed before thy face the way of life, and the way of death: choose what is good, and walk in it." Isaiah too: "If you are willing, and hear me, ye shall eat the good of the land; but if ye be unwilling, and will not hear me, the sword will consume you: for the mouth of the LORD hath spoken it." And in the Psalms: "If My people had heard Me, and Israel had walked in My ways, I would have humbled their enemies to nothing, and laid My hand upon those that afflicted them;" showing that it was in the power of His people to hear and to walk in the ways of God. And the Saviour also, when He commands, "But I say unto you, Resist not evil;" and, "Whosoever shall be angry with his brother, shall be in danger of the judgment;" and, "Whosoever shall look upon a woman to lust after her, hath already committed adultery with her in his heart;" and by any other commandment which He gives, declares that it lies with ourselves to keep what is enjoined, and that we shall reasonably be liable to condemnation if we transgress. And therefore He says in addition: "He that heareth My words, and doeth them, shall be likened to a prudent man, who built his house upon a rock," etc., etc.; "while he that heareth them, but doeth them not, is like a foolish man, who built his house upon the sand," etc. And when He says to those on His right hand, "Come, ye blessed of My Father," etc.; "for I was an hungered, and ye gave Me to eat; I was athirst, and ye gave Me to drink," it is exceedingly manifest that He gives the promises to these as being deserving of praise. But, on the contrary, to the others, as being censurable in comparison with them, He says, "Depart, ye cursed, into everlasting fire!" And let us observe how Paul also converses with us as having freedom of will, and as being ourselves the cause of ruin or salvation, when he says, "Dost thou despise the riches of His goodness, and of His patience, and of His long-suffering; not knowing that the goodness of God leadeth thee to repentance? But, according to thy hardness and impenitent heart, thou art treasuring up for thyself wrath on the day of wrath and revelation of the righteous judgment of God; who will render to every one according to his works: to those who, by patient continuance in well-doing, seek for glory and immortality, eternal life;

while to those who are contentious, and believe not the truth, but who believe iniquity, anger, wrath, tribulation, and distress, on every soul of man that worketh evil; on the Jew first, and on the Greek: but glory, and honour, and peace to every one that worketh good; to the Jew first, and to the Greek." There are, indeed, innumerable passages in the Scriptures which establish with exceeding clearness the existence of freedom of will.

7. But, since certain declarations of the Old Testament and of the New lead to the opposite conclusion—namely, that it does not depend on ourselves to keep the commandments and to be saved, or to transgress them and to be lost—let us adduce them one by one, and see the explanations of them, in order that from those which we adduce, any one selecting in a similar way all the passages that seem to nullify free-will, may consider what is said about them by way of explanation. And now, the statements regarding Pharaoh have troubled many, respecting whom God declared several times, "I will harden Pharaoh's heart." For if he is hardened by God, and commits sin in consequence of being hardened, he is not the cause of sin to himself; and if so, then neither does Pharaoh possess free-will. And some one will say that, in a similar way, they who perish have not free-will, and will not perish of themselves. The declaration also in Ezekiel, "I will take away their stony hearts, and will put in them hearts of flesh, that they may walk in My precepts, and keep My commandments," might lead one to think that it was God who gave the power to walk in His commandments, and to keep His precepts, by His withdrawing the hindrance—the stony heart, and implanting a better—a heart of flesh. And let us look also at the passage in the Gospel—the answer which the Saviour returns to those who inquired why He spake to the multitude in parables. His words are: "That seeing they might not see; and hearing they may hear, and not understand; lest they should be converted, and their sins be forgiven them." The passage also in Paul: "It is not of him that willeth, nor of him that runneth, but of God that showeth mercy." The declarations, too, in other places, that "both to will and to do are of God;" "that God hath mercy upon whom He will have mercy, and whom He will He hardeneth. Thou wilt say then, Why doth He yet find fault? For who hath resisted His will?" "The persuasion is of Him that calleth, and not of us." "Nay, O man, who art thou that repliest against God? Shall the thing formed say to him that hath formed it, Why hast thou made me thus? Hath not the potter power over the clay, of the same lump to make one vessel unto honour, and another unto dishonour?" Now these passages are sufficient of themselves to trouble the multitude, as if man were not possessed of

free-will, but as if it were God who saves and destroys whom He will.

8. Let us begin, then, with what is said about Pharaoh—that he was hardened by God, that he might not send away the people; along with which will be examined also the statement of the apostle, "Therefore hath He mercy on whom He will have mercy, and whom He will He hardeneth." And certain of those who hold different opinions misuse these passages, themselves also almost destroying free-will by introducing ruined natures incapable of salvation, and others saved which it is impossible can be lost; and Pharaoh, they say, as being of a ruined nature, is therefore hardened by God, who has mercy upon the spiritual, but hardens the earthly. Let us see now what they mean. For we shall ask them if Pharaoh was of an earthy nature; and when they answer, we shall say that he who is of an earthy nature is altogether disobedient to God: but if disobedient, what need is there of his heart being hardened, and that not once, but frequently? Unless perhaps, since it was possible for him to obey (in which case he would certainly have obeyed, as not being earthy, when hard pressed by the signs and wonders), God needs him to be disobedient to a greater degree, in order that He may manifest His mighty deeds for the salvation of the multitude, and therefore hardens his heart. This will be our answer to them in the first place, in order to overturn their supposition that Pharaoh was of a ruined nature. And the same reply must be given to them with respect to the statement of the apostle. For whom does God harden? Those who perish, as if they would obey unless they were hardened, or manifestly those who would be saved because they are not of a ruined nature. And on whom has He mercy? Is it on those who are to be saved? And how is there need of a second mercy for those who have been prepared once for salvation, and who will by all means become blessed on account of their nature? Unless perhaps, since they are capable of incurring destruction, if they did not receive mercy, they will obtain mercy, in order that they may not incur that destruction of which they are capable, but may be in the condition of those who are saved. And this is our answer to such persons.

9. But to those who think they understand the term "hardened," we must address the inquiry, What do they mean by saying that God, by His working, hardens the heart, and with what purpose does He do this? For let them observe the conception of a God who is in reality just and good; but if they will not allow this, let it be conceded to them for the present that He is just; and let them show how the good and just God, or the just God only, appears to be just, in hardening the heart of him who perishes because of his being hardened: and how the just God becomes the cause of destruction and disobedience, when

men are chastened by Him on account of their hardness and disobedience. And why does He find fault with him, saying, "Thou wilt not let My people go;" "Lo, I will smite all the first-born in Egypt, even thy first-born;" and whatever else is recorded as spoken from God to Pharaoh through the intervention of Moses? For he who believes that the Scriptures are true, and that God is just, must necessarily endeavour, if he be honest, to show how God, in using such expressions, may be distinctly understood to be just. But if any one should stand, declaring with uncovered head that the Creator of the world was inclined to wickedness, we should need other words to answer them.

10. But since they say that they regard Him as a just God, and we as one who is at the same time good and just, let us consider how the good and just God could harden the heart of Pharaoh. See, then, whether, by an illustration used by the apostle in the Epistle to the Hebrews, we are able to prove that by one operation God has mercy upon one man while He hardens another, although not intending to harden; but, (although) having a good purpose, hardening follows as a result of the inherent principle of wickedness in such persons, and so He is said to harden him who is hardened. "The earth," he says, "which drinketh in the rain that cometh oft upon it, and bringeth forth herbs meet for them for whom it is dressed, receiveth blessing from God; but that which beareth thorns and briers is rejected, and is nigh to cursing, whose end is to be burned." As respects the rain, then, there is one operation; and there being one operation as regards the rain, the ground which is cultivated produces fruit, while that which is neglected and is barren produces thorns. Now, it might seem profane for Him who rains to say, "I produced the fruits, and the thorns that are in the earth;" and yet, although profane, it is true. For, had rain not fallen, there would have been neither fruits nor thorns; but, having fallen at the proper time and in moderation, both were produced. The ground, now, which drank in the rain which often fell upon it, and yet produced thorns and briers, is rejected and nigh to cursing. The blessing, then, of the rain descended even upon the inferior land; but it, being neglected and uncultivated, yielded thorns and thistles. In the same way, therefore, the wonderful works also done by God are, as it were, the rain; while the differing purposes are, as it were, the cultivated and neglected land, being (yet), like earth, of one nature.

11. And as if the sun, uttering a voice, were to say, "I liquefy and dry up," liquefaction and drying up being opposite things, he would not speak falsely as regards the point in question; wax being melted and mud being dried by the same heat; so the same operation, which was

performed through the instrumentality of Moses, proved the hardness of Pharaoh on the one hand, the result of his wickedness, and the yielding of the mixed Egyptian multitude who took their departure with the Hebrews. And the brief statement that the heart of Pharaoh was softened, as it were, when he said, "But ye shall not go far: ye will go a three days' journey, and leave your wives," and anything else which he said, yielding little by little before the signs, proves that the wonders made some impression even upon him, but did not accomplish all (that they might). Yet even this would not have happened, if that which is supposed by the many—the hardening of Pharaoh's heart—had been produced by God Himself. And it is not absurd to soften down such expressions agreeably to common usage: for good masters often say to their slaves, when spoiled by their kindness and forbearance, "I have made you bad, and I am to blame for offences of such enormity." For we must attend to the character and force of the phrase, and not argue sophistically, disregarding the meaning of the expression. Paul accordingly, having examined these points clearly, says to the sinner: "Or despisest thou the riches of His goodness, and forbearance, and long-suffering; not knowing that the goodness of God leadeth thee to repentance? but, after thy hardness and impenitent heart, treasurest up unto thyself wrath against the day of wrath and revelation of the righteous judgment of God." Now, let what the apostle says to the sinner be addressed to Pharaoh, and then the announcements made to him will be understood to have been made with peculiar fitness, as to one who, according to his hardness and unrepentant heart, was treasuring up to himself wrath; seeing that his hardness would not have been proved nor made manifest unless miracles had been performed, and miracles, too, of such magnitude and importance.

12. But since such narratives are slow to secure assent, and are considered to be forced, let us see from the prophetical declarations also, what those persons say, who, although they have experienced the great kindness of God, have not lived virtuously, but have afterwards sinned. "Why, O Lord, hast Thou made us to err from Thy ways? Why hast Thou hardened our heart, so as not to fear Thy name? Return for Thy servants' sake, for the tribes of Thine inheritance, that we may inherit a small portion of Thy holy mountain." And in Jeremiah: "Thou hast deceived me, O Lord, and I was deceived; Thou wert strong, and Thou didst prevail." For the expression, "Why hast Thou hardened our heart, so as not to fear Thy name?" uttered by those who are begging to receive mercy, is in its nature as follows: "Why hast Thou spared us so long, not visiting us because of our sins, but deserting us, until our transgressions come to a height?" Now He leaves the greater part of

men unpunished, both in order that the habits of each one may be examined, so far as it depends upon ourselves, and that the virtuous may be made manifest in consequence of the test applied; while the others, not escaping notice from God—for He knows all things before they exist—but from the rational creation and themselves, may afterwards obtain the means of cure, seeing they would not have known the benefit had they not condemned themselves. It is of advantage to each one, that he perceive his own peculiar nature and the grace of God. For he who does not perceive his own weakness and the divine favour, although he receive a benefit, yet, not having made trial of himself, nor having condemned himself, will imagine that the benefit conferred upon him by the grace of Heaven is his own doing. And this imagination, producing also vanity, will be the cause of a downfall: which, we conceive, was the case with the devil, who attributed to himself the priority which he possessed when in a state of sinlessness. "For every one that exalteth himself shall be abased," and "every one that humbleth himself shall be exalted." And observe, that for this reason divine things have been concealed from the wise and prudent, in order, as says the apostle, that "no flesh should glory in the presence of God;" and they have been revealed to babes, to those who after childhood have come to better things, and who remember that it is not so much from their own effort, as by the unspeakable goodness (of God), that they have reached the greatest possible extent of blessedness.

13. It is not without reason, then, that he who is abandoned, is abandoned to the divine judgment, and that God is long-suffering with certain sinners; but because it will be for their advantage, with respect to the immortality of the soul and the unending world, that they be not quickly brought into a state of salvation, but be conducted to it more slowly, after having experienced many evils. For as physicians, who are able to cure a man quickly, when they suspect that a hidden poison exists in the body, do the reverse of healing, making this more certain through their very desire to heal, deeming it better for a considerable time to retain the patient under inflammation and sickness, in order that he may recover his health more surely, than to appear to produce a rapid recovery, and afterwards to cause a relapse, and (thus) that hasty cure last only for a time; in the same way, God also, who knows the secret things of the heart, and foresees future events, in His long-suffering, permits (certain events to occur), and by means of those things which happen from without extracts the secret evil, in order to cleanse him who through carelessness has received the seeds of sin, that having vomited them forth when they came to the surface,

although he may have been deeply involved in evils, he may afterwards obtain healing after his wickedness, and be renewed. For God governs souls not with reference, let me say, to the fifty years of the present life, but with reference to an illimitable age: for He made the thinking principle immortal in its nature, and kindred to Himself; and the rational soul is not, as in this life, excluded from cure.

14. Come now, and let us use the following image from the Gospel. There is a certain rock, with a little surface-soil, on which, if seeds fall, they quickly spring up; but when sprung up, as not having root, they are burned and withered when the sun has arisen. Now this rock is a human soul, hardened on account of its negligence, and converted to stone because of its wickedness; for no one receives from God a heart created of stone, but it becomes such in consequence of wickedness. If one, then, were to find fault with the husbandman for not sowing his seed sooner upon the rocky soil, when he saw other rocky ground which had received seed flourishing, the husbandman would reply, "I shall sow this ground more slowly, casting in seeds that will be able to retain their hold, this slower method being better for the ground, and more secure than that which receives the seed in a more rapid manner, and more upon the surface." (The person finding fault) would yield his assent to the husbandman, as one who spoke with sound reason, and who acted with skill: so also the great Husbandman of all nature postpones that benefit which might be deemed premature, that it may not prove superficial. But it is probable that here some one may object to us with reference to this: "Why do some of the seeds fall upon the earth that has superficial soil, the soul being, as it were, a rock?" Now we must say, in answer to this, that it was better for this soul, which desired better things precipitately, and not by a way which led to them, to obtain its desire, in order that, condemning itself on this account, it may, after a long time, endure to receive the husbandry which is according to nature. For souls are, as one may say, innumerable; and their habits are innumerable, and their movements, and their purposes, and their assaults, and their efforts, of which there is only one admirable administrator, who knows both the season, and the fitting helps, and the avenues, and the ways, viz., the God and Father of all things, who knows how He conducts even Pharaoh by so great events, and by drowning in the sea, with which latter occurrence His superintendence of Pharaoh does not cease. For he was not annihilated when drowned: "For in the hand of God are both we and our words; all wisdom also, and knowledge of workmanship." And such is a moderate defence with regard to the statement that "Pharaoh's heart was hardened," and that "God hath mercy upon whom He will have

mercy, and whom He will He hardeneth."

15. Let us look also at the declaration in Ezekiel, which says, "I shall take away their stony hearts, and will put in them hearts of flesh, that they may walk in My statutes and keep My precepts." For if God, when He wills, takes away the stony hearts, and implants hearts of flesh, so that His precepts are obeyed and His commandments are observed, it is not in our power to put away wickedness. For the taking away of the stony hearts is nothing else than the taking away of the wickedness, according to which one is hardened, from him from whom God wills to take it; and the implanting of a heart of flesh, so that a man may walk in the precepts of God and keep His commandments, what else is it than to become somewhat yielding and unresistent to the truth, and to be capable of practising virtues? And if God promises to do this, and if, before He takes away the stony hearts, we do not lay them aside, it is manifest that it does not depend upon ourselves to put away wickedness; and if it is not we who do anything towards the production within us of the heart of flesh, but if it is God's doing, it will not be our own act to live agreeably to virtue, but altogether (the result of) divine grace. Such will be the statements of him who, from the mere words (of Scripture), annihilates free-will. But we shall answer, saying, that we ought to understand these passages thus: That as a man, e.g., who happened to be ignorant and uneducated, on perceiving his own defects, either in consequence of an exhortation from his teacher, or in some other way, should spontaneously give himself up to him whom he considers able to introduce him to education and virtue; and, on his yielding himself up, his instructor promises that he will take away his ignorance, and implant instruction, not as if it contributed nothing to his training, and to the avoiding of ignorance, that he brought himself to be healed, but because the instructor promised to improve him who desired improvement; so, in the same way, the Word of God promises to take away wickedness, which it calls a stony heart, from those who come to it, not if they are unwilling, but (only) if they submit themselves to the Physician of the sick, as in the Gospels the sick are found coming to the Saviour, and asking to obtain healing, and so are cured. And, let me say, the recovery of sight by the blind is, so far as their request goes, the act of those who believe that they are capable of being healed; but as respects the restoration of sight, it is the work of our Saviour. Thus, then, does the Word of God promise to implant knowledge in those who come to it, by taking away the stony and hard heart, which is wickedness, in order that one may walk in the divine commandments, and keep the divine injunctions.

. 16. There was after this the passage from the Gospel, where the

Saviour said, that for this reason did He speak to those without in parables, that "seeing they may not see, and hearing they may not understand; lest they should be converted, and their sins be forgiven them." Now, our opponent will say, "If some persons are assuredly converted on hearing words of greater clearness, so that they become worthy of the remission of sins, and if it does not depend upon themselves to hear these words of greater clearness, but upon him who teaches, and he for this reason does not announce them to them more distinctly, lest they should see and understand, it is not within the power of such to be saved; and if so, we are not possessed of free-will as regards salvation and destruction." Effectual, indeed, would be the reply to such arguments, were it not for the addition, "Lest they should be converted, and their sins be forgiven them,"—namely, that the Saviour did not wish those who were not to become good and virtuous to understand the more mystical (parts of His teaching), and for this reason spake to them in parables; but now, on account of the words, "Lest they should be converted, and their sins be forgiven them," the defence is more difficult. In the first place, then, we must notice the passage in its bearing on the heretics, who hunt out those portions from the Old Testament where is exhibited, as they themselves daringly assert, the cruelty of the Creator of the world in His purpose of avenging and punishing the wicked, or by whatever other name they wish to designate such a quality, so speaking only that they may say that goodness does not exist in the Creator; and who do not deal with the New Testament in a similar manner, nor in a spirit of candour, but pass by places similar to those which they consider censurable in the Old Testament. For manifestly, and according to the Gospel, is the Saviour shown, as they assert, by His former words, not to speak distinctly for this reason, that men might not be converted, and, being converted, might become deserving of the remission of sins: which statement of itself is nothing inferior to those passages from the Old Testament which are objected to. And if they seek to defend the Gospel, we must ask them whether they are not acting in a blameworthy manner in dealing differently with the same questions; and, while not stumbling against the New Testament, but seeking to defend it, they nevertheless bring a charge against the Old regarding similar points, whereas they ought to offer a defence in the same way of the passages from the New. And therefore we shall force them, on account of the resemblances, to regard all as the writings of one God. Come, then, and let us, to the best of our ability, furnish an answer to the question submitted to us.

17. We asserted also, when investigating the subject of Pharaoh, that sometimes a rapid cure is not for the advantage of those who are

healed, if, after being seized by troublesome diseases, they should easily get rid of those by which they had been entangled. For, despising the evil as one that is easy of cure, and not being on their guard a second time against falling into it, they will be involved in it (again). Wherefore, in the case of such persons, the everlasting God, the Knower of secrets, who knows all things before they exist, in conformity with His goodness, delays sending them more rapid assistance, and, so to speak, in helping them does not help, the latter course being to their advantage. It is probable, then, that those "without," of whom we are speaking, having been foreseen by the Saviour, according to our supposition, as not (likely) to prove steady in their conversion, if they should hear more clearly the words that were spoken, were (so) treated by the Saviour as not to hear distinctly the deeper (things of His teaching), lest, after a rapid conversion, and after being healed by obtaining remission of sins, they should despise the wounds of their wickedness, as being slight and easy of healing, and should again speedily relapse into them. And perhaps also, suffering punishment for their former transgressions against virtue, which they had committed when they had forsaken her, they had not yet filled up the (full) time; in order that, being abandoned by the divine superintendence, and being filled to a greater degree by their own evils which they had sown, they may afterwards be called to a more stable repentance; so as not to be quickly entangled again in those evils in which they had formerly been involved when they treated with insolence the requirements of virtue, and devoted themselves to worse things. Those, then, who are said to be "without" (manifestly by comparison with those "within"), not being very far from those "within," while those "within" hear clearly, do themselves hear indistinctly, because they are addressed in parables; but nevertheless they do hear. Others, again, of those "without," who are called Tyrians, although it was foreknown that they would have repented long ago, sitting in sackcloth and ashes, had the Saviour come near their borders, do not hear even those words which are heard by those "without" (being, as is probable, very far inferior in merit to those "without"), in order that at another season, after it has been more tolerable for them than for those who did not receive the word (among whom he mentioned also the Tyrians), they may, on hearing the word at a more appropriate time, obtain a more lasting repentance. But observe whether, besides our desire to investigate (the truth), we do not rather strive to maintain an attitude of piety in everything regarding God and His Christ, seeing we endeavour by every means to prove that, in matters so great and so peculiar regarding the varied providence of God, He takes an oversight of the immortal soul.

If, indeed, one were to inquire regarding those things that are objected to, why those who saw wonders and who heard divine words are not benefited, while the Tyrians would have repented if such had been performed and spoken amongst them; and should ask, and say, Why did the Saviour proclaim such to these persons, to their own hurt, that their sin might be reckoned to them as heavier? we must say, in answer to such an one, that He who understands the dispositions of all those who find fault with His providence—(alleging) that it is owing to it that they have not believed, because it did not permit them to see what it enabled others to behold, and did not arrange for them to hear those words by which others, on hearing them, were benefited—wishing to prove that their defence is not founded on reason, He grants those advantages which those who blame His administration asked; in order that, after obtaining them, they may notwithstanding be convicted of the greatest impiety in not having even then yielded themselves to be benefited, and may cease from such audacity; and having been made free in respect to this very point, may learn that God occasionally, in conferring benefits upon certain persons, delays and procrastinates, not conferring the favour of seeing and hearing those things which, when seen and heard, would render the sin of those who did not believe, after acts so great and peculiar, heavier and more serious.

18. Let us look next at the passage: "So, then, it is not of him that willeth, nor of him that runneth, but of God that showeth mercy." For they who find fault say: If "it is not of him that willeth, nor of him that runneth, but of God that showeth mercy," salvation does not depend upon ourselves, but upon the arrangement made by Him who has formed us such as we are, or on the purpose of Him who showeth mercy when he pleases. Now we must ask these persons the following questions: Whether to desire what is good is virtuous or vicious; and whether the desire to run in order to reach the goal in the pursuit of what is good be worthy of praise or censure? And if they shall say that it is worthy of censure, they will return an absurd answer; since the saints desire and run, and manifestly in so acting do nothing that is blameworthy. But if they shall say that it is virtuous to desire what is good, and to run after what is good, we shall ask them how a perishing nature desires better things; for it is like an evil tree producing good fruit, since it is a virtuous act to desire better things. They will give (perhaps) a third answer, that to desire and run after what is good is one of those things that are indifferent, and neither beautiful nor wicked. Now to this we must say, that if to desire and to run after what is good be a thing of indifference, then the opposite also is a thing of indifference, viz., to desire what is evil, and to run after it. But it is not

a thing of indifference to desire what is evil, and to run after it. And therefore also, to desire what is good, and to run after it, is not a thing of indifference. Such, then, is the defence which I think we can offer to the statement, that "it is not of him that willeth, nor of him that runneth, but of God that showeth mercy." Solomon says in the book of Psalms (for the Song of Degrees is his, from which we shall quote the words): "Unless the LORD build the house, they labour in vain that build it; except the LORD keep the city, the watchman waketh in vain:" not dissuading us from building, nor teaching us not to keep watch in order to guard the city in our soul, but showing that what is built without God, and does not receive a guard from Him, is built in vain and watched to no purpose, because God might reasonably be entitled the Lord of the building; and the Governor of all things, the Ruler of the guard of the city. As, then, if we were to say that such a building is not the work of the builder, but of God, and that it was not owing to the successful effort of the watcher, but of the God who is over all, that such a city suffered no injury from its enemies, we should not be wrong, it being understood that something also had been done by human means, but the benefit being gratefully referred to God who brought it to pass; so, seeing that the (mere) human desire is not sufficient to attain the end, and that the running of those who are, as it were, athletes, does not enable them to gain the prize of the high calling of God in Christ Jesus—for these things are accomplished with the assistance of God—it is well said that "it is not of him that willeth, nor of him that runneth, but of God that showeth mercy." As if also it were said with regard to husbandry what also is actually recorded: "I planted, Apollos watered; and God gave the increase. So then neither is he that planteth anything, neither he that watereth; but God that giveth the increase." Now we could not piously assert that the production of full crops was the work of the husbandman, or of him that watered, but the work of God. So also our own perfection is brought about, not as if we ourselves did nothing; for it is not completed by us, but God produces the greater part of it. And that this assertion may be more clearly believed, we shall take an illustration from the art of navigation. For in comparison with the effect of the winds, and the mildness of the air, and the light of the stars, all co-operating in the preservation of the crew, what proportion could the art of navigation be said to bear in the bringing of the ship into harbour?—since even the sailors themselves, from piety, do not venture to assert often that they had saved the ship, but refer all to God; not as if they had done nothing, but because what had been done by Providence was infinitely greater than what had been effected by their art. And in the matter of our salvation, what is done by God is infinitely greater than what is done by ourselves; and therefore, I think, is it said that "it is not of him that willeth, nor of him that runneth, but of God that showeth mercy." For if in the manner which they imagine we must explain the statement, that "it is not of him that willeth, nor of him that runneth, but of God that showeth mercy," the commandments are superfluous; and it is in vain that Paul himself blames some for having fallen away, and approves of others as having remained upright, and enacts laws for the Churches: it is in vain also that we give ourselves up to desire better things, and in vain also (to attempt) to run. But it is not in vain that Paul gives such advice, censuring some and approving of others; nor in vain that we give ourselves up to the desire of better things, and to the chase after things that are pre-eminent. They have accordingly not well explained the meaning of the passage.

19. Besides these, there is the passage, "Both to will and to do are of God." And some assert that, if to will be of God, and to do be of God, and if, whether we will evil or do evil, these (movements) come to us from God, then, if so, we are not possessed of free-will. But again, on the other hand, when we will better things, and do things that are more excellent, seeing that willing and doing are from God, it is not we who have done the more excellent things, but we only appeared (to perform them), while it was God that bestowed them; so that even in this respect we do not possess free-will. Now to this we have to answer, that the language of the apostle does not assert that to will evil is of God, or to will good is of Him (and similarly with respect to doing better and worse); but that to will in a general way, and to run in a general way, (are from Him). For as we have from God (the property) of being living things and human beings, so also have we that of willing generally, and, so to speak, of motion in general. And as, possessing (the property) of life and of motion, and of moving, e.g., these members, the hands or the feet, we could not rightly say that we had from God this species of motion, whereby we moved to strike, or destroy, or take away another's goods, but that we had received from Him simply the generic power of motion, which we employed to better or worse purposes; so we have obtained from God (the power) of acting, in respect of our being living things, and (the power) to will from the Creator while we employ the power of will, as well as that of action, for the noblest objects, or the opposite.

20. Still the declaration of the apostle will appear to drag us to the conclusion that we are not possessed of freedom of will, in which, objecting against himself, he says, "Therefore hath He mercy on whom He will have mercy, and whom He will He hardeneth. Thou wilt say

then unto me, Why doth He yet find fault? For who hath resisted His will? Nay but, O man, who art thou that repliest against God? Shall the thing formed say to him that formed it, Why hast thou made me thus? Hath not the potter power over the clay, of the same lump to make one vessel unto honour, and another unto dishonour?" For it will be said: If the potter of the same lump make some vessels to honour and others to dishonour, and God thus form some men for salvation and others for ruin, then salvation or ruin does not depend upon ourselves, nor are we possessed of free-will. Now we must ask him who deals so with these passages, whether it is possible to conceive of the apostle as contradicting himself. I presume, however, that no one will venture to say so. If, then, the apostle does not utter contradictions, how can he, according to him who so understands him, reasonably find fault, censuring the individual at Corinth who had committed fornication, or those who had fallen away, and had not repented of the licentiousness and impurity of which they had been guilty? And how can he bless those whom he praises as having done well, as he does the house of Onesiphorus in these words: "The Lord give mercy to the house of Onesiphorus; for he oft refreshed me, and was not ashamed of my chain: but, when he was in Rome, he sought me out very diligently, and found me. The Lord grant to him that he may find mercy of the Lord in that day." It is not consistent for the same apostle to blame the sinner as worthy of censure, and to praise him who had done well as deserving of approval; and again, on the other hand, to say, as if nothing depended on ourselves, that the cause was in the Creator why the one vessel was formed to honour, and the other to dishonour. And how is this statement correct: "For we must all appear before the judgment-seat of Christ; that every one may receive the things done in his body, according to that he hath done, whether it be good or bad," since they who have done evil have advanced to this pitch of wickedness because they were created vessels unto dishonour, while they that have lived virtuously have done good because they were created from the beginning for this purpose, and became vessels unto honour? And again, how does not the statement made elsewhere conflict with the view which these persons draw from the words which we have quoted (that it is the fault of the Creator that one vessel is in honour and another in dishonour), viz., "that in a great house there are not only vessels of gold and silver, but also of wood and of earth; and some to honour, and some to dishonour. If a man therefore purge himself, he shall be a vessel unto honour, sanctified, and meet for the Master's use, and prepared unto every good work;" for if he who purges himself becomes a vessel unto honour, and he who allows himself to remain

160

unpurged becomes a vessel unto dishonour, then, so far as these words are concerned, the Creator is not at all to blame. For the Creator makes vessels of honour and vessels of dishonour, not from the beginning according to His foreknowledge, since He does not condemn or justify beforehand according to it; but (He makes) those into vessels of honour who purged themselves, and those into vessels of dishonour who allowed themselves to remain unpurged: so that it results from older causes (which operated) in the formation of the vessels unto honour and dishonour, that one was created for the former condition, and another for the latter. But if we once admit that there were certain older causes (at work) in the forming of a vessel unto honour, and of one unto dishonour, what absurdity is there in going back to the subject of the soul, and (in supposing) that a more ancient cause for Jacob being loved and for Esau being hated existed with respect to Jacob before his assumption of a body, and with regard to Esau before he was conceived in the womb of Rebecca?

21. And at the same time, it is clearly shown that, as far as regards the underlying nature, as there is one (piece of) clay which is under the hands of the potter, from which piece vessels are formed unto honour and dishonour; so the one nature of every soul being in the hands of God, and, so to speak, there being (only) one lump of reasonable beings, certain causes of more ancient date led to some being created vessels unto honour, and others vessels unto dishonour. But if the language of the apostle convey a censure when he says, "Nay but, O man, who art thou that repliest against God?" it teaches us that he who has confidence before God, and is faithful, and has lived virtuously, would not hear the words, "Who art thou that repliest against God?" Such an one, e.g., as Moses was, "For Moses spake, and God answered him with a voice;" and as God answers Moses, so does a saint also answer God. But he who does not possess this confidence, manifestly, either because he has lost it, or because he investigates these matters not from a love of knowledge, but from a desire to find fault, and who therefore says, "Why does He yet find fault? for who hath resisted His will?" would merit the language of censure, which says, "Nay but, O man, who art thou that repliest against God?"

Now to those who introduce different natures, and who make use of the declaration of the apostle (to support their view), the following must be our answer. If they maintain that those who perish and those who are saved are formed of one lump, and that the Creator of those who are saved is the Creator also of them who are lost, and if He is good who creates not only spiritual but also earthy (natures) (for this follows from their view), it is nevertheless possible that he who, in consequence of certain former acts of righteousness, had now been made a vessel of honour, but who had not (afterwards) acted in a similar manner, nor done things befitting a vessel of honour, was converted in another world into a vessel of dishonour; as, on the other hand, it is possible that he who, owing to causes more ancient than the present life, was here a vessel of dishonour, may after reformation become in the new creation "a vessel of honour, sanctified and meet for the Master's use, prepared unto every good work." And perhaps those who are now Israelites, not having lived worthily of their descent, will be deprived of their rank, being changed, as it were, from vessels of honour into those of dishonour; and many of the present Egyptians and Idumeans who came near to Israel, when they shall have borne fruit to a larger extent, shall enter into the Church of the Lord, being no longer accounted Egyptians and Idumeans, but becoming Israelites: so that, according to this view, it is owing to their (varying) purposes that some advance from a worse to a better condition, and others fall from better to worse; while others, again, are preserved in a virtuous course, or ascend from good to better; and others, on the contrary, remain in a course of evil, or from bad become worse, as their wickedness flows on.

22. But since the apostle in one place does not pretend that the becoming of a vessel unto honour or dishonour depends upon God, but refers back the whole to ourselves, saying, "If, then, a man purge himself, he will be a vessel unto honour, sanctified, meet for the Master's use, and prepared unto every good work;" and elsewhere does not even pretend that it is dependent upon ourselves, but appears to attribute the whole to God, saying, "The potter hath power over the clay, of the same lump to make one vessel unto honour and another to dishonour;" and as his statements are not contradictory, we must reconcile them, and extract one complete statement from both. Neither does our own power, apart from the knowledge of God, compel us to make progress; nor does the knowledge of God (do so), unless we ourselves also contribute something to the good result; nor does our own power, apart from the knowledge of God, and the use of the power that worthily belongs to us, make a man become (a vessel) unto honour or dishonour; nor does the will of God alone form a man to honour or to dishonour, unless He hold our will to be a kind of matter that admits of variation, and that inclines to a better or worse course of conduct. And these observations are sufficient to have been made by us on the subject of free-will.

CHAPTER II—ON THE OPPOSING POWERS

1. We have now to notice, agreeably to the statements of Scripture, how the opposing powers, or the devil himself, contends with the human race, inciting and instigating men to sin. And in the first place, in the book of Genesis, the serpent is described as having seduced Eve; regarding whom, in the work entitled *The Ascension of Moses* (a little treatise, of which the Apostle Jude makes mention in his Epistle), the archangel Michael, when disputing with the devil regarding the body of Moses, says that the serpent, being inspired by the devil, was the cause of Adam and Eve's transgression. This also is made a subject of inquiry by some, viz., who the angel was that, speaking from heaven to Abraham, said, "Now I know that thou fearest God, and on my account hast not spared thy beloved son, whom thou lovedst." For he is manifestly described as an angel who said that he knew then that Abraham feared God, and had not spared his beloved son, as the Scripture declares, although he did not say that it was on account of God that Abraham had done this, but on his, that is, the speaker's account. We must also ascertain who that is of whom it is stated in the book of Exodus that he wished to slay Moses, because he was taking his departure for Egypt; and afterwards, also, who he is that is called the destroying angel, as well as he who in the book of Leviticus is called Apopompaeus, i.e., Averter, regarding whom Scripture says, "One lot for the LORD, and one lot for Apopompaeus, i.e., the Averter." In the first book of Kings, also, an evil spirit is said to strangle Saul; and in the third book, Micaiah the prophet says, "I saw the LORD of Israel sitting on His throne, and all the host of heaven standing by Him, on His right hand and on His left. And the LORD said, Who will deceive Achab king of Israel, that he may go up and fall at Ramoth-gilead? And one said on this manner, and another said on that manner. And there came forth a spirit, and stood before the Lord, and said, I will deceive him. And the Lord said to him, Wherewith? And he said, I will go forth, and I will be a lying spirit in the mouth of all his prophets. And He said, Thou shalt deceive him, and prevail also: go forth, and do so quickly. And now therefore the LORD hath put a lying spirit in the mouth of all thy prophets: the LORD hath spoken evil concerning thee." Now by this last quotation it is clearly shown that a certain spirit, from his own (free) will and choice, elected to deceive (Achab), and to work a lie, in order that the Lord might mislead the king to his death, for he deserved to suffer. In the first book of Chronicles also it is said, "The devil, Satan, stood up against Israel, and provoked David to number the people." In the Psalms, moreover, an evil angel is said to harass certain persons.

In the book of Ecclesiastes, too, Solomon says, "If the spirit of the ruler rise up against thee, leave not thy place; for soundness will restrain many transgressions." In Zechariah we read that the devil stood on the right hand of Joshua, and resisted him. Isaiah says that the sword of the Lord arises against the dragon, the crooked serpent. And what shall I say of Ezekiel, who in his second vision prophesies most unmistakeably to the prince of Tyre regarding an opposing power, and who says also that the dragon dwells in the rivers of Egypt? Nay, with what else are the contents of the whole work which is written regarding Job occupied, save with the (doings) of the devil, who asks that power may be given him over all that Job possesses, and over his sons, and even over his person? And yet the devil is defeated through the patience of Job. In that book the Lord has by His answers imparted much information regarding the power of that dragon which opposes us. Such, meanwhile, are the statements made in the Old Testament, so far as we can at present recall them, on the subject of hostile powers being either named in Scripture, or being said to oppose the human race, and to be afterwards subjected to punishment.

Let us now look also to the New Testament, where Satan approaches the Saviour, and tempts Him: wherein also it is stated that evil spirits and unclean demons, which had taken possession of very many, were expelled by the Saviour from the bodies of the sufferers, who are said also to be made free by Him. Even Judas, too, when the devil had already put it in his heart to betray Christ, afterwards received Satan wholly into him; for it is written, that after the sop "Satan entered into him." And the Apostle Paul teaches us that we ought not to give place to the devil; but "put on," he says, "the armour of God, that ye may be able to resist the wiles of the devil:" pointing out that the saints have to "*wrestle* not against flesh and blood, but against principalities, against powers, against the rulers of the darkness of this world, against spiritual wickedness in high places." Nay, he says that the Saviour even was crucified by the princes of this world, who shall come to nought, whose wisdom also, he says, he does not speak. By all this, therefore, holy Scripture teaches us that there are certain invisible enemies that fight against us, and against whom it commands us to arm ourselves. Whence, also, the more simple among the believers in the Lord Christ are of opinion, that all the sins which men have committed are caused by the persistent efforts of these opposing powers exerted upon the minds of sinners, because in that invisible struggle these powers are found to be superior (to man). For if, for example, there were no devil, no single human being would go astray.

2. We, however, who see the reason (of the thing) more clearly, do

not hold this opinion, taking into account those (sins) which manifestly originate as a necessary consequence of our bodily constitution. Must we indeed suppose that the devil is the cause of our feeling hunger or thirst? Nobody, I think, will venture to maintain that. If, then, he is not the cause of our feeling hunger and thirst, wherein lies the difference when each individual has attained the age of puberty, and that period has called forth the incentives of the natural heat? It will undoubtedly follow, that as the devil is not the cause of our feeling hunger and thirst, so neither is he the cause of that appetency which naturally arises at the time of maturity, viz., the desire of sexual intercourse. Now it is certain that this cause is not always so set in motion by the devil that we should be obliged to suppose that bodies would nor possess a desire for intercourse of that kind if the devil did not exist. Let us consider, in the next place, if, as we have already shown, food is desired by human beings, not from a suggestion of the devil, but by a kind of natural instinct, whether, if there were no devil, it were possible for human experience to exhibit such restraint in partaking of food as never to exceed the proper limits; i.e., that no one would either take otherwise than the case required, or more than reason would allow; and so it would result that men, observing due measure and moderation in the matter of eating, would never go wrong. I do not think, indeed, that so great moderation could be observed by men (even if there were no instigation by the devil inciting thereto), as that no individual, in partaking of food, would go beyond due limits and restraint, until he had learned to do so from long usage and experience. What, then, is the state of the case? In the matter of eating and drinking it was possible for us to go wrong, even without any incitement from the devil, if we should happen to be either less temperate or less careful (than we ought); and are we to suppose, then, in our appetite for sexual intercourse, or in the restraint of our natural desires, our condition is not something similar? I am of opinion, indeed, that the same course of reasoning must be understood to apply to other natural movements as those of covetousness, or of anger, or of sorrow, or of all those generally which through the vice of intemperance exceed the natural bounds of moderation. There are therefore manifest reasons for holding the opinion, that as in good things the human will is of itself weak to accomplish any good (for it is by divine help that it is brought to perfection in everything); so also, in things of an opposite nature we receive certain initial elements, and, as it were, seeds of sins, from those things which we use agreeably to nature; but when we have indulged them beyond what is proper, and have not resisted the first movements to intemperance, then the hostile power, seizing the occasion of this first transgression, incites and presses us hard in every way, seeking to extend our sins over a wider field, and furnishing us human beings with occasions and beginnings of sins, which these hostile powers spread far and wide, and, if possible, beyond all limits. Thus, when men at first for a little desire money, covetousness begins to grow as the passion increases, and finally the fall into avarice takes place. And after this, when blindness of mind has succeeded passion, and the hostile powers, by their suggestions, hurry on the mind, money is now no longer desired, but stolen, and acquired by force, or even by shedding human blood. Finally, a confirmatory evidence of the fact that vices of such enormity proceed from demons, may be easily seen in this, that those individuals who are oppressed either by immoderate love, or incontrollable anger, or excessive sorrow, do not suffer less than those who are bodily vexed by devils. For it is recorded in certain histories, that some have fallen into madness from a state of love, others from a state of anger, not a few from a state of sorrow, and even from one of excessive joy; which results, I think, from this, that those opposing powers, i.e., those demons, having gained a lodgment in their minds which has been already laid open to them by intemperance, have taken complete possession of their sensitive nature, especially when no feeling of the glory of virtue has aroused them to resistance.

3. That there are certain sins, however, which do not proceed from the opposing powers, but take their beginnings from the natural movements of the body, is manifestly declared by the Apostle Paul in the passage: "The flesh lusteth against the Spirit, and the Spirit against the flesh: and these are contrary the one to the other; so that ye cannot do the things that ye would." If, then, the flesh lust against the Spirit, and the Spirit against the flesh, we have occasionally to wrestle against flesh and blood, i.e., as being men, and walking according to the flesh, and not capable of being tempted by greater than human temptations; since it is said of us, "There hath no temptation taken you, but such as is common to man: but God is faithful, who will not suffer you to be tempted above that ye are able." For as the presidents of the public games do not allow the competitors to enter the lists indiscriminately or fortuitously, but after a careful examination, pairing in a most impartial consideration either of size or age, this individual with that— boys, e.g., with boys, men with men, who are nearly related to each other either in age or strength; so also must we understand the procedure of divine providence, which arranges on most impartial principles all who descend into the struggles of this human life, according to the nature of each individual's power, which is known only to Him who alone beholds the hearts of men: so that one individual

fights against one temptation of the flesh, another against a second; one is exposed to its influence for so long a period of time, another only for so long; one is tempted by the flesh to this or that indulgence, another to one of a different kind; one has to resist this or that hostile power, another has to combat two or three at the same time; or at one time this hostile influence, at another that; at some particular date having to resist one enemy, and at another a different one; being, after the performance of certain acts, exposed to one set of enemies, after others to a second. And observe whether some such state of things be not indicated by the language of the apostle: "God is faithful, who will not suffer you to be tempted above what ye are able," i.e., each one is tempted in proportion to the amount of his strength or power of resistance. Now, although we have said that it is by the just judgment of God that every one is tempted according to the amount of his strength, we are not therefore to suppose that he who is tempted ought by all means to prove victorious in the struggle; in like manner as he who contends in the lists, although paired with his adversary on a just principle of arrangement, will nevertheless not necessarily prove conqueror. But unless the powers of the combatants are equal, the prize of the victor will not be justly won; nor will blame justly attach to the vanquished, because He allows us indeed to be tempted, but not "beyond what we are able:" for it is in proportion to our strength that we are tempted; and it is not written that, in temptation, He will make also a way to escape so as that we should bear it, but a way to escape so as that we should be able to bear it. But it depends upon ourselves to use either with energy or feebleness this power which He has given us. For there is no doubt that under every temptation we have a power of endurance, if we employ properly the strength that is granted us. But it is not the same thing to possess the *power* of conquering and to be victorious, as the apostle himself has shown in very cautious language, saying, "God will make a way to escape, that you may be *able* to bear it," not that you *will* bear it. For many do not sustain temptation, but are overcome by it. Now God enables us not to sustain (temptation), (otherwise there would appear to be no struggle), but to have the *power* of sustaining it. But this power which is given us to enable us to conquer may be used, according to our faculty of free-will, either in a diligent manner, and then we prove victorious, or in a slothful manner, and then we are defeated. For if such a power were wholly given us as that we must by all means prove victorious, and never be defeated, what further reason for a struggle could remain to him who cannot be overcome? Or what merit is there in a victory, where the power of successful resistance is taken away? But if the possibility of conquering be equally conferred on us all, and if it be in our own power how to use this possibility, i.e., either diligently or slothfully, then will the vanquished be justly censured, and the victor be deservedly lauded. Now from these points which we have discussed to the best of our power, it is, I think, clearly evident that there are certain transgressions which we by no means commit under the pressure of malignant powers; while there are others, again, to which we are incited by instigation on their part to excessive and immoderate indulgence. Whence it follows that we have to inquire how those opposing powers produce these incitements within us.

4. With respect to the thoughts which proceed from our heart, or the recollection of things which we have done, or the contemplation of any things or causes whatever, we find that they sometimes proceed from ourselves, and sometimes are originated by the opposing powers; not seldom also are they suggested by God, or by the holy angels. Now such a statement will perhaps appear incredible, unless it be confirmed by the testimony of holy Scripture. That, then, thoughts arise within ourselves, David testifies in the Psalms, saying, "The thought of a man will make confession to Thee, and the rest of the thought shall observe to Thee a festival day." That this, however, is also brought about by the opposing powers, is shown by Solomon in the book of Ecclesiastes in the following manner: "If the spirit of the ruler rise up against thee, leave not thy place; for soundness restrains great offences." The Apostle Paul also will bear testimony to the same point in the words: "Casting down imaginations, and every high thing that exalted itself against the knowledge of Christ." That it is an effect due to God, nevertheless, is declared by David, when he says in the Psalms, "Blessed is the man whose help is in Thee, O Lord, Thy ascents (are) in his heart." And the apostle says that "God put it into the heart of Titus." That certain thoughts are suggested to men's hearts either by good or evil angels, is shown both by the angel that accompanied Tobias, and by the language of the prophet, where he says, "And the angel who spoke in me answered." The book of the Shepherd declares the same, saying that each individual is attended by two angels; that whenever good thoughts arise in our hearts, they are suggested by the good angel; but when of a contrary kind, they are the instigation of the evil angel. The same is declared by Barnabas in his Epistle, where he says there are two ways, one of light and one of darkness, over which he asserts that certain angels are placed;—the angels of God over the way of light, the angels of Satan over the way of darkness. We are not, however, to imagine that any other result follows from what is suggested to our heart, whether good or bad, save a (mental) commotion only, and an

incitement instigating us either to good or evil. For it is quite within our reach, when a malignant power has begun to incite us to evil, to cast away from us the wicked suggestions, and to resist the vile inducements, and to do nothing that is at all deserving of blame. And, on the other hand, it is possible, when a divine power calls us to better things, not to obey the call; our freedom of will being preserved to us in either case. We said, indeed, in the foregoing pages, that certain recollections of good or evil actions were suggested to us either by the act of divine providence or by the opposing powers, as is shown in the book of Esther, when Artaxerxes had not remembered the services of that just man Mordecai, but, when wearied out with his nightly vigils, had it put into his mind by God to require that the annals of his great deeds should be read to him; whereon, being reminded of the benefits received from Mordecai, he ordered his enemy Haman to be hanged, but splendid honours to be conferred on him, and impunity from the threatened danger to be granted to the whole of the holy nation. On the other hand, however, we must suppose that it was through the hostile influence of the devil that the suggestion was introduced into the minds of the high priests and the scribes which they made to Pilate, when they came and said, "Sir, we remember that that deceiver said, while he was yet alive, After three days I will rise again." The design of Judas, also, respecting the betrayal of our Lord and Saviour, did not originate in the wickedness of his mind alone. For Scripture testifies that the "devil had already put it into his heart to betray Him." And therefore Solomon rightly commanded, saying, "Keep thy heart with all diligence." And the Apostle Paul warns us: "Therefore we ought to give the more earnest heed to the things which we have heard, lest perhaps we should let them slip." And when he says, "Neither give place to the devil," he shows by that injunction that it is through certain acts, or a kind of mental slothfulness, that room is made for the devil, so that, if he once enter our heart, he will either gain possession of us, or at least will pollute the soul, if he has not obtained the entire mastery over it, by casting on us his fiery darts; and by these we are sometimes deeply wounded, and sometimes only set on fire. Seldom indeed, and only in a few instances, are these fiery darts quenched, so as not to find a place where they may wound, i.e., when one is covered by the strong and mighty shield of faith. The declaration, indeed, in the Epistle to the Ephesians, "We wrestle not against flesh and blood, but against principalities, against powers, against the rulers of the darkness of this world, against spiritual wickedness in high places," must be so understood as if "we" meant, "I Paul, and you Ephesians, and all who have not to wrestle against flesh and blood:" for such have to struggle against principalities and powers, against the rulers of the darkness of this world, not like the Corinthians, whose struggle was as yet against flesh and blood, and who had been overtaken by no temptation but such as is common to man.

5. We are not, however, to suppose that each individual has to contend against all these (adversaries). For it is impossible for any man, although he were a saint, to carry on a contest against all of them at the same time. If that indeed were by any means to be the case, as it is certainly impossible it should be so, human nature could not possibly bear it without undergoing entire destruction. But as, for example, if fifty soldiers were to say that they were about to engage with fifty others, they would not be understood to mean that one of them had to contend against the whole fifty, but each one would rightly say that "our battle was against fifty," all against all; so also this is to be understood as the apostle's meaning, that all the athletes and soldiers of Christ have to wrestle and struggle against all the adversaries enumerated,—the struggle having, indeed, to be maintained against all, but by single individuals either with individual powers, or at least in such manner as shall be determined by God, who is the just president of the struggle. For I am of opinion that there is a certain limit to the powers of human nature, although there may be a Paul, of whom it is said, "He is a chosen vessel unto Me;" or a Peter, against whom the gates of hell do not prevail; or a Moses, the friend of God: yet not one of them could sustain, without destruction to himself, the whole simultaneous assault of these opposing powers, unless indeed the might of Him alone were to work in him, who said, "Be of good cheer, I have overcome the world." And therefore Paul exclaims with confidence, "I can do all things through Christ, who strengtheneth me;" and again, "I laboured more abundantly than they all; yet not I, but the grace of God which was with me." On account, then, of this power, which certainly is not of human origin operating and speaking in him, Paul could say, "For I am persuaded that neither death, nor life, nor angels, nor principalities, nor powers, nor things present, nor things to come, nor height, nor depth, nor power, nor any other creature, shall be able to separate us from the love of God, which is in Christ Jesus our Lord." For I do not think that human nature can alone of itself maintain a contest with angels, and with the powers of the height and of the abyss, and with any other creature; but when it feels the presence of the Lord dwelling within it, confidence in the divine help will lead it to say, "The LORD is my light, and my salvation; whom shall I fear? The LORD is the protector of my life; of whom shall I be afraid? When the enemies draw near to me, to eat my flesh, my enemies who trouble me, they

stumbled and fell. Though an host encamp against me, my heart shall not fear; though war should rise against me, in Him shall I be confident." From which I infer that a man perhaps would never be able of himself to vanquish an opposing power, unless he had the benefit of divine assistance. Hence, also, the angel is said to have wrestled with Jacob. Here, however, I understand the writer to mean, that it was not the same thing for the angel to have wrestled *with* Jacob, and to have wrestled *against* him; but the angel that wrestles with him is he who was present with him in order to secure his safety, who, after knowing also his moral progress, gave him in addition the name of Israel, i.e., he is *with* him in the struggle, and assists him in the contest; seeing there was undoubtedly another angel against whom he contended, and against whom he had to carry on a contest. Finally, Paul has not said that we wrestle *with* princes, or *with* powers, but *against* principalities and powers. And hence, although Jacob wrestled, it was unquestionably *against* some one of those powers which, Paul declares, resist and contend with the human race, and especially with the saints. And therefore at last the Scripture says of him that "he wrestled with the angel, and had power with God," so that the struggle is supported by help of the angel, but the prize of success conducts the conqueror to God.

6. Nor are we, indeed, to suppose that struggles of this kind are carried on by the exercise of bodily strength, and of the arts of the wrestling school; but spirit contends with spirit, according to the declaration of Paul, that our struggle is against principalities, and powers, and the rulers of the darkness of this world. Nay, the following is to be understood as the nature of the struggles; when, e.g., losses and dangers befall us, or calumnies and false accusations are brought against us, it not being the object of the hostile powers that we should suffer these (trials) only, but that by means of them we should be driven either to excess of anger or sorrow, or to the last pitch of despair; or at least, which is a greater sin, should be forced, when fatigued and overcome by any annoyances, to make complaints against God, as one who does not administer human life justly and equitably; the consequence of which is, that our faith may be weakened, or our hopes disappointed, or we may be compelled to give up the truth of our opinions, or be led to entertain irreligious sentiments regarding God. For some such things are written regarding Job, after the devil had requested God that power should be given him over his goods. By which also we are taught, that it is not by any accidental attacks that we are assailed, whenever we are visited with any such loss of property, nor that it is owing to chance when one of us is taken prisoner, or when the dwellings in which those

who are dear to us are crushed to death, fall in ruins; for, with respect to all these occurrences, every believer ought to say, "Thou couldst have no power at all against Me, except it were given thee from above." For observe that the house of Job did not fall upon his sons until the devil had first received power against them; nor would the horsemen have made an irruption in three bands, to carry away his camels or his oxen, and other cattle, unless they had been instigated by that spirit to whom they had delivered themselves up as the servants of his will. Nor would that fire, as it seemed to be, or thunderbolt, as it has been considered, have fallen upon the sheep of the patriarch, until the devil had said to God, "Hast Thou not made a hedge about all that is without and within his house and around all the rest of his property? But now put forth Thy hand, and touch all that he hath, (and see) if he do not renounce Thee to Thy face."

7. The result of all the foregoing remarks is to show, that all the occurrences in the world which are considered to be of an intermediate kind, whether they be mournful or otherwise are brought about, not indeed by God, and yet not without Him; while He not only does not prevent those wicked and opposing powers that are desirous to bring about these things (from accomplishing their purpose), but even permits them to do so, although only on certain occasions and to certain individuals, as is said with respect to Job himself, that for a certain time he was made to fall under the power of others, and to have his house plundered by unjust persons. And therefore holy Scripture teaches us to receive all that happens as sent by God, knowing that without Him no event occurs. For how can we doubt that such is the case, viz., that nothing comes to man without (the will of) God, when our Lord and Saviour declares, "Are not two sparrows sold for a farthing? and one of them shall not fall on the ground without your Father who is in heaven." But the necessity of the case has drawn us away in a lengthened digression on the subject of the struggle waged by the hostile powers against men, and of those sadder events which happen to human life, i.e., its temptations—according to the declaration of Job, "Is not the whole life of man upon the earth a temptation?"—in order that the manner of their occurrence, and the spirit in which we should regard them, might be clearly shown. Let us notice next, how men fall away into the sin of false knowledge, or with what object the opposing powers are wont to stir up conflict with us regarding such things.

CHAPTER III—ON THREEFOLD WISDOM

1. The holy apostle, wishing to teach us some great and hidden truth respecting science and wisdom, says, in the first Epistle to the Corinthians: "We speak wisdom among them that are perfect; yet not the wisdom of this world, nor of the princes of the world, that come to nought: but we speak the wisdom of God in a mystery, even the hidden wisdom, which God ordained before the world unto our glory: which none of the princes of the world knew: for had they known it, they would not have crucified the Lord of glory." In this passage, wishing to describe the different kinds of wisdom, he points out that there is a wisdom of this world, and a wisdom of the princes of this world, and another wisdom of God. But when he uses the expression "wisdom of the princes of this world," I do not think that he means a wisdom common to all the princes of this world, but one rather that is peculiar to certain individuals among them. And again, when he says, "We speak the wisdom of God in a mystery, even the hidden wisdom, which God ordained before the world unto our glory," we must inquire whether his meaning be, that this is the same wisdom of God which was hidden from other times and generations, and was not made known to the sons of men, as it has now been revealed to His holy apostles and prophets, and which was also that wisdom of God before the advent of the Saviour, by means of which Solomon obtained his wisdom, and in reference to which the language of the Saviour Himself declared, that what He taught was greater than Solomon, in these words, "Behold, a greater than Solomon is here,"—words which show, that those who were instructed by the Saviour were instructed in something higher than the knowledge of Solomon. For if one were to assert that the Saviour did indeed Himself possess greater knowledge, but did not communicate more to others than Solomon did, how will that agree with the statement which follows: "The queen of the south shall rise up in the judgment, and condemn the men of this generation, because she came from the ends of the earth to hear the wisdom of Solomon; and, behold, a greater than Solomon is here?" There is therefore a wisdom of this world, and also probably a wisdom belonging to each individual prince of this world. But with respect to the wisdom of God alone, we perceive that this is indicated, that it operated to a less degree in ancient and former times, and was (afterwards) more fully revealed and manifested through Christ. We shall inquire, however, regarding the wisdom of God in the proper place.

2. But now, since we are treating of the manner in which the opposing powers stir up those contests, by means of which false

knowledge is introduced into the minds of men, and human souls led astray, while they imagine that they have discovered wisdom, I think it necessary to name and distinguish the wisdom of this world, and of the princes of this world, that by so doing we may discover who are the fathers of this wisdom, nay, even of these kinds of wisdom. I am of opinion, therefore, as I have stated above, that there is another wisdom of this world besides those (different kinds of) wisdom which belong to the princes of this world, by which wisdom those things seem to be understood and comprehended which belong to this world. This wisdom, however, possesses in itself no fitness for forming any opinion either respecting divine things, or the plan of the world's government, or any other subjects of importance, or regarding the training for a good or happy life; but is such as deals wholly with the art of poetry, e.g., or that of grammar, or rhetoric, or geometry, or music, with which also, perhaps, medicine should be classed. In all these subjects we are to suppose that the wisdom of this world is included. The wisdom of the princes of this world, on the other hand, we understand to be such as the secret and occult philosophy, as they call it, of the Egyptians, and the astrology of the Chaldeans and Indians, who make profession of the knowledge of high things, and also that manifold variety of opinion which prevails among the Greeks regarding divine things. Accordingly, in the holy Scriptures we find that there are princes over individual nations; as in Daniel we read that there was a prince of the kingdom of Persia, and another prince of the kingdom of Graecia, who are clearly shown, by the nature of the passage, to be not human beings, but certain powers. In the prophecies of Ezekiel, also, the prince of Tyre is unmistakeably shown to be a kind of spiritual power. When these, then, and others of the same kind, possessing each his own wisdom, and building up his own opinions and sentiments, beheld our Lord and Saviour professing and declaring that He had for this purpose come into the world, that all the opinions of science, falsely so called, might be destroyed, not knowing what was concealed within Him, they forthwith laid a snare for Him: for "the kings of the earth set themselves, and the rulers assembled together, against the Lord and His Christ." But their snares being discovered, and the plans which they had attempted to carry out being made manifest when they crucified the Lord of glory, therefore the apostle says, "We speak wisdom among them that are perfect, but not the wisdom of this world, nor of the princes of this world, who are brought to nought, which none of the princes of this world knew: for had they known it, they would not have crucified the Lord of glory."

3. We must, indeed, endeavour to ascertain whether that wisdom of

the princes of this world, with which they endeavour to imbue men, is introduced into their minds by the opposing powers, with the purpose of ensnaring and injuring them, or only for the purpose of deceiving them, i.e., not with the object of doing any hurt to man; but, as these princes of this world esteem such opinions to be true, they desire to impart to others what they themselves believe to be the truth: and this is the view which I am inclined to adopt. For as, to take an illustration, certain Greek authors, or the leaders of some heretical sect, after having imbibed an error in doctrine instead of the truth, and having come to the conclusion in their own minds that such is the truth, proceed, in the next place, to endeavour to persuade others of the correctness of their opinions; so, in like manner, are we to suppose is the procedure of the princes of this world, in which to certain spiritual powers has been assigned the rule over certain nations, and who are termed on that account the princes of this world. There are besides, in addition to these princes, certain special energies of this world, i.e., spiritual powers, which bring about certain effects, which they have themselves, in virtue of their freedom of will, chosen to produce, and to these belong those princes who practise the wisdom of this world: there being, for example, a peculiar energy and power, which is the inspirer of poetry; another, of geometry; and so a separate power, to remind us of each of the arts and professions of this kind. Lastly, many Greek writers have been of opinion that the art of poetry cannot exist without madness; whence also it is several times related in their histories, that those whom they call poets were suddenly filled with a kind of spirit of madness. And what are we to say also of those whom they call diviners, from whom, by the working of those demons who have the mastery over them, answers are given in carefully constructed verses? Those persons, too, whom they term Magi or Malevolent, frequently, by invoking demons over boys of tender years, have made them repeat poetical compositions which were the admiration and amazement of all. Now these effects we are to suppose are brought about in the following manner: As holy and immaculate souls, after devoting themselves to God with all affection and purity, and after preserving themselves free from all contagion of evil spirits, and after being purified by lengthened abstinence, and imbued with holy and religious training, assume by this means a portion of divinity, and earn the grace of prophecy, and other divine gifts; so also are we to suppose that those who place themselves in the way of the opposing powers, i.e., who purposely admire and adopt their manner of life and habits, receive their inspiration, and become partakers of their wisdom and doctrine. And the result of this is, that they are filled with the working of those spirits to whose service they have subjected themselves.

4. With respect to those, indeed, who teach differently regarding Christ from what the rule of Scripture allows, it is no idle task to ascertain whether it is from a treacherous purpose that these opposing powers, in their struggles to prevent a belief in Christ, have devised certain fabulous and impious doctrines; or whether, on hearing the word of Christ, and not being able to cast it forth from the secrecy of their conscience, nor yet to retain it pure and holy, they have, by means of vessels that were convenient to their use, and, so to speak, through their prophets, introduced various errors contrary to the rule of Christian truth. Now we are to suppose rather that apostate and refugee powers, which have departed from God out of the very wickedness of their mind and will, or from envy of those for whom there is prepared (on their becoming acquainted with the truth) an ascent to the same rank, whence they themselves had fallen, did, in order to prevent any progress of that kind, invent these errors and delusions of false doctrine. It is then clearly established, by many proofs, that while the soul of man exists in this body, it may admit different energies, i.e., operations, from a diversity of good and evil spirits. Now, of wicked spirits there is a twofold mode of operation: i.e., when they either take complete and entire possession of the mind, so as to allow their captives the power neither of understanding nor feeling; as, for instance, is the case with those commonly called possessed, whom we see to be deprived of reason, and insane (such as those were who are related in the Gospel to have been cured by the Saviour); or when by their wicked suggestions they deprave a sentient and intelligent soul with thoughts of various kinds, persuading it to evil, of which Judas is an illustration, who was induced at the suggestion of the devil to commit the crime of treason, according to the declaration of Scripture, that "the devil had already put it into the heart of Judas Iscariot to betray him."

But a man receives the energy, i.e., the working, of a good spirit, when he is stirred and incited to good, and is inspired to heavenly or divine things; as the holy angels and God Himself wrought in the prophets, arousing and exhorting them by their holy suggestions to a better course of life, yet so, indeed, that it remained within the will and judgment of the individual, either to be willing or unwilling to follow the call to divine and heavenly things. And from this manifest distinction, it is seen how the soul is moved by the presence of a better spirit, i.e., if it encounter no perturbation or alienation of mind whatever from the impending inspiration, nor lose the free control of its will; as, for instance, is the case with all, whether prophets or

176

apostles, who ministered to the divine responses without any perturbation of mind. Now, that by the suggestions of a good spirit the memory of man is aroused to the recollection of better things, we have already shown by previous instances, when we mentioned the cases of Mordecai and Artaxerxes.

5. This too, I think, should next be inquired into, viz., what are the reasons why a human soul is acted on at one time by good (spirits), and at another by bad: the grounds of which I suspect to be older than the bodily birth of the individual, as John (the Baptist) showed by his leaping and exulting in his mother's womb, when the voice of the salutation of Mary reached the ears of his mother Elisabeth; and as Jeremiah the prophet declares, who was known to God before he was formed in his mother's womb, and before he was born was sanctified by Him, and while yet a boy received the grace of prophecy. And again, on the other hand it is shown beyond a doubt, that some have been possessed by hostile spirits from the very beginning of their lives: i.e., some were born with an evil spirit; and others, according to credible histories, have practised divination from childhood. Others have been under the influence of the demon called Python, i.e., the ventriloquial spirit, from the commencement of their existence. To all which instances, those who maintain that everything in the world is under the administration of Divine Providence (as is also our own belief), can, as it appears to me, give no other answer, so as to show that no shadow of injustice rests upon the divine government, than by holding that there were certain causes of prior existence, in consequence of which the souls, before their birth in the body, contracted a certain amount of guilt in their sensitive nature, or in their movements, on account of which they have been judged worthy by Divine Providence of being placed in this condition. For a soul is always in possession of free-will, as well when it is in the body as when it is without it; and freedom of will is always directed either to good or evil. Nor can any rational and sentient being, i.e., a mind or soul, exist without some movement either good or bad. And it is probable that these movements furnish grounds for merit even before they do anything in this world; so that on account of these merits or grounds they are, immediately on their birth, and even before it, so to speak, assorted by Divine Providence for the endurance either of good or evil.

Let such, then, be our views respecting those events which appear to befall men, either immediately after birth, or even before they enter upon the light. But as regards the suggestions which are made to the soul, i.e., to the faculty of human thought, by different spirits, and which arouse men to good actions or the contrary, even in such a case we must suppose that there sometimes existed certain causes anterior to bodily birth. For occasionally the mind, when watchful, and casting away from it what is evil, calls to itself the aid of the good; or if it be, on the contrary, negligent and slothful, it makes room through insufficient caution for these spirits, which, lying in wait secretly like robbers, contrive to rush into the minds of men when they see a lodgment made for them by sloth; as the Apostle Peter says, "that our adversary the devil goes about like a roaring lion, seeking whom he may devour." On which account our heart must be kept with all carefulness both by day and night, and no place be given to the devil; but every effort must be used that the ministers of God—those spirits, viz., who were sent to minister to them who are called to be heirs of salvation— may find a place within us, and be delighted to enter into the guest-chamber of our soul, and dwelling within us may guide us by their counsels; if, indeed, they shall find the habitation of our heart adorned by the practice of virtue and holiness. But let that be sufficient which we have said, as we best could, regarding those powers which are hostile to the human race.

CHAPTER IV—ON HUMAN TEMPTATIONS

1. And now the subject of human temptations must not, in my opinion, be passed over in silence, which take their rise sometimes from flesh and blood, or from the wisdom of flesh and blood, which is said to be hostile to God. And whether the statement be true which certain allege, viz., that each individual has as it were two souls, we shall determine after we have explained the nature of those temptations, which are said to be more powerful than any of human origin, i.e., which we sustain from principalities and powers, and from the rulers of the darkness of this world, and from spiritual wickedness in high places, or to which we are subjected from wicked spirits and unclean demons. Now, in the investigation of this subject, we must, I think, inquire according to a logical method whether there be in us human beings, who are composed of soul and body and vital spirit, some other element, possessing an incitement of its own, and evoking a movement towards evil. For a question of this kind is wont to be discussed by some in this way: whether, viz., as two souls are said to co-exist within us, the one is more divine and heavenly and the other inferior; or whether, from the very fact that we inhere in bodily structures which according to their own proper nature are dead, and altogether devoid of life (seeing it is from us, i.e., from our souls, that the material body derives its life, it being contrary and hostile to the spirit), we are drawn

on and enticed to the practice of those evils which are agreeable to the body; or whether, thirdly (which was the opinion of some of the Greek philosophers), although our soul is one in substance, it nevertheless consists of several elements, and one portion of it is called rational and another irrational, and that which is termed the irrational part is again separated into two affections—those of covetousness and passion. These three opinions, then, regarding the soul, which we have stated above, we have found to be entertained by some, but that one of them, which we have mentioned as being adopted by certain Grecian philosophers, viz., that the soul is tripartite, I do not observe to be greatly confirmed by the authority of holy Scripture; while with respect to the remaining two there is found a considerable number of passages in the holy Scriptures which seem capable of application to them.

2. Now, of these opinions, let us first discuss that which is maintained by some, that there is in us a good and heavenly soul, and another earthly and inferior; and that the better soul is implanted within us from heaven, such as was that which, while Jacob was still in the womb, gave him the prize of victory in supplanting his brother Esau, and which in the case of Jeremiah was sanctified from his birth, and in that of John was filled by the Holy Spirit from the womb. Now, that which they term the inferior soul is produced, they allege, along with the body itself out of the seed of the body, whence they say it cannot live or subsist beyond the body, on which account also they say it is frequently termed flesh. For the expression, "The flesh lusteth against the Spirit," they take to be applicable not to the flesh, but to this soul, which is properly the soul of the flesh. From these words, moreover, they endeavour notwithstanding to make good the declaration in Leviticus: "The life of all flesh is the blood thereof." For, from the circumstance that it is the diffusion of the blood throughout the whole flesh which produces life in the flesh, they assert that this soul, which is said to be the life of all flesh, is contained in the blood. This statement, moreover, that the flesh struggles against the spirit, and the spirit against the flesh; and the further statement, that "the life of all flesh is the blood thereof," is, according to these writers, simply calling the wisdom of the flesh by another name, because it is a kind of material spirit, which is not subject to the law of God, nor can be so, because it has earthly wishes and bodily desires. And it is with respect to this that they think the apostle uttered the words: "I see another law in my members, warring against the law of my mind, and bringing me into captivity to the law of sin which is in my members." And if one were to object to them that these words were spoken of the nature of the body, which indeed, agreeably to the peculiarity of its nature, is dead,

but is said to have sensibility, or wisdom which is hostile to God, or which struggles against the spirit; or if one were to say that, in a certain degree, the flesh itself was possessed of a voice, which should cry out against the endurance of hunger, or thirst, or cold, or of any discomfort arising either from abundance or poverty,—they would endeavour to weaken and impair the force of such (arguments), by showing that there were many other mental perturbations which derive their origin in no respect from the flesh, and yet against which the spirit struggles, such as ambition, avarice, emulation, envy, pride, and others like these; and seeing that with these the human mind or spirit wages a kind of contest, they lay down as the cause of all these evils, nothing else than this corporal soul, as it were, of which we have spoken above, and which is generated from the seed by a process of traducianism. They are accustomed also to adduce, in support of their assertion, the declaration of the apostle, "Now the works of the flesh are manifest, which are these, fornication, uncleanness, lasciviousness, idolatry, poisonings, hatred, contentions, emulations, wrath, quarrelling, dissensions, heresies, sects, envyings, drunkenness, revellings, and the like;" asserting that all these do not derive their origin from the habits or pleasures of the flesh, so that all such movements are to be regarded as inherent in that substance which has not a soul, i.e., the flesh. The declaration, moreover, "For ye see your calling, brethren, how that not many wise men among you according to the flesh are called," would seem to require to be understood as if there were one kind of wisdom, carnal and material, and another according to the spirit, the former of which cannot indeed be called wisdom, unless there be a soul of the flesh, which is wise in respect of what is called carnal wisdom. And in addition to these passages they adduce the following: "Since the flesh lusteth against the Spirit, and the Spirit against the flesh, so that we cannot do the things that we would." What are these things now respecting which he says, "that we cannot do the things that we would?" It is certain, they reply, that the spirit cannot be intended; for the will of the spirit suffers no hindrance. But neither can the flesh be meant, because if it has not a soul of its own, neither can it assuredly possess a will. It remains, then, that the will of this soul be intended which is capable of having a will of its own, and which certainly is opposed to the will of the spirit. And if this be the case, it is established that the will of the soul is something intermediate between the flesh and the spirit, undoubtedly obeying and serving that one of the two which it has elected to obey. And if it yield itself up to the pleasures of the flesh, it renders men carnal; but when it unites itself with the spirit, it produces men of the Spirit, and who on that account are termed spiritual. And this seems to be the meaning of the apostle in the words, "But ye are not in the flesh, but in the Spirit."

We have accordingly to ascertain what is this very will (intermediate) between flesh and spirit, besides that will which is said to belong to the flesh or the spirit. For it is held as certain, that everything which is said to be a work of the spirit is (a product of) the will of the spirit, and everything that is called a work of the flesh (proceeds from) the will of the flesh. What else then, besides these, is that will of the soul which receives a separate name, and which will, the apostle being opposed to our executing, says: "Ye cannot do the things that ye would?" By this it would seem to be intended, that it ought to adhere to neither of these two, i.e., to neither flesh nor spirit. But some one will say, that as it is better for the soul to execute its own will than that of the flesh; so, on the other hand, it is better to do the will of the spirit than its own will. How, then, does the apostle say, "that ye cannot do the things that ye would?" Because in that contest which is waged between flesh and spirit, the spirit is by no means certain of victory, it being manifest that in very many individuals the flesh has the mastery.

3. But since the subject of discussion on which we have entered is one of great profundity, which it is necessary to consider in all its bearings, let us see whether some such point as this may not be determined: that as it is better for the soul to follow the spirit when the latter has overcome the flesh, so also, if it seem to be a worse course for the former to follow the flesh in its struggles against the spirit, when the latter would recall the soul to its influence, it may nevertheless appear a more advantageous procedure for the soul to be under the mastery of the flesh than to remain under the power of its own will. For, since it is said to be neither hot nor cold, but to continue in a sort of tepid condition, it will find conversion a slow and somewhat difficult undertaking. If indeed it clung to the flesh, then, satiated at length, and filled with those very evils which it suffers from the vices of the flesh, and wearied as it were by the heavy burdens of luxury and lust, it may sometimes be converted with greater ease and rapidity from the filthiness of matter to a desire for heavenly things, and (to a taste for) spiritual graces. And the apostle must be supposed to have said, that "the Spirit contends against the flesh, and the flesh against the Spirit, so that we cannot do the things that we would" (those things, undoubtedly, which are designated as being beyond the will of the spirit, and the will of the flesh), meaning (as if we were to express it in other words) that it is better for a man to be either in a state of virtue or in one of wickedness, than in neither of these; but that the soul, before its conversion to the spirit, and its union with it, appears during

its adherence to the body, and its meditation of carnal things, to be neither in a good condition nor in a manifestly bad one, but resembles, so to speak, an animal. It is better, however, for it, if possible, to be rendered spiritual through adherence to the spirit; but if that cannot be done, it is more expedient for it to follow even the wickedness of the flesh, than, placed under the influence of its own will, to retain the position of an irrational animal.

These points we have now discussed, in our desire to consider each individual opinion, at greater length than we intended, that those views might not be supposed to have escaped our notice which are generally brought forward by those who inquire whether there is within us any other soul than this heavenly and rational one, which is naturally opposed to the latter, and is called either the flesh, or the wisdom of the flesh, or the soul of the flesh.

4. Let us now see what answer is usually returned to these statements by those who maintain that there is in us one movement, and one life, proceeding from one and the same soul, both the salvation and the destruction of which are ascribed to itself as a result of its own actions. And, in the first place, let us notice of what nature those commotions of the soul are which we suffer, when we feel ourselves inwardly drawn in different directions; when there arises a kind of contest of thoughts in our hearts, and certain probabilities are suggested us, agreeably to which we lean now to this side, now to that, and by which we are sometimes convicted of error, and sometimes approve of our acts. It is nothing remarkable, however, to say of wicked spirits, that they have a varying and conflicting judgment, and one out of harmony with itself, since such is found to be the case in all men, whenever, in deliberating upon an uncertain event, council is taken, and men consider and consult what is to be chosen as the better and more useful course. It is not therefore surprising that, if two probabilities meet, and suggest opposite views, they should drag the mind in contrary directions. For example, if a man be led by reflection to believe and to fear God, it cannot then be said that the flesh contends against the Spirit; but, amidst the uncertainty of what may be true and advantageous, the mind is drawn in opposite directions. So, also, when it is supposed that the flesh provokes to the indulgence of lust, but better counsels oppose allurements of that kind, we are not to suppose that it is one life which is resisting another, but that it is the tendency of the nature of the body, which is eager to empty out and cleanse the places filled with seminal moisture; as, in like manner, it is not to be supposed that it is any opposing power, or the life of another soul, which excites within us the appetite of thirst, and impels us to drink, or which causes us to feel

182

hunger, and drives us to satisfy it. But as it is by the natural movements of the body that food and drink are either desired or rejected, so also the natural seed, collected together in course of time in the various vessels, has an eager desire to be expelled and thrown away, and is so far from never being removed, save by the impulse of some exciting cause, that it is even sometimes spontaneously emitted. When, therefore, it is said that "the flesh struggles against the Spirit," these persons understand the expression to mean that habit or necessity, or the delights of the flesh, arouse a man, and withdraw him from divine and spiritual things. For, owing to the necessity of the body being drawn away, we are not allowed to have leisure for divine things, which are to be eternally advantageous. So again, the soul, devoting itself to divine and spiritual pursuits, and being united to the spirit, is said to fight against the flesh, by not permitting it to be relaxed by indulgence, and to become unsteady through the influence of those pleasures for which it feels a natural delight. In this way, also, they claim to understand the words, "The wisdom of the flesh is hostile to God," not that the flesh really has a soul, or a wisdom of its own. But as we are accustomed to say, by an abuse of language, that the earth is thirsty, and wishes to drink in water, this use of the word "wishes" is not proper, but catachrestic,—as if we were to say again, that this house wants to be rebuilt, and many other similar expressions; so also is the wisdom of the flesh to be understood, or the expression, that "the flesh lusteth against the Spirit." They generally connect with these the expression, "The voice of thy brother's blood crieth unto Me from the ground." For what cries unto the Lord is not properly the blood which was shed; but the blood is said improperly to cry out, vengeance being demanded upon him who had shed it. The declaration also of the apostle, "I see another law in my members, warring against the law of my mind," they so understand as if he had said, That he who wishes to devote himself to the word of God is, on account of his bodily necessities and habits, which like a sort of law are ingrained in the body, distracted, and divided, and impeded, lest, by devoting himself vigorously to the study of wisdom, he should be enabled to behold the divine mysteries.

5. With respect, however, to the following being ranked among the works of the flesh, viz., heresies, and envyings, and contentions, or other (vices), they so understand the passage, that the mind, being rendered grosser in feeling, from its yielding itself to the passions of the body, and being oppressed by the mass of its vices, and having no refined or spiritual feelings, is said to be made flesh, and derives its name from that in which it exhibits more vigour and force of will. They

183

also make this further inquiry, "Who will be found, or who will be said to be, the creator of this evil sense, called the sense of the flesh?" Because they defend the opinion that there is no other creator of soul and flesh than God. And if we were to assert that the good God created anything in His own creation that was hostile to Himself, it would appear to be a manifest absurdity. If, then, it is written, that "carnal wisdom is enmity against God," and if this be declared to be a result of creation, God Himself will appear to have formed a nature hostile to Himself, which cannot be subject to Him nor to His law, as if it were (supposed to be) an animal of which such qualities are predicated. And if this view be admitted, in what respect will it appear to differ from that of those who maintain that souls of different natures are created, which, according to their natures, are destined either to be lost or saved? But this is an opinion of the heretics alone, who, not being able to maintain the justice of God on grounds of piety, compose impious inventions of this kind. And now we have brought forward to the best of our ability, in the person of each of the parties, what might be advanced by way of argument regarding the several views, and let the reader choose out of them for himself that which he thinks ought to be preferred.

CHAPTER V—THAT THE WORLD TOOK ITS BEGINNING IN TIME

1. And now, since there is one of the articles of the Church which is held principally in consequence of our belief in the truth of our sacred history, viz. that this world was created and took its beginning at a certain time, and, in conformity to the cycle of time decreed to all things, is to be destroyed on account of its corruption, there seems no absurdity in re-discussing a few points connected with this subject. And so far, indeed, as the credibility of Scripture is concerned, the declarations on such a matter seem easy of proof. Even the heretics, although widely opposed on many other things, yet on this appear to be at one, yielding to the authority of Scripture.

Concerning, then, the creation of the world, what portion of Scripture can give us more information regarding it, than the account which Moses has transmitted respecting its origin? And although it comprehends matters of profounder significance than the mere historical narrative appears to indicate, and contains very many things that are to be spiritually understood, and employs the letter, as a kind of veil, in treating of profound and mystical subjects; nevertheless the language of the narrator shows that all visible things were created at a certain time. But with regard to the consummation of the world, Jacob is the first who gives any information, in addressing his children in the words: "Gather yourselves together unto me, ye sons of Jacob, that I may tell you what shall be in the last days," or "after the last days." If, then, there be "last days," or a period "succeeding the last days," the days which had a beginning must necessarily come to an end. David, too, declares: "The heavens shall perish, but Thou shalt endure; yea, all of them shall wax old as doth a garment: as a vesture shalt Thou change them, and they shall be changed: but Thou art the same, and Thy years shall have no end." Our Lord and Saviour, indeed, in the words, "He who made them at the beginning, made them male and female," Himself bears witness that the world was created; and again, when He says, "Heaven and earth shall pass away, but My word shall not pass away," He points out that they are perishable, and must come to an end. The apostle, moreover, in declaring that "the creature was made subject to vanity, not willingly, but by reason of Him who hath subjected the same in hope, because the creature itself also shall be delivered from the bondage of corruption into the glorious liberty of the children of God," manifestly announces the end of the world; as he does also when he again says, "The fashion of this world passeth away." Now, by the expression which he employs, "that the creature was made subject to vanity," he shows that there was a beginning to this world: for if the creature were made subject to vanity on account of some hope, it was certainly made subject from a cause; and seeing it was from a cause, it must necessarily have had a beginning: for, without some beginning, the creature could not be subject to vanity, nor could that (creature) hope to be freed from the bondage of corruption, which had not begun to serve. But any one who chooses to search at his leisure, will find numerous other passages in holy Scripture in which the world is both said to have a beginning and to hope for an end.

2. Now, if there be any one who would here oppose either the authority or credibility of our Scriptures, we would ask of him whether he asserts that God can, or cannot, comprehend all things? To assert that He cannot, would manifestly be an act of impiety. If then he answer, as he must, that God comprehends all things, it follows from the very fact of their being capable of comprehension, that they are understood to have a beginning and an end, seeing that which is altogether without any beginning cannot be at all comprehended. For however far understanding may extend, so far is the faculty of comprehending illimitably withdrawn and removed when there is held to be no beginning.

3. But this is the objection which they generally raise: they say, "If

185

the world had its beginning in time, what was God doing before the world began? For it is at once impious and absurd to say that the nature of God is inactive and immoveable, or to suppose that goodness at one time did not do good, and omnipotence at one time did not exercise its power." Such is the objection which they are accustomed to make to our statement that this world had its beginning at a certain time, and that, agreeably to our belief in Scripture, we can calculate the years of its past duration. To these propositions I consider that none of the heretics can easily return an answer that will be in conformity with the nature of their opinions. But we can give a logical answer in accordance with the standard of religion, when we say that not then for the first time did God begin to work when He made this visible world; but as, after its destruction, there will be another world, so also we believe that others existed before the present came into being. And both of these positions will be confirmed by the authority of holy Scripture. For that there will be another world after this, is taught by Isaiah, who says, "There will be new heavens, and a new earth, which I shall make to abide in my sight, saith the Lord;" and that before this world others also existed is shown by Eccelesiastes, in the words: "What is that which hath been? Even that which shall be. And what is that which has been created? Even this which is to be created: and there is nothing altogether new under the sun. Who shall speak and declare, Lo, this is new? It hath already been in the ages which have been before us." By these testimonies it is established both that there were ages before our own, and that there will be others after it. It is not, however, to be supposed that several worlds existed at once, but that, after the end of this present world, others will take their beginning; respecting which it is unnecessary to repeat each particular statement, seeing we have already done so in the preceding pages.

4. This point, indeed, is not to be idly passed by, that the holy Scriptures have called the creation of the world by a new and peculiar name, terming it *katabole*, which has been very improperly translated into Latin by "constitutio;" for in Greek *katabole* signifies rather "dejicere," i.e., to cast downwards,—a word which has been, as we have already remarked, improperly translated into Latin by the phrase "constitutio mundi," as in the Gospel according to John, where the Saviour says, "And there will be tribulation in those days, such as was not since the beginning of the world;" in which passage *katabole* is rendered by beginning (*constitutio*), which is to be understood as above explained. The apostle also, in the Epistle to the Ephesians, has employed the same language, saying, "Who hath chosen us before the foundation of the world;" and this foundation he calls *katabole*, to be

understood in the same sense as before. It seems worth while, then, to inquire what is meant by this new term; and I am, indeed, of opinion that, as the end and consummation of the saints will be in those (ages) which are not seen, and are eternal, we must conclude (as frequently pointed out in the preceding pages), from a contemplation of that very end, that rational creatures had also a similar beginning. And if they had a beginning such as the end for which they hope, they existed undoubtedly from the very beginning in those (ages) which are not seen, and are eternal. And if this is so, then there has been a descent from a higher to a lower condition, on the part not only of those souls who have deserved the change by the variety of their movements, but also on that of those who, in order to serve the whole world, were brought down from those higher and invisible spheres to these lower and visible ones, although against their will—"Because the creature was subjected to vanity, not willingly, but because of Him who subjected the same in hope;" so that both sun, and moon, and stars, and angels might discharge their duty to the world, and to those souls which, on account of their excessive mental defects, stood in need of bodies of a grosser and more solid nature; and for the sake of those for whom this arrangement was necessary, this visible world was also called into being. From this it follows, that by the use of the word *katabole*, a descent from a higher to a lower condition, shared by all in common, would seem to be pointed out. The hope indeed of freedom is entertained by the whole of creation—of being liberated from the corruption of slavery—when the sons of God, who either fell away or were scattered abroad, shall be gathered together into one, or when they shall have fulfilled their other duties in this world, which are known to God alone, the Disposer of all things. We are, indeed, to suppose that the world was created of such quality and capacity as to contain not only all those souls which it was determined should be trained in this world, but also all those powers which were prepared to attend, and serve, and assist them. For it is established by many declarations that all rational creatures are of one nature: on which ground alone could the justice of God in all His dealings with them be defended, seeing every one has the reason in himself, why he has been placed in this or that rank in life.

5. This arrangement of things, then, which God afterwards appointed (for He had, from the very origin of the world, clearly perceived the reasons and causes affecting those who, either owing to mental deficiencies, deserved to enter into bodies, or those who were carried away by their desire for visible things, and those also who, either willingly or unwillingly, were compelled, (by Him who subjected the

187

same in hope), to perform certain services to such as had fallen into that condition), not being understood by some, who failed to perceive that it was owing to preceding causes, originating in free-will, that this variety of arrangement had been instituted by God, they have concluded that all things in this world are directed either by fortuitous movements or by a necessary fate, and that nothing is within the power of our own will. And, therefore, also they were unable to show that the providence of God was beyond the reach of censure.

6. But as we have said that all the souls who lived in this world stood in need of many ministers, or rulers, or assistants; so, in the last times, when the end of the world is already imminent and near, and the whole human race is verging upon the last destruction, and when not only those who were governed by others have been reduced to weakness, but those also to whom had been committed the cares of government, it was no longer such help nor such defenders that were needed, but the help of the Author and Creator Himself was required to restore to the one the discipline of obedience, which had been corrupted and profaned, and to the other the discipline of rule. And hence the only-begotten Son of God, who was the Word and the Wisdom of the Father, when He was in the possession of that glory with the Father, which He had before the world was, divested Himself of it, and, taking the form of a servant, was made obedient unto death, that He might teach obedience to those who could not otherwise than by obedience obtain salvation. He restored also the laws of rule and government which had been corrupted, by subduing all enemies under His feet, that by this means (for it was necessary that He should reign until He had put all enemies under His feet, and destroyed the last enemy—death) He might teach rulers themselves moderation in their government. As He had come, then, to restore the discipline, not only of government, but of obedience, as we have said, accomplishing in Himself first what He desired to be accomplished by others, He became obedient to the Father, not only to the death of the cross, but also, in the end of the world, embracing in Himself all whom He subjects to the Father, and who by Him come to salvation, He Himself, along with them, and in them, is said also to be subject to the Father; all things subsisting in Him, and He Himself being the Head of all things, and in Him being the salvation and the fulness of those who obtain salvation. And this consequently is what the apostle says of Him: "And when all things shall be subjected to Him, then shall the Son also Himself be subject to Him that put all things under Him, that God may be all in all."

7. I know not, indeed, how the heretics, not understanding the meaning of the apostle in these words, consider the term "subjection"

degrading as applied to the Son; for if the propriety of the title be called in question, it may easily be ascertained from making a contrary supposition. Because if it be not good to be in subjection, it follows that the opposite will be good, viz., not to be in subjection. Now the language of the apostle, according to their view, appears to indicate by these words, "And when all things shall be subdued unto Him, then shall the Son also Himself be subject unto Him that put all things under Him," that He, who is not now in subjection to the Father, will become subject to Him when the Father shall have first subdued all things unto Him. But I am astonished how it can be conceived to be the meaning, that He who, while all things are not yet subdued to Him, is not Himself in subjection, should—at a time when all things have been subdued to Him, and when He has become King of all men, and holds sway over all things—be supposed then to be made subject, seeing He was not formerly in subjection; for such do not understand that the subjection of Christ to the Father indicates that our happiness has attained to perfection, and that the work undertaken by Him has been brought to a victorious termination, seeing He has not only purified the power of supreme government over the whole of creation, but presents to the Father the principles of the obedience and subjection of the human race in a corrected and improved condition. If, then, that subjection be held to be good and salutary by which the Son is said to be subject to the Father, it is an extremely rational and logical inference to deduce that the subjection also of enemies, which is said to be made to the Son of God, should be understood as being also salutary and useful; as if, when the Son is said to be subject to the Father, the perfect restoration of the whole of creation is signified, so also, when enemies are said to be subjected to the Son of God, the salvation of the conquered and the restoration of the lost is in that understood to consist.

8. This subjection, however, will be accomplished in certain ways, and after certain training, and at certain times; for it is not to be imagined that the subjection is to be brought about by the pressure of necessity (lest the whole world should then appear to be subdued to God by force), but by word, reason, and doctrine; by a call to a better course of things, by the best systems of training, by the employment also of suitable and appropriate threatenings, which will justly impend over those who despise any care or attention to their salvation and usefulness. In a word, we men also, in training either our slaves or children, restrain them by threats and fear while they are, by reason of their tender age, incapable of using their reason; but when they have begun to understand what is good, and useful, and honourable, the fear of the lash being over, they acquiesce through the suasion of words and

reason in all that is good. But how, consistently with the preservation of freedom of will in all rational creatures, each one ought to be regulated, i.e., who they are whom the word of God finds and trains, as if they were already prepared and capable of it; who they are whom it puts off to a later time; who these are from whom it is altogether concealed, and who are so situated as to be far from hearing it; who those, again, are who despise the word of God when made known and preached to them, and who are driven by a kind of correction and chastisement to salvation, and whose conversion is in a certain degree demanded and extorted; who those are to whom certain opportunities of salvation are afforded, so that sometimes, their faith being proved by an answer alone, they have unquestionably obtained salvation;— from what causes or on what occasions these results take place, or what the divine wisdom sees within them, or what movements of their will leads God so to arrange all these things, is known to Him alone, and to His only-begotten Son, through whom all things were created and restored, and to the Holy Spirit, through whom all things are sanctified, who proceedeth from the Father, to whom be glory for ever and ever. Amen.

CHAPTER VI—ON THE END OF THE WORLD

1. Now, respecting the end of the world and the consummation of all things, we have stated in the preceding pages, to the best of our ability, so far as the authority of holy Scripture enabled us, what we deem sufficient for purposes of instruction; and we shall here only add a few admonitory remarks, since the order of investigation has brought us back to the subject. The highest good, then, after the attainment of which the whole of rational nature is seeking, which is also called the end of all blessings, is defined by many philosophers as follows: The highest good, they say, is to become as like to God as possible. But this definition I regard not so much as a discovery of theirs, as a view derived from holy Scripture. For this is pointed out by Moses, before all other philosophers, when he describes the first creation of man in these words: "And God said, Let Us make man in Our own image, and after Our likeness;" and then he adds the words: "So God created man in His own image: in the image of God created He him; male and female created He them, and He blessed them." Now the expression, "In the image of God created He him," without any mention of the word" likeness," conveys no other meaning than this, that man received the dignity of God's image at his first creation; but that the perfection of his likeness has been reserved for the consummation,—

namely, that he might acquire it for himself by the exercise of his own diligence in the imitation of God, the possibility of attaining to perfection being granted him at the beginning through the dignity of the divine image, and the perfect realization of the divine likeness being reached in the end by the fulfilment of the (necessary) works. Now, that such is the case, the Apostle John points out more clearly and unmistakeably, when he makes this declaration: "Little children, we do not yet know what we shall be; but if a revelation be made to us from the Saviour, ye will say, without any doubt, we shall be like Him." By which expression he points out with the utmost certainty, that not only was the end of all things to be hoped for, which he says was still unknown to him, but also the likeness to God, which will be conferred in proportion to the completeness of our deserts. The Lord Himself, in the Gospel, not only declares that these same results are future, but that they are to be brought about by His own intercession, He Himself deigning to obtain them from the Father for His disciples, saying, "Father, I will that where I am, these also may be with Me; and as Thou and I are one, they also may be one in Us." In which the divine likeness itself already appears to advance, if we may so express ourselves, and from being merely similar, to become the same, because undoubtedly in the consummation or end God is "all and in all." And with reference to this, it is made a question by some whether the nature of bodily matter, although cleansed and purified, and rendered altogether spiritual, does not seem either to offer an obstruction towards attaining the dignity of the (divine) likeness, or to the property of unity, because neither can a corporeal nature appear capable of any resemblance to a divine nature which is certainly incorporeal; nor can it be truly and deservedly designated one with it, especially since we are taught by the truths of our religion that that which alone is one, viz., the Son with the Father, must be referred to a peculiarity of the (divine) nature.

2. Since, then, it is promised that in the end God will be all and in all, we are not, as is fitting, to suppose that animals, either sheep or other cattle, come to that end, lest it should be implied that God dwelt even in animals, whether sheep or other cattle; and so, too, with pieces of wood or stones, lest it should be said that God is in these also. So, again, nothing that is wicked must be supposed to attain to that end, lest, while God is said to be in all things, He may also be said to be in a vessel of wickedness. For if we now assert that God is everywhere and in all things, on the ground that nothing can be empty of God, we nevertheless do not say that He is now "all things" in those in whom He is. And hence we must look more carefully as to what that is which denotes the perfection of blessedness and the end of things, which is

not only said to be God in all things, but also "all in all." Let us then inquire what all those things are which God is to become in all.

3. I am of opinion that the expression, by which God is said to be "all in all," means that He is "all" in each individual person. Now He will be "all" in each individual in this way: when all which any rational understanding, cleansed from the dregs of every sort of vice, and with every cloud of wickedness completely swept away, can either feel, or understand, or think, will be wholly God; and when it will no longer behold or retain anything else than God, but when God will be the measure and standard of all its movements; and thus God will be "all," for there will no longer be any distinction of good and evil, seeing evil nowhere exists; for God is all things, and to Him no evil is near: nor will there be any longer a desire to eat from the tree of the knowledge of good and evil, on the part of him who is always in the possession of good, and to whom God is all. So then, when the end has been restored to the beginning, and the termination of things compared with their commencement, that condition of things will be re-established in which rational nature was placed, when it had no need to eat of the tree of the knowledge of good and evil; so that when all feeling of wickedness has been removed, and the individual has been purified and cleansed, He who alone is the one good God becomes to him "all," and that not in the case of a few individuals, or of a considerable number, but He Himself is "all in all." And when death shall no longer anywhere exist, nor the sting of death, nor any evil at all, then verily God will be "all in all." But some are of opinion that that perfection and blessedness of rational creatures, or natures, can only remain in that same condition of which we have spoken above, i.e., that all things should possess God, and God should be to them all things, if they are in no degree prevented by their union with a bodily nature. Otherwise they think that the glory of the highest blessedness is impeded by the intermixture of any material substance. But this subject we have discussed at greater length, as may be seen in the preceding pages.

4. And now, as we find the apostle making mention of a spiritual body, let us inquire, to the best of our ability, what idea we are to form of such a thing. So far, then, as our understanding can grasp it, we consider a spiritual body to be of such a nature as ought to be inhabited not only by all holy and perfect souls, but also by all those creatures which will be liberated from the slavery of corruption. Respecting the body also, the apostle has said, "We have a house not made with hands, eternal in the heavens," i.e., in the mansions of the blessed. And from this statement we may form a conjecture, how pure, how refined, and how glorious are the qualities of that body, if we compare it with those

which, although they are celestial bodies, and of most brilliant splendour, were nevertheless made with hands, and are visible to our sight. But of that body it is said, that it is a house not made with hands, but eternal in the heavens. Since, then, those things "which are seen are temporal, but those things which are not seen are eternal," all those bodies which we see either on earth or in heaven, and which are capable of being seen, and have been made with hands, but are not eternal, are far excelled in glory by that which is not visible, nor made with hands, but is eternal. From which comparison it may be conceived how great are the comeliness, and splendour, and brilliancy of a spiritual body; and how true it is, that "eye hath not seen, nor ear heard, nor hath it entered into the heart of man to conceive, what God hath prepared for them that love Him." We ought not, however, to doubt that the nature of this present body of ours may, by the will of God, who made it what it is, be raised to those qualities of refinement, and purity, and splendour (which characterize the body referred to), according as the condition of things requires, and the deserts of our rational nature shall demand. Finally, when the world required variety and diversity, matter yielded itself with all docility throughout the diverse appearances and species of things to the Creator, as to its Lord and Maker, that He might educe from it the various forms of celestial and terrestrial beings. But when things have begun to hasten to that consummation that all may be one, as the Father is one with the Son, it may be understood as a rational inference, that where all are one, there will no longer be any diversity.

5. The last enemy, moreover, who is called death, is said on this account to be destroyed, that there may not be anything left of a mournful kind when death does not exist, nor anything that is adverse when there is no enemy. The destruction of the last enemy, indeed, is to be understood, not as if its substance, which was formed by God, is to perish, but because its mind and hostile will, which came not from God, but from itself, are to be destroyed. Its destruction, therefore, will not be its non-existence, but its ceasing to be an enemy, and (to be) death. For nothing is impossible to the Omnipotent, nor is anything incapable of restoration to its Creator: for He made all things that they might exist, and those things which were made for existence cannot cease to be. For this reason also will they admit of change and variety, so as to be placed, according to their merits, either in a better or worse position; but no destruction of substance can befall those things which were created by God for the purpose of permanent existence. For those things which agreeably to the common opinion are believed to perish, the nature either of our faith or of the truth will not permit us to

suppose to be destroyed. Finally, our flesh is supposed by ignorant men and unbelievers to be destroyed after death, in such a degree that it retains no relic at all of its former substance. We, however, who believe in its resurrection, understand that a change only has been produced by death, but that its substance certainly remains; and that by the will of its Creator, and at the time appointed, it will be restored to life; and that a second time a change will take place in it, so that what at first was flesh (formed) out of earthly soil, and was afterwards dissolved by death, and again reduced to dust and ashes ("For dust thou art," it is said, "and to dust shalt thou return"), will be again raised from the earth, and shall after this, according to the merits of the indwelling soul, advance to the glory of a spiritual body.

6. Into this condition, then, we are to suppose that all this bodily substance of ours will be brought, when all things shall be re-established in a state of unity, and when God shall be all in all. And this result must be understood as being brought about, not suddenly, but slowly and gradually, seeing that the process of amendment and correction will take place imperceptibly in the individual instances during the lapse of countless and unmeasured ages, some outstripping others, and tending by a swifter course towards perfection, while others again follow close at hand, and some again a long way behind; and thus, through the numerous and uncounted orders of progressive beings who are being reconciled to God from a state of enmity, the last enemy is finally reached, who is called death, so that he also may be destroyed, and no longer be an enemy. When, therefore, all rational souls shall have been restored to a condition of this kind, then the nature of this body of ours will undergo a change into the glory of a spiritual body. For as we see it not to be the case with rational natures, that some of them have lived in a condition of degradation owing to their sins, while others have been called to a state of happiness on account of their merits; but as we see those same souls who had formerly been sinful, assisted, after their conversion and reconciliation to God, to a state of happiness; so also are we to consider, with respect to the nature of the body, that the one which we now make use of in a state of meanness, and corruption, and weakness, is not a different body from that which we shall possess in incorruption, and in power, and in glory; but that the same body, when it has cast away the infirmities in which it is now entangled, shall be transmuted into a condition of glory, being rendered spiritual, so that what was a vessel of dishonour may, when cleansed, become a vessel unto honour, and an abode of blessedness. And in this condition, also, we are to believe, that by the will of the Creator, it will abide for ever without any change, as is confirmed by the declaration

194

of the apostle, when he says, "We have a house, not made with hands, eternal in the heavens." For the faith of the Church does not admit the view of certain Grecian philosophers, that there is besides the body, composed of four elements, another fifth body, which is different in all its parts, and diverse from this our present body; since neither out of sacred Scripture can any produce the slightest suspicion of evidence for such an opinion, nor can any rational inference from things allow the reception of it, especially when the holy apostle manifestly declares, that it is not new bodies which are given to those who rise from the dead, but that they receive those identical ones which they had possessed when living, transformed from an inferior into a better condition. For his words are: "It is sown an animal body, it will rise a spiritual body; it is sown in corruption, it will arise in incorruption: it is sown in weakness, it will arise in power: it is sown in dishonour, it will arise in glory." As, therefore, there is a kind of advance in man, so that from being first an animal being, and not understanding what belongs to the Spirit of God, he reaches by means of instruction the stage of being made a spiritual being, and of judging all things, while he himself is judged by no one; so also, with respect to the state of the body, we are to hold that this very body which now, on account of its service to the soul, is styled an animal body, will, by means of a certain progress, when the soul, united to God, shall have been made one spirit with Him (the body even then ministering, as it were, to the spirit), attain to a spiritual condition and quality, especially since, as we have often pointed out, bodily nature was so formed by the Creator, as to pass easily into whatever condition he should wish, or the nature of the case demand.

7. The whole of this reasoning, then, amounts to this: that God created two general natures,—a visible, i.e., a corporeal nature; and an invisible nature, which is incorporeal. Now these two natures admit of two different permutations. That invisible and rational nature changes in mind and purpose, because it is endowed with freedom of will, and is on this account found sometimes to be engaged in the practice of good, and sometimes in that of the opposite. But this corporeal nature admits of a change in substance; whence also God, the arranger of all things, has the service of this matter at His command in the moulding, or fabrication, or re-touching of whatever He wishes, so that corporeal nature may be transmuted, and transformed into any forms or species whatever, according as the deserts of things may demand; which the prophet evidently has in view when he says, "It is God who makes and transforms all things."

8. And now the point for investigation is, whether, when God shall be all in all, the whole of bodily nature will, in the consummation of all

things, consist of one species, and the sole quality of body be that which shall shine in the indescribable glory which is to be regarded as the future possession of the spiritual body. For if we rightly understand the matter, this is the statement of Moses in the beginning of his book, when he says, "In the beginning God created the heavens and the earth." For this is the beginning of all creation: to this beginning the end and consummation of all things must be recalled, i.e., in order that that heaven and that earth may be the habitation and resting-place of the pious; so that all the holy ones, and the meek, may first obtain an inheritance in that land, since this is the teaching of the law, and of the prophets, and of the Gospel. In which land I believe there exist the true and living forms of that worship which Moses handed down under the shadow of the law; of which it is said, that "they serve unto the example and shadow of heavenly things"—those, viz., who were in subjection in the law. To Moses himself also was the injunction given, "Look that thou make them after the form and pattern which were showed thee on the mount." From which it appears to me, that as on this earth the law was a sort of schoolmaster to those who by it were to be conducted to Christ, in order that, being instructed and trained by it, they might more easily, after the training of the law, receive the more perfect principles of Christ; so also another earth, which receives into it all the saints, may first imbue and mould them by the institutions of the true and everlasting law, that they may more easily gain possession of those perfect institutions of heaven, to which nothing can be added; in which there will be, of a truth, that Gospel which is called everlasting, and that Testament, ever new, which shall never grow old.

9. In this way, accordingly, we are to suppose that at the consummation and restoration of all things, those who make a gradual advance, and who ascend (in the scale of improvement), will arrive in due measure and order at that land, and at that training which is contained in it, where they may be prepared for those better institutions to which no addition can be made. For, after His agents and servants, the Lord Christ, who is King of all, will Himself assume the kingdom; i.e., after instruction in the holy virtues, He will Himself instruct those who are capable of receiving Him in respect of His being wisdom, reigning in them until He has subjected them to the Father, who has subdued all things to Himself, i.e., that when they shall have been made capable of receiving God, God may be to them all in all. Then accordingly, as a necessary consequence, bodily nature will obtain that highest condition to which nothing more can be added. Having discussed, up to this point, the quality of bodily nature, or of spiritual body, we leave it to the choice of the reader to determine what he shall

consider best. And here we may bring the third book to a conclusion.

BOOK IV

CHAPTER I [FROM THE LATIN OF RUFINUS]—
THAT THE SCRIPTURES ARE DIVINELY INSPIRED

1. BUT as it is not sufficient, in the discussion of matters of such importance, to entrust the decision to the human senses and to the human understanding, and to pronounce on things invisible as if they were seen by us, we must, in order to establish the positions which we have laid down, adduce the testimony of Holy Scripture. And that this testimony may produce a sure and unhesitating belief, either with regard to what we have still to advance, or to what has been already stated, it seems necessary to show, in the first place, that the Scriptures themselves are divine, i.e., were inspired by the Spirit of God. We shall therefore with all possible brevity draw forth from the Holy Scriptures themselves, such evidence on this point as may produce upon us a suitable impression, (making our quotations) from Moses, the first legislator of the Hebrew nation, and from the words of Jesus Christ, the Author and Chief of the Christian religious system. For although there have been numerous legislators among the Greeks and Barbarians, and also countless teachers and philosophers who professed to declare the truth, we do not remember any legislator who was able to produce in the minds of foreign nations an affection and a zeal (for him) such as led them either voluntarily to adopt his laws, or to defend them with all the efforts of their mind. No one, then, has been able to introduce and make known what seemed to himself the truth, among, I do not say many foreign nations, but even amongst the individuals of one single nation, in such a manner that a knowledge and belief of the same should extend to all. And yet there can be no doubt that it was the wish of the legislators that their laws should be observed by all men, if possible; and of the teachers, that what appeared to themselves to be truth, should become known to all. But knowing that they could by no means succeed in producing any such mighty power within them as would lead foreign nations to obey their laws, or have regard to their statements, they did not venture even to essay the attempt, lest the failure of the undertaking should stamp their conduct with the mark of imprudence. And yet there are throughout the whole world—throughout all Greece, and all foreign countries—countless individuals who have abandoned the laws of their country, and those whom they had believed to be gods, and have yielded themselves up to the obedience of the law of Moses, and to the discipleship and worship

of Christ; and have done this, not without exciting against themselves the intense hatred of the worshippers of images, so as frequently to be exposed to cruel tortures from the latter, and sometimes even to be put to death. And yet they embrace, and with all affection preserve, the words and teaching of Christ.

2. And we may see, moreover, how that religion itself grew up in a short time, making progress by the punishment and death of its worshippers, by the plundering of their goods, and by the tortures of every kind which they endured; and this result is the more surprising, that even the teachers of it themselves neither were men of skill, nor very numerous; and yet these words are preached throughout the whole world, so that Greeks and Barbarians, wise and foolish, adopt the doctrines of the Christian religion. From which it is no doubtful inference, that it is not by human power or might that the words of Jesus Christ come to prevail with all faith and power over the understandings and souls of all men. For, that these results were both predicted by Him, and established by divine answers proceeding from Him, is clear from His own words: "Ye shall be brought before governors and kings for My sake, for a testimony against them and the Gentiles." And again: "This Gospel of the kingdom shall be preached among all nations." And again: "Many shall say to Me in that day, Lord, Lord, have we not eaten and drunk in Thy name, and in Thy name cast out devils? And I will say unto them, Depart from Me, ye workers of iniquity, I never knew you." If these sayings, indeed, had been so uttered by Him, and yet if these predictions had not been fulfilled, they might perhaps appear to be untrue, and not to possess any authority. But now, when His declarations do pass into fulfilment, seeing they were predicted with such power and authority, it is most clearly shown to be true that He, when He was made man, delivered to men the precepts of salvation.

3. What, then, are we to say of this, which the prophets had beforehand foretold of Him, that princes would not cease from Judah, nor leaders from between his thighs, until He should come for whom it has been reserved (viz., the kingdom), and until the expectation of the Gentiles should come? For it is most distinctly evident from the history itself, from what is clearly seen at the present day, that from the times of Christ onwards there were no kings amongst the Jews. Nay, even all those objects of Jewish pride, of which they vaunted so much, and in which they exulted, whether regarding the beauty of the temple or the ornaments of the altar, and all those sacerdotal fillets and robes of the high priests, were all destroyed together. For the prophecy was fulfilled which had declared, "For the children of Israel shall abide

many days without king and prince: there shall be no victim, nor altar, nor priesthood, nor answers." These testimonies, accordingly, we employ against those who seem to assert that what is spoken in Genesis by Jacob refers to Judah; and who say that there still remains a prince of the race of Judah—he, viz., who is the prince of their nation, whom they style Patriarch—and that there cannot fail (a ruler) of his seed, who will remain until the advent of that Christ whom they picture to themselves. But if the prophet's words be true, when he says, "The children of Israel shall abide many days without king, without prince; and there shall be no victim, nor altar, nor priesthood;" and if, certainly, since the overthrow of the temple, victims are neither offered, nor any altar found, nor any priesthood exists, it is most certain that, as it is written, princes have departed from Judah, and a leader from between his thighs, until the coming of Him for whom it has been reserved. It is established, then, that He is come for whom it has been reserved, and in whom is the expectation of the Gentiles. And this manifestly seems to be fulfilled in the multitude of those who have believed on God through Christ out of the different nations.

4. In the song of Deuteronomy, also, it is prophetically declared that, on account of the sins of the former people, there was to be an election of a foolish nation,—no other, certainly, than that which was brought about by Christ; for thus the words run: "They have moved Me to anger with their images, and I will stir them up to jealousy; I will arouse them to anger against a foolish nation." We may therefore evidently see how the Hebrews, who are said to have excited God's anger by means of those (idols), which are no gods, and to have aroused His wrath by their images, were themselves also excited to jealousy by means of a foolish nation, which God hath chosen by the advent of Jesus Christ and His disciples. For the following is the language of the apostle: "For ye see your calling, brethren, how that not many wise men among you after the flesh, not many mighty, not many noble (are called): but God has chosen the foolish things of the world, and the things which are not, to destroy the things which formerly existed." Carnal Israel, therefore, should not boast; for such is the term used by the apostle: "No flesh, I say, should glory in the presence of God."

5. What are we to say, moreover, regarding those prophecies of Christ contained in the Psalms, especially the one with the superscription, "A song for the Beloved;" in which it is stated that "His tongue is the pen of a ready writer; fairer than the children of men;" that "grace is poured into His lips?" Now, the indication that grace has been poured upon His lips is this, that, after a short period had elapsed—for He taught only during a year and some months—the

whole world, nevertheless, became filled with His doctrine, and with faith in His religion. There arose, then, "in His days righteous men, and abundance of peace," abiding even to the end, which end is entitled "the taking away of the moon;" and "His dominion shall extend from sea to sea, and from the river to the ends of the earth." There was a sign also given to the house of David. For a virgin conceived, and bare Emmanuel, which, when interpreted, signifies, "God with us: know it, O nations, and be overcome." For we are conquered and overcome, who are of the Gentiles, and remain as a kind of spoils of His victory, who have subjected our necks to His grace. Even the place of His birth was predicted in the prophecies of Micah, who said, "And thou, Bethlehem, land of Judah, art by no means small among the leaders of Judah: for out of thee shall come forth a Leader, who shall rule My people Israel." The weeks of years, also, which the prophet Daniel had predicted, extending to the leadership of Christ, have been fulfilled. Moreover, he is at hand, who in the book of Job is said to be about to destroy the huge beast, who also gave power to his own disciples to tread on serpents and scorpions, and on all the power of the enemy, without being injured by him. But if any one will consider the journeys of Christ's apostles throughout the different places, in which as His messengers they preached the Gospel, he will find that both what they ventured to undertake is beyond the power of man, and what they were enabled to accomplish is from God alone. If we consider how men, on hearing that a new doctrine was introduced by these, were able to receive them; or rather, when desiring often to destroy them, they were prevented by a divine power which was in them, we shall find that in this nothing was effected by human strength, but that the whole was the result of the divine power and providence,—signs and wonders, manifest beyond all doubt, bearing testimony to their word and doctrine.

6. These points now being briefly established, viz., regarding the deity of Christ, and the fulfilment of all that was prophesied respecting Him, I think that this position also has been made good, viz., that the Scriptures themselves, which contained these predictions, were divinely inspired,—those, namely, which had either foretold His advent, or the power of His doctrine, or the bringing over of all nations (to His obedience). To which this remark must be added, that the divinity and inspiration both of the predictions of the prophets and of the law of Moses have been clearly revealed and confirmed, especially since the advent of Christ into the world. For before the fulfilment of those events which were predicted by them, they could not, although true and inspired by God, be shown to be so, because they were as yet

unfulfilled. But the coming of Christ was a declaration that their statements were true and divinely inspired, although it was certainly doubtful before that whether there would be an accomplishment of those things which had been foretold.

If any one, moreover, consider the words of the prophets with all the zeal and reverence which they deserve, it is certain that, in the perusal and careful examination thus given them, he will feel his mind and senses touched by a divine breath, and will acknowledge that the words which he reads were no human utterances, but the language of God; and from his own emotions he will feel that these books were the composition of no human skill, nor of any mortal eloquence, but, so to speak, of a style that is divine. The splendour of Christ's advent, therefore, illuminating the law of Moses by the light of truth, has taken away that veil which had been placed over the letter (of the law), and has unsealed, for every one who believes upon Him, all the blessings which were concealed by the covering of the word.

7. It is, however, a matter attended with considerable labour, to point out, in every instance, how and when the predictions of the prophets were fulfilled, so as to appear to confirm those who are in doubt, seeing it is possible for everyone who wishes to become more thoroughly acquainted with these things, to gather abundant proofs from the records of the truth themselves. But if the sense of the letter, which is beyond man, does not appear to present itself at once, on the first glance, to those who are less versed in divine discipline, it is not at all to be wondered at, because divine things are brought down somewhat slowly to (the comprehension of) men, and elude the view in proportion as one is either sceptical or unworthy. For although it is certain that all things which exist in this world, or take place in it, are ordered by the providence of God, and certain events indeed do appear with sufficient clearness to be under the disposal of His providential government, yet others again unfold themselves so mysteriously and incomprehensibly, that the plan of Divine Providence with regard to them is completely concealed; so that it is occasionally believed by some that particular occurrences do not belong to (the plan of) Providence, because the principle eludes their grasp, according to which the works of Divine Providence are administered with indescribable skill; which principle of administration, however, is not equally concealed from all. For even among men themselves, one individual devotes less consideration to it, another more; while by every man, He who is on earth, whoever is the inhabitant of heaven, is more acknowledged. And the nature of bodies is clear to us in one way, that of trees in another, that of animals in a third; the nature of souls, again,

202

is concealed in a different way; and the manner in which the diverse movements of rational understandings are ordered by Providence, eludes the view of men in a greater degree, and even, in my opinion, in no small degree that of the angels also. But as the existence of divine providence is not refuted by those especially who are certain of its existence, but who do not comprehend its workings or arrangements by the powers of the human mind; so neither will the divine inspiration of holy Scripture, which extends throughout its body, be believed to be non-existent, because the weakness of our understanding is unable to trace out the hidden and secret meaning in each individual word, the treasure of divine wisdom being hid in the vulgar and unpolished vessels of words, as the apostle also points out when he says, "We have this treasure in earthen vessels," that the virtue of the divine power may shine out the more brightly, no colouring of human eloquence being intermingled with the truth of the doctrines. For if our books induced men to believe because they were composed either by rhetorical arts or by the wisdom of philosophy, then undoubtedly our faith would be considered to be based on the art of words, and on human wisdom, and not upon the power of God; whereas it is now known to all that the word of this preaching has been so accepted by numbers throughout almost the whole world, because they understood their belief to rest not on the persuasive words of human wisdom, but on the manifestation of the Spirit and of power. On which account, being led by a heavenly, nay, by a more than heavenly power, to faith and acceptance, that we may worship the sole Creator of all things as our God, let us also do our utmost endeavour, by abandoning the language of the elements of Christ, which are but the first beginnings of wisdom, to go on to perfection, in order that that wisdom which is given to them who are perfect, may be given to us also. For such is the promise of him to whom was entrusted the preaching of this wisdom, in the words: "Howbeit we speak wisdom among them that are perfect; yet not the wisdom of this world, nor of the princes of this world, who will be brought to nought;" by which he shows that this wisdom of ours has nothing in common, so far as regards the beauty of language, with the wisdom of this world. This wisdom, then, will be inscribed more clearly and perfectly on our hearts, if it be made known to us according to the revelation of the mystery which has been hid from eternity, but now is manifest through the Scriptures of prophecy, and the advent of our Lord and Saviour Jesus Christ, to whom be glory for ever. Amen.

Many, not understanding the Scriptures in a spiritual sense, but incorrectly, have fallen into heresies.

8. These particulars, then, being briefly stated regarding the

inspiration of the sacred Scriptures by the Holy Spirit, it seems necessary to explain this point also, viz., how certain persons, not reading them correctly, have given themselves over to erroneous opinions, inasmuch as the procedure to be followed, in order to attain an understanding of the holy writings, is unknown to many. The Jews, in fine, owing to the hardness of their heart, and from a desire to appear wise in their own eyes, have not believed in our Lord and Saviour, judging that those statements which were uttered respecting Him ought to be understood literally, i.e., that He ought in a sensible and visible manner to preach deliverance to the captives, and first build a city which they truly deem the city of God, and cut off at the same time the chariots of Ephraim, and the horse from Jerusalem; that He ought also to eat butter and honey, in order to choose the good before He should come to know how to bring forth evil. They think, also, that it has been predicted that the wolf—that four-footed animal—is, at the coming of Christ, to feed with the lambs, and the leopard to lie down with kids, and the calf and the bull to pasture with lions, and that they are to be led by a little child to the pasture; that the ox and the bear are to lie down together in the green fields, and that their young ones are to be fed together; that lions also will frequent stalls with the oxen, and feed on straw. And seeing that, according to history, there was no accomplishment of any of those things predicted of Him, in which they believed the signs of Christ's advent were especially to be observed, they refused to acknowledge the presence of our Lord Jesus Christ; nay, contrary to all the principles of human and divine law, i.e., contrary to the faith of prophecy, they crucified Him for assuming to Himself the name of Christ. Thereupon the heretics, reading that it is written in the law, "A fire has been kindled in Mine anger;" and that "I the Lord am a jealous (God), visiting the sins of the fathers upon the children unto the third and fourth generation;" and that "it repenteth Me that I anointed Saul to be king;" and, "I am the LORD, who make peace and create evil;" and again, "There is not evil in a city which the LORD hath not done;" and, "Evils came down from the LORD upon the gates of Jerusalem;" and, "An evil spirit from the LORD plagued Saul;" and reading many other passages similar to these, which are found in Scripture, they did not venture to assert that these were not the Scriptures of God, but they considered them to be the words of that creator God whom the Jews worshipped, and who, they judged, ought to be regarded as just only, and not also as good; but that the Saviour had come to announce to us a more perfect God, who, they allege; is not the creator of the world,—there being different and discordant opinions among them even on this very point, because, when they once depart from a belief in God the Creator, who is Lord of all, they have given themselves over to various inventions and fables, devising certain (fictions), and asserting that some things were visible, and made by one (God), and that certain other things were invisible, and were created by another, according to the vain and fanciful suggestions of their own minds. But not a few also of the more simple of those, who appear to be restrained within the faith of the Church, are of opinion that there is no greater God than the Creator, holding in this a correct and sound opinion; and yet they entertain regarding Him such views as would not be entertained regarding the most unjust and cruel of men.

9. Now the reason of the erroneous apprehension of all these points on the part of those whom we have mentioned above, is no other than this, that holy Scripture is not understood by them according to its spiritual, but according to its literal meaning. And therefore we shall endeavour, so far as our moderate capacity will permit, to point out to those who believe the holy Scriptures to be no human compositions, but to be written by inspiration of the Holy Spirit, and to be transmitted and entrusted to us by the will of God the Father, through His only-begotten Son Jesus Christ, what appears to us, who observe things by a right way of understanding, to be the standard and discipline delivered to the apostles by Jesus Christ, and which they handed down in succession to their posterity, the teachers of the holy Church. Now, that there are certain mystical economies indicated in holy Scripture, is admitted by all, I think, even the simplest of believers. But what these are, or of what kind they are, he who is rightly minded, and not overcome with the vice of boasting, will scrupulously acknowledge himself to be ignorant. For if anyone, e.g., were to adduce the case of the daughters of Lot, who seem, contrary to the law of God, to have had intercourse with their father, or that of the two wives of Abraham, or of the two sisters who were married to Jacob, or of the two handmaids who increased the number of his sons, what other answer could be returned than that these were certain mysteries, and forms of spiritual things, but that we are ignorant of what nature they are? Nay, even when we read of the construction of the tabernacle, we deem it certain that the written descriptions are the figures of certain hidden things; but to adapt these to their appropriate standards, and to open up and discuss every individual point, I consider to be exceedingly difficult, not to say impossible. That that description, however, is, as I have said, full of mysteries, does not escape even the common understanding. But all the narrative portion, relating either to the marriages, or to the begetting of the children, or to battles of different kinds, or to any other histories whatever, what else can they be

supposed to be, save the forms and figures of hidden and sacred things? As men, however, make little effort to exercise their intellect, or imagine that they possess knowledge before they really learn, the consequence is that they never begin to have knowledge or if there be no want of a desire, at least, nor of an instructor, and if divine knowledge be sought after, as it ought to be, in a religious and holy spirit, and in the hope that many points will be opened up by the revelation of God—since to human sense they are exceedingly difficult and obscure—then, perhaps, he who seeks in such a manner will find what it is lawful to discover.

10. But lest this difficulty perhaps should be supposed to exist only in the language of the prophets, seeing the prophetic style is allowed by all to abound in figures and enigmas, what do we find when we come to the Gospels? Is there not hidden there also an inner, namely a divine sense, which is revealed by that grace alone which he had received who said, "But we have the mind of Christ, that we might know the things freely given to us by God. Which things also we speak, not in the words which man's wisdom teaches, but which the Spirit teacheth?" And if one now were to read the revelations which were made to John, how amazed would he not be that there should be contained within them so great an amount of hidden, ineffable mysteries, in which it is clearly understood, even by those who cannot comprehend *what* is concealed, that *something* certainly is concealed. And yet are not the Epistles of the Apostles, which seem to some to be plainer, filled with meanings so profound, that by means of them, as by some small receptacle, the clearness of incalculable light appears to be poured into those who are capable of understanding the meaning of divine wisdom? And therefore, because this is the case, and because there are many who go wrong in this life, I do not consider that it is easy to pronounce, without danger, that anyone knows or understands those things, which, in order to be opened up, need the key of knowledge; which key, the Saviour declared, lay with those who were skilled in the law. And here, although it is a digression, I think we should inquire of those who assert that before the advent of the Saviour there was no truth among those who were engaged in the study of the law, how it could be said by our Lord Jesus Christ that the keys of knowledge were with them, who had the books of the prophets and of the law in their hands. For thus did He speak: "Woe unto you, ye teachers of the law, who have taken away the key of knowledge: ye entered not in yourselves, and them who wished to enter in ye hindered."

11. But, as we had begun to observe, the way which seems to us the correct one for the understanding of the Scriptures, and for the

investigation of their meaning, we consider to be of the following kind: for we are instructed by Scripture itself in regard to the ideas which we ought to form of it. In the Proverbs of Solomon we find some such rule as the following laid down, respecting the consideration of holy Scripture: "And do thou," he says, "describe these things to thyself in a threefold manner, in counsel and knowledge, and that thou mayest answer the words of truth to those who have proposed them to thee." Each one, then, ought to describe in his own mind, in a threefold manner, the understanding of the divine letters,—that is, in order that all the more simple individuals may be edified, so to speak, by the very body of Scripture; for such we term that common and historical sense: while, if some have commenced to make considerable progress, and are able to see something more (than that), they may be edified by the very soul of Scripture. Those, again, who are perfect, and who resemble those of whom the apostle says, "We speak wisdom among them that are perfect, but not the wisdom of this world, nor of the princes of this world, who will be brought to nought; but we speak the wisdom of God, hidden in a mystery, which God hath decreed before the ages unto our glory;"—all such as these may be edified by the spiritual law itself (which has a shadow of good things to come), as if by the Spirit. For as man is said to consist of body, and soul, and spirit, so also does sacred Scripture, which has been granted by the divine bounty for the salvation of man; which we see pointed out, moreover, in the little book of *The Shepherd*, which seems to be despised by some, where Hermas is commanded to write two little books, and afterwards to announce to the presbyters of the Church what he learned from the Spirit. For these are the words that are written: "And you will write," he says, "two books; and you will give the one to Clement, and the other to Grapte. And let Grapte admonish the widows and orphans, and let Clement send through all the cities which are abroad, while you will announce to the presbyters of the Church." Grapte, accordingly, who is commanded to admonish the orphans and widows, is the pure understanding of the letter itself; by which those youthful minds are admonished, who have not yet deserved to have God as their Father, and are on that account styled orphans. They, again, are the widows, who have withdrawn themselves from the unjust man, to whom they had been united contrary to law; but who have remained widows, because they have not yet advanced to the stage of being joined to a heavenly Bridegroom. Clement, moreover, is ordered to send into those cities which are abroad what is written to those individuals who already are withdrawing from the letter,—as if the meaning were to those souls who, being built up by this means, have begun to rise above the cares of the body and the desires of the flesh; while he himself, who had learned from the Holy Spirit, is commanded to announce, not by letter nor by book, but by the living voice, to the presbyters of the Church of Christ, i.e., to those who possess a mature faculty of wisdom, capable of receiving spiritual teaching.

12. This point, indeed, is not to be passed by without notice, viz., that there are certain passages of Scripture where this "body," as we termed it, i.e., this inferential historical sense, is not always found, as we shall prove to be the case in the following pages, but where that which we termed "soul" or "spirit" can only be understood. And this, I think, is indicated in the Gospels, where there are said to be placed, according to the manner of purification among the Jews, six water-vessels, containing two or three firkins a-piece; by which, as I have said, the language of the Gospel seems to indicate, with respect to those who are secretly called by the apostle "Jews," that they are purified by the word of Scripture,—receiving indeed sometimes two firkins, i.e., the understanding of the "soul" or "spirit," according to our statement as above; sometimes even three (firkins), when in the reading (of Scripture) the "bodily" sense, which is the "historical," may be preserved for the edification of the people. Now six water-vessels are appropriately spoken of, with regard to those persons who are purified by being placed in the world; for we read that in six days—which is the perfect number—this world and all things in it were finished. How great, then, is the utility of this first "historical" sense which we have mentioned, is attested by the multitude of all believers, who believe with adequate faith and simplicity, and does not need much argument, because it is openly manifest to all; whereas of that sense which we have called above the "soul," as it were, of Scripture, the Apostle Paul has given us numerous examples in the first Epistle to the Corinthians. For we find the expression, "Thou shalt not muzzle the mouth of the ox that treadeth out the corn." And afterwards, when explaining what precept ought to be understood by this, he adds the words: "Doth God take care for oxen? or saith He it altogether for our sakes? For our sakes, no doubt, this is written; that he who plougheth should plough in hope, and he that thresheth, in hope of partaking." Very many other passages also of this nature, which are in this way explained of the law, contribute extensive information to the hearers.

13. Now a "spiritual" interpretation is of this nature: when one is able to point out what are the heavenly things of which these serve as the patterns and shadow, who are Jews "according to the flesh," and of what things future the law contains a shadow, and any other expressions of this kind that may be found in holy Scripture; or when

it is a subject of inquiry, what is that wisdom hidden in a mystery which "God ordained before the world for our glory, which none of the princes of this world knew;" or the meaning of the apostle's language, when, employing certain illustrations from Exodus or Numbers, he says: "These things happened to them in a figure, and they are written on our account, on whom the ends of the ages have come." Now, an opportunity is afforded us of understanding of what those things which happened to them were figures, when he adds: "And they drank of that spiritual Rock which followed them, and that Rock was Christ." In another Epistle also, when referring to the tabernacle, he mentions the direction which was given to Moses: "Thou shalt make (all things) according to the pattern which was showed thee in the mount." And writing to the Galatians, and upbraiding certain individuals who seem to themselves to read the law, and yet without understanding it, because of their ignorance of the fact that an allegorical meaning underlies what is written, he says to them in a certain tone of rebuke: "Tell me, ye who desire to be under the law, do ye not hear the law? For it is written that Abraham had two sons; the one by a bond-maid, the other by a free woman. But he who was of the bond-woman was born according to the flesh; but he of the free woman was by promise. Which things are an allegory: for these are the two covenants." And here this point is to be attended to, viz., the caution with which the apostle employs the expression, "Ye who are under the law, do ye not hear the law?" Do ye not *hear*, i.e., do ye not understand and know? In the Epistle to the Colossians, again, briefly summing up and condensing the meaning of the whole law, he says: "Let no man therefore judge you in meat, or in drink, or in respect of holy days, or of the new moon, or of the Sabbath, which are a shadow of things to come." Writing to the Hebrews also, and treating of those who belong to the circumcision, he says: "Those who serve to the example and shadow of heavenly things." Now perhaps, through these illustrations, no doubt will be entertained regarding the five books of Moses, by those who hold the writings of the apostle, as divinely inspired. And if they require, with respect to the rest of the history, that those events which are contained in it should be considered as having happened for an ensample to those of whom they are written, we have observed that this also has been stated in the Epistle to the Romans, where the apostle adduces an instance from the third book of Kings, saying, "I have left me seven thousand men who have not bowed the knee to Baal;" which expression Paul understood as figuratively spoken of those who are called Israelites according to the election, in order to show that the advent of Christ had not only now been of advantage to the Gentiles, but that very many even of the race of Israel had been called to salvation.

14. This being the state of the case, we shall sketch out, as if by way of illustration and pattern, what may occur to us with regard to the manner in which holy Scripture is to be understood on these several points, repeating in the first instance, and pointing out this fact, that the Holy Spirit, by the providence and will of God, through the power of His only-begotten Word, who was in the beginning God with God, enlightened the ministers of truth, the prophets and apostles, to understand the mysteries of those things or causes which take place among men, or with respect to men. And by "men," I now mean souls that are placed in bodies, who, relating those mysteries that are known to them, and revealed through Christ, as if they were a kind of human transactions, or handing down certain legal observances and injunctions, described them figuratively; not that anyone who pleased might view these expositions as deserving to be trampled under foot, but that he who should devote himself with all chastity, and sobriety, and watchfulness, to studies of this kind, might be able by this means to trace out the meaning of the Spirit of God, which is perhaps lying profoundly buried, and the context, which may be pointing again in another direction than the ordinary usage of speech would indicate. And in this way he might become a sharer in the knowledge of the Spirit, and a partaker in the divine counsel, because the soul cannot come to the perfection of knowledge otherwise than by inspiration of the truth of the divine wisdom. Accordingly, it is of God, i.e., of the Father, and of the Son, and of the Holy Spirit, that these men, filled with the Divine Spirit, chiefly treat; then the mysteries relating to the Son of God—how the Word became flesh, and why He descended even to the assumption of the form of a servant—are the subject, as I have said, of explanation by those persons who are filled with the Divine Spirit. It next followed, necessarily, that they should instruct mortals by divine teaching, regarding rational creatures, both those of heaven and the happier ones of earth; and also (should explain) the differences among souls, and the origin of these differences; and then should tell what this world is, and why it was created; whence also sprung the great and terrible wickedness which extends over the earth. And whether that wickedness is found on this earth only, or in other places, is a point which it was necessary for us to learn from divine teaching. Since, then, it was the intention of the Holy Spirit to enlighten with respect to these and similar subjects, those holy souls who had devoted themselves to the service of the truth, this object was kept in view, in the second place, viz., for the sake of those who either could not or would not give themselves to this labour and toil by which they

might deserve to be instructed in or to recognise things of such value and importance, to wrap up and conceal, as we said before, in ordinary language, under the covering of some history and narrative of visible things, hidden mysteries. There is therefore introduced the narrative of the visible creation, and the creation and formation of the first man; then the offspring which followed from him in succession, and some of the actions which were done by the good among his posterity, are related, and occasionally certain crimes also, which are stated to have been committed by them as being human; and afterwards certain unchaste or wicked deeds also are narrated as being the acts of the wicked. The description of battles, moreover, is given in a wonderful manner, and the alternations of victors and vanquished, by which certain ineffable mysteries are made known to those who know how to investigate statements of that kind. By an admirable discipline of wisdom, too, the law of truth, even of the prophets, is implanted in the Scriptures of the law, each of which is woven by a divine art of wisdom, as a kind of covering and veil of spiritual truths; and this is what we have called the "body" of Scripture, so that also, in this way, what we have called the covering of the letter, woven by the art of wisdom, might be capable of edifying and profiting many, when others would derive no benefit.

15. But as if, in all the instances of this covering (i.e., of this history), the logical connection and order of the law had been preserved, we would not certainly believe, when thus possessing the meaning of Scripture in a continuous series, that anything else was contained in it save what was indicated on the surface; so for that reason divine wisdom took care that certain stumbling-blocks, or interruptions, to the historical meaning should take place, by the introduction into the midst (of the narrative) of certain impossibilities and incongruities; that in this way the very interruption of the narrative might, as by the interposition of a bolt, present an obstacle to the reader, whereby he might refuse to acknowledge the way which conducts to the ordinary meaning; and being thus excluded and debarred from it, we might be recalled to the beginning of another way, in order that, by entering upon a narrow path, and passing to a loftier and more sublime road, he might lay open the immense breadth of divine wisdom. This, however, must not be unnoted by us, that as the chief object of the Holy Spirit is to preserve the coherence of the spiritual meaning, either in those things which ought to be done or which have been already performed, if He anywhere finds that those events which, according to the history, took place, can be adapted to a spiritual meaning, He composed a texture of both kinds in one style of narration, always concealing the

211

hidden meaning more deeply; but where the historical narrative could not be made appropriate to the spiritual coherence of the occurrences, He inserted sometimes certain things which either did not take place or could not take place; sometimes also what might happen, but what did not: and He does this at one time in a few words, which, taken in their "bodily" meaning, seem incapable of containing truth, and at another by the insertion of many. And this we find frequently to be the case in the legislative portions, where there are many things manifestly useful among the "bodily" precepts, but a very great number also in which no principle of utility is at all discernible, and sometimes even things which are judged to be impossibilities. Now all this, as we have remarked, was done by the Holy Spirit in order that, seeing those events which lie on the surface can be neither true nor useful, we may be led to the investigation of that truth which is more deeply concealed, and to the ascertaining of a meaning worthy of God in those Scriptures which we believe to be inspired by Him.

16. Nor was it only with regard to those Scriptures which were composed down to the advent of Christ that the Holy Spirit thus dealt; but as being one and the same Spirit, and proceeding from one God, He dealt in the same way with the evangelists and apostles. For even those narratives which He inspired them to write were not composed without the aid of that wisdom of His, the nature of which we have above explained. Whence also in them were intermingled not a few things by which, the historical order of the narrative being interrupted and broken up, the attention of the reader might be recalled, by the impossibility of the case, to an examination of the inner meaning. But, that our meaning may be ascertained by the facts themselves, let us examine the passages of Scripture. Now who is there, pray, possessed of understanding, that will regard the statement as appropriate, that the first day, and the second, and the third, in which also both evening and morning are mentioned, existed without sun, and moon, and stars— the first day even without a sky? And who is found so ignorant as to suppose that God, as if He had been a husbandman, planted trees in paradise, in Eden towards the east, and a tree of life in it, i.e., a visible and palpable tree of wood, so that anyone eating of it with bodily teeth should obtain life, and, eating again of another tree, should come to the knowledge of good and evil? No one, I think, can doubt that the statement that God walked in the afternoon in paradise, and that Adam lay hid under a tree, is related figuratively in Scripture, that some mystical meaning may be indicated by it. The departure of Cain from the presence of the Lord will manifestly cause a careful reader to inquire what is the presence of God, and how anyone can go out from it. But

not to extend the task which we have before us beyond its due limits, it is very easy for anyone who pleases to gather out of holy Scripture what is recorded indeed as having been done, but what nevertheless cannot be believed as having reasonably and appropriately occurred according to the historical account. The same style of Scriptural narrative occurs abundantly in the Gospels, as when the devil is said to have placed Jesus on a lofty mountain, that he might show Him from thence all the kingdoms of the world, and the glory of them. How could it literally come to pass, either that Jesus should be led up by the devil into a high mountain, or that the latter should show him all the kingdoms of the world (as if they were lying beneath his bodily eyes, and adjacent to one mountain), i.e., the kingdoms of the Persians, and Scythians, and Indians? or how could he show in what manner the kings of these kingdoms are glorified by men? And many other instances similar to this will be found in the Gospels by anyone who will read them with attention, and will observe that in those narratives which appear to be literally recorded, there are inserted and interwoven things which cannot be admitted historically, but which may be accepted in a spiritual signification.

17. In the passages containing the commandments also, similar things are found. For in the law Moses is commanded to destroy every male that is not circumcised on the eighth day, which is exceedingly incongruous; since it would be necessary, if it were related that the law was executed according to the history, to command those parents to be punished who did not circumcise their children, and also those who were the nurses of little children. The declaration of Scripture now is, "The uncircumcised male, i.e., who shall not have been circumcised, shall be cut off from his people." And if we are to inquire regarding the impossibilities of the law, we find an animal called the goat-stag, which cannot possibly exist, but which, as being in the number of clean beasts, Moses commands to be eaten; and a griffin, which no one ever remembers or heard of as yielding to human power, but which the legislator forbids to be used for food. Respecting the celebrated observance of the Sabbath also he thus speaks: "Ye shall sit, everyone in your dwellings; no one shall move from his place on the Sabbath-day." Which precept it is impossible to observe literally; for no man can sit a whole day so as not to move from the place where he sat down. With respect to each one of these points now, those who belong to the circumcision, and all who would have no more meaning to be found in sacred Scripture than what is indicated by the letter, consider that there should be no investigation regarding the goat-stag, and the griffin, and the vulture; and they invent some empty and trifling tales about the

Sabbath, drawn from some traditional sources or other, alleging that everyone's place is computed to him within two thousand cubits. Others, again, among whom is Dositheus the Samaritan, censure indeed expositions of this kind, but themselves lay down something more ridiculous, viz., that each one must remain until the evening in the posture, place, or position in which he found himself on the Sabbath-day; i.e., if found sitting, he is to sit the whole day, or if reclining, he is to recline the whole day. Moreover, the injunction which runs, "Bear no burden on the Sabbath-day," seems to me an impossibility. For the Jewish doctors, in consequence of these (prescriptions), have betaken themselves, as the holy apostle says, to innumerable fables, saying that it is not accounted a burden if a man wear shoes without nails, but that it is a burden if shoes with nails be worn; and that if it be carried on one shoulder, they consider it a burden but if on both, they declare it to be none.

18. And now, if we institute a similar examination with regard to the Gospels, how shall it appear otherwise than absurd to take the injunction literally, "Salute no man by the way?" And yet there are simple individuals, who think that our Saviour gave this command to His apostles! How, also, can it appear possible for such an order as this to be observed, especially in those countries where there is a rigorous winter, attended by frost and ice, viz., that one should possess "neither two coats, nor shoes?" And this, that when one is smitten on the right cheek, he is ordered to present the left also, since everyone who strikes with the *right* hand smites the *left* cheek? This precept also in the Gospels must be accounted among impossibilities, viz., that if the right eye "offend" thee, it is to be plucked out; for even if we were to suppose that bodily eyes were spoken of, how shall it appear appropriate, that when both eyes have the property of sight, the responsibility of the "offence" should be transferred to one eye, and that the right one? Or who shall be considered free of a crime of the greatest enormity, that lays hands upon himself? But perhaps the Epistles of the Apostle Paul will appear to be beyond this. For what is his meaning, when he says, "Is any man called, being circumcised? Let him not become uncircumcised." This expression indeed, in the first place, does not on careful consideration seem to be spoken with reference to the subject of which he was treating at the time, for this discourse consisted of injunctions relating to marriage and to chastity; and these words, therefore, will have the appearance an unnecessary addition to such a subject. In the second place, however, what objection would there be, if, for the sake of avoiding that unseemliness which is caused by circumcision, a man were able to become

uncircumcised? And, in the third place, that is altogether impossible.

The object of all these statements on our part, is to show that it was the design of the Holy Spirit, who deigned to bestow upon us the sacred Scriptures, to show that we were not to be edified by the letter alone, or by everything in it,—a thing which we see to be frequently impossible and inconsistent; for in that way not only absurdities, but impossibilities, would be the result; but that we are to understand that certain occurrences were interwoven in this "visible" history, which, when considered and understood in their inner meaning, give forth a law which is advantageous to men and worthy of God.

19. Let no one, however, entertain the suspicion that we do not believe any history in Scripture to be real, because we suspect certain events related in it not to have taken place; or that no precepts of the law are to be taken literally, because we consider certain of them, in which either the nature or possibility of the case so requires, incapable of being observed; or that we do not believe those predictions which were written of the Saviour to have been fulfilled in a manner palpable to the senses; or that His commandments are not to be literally obeyed. We have therefore to state in answer, since we are manifestly so of opinion, that the truth of the history may and ought to be preserved in the majority of instances. For who can deny that Abraham was buried in the double cave at Hebron, as well as Isaac and Jacob, and each of their wives? Or who doubts that Shechem was given as a portion to Joseph? or that Jerusalem is the metropolis of Judea, on which the temple of God was built by Solomon?—and countless other statements. For the passages which hold good in their historical acceptation are much more numerous than those which contain a purely spiritual meaning. Then, again, who would not maintain that the command to "honour thy father and thy mother, that it may be well with thee," is sufficient of itself without any spiritual meaning, and necessary for those who observe it? especially when Paul also has confirmed the command by repeating it in the same words. And what need is there to speak of the prohibitions, "Thou shalt not commit adultery," "Thou shalt not steal," "Thou shalt not bear false witness," and others of the same kind? And with respect to the precepts enjoined in the Gospels, no doubt can be entertained that very many of these are to be literally observed, as, e.g., when our Lord says, "But I say unto you, Swear not at all;" and when He says, "Whosoever looketh upon a woman to lust after her, hath committed adultery with her already in his heart;" the admonitions also which are found in the writings of the Apostle Paul, "Warn them that are unruly, comfort the feeble-minded, support the weak, be patient towards all men," and very many others.

And yet I have no doubt that an attentive reader will, in numerous instances, hesitate whether this or that history can be considered to be literally true or not; or whether this or that precept ought to be observed according to the letter or no. And therefore great pains and labour are to be employed, until every reader reverentially understand that he is dealing with divine and not human words inserted in the sacred books.

20. The understanding, therefore, of holy Scripture which we consider ought to be deservedly and consistently maintained, is of the following kind. A certain nation is declared by holy Scripture to have been chosen by God upon the earth, which nation has received several names: for sometimes the whole of it is termed Israel, and sometimes Jacob; and it was divided by Jeroboam son of Nebat into two portions; and the ten tribes which were formed under him were called Israel, while the two remaining ones (with which were united the tribe of Levi, and that which was descended from the royal race of David) was named Judah. Now the whole of the country possessed by that nation, which it had received from God, was called Judea, in which was situated the metropolis, Jerusalem; and it is called metropolis, being as it were the mother of many cities, the names of which you will frequently find mentioned here and there in the other books of Scripture, but which are collected together into one catalogue in the book of Joshua the son of Nun.

21. This, then, being the state of the case, the holy apostle desiring to elevate in some degree, and to raise our understanding above the earth, says in a certain place, "Behold Israel after the flesh;" by which he certainly means that there is another Israel which is not according to the flesh, but according to the Spirit. And again in another passage, "For they are not all Israelites who are of Israel."

22. Being taught, then, by him that there is one Israel according to the flesh, and another according to the Spirit, when the Saviour says, "I am not sent but to the lost sheep of the house of Israel," we do not understand these words as those do who savour of earthly things, i.e., the Ebionites, who derive the appellation of "poor" from their very name (for "Ebion" means "poor" in Hebrew); but we understand that there exists a race of souls which is termed "Israel," as is indicated by the interpretation of the name itself: for Israel is interpreted to mean a "mind," or "man seeing God." The apostle, again, makes a similar revelation respecting Jerusalem, saying, "The Jerusalem which is above is free, which is the mother of us all." And in another of his Epistles he says: "But ye are come unto mount Zion, and to the city of the living God, and to the heavenly Jerusalem, and to an innumerable company

216

of angels, and to the Church of the first-born which is written in heaven." If, then, there are certain souls in this world who are called Israel, and a city in heaven which is called Jerusalem, it follows that those cities which are said to belong to the nation of Israel have the heavenly Jerusalem as their metropolis; and that, agreeably to this, we understand as referring to the whole of Judah (of which also we are of opinion that the prophets have spoken in certain mystical narratives), any predictions delivered either regarding Judea or Jerusalem, or invasions of any kind, which the sacred histories declare to have happened to Judea or Jerusalem. Whatever, then, is either narrated or predicted of Jerusalem, must, if we accept the words of Paul as those of Christ speaking in him, be understood as spoken in conformity with his opinion regarding that city which he calls the heavenly Jerusalem, and all those places or cities which are said to be cities of the holy land, of which Jerusalem is the metropolis. For we are to suppose that it is from these very cities that the Saviour, wishing to raise us to a higher grade of intelligence, promises to those who have well managed the money entrusted to them by Himself, that they are to have power over ten or five cities. If, then, the prophecies delivered concerning Judea, and Jerusalem, and Judah, and Israel, and Jacob, not being understood by us in a carnal sense, signify certain divine mysteries, it certainly follows that those prophecies also which were delivered either concerning Egypt or the Egyptians, or Babylonia and the Babylonians, and Sidon and the Sidonians, are not to be understood as spoken of that Egypt which is situated on the earth, or of the earthly Babylon, Tyre, or Sidon. Nor can those predictions which the prophet Ezekiel delivered concerning Pharaoh king of Egypt, apply to any man who may seem to have reigned over Egypt, as the nature of the passage itself declares. In a similar manner also, what is spoken of the prince of Tyre cannot be understood of any man or king of Tyre. And how could we possibly accept, as spoken of a man, what is related in many passages of Scripture, and especially in Isaiah, regarding Nebuchadnezzar? For he is not a man who is said to have "fallen from heaven," or who was "Lucifer," or who "arose in the morning." But with respect to those predictions which are found in Ezekiel concerning Egypt, such as that it is to be destroyed in forty years, so that the foot of man should not be found within it, and that it should suffer such devastation, that throughout the whole land the blood of men should rise to the knees, I do not know that anyone possessed of understanding could refer this to that earthly Egypt which adjoins Ethiopia. But let us see whether it may not be understood more fittingly in the following manner: viz., that as there is a heavenly Jerusalem and Judea, and a nation undoubtedly which inhabits it, and is named Israel; so also it is possible that there are certain localities near to these which may seem to be called either Egypt, or Babylon, or Tyre, or Sidon, and that the princes of these places, and the souls, if there be any, that inhabit them, are called Egyptians, Babylonians, Tyrians, and Sidonians. From whom also, according to the mode of life which they lead there, a sort of captivity would seem to result, in consequence of which they are said to have fallen from Judea into Babylonia or Egypt, from a higher and better condition, or to have been scattered into other countries.

23. For perhaps as those who, departing this world in virtue of that death which is common to all, are arranged, in conformity with their actions and deserts—according as they shall be deemed worthy—some in the place which is called "hell," others in the bosom of Abraham, and in different localities or mansions; so also from those places, as if dying there, if the expression can be used, do they come down from the "upper world" to this "hell." For that "hell" to which the souls of the dead are conducted from this world, is, I believe, on account of this distinction, called the "lower hell" by Scripture, as is said in the book of Psalms: "Thou hast delivered my soul from the lowest hell." Everyone, accordingly, of those who descend to the earth is, according to his deserts, or agreeably to the position which he occupied there, ordained to be born in this world, in a different country, or among a different nation, or in a different mode of life, or surrounded by infirmities of a different kind, or to be descended from religious parents, or parents who are not religious; so that it may sometimes happen that an Israelite descends among the Scythians, and a poor Egyptian is brought down to Judea. And yet our Saviour came to gather together the lost sheep of the house of Israel; and as many of the Israelites did not accept His teaching, those who belonged to the Gentiles were called. From which it will appear to follow, that those prophecies which are delivered to the individual nations ought to be referred rather to the souls, and to their different heavenly mansions. Nay, the narratives of the events which are said to have happened either to the nation of Israel, or to Jerusalem, or to Judea, when assailed by this or that nation, cannot in many instances be understood as having actually occurred, and are much more appropriate to those nations of souls who inhabit that heaven which is said to pass away, or who even now are supposed to be inhabitants of it.

If now anyone demand of us clear and distinct declarations on these points out of holy Scripture, we must answer that it was the design of the Holy Spirit, in those portions which appear to relate the history of events, rather to cover and conceal the meaning: in those passages, e.g., where they are said to go down into Egypt, or to be carried captive to Babylonia, or when in these very countries some are said to be brought to excessive humiliation, and to be placed under bondage to their masters; while others, again, in these very countries of their captivity, were held in honour and esteem, so as to occupy positions of rank and power, and were appointed to the government of provinces;—all which things, as we have said, are kept hidden and covered in the narratives of holy Scripture, because "the kingdom of heaven is like a treasure hid in a field; which when a man findeth, he hideth it, and for joy thereof goeth away and selleth all that he hath, and buyeth that field." By which similitude, consider whether it be not pointed out that the very soil and surface, so to speak, of Scripture—that is, the literal meaning—is the field, filled with plants and flowers of all kinds; while that deeper and profounder "spiritual" meaning are the very hidden treasures of wisdom and knowledge which the Holy Spirit by Isaiah calls the dark and invisible and hidden treasures, for the finding out of which the divine help is required: for God alone can burst the brazen gates by which they are enclosed and concealed, and break in pieces the iron bolts and levers by which access is prevented to all those things which are written and concealed in Genesis respecting the different kinds of souls, and of those seeds and generations which either have a close connection with Israel or are widely separated from his descendants; as well as what is that descent of seventy souls into Egypt, which seventy souls became in that land as the stars of heaven in multitude. But as not all of them were the light of this world—"for all who are of Israel are not Israel"—they grow from being seventy souls to be an important people, and as the "sand by the sea-shore innumerable."

CHAPTER I [FROM THE GREEK]—ON THE INSPIRATION OF HOLY SCRIPTURE, AND HOW THE SAME IS TO BE READ AND UNDERSTOOD, AND WHAT IS THE REASON OF THE UNCERTAINTY IN IT; AND OF THE IMPOSSIBILITY OR IRRATIONALITY OF CERTAIN THINGS IN IT, TAKEN ACCORDING TO THE LETTER

[The translation from the Greek is designedly literal, that the difference between the original and the paraphrase of Rufinus may be more clearly seen.]

1. Since, in our investigation of matters of such importance, not satisfied with the common opinions, and with the clear evidence of visible things, we take in addition, for the proof of our statements, testimonies from what are believed by us to be divine writings, viz., from that which is called the Old Testament, and that which is styled the New, and endeavour by reason to confirm our faith; and as we have not yet spoken of the Scriptures as divine, come and let us, as if by way of an epitome, treat of a few points respecting them, laying down those reasons which lead us to regard them as divine writings. And before making use of the words of the writings themselves, and of the things which are exhibited in them, we must make the following statement regarding Moses and Jesus Christ,—the lawgiver of the Hebrews, and the Introducer of the saving doctrines according to Christianity. For, although there have been very many legislators among the Greeks and Barbarians, and teachers who announced opinions which professed to be the truth, we have heard of no legislator who was able to imbue other nations with a zeal for the reception of his words; and although those who professed to philosophize about truth brought forward a great apparatus of apparent logical demonstration, no one has been able to impress what was deemed by him the truth upon other nations, or even on any number of persons worth mentioning in a single nation. And yet not only would the legislators have liked to enforce those laws which appeared to be good, if possible, upon the whole human race, but the teachers also to have spread what they imagined to be truth everywhere throughout the world. But as they were unable to call men of other languages and from many nations to observe their laws, and accept their teaching, they did not at all attempt to do this, considering not unwisely the impossibility of such a result happening to them. Whereas all Greece, and the barbarous part of our world, contains innumerable zealots, who have deserted the laws of their fathers and the established gods, for the observance of the laws of Moses and the discipleship of the words of Jesus Christ; although those who clave to the law of Moses were hated by the worshippers of images, and those who accepted the words of Jesus Christ were exposed, in addition, to the danger of death.

2. And if we observe how powerful the word has become in a very few years, notwithstanding that against those who acknowledged Christianity conspiracies were formed, and some of them on its account put to death, and others of them lost their property, and that, notwithstanding the small number of its teachers, it was preached everywhere throughout the world, so that Greeks and Barbarians, wise and foolish, gave themselves up to the worship that is through Jesus,

we have no difficulty in saying that the result is beyond any human power, Jesus having taught with all authority and persuasiveness that His word should not be overcome; so that we may rightly regard as oracular responses those utterances of His, such as, "Ye shall be brought before governors and kings for My sake, for a testimony against them and the Gentiles;" and, "Many shall say unto Me in that day, Lord, Lord, have we not eaten in Thy name, and drunk in Thy name, and in Thy name cast out devils? And I shall say unto them, Depart from Me, ye workers of iniquity, I never knew you." Now it was perhaps (once) probable that, in uttering these words, He spoke them in vain, so that they were not true; but when that which was delivered with so much authority *has* come to pass, it shows that God, having really become man, delivered to men the doctrines of salvation.

3. And what need is there to mention also that it was predicted of Christ that then would the rulers fail from Judah, and the leaders from his thighs, when He came for whom it is reserved (the kingdom, namely); and that the expectation of the Gentiles should dwell in the land? For it is clearly manifest from the history, and from what is seen at the present day, that from the times of Jesus there were no longer any who were called kings of the Jews; all those Jewish institutions on which they prided themselves—I mean those arrangements relating to the temple and the altar, and the offering of the service, and the robes of the high priest having been destroyed. For the prophecy was fulfilled which said, "The children of Israel shall sit many days, there being no king, nor ruler, nor sacrifice, nor altar, nor priesthood, nor responses." And these predictions we employ to answer those who, in their perplexity as to the words spoken in Genesis by Jacob to Judah, assert that the Ethnarch, being of the race of Judah, is the ruler of the people, and that there will not fail some of his seed, until the advent of that Christ whom they figure to their imagination. But if "the children of Israel are to sit many days without a king, or ruler, or altar, or priesthood, or responses;" and if, since the temple was destroyed, there exists no longer sacrifice, nor altar, nor priesthood, it is manifest that the ruler *has* failed out of Judah, and the leader from between his thighs. And since the prediction declares that "the ruler shall not fail from Judah, and the leader from between his thighs, until what is reserved for Him shall come," it is manifest that He is come to whom (belongs) what is reserved—the expectation of the Gentiles. And this is clear from the multitude of the heathen who have believed on God through Jesus Christ.

4. And in the song in Deuteronomy, also, it is prophetically made known that, on account of the sins of the former people, there was to

be an election of foolish nations, which has been brought to pass by no other than by Jesus. "For they," He says, "moved Me to jealousy with that which is not God, they have provoked Me to anger with their idols; and I will move them to jealousy with those which are not a people, and will provoke them to anger with a foolish nation." Now it is possible to understand with all clearness how the Hebrews, who are said to have moved God to jealousy by that which is not God, and to have provoked Him to anger by their idols, were (themselves) aroused to jealousy by that which was not a people—the foolish nation, namely, which God chose by the advent of Jesus Christ and His disciples. We see, indeed, "our calling, that not many wise men after the flesh, not many mighty, not many noble (are called); but God hath chosen the foolish things of the world to confound the wise; and base things, and things that are despised, hath God chosen, and things that are not, to bring to nought the things which formerly existed;" and let not the Israel according to the flesh, which is called by the apostle "flesh," boast in the presence of God.

5. And what are we to say regarding the prophecies of Christ in the Psalms, there being a certain ode with the superscription "For the Beloved," whose" tongue" is said to be the "pen of a ready writer, who is fairer than the sons of men," since "grace was poured on His lips?" For a proof that grace was poured on His lips is this, that although the period of His teaching was short—for He taught somewhere about a year and a few months—the world has been filled with his teaching, and with the worship of God (established) through Him. For there arose "in His days righteousness and abundance of peace," which abides until the consummation, which has been called the taking away of the moon; and He continues "ruling from sea to sea, and from the rivers to the ends of the earth." And to the house of David has been given a sign: for the Virgin bore, and was pregnant, and brought forth a son, and His name is Emmanuel, which is, "God with us;" and as the same prophet says, the prediction has been fulfilled, "God (is) with us; know it, O nations, and be overcome; ye who are strong, be vanquished:" for we of the heathen have been overcome and vanquished, we who have been taken by the grace of His teaching. The place also of His birth has been foretold in (the prophecies of) Micah: "For thou, Bethlehem," he says, "land of Judah, art by no means the least among the rulers of Judah; for out of thee shall come forth a Ruler, who shall rule My people Israel." And according to Daniel, seventy weeks were fulfilled until (the coming of) Christ the Ruler. And He came, who, according to Job, has subdued the great fish, and has given power to His true disciples to tread upon serpents and scorpions, and

all the power of the enemy, without sustaining any injury from them. And let one notice also the universal advent of the apostles sent by Jesus to announce the Gospel, and he will see both that the undertaking was beyond human power, and that the commandment came from God. And if we examine how men, on hearing new doctrines, and strange words, yielded themselves up to these teachers, being overcome, amid the very desire to plot against them, by a divine power that watched over these (teachers), we shall not be incredulous as to whether they also wrought miracles, God bearing witness to their words both by signs, and wonders, and divers miracles.

6. And while we thus briefly demonstrate the deity of Christ, and (in so doing) make use of the prophetic declarations regarding Him, we demonstrate at the same time that the writings which prophesied of Him were divinely inspired; and that those documents which announced His coming and His doctrine were given forth with all power and authority, and that on this account they obtained the election from the Gentiles. We must say, also, that the divinity of the prophetic declarations, and the spiritual nature of the law of Moses, shone forth after the advent of Christ. For before the advent of Christ it was not altogether possible to exhibit manifest proofs of the divine inspiration of the ancient Scripture; whereas His coming led those who might suspect the law and the prophets not to be divine, to the clear conviction that they were composed by (the aid of) heavenly grace. And he who reads the words of the prophets with care and attention, feeling by the very perusal the traces of the divinity that is in them, will be led by his own emotions to believe that those words which have been deemed to be the words of God are not the compositions of men. The light, moreover, which was contained in the law of Moses, but which had been concealed by a veil, shone forth at the advent of Jesus, the veil being taken away, and those blessings, the shadow of which was contained in the letter, coming forth gradually to the knowledge (of men).

7. It would be tedious now to enumerate the most ancient prophecies respecting each future event, in order that the doubter, being impressed by their divinity, may lay aside all hesitation and distraction, and devote himself with his whole soul to the words of God. But if in every part of the Scriptures the superhuman element of thought does not seem to present itself to the uninstructed, that is not at all wonderful for, with respect to the works of that providence which embraces the whole world, some show with the utmost clearness that they are works of providence, while others are so concealed as to seem to furnish ground for unbelief with respect to that God who orders all

things with unspeakable skill and power. For the artistic plan of a providential Ruler is not so evident in those matters belonging to the earth, as in the case of the sun, and moon, and stars; and not so clear in what relates to human occurrences, as it is in the souls and bodies of animals,—the object and reason of the impulses, and phantasies and natures of animals, and the structure of their bodies, being carefully ascertained by those who attend to these things. But as (the doctrine of) providence is not at all weakened (on account of those things which are not understood) in the eyes of those who have once honestly accepted it, so neither is the divinity of Scripture, which extends to the whole of it, (lost) on account of the inability of our weakness to discover in every expression the hidden splendour of the doctrines veiled in common and unattractive phraseology. For we have the treasure in earthen vessels, that the excellency of the power of God may shine forth, and that it may not be deemed to proceed from us (who are but) human beings. For if the hackneyed methods of demonstration (common) among men, contained in the books (of the Bible), had been successful in producing conviction; then our faith would rightly have been supposed to rest on the wisdom of men, and not on the power of God; but now it is manifest to everyone who lifts up his eyes, that the word and preaching have not prevailed among the multitude "by persuasive words of wisdom, but by demonstration of the Spirit and of power." Wherefore, since a celestial or even a super-celestial power compels us to worship the only Creator, let us leave the doctrine of the beginning of Christ, i.e., the elements, and endeavour to go on to perfection, in order that the wisdom spoken to the perfect may be spoken to us also. For he who possesses it promises to speak wisdom among them that are perfect, but another wisdom than that of this world, and of the rulers of this world, which is brought to nought. And this wisdom will be distinctly stamped upon us, and will produce a revelation of the mystery that was kept silent in the eternal ages, but now has been manifested through the prophetic Scriptures, and the appearance of our Lord and Saviour Jesus Christ, to whom be glory for ever and ever. Amen.

8. Having spoken thus briefly on the subject of the divine inspiration of the holy Scriptures, it is necessary to proceed to the (consideration of the) manner in which they are to be read and understood, seeing numerous errors have been committed in consequence of the method in which the holy documents ought to be examined; not having been discovered by the multitude. For both the hardened in heart, and the ignorant persons belonging to the circumcision, have not believed on our Saviour, thinking that they are following the language of the

prophecies respecting Him, and not perceiving in a manner palpable to their senses that He had proclaimed liberty to the captives, nor that He had built up what they truly consider the city of God, nor cut off "the chariots of Ephraim, and the horse from Jerusalem," nor eaten butter and honey, and, before knowing or preferring the evil, had selected the good. And thinking, moreover, that it was prophesied that the wolf—the four-footed animal—was to feed with the lamb, and the leopard to lie down with the kid, and the calf and bull and lion to feed together, being led by a little child, and that the ox and bear were to pasture together, their young ones growing up together, and that the lion was to eat straw like the ox: seeing none of these things visibly accomplished during the advent of Him who is believed by us to be Christ, they did not accept our Lord Jesus; but, as having called Himself Christ improperly, they crucified Him. And those belonging to heretical sects reading this (statement), "A fire has been kindled in Mine anger;" and this, "I am a jealous God, visiting the iniquities of the fathers upon the children unto the third and fourth generation;" and this, "I repent of having anointed Saul to be king;" and this, "I am a God that maketh peace, and createth evil;" and, among others, this, "There is not wickedness in the city which the LORD hath not done;" and again this, "Evils came down from the LORD upon the gates of Jerusalem;" and, "An evil spirit from the LORD plagued Saul;" and countless other passages like these—they have not ventured to disbelieve these as the Scriptures of God; but believing them to be the (words) of the Demiurge, whom the Jews worship, they thought that as the Demiurge was an imperfect and unbenevolent God, the Saviour had come to announce a more perfect Deity, who, they say, is not the Demiurge, being of different opinions regarding Him; and having once departed from the Demiurge, who is the only uncreated God, they have given themselves up to fictions, inventing to themselves hypotheses, according to which they imagine that there are some things which are visible, and certain other things which are not visible, all which are the fancies of their own minds. And yet, indeed, the more simple among those who profess to belong to the Church have supposed that there is no deity greater than the Demiurge, being right in so thinking, while they imagine regarding Him such things as would not be believed of the most savage and unjust of mankind.

9. Now the cause, in all the points previously enumerated, of the false opinions, and of the impious statements or ignorant assertions about God, appears to be nothing else than the not understanding the Scripture according to its spiritual meaning, but the interpretation of it agreeably to the mere letter. And therefore, to those who believe that

the sacred books are not the compositions of men, but that they were composed by inspiration of the Holy Spirit, agreeably to the will of the Father of all things through Jesus Christ, and that they have come down to us, we must point out the ways (of interpreting them) which appear (correct) to us, who cling to the standard of the heavenly Church of Jesus Christ according to the succession of the apostles. Now, that there are certain mystical economies made known by the holy Scriptures, all—even the most simple of those who adhere to the word—have believed; but what these are, candid and modest individuals confess that they know not. If, then, one were to be perplexed about the intercourse of Lot with his daughters, and about the two wives of Abraham, and the two sisters married to Jacob, and the two handmaids who bore him children, they can return no other answer than this, that these are mysteries not understood by us. Nay, also, when the (description of the) fitting out of the tabernacle is read, believing that what is written is a type, they seek to adapt what they can to each particular related about the tabernacle,—not being wrong so far as regards their belief that the tabernacle is a type of *something*, but erring sometimes in adapting the description of that of which the tabernacle is a type, to some special thing in a manner worthy of Scripture. And all the history that is considered to tell of marriages, or the begetting of children, or of wars, or any histories whatever that are in circulation among the multitude, they declare to be types; but of what in each individual instance, partly owing to their habits not being thoroughly exercised—partly, too, owing to their precipitation— sometimes, even when an individual does happen to be well trained and clear-sighted, owing to the excessive difficulty of discovering things on the part of men,—the nature of each particular regarding these (types) is not clearly ascertained.

10. And what need is there to speak of the prophecies, which we all know to be filled with enigmas and dark sayings? And if we come to the Gospels, the exact understanding of these also, as being the mind of Christ, requires the grace that was given to him who said, "But we have the mind of Christ, that we might know the things freely given to us by God. Which things also we speak, not in the words which man's wisdom teacheth, but which the Spirit teacheth." And who, on reading the revelations made to John, would not be amazed at the unspeakable mysteries therein concealed, and which are evident (even) to him who does not comprehend what is written? And to what person, skilful in investigating words, would the Epistles of the Apostles seem to be clear and easy of understanding, since even in them there are countless numbers of most profound ideas, which, (issuing forth) as by an

aperture, admit of no rapid comprehension? And therefore, since these things are so, and since innumerable individuals fall into mistakes, it is not safe in reading (the Scriptures) to declare that one easily understands what needs the key of knowledge, which the Saviour declares is with the lawyers. And let those answer who will not allow that the truth was with these before the advent of Christ, how the key of knowledge is said by our Lord Jesus Christ to be with those who, as they allege, had not the books which contain the secrets of knowledge, and perfect mysteries. For His words run thus: "Woe unto you, ye lawyers! for ye have taken away the key of knowledge: ye have not entered in yourselves, and them that were entering in ye hindered."

11. The way, then, as it appears to us, in which we ought to deal with the Scriptures, and extract from them their meaning, is the following, which has been ascertained from the Scriptures themselves. By Solomon in the Proverbs we find some such rule as this enjoined respecting the divine doctrines of Scripture: "And do thou portray them in a threefold manner, in counsel and knowledge, to answer words of truth to them who propose them to thee." The individual ought, then, to portray the ideas of holy Scripture in a threefold manner upon his own soul; in order that the simple man may be edified by the "flesh," as it were, of the Scripture, for so we name the obvious sense; while he who has ascended a certain way (may be edified) by the "soul," as it were. The perfect man, again, and he who resembles those spoken of by the apostle, when he says, "We speak wisdom among them that are perfect, but not the wisdom of the world, nor of the rulers of this world, who come to nought; but we speak the wisdom of God in a mystery, the hidden wisdom, which God hath ordained before the ages, unto our glory," (may receive edification) from the spiritual law, which has a shadow of good things to come. For as man consists of body, and soul, and spirit, so in the same way does Scripture, which has been arranged to be given by God for the salvation of men. And therefore we deduce this also from a book which is despised by some—*The Shepherd*—in respect of the command given to Hermas to write two books, and after so doing to announce to the presbyters of the Church what he had learned from the Spirit. The words are as follows: "You will write two books, and give one to Clement, and one to Grapte. And Grapte shall admonish the widows and the orphans, and Clement will send to the cities abroad, while you will announce to the presbyters of the Church." Now Grapte, who admonishes the widows and the orphans, is the mere letter (of Scripture), which admonishes those who are yet children in soul, and not able to call God their Father, and who are on that account styled orphans,—admonishing, moreover, those

who no longer have an unlawful bridegroom, but who remain widows, because they have not yet become worthy of the (heavenly) Bridegroom; while Clement, who is already beyond the letter, is said to send what is written to the cities abroad, as if we were to call these the "souls," who are above (the influence of) bodily (affections) and degraded ideas,—the disciple of the Spirit himself being enjoined to make known, no longer by letters, but by living words, to the presbyters of the whole Church of God, who have become grey through wisdom.

12. But as there are certain passages of Scripture which do not at all contain the "corporeal" sense, as we shall show in the following (paragraphs), there are also places where we must seek only for the "soul," as it were, and "spirit" of Scripture. And perhaps on this account the water-vessels containing two or three firkins a-piece are said to lie for the purification of the Jews, as we read in the Gospel according to John: the expression darkly intimating, with respect to those who (are called) by the apostle "Jews" secretly, that they are purified by the word of Scripture, receiving sometimes two firkins, i.e., so to speak, the "psychical" and "spiritual" sense; and sometimes three firkins, since some have, in addition to those already mentioned, also the "corporeal" sense, which is capable of (producing) edification. And six water-vessels are reasonably (appropriate) to those who are purified in the world, which was made in six days—the perfect number. That the first "sense," then, is profitable in this respect, that it is capable of imparting edification, is testified by the multitudes of genuine and simple believers; while of that interpretation which is referred back to the "soul," there is an illustration in Paul's first Epistle to the Corinthians. The expression is, "Thou shalt not muzzle the mouth of the ox that treadeth out the corn;" to which he adds, "Doth God take care of oxen? or saith He it altogether for our sakes? For our sakes, no doubt, this was written: that he that plougheth should plough in hope, and that he who thresheth, in hope of partaking." And there are numerous interpretations adapted to the multitude which are in circulation, and which edify those who are unable to understand profounder meanings, and which have somewhat the same character.

13. But the interpretation is "spiritual," when one is able to show of what heavenly things the Jews "according to the flesh" served as an example and a shadow, and of what future blessings the law contains a shadow. And, generally, we must investigate, according to the apostolic promise, "the wisdom in a mystery, the hidden wisdom which God ordained before the world for the glory" of the just, which "none of the princes of this world knew." And the same apostle says somewhere, after referring to certain events mentioned as occurring in Exodus and

Numbers, "that these things happened to them figuratively, but that they were written on our account, on whom the ends of the world are come." And he gives an opportunity for ascertaining of what things these were patterns, when he says: "For they drank of the spiritual Rock that followed them, and that Rock was Christ." And in another Epistle, when sketching the various matters relating to the tabernacle, he used the words: "Thou shalt make everything according to the pattern showed thee in the mount." Moreover, in the Epistle to the Galatians, as if upbraiding those who think that they read the law, and yet do not understand it, judging that those do not understand it who do not reflect that allegories are contained under what is written, he says: "Tell me, ye that desire to be under the law, do ye not hear the law? For it is written, Abraham had two sons; the one by the bond-maid, the other by the free woman. But he who was by the bond-maid was born according to the flesh; but he of the free woman was by promise. Which things are an allegory: for these are the two covenants," and so on. Now we must carefully observe each word employed by him. He says: "Ye who desire to be under the law," not "Ye that are under the law;" and, "Do ye not *hear* the law?"—"hearing" being understood to mean "*comprehending*" and "*knowing*." And in the Epistle to the Colossians, briefly abridging the meaning of the whole legislation, he says: "Let no man therefore judge you in meat, or in drink, or in respect of a festival, or of a new moon, or of Sabbaths, which are a shadow of things to come." Moreover, in the Epistle to the Hebrews, discoursing of those who belong to the circumcision, he writes: "who serve for an ensample and shadow of heavenly things." Now it is probable that, from these illustrations, those will entertain no doubt with respect to the five books of Moses, who have once given in their adhesion to the apostle, as divinely inspired; but do you wish to know, with regard to the rest of the history, if it also happened as a pattern? We must note, then, the expression in the Epistle to the Romans, "I have left to myself seven thousand men, who have not bowed the knee to Baal," quoted from the third book of Kings, which Paul has understood as equivalent (in meaning) to those who are Israelites according to election, because not only were the Gentiles benefited by the advent of Christ, but also certain of the race of God.

14. This being the state of the case, we have to sketch what seem to us to be the marks of the (true) understanding of Scriptures. And, in the first place, this must be pointed out, that the object of the Spirit, which by the providence of God, through the Word who was in the beginning with God, illuminated the ministers of truth, the prophets and apostles, was especially (the communication) of ineffable mysteries

regarding the affairs of men (now by men I mean those souls that make use of bodies), in order that he who is capable of instruction may by investigation, and by devoting himself to the study of the profundities of meaning contained in the words, become a participator of all the doctrines of his counsel. And among those matters which relate to souls (who cannot otherwise obtain perfection apart from the rich and wise truth of God), the (doctrines) belonging to God and His only-begotten Son are necessarily laid down as primary, viz., of what nature He is, and in what manner He is the Son of God, and what are the causes of His descending even to (the assumption of) human flesh, and of complete humanity; and what, also, is the operation of this (Son), and upon whom and when exercised. And it was necessary also that the subject of kindred beings, and other rational creatures, both those who are divine and those who have fallen from blessedness, together with the reasons of their fall, should be contained in the divine teaching; and also that of the diversities of souls, and of the origin of these diversities, and of the nature of the world, and the cause of its existence. We must learn also the origin of the great and terrible wickedness which overspreads the earth, and whether it is confined to this earth only, or prevails elsewhere. Now, while these and similar objects were present to the Spirit, who enlightened the souls of the holy ministers of the truth, there was a second object, for the sake of those who were unable to endure the fatigue of investigating matters so important, viz., to conceal the doctrine relating to the previously mentioned subjects, in expressions containing a narrative which conveyed an announcement regarding the things of the visible creation, the creation of man, and the successive descendants of the first men until they became numerous; and other histories relating the acts of just men, and the sins occasionally committed by these same men as being human beings, and the wicked deeds, both of unchastity and vice, committed by sinful and ungodly men. And what is most remarkable, by the history of wars, and of the victors, and the vanquished, certain mysteries are indicated to those who are able to test these statements. And more wonderful still, the laws of truth are predicted by the written legislation;—all these being described in a connected series, with a power which is truly in keeping with the wisdom of God. For it was intended that the covering also of the spiritual truths—I mean the "bodily" part of Scripture—should not be without profit in many cases, but should be capable of improving the multitude, according to their capacity.

15. But since, if the usefulness of the legislation, and the sequence and beauty of the history, were universally evident of itself, we should not believe that any other thing could be understood in the Scriptures

save what was obvious, the word of God has arranged that certain stumbling-blocks, as it were, and offences, and impossibilities, should be introduced into the midst of the law and the history, in order that we may not, through being drawn away in all directions by the merely attractive nature of the language, either altogether fall away from the (true) doctrines, as learning nothing worthy of God, or, by not departing from the letter, come to the knowledge of nothing more divine. And this also we must know, that the principal aim being to announce the "spiritual" connection in those things that are done, and that ought to be done, where the Word found that things done according to the history could be adapted to these mystical senses, He made use of them, concealing from the multitude the deeper meaning; but where, in the narrative of the development of super-sensual things, there did not follow the performance of those certain events, which was already indicated by the mystical meaning, the Scripture interwove in the history (the account of) some event that did not take place, sometimes what could not have happened; sometimes what could, but did not. And sometimes a few words are interpolated which are not true in their literal acceptation, and sometimes a larger number. And a similar practice also is to be noticed with regard to the legislation, in which is often to be found what is useful in itself, and appropriate to the times of the legislation; and sometimes also what does not appear to be of utility; and at other times impossibilities are recorded for the sake of the more skilful and inquisitive, in order that they may give themselves to the toil of investigating what is written, and thus attain to a becoming conviction of the manner in which a meaning worthy of God must be sought out in such subjects.

16. It was not only, however, with the (Scriptures composed) before the advent (of Christ) that the Spirit thus dealt; but as being the same Spirit, and (proceeding) from the one God, He did the same thing both with the evangelists and the apostles,—as even these do not contain throughout a pure history of events, which are interwoven indeed according to the letter, but which did not actually occur. Nor even do the law and the commandments wholly convey what is agreeable to reason. For who that has understanding will suppose that the first, and second, and third day, and the evening and the morning, existed without a sun, and moon, and stars? and that the first day was, as it were, also without a sky? And who is so foolish as to suppose that God, after the manner of a husbandman, planted a paradise in Eden, towards the east, and placed in it a tree of life, visible and palpable, so that one tasting of the fruit by the bodily teeth obtained life? and again, that one was a partaker of good and evil by masticating what was taken from the

tree? And if God is said to walk in the paradise in the evening, and Adam to hide himself under a tree, I do not suppose that anyone doubts that these things figuratively indicate certain mysteries, the history having taken place in appearance, and not literally. Cain also, when going forth from the presence of God, certainly appears to thoughtful men as likely to lead the reader to inquire what is the presence of God, and what is the meaning of going out from Him. And what need is there to say more, since those who are not altogether blind can collect countless instances of a similar kind recorded as having occurred, but which did not literally take place? Nay, the Gospels themselves are filled with the same kind of narratives; e.g., the devil leading Jesus up into a high mountain, in order to show him from thence the kingdoms of the whole world, and the glory of them. For who is there among those who do not read such accounts carelessly, that would not condemn those who think that with the eye of the body—which requires a lofty height in order that the parts lying (immediately) under and adjacent may be seen—the kingdoms of the Persians, and Scythians, and Indians, and Parthians, were beheld, and the manner in which their princes are glorified among men? And the attentive reader may notice in the Gospels innumerable other passages like these, so that he will be convinced that in the histories that are literally recorded, circumstances that did not occur are inserted.

17. And if we come to the legislation of Moses, many of the laws manifest the irrationality, and others the impossibility, of their literal observance. The irrationality (in this), that the people are forbidden to eat vultures, although no one even in the direst famines was (ever) driven by want to have recourse to this bird; and that children eight days old, which are uncircumcised, are ordered to be exterminated from among their people, it being necessary, if the law were to be carried out at all literally with regard to these, that their fathers, or those with whom they are brought up, should be commanded to be put to death. Now the Scripture says: "Every male that is uncircumcised, who shall not be circumcised on the eighth day, shall be cut off from among his people." And if you wish to see impossibilities contained in the legislation, let us observe that the goat-stag is one of those animals that cannot exist, and yet Moses commands us to offer it as being a clean beast; whereas a griffin, which is not recorded ever to have been subdued by man, the lawgiver forbids to be eaten. Nay, he who carefully considers (the famous injunction relating to) the Sabbath, "Ye shall sit each one in your dwellings: let no one go out from his place on the seventh day," will deem it impossible to be literally observed: for no living being is able to sit throughout a whole day, and remain without moving from a

sitting position. And therefore those who belong to the circumcision, and all who desire that no meaning should be exhibited, save the literal one, do not investigate at all such subjects as those of the goat-stag and griffin and vulture, but indulge in foolish talk on certain points, multiplying words and adducing tasteless traditions; as, for example, with regard to the Sabbath, saying that two thousand cubits is each one's limit. Others, again, among whom is Dositheus the Samaritan, condemning such an interpretation, think that in the position in which a man is found on the Sabbath-day, he is to remain until evening. Moreover, the not carrying of a burden on the Sabbath-day is an impossibility; and therefore the Jewish teachers have fallen into countless absurdities, saying that a shoe of such a kind was a burden, but not one of another kind; and that a sandal which had nails was a burden, but not one that was without them; and in like manner what was borne on one shoulder (was a load), but not that which was carried on both.

18. And if we go to the Gospel and institute a similar examination, what would be more irrational than (to take literally the injunction), "Salute no man by the way," which simple persons think the Saviour enjoined on the apostles? The command, moreover, that the right cheek should be smitten, is most incredible, since everyone who strikes, unless he happen to have some bodily defect, smites the *left* cheek with his *right* hand. And it is impossible to take (literally, the statement) in the Gospel about the "offending" of the right eye. For, to grant the possibility of one being "offended" by the sense of sight, how, when there are two eyes that see, should the blame be laid upon the right eye? And who is there that, condemning himself for having looked upon a woman to lust after her, would rationally transfer the blame to the right eye alone, and throw *it* away? The apostle, moreover, lays down the law, saying, "Is any man called, being circumcised? Let him not become uncircumcised." In the first place, anyone will see that he does not utter these words in connection with the subject before him. For, when laying down precepts on marriage and purity, how will it not appear that he has introduced these words at random? But, in the second place, who will say that a man does wrong who endeavours to become uncircumcised, if that be possible, on account of the disgrace that is considered by the multitude to attach to circumcision.

All these statements have been made by us, in order to show that the design of that divine power which gave us the sacred Scriptures is, that we should not receive what is presented by the letter alone (such things being sometimes not true in their literal acceptation, but absurd and impossible), but that certain things have been introduced into the actual history and into the legislation that are useful in their literal sense.

19. But that no one may suppose that we assert respecting the whole that no history is real because a certain one is not; and that no law is to be literally observed, because a certain one, (understood) according to the letter, is absurd or impossible; or that the statements regarding the Saviour are not true in a manner perceptible to the senses; or that no commandment and precept of His ought to be obeyed;—we have to answer that, with regard to certain things, it is perfectly clear to us that the historical account is true; as that Abraham was buried in the double cave at Hebron, as also Isaac and Jacob, and the wives of each of them; and that Shechem was given as a portion to Joseph; and that Jerusalem is the metropolis of Judea, in which the temple of God was built by Solomon; and innumerable other statements. For the passages that are true in their historical meaning are much more numerous than those which are interspersed with a purely spiritual signification. And again, who would not say that the command which enjoins to "honour thy father and thy mother, that it may be well with thee," is useful, apart from all allegorical meaning, and ought to be observed, the Apostle Paul also having employed these very same words? And what need is there to speak of the (prohibitions), "Thou shalt not commit adultery," "Thou shalt not kill," "Thou shalt not steal," "Thou shalt not bear false witness?" And again, there are commandments contained in the Gospel which admit of no doubt whether they are to be observed according to the letter or not; e.g., that which says, "But I say unto you, Whoever is angry with his brother," and so on. And again, "But I say unto you, Swear not at all." "And in the writings of the apostle the literal sense is to be retained: "Warn them that are unruly, comfort the feeble-minded, support the weak, be patient towards all men;" although it is possible for those ambitious of a deeper meaning to retain the profundities of the wisdom of God, without setting aside the commandment in its literal meaning. The careful (reader), however, will be in doubt as to certain points, being unable to show without long investigation whether this history so deemed literally occurred or not, and whether the literal meaning of this law is to be observed or not. And therefore the exact reader must, in obedience to the Saviour's injunction to "search the Scriptures," carefully ascertain in how far the literal meaning is true, and in how far impossible; and so far as he can, trace out, by means of similar statements, the meaning everywhere scattered through Scripture of that which cannot be understood in a literal signification.

20. Since, therefore, as will be clear to those who read, the connection taken literally is impossible, while the sense preferred is not impossible, but even the true one, it must be our object to grasp the

whole meaning, which connects the account of what is literally impossible in an intelligible manner with what is not only not impossible, but also historically true, and which is allegorically understood, in respect of its not having literally occurred. For, with respect to holy Scripture, our opinion is that the whole of it has a "spiritual," but not the whole a "bodily" meaning, because the bodily meaning is in many places proved to be impossible. And therefore great attention must be bestowed by the cautious reader on the divine books, as being divine writings; the manner of understanding which appears to us to be as follows:—The Scriptures relate that God chose a certain nation upon the earth, which they call by several names. For the whole of this nation is termed Israel, and also Jacob. And when it was divided in the times of Jeroboam the son of Nebat, the ten tribes related as being subject to him were called Israel; and the remaining two, along with the tribe of Levi, being ruled over by the descendants of David, were named Judah. And the whole of the territory which the people of this nation inhabited, being given them by God, receives the name of Judah, the metropolis of which is Jerusalem,—a metropolis, namely, of numerous cities, the names of which lie scattered about in many other passages (of Scripture), but are enumerated together in the book of Joshua the son of Nun.

21. Such, then, being the state of the case, the apostle, elevating our power of discernment (above the letter), says somewhere, "Behold Israel after the flesh," as if there were an Israel "according to the Spirit." And in another place he says, "For they who are the children of the flesh are not the children of God;" nor are "they all Israel who are of Israel;" nor is "he a Jew who is one outwardly, nor is that 'circumcision' which is outward in the flesh: but he is a Jew who is one 'inwardly;' and circumcision is that of the heart, in the spirit, and not in the letter." For if the judgment respecting the "Jew inwardly" be adopted, we must understand that, as there is a "bodily" race of Jews, so also is there a race of "Jews inwardly," the soul having acquired this nobility for certain mysterious reasons. Moreover, there are many prophecies which predict regarding Israel and Judah what is about to befall them. And do not such promises as are written concerning them, in respect of their being mean in expression, and manifesting no elevation (of thought), nor anything worthy of the promise of God, need a mystical interpretation? And if the "spiritual" promises are announced by visible signs, then they to whom the promises are made are not "corporeal." And not to linger over the point of the Jew who is a Jew "inwardly," nor over that of the Israelite according to the "inner man"—these statements being sufficient for those who are not devoid of

understanding—we return to our subject, and say that Jacob is the father of the twelve patriarchs, and they of the rulers of the people; and these, again, of the other Israelites. Do not, then, the "corporeal" Israelites refer their descent to the rulers of the people, and the rulers of the people to the patriarchs, and the patriarchs to Jacob, and those still higher up; while are not the "spiritual" Israelites, of whom the "corporeal" Israelites were the type, sprung from the families, and the families from the tribes, and the tribes from some one individual whose descent is not of a "corporeal" but of a better kind,—he, too, being born of Isaac, and he of Abraham,—all going back to Adam, whom the apostle declares to be Christ? For every beginning of those families which have relation to God as to the Father of all, took its commencement lower down with Christ, who is next to the God and Father of all, being thus the Father of every soul, as Adam is the father of all men. And if Eve also is intended by the apostle to refer to the Church, it is not surprising that Cain, who was born of Eve, and all after him, whose descent goes back to Eve, should be types of the Church, inasmuch as in a pre-eminent sense they are all descended from the Church.

22. Now, if the statements made to us regarding Israel, and its tribes and its families, are calculated to impress us, when the Saviour says, "I was not sent but to the lost sheep of the house of Israel," we do not understand the expression as the Ebionites do, who are poor in understanding (deriving their name from the poverty of their intellect—"Ebion" signifying "poor" in Hebrew), so as to suppose that the Saviour came specially to the "carnal" Israelites; for "they who are the children of the flesh are not the children of God." Again, the apostle teaches regarding Jerusalem as follows: "The Jerusalem which is above is free, which is the mother of us all." And in another Epistle: "But ye are come unto mount Zion, and to the city of the living God, to the heavenly Jerusalem, and to an innumerable company of angels, to the general assembly and to the Church of the first-born which are written in heaven." If, then, Israel is among the race of souls, and if there is in heaven a city of Jerusalem, it follows that the cities of Israel have for their metropolis the heavenly Jerusalem, and it consequently is the metropolis of all Judea. Whatever, therefore, is predicted of Jerusalem, and spoken of it, if we listen to the words of Paul as those of God, and of one who utters wisdom, we must understand the Scriptures as speaking of the heavenly city, and of the whole territory included within the cities of the holy land. For perhaps it is to these cities that the Saviour refers us, when to those who have gained credit by having managed their "pounds" well, He assigns the presidency over

236

five or ten cities. If, therefore, the prophecies relating to Judea, and Jerusalem, and Israel, and Judah, and Jacob, not being understood by us in a "carnal" sense, indicate some such mysteries (as already mentioned), it will follow also that the predictions concerning Egypt and the Egyptians, Babylon and the Babylonians, Tyre and the Tyrians, Sidon and the Sidonians, or the other nations, are spoken not only of these "bodily" Egyptians, and Babylonians, and Tyrians, and Sidonians, but also of their "spiritual" (counterparts). For if there be "spiritual" Israelites, it follows that there are also "spiritual" Egyptians and Babylonians. For what is related in Ezekiel concerning Pharaoh king of Egypt does not at all apply to the case of a certain man who ruled or was said to rule over Egypt, as will be evident to those who give it careful consideration. Similarly, what is said about the ruler of Tyre cannot be understood of a certain man who ruled over Tyre. And what is said in many places, and especially in Isaiah, of Nebuchadnezzar, cannot be explained of that individual. For the man Nebuchadnezzar neither fell from heaven, nor was he the morning star, nor did he arise upon the earth in the morning. Nor would any man of understanding interpret what is said in Ezekiel about Egypt—viz., that in forty years it should be laid desolate, so that the footstep of man should not be found thereon, and that the ravages of war should be so great that the blood should run throughout the whole of it, and rise to the knees— of that Egypt which is situated beside the Ethiopians whose bodies are blackened by the sun.

23. And perhaps as those here, dying according to the death common to all, are, in consequence of the deeds done here, so arranged as to obtain different places according to the proportion of their sins, if they should be deemed worthy of the place called Hades; so those there dying, so to speak, descend into this Hades, being judged deserving of different abodes—better or worse—throughout all this space of earth, and (of being descended) from parents of different kinds, so that an Israelite may sometimes fall among Scythians, and an Egyptian descend into Judea. And yet the Saviour came to gather together the lost sheep of the house of Israel; but many of the Israelites not having yielded to His teaching, those from the Gentiles were called. . . . And these points, as we suppose, have been concealed in the histories. For "the kingdom of heaven is like a treasure hid in a field; the which when a man hath found, he hideth, and for joy thereof goeth and selleth all that he hath, and buyeth that field." Let us notice, then, whether the apparent and superficial and obvious meaning of Scripture does not resemble a field filled with plants of every kind, while the things lying in it, and not visible to all, but buried, as it were, under the

plants that are seen, are the hidden treasures of wisdom and knowledge; which the Spirit through Isaiah calls dark and invisible and concealed, God alone being able to break the brazen gates that conceal them, and to burst the iron bars that are upon the gates, in order that all the statements in the book of Genesis may be discovered which refer to the various genuine kinds, and seeds, as it were, of souls, which stand nearly related to Israel, or at a distance from it; and the descent into Egypt of the seventy souls, that they may there become as the "stars of heaven in multitude." But since not all who are of them are the light of the world—"for not all who are of Israel are Israel"—they become from seventy souls as the "sand that is beside the sea-shore innumerable."

CHAPTER I CONTINUED [FROM THE LATIN]

24. This descent of the holy fathers into Egypt will appear as granted to this world by the providence of God for the illumination of others, and for the instruction of the human race, that so by this means the souls of others might be assisted in the work of enlightenment. For to them was first granted the privilege of converse with God, because theirs is the only race which is said to see God; this being the meaning, by interpretation, of the word "Israel." And now it follows that, agreeably to this view, ought the statement to be accepted and explained that Egypt was scourged with ten plagues, to allow the people of God to depart, or the account of what was done with the people in the wilderness, or of the building of the tabernacle by means of contributions from all the people, or of the wearing of the priestly robes, or of the vessels of the public service, because, as it is written, they truly contain within them the "shadow and form of heavenly things." For Paul openly says of them, that "they serve unto the example and shadow of heavenly things." There are, moreover, contained in this same law the precepts and institutions, according to which men are to live in the holy land. Threatenings also are held out as impending over those who shall transgress the law; different kinds of purifications are moreover prescribed for those who required purification, as being persons who were liable to frequent pollution, that by means of these they may arrive at last at that one purification after which no further pollution is permitted. The very people are numbered, though not all; for the souls of children are not yet old enough to be numbered according to the divine command: nor are those souls who cannot become the head of another, but are themselves subordinated to others as to a head, who are called

"women," who certainly are not included in that numbering which is enjoined by God; but they alone are numbered who are called "men," by which it might be shown that the women could not be counted separately, but were included in those called men. Those, however, especially belong to the sacred number, who are prepared to go forth to the battles of the Israelites, and are able to fight against those public and private enemies whom the Father subjects to the Son, who sits on His right hand that He may destroy all principality and power, and by means of these bands of His soldiery, who, being engaged in a warfare for God, do not entangle themselves in secular business, He may overturn the Kingdom of His adversary; by whom the shields of faith are borne, and the weapons of wisdom brandished; among whom also the helmet of hope and salvation gleams forth, and the breastplate of brightness fortifies the breast that is filled with God. Such soldiers appear to me to be indicated, and to be prepared for wars of this kind, in those persons who in the sacred books are ordered by God's command to be numbered. But of these, by far the more perfect and distinguished are shown to be those of whom the very hairs of the head are said to be numbered. Such, indeed, as were punished for their sins, whose bodies fell in the wilderness, appear to possess a resemblance to those who had made indeed no little progress, but who could not at all, for various reasons, attain to the end of perfection; because they are reported either to have murmured, or to have worshipped idols, or to have committed fornication, or to have done some evil work which the mind ought not even to conceive. I do not consider the following even to be without some mystical meaning, viz., that certain (of the Israelites), possessing many flocks and animals, take possession by anticipation of a country adapted for pasture and the feeding of cattle, which was the very first that the right hand of the Hebrews had secured in war. For, making a request of Moses to receive this region, they are divided off by the waters of the Jordan, and set apart from any possession in the holy land. And this Jordan, according to the form of heavenly things, may appear to water and irrigate thirsty souls, and the senses that are adjacent to it. In connection with which, even this statement does not appear superfluous, that Moses indeed hears from God what is described in the book of Leviticus, while in Deuteronomy it is the people that are the auditors of Moses, and who learn from him what they could not hear from God. For as Deuteronomy is called, as it were, the second law, which to some will appear to convey this signification, that when the first law which was given through Moses had come to an end, so a second legislation seems to have been enacted, which was specially transmitted by Moses to his successor Joshua, who is certainly believed to embody a type of our Saviour, by whose second law—that is, the precepts of the Gospel—all things are brought to perfection.

25. We have to see, however, whether this deeper meaning may not perhaps be indicated, viz., that as in Deuteronomy the legislation is made known with greater clearness and distinctness than in those books which were first written, so also by that advent of the Saviour which He accomplished in His state of humiliation, when He assumed the form of a servant, that more celebrated and renowned second advent in the glory of His Father may not be pointed out, and in it the types of Deuteronomy may be fulfilled, when in the kingdom of heaven all the saints shall live according to the laws of the everlasting Gospel; and as in His coming now He fulfilled that law which has a shadow of good things to come, so also by that (future) glorious advent will be fulfilled and brought to perfection the shadows of the present advent. For thus spake the prophet regarding it: "The breath of our countenance, Christ the Lord, to whom we said, that under Thy shadow we shall live among the nations;" at the time, viz., when He will more worthily transfer all the saints from a temporal to an everlasting Gospel, according to the designation, employed by John in the Apocalypse, of "an everlasting Gospel."

26. But let it be sufficient for us in all these matters to adapt our understanding to the rule of religion, and so to think of the words of the Holy Spirit as not to deem the language the ornate composition of feeble human eloquence, but to hold, according to the scriptural statement, that "all the glory of the King is within," and that the treasure of divine meaning is enclosed within the frail vessel of the common letter. And if any curious reader were still to ask an explanation of individual points, let him come and hear, along with ourselves, how the Apostle Paul, seeking to penetrate by help of the Holy Spirit, who searches even the "deep things" of God, into the depths of divine wisdom and knowledge, and yet, unable to reach the end, so to speak, and to come to a thorough knowledge, exclaims in despair and amazement, "Oh the depth of the riches of the knowledge and wisdom of God!" Now, that it was from despair of attaining a perfect understanding that he uttered this exclamation, listen to his own words: "How unsearchable are God's judgments! and His ways, how past finding out!" For he did not say that God's judgments were difficult to discover, but that they were altogether inscrutable; nor that it was (simply) difficult to trace out His ways, but that they were altogether past finding out. For however far a man may advance in his investigations, and how great soever the progress that he may make by

unremitting study, assisted even by the grace of God, and with his mind enlightened, he will not be able to attain to the end of those things which are the object of his inquiries. Nor can any created mind deem it possible in any way to attain a full comprehension (of things); but after having discovered certain of the objects of its research, it sees again others which have still to be sought out. And even if it should succeed in mastering these, it will see again many others succeeding them which must form the subject of investigation. And on this account, therefore, Solomon, the wisest of men, beholding by his wisdom the nature of things, says, "I said, I will become wise; and wisdom herself was made far from me, far further than it was; and a profound depth, who shall find?" Isaiah also, knowing that the beginnings of things could not be discovered by a mortal nature, and not even by those natures which, although more divine than human, were nevertheless themselves created or formed; knowing then, that by none of these could either the beginning or the end be discovered, says, "Tell the former things which have been, and we know that ye are gods; or announce what are the last things, and then we shall see that ye are gods." For my Hebrew teacher also used thus to teach, that as the beginning or end of all things could be comprehended by no one, save only our Lord Jesus Christ and the Holy Spirit, so under the form of a vision Isaiah spake of two seraphim alone, who with two wings cover the countenance of God, and with two His feet, and with two do fly, calling to each other alternately, and saying, "Holy, holy, holy is the LORD God of Sabaoth; the whole earth is full of Thy glory." That the seraphim alone have both their wings over the face of God, and over His feet, we venture to declare as meaning that neither the hosts of holy angels, nor the "holy seats," nor the "dominions," nor the "principalities," nor the "powers," can fully understand the beginning of all things, and the limits of the universe. But we are to understand that those "saints" whom the Spirit has enrolled, and the "virtues," approach very closely to those very beginnings, and attain to a height which the others cannot reach; and yet whatever it be that these "virtues" have learned through revelation from the Son of God and from the Holy Spirit—and they will certainly be able to learn very much, and those of higher rank much more than those of a lower— nevertheless it is impossible for them to comprehend all things, according to the statement, "The most part of the works of God are hid." And therefore also it is to be desired that every one, according to his strength, should ever stretch out to those things that are before, "forgetting the things that are behind," both to better works and to a clearer apprehension and understanding, through Jesus Christ our

241

Saviour, to whom be glory for ever!

27. Let every one, then, who cares for truth, be little concerned about words and language, seeing that in every nation there prevails a different usage of speech; but let him rather direct his attention to the meaning conveyed by the words, than to the nature of the words that convey the meaning, especially in matters of such importance and difficulty: as, e.g., when it is an object of investigation whether there is any "substance" in which neither colour, nor form, nor touch, nor magnitude is to be understood as existing visible to the mind alone, which any one names as he pleases; for the Greeks call such *asomaton,* i.e., "incorporeal," while holy Scripture declares it to be "invisible," for Paul calls Christ the "image of the invisible God," and says again, that by Christ were created all things "visible and invisible." And by this it is declared that there are, among created things, certain "substances" that are, according to their peculiar nature, invisible. But although these are not themselves "corporeal," they nevertheless make use of bodies, while they are themselves better than any bodily substances. But that "substance" of the Trinity which is the beginning and cause of all things, "from which are all things, and through which are all things, and in which are all things," cannot be believed to be either a body or in a body, but is altogether incorporeal. And now let it suffice to have spoken briefly on these points (although in a digression, caused by the nature of the subject), in order to show that there are certain things, the meaning of which cannot be unfolded at all by any words of human language, but which are made known more through simple apprehension than by any properties of words. And under this rule must be brought also the understanding of the sacred Scripture, in order that its statements may be judged not according to the worthlessness of the letter, but according to the divinity of the Holy Spirit, by whose inspiration they were caused to be written.

SUMMARY (OF DOCTRINE) REGARDING THE FATHER, THE SON, AND THE HOLY SPIRIT, AND THE OTHER TOPICS DISCUSSED IN THE PRECEDING PAGES.

28. It is now time, after the rapid consideration which to the best of our ability we have given to the topics discussed, to recapitulate, by way of summing up what we have said in different places, the individual points, and first of all to restate our conclusions regarding the Father, and the Son, and the Holy Spirit.

Seeing God the Father is invisible and inseparable from the Son, the Son is not generated from Him by "prolation," as some suppose. For if the Son be a "prolation" of the Father (the term "prolation" being used to signify such a generation as that of animals or men usually is), then, of necessity, both He who "prolated" and He who *was* "prolated" are corporeal. For we do not say, as the heretics suppose, that some part of the substance of God was converted into the Son, or that the Son was procreated by the Father out of things non-existent, i.e., beyond His own substance, so that there once was a time when He did not exist; but, putting away all corporeal conceptions, we say that the Word and Wisdom was begotten out of the invisible and incorporeal without any corporeal feeling, as if it were an act of the will proceeding from the understanding. Nor, seeing He is called the Son of (His) love, will it appear absurd if in this way He be called the Son of (His) will. Nay, John also indicates that "God is Light," and Paul also declares that the Son is the splendour of everlasting light. As light, accordingly, could never exist without splendour, so neither can the Son be understood to exist without the Father; for He is called the "express image of His person," and the Word and Wisdom. How, then, can it be asserted that there once was a time when He was not the Son? For that is nothing else than to say that there was once a time when He was not the Truth, nor the Wisdom, nor the Life, although in all these He is judged to be the perfect essence of God the Father; for these things cannot be severed from Him, or even be separated from His essence. And although these qualities are said to be many in understanding, yet in their nature and essence they are one, and in them is the fulness of divinity. Now this expression which we employ—"that there never was a time when He did not exist"—is to be understood with an allowance. For these very words "when" or "never" have a meaning that relates to time, whereas the statements made regarding Father, Son, and Holy Spirit are to be understood as transcending all time, all ages, and all eternity. For it is the Trinity alone which exceeds the comprehension not only of temporal but even of eternal intelligence; while other things which are not included in it are to be measured by times and ages. This Son of God, then, in respect of the Word being God, which was in the beginning with God, no one will logically suppose to be contained in any place; nor yet in respect of His being "Wisdom," or "Truth," or the "Life," or "Righteousness," or "Sanctification," or "Redemption:" for all these properties do not require space to be able to act or to operate, but each one of them is to be understood as meaning those individuals who participate in His virtue and working.

29. Now, if any one were to say that, through those who are partakers of the "Word" of God, or of His "Wisdom," or His "Truth," or His "Life," the Word and Wisdom itself appeared to be contained

in a place, we should have to say to him in answer, that there is no doubt that Christ, in respect of being the "Word" or "Wisdom," or all other things, was in Paul, and that he therefore said, "Do you seek a proof of Christ speaking in me?" and again, "I live, yet not I, but Christ liveth in me." Seeing, then, He was in Paul, who will doubt that He was in a similar manner in Peter and in John, and in each one of the saints; and not only in those who are upon the earth, but in those also who are in heaven? For it is absurd to say that Christ was in Peter and in Paul, but not in Michael the archangel, nor in Gabriel. And from this it is distinctly shown that the divinity of the Son of God was not shut up in some place; otherwise it would have been in it only, and not in another. But since, in conformity with the majesty of its incorporeal nature, it is confined to no place; so, again, it cannot be understood to be wanting in any. But this is understood to be the sole difference, that although He is in different individuals as we have said—as Peter, or Paul, or Michael, or Gabriel—He is not in a similar way in all beings whatever. For He is more fully and clearly, and, so to speak, more openly in archangels than in other holy men. And this is evident from the statement, that when all who are saints have arrived at the summit of perfection, they are said to be made like, or equal to, the angels, agreeably to the declaration in the Gospels. Whence it is clear that Christ is in each individual in as great a degree as the amount of his deserts allows.

30. Having, then, briefly restated these points regarding the nature of the Trinity, it follows that we notice shortly this statement also, that "by the Son" are said to be created "all things that are in heaven, and that are in earth, visible and invisible, whether they be thrones, or dominions, or principalities, or powers: all things were created by Him, and for Him; and He is before all, and all things consist by Him, who is the Head." In conformity with which John also in his Gospel says: "All things were created by Him; and without Him was not anything made." And David, intimating that the mystery of the entire Trinity was (concerned) in the creation of all things, says: "By the Word of the LORD were the heavens made; and all the host of them by the Spirit of His mouth."

After these points we shall appropriately remind (the reader) of the bodily advent and incarnation of the only-begotten Son of God, with respect to whom we are not to suppose that all the majesty of His divinity is confined within the limits of His slender body, so that all the "word" of God, and His "wisdom," and "essential truth," and "life," was either rent asunder from the Father, or restrained and confined within the narrowness of His bodily person, and is not to be considered to have operated anywhere besides; but the cautious acknowledgment of a religious man ought to be between the two, so that it ought neither to be believed that anything of divinity was wanting in Christ, nor that any separation at all was made from the essence of the Father, which is everywhere. For some such meaning seems to be indicated by John the Baptist, when he said to the multitude in the bodily absence of Jesus, "There standeth one among you whom ye know not: He it is who cometh after me, the latchet of whose shoes I am not worthy to unloose." For it certainly could not be said of Him, who was absent, so far as His bodily presence is concerned, that He was standing in the midst of those among whom the Son of God was not bodily present.

31. Let no one, however, suppose that by this we affirm that some portion of the divinity of the Son of God was in Christ, and that the remaining portion was elsewhere or everywhere, which may be the opinion of those who are ignorant of the nature of an incorporeal and invisible essence. For it is impossible to speak of the parts of an incorporeal being, or to make any division of them; but He is in all things, and through all things, and above all things, in the manner in which we have spoken above, i.e., in the manner in which He is understood to be either "wisdom," or the "word," or the "life," or the "truth," by which method of understanding all confinement of a local kind is undoubtedly excluded. The Son of God, then, desiring for the salvation of the human race to appear unto men, and to sojourn among them, assumed not only a human body, as some suppose, but also a soul resembling our souls indeed in nature, but in will and power resembling Himself, and such as might unfailingly accomplish all the desires and arrangements of the "word" and "wisdom." Now, that He had a soul, is most clearly shown by the Saviour in the Gospels, when He said, "No man taketh my life from me, but I lay it down of myself. I have power to lay down my life, and I have power to take it again." And again, "My soul is sorrowful even unto death." And again, "Now is my soul troubled." For the "Word" of God is not to be understood to be a "sorrowful and troubled" soul, because with the authority of divinity He says, "I have power to lay down my life." Nor yet do we assert that the Son of God was in that soul as he was in the soul of Paul or Peter and the other saints, in whom Christ is believed to speak as He does in Paul. But regarding all these we are to hold, as Scripture declares, "No one is clean from filthiness, not even if his life lasted but a single day." But this soul which was in Jesus, before it knew the evil, selected the good; and because He loved righteousness, and hated iniquity, therefore God "anointed Him with the oil of gladness above His fellows." He is anointed, then, with the oil of gladness when He is

united to the "word" of God in a stainless union, and by this means alone of all souls was incapable of sin, because it was capable of (receiving) well and fully the Son of God; and therefore also it is one with Him, and is named by His titles, and is called Jesus Christ, by whom all things are said to be made. Of which soul, seeing it had received into itself the whole wisdom of God, and the truth, and the life, I think that the apostle also said this: "Our life is hidden with Christ in God; but when Christ, who is our life, shall appear, then shall we also appear with him in glory." For what other Christ can be here understood, who is said to be hidden in God, and who is afterwards to appear, except Him who is related to have been anointed with the oil of gladness, i.e., to have been filled with God essentially, in whom he is now said to be hidden? For on this account is Christ proposed as an example to all believers, because as He always, even before he knew evil at all, selected the good, and loved righteousness, and hated iniquity, and therefore God anointed Him with the oil of gladness; so also ought each one, after a lapse or sin, to cleanse himself from his stains, making Him his example, and, taking Him as the guide of his journey, enter upon the steep way of virtue, that so perchance by this means, as far as possible we may, by imitating Him, be made partakers of the divine nature, according to the words of Scripture: "He that saith that he believeth in Christ, ought so to walk, as He also walked."

This "word," then, and this "wisdom," by the imitation of which we are said to be either wise or rational (beings), becomes "all things to all men, that it may gain all;" and because it is made weak, it is therefore said of it, "Though He was crucified through weakness, yet He liveth by the power of God." Finally, to the Corinthians who were weak, Paul declares that he "knew nothing, save Jesus Christ, and Him crucified."

32. Some, indeed, would have the following language of the apostle applied to the soul itself, as soon as it had assumed flesh from Mary, viz., "Who, being in the form of God, thought it not robbery to be equal with God, but divested Himself (of His glory) taking upon Himself the form of a servant;" since He undoubtedly restored it to the form of God by means of better examples and training, and recalled it to that fulness of which He had divested Himself.

As now by participation in the Son of God one is adopted as a son, and by participating in that wisdom which is in God is rendered wise, so also by participation in the Holy Spirit is a man rendered holy and spiritual. For it is one and the same thing to have a share in the Holy Spirit, which is (the Spirit) of the Father and the Son, since the nature of the Trinity is one and incorporeal. And what we have said regarding the participation of the soul is to be understood of angels and heavenly powers in a similar way as of souls, because every rational creature needs a participation in the Trinity.

Respecting also the plan of this visible world—seeing one of the most important questions usually raised is as to the manner of its existence—we have spoken to the best of our ability in the preceding pages, for the sake of those who are accustomed to seek the grounds of their belief in our religion, and also for those who stir against us heretical questions, and who are accustomed to bandy about the word "matter," which they have not yet been able to understand; of which subject I now deem it necessary briefly to remind (the reader).

33. And, in the first place, it is to be noted that we have nowhere found in the canonical Scriptures, up to the present time, the word "matter" used for that substance which is said to underlie bodies. For in the expression of Isaiah, "And he shall devour *hule*," i.e., matter, "like hay," when speaking of those who were appointed to undergo their punishments, the word "matter" was used instead of "sins." And if this word "matter" should happen to occur in any other passage, it will never be found, in my opinion, to have the signification of which we are now in quest, unless perhaps in the book which is called the Wisdom of Solomon, a work which is certainly not esteemed authoritative by all. In that book, however, we find written as follows: "For thy almighty hand, that made the world out of shapeless matter, wanted not means to send among them a multitude of bears and fierce lions." Very many, indeed, are of opinion that the matter of which things are made is itself signified in the language used by Moses in the beginning of Genesis: "In the beginning God made heaven and earth; and the earth was invisible, and not arranged:" for by the words "invisible and not arranged" Moses would seem to mean nothing else than shapeless matter. But if this be truly matter, it is clear then that the original elements of bodies are not incapable of change. For those who posited "atoms"—either those particles which are incapable of subdivision, or those which are subdivided into equal parts—or any one element, as the principles of bodily things, could not posit the word "matter" in the proper sense of the term among the first principles of things. For if they will have it that matter underlies every body—a substance convertible or changeable, or divisible in all its parts—they will not, as is proper, assert that it exists without qualities. And with them we agree, for we altogether deny that matter ought to be spoken of as "unbegotten" or "uncreated," agreeably to our former statements, when we pointed out that from water, and earth, and air or heat, different kinds of fruits were produced by different kinds of trees; or when we showed that fire, and air, and water, and earth were alternately

converted into each other, and that one element was resolved into another by a kind of mutual consanguinity; and also when we proved that from the food either of men or animals the substance of the flesh was derived, or that the moisture of the natural seed was converted into solid flesh and bones;—all which go to prove that the substance of the body is changeable, and may pass from one quality into all others.

34. Nevertheless we must not forget that a substance never exists without a quality, and that it is by an act of the understanding alone that this (substance) which underlies bodies, and which is capable of quality, is discovered to be matter. Some indeed, in their desire to investigate these subjects more profoundly, have ventured to assert that bodily nature is nothing else than qualities. For if hardness and softness, heat and cold, moisture and aridity, be qualities; and if, when these or other (qualities) of this sort be cut away, nothing else is understood to remain, then all things will appear to be "qualities." And therefore also those persons who make these assertions have endeavoured to maintain, that since all who say that matter was uncreated will admit that qualities were created by God, it may be in this way shown that even according to them matter was not uncreated; since qualities constitute everything, and these are declared by all without contradiction to have been made by God. Those, again, who would make out that qualities are superimposed from without upon a certain underlying matter, make use of illustrations of this kind: e.g., Paul undoubtedly is either silent, or speaks, or watches, or sleeps, or maintains a certain attitude of body; for he is either in a sitting, or standing, or recumbent position. For these are "accidents" belonging to men, without which they are almost never found. And yet our conception of man does not lay down any of these things as a definition of him; but we so understand and regard him by their means, that we do not at all take into account the reason of his (particular) condition either in watching, or in sleeping, or in speaking, or in keeping silence, or in any other action that must necessarily happen to men. If any one, then, can regard Paul as being without all these things which are capable of happening, he will in the same way also be able to understand this underlying (substance) without qualities. When, then, our mind puts away all qualities from its conception, and gazes, so to speak, upon the underlying element alone, and keeps its attention closely upon it, without any reference to the softness or hardness, or heat or cold, or humidity or aridity of the substance, then by means of this somewhat simulated process of thought it will appear to behold matter clear from qualities of every kind.

35. But some one will perhaps inquire whether we can obtain out of Scripture any grounds for such an understanding of the subject. Now I

think some such view is indicated in the Psalms, when the prophet says, "Mine eyes have seen thine imperfection;" by which the mind of the prophet, examining with keener glance the first principles of things, and separating in thought and imagination only between matter and its qualities, perceived the imperfection of God, which certainly is understood to be perfected by the addition of qualities. Enoch also, in his book, speaks as follows: "I have walked on even to imperfection;" which expression I consider may be understood in a similar manner, viz., that the mind of the prophet proceeded in its scrutiny and investigation of all visible things, until it arrived at that first beginning in which it beheld imperfect matter (existing) without "qualities." For it is written in the same book of Enoch, "I beheld the whole of matter;" which is so understood as if he had said: "I have clearly seen all the divisions of matter which are broken up from one into each individual species either of men, or animals, or of the sky, or of the sun, or of all other things in this world." After these points, now, we proved to the best of our power in the preceding pages that all things which exist were made by God, and that there was nothing which was not made, save the nature of the Father, and the Son, and the Holy Spirit; and that God, who is by nature good, desiring to have those upon whom He might confer benefits, and who might rejoice in receiving His benefits, created creatures worthy (of this), i.e., who were capable of receiving Him in a worthy manner, who, He says, are also begotten by Him as his sons. He made all things, moreover, by number and measure. For there is nothing before God without either limit or measure. For by His power He comprehends all things, and He Himself is comprehended by the strength of no created thing, because that nature is known to itself alone. For the Father alone knoweth the Son, and the Son alone knoweth the Father, and the Holy Spirit alone searcheth even the deep things of God. All created things, therefore, i.e., either the number of rational beings or the measure of bodily matter, are distinguished by Him as being within a certain number or measurement; since, as it was necessary for an intellectual nature to employ bodies, and this nature is shown to be changeable and convertible by the very condition of its being created (for what did not exist, but began to exist, is said by this very circumstance to be of mutable nature), it can have neither goodness nor wickedness as an essential, but only as an accidental attribute of its being. Seeing, then, as we have said, that rational nature was mutable and changeable, so that it made use of a different bodily covering of this or that sort of quality, according to its merits, it was necessary, as God foreknew there would be diversities in souls or spiritual powers, that He should create also a bodily nature the qualities of which might be changed at the will of the Creator into all that was required. And this bodily nature must last as long as those things which require it as a covering: for there will be always rational natures which need a bodily covering; and there will therefore always be a bodily nature whose coverings must necessarily be used by rational creatures, unless some one be able to demonstrate by arguments that a rational nature can live without a body. But how difficult—nay, how almost impossible—this is for our understanding, we have shown in the preceding pages, in our discussion of the individual topics.

36. It will not, I consider, be opposed to the nature of our undertaking, if we restate with all possible brevity our opinions on the immortality of rational natures. Every one who participates in anything, is unquestionably of one essence and nature with him who is partaker of the same thing. For example, as all eyes participate in the light, so accordingly all eyes which partake of the light are of one nature; but although every eye partakes of the light, yet, inasmuch as one sees more clearly, and another more obscurely, every eye does not equally share in the light. And again, all hearing receives voice or sound, and therefore all hearing is of one nature; but each one hears more rapidly or more slowly, according as the quality of his hearing is clear and sound. Let us pass now from these sensuous illustrations to the consideration of intellectual things. Every mind which partakes of intellectual light ought undoubtedly to be of one nature with every mind which partakes in a similar manner of intellectual light. If the heavenly virtues, then, partake of intellectual light, i.e., of divine nature, because they participate in wisdom and holiness, and if human souls, have partaken of the same light and wisdom, and thus are mutually of one nature and of one essence,—then, since the heavenly virtues are incorruptible and immortal, the essence of the human soul will also be immortal and incorruptible. And not only so, but because the nature of Father, and Son, and Holy Spirit, whose intellectual light alone all created things have a share, is incorruptible and eternal, it is altogether consistent and necessary that every substance which partakes of that eternal nature should last for ever, and be incorruptible and eternal, so that the eternity of divine goodness may be understood also in this respect, that they who obtain its benefits are also eternal. But as, in the instances referred to, a diversity in the participation of the light was observed, when the glance of the beholder was described as being duller or more acute, so also a diversity is to be noted in the participation of Father, Son, and Holy Spirit, varying with the degree of zeal or capacity of mind. If such were not the case, we have to consider whether it would not seem to be an act of impiety to say that

250

the mind which is capable of (receiving) God should admit of a destruction of its essence; as if the very fact that it is able to feel and understand God could not suffice for its perpetual existence, especially since, if even through neglect the mind fall away from a pure and complete reception of God, it nevertheless contains within it certain seeds of restoration and renewal to a better understanding, seeing the "inner," which is also called the "rational" man, is renewed after "the image and likeness of God, who created him." And therefore the prophet says, "All the ends of the earth shall remember, and turn unto the LORD; and all the kindreds of the nations shall worship before Thee."

37. If any one, indeed, venture to ascribe essential corruption to Him who was made after the image and likeness of God, then, in my opinion, this impious charge extends even to the Son of God Himself, for He is called in Scripture the image of God. Or he who holds this opinion would certainly impugn the authority of Scripture, which says that man was made in the image of God; and in him are manifestly to be discovered traces of the divine image, not by any appearance of the bodily frame, which is corruptible, but by mental wisdom, by justice, moderation, virtue, wisdom, discipline; in fine, by the whole band of virtues, which are innate in the essence of God, and which may enter into man by diligence and imitation of God; as the Lord also intimates in the Gospel, when He says, "Be ye therefore merciful, as your Father also is merciful;" and, "Be ye perfect, even as your Father also is perfect." From which it is clearly shown that all these virtues are perpetually in God, and that they can never approach to or depart from Him, whereas by men they are acquired only slowly, and one by one. And hence also by these means they seem to have a kind of relationship with God; and since God knows all things, and none of things intellectual in themselves can elude His notice (for God the Father alone, and His only-begotten Son, and the Holy Spirit, not only possess a knowledge of those things which they have created, but also of themselves), a rational understanding also, advancing from small things to great, and from things visible to things invisible, may attain to a more perfect knowledge. For it is placed in the body, and advances from sensible things themselves, which are corporeal, to things that are intellectual. But lest our statement that things intellectual are not cognisable by the senses should appear unbecoming, we shall employ the instance of Solomon, who says, "You will find also a divine sense;" by which he shows that those things which are intellectual are to be sought out not by means of a bodily sense, but by a certain other which he calls "divine." And with this sense must we look on each of those

rational beings which we have enumerated above; and with this sense are to be understood those words which we speak, and those statements to be weighed which we commit to writing. For the divine nature knows even those thoughts which we revolve within us in silence. And on those matters of which we have spoken, or on the others which follow from them, according to the rule above laid down, are our opinions to be formed.

LETTERS

A LETTER TO ORIGEN FROM AFRICANUS ABOUT THE HISTORY OF SUSANNA

GREETING, my lord and son, most worthy Origen, from Africanus. In your sacred discussion with Agnomon you referred to that prophecy of Daniel which is related of his youth. This at that time, as was meet, I accepted as genuine. Now, however, I cannot understand how it escaped you that this part of the book is spurious. For, in sooth, this section, although apart from this it is elegantly written, is plainly a more modern forgery. There are many proofs of this. When Susanna is condemned to die, the prophet is seized by the Spirit, and cries out that the sentence is unjust. Now, in the first place, it is always in some other way that Daniel prophesies—by visions, and dreams, and an angel appearing to him, never by prophetic inspiration. Then, after crying out in this extraordinary fashion, he detects them in a way no less incredible, which not even Philistion the play-writer would have resorted to. For, not satisfied with rebuking them through the Spirit, he placed them apart, and asked them severally where they saw her committing adultery. And when the one said, "Under a holm-tree" (*prinos*), he answered that the angel would saw him asunder (*prisein*); and in a similar fashion menaced the other who said, "Under a mastich-tree" (*schinos*), with being rent asunder (*schisthenai*). Now, in Greek, it happens that "holm-tree" and "saw asunder," and "rend" and "mastich-tree" sound alike; but in Hebrew they are quite distinct. But all the books of the Old Testament have been translated from Hebrew into Greek.

2. Moreover, how is it that they who were captives among the Chaldaeans, lost and won at play, thrown out unburied on the streets, as was prophesied of the former captivity, their sons torn from them to be eunuchs, and their daughters to be concubines, as had been prophesied; how is it that such could pass sentence of death, and that on the wife of their king Joakim, whom the king of the Babylonians had made partner of his throne? Then if it was not this Joakim, but some other from the common people, whence had a captive such a mansion and spacious garden? But a more fatal objection is, that this section, along with the other two at the end of it, is not contained in the Daniel received among the Jews. And add that, among all the many prophets who had been before, there is no one who has quoted from another word for word. For they had no need to go a-begging for

255

words, since their own were true; but this one, in rebuking one of those men, quotes the words of the Lord: "The innocent and righteous shalt thou not slay." From all this I infer that this section is a later addition. Moreover, the style is different. I have struck the blow; do you give the echo; answer, and instruct me. Salute all my masters. The learned all salute thee. With all my heart I pray for your and your circle's health.

A LETTER FROM ORIGEN TO AFRICANUS

ORIGEN to Africanus, a beloved brother in God the Father, through Jesus Christ, His holy Child, greeting. Your letter, from which I learn what you think of the Susanna in the Book of Daniel, which is used in the Churches, although apparently somewhat short, presents in its few words many problems, each of which demands no common treatment, but such as oversteps the character of a letter, and reaches the limits of a discourse. And I, when I consider, as best I can, the measure of my intellect, that I may know myself, am aware that I am wanting in the accuracy necessary to reply to your letter; and that the more, that the few days I have spent in Nicomedia have been far from sufficient to send you an answer to all your demands and queries even after the fashion of the present epistle. Wherefore pardon my little ability, and the little time I had, and read this letter with all indulgence, supplying anything I may omit.

2. You begin by saying, that when, in my discussion with our friend Bassus, I used the Scripture which contains the prophecy of Daniel when yet a young man in the affair of Susanna, I did this as if it had escaped me that this part of the book was spurious. You say that you praise this passage as elegantly written, but find fault with it as a more modern composition, and a forgery; and you add that the forger has had recourse to something which not even Philistion the play-writer would have used in his puns between *prinos* and *prisein*, *schinos* and *schisis*, which words as they sound in Greek can be used in this way, but not in Hebrew. In answer to this, I have to tell you what it behoves us to do in the cases not only of the History of Susanna, which is found in every Church of Christ in that Greek copy which the Greeks use, but is not in the Hebrew, or of the two other passages you mention at the end of the book containing the history of Bel and the Dragon, which likewise are not in the Hebrew copy of Daniel; but of thousands of other passages also which I found in many places when with my little strength I was collating the Hebrew copies with ours. For in Daniel itself I found the word "bound" followed in our versions by very many verses which are not in the Hebrew at all, beginning (according to one of the copies which circulate in the Churches) thus: "Ananias, and Azarias, and Misael prayed and sang unto God," down to "O, all ye that worship the Lord, bless ye the God of gods. Praise Him, and say that His mercy endureth for ever and ever. And it came to pass, when

the king heard them singing, and saw them that they were alive." Or, as in another copy, from "And they walked in the midst of the fire, praising God and blessing the Lord," down to "O, all ye that worship the Lord, bless ye the God of gods. Praise Him, and say that His mercy endureth to all generations." But in the Hebrew copies the words, "And these three men, Sedrach, Misach, and Abednego fell down bound into the midst of the fire," are immediately followed by the verse, "Nabouchodonosor the king was astonished, and rose up in haste, and spake, and said unto his counsellors." For so Aquila, following the Hebrew reading, gives it, who has obtained the credit among the Jews of having interpreted the Scriptures with no ordinary care, and whose version is most commonly used by those who do not know Hebrew, as the one which has been most successful. Of the copies in my possession whose readings I gave, one follows the Seventy, and the other Theodotion; and just as the History of Susanna which you call a forgery is found in both, together with the passages at the end of Daniel, so they give also these passages, amounting, to make a rough guess, to more than two hundred verses.

3. And in many other of the sacred books I found sometimes more in our copies than in the Hebrew, sometimes less. I shall adduce a few examples, since it is impossible to give them all. Of the Book of Esther neither the prayer of Mardochaios nor that of Esther, both fitted to edify the reader, is found in the Hebrew. Neither are the letters; nor the one written to Amman about the rooting up of the Jewish nation, nor that of Mardochaios in the name of Artaxerxes delivering the nation from death. Then in Job, the words from "It is written, that he shall rise again with those whom the Lord raises," to the end, are not in the Hebrew, and so not in Aquila's edition; while they are found in the Septuagint and in Theodotion's version, agreeing with each other at least in sense. And many other places I found in Job where our copies have more than the Hebrew ones, sometimes a little more, and sometimes a great deal more: a little more, as when to the words, "Rising up in the morning, he offered burnt-offerings for them according to their number," they add, "one heifer for the sin of their soul;" and to the words, "The angels of God came to present themselves before God, and the devil came with them," "from going to and fro in the earth, and from walking up and down in it." Again, after "The LORD gave, the LORD has taken away," the Hebrew has not, "It was so, as seemed good to the Lord." Then our copies are very much fuller than the Hebrew, when Job's wife speaks to him, from "How long wilt thou hold out? And he said, Lo, I wait yet a little while, looking for the hope of my salvation," down to "that I may cease from

my troubles, and my sorrows which compass me." For they have only these words of the woman, "But say a word against God, and die."

4. Again, through the whole of Job there are many passages in the Hebrew which are wanting in our copies, generally four or five verses, but sometimes, however, even fourteen, and nineteen, and sixteen. But why should I enumerate all the instances I collected with so much labour, to prove that the difference between our copies and those of the Jews did not escape me? In Jeremiah I noticed many instances, and indeed in that book I found much transposition and variation in the readings of the prophecies. Again, in Genesis, the words, "God saw that it was good," when the firmament was made, are not found in the Hebrew, and there is no small dispute among them about this; and other instances are to be found in Genesis, which I marked, for the sake of distinction, with the sign the Greeks call an obelisk, as on the other hand I marked with an asterisk those passages in our copies which are not found in the Hebrew. What needs there to speak of Exodus, where there is such diversity in what is said about the tabernacle and its court, and the ark, and the garments of the high priest and the priests, that sometimes the meaning even does not seem to be akin? And, forsooth, when we notice such things, we are forthwith to reject as spurious the copies in use in our Churches, and enjoin the brotherhood to put away the sacred books current among them, and to coax the Jews, and persuade them to give us copies which shall be untampered with, and free from forgery! Are we to suppose that that Providence which in the sacred Scriptures has ministered to the edification of all the Churches of Christ, had no thought for those bought with a price, for whom Christ died; whom, although His Son, God who is love spared not, but gave Him up for us all, that with Him He might freely give us all things?

5. In all these cases consider whether it would not be well to remember the words, "Thou shalt not remove the ancient landmarks which thy fathers have set." Nor do I say this because I shun the labour of investigating the Jewish Scriptures, and comparing them with ours, and noticing their various readings. This, if it be not arrogant to say it, I have already to a great extent done to the best of my ability, labouring hard to get at the meaning in all the editions and various readings; while I paid particular attention to the interpretation of the Seventy, lest I might to be found to accredit any forgery to the Churches which are under heaven, and give an occasion to those who seek such a starting-point for gratifying their desire to slander the common brethren, and to bring some accusation against those who shine forth in our community. And I make it my endeavour not to be ignorant of their

259

various readings, lest in my controversies with the Jews I should quote to them what is not found in their copies, and that I may make some use of what is found there, even although it should not be in our Scriptures. For if we are so prepared for them in our discussions, they will not, as is their manner, scornfully laugh at Gentile believers for their ignorance of the true reading as they have them. So far as to the History of Susanna not being found in the Hebrew.

6. Let us now look at the things you find fault with in the story itself. And here let us begin with what would probably make any one averse to receiving the history: I mean the play of words between *prinos* and *prisis*, *schinos* and *schisis*. You say that you can see how this can be in Greek, but that in Hebrew the words are altogether distinct. On this point, however, I am still in doubt; because, when I was considering this passage (for I myself saw this difficulty), I consulted not a few Jews about it, asking them the Hebrew words for *prinos* and *prisein*, and how they would translate *schinos* the tree, and how *schisis*. And they said that they did not know these Greek words *prinos* and *schinos*, and asked me to show them the trees, that they might see what they called them. And I at once (for the truth's dear sake) put before them pieces of the different trees. One of them then said, that he could not with any certainty give the Hebrew name of anything not mentioned in Scripture, since, if one was at a loss, he was prone to use the Syriac word instead of the Hebrew one; and he went on to say, that some words the very wisest could not translate. "If, then," said he, "you can adduce a passage in any Scripture where the *schinos* is mentioned, or the *prinos*, you will find there the words you seek, together with the words which have the same sound; but if it is nowhere mentioned, we also do not know it." This, then, being what the Hebrews said to whom I had recourse, and who were acquainted with the history, I am cautious of affirming whether or not there is any correspondence to this play of words in the Hebrew. Your reason for affirming that there is not, you yourself probably know.

7. Moreover, I remember hearing from a learned Hebrew, said among themselves to be the son of a wise man, and to have been specially trained to succeed his father, with whom I had intercourse on many subjects, the names of these elders, just as if he did not reject the History of Susanna, as they occur in Jeremias as follows: "The LORD make thee like Zedekias and Achiab, whom the king of Babylon roasted in the fire, for the iniquity they did in Israel." How, then, could the one be sawn asunder by an angel, and the other rent in pieces? The answer is, that these things were prophesied not of this world, but of the judgment of God, after the departure from this world. For as the lord

of that wicked servant who says, "My lord delayeth his coming," and so gives himself up to drunkenness, eating and drinking with drunkards, and smiting his fellow-servants, shall at his coming "cut him asunder, and appoint him his portion with the unbelievers," even so the angels appointed to punish will accomplish these things (just as they will cut asunder the wicked steward of that passage) on these men, who were called indeed elders, but who administered their stewardship wickedly. One will saw asunder him who was waxen old in wicked days, who had pronounced false judgment, condemning the innocent, and letting the guilty go free; and another will rend in pieces him of the seed of Chanaan, and not of Judah, whom beauty had deceived, and whose heart lust had perverted.

8. And I knew another Hebrew, who told about these elders such traditions as the following: that they pretended to the Jews in captivity, who were hoping by the coming of Christ to be freed from the yoke of their enemies, that they could explain clearly the things concerning Christ,. . . . and that they so deceived the wives of their countrymen. Wherefore it is that the prophet Daniel calls the one "waxen old in wicked days," and says to the other, "Thus have ye dealt with the children of Israel; but the daughters of Juda would not abide your wickedness."

9. But probably to this you will say, Why then is the "History" not in their Daniel, if, as you say, their wise men hand down by tradition such stories? The answer is, that they hid from the knowledge of the people as many of the passages which contained any scandal against the elders, rulers, and judges, as they could, some of which have been preserved in uncanonical writings (Apocrypha). As an example, take the story told about Esaias; and guaranteed by the Epistle to the Hebrews, which is found in none of their public books. For the author of the Epistle to the Hebrews, in speaking of the prophets, and what they suffered, says, "They were stoned, they were sawn asunder, they were slain with the sword." To whom, I ask, does the "sawn asunder" refer (for by an old idiom, not peculiar to Hebrew, but found also in Greek, this is said in the plural, although it refers to but one person)? Now we know very well that tradition says that Esaias the prophet was sawn asunder; and this is found in some apocryphal work, which probably the Jews have purposely tampered with, introducing some phrases manifestly incorrect, that discredit might be thrown on the whole.

However, some one hard pressed by this argument may have recourse to the opinion of those who reject this Epistle as not being Paul's; against whom I must at some other time use other arguments

261

to prove that it is Paul's. At present I shall adduce from the Gospel what Jesus Christ testifies concerning the prophets, together with a story which He refers to, but which is not found in the Old Testament, since in it also there is a scandal against unjust judges in Israel. The words of our Saviour run thus: "Woe unto you, scribes and Pharisees, hypocrites because ye build the tombs of the prophets, and garnish the sepulchres of the righteous, and say, If we had been in the days of our fathers, we would not have been partaken with them in the blood of the prophets. Wherefore be ye witnesses unto yourselves, that ye are the children of them which killed the prophets. Fill ye up then the measure of your fathers. Ye serpents, ye generation of vipers, how can ye escape the damnation of Gehenna? Wherefore, behold, I send unto you prophets, and wise men, and scribes; and some of them ye shall kill and crucify; and some of them shall ye scourge in your synagogues, and persecute them from city to city: that upon you may come all the righteous blood shed upon the earth, from the blood of righteous Abel unto the blood of Zacharias, son of Barachias, whom ye slew between the temple and the altar. Verily I say unto you, All these things shall come upon this generation." And what follows is of the same tenor: "O Jerusalem, Jerusalem, thou that killest the prophets, and stonest them which are sent unto thee, how often would I have gathered thy children together, even as a hen gathereth her chickens under her wings, and ye would not! Behold, your house is left unto you desolate."

Let us see now if in these cases we are not forced to the conclusion, that while the Saviour gives a true account of them, none of the Scriptures which could prove what He tells are to be found. For they who build the tombs of the prophets and garnish the sepulchres of the righteous, condemning the crimes their fathers committed against the righteous and the prophets, say, "If we had been in the days of our fathers, we would not have been partakers with them in the blood of the prophets." In the blood of what prophets, can any one tell me? For where do we find anything like this written of Esaias, or Jeremias, or any of the twelve, or Daniel? Then about Zacharias the son of Barachias, who was slain between the temple and the altar, we learn from Jesus only, not knowing it otherwise from any Scripture. Wherefore I think no other supposition is possible, than that they who had the reputation of wisdom, and the rulers and elders, took away from the people every passage which might bring them into discredit among the people. We need not wonder, then, if this history of the evil device of the licentious elders against Susanna is true, but was concealed and removed from the Scriptures by men themselves not very far removed from the counsel of these elders.

In the Acts of the Apostles also, Stephen, in his other testimony, says, "Which of the prophets have not your fathers persecuted? And they have slain them which showed before of the coming of the Just One; of whom ye have been now the betrayers and murderers." That Stephen speaks the truth, every one will admit who receives the Acts of the Apostles; but it is impossible to show from the extant books of the Old Testament how with any justice he throws the blame of having persecuted and slain the prophets on the fathers of those who believed not in Christ. And Paul, in the first Epistle to the Thessalonians, testifies this concerning the Jews: "For ye, brethren, became followers of the Churches of God which in Judea are in Christ Jesus: for ye also have suffered like things of your own countrymen, even as they have of the Jews; who both killed the Lord Jesus and their own prophets, and have persecuted us; and they please not God, and are contrary to all men." What I have said is, I think, sufficient to prove that it would be nothing wonderful if this history were true, and the licentious and cruel attack was actually made on Susanna by those who were at that time elders, and written down by the wisdom of the Spirit, but removed by these rulers of Sodom, as the Spirit would call them.

10. Your next objection is, that in this writing Daniel is said to have been seized by the Spirit, and to have cried out that the sentence was unjust; while in that writing of his which is universally received he is represented as prophesying in quite another manner, by visions and dreams, and an angel appearing to him, but never by prophetic inspiration. You seem to me to pay too little heed to the words, "At sundry times, and in divers manners, God spake in time past unto the fathers by the prophets." This is true not only in the general, but also of individuals. For if you notice, you will find that the same saints have been favoured with divine dreams and angelic appearances and (direct) inspirations. For the present it will suffice to instance what is testified concerning Jacob. Of dreams from God he speaks thus: "And it came to pass, at the time that the cattle conceived, that I saw them before my eyes in a dream, and, behold, the rams and he-goats which leaped upon the sheep and the goats, white-spotted, and speckled, and grisled. And the angel of God spake unto me in a dream, saying, Jacob. And I said, What is it? And he said, Lift up thine eyes and see, the goats and rams leaping on the goats and sheep, white-spotted, and speckled, and grisled: for I have seen all that Laban doeth unto thee. I am God, who appeared unto thee in the place of God, where thou anointedst to Me there a pillar, and vowedst a vow there to Me: now arise, get thee out from this land, and return unto the land of thy kindred."

And as to an appearance (which is better than a dream), he speaks as follows about himself: "And Jacob was left alone; and there wrestled a man with him until the breaking of the day. And he saw that he prevailed not against him, and he touched the breadth of his thigh; and the breadth of Jacob's thigh grew stiff while he was wrestling with him. And he said to him, Let me go, for the day breaketh. And he said, I will not let thee go, except thou bless me. And he said unto him, What is thy name? And he said, Jacob. And he said to him, Thy name shall be called no more Jacob, but Israel shall be thy name: for thou hast prevailed with God, and art powerful with men. And Jacob asked him, and said, Tell me thy name. And he said, Wherefore is it that thou dost ask after my name? And he blessed him there. And Jacob called the name of the place Vision of God: for I have seen God face to face, and my life is preserved. And the sun rose, when the vision of God passed by." And that he also prophesied by inspiration, is evident from this passage: "And Jacob called unto his sons, and said, Gather yourselves together, that I may tell you what shall befall you in the last days. Gather yourselves together, and hear, ye sons of Jacob; and hearken unto Israel your father. Reuben, my first-born, my might, and the beginning of my children, hard to be born, hard and stubborn. Thou wert wanton, boil not over like water; because thou wentest up to thy father's bed; then defiledst thou the couch to which thou wentest up." And so with the rest: it was by inspiration that the prophetic blessings were pronounced. We need not wonder, then, that Daniel sometimes prophesied by inspiration, as when he rebuked the elders sometimes, as you say, by dreams and visions, and at other times by an angel appearing unto him.

11. Your other objections are stated, as it appears to me, somewhat irreverently, and without the becoming spirit of piety. I cannot do better than quote your very words: "Then, after crying out in this extraordinary fashion, he detects them in a way no less incredible, which not even Philistion the play-writer would have resorted to. For, not satisfied with rebuking them through the Spirit, he placed them apart, and asked them severally where they saw her committing adultery; and when the one said, 'Under a holm-tree' (*prinos*) he answered that the angel would saw him asunder (*prisein*); and in a similar fashion threatened the other, who said, 'Under a mastich-tree' (*schinos*), with being rent asunder."

You might as reasonably compare to Philistion the play-writer, a story somewhat like this one, which is found in the third book of Kings, which you yourself will admit to be well written. Here is what we read in Kings:—

"Then there appeared two women that were harlots before the king, and stood before him. And the one woman said, To me, my lord, I and

264

this woman dwell in one house; and we were delivered in the house. And it came to pass, the third day after that I was delivered, that this woman was delivered also: and we were together; there is no one in our house except us two. And this woman's child died in the night; because she overlaid it. And she arose at midnight, and took my son from my arms. And thine handmaid slept. And she laid it in her bosom, and laid her dead child in my bosom. And I arose in the morning to give my child suck, and he was dead; but when I had considered it in the morning, behold, it was not my son which I did bear. And the other woman said, Nay; the dead is thy son, but the living is my son. And the other said, No; the living is my son, but the dead is thy son. Thus they spake before the king. Then said the king, Thou sayest, This is my son that liveth, and thy son is the dead: and thou sayest, Nay; but thy son is the dead, and my son is the living. And the king said, Bring me a sword. And they brought a sword before the king. And the king said, Divide the living child in two, and give half to the one, and half to the other. Then spake the woman whose the living child was unto the king (for her bowels yearned after her son), and she said, To me, my lord, give her the living child, and in no wise slay it. But the other said, Let it be neither mine nor thine, but divide it. Then the king answered and said, Give the child to her which said, Give her the living child, and in no wise slay it: for she is the mother of it. And all Israel heard of the judgment which the king had judged; and they feared the face of the king: for they saw that the wisdom of God was in him to do judgment."

For if we were at liberty to speak in this scoffing way of the Scriptures in use in the Churches, we should rather compare this story of the two harlots to the play of Philistion than that of the chaste Susanna. And just as the people would not have been persuaded if Solomon had merely said, "Give this one the living child, for she is the mother of it;" so Daniel's attack on the elders would not have been sufficient had there not been added the condemnation from their own mouth, when both said that they had seen her lying with the young man under a tree, but did not agree as to what kind of tree it was. And since you have asserted, as if you knew for certain, that Daniel in this matter judged by inspiration (which may or may not have been the case), I would have you notice that there seem to me to be some analogies in the story of Daniel to the judgment of Solomon, concerning whom the Scripture testifies that the people saw that the wisdom of God was in him to do judgment. This might be said also of Daniel, for it was because wisdom was in him to do judgment that the elders were judged in the manner described.

12. I had nearly forgotten an additional remark I have to make about

the *prino-prisein* and *schino-schisein* difficulty; that is, that in our Scriptures there are many etymological fancies, so to call them, which in the Hebrew are perfectly suitable, but not in the Greek. It need not surprise us, then, if the translators of the History of Susanna contrived it so that they found out some Greek words, derived from the same root, which either corresponded exactly to the Hebrew form (though this I hardly think possible), or presented some analogy to it. Here is an instance of this in our Scripture. When the woman was made by God from the rib of the man, Adam says, "She shall be called woman, because she was taken out of her husband." Now the Jews say that the woman was called "*Essa*," and that "taken" is a translation of this word as is evident from "*chos isouoth essa*," which means, "I have taken the cup of salvation;" and that "*is*" means "man," as we see from "*Hesre ais*," which is, "Blessed is the man." According to the Jews, then, "*is*" is "man," and "*essa*," "woman," because she was taken out of her husband (*is*). It need not then surprise us if some interpreters of the Hebrew "Susanna," which had been concealed among them at a very remote date, and had been preserved only by the more learned and honest, should have either given the Hebrew word for word, or hit upon some analogy to the Hebrew forms, that the Greeks might be able to follow them. For in many other passages we can find traces of this kind of contrivance on the part of the translators, which I noticed when I was collating the various editions.

13. You raise another objection, which I give in your own words: "Moreover, how is it that they, who were captives among the Chaldeans, lost and won at play, thrown out unburied on the streets, as was prophesied of the former captivity, their sons torn from them to be eunuchs, and their daughters to be concubines, as had been prophesied; how is it that such could pass sentence of death, and that on the wife of their king Joakim, whom the king of the Babylonians had made partner of his throne? Then, if it was not this Joakim, but some other from the common people, whence had a captive such a mansion and spacious garden?"

Where you get your "lost and won at play, and thrown out unburied on the streets," I know not, unless it is from Tobias; and Tobias (as also Judith), we ought to notice, the Jews do not use. They are not even found in the Hebrew Apocrypha, as I learned from the Jews themselves. However, since the Churches use Tobias, you must know that even in the captivity some of the captives were rich and well to do. Tobias himself says, "Because I remembered God with all my heart; and the Most High gave me grace and beauty in the eyes of Nemessarus, and I was his purveyor; and I went into Media, and left in trust with Gabael, the brother of Gabrias, at Ragi, a city of Media, ten talents of silver." And he adds, as if he were a rich man, "In the days of Nemessarus I gave many alms to my brethren. I gave my bread to the hungry, and my clothes to the naked: and if I saw any of my nation dead, and cast outside the walls of Nineve, I buried him; and if king Senachereim had slain any when he came fleeing from Judea, I buried them privily (for in his wrath he killed many)." Think whether this great catalogue of Tobias's good deeds does not betoken great wealth and much property, especially when he adds, "Understanding that I was sought for to be put to death, I withdrew myself for fear, and all my goods were forcibly taken away."

And another captive, Dachiacharus, the son of Ananiel, the brother of Tobias, was set over all the exchequer of the kingdom of king Acherdon; and we read, "Now Achiacharus was cup-bearer and keeper of the signet, and steward and overseer of the accounts."

Mardochaios, too, frequented the court of the king, and had such boldness before him, that he was inscribed among the benefactors of Artaxerxes.

Again we read in Esdras, that Neemias, a cup-bearer and eunuch of the king, of Hebrew race, made a request about the rebuilding of the temple, and obtained it; so that it was granted to him, with many more, to return and build the temple again. Why then should we wonder that one Joakim had garden, and house, and property, whether these were very expensive or only moderate, for this is not clearly told us in the writing?

14. But you say, "How could they who were in captivity pass sentence of death?" asserting, I know not on what grounds, that Susanna was the wife of a king, because of the name Joakim. The answer is, that it is no uncommon thing, when great nations become subject, that the king should allow the captives to use their own laws and courts of justice. Now, for instance, that the Romans rule, and the Jews pay the half-shekel to them, how great power by the concession of Caesar the ethnarch has; so that we, who have had experience of it, know that he differs in little from a true king! Private trials are held according to the law, and some are condemned to death. And though there is not full licence for this, still it is not done without the knowledge of the ruler, as we learned and were convinced of when we spent much time in the country of that people. And yet the Romans only take account of two tribes, while at that time besides Judah there were the ten tribes of Israel. Probably the Assyrians contented themselves with holding them in subjection, and conceded to them their own judicial processes.

15. I find in your letter yet another objection in these words: "And add, that among all the many prophets who had been before, there is no one who has quoted from another word for word. For they had no need to go a-begging for words, since their own were true. But this one, in rebuking one of these men, quotes the words of the Lord, 'The innocent and righteous shalt thou not slay.'" I cannot understand how, with all your exercise in investigating and meditating on the Scriptures, you have not noticed that the prophets continually quote each other almost word for word. For who of all believers does not know the words in Esaias? "And in the last days the mountain of the LORD shall be manifest, and the house of the LORD on the top of the mountains, and it shall be exalted above the hills; and all nations shall come unto it. And many people shall go and say, Come ye, and let us go up to the mountain of the LORD, unto the house of the God of Jacob; and He will teach us His way, and we will walk in it: for out of Zion shall go forth a law, and a word of the LORD from Jerusalem. And He shall judge among the nations, and shall rebuke many people; and they shall beat their swords into ploughshares, and their spears into pruning-hooks: nation shall not lift up sword against nation; neither shall they learn war any more."

But in Micah we find a parallel passage, which is almost word for word: "And in the last days the mountain of the LORD shall be manifest, established on the top of the mountains, and it shall be exalted above the hills; and people shall hasten unto it. And many nations shall come, and say, Come, let us go up to the mountain of the LORD, to the house of the God of Jacob; and they will teach us His way, and we will walk in His paths: for a law shall go forth from Zion, and a word of the LORD from Jerusalem. And He shall judge among many people, and rebuke strong nations; and they shall beat their swords into ploughshares, and their spears into pruning-hooks: nation shall not lift up a sword against nation, neither shall they learn war any more."

Again, in First Chronicles, the psalm which is put in the hands of Asaph and his brethren to praise the Lord, beginning, "Give thanks unto the LORD, call upon His name," is in the beginning almost identical with Psalm cv., down to "and do my prophets no harm;" and after that it is the same as Psalm xcvi., from the beginning of that psalm, which is something like this, "Praise the Lord all the earth," down to "For He cometh to judge the earth." (It would have taken up too much time to quote more fully; so I have given these short references, which are sufficient for the matter before us.) And you will find the law about not bearing a burden on the Sabbath-day in Jeremias, as well as in

Moses. And the rules about the passover, and the rules for the priests, are not only in Moses, but also at the end of Ezekiel. I would have quoted these, and many more, had I not found that from the shortness of my stay in Nicomedia my time for writing you was already too much restricted.

Your last objection is, that the style is different. This I cannot see.

This, then, is my defence. I might, especially after all these accusations, speak in praise of this history of Susanna, dwelling on it word by word, and expounding the exquisite nature of the thoughts. Such an encomium, perhaps, some of the learned and able students of divine things may at some other time compose. This, however, is my answer to your strokes, as you call them. Would that I could instruct you! But I do not now arrogate that to myself. My lord and dear brother Ambrosius, who has written this at my dictation, and has, in looking over it, corrected as he pleased, salutes you. His faithful spouse, Marcella, and her children, also salute you. Also Anicetus. Do you salute our dear father Apollinarius, and all our friends.

A LETTER FROM ORIGEN TO GREGORY

1. GREETING in God, my most excellent sir, and venerable son Gregory, from Origen. A natural readiness of comprehension, as you well know, may, if practice be added, contribute somewhat to the contingent end, if I may so call it, of that which any one wishes to practise. Thus, your natural good parts might make of you a finished Roman lawyer or a Greek philosopher, so to speak, of one of the schools in high reputation. But I am anxious that you should devote all the strength of your natural good parts to Christianity for your end; and in order to this, I wish to ask you to extract from the philosophy of the Greeks what may serve as a course of study or a preparation for Christianity, and from geometry and astronomy what will serve to explain the sacred Scriptures, in order that all that the sons of the philosophers are wont to say about geometry and music, grammar, rhetoric, and astronomy, as fellow-helpers to philosophy, we may say about philosophy itself, in relation to Christianity.

2. Perhaps something of this kind is shadowed forth in what is written in Exodus from the mouth of God, that the children of Israel were commanded to ask from their neighbours, and those who dwelt with them, vessels of silver and gold, and raiment, in order that, by spoiling the Egyptians, they might have material for the preparation of the things which pertained to the service of God. For from the things which the children of Israel took from the Egyptians the vessels in the holy of holies were made,—the ark with its lid, and the Cherubim, and the mercy-seat, and the golden coffer, where was the manna, the angels' bread. These things were probably made from the best of the Egyptian gold. An inferior kind would be used for the solid golden candlestick near the inner veil, and its branches, and the golden table on which were the pieces of shewbread, and the golden censer between them. And if there was a third and fourth quality of gold, from it would be made the holy vessels; and the other things would be made of Egyptian silver. For when the children of Israel dwelt in Egypt, they gained this from their dwelling there, that they had no lack of such precious material for the utensils of the service of God. And of the Egyptian raiment were probably made all those things which, as the Scripture mentions, needed sewed and embroidered work, sewed with the wisdom of God, the one to the other, that the veils might be made, and the inner and the outer courts. And why should I go on, in this untimely

270

digression, to set forth how useful to the children of Israel were the things brought from Egypt, which the Egyptians had not put to a proper use, but which the Hebrews, guided by the wisdom of God, used for God's service? Now the sacred Scripture is wont to represent as an evil the going down from the land of the children of Israel into Egypt, indicating that certain persons get harm from sojourning among the Egyptians, that is to say, from meddling with the knowledge of this world, after they have subscribed to the law of God, and the Israelitish service of Him. Ader at least, the Idumaean; so long as he was in the land of Israel, and had not tasted the bread of the Egyptians, made no idols. It was when he fled from the wise Solomon, and went down into Egypt, as it were flying from the wisdom of God, and was made a kinsman of Pharaoh by marrying his wife's sister, and begetting a child, who was brought up with the children of Pharaoh, that he did this. Wherefore, although he did return to the land of Israel, he returned only to divide the people of God, and to make them say to the golden calf, "These be thy gods, O Israel, which brought thee up from the land of Egypt." And I may tell you from my experience, that not many take from Egypt only the useful, and go away and use it for the service of God; while Ader the Idumaean has many brethren. These are they who, from their Greek studies, produce heretical notions, and set them up, like the golden calf, in Bethel, which signifies "God's house." In these words also there seems to me an indication that they have set up their own imaginations in the Scriptures, where the word of God dwells, which is called in a figure Bethel. The other figure, the word says, was set up in Dan. Now the borders of Dan are the most extreme, and nearest the borders of the Gentiles, as is clear from what is written in Joshua, the son of Nun. Now some of the devices of these brethren of Ader, as we call them, are also very near the borders of the Gentiles.

3. Do you then, my son, diligently apply yourself to the reading of the sacred Scriptures. Apply yourself, I say. For we who read the things of God need much application, lest we should say or think anything too rashly about them. And applying yourself thus to the study of the things of God, with faithful prejudgments such as are well pleasing to God, knock at its locked door, and it will be opened to you by the porter, of whom Jesus says, "To him the porter opens." And applying yourself thus to the divine study, seek aright, and with unwavering trust in God, the meaning of the holy Scriptures, which so many have missed. Be not satisfied with knocking and seeking; for prayer is of all things indispensable to the knowledge of the things of God. For to this the Saviour exhorted, and said not only, "Knock, and it shall be opened to you; and seek, and ye shall find," but also, "Ask, and it shall be given

unto you." My fatherly love to you has made me thus bold; but whether my boldness be good, God will know, and His Christ, and all partakers of the Spirit of God and the Spirit of Christ. May you also be a partaker, and be ever increasing your inheritance, that you may say not only, "We are become partakers of Christ," but also partakers of God.

AGAINST CELSUS

BOOK I

PREFACE

1. WHEN false witnesses testified against our Lord and Saviour Jesus Christ, He remained silent; and when unfounded charges were brought against Him, He returned no answer, believing that His whole life and conduct among the Jews were a better refutation than any answer to the false testimony, or than any formal defence against the accusations. And I know not, my pious Ambrosius, why you wished me to write a reply to the false charges brought by Celsus against the Christians, and to his accusations directed against the faith of the Churches in his treatise; as if the facts themselves did not furnish a manifest refutation, and the doctrine a better answer than any writing, seeing it both disposes of the false statements, and does not leave to the accusations any credibility or validity. Now, with respect to our Lord's silence when false witness was borne against Him, it is sufficient at present to quote the words of Matthew, for the testimony of Mark is to the same effect. And the words of Matthew are as follow: "And the high priest and the council sought false witness against Jesus to put Him to death, but found none, although many false witnesses came forward. At last two false witnesses came and said, This fellow said, I am able to destroy the temple of God, and after three days to build it up. And the high priest arose, and said to Him, Answerest thou nothing to what these witness against thee? But Jesus held His peace." And that He returned no answer when falsely accused, the following is the statement: "And Jesus stood before the governor; and he asked Him, saying, Art Thou the King of the Jews? And Jesus said to him, Thou sayest. And when He was accused of the chief priests and elders, He answered nothing. Then said Pilate unto Him, Hearest thou not how many things they witness against Thee? And He answered him to never a word, insomuch that the governor marvelled greatly."

2. It was, indeed, matter of surprise to men even of ordinary intelligence, that one who was accused and assailed by false testimony, but who was able to defend Himself, and to show that He was guilty of none of the charges (alleged), and who might have enumerated the praiseworthy deeds of His own life, and His miracles wrought by divine power, so as to give the judge an opportunity of delivering a more honourable judgment regarding Him, should not have done this, but should have disdained such a procedure, and in the nobleness of His nature have contemned His accusers. That the judge would, without

any hesitation, have set Him at liberty if He had offered a defence, is clear from what is related of him when he said, "Which of the two do ye wish that I should release unto you, Barabbas or Jesus, who is called Christ?" and from what the Scripture adds, "For he knew that for envy they had delivered Him." Jesus, however, is at all times assailed by false witnesses, and, while wickedness remains in the world, is ever exposed to accusation. And yet even now He continues silent before these things, and makes no audible answer, but places His defence in the lives of His genuine disciples, which are a pre-eminent testimony, and one that rises superior to all false witness, and refutes and overthrows all unfounded accusations and charges.

3. I venture, then, to say that this "apology" which you require me to compose will somewhat weaken that defence (of Christianity) which rests on facts, and that power of Jesus which is manifest to those who are not altogether devoid of perception. Notwithstanding, that we may not have the appearance of being reluctant to undertake the task which you have enjoined, we have endeavoured, to the best of our ability, to suggest, by way of answer to each of the statements advanced by Celsus, what seemed to us adapted to refute them, although his arguments have no power to shake the faith of any (true) believer. And forbid, indeed, that any one should be found who, after having been a partaker in such a love of God as was (displayed) in Christ Jesus, could be shaken in his purpose by the arguments of Celsus, or of any such as he. For Paul, when enumerating the innumerable causes which generally separate men from the love of Christ and from the love of God in Christ Jesus (to all of which, the love that was in himself rose superior), did not set down argument among the grounds of separation. For observe that he says, firstly: "Who shall separate us from the love of Christ? Shall tribulation, or distress, or persecution, or famine, or nakedness, or peril, or sword? (as it is written, For Thy sake we are killed all the day long; we are accounted as sheep for the slaughter.) Nay, in all these things we are more than conquerors through Him that loved us." And secondly, when laying down another series of causes which naturally tend to separate those who are not firmly grounded in their religion, he says: "For I am persuaded that neither death, nor life, nor angels, nor principalities, nor powers, nor things present, nor things to come, nor height, nor depth, nor any other creature, shall be able to separate us from the love of God, which is in Christ Jesus our Lord."

4. Now, truly, it is proper that *we* should feel elated because afflictions, or those other causes enumerated by Paul, do not separate us (from Christ); but not that Paul and the other apostles, and any other resembling them, (should entertain that feeling), because they were far

exalted above such things when they said, "In all these things we are *more* than conquerors through Him that loved us," which is a stronger statement than that they are simply "conquerors." But if it be proper for apostles to entertain a feeling of elation in not being separated from the love of God that is in Christ Jesus our Lord, that feeling will be entertained by them, because neither death, nor life, nor angels, nor principalities, nor any of the things that follow, can separate them from the love of God which is in Christ Jesus our Lord. And therefore I do not congratulate that believer in Christ whose faith can be shaken by Celsus—who no longer shares the common life of men, but has long since departed—or by any apparent plausibility of argument. For I do not know in what rank to place him who has need of arguments written in books in answer to the charges of Celsus against the Christians, in order to prevent him from being shaken in his faith, and confirm him in it. But nevertheless, since in the multitude of those who are considered believers some such persons might be found as would have their faith shaken and overthrown by the writings of Celsus, but who might be preserved by a reply to them of such a nature as to refute his statements and to exhibit the truth, we have deemed it right to yield to your injunction, and to furnish an answer to the treatise which you sent us, but which I do not think that any one, although only a short way advanced in philosophy, will allow to be a "True Discourse," as Celsus has entitled it.

5. Paul, indeed, observing that there are in Greek philosophy certain things not to be lightly esteemed, which are plausible in the eyes of the many, but which represent falsehood as truth, says with regard to such: "Beware lest any man spoil you through philosophy and vain deceit, after the tradition of men, after the rudiments of the world, and not after Christ." And seeing that there was a kind of greatness manifest in the words of the world's wisdom, he said that the words of the philosophers were "according to the rudiments of the world." No man of sense, however, would say that those of Celsus were "according to the rudiments of the world." Now those words, which contained some element of deceitfulness, the apostle named "vain deceit," probably by way of distinction from a deceit that was not "vain;" and the prophet Jeremiah observing this, ventured to say to God, "O LORD, Thou hast deceived me, and I was deceived; Thou art stronger than I, and hast prevailed." But in the language of Celsus there seems to me to be no deceitfulness at all, not even that which is "vain;" such deceitfulness, viz., as is found in the language of those who have founded philosophical sects, and who have been endowed with no ordinary talent for such pursuits. And as no one would say that any ordinary

error in geometrical demonstrations was intended to deceive, or would describe it for the sake of exercise in such matters; so those opinions which are to be styled "vain deceit," and the "tradition of men," and "according to the rudiments of the world," must have some resemblance to the views of those who have been the founders of philosophical sects, (if such titles are to be appropriately applied to them).

6. After proceeding with this work as far as the place where Celsus introduces the Jew disputing with Jesus, I resolved to prefix this preface to the beginning (of the treatise), in order that the reader of our reply to Celsus might fall in with it first, and see that this book has been composed not for those who are thorough believers, but for such as are either wholly unacquainted with the Christian faith, or for those who, as the apostle terms them, are "weak in the faith;" regarding whom he says, "Him that is weak in the faith receive ye." And this preface must be my apology for beginning my answer to Celsus on one plan, and carrying it on on another. For my first intention was to indicate his principal objections, and then briefly the answers that were returned to them, and subsequently to make a systematic treatise of the whole discourse. But afterwards, circumstances themselves suggested to me that I should be economical of my time, and that, satisfied with what I had already stated at the commencement, I should in the following part grapple closely, to the best of my ability, with the charges of Celsus. I have therefore to ask indulgence for those portions which follow the preface towards the beginning of the book. And if you are not impressed by the powerful arguments which succeed, then, asking similar indulgence also with respect to them, I refer you, if you still desire an argumentative solution of the objections of Celsus, to those men who are wiser than myself, and who are able by words and treatises to overthrow the charges which he brings against us. But better is the man who, although meeting with the work of Celsus, needs no answer to it at all, but who despises all its contents, since they are contemned, and with good reason, by every believer in Christ, through the Spirit that is in him.

CHAPTER I

The first point which Celsus brings forward, in his desire to throw discredit upon Christianity, is, that the Christians entered into secret associations with each other contrary to law, saying, that "of associations some are public, and that these are in accordance with the laws; others, again, secret, and maintained in violation of the laws." And his wish is to bring into disrepute what are termed the "love-feasts" of the Christians, as if they had their origin in the common danger, and were more binding than any oaths. Since, then, he babbles about the public law, alleging that the associations of the Christians are in violation of it, we have to reply, that if a man were placed among Scythians, whose laws were unholy, and having no opportunity of escape, were compelled to live among them, such an one would with good reason, for the sake of the law of truth, which the Scythians would regard as wickedness, enter into associations contrary to their laws, with those like-minded with himself; so, if truth is to decide, the laws of the heathens which relate to images, and an atheistical polytheism, are "Scythian" laws, or more impious even than these, if there be any such. It is not irrational, then, to form associations in opposition to existing laws, if done for the sake of the truth. For as those persons would do well who should enter into a secret association in order to put to death a tyrant who had seized upon the liberties of a state, so Christians also, when tyrannized over by him who is called the devil, and by falsehood, form leagues contrary to the laws of the devil, against his power, and for the safety of those others whom they may succeed in persuading to revolt from a government which is, as it were, "Scythian," and despotic.

CHAPTER II

Celsus next proceeds to say, that the system of doctrine, viz., Judaism, upon which Christianity depends, was barbarous in its origin. And with an appearance of fairness, he does not reproach Christianity because of its origin among barbarians, but gives the latter credit for their ability in discovering (such) doctrines. To this, however, he adds the statement, that the Greeks are more skilful than any others in judging, establishing, and reducing to practice the discoveries of barbarous nations. Now this is our answer to his allegations, and our defence of the truths contained in Christianity, that if any one were to come from the study of Grecian opinions and usages to the Gospel, he would not only decide that its doctrines were true, but would by practice establish their truth, and supply whatever seemed wanting, from a Grecian point of view, to their demonstration, and thus confirm the truth of Christianity. We have to say, moreover, that the Gospel has a demonstration of its own, more divine than any established by Grecian dialectics. And this diviner method is called by the apostle the "manifestation of the Spirit and of power:" of "the Spirit," on account of the prophecies, which are sufficient to produce faith in any one who reads them, especially in those things which relate to Christ; and of "power," because of the signs and wonders which we must believe to have been performed, both on many other grounds, and on this, that traces of them are still preserved among those who regulate their lives by the precepts of the Gospel.

CHAPTER III

After this, Celsus proceeding to speak of the Christians teaching and practising their favourite doctrines in secret, and saying that they do this to some purpose, seeing they escape the penalty of death which is imminent, he compares their dangers with those which were encountered by such men as Socrates for the sake of philosophy; and here he might have mentioned Pythagoras as well, and other philosophers. But our answer to this is, that in the case of Socrates the Athenians immediately afterwards repented; and no feeling of bitterness remained in their minds regarding him, as also happened in the history of Pythagoras. The followers of the latter, indeed, for a considerable time established their schools in that part of Italy called Magna Graecia; but in the case of the Christians, the Roman Senate, and the princes of the time, and the soldiery, and the people, and the relatives of those who had become converts to the faith, made war upon their doctrine, and would have prevented (its progress), overcoming it by a confederacy of so powerful a nature, had it not, by the help of God, escaped the danger, and risen above it, so as (finally) to defeat the whole world in its conspiracy against it.

CHAPTER IV

Let us notice also how he thinks to cast discredit upon our system of morals, alleging that it is only common to us with other philosophers, and no venerable or new branch of instruction. In reply to which we have to say, that unless all men had naturally impressed upon their minds sound ideas of morality, the doctrine of the punishment of sinners would have been excluded by those who bring upon themselves the righteous judgments of God. It is not therefore matter of surprise that the same God should have sown in the hearts of all men those truths which He taught by the prophets and the Saviour, in order that at the divine judgment every man may be without excuse, having the "requirements of the law written upon his heart,"— a truth obscurely alluded to by the Bible in what the Greeks regard as a myth, where it represents God as having with His own finger written down the commandments, and given them to Moses, and which the wickedness of the worshippers of the calf made him break in pieces, as if the flood of wickedness, so to speak, had swept them away. But Moses having again hewn tables of stone, God wrote the commandments a second time, and gave them to him; the prophetic word preparing the soul, as it were, after the first transgression, for the writing of God a second time.

CHAPTER V

Treating of the regulations respecting idolatry as being peculiar to Christianity, Celsus establishes their correctness, saying that the Christians do not consider those to be gods that are made with hands, on the ground that it is not in conformity with right reason (to suppose) that images, fashioned by the most worthless and depraved of workmen, and in many instances also provided by wicked men, can be (regarded as) gods. In what follows, however, wishing to show that this is a common opinion, and one not first discovered by Christianity, he quotes a saying of Heraclitus to this effect: "That those who draw near to lifeless images, as if they were gods, act in a similar manner to those who would enter into conversation with houses." Respecting this, then, we have to say, that ideas were implanted in the minds of men like the principles of morality, from which not only Heraclitus, but any other Greek or barbarian, might by reflection have deduced the same conclusion; for he states that the Persians also were of the same opinion, quoting Herodotus as his authority. We also can add to these Zeno of Citium, who in his *Polity*, says: "And there will be no need to build temples, for nothing ought to be regarded as sacred, or of much value, or holy, which is the work of builders and of mean men." It is evident, then, with respect to this opinion (as well as others), that there has been engraven upon the hearts of men by the finger of God a sense of the duty that is required.

CHAPTER VI

After this, through the influence of some motive which is unknown to me, Celsus asserts that it is by the names of certain demons, and by the use of incantations, that the Christians appear to be possessed of (miraculous) power; hinting, I suppose, at the practices of those who expel evil spirits by incantations. And here he manifestly appears to malign the Gospel. For it is not by incantations that Christians seem to prevail (over evil spirits), but by the name of Jesus, accompanied by the announcement of the narratives which relate to Him; for the repetition of these has frequently been the means of driving demons out of men, especially when those who repeated them did so in a sound and genuinely believing spirit. Such power, indeed, does the name of Jesus possess over evil spirits, that there have been instances where it was effectual, when it was pronounced even by bad men, which Jesus Himself taught (would be the case), when He said: "Many shall say to Me in that day, In Thy name we have cast out devils, and done many wonderful works." Whether Celsus omitted this from intentional malignity, or from ignorance, I do not know. And he next proceeds to bring a charge against the Saviour Himself, alleging that it was by means of sorcery that He was able to accomplish the wonders which He performed; and that foreseeing that others would attain the same knowledge, and do the same things, making a boast of doing them by help of the power of God, He excludes such from His kingdom. And his accusation is, that if they are justly excluded, while He Himself is guilty of the same practices, He is a wicked man; but if He is not guilty of wickedness in doing such things, neither are they who do the same as He. But even if it be impossible to show by what power Jesus wrought these miracles, it is clear that Christians employ no spells or incantations, but the simple name of Jesus, and certain other words in which they repose faith, according to the holy Scriptures.

CHAPTER VII

Moreover, since he frequently calls the Christian doctrine a secret system (of belief), we must confute him on this point also, since almost the entire world is better acquainted with what Christians preach than with the favourite opinions of philosophers. For who is ignorant of the statement that Jesus was born of a virgin, and that He was crucified, and that His resurrection is an article of faith among many, and that a general judgment is announced to come, in which the wicked are to be punished according to their deserts, and the righteous to be duly rewarded? And yet the mystery of the resurrection, not being understood, is made a subject of ridicule among unbelievers. In these circumstances, to speak of the Christian doctrine as a *secret* system, is altogether absurd. But that there should be certain doctrines, not made known to the multitude, which are (revealed) after the exoteric ones have been taught, is not a peculiarity of Christianity alone, but also of philosophic systems, in which certain truths are exoteric and others esoteric. Some of the hearers of Pythagoras were content with his *ipse dixit*; while others were taught in secret those doctrines which were not deemed fit to be communicated to profane and insufficiently prepared ears. Moreover, all the mysteries that are celebrated everywhere throughout Greece and barbarous countries, although held in secret, have no discredit thrown upon them, so that it is in vain that he endeavours to calumniate the secret doctrines of Christianity, seeing he does not correctly understand its nature.

CHAPTER VIII

It is with a certain eloquence, indeed, that he appears to advocate the cause of those who bear witness to the truth of Christianity by their death, in the following words: "And I do not maintain that if a man, who has adopted a system of good doctrine, is to incur danger from men on that account, he should either apostatize, or feign apostasy, or openly deny his opinions." And he condemns those who, while holding the Christian views, either pretend that they do not, or deny them, saying that "he who holds a certain opinion ought not to feign recantation, or publicly disown it." And here Celsus must be convicted of self-contradiction. For from other treatises of his it is ascertained that he was an Epicurean; but here, because he thought that he could assail Christianity with better effect by not professing the opinions of Epicurus, he pretends that there is a something better in man than the earthly part of his nature, which is akin to God, and says that "they in whom this element, viz., the soul, is in a healthy condition, are ever seeking after their kindred nature, meaning God, and are ever desiring to hear something about Him, and to call it to remembrance." Observe now the insincerity of his character! Having said a little before, that "the man who had embraced a system of good doctrine ought not, even if exposed to danger on that account from men, to disavow it, or pretend that he had done so, nor yet openly disown it," he now involves himself in all manner of contradictions. For he knew that if he acknowledged himself an Epicurean, he would not obtain any credit when accusing those who, in any degree, introduce the doctrine of Providence, and who place a God over the world. And we have heard that there were two individuals of the name of Celsus, both of whom were Epicureans; the earlier of the two having lived in the time of Nero, but this one in that of Adrian, and later.

CHAPTER IX

He next proceeds to recommend, that in adopting opinions we should follow reason and a rational guide, since he who assents to opinions without following this course is very liable to be deceived.

And he compares inconsiderate believers to Metragyrtae, and soothsayers, and Mithrae, and Sabbadians, and to anything else that one may fall in with, and to the phantoms of Hecate, or any other demon or demons. For as amongst such persons are frequently to be found wicked men, who, taking advantage of the ignorance of those who are easily deceived, lead them away whither they will, so also, he says, is the case among Christians. And he asserts that certain persons who do not wish either to give or receive a reason for their belief, keep repeating, "Do not examine, but believe!" and, "Your faith will save you!" And he alleges that such also say, "The wisdom of this life is bad, but that foolishness is a good thing!" To which we have to answer, that if it were possible for all to leave the business of life, and devote themselves to philosophy, no other method ought to be adopted by any one, but this alone. For in the Christian system also it will be found that there is, not to speak at all arrogantly, at least as much of investigation into articles of belief, and of explanation of dark sayings, occurring in the prophetical writings, and of the parables in the Gospels, and of countless other things, which either were narrated or enacted with a symbolical signification, (as is the case with other systems). But since the course alluded to is impossible, partly on account of the necessities of life, partly on account of the weakness of men, as only a very few individuals devote themselves earnestly to study, what better method could be devised with a view of assisting the multitude, than that which was delivered by Jesus to the heathen? And let us inquire, with respect to the great multitude of believers, who have washed away the mire of wickedness in which they formerly wallowed, whether it were better for them to believe without a reason, and (so) to have become reformed and improved in their habits, through the belief that men are chastised for sins, and honoured for good works or not to have allowed themselves to be converted on the strength of mere faith, but (to have waited) until they could give themselves to a thorough examination of the (necessary) reasons. For it is manifest that, (on such a plan), all men, with very few exceptions, would not obtain this (amelioration of conduct) which they have obtained through a simple faith, but would continue to remain in the practice of a wicked life. Now, whatever other evidence can be furnished of the fact, that it was not without divine intervention that the philanthropic scheme of Christianity was introduced among men, this also must be added. For a pious man will not believe that even a physician of the body, who restores the sick to better health, could take up his abode in any city or country without divine permission, since no good happens to men without the help of God. And if he who has cured the *bodies* of many, or restored them to

284

better health, does not effect his cures without the help of God, how much more He who has healed the *souls* of many, and has turned them (to virtue), and improved their nature, and attached them to God who is over all things, and taught them to refer every action to His good pleasure, and to shun all that is displeasing to Him, even to the least of their words or deeds, or even of the thoughts of their hearts?

CHAPTER X

In the next place, since our opponents keep repeating those statements about faith, we must say that, considering it as a useful thing for the multitude, we admit that we teach those men to believe without reasons, who are unable to abandon all other employments, and give themselves to an examination of arguments; and our opponents, although they do not acknowledge it, yet practically do the same. For who is there that, on betaking himself to the study of philosophy, and throwing himself into the ranks of some sect, either by chance, or because he is provided with a teacher of that school, adopts such a course for any other reason, except that he *believes* his particular sect to be superior to any other? For, not waiting to hear the arguments of all the other philosophers, and of all the different sects, and the reasons for condemning one system and for supporting another, he in this way elects to become a Stoic, e.g., or a Platonist, or a Peripatetic, or an Epicurean, or a follower of some other school, and is thus borne, although they will not admit it, by a kind of irrational impulse to the practice, say of Stoicism, to the disregard of the others; despising either Platonism, as being marked by greater humility than the others; or Peripateticism, as more human, and as admitting with more fairness than other systems the blessings of human life. And some also, alarmed at first sight about the doctrine of providence, from seeing what happens in the world to the vicious and to the virtuous, have rashly concluded that there is no divine providence at all, and have adopted the views of Epicurus and Celsus.

CHAPTER XI

Since, then, as reason teaches, we must repose faith in some one of those who have been the introducers of sects among the Greeks or Barbarians, why should we not rather believe in God who is over all things, and in Him who teaches that worship is due to God alone, and that other things are to be passed by, either as non-existent, or as existing indeed, and worthy of honour, but not of worship and reverence? And respecting these things, he who not only believes, but who contemplates things with the eye of reason, will state the demonstrations that occur to him, and which are the result of careful investigation. And why should it not be more reasonable, seeing all human things are dependent upon faith, to believe God rather than them? For who enters on a voyage, or contracts a marriage, or becomes the father of children, or casts seed into the ground, without believing that better things will result from so doing, although the contrary might and sometimes does happen? And yet the belief that better things, even agreeably to their wishes, will follow, makes all men venture upon uncertain enterprises, which may turn out differently from what they expect. And if the hope and belief of a better future be the support of life in every uncertain enterprise, why shall not this faith rather be rationally accepted by him who believes on better grounds than he who sails the sea, or tills the ground, or marries a wife, or engages in any other human pursuit, in the existence of a God who was the Creator of all these things, and in Him who with surpassing wisdom and divine greatness of mind dared to make known this doctrine to men in every part of the world, at the cost of great danger, and of a death considered infamous, which He underwent for the sake of the human race; having also taught those who were persuaded to embrace His doctrine at the first, to proceed, under the peril of every danger, and of ever impending death, to all quarters of the world to ensure the salvation of men?

CHAPTER XII

In the next place, when Celsus says in express words, "If they would answer me, not as if I were asking for information, for I am acquainted with all their opinions, but because I take an equal interest in them all, it would be well. And if they will not, but will keep reiterating, as they generally do, 'Do not investigate,' etc., they must, he continues, "explain to me at least of what nature these things are of which they speak, and whence they are derived," etc. Now, with regard to his statement that he "is acquainted with all our doctrines," we have to say that this is a boastful and daring assertion; for if he had read the prophets in particular, which are full of acknowledged difficulties, and of declarations that are obscure to the multitude, and if he had perused the parables of the Gospels, and the other writings of the law and of the Jewish history, and the utterances of the apostles, and had read them candidly, with a desire to enter into their meaning, he would not have expressed himself with such boldness, nor said that he "was acquainted with all their doctrines." Even we ourselves, who have devoted much study to these writings, would not say that "we were acquainted with everything," for we have a regard for truth. Not one of us will assert, "I know all the doctrines of Epicurus," or will be confident that he knows all those of Plato, in the knowledge of the fact that so many differences of opinion exist among the expositors of these systems. For who is so daring as to say that he knows all the opinions of the Stoics or of the Peripatetics? Unless, indeed, it should be the case that he has heard this boast, "I know them all," from some ignorant and senseless individuals, who do not perceive their own ignorance, and should thus imagine, from having had such persons as his teachers, that he was acquainted with them all. Such an one appears to me to act very much as a person would do who had visited Egypt (where the Egyptian *savans*, learned in their country's literature, are greatly given to philosophizing about those things which are regarded among them as divine, but where the vulgar, hearing certain myths, the reasons of which they do not understand, are greatly elated because of their fancied knowledge), and who should imagine that he is acquainted with the whole circle of Egyptian knowledge, after having been a disciple of the ignorant alone, and without having associated with any of the priests, or having learned the mysteries of the Egyptians from any other source. And what I have said regarding the learned and ignorant among the Egyptians, I might have said also of the Persians; among whom there are mysteries, conducted on rational principles by the learned among them, but understood in a symbolical sense by the more superficial of the multitude. And the same remark applies to the Syrians, and Indians, and to all those who have a literature and a mythology.

CHAPTER XIII

But since Celsus has declared it to be a saying of many Christians, that "the wisdom of this life is a bad thing, but that foolishness is good," we have to answer that he slanders the Gospel, not giving the words as they actually occur in the writings of Paul, where they run as follow: "If any one among you seemeth to be wise in this world, let him become a fool, that he may become wise. For the wisdom of this world is foolishness with God." The apostle, therefore, does not say simply that "wisdom is foolishness with God," but "the wisdom of *this world*." And again, not, "If any one among you seemeth to be wise, let him become a fool universally;" but, "let him become a fool *in this world*, that he may become wise." We term, then, "the wisdom of this world," every false system of philosophy, which, according to the Scriptures, is brought to nought; and we call foolishness good, not without restriction, but when a man becomes foolish as to *this world*. As if we were to say that the Platonist, who believes in the immortality of the soul, and in the doctrine of its metempsychosis, incurs the charge of folly with the Stoics, who discard this opinion; and with the Peripatetics, who babble about the subtleties of Plato; and with the Epicureans, who call it superstition to introduce a providence, and to place a God over all things. Moreover, that it is in agreement with the spirit of Christianity, of much more importance to give our assent to doctrines upon grounds of reason and wisdom than on that of faith merely, and that it was only in certain circumstances that the latter course was desired by Christianity, in order not to leave men altogether without help, is shown by that genuine disciple of Jesus, Paul, when he says: "For after that, in the wisdom of God, the world by wisdom knew not God, it pleased God by the foolishness of preaching to save them that believe." Now by these words it is clearly shown that it is by the wisdom of God that God ought to be known. But as this result did not follow, it pleased God a second time to save them that believe, not by "folly" *universally*, but by such foolishness as depended on preaching. For the preaching of Jesus Christ as crucified is the "foolishness" of preaching, as Paul also perceived, when he said, "But we preach Christ crucified, to the Jews a stumbling-block, and to the Greeks foolishness; but to them who are called, both Jews and Greeks, Christ the power of God, and wisdom of God."

CHAPTER XIV

Celsus, being of opinion that there is to be found among many nations a general relationship of doctrine, enumerates all the nations which gave rise to such and such opinions; but for some reason, unknown to me, he casts a slight upon the Jews, not including them amongst the others, as having either laboured along with them, and arrived at the same conclusions, or as having entertained similar opinions on many subjects. It is proper, therefore, to ask him why he gives credence to the histories of Barbarians and Greeks respecting the antiquity of those nations of whom he speaks, but stamps the histories of this nation alone as false. For if the respective writers related the events which are found in these works in the spirit of truth, why should we distrust the prophets of the Jews alone? And if Moses and the prophets have recorded many things in their history from a desire to favour their own system, why should we not say the same of the historians of other countries? Or, when the Egyptians or their histories speak evil of the Jews, are they to be believed on that point; but the Jews, when saying the same things of the Egyptians, and declaring that they had suffered great injustice at their hands, and that on this account they had been punished by God, are to be charged with falsehood? And this applies not to the Egyptians alone, but to others; for we shall find that there was a connection between the Assyrians and the Jews, and that this is recorded in the ancient histories of the Assyrians. And so also the Jewish historians (I avoid using the word "prophets," that I may not appear to prejudge the case) have related that the Assyrians were enemies of the Jews. Observe at once, then, the arbitrary procedure of this individual, who believes the histories of these nations on the ground of their being learned, and condemns others as being wholly ignorant. For listen to the statement of Celsus: "There is," he says, "an authoritative account from the very beginning, respecting which there is a constant agreement among all the most learned nations, and cities, and men." And yet he will not call the Jews a learned nation in the same way in which he does the Egyptians, and Assyrians, and Indians, and Persians, and Odrysians, and Samothracians, and Eleusinians.

CHAPTER XV

How much more impartial than Celsus is Numenius the Pythagorean, who has given many proofs of being a very eloquent man, and who has carefully tested many opinions, and collected together from many sources what had the appearance of truth; for, in the first book of his treatise *On the Good*, speaking of those nations who have adopted the opinion that God is incorporeal, he enumerates the Jews also among those who hold this view; not showing any reluctance to use even the language of their prophets in his treatise, and to give it a metaphorical signification. It is said, moreover, that Hermippus has recorded in his first book, *On Lawgivers*, that it was from the Jewish people that Pythagoras derived the philosophy which he introduced among the Greeks. And there is extant a work by the historian Hecataeus, treating of the Jews, in which so high a character is bestowed upon that nation for its learning, that Herennius Philo, in his treatise on the Jews, has doubts in the first place, whether it is really the composition of the historian; and says, in the second place, that if really his, it is probable that he was carried away by the plausible nature of the Jewish history, and so yielded his assent to their system.

CHAPTER XVI

I must express my surprise that Celsus should class the Odrysians, and Samothracians, and Eleusinians, and Hyperboreans among the most ancient and learned nations, and should not deem the Jews worthy of a place among such, either for their learning or their antiquity, although there are many treatises in circulation among the Egyptians, and Phoenicians, and Greeks, which testify to their existence as an ancient people, but which I have considered it unnecessary to quote. For any one who chooses may read what Flavius Josephus has recorded in his two books, *On the Antiquity of the Jews*, where he brings together a great collection of writers, who bear witness to the antiquity of the Jewish people; and there exists the *Discourse to the Greeks* of Tatian the younger, in which with very great learning he enumerates those historians who have treated of the antiquity of the Jewish nation and of Moses. It seems, then, to be not from a love of truth, but from a spirit of hatred, that Celsus makes these statements, his object being to asperse the origin of Christianity, which is connected with Judaism. Nay, he styles the Galactophagi of Homer, and the Druids of the Gauls, and the Getae, most learned and ancient tribes, on account of the resemblance between their traditions and those of the Jews, although I know not whether any of their histories survive; but the Hebrews alone, as far as in him lies, he deprives of the honour both of antiquity and learning. And again, when making a list of ancient and learned men who have conferred benefits upon their contemporaries (by their deeds), and upon posterity by their writings, he excluded Moses from the number; while of Linus, to whom Celsus assigns a foremost place in his list, there exists neither laws nor discourses which produced a change for the better among any tribes; whereas a whole nation, dispersed throughout the entire world, obey the laws of Moses. Consider, then, whether it is not from open malevolence that he has expelled Moses from his catalogue of learned men, while asserting that Linus, and Musaeus, and Orpheus, and Pherecydes, and the Persian Zoroaster, and Pythagoras, discussed these topics, and that their opinions were deposited in books, and have thus been preserved down to the present time. And it is intentionally also that he has omitted to take notice of the myth, embellished chiefly by Orpheus, in which the gods are described as affected by human weaknesses and passions.

CHAPTER XVII

In what follows, Celsus, assailing the Mosaic history, finds fault with those who give it a tropical and allegorical signification. And here one might say to this great man, who inscribed upon his own work the title of a *True Discourse*, "Why, good sir, do you make it a boast to have it recorded that the gods should engage in such adventures as are described by your learned poets and philosophers, and be guilty of abominable intrigues, and of engaging in wars against their own fathers, and of cutting off their secret parts, and should dare to commit and to suffer such enormities; while Moses, who gives no such accounts respecting God, nor even regarding the holy angels, and who relates deeds of far less atrocity regarding men (for in his writings no one ever ventured to commit such crimes as Kronos did against Uranus, or Zeus against his father, or that of the father of men and gods, who had intercourse with his own daughter), should be considered as having deceived those who were placed under his laws, and to have led them into error?" And here Celsus seems to me to act somewhat as Thrasymachus the Platonic philosopher did, when he would not allow Socrates to answer regarding justice, as he wished, but said, "Take care not to say that utility is justice, or duty, or anything of that kind." For in like manner Celsus assails (as he thinks) the Mosaic histories, and finds fault with those who understand them allegorically, at the same time bestowing also some praise upon those who do so, to the effect that they are more impartial (than those who do not); and thus, as it were, he prevents by his cavils those who are able to show the true state of the case from offering such a defence as they would wish to offer.

CHAPTER XVIII

And challenging a comparison of book with book, I would say, "Come now, good sir, take down the poems of Linus, and of Musaeus, and of Orpheus, and the writings of Pherecydes, and carefully compare these with the laws of Moses—histories with histories, and ethical discourses with laws and commandments—and see which of the two are the better fitted to change the character of the hearer on the very spot, and which to harden him in his wickedness; and observe that your series of writers display little concern for those readers who are to peruse them at once unaided, but have composed their philosophy (as you term it) for those who are able to comprehend its metaphorical and allegorical signification; whereas Moses, like a distinguished orator who meditates some figure of Rhetoric, and who carefully introduces in every part language of twofold meaning, has done this in his five books: neither affording, in the portion which relates to morals, any handle to his Jewish subjects for committing evil; nor yet giving to the few individuals who were endowed with greater wisdom, and who were capable of investigating his meaning, a treatise devoid of material for speculation. But of your learned poets the very writings would seem no longer to be preserved, although they would have been carefully treasured up if the readers had perceived any benefit (likely to be derived from them); whereas the works of Moses have stirred up many, who were even aliens to the manners of the Jews, to the belief that, as these writings testify, the first who enacted these laws and delivered them to Moses, was the God who was the Creator of the world. For it became the Creator of the universe, after laying down laws for its government, to confer upon His words a power which might subdue all men in every part of the earth. And this I maintain, having as yet entered into no investigation regarding Jesus, but still demonstrating that Moses, who is far inferior to the Lord, is, as the *Discourse* will show, greatly superior to your wise poets and philosophers."

CHAPTER XIX

After these statements, Celsus, from a secret desire to cast discredit upon the Mosaic account of the creation, which teaches that the world is not yet ten thousand years old, but very much under that, while concealing his wish, intimates his agreement with those who hold that the world is uncreated. For, maintaining that there have been, from all eternity, many conflagrations and many deluges, and that the flood which lately took place in the time of Deucalion is comparatively modern, he clearly demonstrates to those who are able to understand him, that, in his opinion, the world was uncreated. But let this assailant of the Christian faith tell us by what arguments he was compelled to accept the statement that there have been many conflagrations and many cataclysms, and that the flood which occurred in the time of Deucalion, and the conflagration in that of Phaethon, were more recent than any others. And if he should put forward the dialogues of Plato (as evidence) on these subjects, we shall say to him that it is allowable for us also to believe that there resided in the pure and pious soul of Moses, who ascended above all created things, and united himself to the Creator of the universe, and who made known divine things with far greater clearness than Plato, or those other wise men (who lived) among the Greeks and Romans, a spirit which was divine. And if he demands of us our reasons for such a belief, let him first give grounds for his own unsupported assertions, and then we shall show that this view of ours is the correct one.

CHAPTER XX

And yet, against his will, Celsus is entangled into testifying that the world is comparatively modern, and not yet ten thousand years old, when he says that the Greeks consider those things as ancient, because, owing to the deluges and conflagrations, they have not beheld or received any memorials of older events. But let Celsus have, as his authorities for the myth regarding the conflagrations and inundations, those persons who, in his opinion, are the most learned of the Egyptians, traces of whose wisdom are to be found in the worship of irrational animals, and in arguments which prove that such a worship of God is in conformity with reason, and of a secret and mysterious character. The Egyptians, then, when they boastfully give their own account of the divinity of animals, are to be considered wise; but if any Jew, who has signified his adherence to the law and the lawgiver, refer everything to the Creator of the universe, and the only God, he is, in the opinion of Celsus and those like him, deemed inferior to him who degrades the Divinity not only to the level of rational and mortal animals, but even to that of irrational also!—a view which goes far beyond the mythical doctrine of transmigration, according to which the soul falls down from the summit of heaven, and enters into the body of brute beasts, both tame and savage! And if the Egyptians related fables of this kind, they are believed to convey a philosophical meaning by their enigmas and mysteries; but if Moses compose and leave behind him histories and laws for an entire nation, they are to be considered as empty fables, the language of which admits of no allegorical meaning!

CHAPTER XXI

The following is the view of Celsus and the Epicureans: "Moses having," he says, "learned the doctrine which is to be found existing among wise nations and eloquent men, obtained the reputation of divinity." Now, in answer to this we have to say, that it may be allowed him that Moses did indeed hear a somewhat ancient doctrine, and transmitted the same to the Hebrews; that if the doctrine which he heard was false, and neither pious nor venerable, and if notwithstanding, he received it and handed it down to those under his authority, he is liable to censure; but if, as you assert, he gave his adherence to opinions that were wise and true, and educated his people by means of them, what, pray, has he done deserving of condemnation? Would, indeed, that not only Epicurus, but Aristotle, whose sentiments regarding providence are not so impious (as those of the former), and the Stoics, who assert that God is a body, had heard such a doctrine! Then the world would not have been filled with opinions which either disallow or enfeeble the action of providence, or introduce a corrupt corporeal principle, according to which the god of the Stoics is a body, with respect to whom they are not afraid to say that he is capable of change, and may be altered and transformed in all his parts, and, generally, that he is capable of corruption, if there be any one to corrupt him, but that he has the good fortune to escape corruption, because there is none to corrupt. Whereas the doctrine of the Jews and Christians, which preserves the immutability and unalterableness of the divine nature, is stigmatized as impious, because it does not partake of the profanity of those whose notions of God are marked by impiety, but because it says in the supplication addressed to the Divinity, "Thou art the same," it being, moreover, an article of faith that God has said, "I change not."

CHAPTER XXII

After this, Celsus, without condemning circumcision as practised by the Jews, asserts that this usage was derived from the Egyptians; thus believing the Egyptians rather than Moses, who says that Abraham was the first among men who practised the rite. And it is not Moses alone who mentions the name of Abraham, assigning to him great intimacy with God; but many also of those who give themselves to the practice of the conjuration of evil spirits, employ in their spells the expression "God of Abraham," pointing out by the very name the friendship (that existed) between that just man and God. And yet, while making use of the phrase "God of Abraham," they do not know who Abraham is! And the same remark applies to Isaac, and Jacob, and Israel; which names, although confessedly Hebrew, are frequently introduced by those Egyptians who profess to produce some wonderful result by means of their knowledge. The rite of circumcision, however, which began with Abraham, and was discontinued by Jesus, who desired that His disciples should not practise it, is not before us for explanation; for the present occasion does not lead us to speak of such things, but to make an effort to refute the charges brought against the doctrine of the Jews by Celsus, who thinks that he will be able the more easily to establish the falsity of Christianity, if, by assailing its origin in Judaism, he can show that the latter also is untrue.

CHAPTER XXIII

After this, Celsus next asserts that "Those herdsmen and shepherds who followed Moses as their leader, had their minds deluded by vulgar deceits, and so supposed that there was one God." Let him show, then, how, after this irrational departure, as he regards it, of the herdsmen and shepherds from the worship of many gods, he himself is able to establish the multiplicity of deities that are found amongst the Greeks, or among those other nations that are called Barbarian. Let him establish, therefore, the existence of Mnemosyne, the mother of the Muses by Zeus; or of Themis, the parent of the Hours; or let him prove that the ever naked Graces can have a real, substantial existence. But he will not be able to show, from any actions of theirs, that these fictitious representations of the Greeks, which have the appearance of being invested with bodies, are (really) gods. And why should the fables of the Greeks regarding the gods be true, any more than those of the Egyptians for example, who in their language know nothing of a Mnemosyne, mother of the nine Muses; nor of a Themis, parent of the Hours; nor of a Euphrosyne, one of the Graces; nor of any other of these names? How much more manifest (and how much better than all these inventions!) is it that, convinced by what we see, in the admirable order of the world, we should worship the Maker of it as the one Author of one effect, and which, as being wholly in harmony with itself, cannot on that account have been the work of many makers; and that we should believe that the whole heaven is not held together by the movements of many souls, for one is enough, which bears the whole of the non-wandering sphere from east to west, and embraces within it all things which the world requires, and which are not self-existing! For all are parts of the world, while God is no part of the whole. But God cannot be imperfect, as a part is imperfect. And perhaps profounder consideration will show, that as God is not a part, so neither is He properly the whole, since the whole is composed of parts; and reason will not allow us to believe that the God who is over all is composed of parts, each one of which cannot do what all the other parts can.

CHAPTER XXIV

After this he continues: "These herdsmen and shepherds concluded that there was but one God, named either the Highest, or Adonai, or the Heavenly, or Sabaoth, or called by some other of those names which they delight to give this world; and they knew nothing beyond that." And in a subsequent part of his work he says, that "It makes no difference whether the God who is over all things be called by the name of Zeus, which is current among the Greeks, or by that, e.g., which is in use among the Indians or Egyptians." Now, in answer to this, we have to remark that this involves a deep and mysterious subject—that, viz., respecting the nature of names: it being a question whether, as Aristotle thinks, names were bestowed by arrangement, or, as the Stoics hold, by nature; the first words being imitations of things, agreeably to which the names were formed, and in conformity with which they introduce certain principles of etymology; or whether, as Epicurus teaches (differing in this from the Stoics), names were given by nature,—the first men having uttered certain words varying with the circumstances in which they found themselves. If, then, we shall be able to establish, in reference to the preceding statement, the nature of powerful names, some of which are used by the learned amongst the Egyptians, or by the Magi among the Persians, and by the Indian philosophers called Brahmans, or by the Samanaeans, and others in different countries; and shall be able to make out that the so-called magic is not, as the followers of Epicurus and Aristotle suppose, an altogether uncertain thing, but is, as those skilled in it prove, a consistent system, having words which are known to exceedingly few; then we say that the name Sabaoth, and Adonai, and the other names treated with so much reverence among the Hebrews, are not applicable to any ordinary created things, but belong to a secret theology which refers to the Framer of all things. These names, accordingly, when pronounced with that attendant train of circumstances which is appropriate to their nature, are possessed of great power; and other names, again, current in the Egyptian tongue, are efficacious against certain demons who can only do certain things; and other names in the Persian language have corresponding power over other spirits; and so on in every individual nation, for different purposes. And thus it will be found that, of the various demons upon the earth, to whom different localities have been assigned, each one bears a name appropriate to the several dialects of place and country. He, therefore, who has a nobler idea, however small, of these matters, will be careful not to apply differing names to different things; lest he should resemble those who mistakenly apply the name of God to lifeless matter, or who drag down the title of "the Good" from the First Cause, or from virtue and excellence, and apply it to blind Plutus, and to a healthy and well-proportioned mixture of flesh and blood and bones, or to what is considered to be noble birth.

CHAPTER XXV

And perhaps there is a danger as great as that which degrades the name of "God," or of "the Good," to improper objects, in changing the name of God according to a secret system, and applying those which belong to inferior beings to greater, and *vice versa.* And I do not dwell on this, that when the name of Zeus is uttered, there is heard at the same time that of the son of Kronos and Rhea, and the husband of Hera, and brother of Poseidon, and father of Athene, and Artemis, who was guilty of incest with his own daughter Persephone; or that Apollo immediately suggests the son of Leto and Zeus, and the brother of Artemis, and half-brother of Hermes; and so with all the other names invented by these wise men of Celsus, who are the parents of these opinions, and the ancient theologians of the Greeks. For what are the grounds for deciding that he should on the one hand be properly called Zeus, and yet on the other should not have Kronos for his father and Rhea for his mother? And the same argument applies to all the others that are called gods. But this charge does not at all apply to those who, for some mysterious reason, refer the word Sabaoth, or Adonai, or any of the other names to the (true) God. And when one is able to philosophize about the mystery of names, he will find much to say respecting the titles of the angels of God, of whom one is called Michael, and another Gabriel, and another Raphael, appropriately to the duties which they discharge in the world, according to the will of the God of all things. And a similar philosophy of names applies also to our Jesus, whose name has already been seen, in an unmistakeable manner, to have expelled myriads of evil spirits from the souls and bodies (of men), so great was the power which it exerted upon those from whom the spirits were driven out. And while still upon the subject of names, we have to mention that those who are skilled in the use of incantations, relate that the utterance of the same incantation in its proper language can accomplish what the spell professes to do; but when translated into any other tongue, it is observed to become inefficacious and feeble. And thus it is not the things signified, but the qualities and peculiarities of words, which possess a certain power for this or that purpose. And so on such grounds as these we defend the conduct of the Christians, when they struggle even to death to avoid calling God by the name of Zeus, or to give Him a name from any other language. For they either use the common name—God—indefinitely, or with some such addition as that of the "Maker of all things," "the Creator of heaven and earth"—He who sent down to the human race those good men, to whose names that of God being added, certain mighty works are wrought among men. And much more besides might be said on the subject of names, against those who think that we ought to be indifferent as to our use of them. And if the remark of Plato in the *Philebus* should surprise us, when he says, "My fear, O Protagoras, about the names of the gods is no small one," seeing Philebus in his discussion with Socrates had called pleasure a "god," how shall we not rather approve the piety of the Christians, who apply none of the names used in the mythologies to the Creator of the world? And now enough on this subject for the present.

CHAPTER XXVI

But let us see the manner in which this Celsus, who professes to know everything, brings a false accusation against the Jews, when he alleges that "they worship angels, and are addicted to sorcery, in which Moses was their instructor." Now, in what part of the writings of Moses he found the lawgiver laying down the worship of angels, let him tell, who professes to know all about Christianity and Judaism; and let him show also how sorcery can exist among those who have accepted the Mosaic law, and read the injunction, "Neither seek after wizards, to be defiled by them." Moreover, he promises to show afterwards "how it was through ignorance that the Jews were deceived and led into error." Now, if he had discovered that the ignorance of the Jews regarding Christ was the effect of their not having heard the prophecies about Him, he would show with truth how the Jews fell into error. But without any wish whatever that this should appear, he views as Jewish errors what are no errors at all. And Celsus having promised to make us acquainted, in a subsequent part of his work, with the doctrines of Judaism, proceeds in the first place to speak of our Saviour as having been the leader of our generation, in so far as we are Christians, and says that "a few years ago he began to teach this doctrine, being regarded by Christians as the Son of God." Now, with respect to this point—His prior existence a few years ago—we have to remark as follows. Could it have come to pass without divine assistance, that Jesus, desiring during these years to spread abroad His words and teaching, should have been so successful, that everywhere throughout the world, not a few persons, Greeks as well as Barbarians, learned as well as ignorant, adopted His doctrine, so that they struggled, even to death in its defence, rather than deny it, which no one is ever related to have done for any other system? I indeed, from no wish to flatter Christianity, but from a desire thoroughly to examine the facts, would say that even those who are engaged in the healing of numbers of sick persons, do not attain their object—the cure of the body—without divine help; and if one were to succeed in delivering souls from a flood of wickedness, and excesses, and acts of injustice, and from a contempt of God, and were to show, as evidence of such a result, one hundred persons improved in their natures (let us suppose the number to be so large), no one would reasonably say that it was without divine assistance that he had implanted in those hundred individuals a doctrine capable of removing so many evils. And if any one, on a candid consideration of these things, shall admit that no improvement ever takes place among men without divine help, how much more confidently shall he make the same assertion regarding Jesus, when he compares the former lives of many converts to His doctrine with their after conduct, and reflects in what acts of licentiousness and injustice and covetousness they formerly indulged, until, as Celsus, and they who think with him, allege, "they were deceived," and accepted a doctrine which, as these individuals assert, is destructive of the life of men; but who, from the time that they adopted it, have become in some way meeker, and more religious, and more consistent, so that certain among them, from a desire of exceeding chastity, and a wish to worship God with greater purity, abstain even from the permitted indulgences of (lawful) love.

CHAPTER XXVII

Any one who examines the subject will see that Jesus attempted and successfully accomplished works beyond the reach of human power. For although, from the very beginning, all things opposed the spread of His doctrine in the world,—both the princes of the times, and their chief captains and generals, and all, to speak generally, who were possessed of the smallest influence, and in addition to these, the rulers of the different cities, and the soldiers, and the people,—yet it proved victorious, as being the Word of God, the nature of which is such that it cannot be hindered; and becoming more powerful than all such adversaries, it made itself master of the whole of Greece, and a considerable portion of Barbarian lands, and convened countless numbers of souls to His religion. And although, among the multitude of converts to Christianity, the simple and ignorant necessarily outnumbered the more intelligent, as the former class always does the latter, yet Celsus, unwilling to take note of this, thinks that this philanthropic doctrine, which reaches to every soul under the sun, is vulgar, and on account of its vulgarity and its want of reasoning power, obtained a hold only over the ignorant. And yet he himself admits that it was not the simple alone who were led by the doctrine of Jesus to adopt His religion; for he acknowledges that there were amongst them some persons of moderate intelligence, and gentle disposition, and possessed of understanding, and capable of comprehending allegories.

CHAPTER XXVIII

And since, in imitation of a rhetorician training a pupil, he introduces a Jew, who enters into a personal discussion with Jesus, and speaks in a very childish manner, altogether unworthy of the grey hairs of a philosopher, let me endeavour, to the best of my ability, to examine his statements, and show that he does not maintain, throughout the discussion, the consistency due to the character of a Jew. For he represents him disputing with Jesus, and confuting Him, as he thinks, on many points; and in the first place, he accuses Him of having "invented his birth from a virgin," and upbraids Him with being "born in a certain Jewish village, of a poor woman of the country, who gained her subsistence by spinning, and who was turned out of doors by her husband, a carpenter by trade, because she was convicted of adultery; that after being driven away by her husband, and wandering about for a time, she disgracefully gave birth to Jesus, an illegitimate child, who having hired himself out as a servant in Egypt on account of his poverty, and having there acquired some miraculous powers, on which the Egyptians greatly pride themselves, returned to his own country, highly elated on account of them, and by means of these proclaimed himself a God." Now, as I cannot allow anything said by unbelievers to remain unexamined, but must investigate everything from the beginning, I give it as my opinion that all these things worthily harmonize with the predictions that Jesus is the Son of God.

CHAPTER XXIX

For birth is an aid towards an individual's becoming famous, and distinguished, and talked about; viz., when a man's parents happen to be in a position of rank and influence, and are possessed of wealth, and are able to spend it upon the education of their son, and when the country of one's birth is great and illustrious; but when a man having all these things against him is able, notwithstanding these hindrances, to make himself known, and to produce an impression on those who hear of him, and to become distinguished and visible to the whole world, which speaks of him as it did not do before, how can we help admiring such a nature as being both noble in itself, and devoting itself to great deeds, and possessing a courage which is not by any means to be despised? And if one were to examine more fully the history of such an individual, why should he not seek to know in what manner, after being reared up in frugality and poverty, and without receiving any complete education, and without having studied systems and opinions by means of which he might have acquired confidence to associate with multitudes, and play the demagogue, and attract to himself many hearers, he nevertheless devoted himself to the teaching of new opinions, introducing among men a doctrine which not only subverted the customs of the Jews, while preserving due respect for their prophets, but which especially overturned the established observances of the Greeks regarding the Divinity? And how could such a person— one who had been so brought up, and who, as his calumniators admit, had learned nothing great from men—have been able to teach, in a manner not at all to be despised, such doctrines as he did regarding the divine judgment, and the punishments that are to overtake wickedness, and the rewards that are to be conferred upon virtue; so that not only rustic and ignorant individuals were won by his words, but also not a few of those who were distinguished by their wisdom, and who were able to discern the hidden meaning in those more common doctrines, as they were considered, which were in circulation, and which secret meaning enwrapped, so to speak, some more recondite signification still? The Seriphian, in Plato, who reproaches Themistocles after he had become celebrated for his military skill, saying that his reputation was due not to his own merits, but to his good fortune in having been born in the most illustrious country in Greece, received from the good-natured Athenian, who saw that his native country did contribute to his renown, the following reply: "Neither would I, had I been a Seriphian, have been so distinguished as I am, nor would you have been a Themistocles, even if you had had the good fortune to be an Athenian!" And now, our Jesus, who is reproached with being born in a village, and that not a Greek one, nor belonging to any nation widely esteemed, and being despised as the son of a poor labouring woman, and as having on account of his poverty left his native country and hired himself out in Egypt, and being, to use the instance already quoted, not only a Seriphian, as it were, a native of a very small and undistinguished island, but even, so to speak, the meanest of the Seriphians, has yet been able to shake the whole inhabited world not only to a degree far above what Themistocles the Athenian ever did, but beyond what even Pythagoras, or Plato, or any other wise man in any part of the world whatever, or any prince or general, ever succeeded in doing.

CHAPTER XXX

Now, would not any one who investigated with ordinary care the nature of these facts, be struck with amazement at this man's victory?—with his complete success in surmounting by his reputation all causes that tended to bring him into disrepute, and with his superiority over all other illustrious individuals in the world? And yet it is a rare thing for distinguished men to succeed in acquiring a reputation for several things at once. For one man is admired on account of his wisdom, another for his military skill, and some of the Barbarians for their marvellous powers of incantation, and some for one quality, and others for another; but not many have been admired and acquired a reputation for many things at the same time; whereas this man, in addition to his other merits, is an object of admiration both for his wisdom, and for his miracles, and for his powers of government. For he persuaded some to withdraw themselves from their laws, and to secede to him, not as a tyrant would do, nor as a robber, who arms his followers against men; nor as a rich man, who bestows help upon those who come to him; nor as one of those who confessedly are deserving of censure; but as a teacher of the doctrine regarding the God of all things, and of the worship which belongs to Him, and of all moral precepts which are able to secure the favour of the Supreme God to him who orders his life in conformity therewith. Now, to Themistocles, or to any other man of distinction, nothing happened to prove a hindrance to their reputation; whereas to this man, besides what we have already enumerated, and which are enough to cover with dishonour the soul of a man even of the most noble nature, there was that apparently infamous death of crucifixion, which was enough to efface his previously acquired glory, and to lead those who, as they who disavow his doctrine assert, were formerly deluded by him to abandon their delusion, and to pass condemnation upon their deceiver.

CHAPTER XXXI

And besides this, one may well wonder how it happened that the disciples—if, as the calumniators of Jesus say, they did not see Him after His resurrection from the dead, and were not persuaded of His divinity—were not afraid to endure the same sufferings with their Master, and to expose themselves to danger, and to leave their native country to teach, according to the desire of Jesus, the doctrine delivered to them by Him. For I think that no one who candidly examines the facts would say that these men devoted themselves to a life of danger for the sake of the doctrine of Jesus, without profound belief which He had wrought in their minds of its truth, not only teaching them to conform to His precepts, but others also, and to conform, moreover, when manifest destruction to life impended over him who ventured to introduce these new opinions into all places and before all audiences, and who could retain as his friend no human being who adhered to the former opinions and usages. For did not the disciples of Jesus see, when they ventured to prove not only to the Jews from their prophetic Scriptures that this is He who was spoken of by the prophets, but also to the other heathen nations, that He who was crucified yesterday or the day before underwent this death voluntarily on behalf of the human race,—that this was analogous to the case of those who have died for their country in order to remove pestilence, or barrenness, or tempests? For it is probable that there is in the nature of things, for certain mysterious reasons which are difficult to be understood by the multitude, such a virtue that one just man, dying a voluntary death for the common good, might be the means of removing wicked spirits, which are the cause of plagues, or barrenness, or tempests, or similar calamities. Let those, therefore, who would disbelieve the statement that Jesus died on the cross on behalf of men, say whether they also refuse to accept the many accounts current both among Greeks and Barbarians, of persons who have laid down their lives for the public advantage, in order to remove those evils which had fallen upon cities and countries? Or will they say that such events actually happened, but that no credit is to be attached to that account which makes this so-called man to have died to ensure the destruction of a mighty evil spirit, the ruler of evil spirits, who had held in subjection the souls of all men upon earth? And the disciples of Jesus, seeing this and much more (which, it is probable, they learned from Jesus in private), and being filled, moreover, with a divine power (since it was no mere poetical virgin that endowed them with strength and courage, but the true wisdom and understanding of God), exerted all their efforts "to become distinguished among all men," not only among the Argives, but among all the Greeks and Barbarians alike, and "so bear away for themselves a glorious renown."

CHAPTER XXXII

But let us now return to where the Jew is introduced, speaking of the mother of Jesus, and saying that "when she was pregnant she was turned out of doors by the carpenter to whom she had been betrothed, as having been guilty of adultery, and that she bore a child to a certain soldier named Panthera;" and let us see whether those who have blindly concocted these fables about the adultery of the Virgin with Panthera, and her rejection by the carpenter, did not invent these stories to overturn His miraculous conception by the Holy Ghost: for they could have falsified the history in a different manner, on account of its extremely miraculous character, and not have admitted, as it were against their will, that Jesus was born of no ordinary human marriage. It was to be expected, indeed, that those who would not believe the miraculous birth of Jesus would invent some falsehood. And their not doing this in a credible manner, but (their) preserving the fact that it was not by Joseph that the Virgin conceived Jesus, rendered the falsehood very palpable to those who can understand and detect such inventions. Is it at all agreeable to reason, that he who dared to do so much for the human race, in order that, as far as in him lay, all the Greeks and Barbarians, who were looking for divine condemnation, might depart from evil, and regulate their entire conduct in a manner pleasing to the Creator of the world, should not have had a miraculous birth, but one the vilest and most disgraceful of all? And I will ask of them as Greeks, and particularly of Celsus, who either holds or not the sentiments of Plato, and at any rate quotes them, whether He who sends souls down into the bodies of men, degraded Him who was to dare such mighty acts, and to teach so many men, and to reform so many from the mass of wickedness in the world, to a birth more disgraceful than any other, and did not rather introduce Him into the world through a lawful marriage? Or is it not more in conformity with reason, that every soul, for certain mysterious reasons (I speak now according to the opinion of Pythagoras, and Plato, and Empedocles, whom Celsus frequently names), is introduced into a body, and introduced according to its deserts and former actions? It is probable, therefore, that this soul also, which conferred more benefit by its residence in the flesh than that of many men (to avoid prejudice, I do not say "all"), stood in need of a body not only superior to others, but invested with all excellent qualities.

CHAPTER XXXIII

Now if a particular soul, for certain mysterious reasons, is not deserving of being placed in the body of a wholly irrational being, nor yet in that of one purely rational, but is clothed with a monstrous body, so that reason cannot discharge its functions in one so fashioned, which has the head disproportioned to the other parts, and altogether too short; and another receives such a body that the soul is a little more rational than the other; and another still more so, the nature of the body counteracting to a greater or less degree the reception of the reasoning principle; why should there not be also some soul which receives an altogether miraculous body, possessing some qualities common to those of other men, so that it may be able to pass through life with them, but possessing also some quality of superiority, so that the soul may be able to remain untainted by sin? And if there be any truth in the doctrine of the physiognomists, whether Zopyrus, or Loxus, or Polemon, or any other who wrote on such a subject, and who profess to know in some wonderful way that all bodies are adapted to the habits of the souls, must there have been for that soul which was to dwell with miraculous power among men, and work mighty deeds, a body produced, as Celsus thinks, by an act of adultery between Panthera and the Virgin?! Why, from such unhallowed intercourse there must rather have been brought forth some fool to do injury to mankind,—a teacher of licentiousness and wickedness, and other evils; and not of temperance, and righteousness, and the other virtues!

CHAPTER XXXIV

But it was, as the prophets also predicted, from a virgin that there was to be born, according to the promised sign, one who was to give His name to the fact, showing that at His birth God was to be with man. Now it seems to me appropriate to the character of a Jew to have quoted the prophecy of Isaiah, which says that Immanuel was to be born of a virgin. This, however, Celsus, who professes to know everything, has not done, either from ignorance or from an unwillingness (if he had read it and voluntarily passed it by in silence) to furnish an argument which might defeat his purpose. And the prediction runs thus: "And the LORD spake again unto Ahaz, saying, Ask thee a sign of the LORD thy God; ask it either in the depth or in the height above. But Ahaz said, I will not ask, neither will I tempt the LORD. And he said, Hear ye now, O house of David; is it a small thing for you to weary men, but will ye weary my God also? Therefore the Lord Himself shall give you a sign. Behold, a virgin shall conceive, and bear a son, and shall call His name Immanuel, which is, being interpreted, God with us." And that it was from intentional malice that Celsus did not quote this prophecy, is clear to me from this, that although he makes numerous quotations from the Gospel according to Matthew, as of the star that appeared at the birth of Christ, and other miraculous occurrences, he has made no mention at all of this. Now, if a Jew should split words, and say that the words are not, "Lo, a virgin," but, "Lo, a young woman," we reply that the word "Olmah"—which the Septuagint have rendered by "a virgin," and others by "a young woman"—occurs, as they say, in Deuteronomy, as applied to a "virgin," in the following connection: "If a damsel that is a virgin be betrothed unto an husband, and a man find her in the city, and lie with her; then ye shall bring them both out unto the gate of that city, and ye shall stone them with stones that they die; the damsel, because she cried not, being in the city; and the man, because he humbled his neighbour's wife." And again: "But if a man find a betrothed damsel in a field, and the man force her, and lie with her: then the man only that lay with her shall die: but unto the damsel ye shall do nothing; there is in her no sin worthy of death."

CHAPTER XXXV

But that we may not seem, because of a Hebrew word, to endeavour to persuade those who are unable to determine whether they ought to believe it or not, that the prophet spoke of this man being born of a virgin, because at his birth these words, "God with us," were uttered, let us make good our point from the words themselves. The Lord is related to have spoken to Ahaz thus: "Ask a sign for thyself from the LORD thy God, either in the depth or height above;" and afterwards the sign is given, "Behold, a virgin shall conceive, and bear a son." What kind of sign, then, would that have been—a young woman who was not a virgin giving birth to a child? And which of the two is the more appropriate as the mother of Immanuel (i.e., "God with us"),— whether a woman who has had intercourse with a man, and who has conceived after the manner of women, or one who is still a pure and holy virgin? Surely it is appropriate only to the latter to produce a being at whose birth it is said, "God with us." And should he be so captious as to say that it is to Ahaz that the command is addressed, "Ask for thyself a sign from the LORD thy God," we shall ask in return, who in the times of Ahaz bore a son at whose birth the expression is made use of, "Immanuel," i.e., "God with us?" And if no one can be found, then manifestly what was said to Ahaz was said to the house of David, because it is written that the Saviour was born of the house of David according to the flesh; and this sign is said to be "in the depth or in the height," since "He that descended is the same also that ascended up far above all heavens, that He might fill all things." And these arguments I employ as against a Jew who believes in prophecy. Let Celsus now tell me, or any of those who think with him, with what meaning the prophet utters either these statements about the future, or the others which are contained in the prophecies? Is it with any foresight of the future or not? If with a foresight of the future, then the prophets were divinely inspired; if with no foresight of the future, let him explain the meaning of one who speaks thus boldly regarding the future, and who is an object of admiration among the Jews because of his prophetic powers.

CHAPTER XXXVI

And now, since we have touched upon the subject of the prophets, what we are about to advance will be useful not only to the Jews, who believe that they spake by divine inspiration, but also to the more candid among the Greeks. To these we say that we must necessarily admit that the Jews had prophets, if they were to be kept together under that system of law which had been given them, and were to believe in the Creator of the world, as they had learned, and to be without pretexts, so far as the law was concerned, for apostatizing to the polytheism of the heathen. And we establish this necessity in the following manner. "For the nations," as it is written in the law of the Jews itself, "shall hearken unto observers of times, and diviners;" but to that people it is said: "But as for thee, the LORD thy God hath not suffered thee so to do." And to this is subjoined the promise: "A prophet shall the LORD thy God raise up unto thee from among thy brethren." Since, therefore, the heathen employ modes of divination either by oracles or by omens, or by birds, or by ventriloquists, or by those who profess the art of sacrifice, or by Chaldean genealogists—all which practices were forbidden to the Jews—this people, if they had no means of attaining a knowledge of futurity, being led by the passion common to humanity of ascertaining the future would have despised their own prophets, as not having in them any particle of divinity; and would not have accepted any prophet after Moses, nor committed their words to writing, but would have spontaneously betaken themselves to the divining usages of the heathen, or attempted to establish some such practices amongst themselves. There is therefore no absurdity in their prophets having uttered predictions even about events of no importance, to soothe those who desire such things, as when Samuel prophesies regarding three she-asses which were lost, or when mention is made in the third book of Kings respecting the sickness of a king's son. And why should not those who desired to obtain auguries from idols be severely rebuked by the administrators of the law among the Jews?—as Elijah is found rebuking Ahaziah, and saying, "Is it because there is not a God in Israel that ye go to inquire of Baalzebub, god of

Ekron?"

CHAPTER XXXVII

I think, then, that it has been pretty well established not only that our Saviour was to be born of a virgin, but also that there were prophets among the Jews who uttered not merely general predictions about the future,—as, e.g., regarding Christ and the kingdoms of the world, and the events that were to happen to Israel, and those nations which were to believe on the Saviour, and many other things concerning Him,— but also prophecies respecting particular events; as, for instance, how the asses of Kish, which were lost, were to be discovered, and regarding the sickness which had fallen upon the son of the king of Israel, and any other recorded circumstance of a similar kind. But as a further answer to the Greeks, who do not believe in the birth of Jesus from a virgin, we have to say that the Creator has shown, by the generation of several kinds of animals, that what He has done in the instance of one animal, He could do, if it pleased Him, in that of others, and also of man himself. For it is ascertained that there is a certain female animal which has no intercourse with the male (as writers on animals say is the case with vultures), and that this animal, without sexual intercourse, preserves the succession of race. What incredibility, therefore, is there in supposing that, if God wished to send a divine teacher to the human race, He caused Him to be born in some manner different from the common! Nay, according to the Greeks themselves, all men were not born of a man and woman. For if the world has been created, as many even of the Greeks are pleased to admit, then the first men must have been produced not from sexual intercourse, but from the earth, in which spermatic elements existed; which, however, I consider more incredible than that Jesus was born like other men, so far as regards the half of his birth. And there is no absurdity in employing Grecian histories to answer Greeks, with the view of showing that we are not the only persons who have recourse to miraculous narratives of this kind. For some have thought fit, not in regard to ancient and heroic narratives, but in regard to events of very recent occurrence, to relate as a possible thing that Plato was the son of Amphictione, Ariston being prevented from having marital intercourse with his wife until she had given birth to him with whom she was pregnant by Apollo. And yet these are veritable fables, which have led to the invention of such stories concerning a man whom they regarded as possessing greater wisdom and power than the multitude, and as having received the beginning of his corporeal substance from better and diviner elements than others, because they thought that this was appropriate to persons who were too great to be human beings. And since Celsus has introduced the Jew disputing with Jesus, and tearing in pieces, as he imagines, the fiction of His birth from a virgin, comparing the Greek fables about Danae, and Melanippe, and Auge, and Antiope, our answer is, that such language becomes a buffoon, and not one who is writing in a serious tone.

CHAPTER XXXVIII

But, moreover, taking the history, contained in the Gospel according to Matthew, of our Lord's descent into Egypt, he refuses to believe the miraculous circumstances attending it, viz., either that the angel gave the divine intimation, or that our Lord's quitting Judea and residing in Egypt was an event of any significance; but he invents something altogether different, admitting somehow the miraculous works done by Jesus, by means of which He induced the multitude to follow Him as the Christ. And yet he desires to throw discredit on them, as being done by help of magic and not by divine power; for he asserts "that he (Jesus), having been brought up as an illegitimate child, and having served for hire in Egypt, and then coming to the knowledge of certain miraculous powers, returned from thence to his own country, and by means of those powers proclaimed himself a god." Now I do not understand how a magician should exert himself to teach a doctrine which persuades us always to act as if God were to judge every man for his deeds; and should have trained his disciples, whom he was to employ as the ministers of his doctrine, in the same belief. For did the latter make an impression upon their hearers, after they had been so taught to work miracles; or was it without the aid of these? The assertion, therefore, that they did no miracles at all, but that, after yielding their belief to arguments which were not at all convincing, like the wisdom of Grecian dialectics, they gave themselves up to the task of teaching the new doctrine to those persons among whom they happened to take up their abode, is altogether absurd. For in what did they place their confidence when they taught the doctrine and disseminated the new opinions? But if they indeed wrought miracles, then how can it be believed that magicians exposed themselves to such hazards to introduce a doctrine which forbade the practice of magic?

CHAPTER XXXIX

I do not think it necessary to grapple with an argument advanced not in a serious but in a scoffing spirit, such as the following: "If the mother of Jesus was beautiful, then the god whose nature is not to love a corruptible body, had intercourse with her because she was beautiful;" or, "It was improbable that the god would entertain a passion for her, because she was neither rich nor of royal rank, seeing no one, even of her neighbours, knew her." And it is in the same scoffing spirit that he adds: "When hated by her husband, and turned out of doors, she was not saved by divine power, nor was her story believed. Such things," he says, "have no connection with the kingdom of heaven." In what respect does such language differ from that of those who pour abuse on others on the public streets, and whose words are unworthy of any serious attention?

CHAPTER XL

After these assertions, he takes from the Gospel of Matthew, and perhaps also from the other Gospels, the account of the dove alighting upon our Saviour at His baptism by John, and desires to throw discredit upon the statement, alleging that the narrative is a fiction. Having completely disposed, as he imagined, of the story of our Lord's birth from a virgin, he does not proceed to deal in an orderly manner with the accounts that follow it; since passion and hatred observe no order, but angry and vindictive men slander those whom they hate, as the feeling comes upon them, being prevented by their passion from arranging their accusations on a careful and orderly plan. For if he had observed a proper arrangement, he would have taken up the Gospel, and, with the view of assailing it, would have objected to the first narrative, then passed on to the second, and so on to the others. But now, after the birth from a virgin, this Celsus, who professes to be acquainted with all our history, attacks the account of the appearance of the Holy Spirit in the form of a dove at the baptism. He then, after that, tries to throw discredit upon the prediction that our Lord was to come into the world. In the next place, he runs away to what immediately follows the narrative of the birth of Jesus—the account of the star, and of the wise men who came from the east to worship the child. And you yourself may find, if you take the trouble, many confused statements made by Celsus throughout his whole book; so that even in this account he may, by those who know how to observe and require an orderly method of arrangement, be convicted of great rashness and boasting, in having inscribed upon his work the title of *A True Discourse*,—a thing which is never done by a learned philosopher. For Plato says, that it is not an indication of an intelligent man to make strong assertions respecting those matters which are somewhat uncertain; and the celebrated Chrysippus even, who frequently states the reasons by which he is decided, refers us to those whom we shall find to be abler speakers than himself. This man, however, who is wiser than those already named, and than all the other Greeks, agreeably to his assertion of being acquainted with everything, inscribed upon his book the words, *A True Discourse*!

CHAPTER XLI

But, that we may not have the appearance of intentionally passing by his charges through inability to refute them, we have resolved to answer each one of them separately according to our ability, attending not to the connection and sequence of the nature of the things themselves, but to the arrangement of the subjects as they occur in this book. Let us therefore notice what he has to say by way of impugning the bodily appearance of the Holy Spirit to our Saviour in the form of a dove. And it is a Jew who addresses the following language to Him whom we acknowledge to be our Lord Jesus: "When you were bathing," says the Jew, "beside John, you say that what had the appearance of a bird from the air alighted upon you." And then this same Jew of his, continuing his interrogations, asks, "What credible witness beheld this appearance? or who heard a voice from heaven declaring you to be the Son of God? What proof is there of it, save your own assertion, and the statement of another of those individuals who have been punished along with you?"

CHAPTER XLII

Before we begin our reply, we have to remark that the endeavour to show, with regard to almost any history, however true, that it actually occurred, and to produce an intelligent conception regarding it, is one of the most difficult undertakings that can be attempted, and is in some instances an impossibility. For suppose that some one were to assert that there never had been any Trojan war, chiefly on account of the impossible narrative interwoven therewith, about a certain Achilles being the son of a sea-goddess Thetis and of a man Peleus, or Sarpedon being the son of Zeus, or Ascalaphus and Ialmenus the sons of Ares, or Aeneas that of Aphrodite, how should we prove that such was the case, especially under the weight of the fiction attached, I know not how, to the universally prevalent opinion that there was really a war in Ilium between Greeks and Trojans? And suppose, also, that some one disbelieved the story of Oedipus and Jocasta, and of their two sons Eteocles and Polynices, because the sphinx, a kind of half-virgin, was introduced into the narrative, how should we demonstrate the reality of such a thing? And in like manner also with the history of the Epigoni, although there is no such marvellous event interwoven with it, or with the return of the Heracleidae, or countless other historical events. But he who deals candidly with histories, and would wish to keep himself also from being imposed upon by them, will exercise his judgment as to what statements he will give his assent to, and what he will accept figuratively, seeking to discover the meaning of the authors of such inventions, and from what statements he will withhold his belief, as having been written for the gratification of certain individuals. And we have said this by way of anticipation respecting the whole history related in the Gospels concerning Jesus, not as inviting men of acuteness to a simple and unreasoning faith, but wishing to show that there is need of candour in those who are to read, and of much investigation, and, so to speak, of insight into the meaning of the writers, that the object with which each event has been recorded may be discovered.

CHAPTER XLIII

We shall therefore say, in the first place, that if he who disbelieves the appearance of the Holy Spirit in the form of a dove had been described as an Epicurean, or a follower of Democritus, or a Peripatetic, the statement would have been in keeping with the character of such an objector. But now even this Celsus, wisest of all men, did not perceive that it is to a Jew, who believes more incredible things contained in the writings of the prophets than the narrative of the appearance of the dove, that he attributes such an objection! For one might say to the Jew, when expressing his disbelief of the appearance, and thinking to assail it as a fiction, "How are you able to prove, sir, that the Lord spake to Adam, or to Eve, or to Cain, or to Noah, or to Abraham, or to Isaac, or to Jacob, those words which He is recorded to have spoken to these men?" And, to compare history with history, I would say to the Jew, "Even your own Ezekiel writes, saying, 'The heavens were opened, and I saw a vision of God.' After relating which, he adds, 'This was the appearance of the likeness of the glory of the LORD; and He said to me,'" etc. Now, if what is related of Jesus be false, since we cannot, as you suppose, clearly prove it to be true, it being seen or heard by Himself alone, and, as you appear to have observed, also by one of those who were punished, why should we not rather say that Ezekiel also was dealing in the marvellous when he said, "The heavens were opened," etc.? Nay, even Isaiah asserts, "I saw the Lord of hosts sitting on a throne, high and lifted up; and the seraphim stood round about it: the one had six wings, and the other had six wings." How can we tell whether he really saw them or not? Now, O Jew, you have believed these visions to be true, and to have been not only shown to the prophet by a diviner Spirit, but also to have been both spoken and recorded by the same. And who is the more worthy of belief, when declaring that the heavens were opened before him, and that he heard a voice, or beheld the Lord of Sabaoth sitting upon a throne high and lifted up,—whether Isaiah and Ezekiel or Jesus? Of the former, indeed, no work has been found equal to those of the latter; whereas the good deeds of Jesus have not been confined solely to the period of His tabernacling in the flesh, but up to the present time His power still produces conversion and amelioration of life in those who believe in God through Him. And a manifest proof that these things are done by His power, is the fact that, although, as He Himself said, and as is admitted, there are not labourers enough to gather in the harvest of souls, there really is nevertheless such a great harvest of those who are gathered together and conveyed into the everywhere existing threshing-floors and Churches of God.

CHAPTER XLIV

And with these arguments I answer the Jew, not disbelieving, I who am a Christian, Ezekiel and Isaiah, but being very desirous to show, on the footing of our common belief, that this man is far more worthy of credit than they are when He says that He beheld such a sight, and, as is probable, related to His disciples the vision which He saw, and told them of the voice which He heard. But another party might object, that not all those who have narrated the appearance of the dove and the voice from heaven heard the accounts of these things from Jesus, but that that Spirit which taught Moses the history of events before his own time, beginning with the creation, and descending down to Abraham his father, taught also the writers of the Gospel the miraculous occurrence which took place at the time of Jesus' baptism. And he who is adorned with the spiritual gift, called the "word of wisdom," will explain also the reason of the heavens opening, and the dove appearing, and why the Holy Spirit appeared to Jesus in the form of no other living thing than that of a dove. But our present subject does not require us to explain this, our purpose being to show that Celsus displayed no sound judgment in representing a Jew as disbelieving, on such grounds, a fact which has greater probability in its favour than many events in which he firmly reposes confidence.

CHAPTER XLV

And I remember on one occasion, at a disputation held with certain Jews who were reputed learned men, having employed the following argument in the presence of many judges: "Tell me, sirs," I said, "since there are two individuals who have visited the human race, regarding whom are related marvellous works surpassing human power—Moses, viz., your own legislator, who wrote about himself, and Jesus our teacher, who has left no writings regarding Himself, but to whom testimony is borne by the disciples in the Gospels—what are the grounds for deciding that Moses is to be believed as speaking the truth, although the Egyptians slander him as a sorcerer, and as appearing to have wrought his mighty works by jugglery, while Jesus is not to be believed because you are His accusers? And yet there are nations which bear testimony in favour of both: the Jews to Moses; and the Christians, who do not deny the prophetic mission of Moses, but proving from that very source the truth of the statement regarding Jesus, accept as true the miraculous circumstances related of Him by His disciples. Now, if ye ask us for the reasons of our faith in Jesus, give yours first for believing in Moses, who lived before Him, and then we shall give you ours for accepting the latter. But if you draw back, and shirk a demonstration, then we, following your own example, decline for the present to offer any demonstration likewise. Nevertheless, admit that ye have no proof to offer for Moses, and then listen to our defence of Jesus derived from the law and the prophets. And now observe what is almost incredible! It is shown from the declarations concerning Jesus, contained in the law and the prophets, that both Moses and the prophets were truly prophets of God."

CHAPTER XLVI

For the law and the prophets are full of marvels similar to those recorded of Jesus at His baptism, viz., regarding the dove and the voice from heaven. And I think the wonders wrought by Jesus are a proof of the Holy Spirit's having then appeared in the form of a dove, although Celsus, from a desire to cast discredit upon them, alleges that He performed only what He had learned among the Egyptians. And I shall refer not only to His miracles, but, as is proper, to those also of the apostles of Jesus. For they could not without the help of miracles and wonders have prevailed on those who heard their new doctrines and new teachings to abandon their national usages, and to accept their instructions at the danger to themselves even of death. And there are still preserved among Christians traces of that Holy Spirit which appeared in the form of a dove. They expel evil spirits, and perform many cures, and foresee certain events, according to the will of the Logos. And although Celsus, or the Jew whom he has introduced, may treat with mockery what I am going to say, I shall say it nevertheless,— that many have been converted to Christianity as if against their will, some sort of spirit having suddenly transformed their minds from a hatred of the doctrine to a readiness to die in its defence, and having appeared to them either in a waking vision or a dream of the night. Many such instances have we known, which, if we were to commit to writing, although they were seen and witnessed by ourselves, we should afford great occasion for ridicule to unbelievers, who would imagine that we, like those whom they suppose to have invented such things, had ourselves also done the same. But God is witness of our conscientious desire, not by false statements, but by testimonies of different kinds, to establish the divinity of the doctrine of Jesus. And as it is a Jew who is perplexed about the account of the Holy Spirit having descended upon Jesus in the form of a dove, we would say to him, "Sir, who is it that says in Isaiah, 'And now the Lord hath sent me and His Spirit?'" In which sentence, as the meaning is doubtful—viz., whether the Father and the Holy Spirit sent Jesus, or the Father sent both Christ and the Holy Spirit—the latter is correct. For, because the Saviour was sent, afterwards the Holy Spirit was sent also, that the prediction of the prophet might be fulfilled; and as it was necessary that the fulfilment of the prophecy should be known to posterity, the disciples of Jesus for that reason committed the result to writing.

CHAPTER XLVII

I would like to say to Celsus, who represents the Jew as accepting somehow John as a Baptist, who baptized Jesus, that the existence of John the Baptist, baptizing for the remission of sins, is related by one who lived no great length of time after John and Jesus. For in the 18th book of his *Antiquities of the Jews*, Josephus bears witness to John as having been a Baptist, and as promising purification to those who underwent the rite. Now this writer, although not believing in Jesus as the Christ, in seeking after the cause of the fall of Jerusalem and the destruction of the temple, whereas he ought to have said that the conspiracy against Jesus was the cause of these calamities befalling the people, since they put to death Christ, who was a prophet, says nevertheless—being, although against his will, not far from the truth—that these disasters happened to the Jews as a punishment for the death of James the Just, who was a brother of Jesus (called Christ),—the Jews having put him to death, although he was a man most distinguished for his justice. Paul, a genuine disciple of Jesus, says that he regarded this James as a brother of the Lord, not so much on account of their relationship by blood, or of their being brought up together, as because of his virtue and doctrine. If, then, he says that it was on account of James that the desolation of Jerusalem was made to overtake the Jews, how should it not be more in accordance with reason to say that it happened on account (of the death) of Jesus Christ, of whose divinity so many Churches are witnesses, composed of those who have been convened from a flood of sins, and who have joined themselves to the Creator, and who refer all their actions to His good pleasure.

CHAPTER XLVIII

Although the Jew, then, may offer no defence for himself in the instances of Ezekiel and Isaiah, when we compare the opening of the heavens to Jesus, and the voice that was heard by Him, to the similar cases which we find recorded in Ezekiel and Isaiah, or any other of the prophets, we nevertheless, so far as we can, shall support our position, maintaining that, as it is a matter of belief that in a *dream* impressions have been brought before the minds of many, some relating to divine things, and others to future events of this life, and this either with clearness or in an enigmatic manner,—a fact which is manifest to all who accept the doctrine of providence; so how is it absurd to say that the mind which could receive impressions in a *dream* should be impressed also in a waking vision, for the benefit either of him on whom the impressions are made, or of those who are to hear the account of them from him? And as in a dream we fancy that we hear, and that the organs of hearing are actually impressed, and that we see with our eyes—although neither the bodily organs of sight nor hearing are affected, but it is the mind alone which has these sensations—so there is no absurdity in believing that similar things occurred to the prophets, when it is recorded that they witnessed occurrences of a rather wonderful kind, as when they either heard the words of the Lord or beheld the heavens opened. For I do not suppose that the visible heaven was actually opened, and its physical structure divided, in order that Ezekiel might be able to record such an occurrence. Should not, therefore, the same be believed of the Saviour by every intelligent hearer of the Gospels?—although such an occurrence may be a stumbling-block to the simple, who in their simplicity would set the whole world in movement, and split in sunder the compact and mighty body of the whole heavens. But he who examines such matters more profoundly will say, that there being, as the Scripture calls it, a kind of general divine perception which the blessed man alone knows how to discover, according to the saying of Solomon, "Thou shalt find the knowledge of God;" and as there are various forms of this perceptive power, such as a faculty of vision which can naturally see things that are better than bodies, among which are ranked the cherubim and seraphim; and a faculty of hearing which can perceive voices which have not their being in the air; and a sense of taste which can make use of living bread that has come down from heaven, and that giveth life unto the world; and so also a sense of smelling, which scents such things as leads Paul to say that he is a sweet savour of Christ unto God; and a sense of touch, by which John says that he "handled with his hands of the Word of life;"—the blessed prophets having discovered this divine perception, and seeing and hearing in this divine manner, and tasting likewise, and smelling, so to speak, with no sensible organs of perception, and laying hold on the Logos by faith, so that a healing effluence from it comes upon them, saw in this manner what they record as having seen, and heard what they say they heard, and were affected in a similar manner to what they describe when eating the roll of a book that was given them. And so also Isaac smelled the savour of his son's divine garments, and added to the spiritual blessing these words: "See, the savour of my son is as the savour of a full field which the LORD blessed." And similarly to this, and more as a matter to be understood by the mind than to be perceived by the senses, Jesus touched the leper, to cleanse him, as I think, in a twofold sense,— freeing him not only, as the multitude heard, from the visible leprosy by visible contact, but also from that other leprosy, by His truly divine touch. It is in this way, accordingly, that John testifies when he says, "I beheld the Spirit descending from heaven like a dove, and it abode upon Him. And I knew Him not; but He that sent me to baptize with water, the same said to me, Upon whom you will see the Spirit descending, and abiding on Him, the same is He that baptizeth with the Holy Ghost. And I saw, and bear witness, that this is the Son of God." Now it was to Jesus that the heavens were opened; and on that occasion no one except John is recorded to have seen them opened. But with respect to this opening of the heavens, the Saviour, foretelling to His disciples that it would happen, and that they would see it, says, "Verily, verily, I say unto you, Ye shall see the heavens opened, and the angels of God ascending and descending upon the Son of man." And so Paul was carried away into the third heaven, having previously seen it opened, since he was a disciple of Jesus. It does not, however, belong to our present object to explain why Paul says, "Whether in the body, I know not; or whether out of the body, I know not: God knoweth." But I shall add to my argument even those very points which Celsus imagines, viz., that Jesus Himself related the account of the opening of the heavens, and the descent of the Holy Spirit upon Him at the Jordan in the form of a dove, although the Scripture does not assert that He said that He saw it. For this great man did not perceive that it was not in keeping with Him who commanded His disciples on the occasion of the vision on the mount, "Tell what ye have seen to no man, until the Son of man be risen from the dead," to have related to His disciples what was seen and heard by John at the Jordan. For it may be observed as a trait of the character of Jesus, that He on all occasions avoided unnecessary talk about Himself; and on that account said, "If I speak of Myself, My witness is not true." And since He avoided unnecessary talk about Himself, and preferred to show by acts rather than words that He was the Christ, the Jews for that reason said to Him, "If Thou art the Christ, tell us plainly." And as it is a Jew who, in the work of Celsus, uses the language to Jesus regarding the appearance of the Holy Spirit in the form of a dove, "This is your own testimony, unsupported save by one of those who were sharers of your punishment, whom you adduce," it is necessary for us to show him that such a statement is not appropriately placed in the mouth of a Jew. For the Jews do not connect John with Jesus, nor the punishment of John with that of Christ. And by this instance, this man who boasts of universal knowledge is convicted of not knowing what words he ought to ascribe to a Jew engaged in a disputation with Jesus.

CHAPTER XLIX

After this he wilfully sets aside, I know not why, the strongest evidence in confirmation of the claims of Jesus, viz., that His coming was predicted by the Jewish prophets—Moses, and those who succeeded as well as preceded that legislator—from inability, as I think, to meet the argument that neither the Jews nor any other heretical sect refuse to believe that Christ was the subject of prophecy. But perhaps he was unacquainted with the prophecies relating to Christ. For no one who was acquainted with the statements of the Christians, that many prophets foretold the advent of the Saviour, would have ascribed to a Jew sentiments which it would have better befitted a Samaritan or a

Sadducee to utter; nor would the Jew in the dialogue have expressed himself in language like the following: "But my prophet once declared in Jerusalem, that the Son of God will come as the Judge of the righteous and the Punisher of the wicked." Now it is not one of the prophets merely who predicted the advent of Christ. But although the Samaritans and Sadducees, who receive the books of Moses alone, would say that there were contained in them predictions regarding Christ, yet certainly not in Jerusalem, which is not even mentioned in the times of Moses, was the prophecy uttered. It were indeed to be desired, that all the accusers of Christianity were equally ignorant with Celsus, not only of the facts, but of the bare letter of Scripture, and would so direct their assaults against it, that their arguments might not have the least available influence in shaking, I do not say the faith, but the little faith of unstable and temporary believers. A Jew, however, would not admit that any prophet used the expression, "The Son of God' will come;" for the term which they employ is, "The Christ of God' will come." And many a time indeed do they directly interrogate us about the "Son of God," saying that no such being exists, or was made the subject of prophecy. We do not of course assert that the "Son of God" is not the subject of prophecy; but we assert that he most inappropriately attributes to the Jewish disputant, who would not allow that He was, such language as, "My prophet once declared in Jerusalem that the Son of God' will come."

CHAPTER L

In the next place, as if the only event predicted were this, that He was to be "the Judge of the righteous and the Punisher of the wicked," and as if neither the place of His birth, nor the sufferings which He was to endure at the hands of the Jews, nor His resurrection, nor the wonderful works which He was to perform, had been made the subject of prophecy, he continues: "Why should it be you alone, rather than innumerable others, who existed after the prophecies were published, to whom these predictions are applicable?" And desiring, I know not how, to suggest to others the possibility of the notion that they themselves were the persons referred to by the prophets, he says that "some, carried away by enthusiasm, and others having gathered a multitude of followers, give out that the Son of God is come down from heaven." Now we have not ascertained that such occurrences are admitted to have taken place among the Jews. We have to remark then, in the first place, that many of the prophets have uttered predictions in all kinds of ways regarding Christ; some by means of dark sayings, others in allegories or in some other manner, and some also in express words. And as in what follows he says, in the character of the Jew addressing the converts from his own nation, and repeating emphatically and malevolently, that "the prophecies referred to the events of his life may also suit other events as well," we shall state a few of them out of a greater number; and with respect to these, any one who chooses may say what he thinks fitted to ensure a refutation of them, and which may turn away intelligent believers from the faith.

CHAPTER LI

Now the Scripture speaks, respecting the place of the Saviour's birth—that the Ruler was to come forth from Bethlehem—in the following manner: "And thou Bethlehem, house of Ephrata, art not the least among the thousands of Judah: for out of thee shall He come forth unto Me who is to be Ruler in Israel; and His goings forth have been of old, from everlasting." Now this prophecy could not suit any one of those who, as Celsus' Jew says, were fanatics and mob-leaders, and who gave out that they had come from heaven, unless it were clearly shown that He had been born in Bethlehem, or, as another might say, had come forth from Bethlehem to be the leader of the people. With respect to the birth of Jesus in Bethlehem, if any one desires, after the prophecy of Micah and after the history recorded in the Gospels by the disciples of Jesus, to have additional evidence from other sources, let him know that, in conformity with the narrative in the Gospel regarding His birth, there is shown at Bethlehem the cave where He was born, and the manger in the cave where He was wrapped in swaddling-clothes. And this sight is greatly talked of in surrounding places, even among the enemies of the faith, it being said that in this cave was born that Jesus who is worshipped and reverenced by the Christians. Moreover, I am of opinion that, before the advent of Christ, the chief priests and scribes of the people, on account of the distinctness and clearness of this prophecy, taught that in Bethlehem the Christ was to be born. And this opinion had prevailed also extensively among the Jews; for which reason it is related that Herod, on inquiring at the chief priests and scribes of the people, heard from them that the Christ was to be born in Bethlehem of Judea, "whence David was." It is stated also in the Gospel according to John, that the Jews declared that the Christ was to be born in Bethlehem, "whence David was." But after our Lord's coming, those who busied themselves with overthrowing the belief that the place of His birth had been the subject of prophecy from the beginning, withheld such teaching from the people; acting in a similar manner to those individuals who won over those soldiers of the guard stationed around the tomb who had seen Him arise from the dead, and who instructed these eye-witnesses to report as follows: "Say that His disciples, while we slept, came and stole Him away. And if this come to the governor's ears, we shall persuade him, and secure you."

CHAPTER LII

Strife and prejudice are powerful instruments in leading men to disregard even those things which are abundantly clear; so that they who have somehow become familiar with certain opinions, which have deeply imbued their minds, and stamped them with a certain character, will not give them up. For a man will abandon his habits in respect to other things, although it may be difficult for him to tear himself from them, more easily than he will surrender his opinions. Nay, even the former are not easily put aside by those who have become accustomed to them; and so neither houses, nor cities, nor villages, nor intimate acquaintances, are willingly forsaken when we are prejudiced in their favour. This, therefore, was a reason why many of the Jews at that time disregarded the clear testimony of the prophecies, and miracles which Jesus wrought, and of the sufferings which He is related to have endured. And that human nature is thus affected, will be manifest to those who observe that those who have once been prejudiced in favour of the most contemptible and paltry traditions of their ancestors and fellow-citizens, with difficulty lay them aside. For example, no one could easily persuade an Egyptian to despise what he had learned from his fathers, so as no longer to consider this or that irrational animal as a god, or not to guard against eating, even under the penalty of death, of the flesh of such an animal. Now, if in carrying our examination of this subject to a considerable length, we have enumerated the points respecting Bethlehem, and the prophecy regarding it, we consider that we were obliged to do this, by way of defence against those who would assert that if the prophecies current among the Jews regarding Jesus were so clear as we represent them, why did they not at His coming give in their adhesion to His doctrine, and betake themselves to the better life pointed out by Him? Let no one, however, bring such a reproach against believers, since he may see that reasons of no light weight are assigned by those who have learned to state them, for their faith in Jesus.

CHAPTER LIII

And if we should ask for a second prophecy, which may appear to us to have a clear reference to Jesus, we would quote that which was written by Moses very many years before the advent of Christ, when he makes Jacob, on his departure from this life, to have uttered predictions regarding each of his sons, and to have said of Judah along with the others: "The ruler will not fail from Judah, and the governor from his loins, until that which is reserved for him come." Now, any one meeting with this prophecy, which is in reality much older than Moses, so that one who was not a believer might suspect that it was not written by him, would be surprised that Moses should be able to predict that the princes of the Jews, seeing there are among them twelve tribes, should be born of the tribe of Judah, and should be the rulers of the people; for which reason also the whole nation are called Jews, deriving their name from the ruling tribe. And, in the second place, one who candidly considers the prophecy, would be surprised how, after declaring that the rulers and governors of the people were to proceed from the tribe of Judah, he should determine also the limit of their rule, saying that "the ruler should not fail from Judah, nor the governor from his loins, until there should come that which was reserved for him, and that He is the expectation of the Gentiles." For He came for whom these things were reserved, viz., the Christ of God, the ruler of the promises of God. And manifestly He is the only one among those who preceded, and, I might make bold to say, among those also who followed Him, who was the expectation of the Gentiles; for converts from among all the Gentile nations have believed on God through Him, and that in conformity with the prediction of Isaiah, that in His name the Gentiles had hoped: "In Thy name shall the Gentiles hope." And this man said also to those who are in prison, as every man is a captive to the chains of his sins, "Come forth;" and to the ignorant, "Come into the light:" these things also having been thus foretold: "I have given Thee for a covenant of the people, to establish the earth, to cause to inherit the desolate heritage; saying to the prisoners, Go forth; and to them that are in darkness, Show yourselves." And we may see at the appearing of this man, by means of those who everywhere throughout the world have reposed a simple faith in Him, the fulfilment of this prediction: "They shall feed in the ways, and their pastures shall be in all the beaten tracks."

CHAPTER LIV

And since Celsus, although professing to know all about the Gospel, reproaches the Saviour because of His sufferings, saying that He received no assistance from the Father, or was unable to aid Himself; we have to state that His sufferings were the subject of prophecy, along with the cause of them; because it was for the benefit of mankind that He should die on their account, and should suffer stripes because of His condemnation. It was predicted, moreover, that some from among the Gentiles would come to the knowledge of Him (among whom the prophets are not included); and it had been declared that He would be seen in a form which is deemed dishonourable among men. The words of prophecy run thus: "Lo, my Servant shall have understanding, and shall be exalted and glorified, and raised exceedingly high. In like manner, many shall be astonished at Thee; so Thy form shall be in no reputation among men, and Thy glory among the sons of men. Lo, many nations shall marvel because of Him; and kings shall close their mouths: because they, to whom no message about Him was sent, shall see Him; and they who have not heard of Him, shall have knowledge of Him." "Lord, who hath believed our report? and to whom was the arm of the LORD revealed? We have reported, as a child before Him, as a root in a thirsty ground. He has no form nor glory; and we beheld Him, and He had not any form nor beauty: but His appearance was without honour, and deficient more than that of all men. He was a man under suffering, and who knew how to bear sickness: because His countenance was averted, He was treated with disrespect, and was made of no account. This man bears our sins, and suffers pain on our behalf; and we regarded Him as in trouble, and in suffering, and as ill-treated. But He was wounded for our sins, and bruised for our iniquities. The chastisement of our peace was upon Him; by His stripes we were healed. We all, like sheep, wandered from the way. A man wandered in his way, and the Lord delivered Him on account of our sins; and He, because of His evil treatment, opens not His mouth. As a sheep was He led to slaughter; and as a lamb before her shearer is dumb, so He opens not His mouth. In His humiliation His judgment was taken away. And who shall describe His generation? because His life is taken away from the earth; because of the iniquities of My people was He led unto death."

CHAPTER LV

Now I remember that, on one occasion, at a disputation held with certain Jews, who were reckoned wise men, I quoted these prophecies; to which my Jewish opponent replied, that these predictions bore reference to the whole people, regarded as *one individual*, and as being in a state of dispersion and suffering, in order that many proselytes might be gained, on account of the dispersion of the Jews among numerous heathen nations. And in this way he explained the words, "Thy form shall be of no reputation among men;" and then, "They to whom no message was sent respecting him shall see;" and the expression, "A man under suffering." Many arguments were employed on that occasion during the discussion to prove that these predictions regarding one particular person were not rightly applied by them to the whole nation. And I asked to what character the expression would be appropriate, "This man bears our sins, and suffers pain on our behalf;" and this, "But He was wounded for our sins, and bruised for our iniquities;" and to whom the expression properly belonged, "By His stripes were we healed." For it is manifest that it is they who had been sinners, and had been healed by the Saviour's sufferings (whether belonging to the Jewish nation or converts from the Gentiles), who use such language in the writings of the prophet who foresaw these events, and who, under the influence of the Holy Spirit, applied these words to a person. But we seemed to press them hardest with the expression, "Because of the iniquities of My people was He led away unto death." For if the people, according to them, are the subject of the prophecy, how is the man said to be led away to death because of the iniquities of the people of God, unless he be a different person from that people of God? And who is this person save Jesus Christ, by whose stripes they who believe on Him are healed, when "He had spoiled the principalities and powers (that were over us), and had made a show of them openly on His cross?" At another time we may explain the several parts of the prophecy, leaving none of them unexamined. But these matters have been treated at greater length, necessarily as I think, on account of the language of the Jew, as quoted in the work of Celsus.

CHAPTER LVI

Now it escaped the notice of Celsus, and of the Jew whom he has introduced, and of all who are not believers in Jesus, that the prophecies speak of two advents of Christ: the former characterized by human suffering and humility, in order that Christ, being with men, might make known the way that leads to God, and might leave no man in this life a ground of excuse, in saying that he knew not of the judgment to come; and the latter, distinguished only by glory and divinity, having no element of human infirmity intermingled with its divine greatness. To quote the prophecies at length would be tedious; and I deem it sufficient for the present to quote a part of the forty-fifth Psalm, which has this inscription, in addition to others, "A Psalm for the Beloved," where God is evidently addressed in these words: "Grace is poured into Thy lips: therefore God will bless Thee for ever and ever. Gird Thy sword on Thy thigh, O mighty One, with Thy beauty and Thy majesty. And stretch forth, and ride prosperously, and reign, because of Thy truth, and meekness, and righteousness; and Thy right hand shall lead Thee marvellously. Thine arrows are pointed, O mighty One; the people will fall under Thee in the heart of the enemies of the King." But attend carefully to what follows, where He is called God: "For Thy throne, O God, is for ever and ever: a sceptre of righteousness is the sceptre of Thy kingdom. Thou hast loved righteousness, and hated iniquity: therefore God, even Thy God, hath anointed Thee with the oil of gladness above Thy fellows." And observe that the prophet, speaking familiarly to God, whose "throne is for ever and ever," and "a sceptre of righteousness the sceptre of His kingdom," says that this God has been anointed by a God who was His God, and anointed, because more than His fellows He had loved righteousness and hated iniquity. And I remember that I pressed the Jew, who was deemed a learned man, very hard with this passage; and he, being perplexed about it, gave such an answer as was in keeping with his Judaistic views, saying that the words, "Thy throne, O God, is for ever and ever: a sceptre of righteousness is the sceptre of Thy kingdom," are spoken of the God of all things; and these, "Thou hast loved righteousness and hated iniquity, therefore Thy God hath anointed Thee," etc., refer to the Messiah.

CHAPTER LVII

The Jew, moreover, in the treatise, addresses the Saviour thus: "If you say that every man, born according to the decree of Divine Providence, is a son of God, in what respect should you differ from another?" In reply to whom we say, that every man who, as Paul expresses it, is no longer under fear, as a schoolmaster, but who chooses good for its own sake, is "a son of God;" but this man is distinguished far and wide above every man who is called, on account of his virtues, a son of God, seeing He is, as it were, a kind of source and beginning of all such. The words of Paul are as follow: "For ye have not received the spirit of bondage again to fear; but ye have received the Spirit of adoption, whereby we cry, Abba, Father." But, according to the Jew of Celsus, "countless individuals will convict Jesus of falsehood, alleging that those predictions which were spoken of him were intended of them." We are not aware, indeed, whether Celsus knew of any who, after coming into this world, and having desired to act as Jesus did, declared themselves to be also the "sons of God," or the "power" of God. But since it is in the spirit of truth that we examine each passage, we shall mention that there was a certain Theudas among the Jews before the birth of Christ, who gave himself out as some great one, after whose death his deluded followers were completely dispersed. And after him, in the days of the census, when Jesus appears to have been born, one Judas, a Galilean, gathered around him many of the Jewish people, saying he was a wise man, and a teacher of certain new doctrines. And when he also had paid the penalty of his rebellion, his doctrine was overturned, having taken hold of very few persons indeed, and these of the very humblest condition. And after the times of Jesus, Dositheus the Samaritan also wished to persuade the Samaritans that he was the Christ predicted by Moses; and he appears to have gained over some to his views. But it is not absurd, in quoting the extremely wise observation of that Gamaliel named in the book of Acts, to show how those persons above mentioned were strangers to the promise, being neither "sons of God" nor "powers" of God, whereas Christ Jesus was truly the Son of God. Now Gamaliel, in the passage referred to, said: "If this counsel or this work be of men, it will come to nought" (as also did the designs of those men already mentioned after their death); "but if it be of God, ye cannot overthrow this doctrine, lest haply ye be found even to fight against God." There was also Simon the Samaritan magician, who wished to draw away certain by his magical arts. And on that occasion he was successful; but now-a-days it is impossible to find, I suppose, thirty of his followers in the entire world, and probably I have even overstated the number. There are exceedingly few in Palestine; while in the rest of the world, through which he desired to spread the glory of his name, you find it nowhere mentioned. And where it is found, it is found quoted from the Acts of the Apostles; so that it is to Christians that he owes this mention of himself, the unmistakeable result having proved that Simon was in no respect divine.

CHAPTER LVIII

After these matters this Jew of Celsus, instead of the Magi mentioned in the Gospel, says that "Chaldeans are spoken of by Jesus as having been induced to come to him at his birth, and to worship him while yet an infant as a God, and to have made this known to Herod the tetrarch; and that the latter sent and slew all the infants that had been born about the same time, thinking that in this way he would ensure his death among the others; and that he was led to do this through fear that, if Jesus lived to a sufficient age, he would obtain the throne." See now in this instance the blunder of one who cannot distinguish between Magi and Chaldeans, nor perceive that what they profess is different, and so has falsified the Gospel narrative. I know not, moreover, why he has passed by in silence the cause which led the Magi to come, and why he has not stated, according to the scriptural account, that it was a star seen by them in the east. Let us see now what answer we have to make to these statements. The star that was seen in the east we consider to have been a new star, unlike any of the other well-known planetary bodies, either those in the firmament above or those among the lower orbs, but partaking of the nature of those celestial bodies which appear at times, such as comets, or those meteors which resemble beams of wood, or beards, or wine jars, or any of those other names by which the Greeks are accustomed to describe their varying appearances. And we establish our position in the following manner.

CHAPTER LIX

It has been observed that, on the occurrence of great events, and of mighty changes in terrestrial things, such stars are wont to appear, indicating either the removal of dynasties or the breaking out of wars, or the happening of such circumstances as may cause commotions upon the earth. But we have read in the *Treatise on Comets* by Chaeremon the Stoic, that on some occasions also, when *good* was to happen, comets made their appearance; and he gives an account of such instances. If, then, at the commencement of new dynasties, or on the occasion of other important events, there arises a comet so called, or any similar celestial body, why should it be matter of wonder that at the birth of Him who was to introduce a new doctrine to the human race, and to make known His teaching not only to Jews, but also to Greeks, and to many of the barbarous nations besides, a star should have arisen? Now I would say, that with respect to comets there is no prophecy in circulation to the effect that such and such a comet was to arise in connection with a particular kingdom or a particular time; but with respect to the appearance of a star at the birth of Jesus there is a prophecy of Balaam recorded by Moses to this effect: "There shall arise a star out of Jacob, and a man shall rise up out of Israel." And now, if it shall be deemed necessary to examine the narrative about the Magi, and the appearance of the star at the birth of Jesus, the following is what we have to say, partly in answer to the Greeks, and partly to the Jews.

CHAPTER LX

To the Greeks, then, I have to say that the Magi, being on familiar terms with evil spirits, and invoking them for such purposes as their knowledge and wishes extend to, bring about such results only as do not appear to exceed the superhuman power and strength of the evil spirits, and of the spells which invoke them, to accomplish; but should some greater manifestation of divinity be made, then the powers of the evil spirits are overthrown, being unable to resist the light of divinity. It is probable, therefore, that since at the birth of Jesus "a multitude of the heavenly host," as Luke records, and as I believe, "praised God, saying, Glory to God in the highest, and on earth peace, good-will towards men," the evil spirits on that account became feeble, and lost their strength, the falsity of their sorcery being manifested, and their power being broken; this overthrow being brought about not only by the angels having visited the terrestrial regions on account of the birth of Jesus, but also by the power of Jesus Himself, and His innate divinity. The Magi, accordingly, wishing to produce the customary results, which formerly they used to perform by means of certain spells and sorceries, sought to know the reason of their failure, conjecturing the cause to be a great one; and beholding a divine sign in the heaven, they desired to learn its signification. I am therefore of opinion that, possessing as they did the prophecies of Balaam, which Moses also records, inasmuch as Balaam was celebrated for such predictions, and finding among them the prophecy about the star, and the words, "I shall show him to him, but not now; I deem him happy, although he will not be near," they conjectured that the man whose appearance had been foretold along with that of the star, had actually come into the world; and having predetermined that he was superior in power to all demons, and to all common appearances and powers, they resolved to offer him homage. They came, accordingly, to Judea, persuaded that some king had been born; but not knowing over what kingdom he was to reign, and being ignorant also of the place of his birth, bringing gifts, which they offered to him as one whose nature partook, if I may so speak, both of God and of a mortal man,—gold, viz., as to a king; myrrh, as to one who was mortal; and incense, as to a God; and they brought these offerings after they had learned the place of His birth.

But since He was a God, the Saviour of the human race, raised far above all those angels which minister to men, an angel rewarded the piety of the Magi for their worship of Him, by making known to them that they were not to go back to Herod, but to return to their own homes by another way.

CHAPTER LXI

That Herod conspired against the Child (although the Jew of Celsus does not believe that this really happened), is not to be wondered at. For wickedness is in a certain sense blind, and would desire to defeat fate, as if it were stronger than it. And this being Herod's condition, he both believed that a king of the Jews had been born, and yet cherished a purpose contradictory of such a belief; not seeing that the Child is assuredly either a king and will come to the throne, or that he is not to be a king, and that his death, therefore, will be to no purpose. He desired accordingly to kill Him, his mind being agitated by contending passions on account of his wickedness, and being instigated by the blind and wicked devil who from the very beginning plotted against the Saviour, imagining that He was and would become some mighty one. An angel, however, perceiving the course of events, intimated to Joseph, although Celsus may not believe it, that he was to withdraw with the Child and His mother into Egypt, while Herod slew all the infants that were in Bethlehem and the surrounding borders, in the hope that he would thus destroy Him also who had been born King of the Jews. For he saw not the sleepless guardian power that is around those who deserve to be protected and preserved for the salvation of men, of whom Jesus is the first, superior to all others in honour and excellence, who was to be a King indeed, but not in the sense that Herod supposed, but in that in which it became God to bestow a kingdom,—for the benefit, viz., of those who were to be under His sway, who was to confer no ordinary and unimportant blessings, so to speak, upon His subjects, but who was to train them and to subject them to laws that were truly from God. And Jesus, knowing this well, and denying that He was a king in the sense that the multitude expected, but declaring the superiority of His kingdom, says: "If My kingdom were of this world, then would My servants fight, that I should not be delivered to the Jews: but now is My kingdom not of this world." Now, if Celsus had seen this, he would not have said: "But if, then, this was done in order that you might not reign in his stead when you had grown to man's estate; why, after you did reach that estate, do you not become a king, instead of you, the Son of God, wandering about in so mean a

329

condition, hiding yourself through fear, and leading a miserable life up and down?" Now, it is not dishonourable to avoid exposing one's self to dangers, but to guard carefully against them, when this is done, not through fear of death, but from a desire to benefit others by remaining in life, until the proper time come for one who has assumed human nature to die a death that will be useful to mankind. And this is plain to him who reflects that Jesus died for the sake of men,—a point of which we have spoken to the best of our ability in the preceding pages.

CHAPTER LXII

And after such statements, showing his ignorance even of the number of the apostles, he proceeds thus: "Jesus having gathered around him ten or eleven persons of notorious character, the very wickedest of tax-gatherers and sailors, fled in company with them from place to place, and obtained his living in a shameful and importunate manner." Let us to the best of our power see what truth there is in such a statement. It is manifest to us all who possess the Gospel narratives, which Celsus does not appear even to have read, that Jesus selected twelve apostles, and that of these Matthew alone was a tax-gatherer; that when he calls them indiscriminately sailors, he probably means James and John, because they left their ship and their father Zebedee, and followed Jesus; for Peter and his brother Andrew, who employed a net to gain their necessary subsistence, must be classed not as sailors, but as the Scripture describes them, as fishermen. The Lebes also, who was a follower of Jesus, may have been a tax-gatherer; but he was not of the number of the apostles, except according to a statement in one of the copies of Mark's Gospel. And we have not ascertained the employments of the remaining disciples, by which they earned their livelihood before becoming disciples of Jesus. I assert, therefore, in answer to such statements as the above, that it is clear to all who are able to institute an intelligent and candid examination into the history of the apostles of Jesus, that it was by help of a divine power that these men taught Christianity, and succeeded in leading others to embrace the word of God. For it was not any power of speaking, or any orderly arrangement of their message, according to the arts of Grecian dialectics or rhetoric, which was in them the effective cause of converting their hearers. Nay, I am of opinion that if Jesus had selected some individuals who were wise according to the apprehension of the multitude, and who were fitted both to think and speak so as to please them, and had used such as the ministers of His doctrine, He would most justly have been suspected of employing artifices, like those philosophers who are the leaders of certain sects, and consequently the promise respecting the divinity of His doctrine would not have manifested itself; for had the doctrine and the preaching consisted in the persuasive utterance and arrangement of words, then faith also, like that of the philosophers of the world in their opinions, would have been through the wisdom of men, and not through the power of God. Now, who is there on seeing fishermen and tax-gatherers, who had not acquired even the merest elements of learning (as the Gospel relates of them, and in respect to which Celsus believes that they speak the truth, inasmuch as it is their own ignorance which they record), discoursing boldly not only among the Jews of faith in Jesus, but also preaching Him with success among other nations, would not inquire whence they derived this power of persuasion, as theirs was certainly not the common method followed by the multitude? And who would not say that the promise, "Follow Me, and I will make you fishers of men," had been accomplished by Jesus in the history of His apostles by a sort of divine power? And to this also, Paul, referring in terms of commendation, as we have stated a little above, says: "And my speech and my preaching was not with enticing words of man's wisdom, but in demonstration of the Spirit and of power; that your faith should not stand in the wisdom of men, but in the power of God." For, according to the predictions in the prophets, foretelling the preaching of the Gospel, "the Lord gave the word in great power to them who preached it, even the King of the powers of the Beloved," in order that the prophecy might be fulfilled which said, "His words shall run very swiftly." And we see that "the voice of the apostles of Jesus has gone forth into all the earth, and their words to the end of the world." On this account are they who hear the word powerfully proclaimed filled with power, which they manifest both by their dispositions and their lives, and by struggling even to death on behalf of the truth; while some are altogether empty, although they profess to believe in God through Jesus, inasmuch as, not possessing any divine power, they have the appearance only of being converted to the word of God. And although I have previously mentioned a Gospel declaration uttered by the Saviour, I shall nevertheless quote it again, as appropriate to the present occasion, as it confirms both the divine manifestation of our Saviour's foreknowledge regarding the preaching of His Gospel, and the power of His word, which without the aid of teachers gains the mastery over those who yield their assent to persuasion accompanied with divine power; and the words of Jesus referred to are, "The harvest is plenteous, but the labourers are few; pray ye therefore the Lord of the harvest, that He will send forth labourers into His harvest."

CHAPTER LXIII

And since Celsus has termed the apostles of Jesus men of infamous notoriety, saying that they were tax-gatherers and sailors of the vilest character, we have to remark, with respect to this charge, that he seems, in order to bring an accusation against Christianity, to believe the Gospel accounts only where he pleases, and to express his disbelief of them, in order that he may not be forced to admit the manifestations of Divinity related in these same books; whereas one who sees the spirit of truth by which the writers are influenced, ought, from their narration of things of inferior importance, to believe also the account of divine things. Now in the general Epistle of Barnabas, from which perhaps Celsus took the statement that the apostles were notoriously wicked men, it is recorded that "Jesus selected His own apostles, as persons who were more guilty of sin than all other evildoers." And in the Gospel according to Luke, Peter says to Jesus, "Depart from me, O Lord, for I am a sinful man." Moreover, Paul, who himself also at a later time became an apostle of Jesus, says in his Epistle to Timothy, "This is a faithful saying, that Jesus Christ came into the world to save sinners, of whom I am the chief." And I do not know how Celsus should have forgotten or not have thought of saying something about Paul, the founder, after Jesus, of the Churches that are in Christ. He saw, probably, that anything he might say about that apostle would require to be explained, in consistency with the fact that, after being a persecutor of the Church of God, and a bitter opponent of believers, who went so far even as to deliver over the disciples of Jesus to death, so great a change afterwards passed over him, that he preached the Gospel of Jesus from Jerusalem round about to Illyricum, and was ambitious to carry the glad tidings where he needed not to build upon another man's foundation, but to places where the Gospel of God in Christ had not been proclaimed at all. What absurdity, therefore, is there, if Jesus, desiring to manifest to the human race the power which He possesses to heal souls, should have selected notorious and wicked men, and should have raised them to such a degree of moral excellence, that they became a pattern of the purest virtue to all who were converted by their instrumentality to the Gospel of Christ?

CHAPTER LXIV

But if we were to reproach those who have been converted with their former lives, then we would have occasion to accuse Phaedo also, even after he became a philosopher; since, as the history relates, he was drawn away by Socrates from a house of bad fame to the pursuits of philosophy. Nay, even the licentious life of Polemo, the successor of Xenocrates, will be a subject of reproach to philosophy; whereas even in these instances we ought to regard it as a ground of praise, that reasoning was enabled, by the persuasive power of these men, to convert from the practice of such vices those who had been formerly entangled by them. Now among the Greeks there was only one Phaedo, I know not if there were a second, and one Polemo, who betook themselves to philosophy, after a licentious and most wicked life; while with Jesus there were not only at the time we speak of, the twelve disciples, but many more at all times, who, becoming a band of temperate men, speak in the following terms of their former lives: "For we ourselves also were sometimes foolish, disobedient, deceived, serving divers lusts and pleasures, living in malice and envy, hateful, and hating one another. But after that the kindness and love of God our Saviour towards man appeared, by the washing of regeneration, and renewing of the Holy Ghost, which He shed upon us richly," we became such as we are. For "God sent forth His Word and healed them, and delivered them from their destructions," as the prophet taught in the book of Psalms. And in addition to what has been already said, I would add the following: that Chrysippus, in his treatise on the *Cure of the Passions*, in his endeavours to restrain the passions of the human soul, not pretending to determine what opinions are the true ones, says that according to the principles of the different sects are those to be cured who have been brought under the dominion of the passions, and continues: "And if pleasure be an end, then by it must the passions be healed; and if there be three kinds of chief blessings, still, according to this doctrine, it is in the same way that those are to be freed from their passions who are under their dominion;" whereas the assailants of Christianity do not see in how many persons the passions have been brought under restraint, and the flood of wickedness checked, and savage manners softened, by means of the Gospel. So that it well became those who are ever boasting of their zeal for the public good, to make a public acknowledgement of their thanks to that doctrine which by a new method led men to abandon many vices, and to bear their testimony at least to it, that even though not the truth, it has at all events been productive of benefit to the human race.

CHAPTER LXV

And since Jesus, in teaching His disciples not to be guilty of rashness, gave them the precept, "If they persecute you in this city, flee ye into another; and if they persecute you in the other, flee again into a third," to which teaching He added the example of a consistent life, acting so as not to expose Himself to danger rashly, or unseasonably, or without good grounds; from this Celsus takes occasion to bring a malicious and slanderous accusation,—the Jew whom he brings forward saying to Jesus, "In company with your disciples you go and hide yourself in different places." Now similar to what has thus been made the ground of a slanderous charge against Jesus and His disciples, do we say was the conduct recorded of Aristotle. This philosopher, seeing that a court was about to be summoned to try him, on the ground of his being guilty of impiety on account of certain of his philosophical tenets which the Athenians regarded as impious, withdrew from Athens, and fixed his school in Chalcis, defending his course of procedure to his friends by saying, "Let us depart from Athens, that we may not give the Athenians a handle for incurring guilt a second time, as formerly in the case of Socrates, and so prevent them from committing a second act of impiety against philosophy." He further says, "that Jesus went about with His disciples, and obtained His livelihood in a disgraceful and importunate manner." Let him show wherein lay the disgraceful and importunate element in their manner of subsistence. For it is related in the Gospels, that there were certain women who had been healed of their diseases, among whom also was Susanna, who from their own possessions afforded the disciples the means of support. And who is there among philosophers, that, when devoting himself to the service of his acquaintances, is not in the habit of receiving from them what is needful for his wants? Or is it only in them that such acts are proper and becoming; but when the disciples of Jesus do the same, they are accused by Celsus of obtaining their livelihood by disgraceful importunity?

CHAPTER LXVI

And in addition to the above, this Jew of Celsus afterwards addresses Jesus: "What need, moreover, was there that you, while still an infant, should be conveyed into Egypt? Was it to escape being murdered? But then it was not likely that a God should be afraid of death; and yet an angel came down from heaven, commanding you and your friends to flee, lest ye should be captured and put to death! And was not the great God, who had already sent two angels on your account, able to keep you, His only Son, there in safety?" From these words Celsus seems to think that there was no element of divinity in the human body and soul of Jesus, but that His body was not even such as is described in the fables of Homer; and with a taunt also at the blood of Jesus which was shed upon the cross, he adds that it was not

"Ichor, such as flows in the veins of the blessed gods."

We now, believing Jesus Himself, when He says respecting His divinity, "I am the way, and the truth, and the life," and employs other terms of similar import; and when He says respecting His being clothed with a human body, "And now ye seek to kill Me, a man that hath told you the truth," conclude that He was a kind of compound being. And so it became Him who was making provision for His sojourning in the world as a human being, not to expose Himself unseasonably to the danger of death. And in like manner it was necessary that He should be taken away by His parents, acting under the instructions of an angel from heaven, who communicated to them the divine will, saying on the first occasion, "Joseph, thou son of David, fear not to take unto thee Mary thy wife; for that which is conceived in her is of the Holy Ghost;" and on the second, "Arise, and take the young Child, and His mother, and flee into Egypt; and be thou there until I bring thee word: for Herod will seek the young Child to destroy Him." Now, what is recorded in these words appears to me to be not at all marvellous. For in either passage of Scripture it is stated that it was in a dream that the angel spoke these words; and that in a dream certain persons may have certain things pointed out to them to do, is an event of frequent occurrence to many individuals,—the impression on the mind being produced either by an angel or by some other thing. Where, then, is the absurdity in believing that He who had once become incarnate, should be led also by human guidance to keep out of the way of dangers? Not indeed from any impossibility that it should be otherwise, but from the moral fitness that ways and means should be made use of to ensure the safety of Jesus. And it was certainly better that the Child Jesus should escape the snare of Herod, and should reside with His parents in Egypt until the death of the conspirator, than that Divine Providence should hinder the free-will of Herod in his wish to put the Child to death, or that the fabled poetic helmet of Hades should have been employed, or anything of a similar kind done with respect to Jesus, or that they who came to destroy Him should have been smitten with blindness like the people of Sodom. For the sending of help to Him in a very miraculous and unnecessarily public manner, would not have been of any service to Him who wished to show that as a man, to whom witness was borne by God, He possessed within that form which was seen by the eyes of men some higher element of divinity,—that which was properly the

335

Son of God—God the Word—the power of God, and the wisdom of God—He who is called the Christ. But this is not a suitable occasion for discussing the composite nature of the incarnate Jesus; the investigation into such a subject being for believers, so to speak, a sort of private question.

CHAPTER LXVII

After the above, this Jew of Celsus, as if he were a Greek who loved learning, and were well instructed in Greek literature, continues: "The old mythological fables, which attributed a divine origin to Perseus, and Amphion, and Aeacus, and Minos, were not believed by us. Nevertheless, that they might not appear unworthy of credit, they represented the deeds of these personages as great and wonderful, and truly beyond the power of man; but what hast thou done that is noble or wonderful either in deed or in word? Thou hast made no manifestation to us, although they challenged you in the temple to exhibit some unmistakeable sign that you were the Son of God." In reply to which we have to say: Let the Greeks show to us, among those who have been enumerated, any one whose deeds have been marked by a utility and splendour extending to after generations, and which have been so great as to produce a belief in the fables which represented them as of divine descent. But these Greeks can show us nothing regarding those men of whom they speak, which is even inferior by a great degree to what Jesus did; unless they take us back to their fables and histories, wishing us to believe them without any reasonable grounds, and to discredit the Gospel accounts even after the clearest evidence. For we assert that the whole habitable world contains evidence of the works of Jesus, in the existence of those Churches of God which have been founded through Him by those who have been converted from the practice of innumerable sins. And the name of Jesus can still remove distractions from the minds of men, and expel demons, and also take away diseases; and produce a marvellous meekness of spirit and complete change of character, and a humanity, and goodness, and gentleness in those individuals who do not feign themselves to be Christians for the sake of subsistence or the supply of any mortal wants, but who have honestly accepted the doctrine concerning God and Christ, and the judgment to come.

CHAPTER LXVIII

But after this, Celsus, having a suspicion that the great works performed by Jesus, of which we have named a few out of a great number, would be brought forward to view, affects to grant that those statements may be true which are made regarding His cures, or His resurrection, or the feeding of a multitude with a few loaves, from which many fragments remained over, or those other stories which Celsus thinks the disciples have recorded as of a marvellous nature; and he adds: "Well, let us believe that these were actually wrought by you." But then he immediately compares them to the tricks of jugglers, who profess to do more wonderful things, and to the feats performed by those who have been taught by Egyptians, who in the middle of the market-place, in return for a few obols, will impart the knowledge of their most venerated arts, and will expel demons from men, and dispel diseases, and invoke the souls of heroes, and exhibit expensive banquets, and tables, and dishes, and dainties having no real existence, and who will put in motion, as if alive, what are not really living animals, but which have only the appearance of life. And he asks, "Since, then, these persons can perform such feats, shall we of necessity conclude that they are 'sons of God,' or must we admit that they are the proceedings of wicked men under the influence of an evil spirit?" You see that by these expressions he allows, as it were, the existence of magic. I do not know, however, if he is the same who wrote several books against it. But, as it helped his purpose, he compares the (miracles) related of Jesus to the results produced by magic. There would indeed be a resemblance between them, if Jesus, like the dealers in magical arts, had performed His works only for show; but now there is not a single juggler who, by means of his proceedings, invites his spectators to reform their manners, or trains those to the fear of God who are amazed at what they see, nor who tries to persuade them so to live as men who are to be justified by God. And jugglers do none of these things, because they have neither the power nor the will, nor any desire to busy themselves about the reformation of men, inasmuch as their own lives are full of the grossest and most notorious sins. But how should not He who, by the miracles which He did, induced those who beheld the excellent results to undertake the reformation of their characters, manifest Himself not only to His genuine disciples, but also to others, as a pattern of most virtuous life, in order that His disciples might devote themselves to the work of instructing men in the will of God, and that the others, after being more fully instructed by His word and character than by His miracles, as to how they were to direct their lives, might in all their conduct have a constant reference to the good pleasure of the universal God? And if such were the life of Jesus, how could any one with reason compare Him with the sect of impostors, and not, on the contrary, believe, according to the promise, that He was God, who appeared in human form to do good to our race?

CHAPTER LXIX

After this, Celsus, confusing together the Christian doctrine and the opinions of some heretical sect, and bringing them forward as charges that were applicable to all who believe in the divine word, says: "Such a body as yours could not have belonged to God." Now, in answer to this, we have to say that Jesus, on entering into the world, assumed, as one born of a woman, a human body, and one which was capable of suffering a natural death. For which reason, in addition to others, we say that He was also a great wrestler; having, on account of His human body, been tempted in all respects like other men, but no longer as men, with sin as a consequence, but being altogether without sin. For it is distinctly clear to us that "He did no sin, neither was guile found in His mouth; and as one who knew no sin," God delivered Him up as pure for all who had sinned. Then Celsus says: "The body of god would not have been so generated as you, O Jesus, were." He saw, besides, that if, as it is written, it had been born, His body somehow might be even more divine than that of the multitude, and in a certain sense a body of god. But he disbelieves the accounts of His conception by the Holy Ghost, and believes that He was begotten by one Panthera, who corrupted the Virgin, "because a god's body would not have been so generated as you were." But we have spoken of these matters at greater length in the preceding pages.

CHAPTER LXX

He asserts, moreover, that "the body of a god is not nourished with such food (as was that of Jesus)," since he is able to prove from the Gospel narratives both that He partook of food, and food of a particular kind. Well, be it so. Let him assert that He ate the passover with His disciples, when He not only used the words, "With desire have I desired to eat this passover with you," but also actually partook of the same. And let him say also, that He experienced the sensation of thirst beside the well of Jacob, and drank of the water of the well. In what respect do these facts militate against what we have said respecting the nature of His body? Moreover, it appears indubitable that after His resurrection He ate a piece of fish; for, according to our view, He assumed a (true) body, as one born of a woman. "But," objects Celsus, "the body of a god does not make use of such a voice as that of Jesus, nor employ such a method of persuasion as he." These are, indeed, trifling and altogether contemptible objections. For our reply to him will be, that he who is believed among the Greeks to be a god, viz., the Pythian and Didymean Apollo, makes use of such a voice for his Pythian priestess at Delphi, and for his prophetess at Miletus; and yet neither the Pythian nor Didymean is charged by the Greeks with not being a god, nor any other Grecian deity whose worship is established in one place. And it was far better, surely, that a god should employ a voice which, on account of its being uttered with power, should produce an indescribable sort of persuasion in the minds of the hearers.

CHAPTER LXXI

Continuing to pour abuse upon Jesus as one who, on account of his impiety and wicked opinions, was, so to speak, hated by God, he asserts that "these tenets of his were those of a wicked and God-hated sorcerer." And yet, if the name and the thing be properly examined, it will be found an impossibility that man should be hated by God, seeing God loves all existing things, and "hateth nothing of what He has made," for He created nothing in a spirit of hatred. And if certain expressions in the prophets convey such an impression, they are to be interpreted in accordance with the general principle by which Scripture employs such language with regard to God as if He were subject to human affections. But what reply need be made to him who, while professing to bring foreward credible statements, thinks himself bound to make use of calumnies and slanders against Jesus, as if He were a wicked sorcerer? Such is not the procedure of one who seeks to make good his case, but of one who is in an ignorant and unphilosophic state of mind, inasmuch as the proper course is to state the case, and candidly to investigate it; and, according to the best of his ability, to bring forward what occurs to him with regard to it. But as the Jew of Celsus has, with the above remarks, brought to a close his charges against Jesus, so we also shall here bring to a termination the contents of our first book in reply to him. And if God bestow the gift of that truth which destroys all falsehood, agreeably to the words of the prayer, "Cut them off in thy truth," we shall begin, in what follows, the consideration of the second appearance of the Jew, in which he is represented by Celsus as addressing those who have become converts to Jesus.

BOOK II

CHAPTER I

THE first book of our answer to the treatise of Celsus, entitled *A True Discourse*, which concluded with the representation of the Jew addressing Jesus, having now extended to a sufficient length, we intend the present part as a reply to the charges brought by him against those who have been converted from Judaism to Christianity. And we call attention, in the first place, to this special question, viz., why Celsus, when he had once resolved upon the introduction of individuals upon the stage of his book, did not represent the Jew as addressing the converts from heathenism rather than those from Judaism, seeing that his discourse, if directed to us, would have appeared more likely to produce an impression. But probably this claimant to universal knowledge does not know what is appropriate in the matter of such representations; and therefore let us proceed to consider what he has to say to the converts from Judaism. He asserts that "they have forsaken the law of their fathers, in consequence of their minds being led captive by Jesus; that they have been most ridiculously deceived, and that they have become deserters to another name and to another mode of life." Here he has not observed that the Jewish converts have not deserted the law of their fathers, inasmuch as they live according to its prescriptions, receiving their very name from the poverty of the law, according to the literal acceptation of the word; for Ebion signifies "poor" among the Jews, and those Jews who have received Jesus as Christ are called by the name of Ebionites. Nay, Peter himself seems to have observed for a considerable time the Jewish observances enjoined by the law of Moses, not having yet learned from Jesus to ascend from the law that is regulated according to the letter, to that which is interpreted according to the spirit,—a fact which we learn from the Acts of the Apostles. For on the day after the angel of God appeared to Cornelius, suggesting to him "to send to Joppa, to Simon surnamed Peter," Peter "went up into the upper room to pray about the sixth hour. And he became very hungry, and would have eaten: but while they made ready he fell into a trance, and saw heaven opened, and a certain vessel descending unto him, as it had been a great sheet knit at the four corners, and let down to the earth; wherein were all manner of four-footed beasts, and creeping things of the earth, and fowls of the air. And there came a voice to him, Rise, Peter; kill, and eat. But Peter said, Not so, Lord; for I have never eaten anything that is common or unclean. And the voice spake unto him again the second time, What God hath cleansed, that call thou not common." Now observe how, by this instance, Peter is represented as still observing the Jewish customs respecting clean and unclean animals. And from the narrative that follows, it is manifest that he, as being yet a Jew, and living according to their traditions, and despising those who were beyond the pale of Judaism, stood in need of a vision to lead him to communicate to Cornelius (who was not an Israelite according to the flesh), and to those who were with him, the word of faith. Moreover, in the Epistle to the Galatians, Paul states that Peter, still from fear of the Jews, ceased upon the arrival of James to eat with the Gentiles, and "separated himself from them, fearing them that were of the circumcision;" and the rest of the Jews, and Barnabas also, followed the same course. And certainly it was quite consistent that those should not abstain from the observance of Jewish usages who were sent to minister to the circumcision, when they who "seemed to be pillars" gave the right hand of fellowship to Paul and Barnabas, in order that, while devoting themselves to the circumcision, the latter might preach to the Gentiles. And why do I mention that they who preached to the circumcision withdrew and separated themselves from the heathen, when even Paul himself "became as a Jew to the Jews, that he might gain the Jews?" Wherefore also in the Acts of the Apostles it is related that he even brought an offering to the altar, that he might satisfy the Jews that he was no apostate from their law. Now, if Celsus had been acquainted with all these circumstances, he would not have represented the Jew holding such language as this to the converts from Judaism: "What induced you, my fellow-citizens, to abandon the law of your fathers, and to allow your minds to be led captive by him with whom we have just conversed, and thus be most ridiculously deluded, so as to become deserters from us to another name, and to the practices of another life?"

CHAPTER II

Now, since we are upon the subject of Peter, and of the teachers of Christianity to the circumcision, I do not deem it out of place to quote a certain declaration of Jesus taken from the Gospel according to John, and to give the explanation of the same. For it is there related that Jesus said: "I have yet many things to say unto you, but ye cannot bear them now. Howbeit when He, the Spirit of truth, is come, He will guide you into all the truth: for He shall not speak of Himself; but whatsoever He shall hear, that shall He speak." And when we inquire what were the

341

"many things" referred to in the passage which Jesus had to say to His disciples, but which they were not then able to bear, I have to observe that, probably because the apostles were Jews, and had been trained up according to the letter of the Mosaic law, He was unable to tell them what was the true law, and how the Jewish worship consisted in the pattern and shadow of certain heavenly things, and how future blessings were foreshadowed by the injunctions regarding meats and drinks, and festivals, and new moons, and sabbaths. These were many of the subjects which He had to explain to them; but as He saw that it was a work of exceeding difficulty to root out of the mind opinions that have been almost born with a man, and amid which he has been brought up till he reached the period of maturity, and which have produced in those who have adopted them the belief that they are divine, and that it is an act of impiety to overthrow them; and to demonstrate by the superiority of Christian doctrine, that is, by the truth, in a manner to convince the hearers, that such opinions were but "loss and dung," He postponed such a task to a future season—to that, namely, which followed His passion and resurrection. For the bringing of aid unseasonably to those who were not yet capable of receiving it, might have overturned the idea which they had already formed of Jesus, as the Christ, and the Son of the living God. And see if there is not some well-grounded reason for such a statement as this, "I have many things to say unto you, but ye cannot hear them now;" seeing there are many points in the law which require to be explained and cleared up in a spiritual sense, and these the disciples were in a manner unable to bear, having been born and brought up amongst Jews. I am of opinion, moreover, that since these rites were typical, and the truth was that which was to be taught them by the Holy Spirit, these words were added, "When He is come who is the Spirit of truth, He will lead you into all the truth;" as if He had said, into all the truth about those things which, being to you but types, ye believed to constitute a true worship which ye rendered unto God. And so, according to the promise of Jesus, the Spirit of truth came to Peter, saying to him, with regard to the four-footed beasts, and creeping things of the earth, and fowls of the air: "Arise, Peter; kill, and eat." And the Spirit came to him while he was still in a state of superstitious ignorance; for he said, in answer to the divine command, "Not so Lord; for I have never yet eaten anything common or unclean." He instructed him, however, in the true and spiritual meaning of meats, by saying, "What God hath cleansed, that call not thou common." And so, after that vision, the Spirit of truth, which conducted Peter into all the truth, told him the many things which he was unable to bear when Jesus was still with him in the

342

flesh. But I shall have another opportunity of explaining those matters, which are connected with the literal acceptation of the Mosaic law.

CHAPTER III

Our present object, however, is to expose the ignorance of Celsus, who makes this Jew of his address his fellow-citizen and the Israelitish converts in the following manner: "What induced you to abandon the law of your fathers?" etc. Now, how should they have abandoned the law of their fathers, who are in the habit of rebuking those who do not listen to its commands, saying, "Tell me, ye who read the law, do ye not hear the law? For it is written, that Abraham had two sons;" and so on, down to the place, "which things are an allegory," etc.? And how have they abandoned the law of their fathers, who are ever speaking of the usages of their fathers in such words as these: "Or does not the law say these things also? For it is written in the law of Moses, Thou shalt not muzzle the mouth of the ox that treadeth out the corn. Doth God care for oxen? or saith He it altogether for our sakes? for for our sakes it was written," and so on? Now, how confused is the reasoning of the Jew in regard to these matters (although he had it in his power to speak with greater effect) when he says: "Certain among you have abandoned the usages of our fathers under a pretence of explanations and allegories; and some of you, although, as ye pretend, interpreting them in a spiritual manner, nevertheless do observe the customs of our fathers; and some of you, without any such interpretation, are willing to accept Jesus as the subject of prophecy, and to keep the law of Moses according to the customs of the fathers, as having in the words the whole mind of the Spirit." Now how was Celsus able to see these things so clearly in this place, when in the subsequent parts of his work he makes mention of certain godless heresies altogether alien from the doctrine of Jesus, and even of others which leave the Creator out of account altogether, and does not appear to know that there are Israelites who are converts to Christianity, and who have not abandoned the law of their fathers? It was not his object to investigate everything here in the spirit of truth, and to accept whatever he might find to be useful; but he composed these statements in the spirit of an enemy, and with a desire to overthrow everything as soon as he heard it.

CHAPTER IV

The Jew, then, continues his address to converts from his own nation thus: "Yesterday and the day before, when we visited with punishment the man who deluded you, ye became apostates from the law of your fathers;" showing by such statements (as we have just demonstrated) anything but an exact knowledge of the truth. But what he advances afterwards seems to have some force, when he says: "How is it that you take the beginning of your system from our worship, and when you have made some progress you treat it with disrespect, although you have no other foundation to show for your doctrines than our law?" Now, certainly the introduction to Christianity is through the Mosaic worship and the prophetic writings; and after the introduction, it is in the interpretation and explanation of these that progress takes place, while those who are introduced prosecute their investigations into "the mystery according to revelation, which was kept secret since the world began, but now is made manifest in the Scriptures of the prophets," and by the appearance of our Lord Jesus Christ. But they who advance in the knowledge of Christianity do not, as ye allege, treat the things written in the law with disrespect. On the contrary, they bestow upon them greater honour, showing what a depth of wise and mysterious reasons is contained in these writings, which are not fully comprehended by the Jews, who treat them superficially, and as if they were in some degree even fabulous. And what absurdity should there be in our system—that is, the Gospel—having the law for its foundation, when even the Lord Jesus Himself said to those who would not believe upon Him: "If ye had believed Moses, ye would have believed Me, for he wrote of Me. But if ye do not believe his writings, how shall ye believe My words?" Nay, even one of the evangelists— Mark—says: "The beginning of the Gospel of Jesus Christ, as it is written in the prophet Isaiah, Behold, I send My messenger before Thy face, who shall prepare Thy way before Thee," which shows that the beginning of the Gospel is connected with the Jewish writings. What force, then, is there in the objection of the Jew of Celsus, that "if any one predicted to us that the Son of God was to visit mankind, he was one of our prophets, and the prophet of our God?" Or how is it a charge against Christianity, that John, who baptized Jesus, was a Jew? For although He was a Jew, it does not follow that every believer, whether a convert from heathenism or from Judaism, must yield a literal obedience to the law of Moses.

CHAPTER V

After these matters, although Celsus becomes tautological in his statements about Jesus, repeating for the second time that "he was punished by the Jews for his crimes," we shall not again take up the defence, being satisfied with what we have already said. But, in the next place, as this Jew of his disparages the doctrine regarding the resurrection of the dead, and the divine judgment, and of the rewards to be bestowed upon the just, and of the fire which is to devour the wicked, as being stale opinions, and thinks that he will overthrow Christianity by asserting that there is nothing new in its teaching upon these points, we have to say to him, that our Lord, seeing the conduct of the Jews not to be at all in keeping with the teaching of the prophets, inculcated by a parable that the kingdom of God would be taken from them, and given to the converts from heathenism. For which reason, now, we may also see of a truth that all the doctrines of the Jews of the present day are mere trifles and fables, since they have not the light that proceeds from the knowledge of the Scriptures; whereas those of the Christians are the truth, having power to raise and elevate the soul and understanding of man, and to persuade him to seek a citizenship, not like the earthly Jews here below, but in heaven. And this result shows itself among those who are able to see the grandeur of the ideas contained in the law and the prophets, and who are able to commend them to others.

CHAPTER VI

But let it be granted that Jesus observed all the Jewish usages, including even their sacrificial observances, what does that avail to prevent our recognising Him as the Son of God? Jesus, then, is the Son of God, who gave the law and the prophets; and we, who belong to the Church, do not transgress the law, but have escaped the mythologizings of the Jews, and have our minds chastened and educated by the mystical contemplation of the law and the prophets. For the prophets themselves, as not resting the sense of these words in the plain history which they relate, nor in the legal enactments taken according to the word and letter, express themselves somewhere, when about to relate histories, in words like this, "I will open my mouth in parables, I will utter hard sayings of old;" and in another place, when offering up a prayer regarding the law as being obscure, and needing divine help for its comprehension, they offer up this prayer, "Open Thou mine eyes, that I may behold wondrous things out of Thy law."

CHAPTER VII

Moreover, let them show where there is to be found even the

appearance of language dictated by arrogance and proceeding from Jesus. For how could an arrogant man thus express himself, "Learn of Me, for I am meek and lowly of heart, and you shall find rest for your souls?" or how can He be styled arrogant, who after supper laid aside His garments in the presence of His disciples, and, after girding Himself with a towel, and pouring water into a basin, proceeded to wash the feet of each disciple, and rebuked him who was unwilling to allow them to be washed, with the words, "Except I wash thee, thou hast no part with Me?" Or how could He be called such who said, "I was amongst you, not as he that sitteth at meat, but as he that serveth?" And let any one show what were the falsehoods which He uttered, and let him point out what are great and what are small falsehoods, that he may prove Jesus to have been guilty of the former. And there is yet another way in which we may confute him. For as one falsehood is not less or more false than another, so one truth is not less or more true than another. And what charges of impiety he has to bring against Jesus, let the Jew of Celsus especially bring forward. Was it impious to abstain from corporeal circumcision, and from a literal Sabbath, and literal festivals, and literal new moons, and from clean and unclean meats, and to turn the mind to the good and true and spiritual law of God, while at the same time he who was an ambassador for Christ knew how to become to the Jews as a Jew, that he might gain the Jews, and to those who are under the law, as under the law, that he might gain those who are under the law?

CHAPTER VIII

He says, further, that "many other persons would appear such as Jesus was, to those who were willing to be deceived." Let this Jew of Celsus then show us, not many persons, nor even a few, but a single individual, such as Jesus was, introducing among the human race, with the power that was manifested in Him, a system of doctrine and opinions beneficial to human life, and which converts men from the practice of wickedness. He says, moreover, that this charge is brought against the Jews by the Christian converts, that they have not believed in Jesus as in God. Now on this point we have, in the preceding pages, offered a preliminary defence, showing at the same time in what respects we understand Him to be God, and in what we take Him to be man. "How should we," he continues, "who have made known to all men that there is to come from God one who is to punish the wicked, treat him with disregard when he came?" And to this, as an exceedingly silly argument, it does not seem to me reasonable to offer any answer. It is as if some one were to say, "How could we, who teach temperance, commit any act of licentiousness? or we, who are ambassadors for righteousness, be guilty of any wickedness?" For as these inconsistencies are found among men, so, to say that they believed the prophets when speaking of the future advent of Christ, and yet refused their belief to Him when He came, agreeably to prophetic statement, was quite in keeping with human nature. And since we must add another reason, we shall remark that this very result was foretold by the prophets. Isaiah distinctly declares: "Hearing ye shall hear, and shall not understand; and seeing ye shall see, and shall not perceive: for the heart of this people has become fat," etc. And let them explain why it was predicted to the Jews, that although they both heard and saw, they would not understand what was said, nor perceive what was seen as they ought. For it is indeed manifest, that when they beheld Jesus they did not see who He was; and when they heard Him, they did not understand from His words the divinity that was in Him, and which transferred God's providential care, hitherto exercised over the Jews, to His converts from the heathen. Therefore we may see, that after the advent of Jesus the Jews were altogether abandoned, and possess now none of what were considered their ancient glories, so that there is no indication of any Divinity abiding amongst them. For they have no longer prophets nor miracles, traces of which to a considerable extent are still found among Christians, and some of them more remarkable than any that existed among the Jews; and these we ourselves have witnessed, if our testimony may be received. But the Jew of Celsus exclaims: "Why did we treat him, whom we announced beforehand, with dishonour? Was it that we might be chastised more than others?" To which we have to answer, that on account of their unbelief, and the other insults which they heaped upon Jesus, the Jews will not only suffer more than others in that judgment which is believed to impend over the world, but have even already endured such sufferings. For what nation is an exile from their own metropolis, and from the place sacred to the worship of their fathers, save the Jews alone? And these calamities they have suffered, because they were a most wicked nation, which, although guilty of many other sins, yet has been punished so severely for none, as for those that were committed against our Jesus.

CHAPTER IX

The Jew continues his discourse thus: "How should we deem him to be a God, who not only in other respects, as was currently reported, performed none of his promises, but who also, after we had convicted him, and condemned him as deserving of punishment, was found attempting to conceal himself, and endeavouring to escape in a most disgraceful manner, and who was betrayed by those whom he called disciples? And yet," he continues, "he who was a God could neither flee nor be led away a prisoner; and least of all could he be deserted and delivered up by those who had been his associates, and had shared all things in common, and had had him for their teacher, who was deemed to be a Saviour, and a son of the greatest God, and an angel." To which we reply, that even we do not suppose the body of Jesus, which was then an object of sight and perception, to have been God. And why do I say His body? Nay, not even His soul, of which it is related, "My soul is exceeding sorrowful, even unto death." But as, according to the Jewish manner of speaking, "I am the Lord, the God of all flesh," and, "Before Me there was no God formed, neither shall there be after Me," God is believed to be He who employs the soul and body of the prophet as an instrument; and as, according to the Greeks, he who says,

"I know both the number of the sand, and the measures of the sea,
And I understand a dumb man, and hear him who does not speak,"

is considered to be a god when speaking, and making himself heard through the Pythian priestess; so, according to our view, it was the Logos God, and Son of the God of all things, who spake in Jesus these words, "I am the way, and the truth, and the life;" and these, "I am the door;" and these, "I am the living bread that came down from heaven;" and other expressions similar to these. We therefore charge the Jews with not acknowledging Him to be God, to whom testimony was borne in many passages by the prophets, to the effect that He was a mighty power, and a God next to the God and Father of all things. For we assert that it was to Him the Father gave the command, when in the Mosaic account of the creation He uttered the words, "Let there be light," and "Let there be a firmament," and gave the injunctions with regard to those other creative acts which were performed; and that to Him also were addressed the words, "Let Us make man in Our own image and likeness;" and that the Logos, when commanded, obeyed all the Father's will. And we make these statements not from our own conjectures, but because we believe the prophecies circulated among the Jews, in which it is said of God, and of the works of creation, in express words, as follows: "He spake, and they were made; He commanded, and they were created." Now if God gave the command, and the creatures were formed, who, according to the view of the spirit of prophecy, could He be that was able to carry out such commands of the Father, save Him who, so to speak, is the living Logos and the Truth? And that the Gospels do not consider him who in Jesus said these words, "I am the way, and the truth, and the life," to have been of so circumscribed a nature as to have an existence nowhere out of the soul and body of Jesus, is evident both from many considerations, and from a few instances of the following kind which we shall quote. John the Baptist, when predicting that the Son of God was to appear immediately, not in that body and soul, but as manifesting Himself everywhere, says regarding Him: "There stands in the midst of you One whom ye know not, who cometh after me." For if he had thought that the Son of God was only there, where was the visible body of Jesus, how could he have said, "There stands in the midst of you One whom ye know not?" And Jesus Himself, in raising the minds of His disciples to higher thoughts of the Son of God, says: "Where two or three are gathered together in My name, there am I in the midst of you." And of the same nature is His promise to His disciples: "Lo, I am with you alway, even to the end of the world." And we quote these passages, making no distinction between the Son of God and Jesus. For the soul and body of Jesus formed, after the *oikonomia*, one being with the Logos of God. Now if, according to Paul's teaching, "he that is joined unto the Lord is one spirit," every one who understands what being joined to the Lord is, and who has been actually joined to Him, is one spirit with the Lord; how should not that being be one in a far greater and more divine degree, which was once united with the Logos of God? He, indeed, manifested Himself among the Jews as the power of God, by the miracles which He performed, which Celsus suspected were accomplished by sorcery, but which by the Jews of that time were attributed I know not why, to Beelzebub, in the words: "He casteth out devils through Beelzebub, the prince of the devils." But these our Saviour convicted of uttering the greatest absurdities, from the fact that the kingdom of evil was not yet come to an end. And this will be evident to all intelligent readers of the Gospel narrative, which it is not now the time to explain.

CHAPTER X

But what promise did Jesus make which He did not perform? Let Celsus produce any instance of such, and make good his charge. But he will be unable to do so, especially since it is from mistakes, arising either from misapprehension of the Gospel narratives, or from Jewish stories, that he thinks to derive the charges which he brings against Jesus or against ourselves. Moreover, again, when the Jew says, "We both found him guilty, and condemned him as deserving of death," let them show how they who sought to concoct false witness against Him proved Him to be guilty. Was not the great charge against Jesus, which His accusers brought forward, this, that He said, "I am able to destroy the temple of God, and after three days to raise it up again?" But in so saying, He spake of the temple of His body; while they thought, not being able to understand the meaning of the speaker, that His reference was to the temple of stone, which was treated by the Jews with greater respect than He was who ought to have been honoured as the true Temple of God—the Word, and the Wisdom, and the Truth. And who can say that "Jesus attempted to make His escape by disgracefully concealing Himself?" Let any one point to an act deserving to be called disgraceful. And when he adds, "he was taken prisoner," I would say that, if to be taken prisoner implies an act done against one's will, then Jesus was not taken prisoner; for at the fitting time He did not prevent Himself falling into the hands of men, as the Lamb of God, that He might take away the sin of the world. For, knowing all things that were to come upon Him, He went forth, and said to them, "Whom seek ye?" and they answered, "Jesus of Nazareth;" and He said unto them, "I am He." And Judas also, who betrayed Him, was standing with them. When, therefore, He had said to them, "I am He," they went backwards and fell to the ground. Again He asked them, "Whom seek ye?" and they said again, "Jesus of Nazareth." Jesus said to them, "I told you I am He; if then ye seek Me, let these go away." Nay, even to Him who wished to help Him, and who smote the high priest's servant, and cut off his ear, He said: "Put up thy sword into its sheath: for all they who draw the sword shall perish by the sword. Thinkest thou that I cannot even now pray to My Father, and He will presently give Me more than twelve legions of angels? But how then should the Scriptures be fulfilled, that thus it must be?" And if any one imagines these statements to be inventions of the writers of the Gospels, why should not those statements rather be regarded as inventions which proceeded from a spirit of hatred and hostility against Jesus and the Christians? and these the truth, which proceed from those who manifest the sincerity of their feelings towards Jesus, by enduring everything, whatever it may be, for the sake of His words? For the reception by the disciples of such power of endurance and resolution continued even to death, with a disposition of mind that would not invent regarding their Teacher what was not true, is a very evident proof to all candid judges that they were fully persuaded of the truth of what they wrote, seeing they submitted to trials so numerous and so severe, for the sake of Him whom they believed to be the Son of God.

CHAPTER XI

In the next place, that He was betrayed by those whom He called His disciples, is a circumstance which the Jew of Celsus learned from the Gospels; calling the one Judas, however, "many disciples," that he might seem to add force to the accusation. Nor did he trouble himself to take note of all that is related concerning Judas; how this Judas, having come to entertain opposite and conflicting opinions regarding his Master neither opposed Him with his whole soul, nor yet with his whole soul preserved the respect due by a pupil to his teacher. For he that betrayed Him gave to the multitude that came to apprehend Jesus, a sign, saying, "Whomsoever I shall kiss, it is he; seize ye him,"—retaining still some element of respect for his Master: for unless he had done so, he would have betrayed Him, even publicly, without any pretence of affection. This circumstance, therefore, will satisfy all with regard to the purpose of Judas, that along with his covetous disposition, and his wicked design to betray his Master, he had still a feeling of a mixed character in his mind, produced in him by the words of Jesus, which had the appearance (so to speak) of some remnant of good. For it is related that, "when Judas, who betrayed Him, knew that He was condemned, he repented, and brought back the thirty pieces of silver to the high priest and elders, saying, I have sinned, in that I have betrayed the innocent blood. But they said, What is that to us? see thou to that;"—and that, having thrown the money down in the temple, he departed, and went and hanged himself. But if this covetous Judas, who also stole the money placed in the bag for the relief of the poor, repented, and brought back the thirty pieces of silver to the chief priests and elders, it is clear that the instructions of Jesus had been able to produce some feeling of repentance in his mind, and were not altogether despised and loathed by this traitor. Nay, the declaration, "I have sinned, in that I have betrayed the innocent blood," was a public acknowledgment of his crime. Observe, also, how exceedingly passionate was the sorrow for his sins that proceeded from that repentance, and which would not suffer him any longer to live; and how, after he had cast the money down in the temple, he withdrew, and went away and hanged himself: for he passed sentence upon himself, showing what a power the teaching of Jesus had over this sinner Judas, this thief and traitor, who could not always treat with contempt what he had learned from Jesus. Will Celsus and his friends now say that those proofs which show that the apostasy of Judas was not a complete apostasy, even after his attempts against his Master, are inventions, and that this alone is true, viz., that one of His disciples betrayed Him; and will they add to the Scriptural account that he betrayed Him also with his whole heart? To act in this spirit of hostility with the same writings, both as to what we are to believe and what we are not to believe, is absurd. And if we must make a statement regarding Judas which may overwhelm our opponents with shame, we would say that, in the book of Psalms, the whole of the 108th contains a prophecy about Judas, the beginning of which is this: "O God, hold not Thy peace before my praise; for the mouth of the sinner, and the mouth of the crafty man, are opened against me." And it is predicted in this psalm, both that Judas separated himself from the number of the apostles on account of his sins, and that another was selected in his place; and this is shown by the words: "And his bishopric let another take." But suppose now that He had been betrayed by some one of His disciples, who was possessed by a worse spirit than Judas, and who had completely poured out, as it were, all the words which he had heard from Jesus, what would this contribute to an accusation against Jesus or the Christian religion? And how will this demonstrate its doctrine to be false? We have replied in the preceding chapter to the statements which follow this, showing that Jesus was not taken prisoner when attempting to flee, but that He gave Himself up voluntarily for the sake of us all. Whence it follows, that even if He were bound, He was bound agreeably to His own will; thus teaching us the lesson that we should undertake similar things for the sake of religion in no spirit of unwillingness.

CHAPTER XII

And the following appear to me to be childish assertions, viz., that "no good general and leader of great multitudes was ever betrayed; nor even a wicked captain of robbers and commander of very wicked men, who seemed to be of any use to his associates; but Jesus, having been betrayed by his subordinates, neither governed like a good general, nor, after deceiving his disciples, produced in the minds of the victims of his deceit that feeling of good-will which, so to speak, would be manifested towards a brigand chief." Now one might find many accounts of generals who were betrayed by their own soldiers, and of robber chiefs who were captured through the instrumentality of those who did not keep their bargains with them. But grant that no general or robber chief was ever betrayed, what does that contribute to the establishment of the fact as a charge against Jesus, that one of His disciples became His betrayer? And since Celsus makes an ostentatious exhibition of philosophy, I would ask of him, If, then, it was a charge against Plato, that Aristotle, after being his pupil for twenty years, went away and assailed his doctrine of the immortality of the soul, and styled the ideas of Plato the merest trifling? And if I were still in doubt, I would continue thus: Was Plato no longer mighty in dialectics, nor able to defend his views, after Aristotle had taken his departure; and, on that account, are the opinions of Plato false? Or may it not be, that while Plato is true, as the pupils of his philosophy would maintain, Aristotle was guilty of wickedness and ingratitude towards his teacher? Nay, Chrysippus also, in many places of his writings, appears to assail Cleanthes, introducing novel opinions opposed to his views, although the latter had been his teacher when he was a young man, and began the study of philosophy. Aristotle, indeed, is said to have been Plato's pupil for twenty years, and no inconsiderable period was spent by Chrysippus in the school of Cleanthes; while Judas did not remain so much as three years with Jesus. But from the narratives of the lives of philosophers we might take many instances similar to those on which Celsus founds a charge against Jesus on account of Judas. Even the Pythagoreans erected cenotaphs to those who, after betaking themselves to philosophy, fell back again into their ignorant mode of life; and yet neither was Pythagoras nor his followers, on that account, weak in argument and demonstration.

CHAPTER XIII

This Jew of Celsus continues, after the above, in the following fashion: "Although he could state many things regarding the events of the life of Jesus which are true, and not like those which are recorded by the disciples, he willingly omits them." What, then, are those true statements, unlike the accounts in the Gospels, which the Jew of Celsus passes by without mention? Or is he only employing what appears to be a figure of speech, in pretending to have something to say, while in reality he had nothing to produce beyond the Gospel narrative which could impress the hearer with a feeling of its truth, and furnish a clear ground of accusation against Jesus and His doctrine? And he charges the disciples with having invented the statement that Jesus foreknew and foretold all that happened to Him; but the truth of this statement we shall establish, although Celsus may not like it, by means of many other predictions uttered by the Saviour, in which He foretold what would befall the Christians in after generations. And who is there who would not be astonished at this prediction: "Ye shall be brought before governors and kings for My sake, for a testimony against them and the Gentiles;" and at any others which He may have delivered respecting the future persecution of His disciples? For what system of opinions ever existed among men on account of which others are punished, so that any one of the accusers of Jesus could say that, foreseeing the impiety or falsity of his opinions to be the ground of an accusation against them he thought that this would redound to his credit, that he had so predicted regarding it long before? Now if any deserve to be brought, on account of their opinions, before governors and kings, what others are they, save the Epicureans, who altogether deny the existence of providence? And also the Peripatetics, who say that prayers are of no avail, and sacrifices offered as to the Divinity? But some one will say that the Samaritans suffer persecution because of their religion. In answer to whom we shall state that the Sicarians, on account of the practice of circumcision, as mutilating themselves contrary to the established laws and the customs permitted to the Jews alone, are put to death. And you never hear a judge inquiring whether a Sicarian who strives to live according to this established religion of his will be released from punishment if he apostatizes, but will be led away to death if he continues firm; for the evidence of the circumcision is sufficient to ensure the death of him who has undergone it. But Christians alone, according to the prediction of their Saviour, "Ye shall be brought before governors and kings for My sake," are urged up to their last breath by their judges to deny Christianity, and to sacrifice according to the public customs; and after the oath of abjuration, to return to their homes, and to live in safety. And observe whether it is not with great authority that this declaration is uttered: "Whosoever therefore shall confess Me before men, him will I confess also before My Father who is in heaven. And whosoever shall deny Me before men," etc. And go back with me in thought to Jesus when He uttered these words, and see His predictions not yet accomplished. Perhaps you will say, in a spirit of incredulity, that he is talking folly, and speaking to no purpose, for his words will have no fulfilment; or, being in doubt about assenting to his words, you will say, that if these predictions be fulfilled, and the doctrine of Jesus be established, so that governors and kings think of destroying those who acknowledge Jesus, then we shall believe that he utters these prophecies as one who has received great power from God to implant this doctrine among the human race, and as believing that it will prevail. And who will not be filled with wonder, when he goes back in thought to Him who then taught and said, "This Gospel shall be preached throughout the whole world, for a testimony against them and the Gentiles," and beholds, agreeably to His words, the Gospel of Jesus Christ preached in the whole world under heaven to Greeks and Barbarians, wise and foolish alike? For the word, spoken with power, has gained the mastery over men of all sorts of nature, and it is impossible to see any race of men which has escaped accepting the teaching of Jesus. But let this Jew of Celsus, who does not believe that He foreknew all that happened to Him, consider how, while Jerusalem was still standing, and the whole Jewish worship celebrated in it, Jesus foretold what would befall it from the hand of the Romans. For they will not maintain that the acquaintances and pupils of Jesus Himself handed down His teaching contained in the Gospels without committing it to writing, and left His disciples without the memoirs of Jesus contained in their works. Now in these it is recorded, that "when ye shall see Jerusalem compassed about with armies, then shall ye know that the desolation thereof is nigh." But at that time there were no armies around Jerusalem, encompassing and enclosing and besieging it; for the siege began in the reign of Nero, and lasted till the government of Vespasian, whose son Titus destroyed Jerusalem, on account, as Josephus says, of James the Just, the brother of Jesus who was called Christ, but in reality, as the truth makes clear, on account of Jesus Christ the Son of God.

CHAPTER XIV

Celsus, however, accepting or granting that Jesus foreknew what would befall Him, might think to make light of the admission, as he did in the case of the miracles, when he alleged that they were wrought by means of sorcery; for he might say that many persons by means of divination, either by auspices, or auguries, or sacrifices, or nativities, have come to the knowledge of what was to happen. But this concession he would not make, as being too great a one; and although he somehow granted that Jesus worked miracles, he thought to weaken the force of this by the charge of sorcery. Now Phlegon, in the thirteenth or fourteenth book, I think, of his Chronicles, not only ascribed to Jesus a knowledge of future events (although falling into confusion about some things which refer to Peter, as if they referred to Jesus), but also testified that the result corresponded to His predictions. So that he also, by these very admissions regarding foreknowledge, as if against his will, expressed his opinion that the doctrines taught by the fathers of our system were not devoid of divine power.

CHAPTER XV

Celsus continues: "The disciples of Jesus, having no undoubted fact on which to rely, devised the fiction that he foreknew everything before it happened;" not observing, or not wishing to observe, the love of truth which actuated the writers, who acknowledged that Jesus had told His disciples beforehand, "All ye shall be offended because of Me this night,"—a statement which was fulfilled by their all being offended; and that He predicted to Peter, "Before the cock crow, thou shalt deny Me thrice," which was followed by Peter's threefold denial. Now if they had not been lovers of truth, but, as Celsus supposes, inventors of fictions, they would not have represented Peter as denying, nor His disciples as being offended. For although these events actually happened, who could have proved that they turned out in that manner? And yet, according to all probability, these were matters which ought to have been passed over in silence by men who wished to teach the readers of the Gospels to despise death for the sake of confessing Christianity. But now, seeing that the word, by its power, will gain the mastery over men, they related those facts which they have done, and which, I know not how, were neither to do any harm to their readers, nor to afford any pretext for denial.

CHAPTER XVI

Exceedingly weak is his assertion, that "the disciples of Jesus wrote such accounts regarding him, by way of extenuating the charges that told against him: as if," he says, "any one were to say that a certain person was a just man, and yet were to show that he was guilty of injustice; or that he was pious, and yet had committed murder; or that he was immortal, and yet was dead; subjoining to all these statements the remark that he had foretold all these things." Now his illustrations are at once seen to be inappropriate; for there is no absurdity in Him who had resolved that He would become a living pattern to men, as to the manner in which they were to regulate their lives, showing also how they ought to die for the sake of their religion, apart altogether from the fact that His death on behalf of men was a benefit to the whole world, as we proved in the preceding book. He imagines, moreover, that the whole of the confession of the Saviour's sufferings confirms his objection instead of weakening it. For he is not acquainted either with the philosophical remarks of Paul, or the statements of the prophets, on this subject. And it escaped him that certain heretics have declared that Jesus underwent His sufferings in appearance, not in reality. For had he known, he would not have said: "For ye do not even allege this, that he seemed to wicked men to suffer this punishment, though not undergoing it in reality; but, on the contrary, ye acknowledge that he openly suffered." But we do not view His sufferings as having been merely in appearance, in order that His resurrection also may not be a false, but a real event. For he who really died, actually arose, if he did arise; whereas he who appeared only to have died, did not in reality arise. But since the resurrection of Jesus Christ is a subject of mockery to unbelievers, we shall quote the words of Plato, that Erus the son of Armenius rose from the funeral pile twelve days after he had been laid upon it, and gave an account of what he had seen in Hades; and as we are replying to unbelievers, it will not be altogether useless to refer in this place to what Heraclides relates respecting the woman who was deprived of life. And many persons are recorded to have risen from their tombs, not only on the day of their burial, but also on the day following. What wonder is it, then, if in the case of One who performed many marvellous things, both beyond the power of man and with such fulness of evidence, that he who could not deny their performance, endeavoured to calumniate them by comparing them to acts of sorcery, should have manifested also in His death some greater display of divine power, so that His soul, if it pleased, might leave its body, and having performed certain offices out of it, might return again at pleasure? And such a declaration is Jesus said to have made in the Gospel of John, when He said: "No man taketh My life from Me, but I lay it down of Myself. I have power to lay it down, and I have power to take it again." And perhaps it was on this account that He hastened His departure from the body, that He might preserve it, and that His legs might not be broken, as were those of the robbers who were crucified with Him. "For the soldiers brake the legs of the first, and of the other who was crucified with Him; but when they came to Jesus, and saw that He was dead, they brake not His legs." We have accordingly answered the question, "How is it credible that Jesus could have predicted these things?" And with respect to this, "How could the dead man be immortal?" let him who wishes to understand know, that it is not the dead man who is immortal, but He who rose from the dead. So far, indeed, was the dead man from being immortal, that even the Jesus before His decease—the compound being, who was to suffer death—was not immortal. For no one is immortal who is destined to die; but he is immortal when he shall no longer be subject to death. But "Christ, being raised from the dead, dieth no more: death hath no more dominion over Him;" although those may be unwilling to admit this who cannot understand how such things should be said.

CHAPTER XVII

Extremely foolish also is his remark, "What god, or spirit, or prudent man would not, on foreseeing that such events were to befall him, avoid them if he could; whereas he threw himself headlong into those things which he knew beforehand were to happen?" And yet Socrates knew that he would die after drinking the hemlock, and it was in his power, if he had allowed himself to be persuaded by Crito, by escaping from prison, to avoid these calamities; but nevertheless he decided, as it appeared to him consistent with right reason, that it was better for him to die as became a philosopher, than to retain his life in a manner unbecoming one. Leonidas also, the Lacedaemonian general, knowing that he was on the point of dying with his followers at Thermopylae, did not make any effort to preserve his life by disgraceful means but said to his companions, "Let us go to breakfast, as we shall sup in Hades." And those who are interested in collecting stories of this kind will find numbers of them. Now, where is the wonder if Jesus, knowing all things that were to happen, did not avoid them, but encountered what He foreknew; when Paul, His own disciple, having heard what would befall him when he went up to Jerusalem, proceeded to face the danger, reproaching those who were weeping around him, and endeavouring to prevent him from going up to Jerusalem? Many also of our contemporaries, knowing well that if they made a confession of Christianity they would be put to death, but that if they denied it they would be liberated, and their property restored, despised life, and voluntarily selected death for the sake of their religion.

CHAPTER XVIII

After this the Jew makes another silly remark, saying, "How is it that, if Jesus pointed out beforehand both the traitor and the perjurer, they did not fear him as a God, and cease, the one from his intended treason, and the other from his perjury?" Here the learned Celsus did not see the contradiction in his statement: for if Jesus foreknew events as a God, then it was impossible for His foreknowledge to prove untrue; and therefore it was impossible for him who was known to Him as going to betray Him not to execute his purpose, nor for him who was rebuked as going to deny Him not to have been guilty of that crime. For if it had been possible for the one to abstain from the act of betrayal, and the other from that of denial, as having been warned of the consequences of these actions beforehand, then His words were no longer true, who predicted that the one would betray Him and the other deny Him. For if He had foreknowledge of the traitor, He knew the wickedness in which the treason originated, and this wickedness was by no means taken away by the foreknowledge. And, again, if He had ascertained that one would deny Him, He made that prediction from seeing the weakness out of which that act of denial would arise, and yet this weakness was not to be taken away thus at once by the foreknowledge. But whence he derived the statement, "that these persons betrayed and denied him without manifesting any concern about him," I know not; for it was proved, with respect to the traitor, that it is false to say that he betrayed his master without an exhibition of anxiety regarding Him. And this was shown to be equally true of him who denied Him; for he went out, after the denial, and wept bitterly.

CHAPTER XIX

Superficial also is his objection, that "it is always the case when a man against whom a plot is formed, and who comes to the knowledge of it, makes known to the conspirators that he is acquainted with their design, that the latter are turned from their purpose, and keep upon their guard." For many have continued to plot even against those who were acquainted with their plans. And then, as if bringing his argument to a conclusion, he says: "Not because these things were predicted did they come to pass, for that is impossible; but since they have come to pass, their being predicted is shown to be a falsehood: for it is altogether impossible that those who heard beforehand of the discovery of their designs, should carry out their plans of betrayal and denial!" But if his premises are overthrown, then his conclusion also falls to the ground, viz., "that we are not to believe, because these things were predicted, that they have come to pass." Now we maintain that they not only came to pass as being possible, but also that, because they came to pass, the fact of their being predicted is shown to be true; for the truth regarding future events is judged of by results. It is false, therefore, as asserted by him, that the prediction of these events is proved to be untrue; and it is to no purpose that he says, "It is altogether impossible for those who heard beforehand that their designs were discovered, to carry out their plans of betrayal and denial."

CHAPTER XX

Let us see how he continues after this: "These events," he says, "he predicted as being a God, and the prediction must by all means come to pass. God, therefore, who above all others ought to do good to men, and especially to those of his own household, led on his own disciples and prophets, with whom he was in the habit of eating and drinking, to such a degree of wickedness, that they became impious and unholy men. Now, of a truth, he who shared a man's table would not be guilty of conspiring against him; but after banqueting with God, he became a conspirator. And, what is still more absurd, God himself plotted against the members of his own table, by converting them into traitors and villains!" Now, since you wish me to answer even those charges of Celsus which seem to me frivolous, the following is our reply to such statements. Celsus imagines that an event, predicted through foreknowledge, comes to pass because it was predicted; but we do not grant this, maintaining that he who foretold it was not the cause of its happening, because he foretold it would happen; but the future event itself, which would have taken place though not predicted, afforded the occasion to him, who was endowed with foreknowledge, of foretelling its occurrence. Now, certainly this result is present to the foreknowledge of him who predicts an event, when it is possible that it may or may not happen, viz., that one or other of these things will take place. For we do not assert that he who foreknows an event, by secretly taking away the possibility of its happening or not, makes any such declaration as this: "This shall infallibly happen, and it is impossible that it can be otherwise." And this remark applies to all the foreknowledge of events dependent upon ourselves, whether contained in the sacred Scriptures or in the histories of the Greeks. Now, what is called by logicians an "idle argument," which is a sophism, will be no sophism as far as Celsus can help, but according to sound reasoning it is a sophism. And that this may be seen, I shall take from the Scriptures the predictions regarding Judas, or the foreknowledge of our Saviour regarding him as the traitor; and from the Greek histories the oracle that was given to Laius, conceding for the present its truth, since it does not affect the argument. Now, in Ps. cviii., Judas is spoken of by the mouth of the Saviour, in words beginning thus: "Hold not Thy peace, O God of my praise; for the mouth of the wicked and the mouth of the deceitful are opened against me." Now, if you carefully observe the contents of the psalm, you will find that, as it was foreknown that he would betray the Saviour, so also was he considered to be himself the cause of the betrayal, and deserving, on account of his wickedness, of the imprecations contained in the prophecy. For let him suffer these things, "because," says the psalmist, "he remembered not to show mercy, but persecuted the poor and needy man." Wherefore it was possible for him to show mercy, and not to persecute him whom he did persecute. But although he might have done these things, he did not do them, but carried out the act of treason, so as to merit the curses pronounced against him in the prophecy.

And in answer to the Greeks we shall quote the following oracular response to Laius, as recorded by the tragic poet, either in the exact words of the oracle or in equivalent terms. Future events are thus made known to him by the oracle: "Do not try to beget children against the will of the gods. For if you beget a son, your son shall murder you; and all your household shall wade in blood." Now from this it is clear that it was within the power of Laius not to try to beget children, for the oracle would not have commanded an impossibility; and it was also in his power to do the opposite, so that neither of these courses was compulsory. And the consequence of his not guarding against the begetting of children was, that he suffered from so doing the calamities described in the tragedies relating to Oedipus and Jocasta and their sons. Now that which is called the "idle argument," being a quibble, is such as might be applied, say in the case of a sick man, with the view of sophistically preventing him from employing a physician to promote his recovery; and it is something like this: "If it is decreed that you should recover from your disease, you will recover whether you call in a physician or not; but if it is decreed that you should not recover, you will not recover whether you call in a physician or no. But it is certainly decreed either that you should recover, or that you should not recover; and therefore it is in vain that you call in a physician." Now with this argument the following may be wittily compared: "If it is decreed that you should beget children, you will beget them, whether you have intercourse with a woman or not. But if it is decreed that you should not beget children, you will not do so, whether you have intercourse with a woman or no. Now, certainly, it is decreed either that you should beget children or not; therefore it is in vain that you have intercourse with a woman." For, as in the latter instance, intercourse with a woman is not employed in vain, seeing it is an utter impossibility for him who does not use it to beget children; so, in the former, if recovery from disease is to be accomplished by means of the healing art, of necessity the physician is summoned, and it is therefore false to say that "in vain do you call in a physician." We have brought forward all these illustrations on account of the assertion of this learned Celsus, that "being a God He predicted these things, and the predictions must *by all means* come to pass." Now, if by "*by all means*" he means "*necessarily*," we cannot admit this. For it was quite possible, also, that they might *not* come to pass. But if he uses "*by all means*" in the sense of "*simple futurity*," which nothing hinders from being true (although it was possible that they might not happen), he does not at all touch my argument; nor did it follow, from Jesus having predicted the acts of the traitor or the perjurer, that it was the same thing with His being the cause of such impious and unholy proceedings. For He who was amongst us, and knew what was in man, seeing his evil disposition, and foreseeing what he would attempt from his spirit of covetousness, and from his want of stable ideas of duty towards his Master, along with many other declarations, gave utterance to this also: "He that dippeth his hand with Me in the dish, the same shall betray Me."

CHAPTER XXI

Observe also the superficiality and manifest falsity of such a statement of Celsus, when he asserts "that he who was partaker of a man's table would not conspire against him; and if he would not conspire against a man, much less would he plot against a God after banqueting with him." For who does not know that many persons, after partaking of the salt on the table, have entered into a conspiracy against their entertainers? The whole of Greek and Barbarian history is full of such instances. And the Iambic poet of Paros, when upbraiding Lycambes with having violated covenants confirmed by the salt of the table, says to him:—

"But thou hast broken a mighty oath—that, viz., by the salt of the table."

And they who are interested in historical learning, and who give themselves wholly to it, to the neglect of other branches of knowledge more necessary for the conduct of life, can quote numerous instances, showing that they who shared in the hospitality of others entered into conspiracies against them.

CHAPTER XXII

He adds to this, as if he had brought together an argument with conclusive demonstrations and consequences, the following: "And, which is still more absurd, God himself conspired against those who sat at his table, by converting them into traitors and impious men." But how Jesus could either conspire or convert His disciples into traitors or impious men, it would be impossible for him to prove, save by means of such a deduction as any one could refute with the greatest ease.

CHAPTER XXIII

He continues in this strain: "If he had determined upon these things, and underwent chastisement in obedience to his Father, it is manifest that, being a God, and submitting voluntarily, those things that were done agreeably to his own decision were neither painful nor distressing." But he did not observe that here he was at once contradicting himself. For if he granted that He was chastised because He had determined upon these things, and had submitted Himself to His Father, it is clear that He actually suffered punishment, and it was impossible that what was inflicted on Him by His chastisers should not be painful, because pain is an involuntary thing. But if, because He was willing to suffer, His inflictions were neither painful nor distressing, how did He grant that "He was chastised?" He did not perceive that when Jesus had once, by His birth, assumed a body, He assumed one which was capable both of suffering pains, and those distresses incidental to humanity, if we are to understand by distresses what no one voluntarily chooses. Since, therefore, He voluntarily assumed a body, not wholly of a different nature from that of human flesh, so along with His body He assumed also its sufferings and distresses, which it was not in His power to avoid enduring, it being in the power of those who inflicted them to send upon Him things distressing and painful. And in the preceding pages we have already shown, that He would not have come into the hands of men had He not so willed. But He did come, because He was willing to come, and because it was manifest beforehand that His dying upon behalf of men would be of advantage to the whole human race.

CHAPTER XXIV

After this, wishing to prove that the occurrences which befell Him were painful and distressing, and that it was impossible for Him, had He wished, to render them otherwise, he proceeds: "Why does he mourn, and lament, and pray to escape the fear of death, expressing himself in terms like these: 'O Father, if it be possible, let this cup pass from Me?'" Now in these words observe the malignity of Celsus, how not accepting the love of truth which actuates the writers of the Gospels (who might have passed over in silence those points which, as Celsus thinks, are censurable, but who did not omit them for many reasons, which any one, in expounding the Gospel, can give in their proper place), he brings an accusation against the Gospel statement, grossly exaggerating the facts, and quoting what is not written in the

Gospels, seeing it is nowhere found that Jesus lamented. And he changes the words in the expression, "Father, if it be possible, let this cup pass from Me," and does not give what follows immediately after, which manifests at once the ready obedience of Jesus to His Father, and His greatness of mind, and which runs thus: "Nevertheless, not as I will, but as Thou wilt." Nay, even the cheerful obedience of Jesus to the will of His Father in those things which He was condemned to suffer, exhibited in the declaration, "If this cup cannot pass from Me except I drink it, Thy will be done," he pretends not to have observed, acting here like those wicked individuals who listen to the Holy Scriptures in a malignant spirit, and "who talk wickedness with lofty head." For they appear to have heard the declaration, "I kill," and they often make it to us a subject of reproach; but the words, "I will make alive," they do not remember,—the whole sentence showing that those who live amid public wickedness, and who work wickedly, are put to death by God, and that a better life is infused into them instead, even one which God will give to those who have died to sin. And so also these men have heard the words, "I will smite;" but they do not see these, "and I will heal," which are like the words of a physician, who cuts bodies asunder, and inflicts severe wounds, in order to extract from them substances that are injurious and prejudicial to health, and who does not terminate his work with pains and lacerations, but by his treatment restores the body to that state of soundness which he has in view. Moreover, they have not heard the whole of the announcement, "For He maketh sore, and again bindeth up;" but only this part, "He maketh sore." So in like manner acts this Jew of Celsus who quotes the words, "O Father, would that this cup might pass from Me;" but who does not add what follows, and which exhibits the firmness of Jesus, and His preparedness for suffering. But these matters, which afford great room for explanation from the wisdom of God, and which may reasonably be pondered over by those whom Paul calls "perfect" when he said, "We speak wisdom among them who are perfect," we pass by for the present, and shall speak for a little of those matters which are useful for our present purpose.

CHAPTER XXV

We have mentioned in the preceding pages that there are some of the declarations of Jesus which refer to that Being in Him which was the "first-born of every creature," such as, "I am the way, and the truth, and the life," and such like; and others, again, which belong to that in Him which is understood to be man, such as, "But now ye seek to kill

Me, a man that hath told you the truth which I have heard of the Father." And here, accordingly, he describes the element of weakness belonging to human flesh, and that of readiness of spirit which existed in His humanity: the element of weakness in the expression, "Father, if it be possible, let this cup pass from Me;" the readiness of the spirit in this, "Nevertheless, not as I will, but as Thou wilt." And since it is proper to observe the order of our quotations, observe that, in the first place, there is mentioned only the single instance, as one would say, indicating the weakness of the flesh; and afterwards those other instances, greater in number, manifesting the willingness of the spirit. For the expression, "Father, if it be possible, let this cup pass from Me," is only one: whereas more numerous are those others, viz., "Not as I will, but as Thou wilt;" and, "O My Father, if this cup cannot pass from Me except I drink it, Thy will be done." It is to be noted also, that the words are not, "let this cup depart from Me;" but that the whole expression is marked by a tone of piety and reverence, "Father, if it be possible, let this cup pass from Me." I know, indeed, that there is another explanation of this passage to the following effect:—The Saviour, foreseeing the sufferings which the Jewish people and the city of Jerusalem were to undergo in requital of the wicked deeds which the Jews had dared to perpetrate upon Him, from no other motive than that of the purest philanthropy towards them, and from a desire that they might escape the impending calamities, gave utterance to the prayer, "Father, if it be possible, let this cup pass from Me." It is as if He had said, "Because of My drinking this cup of punishment, the whole nation will be forsaken by Thee, I pray, if it be possible, that this cup may pass from Me, in order that Thy portion, which was guilty of such crimes against Me, may not be altogether deserted by Thee." But if, as Celsus would allege, "nothing at that time was done to Jesus which was either painful or distressing," how could men afterwards quote the example of Jesus as enduring sufferings for the sake of religion, if He did *not* suffer what are human sufferings, but only had the *appearance* of so doing?

CHAPTER XXVI

This Jew of Celsus still accuses the disciples of Jesus of having invented these statements, saying to them: "Even although guilty of falsehood, ye have not been able to give a colour of credibility to your inventions." In answer to which we have to say, that there was an easy method of concealing these occurrences,—that, viz., of not recording them at all. For if the Gospels had not contained the accounts of these things, who could have reproached us with Jesus having spoken such words during His stay upon the earth? Celsus, indeed, did not see that it was an inconsistency for the same persons both to be deceived regarding Jesus, believing Him to be God, and the subject of prophecy, and to invent fictions about Him, knowing manifestly that these statements were false. Of a truth, therefore, they were not guilty of inventing untruths, but such were their real impressions, and they recorded them truly; or else they were guilty of falsifying the histories, and did not entertain these views, and were not deceived when they acknowledged Him to be God.

CHAPTER XXVII

After this he says, that certain of the Christian believers, like persons who in a fit of drunkenness lay violent hands upon themselves, have corrupted the Gospel from its original integrity, to a threefold, and fourfold, and many-fold degree, and have remodelled it, so that they might be able to answer objections. Now I know of no others who have altered the Gospel, save the followers of Marcion, and those of Valentinus, and, I think, also those of Lucian. But such an allegation is no charge against the Christian system, but against those who dared so to trifle with the Gospels. And as it is no ground of accusation against philosophy, that there exist Sophists, or Epicureans, or Peripatetics, or any others, whoever they may be, who hold false opinions; so neither is it against genuine Christianity that there are some who corrupt the Gospel histories, and who introduce heresies opposed to the meaning of the doctrine of Jesus.

CHAPTER XXVIII

And since this Jew of Celsus makes it a subject of reproach that Christians should make use of the prophets, who predicted the events of Christ's life, we have to say, in addition to what we have already advanced upon this head, that it became him to spare individuals, as he says, and to expound the prophecies themselves, and after admitting the probability of the Christian interpretation of them, to show how the use which they make of them may be overturned. For in this way he would not appear hastily to assume so important a position on small grounds, and particularly when he asserts that the "prophecies agree with ten thousand other things more credibly than with Jesus." And he ought to have carefully met this powerful argument of the Christians, as being the strongest which they adduce, and to have demonstrated with regard to each particular prophecy, that it can apply to other events with greater probability than to Jesus. He did not, however, perceive that this was a plausible argument to be advanced against the Christians only by one who was an opponent of the prophetic writings; but Celsus has here put in the mouth of a Jew an objection which a Jew would not have made. For a Jew will not admit that the prophecies may be applied to countless other things with greater probability than to Jesus; but he will endeavour, after giving what appears to him the meaning of each, to oppose the Christian interpretation, not indeed by any means adducing convincing reasons, but only attempting to do so.

CHAPTER XXIX

In the preceding pages we have already spoken of this point, viz., the prediction that there were to be two advents of Christ to the human race, so that it is not necessary for us to reply to the objection, supposed to be urged by a Jew, that "the prophets declare the coming one to be a mighty potentate, Lord of all nations and armies." But it is in the spirit of a Jew, I think, and in keeping with their bitter animosity, and baseless and even improbable calumnies against Jesus, that he adds: "Nor did the prophets predict such a pestilence." For neither Jews, nor Celsus, nor any other, can bring any argument to prove that a pestilence converts men from the practice of evil to a life which is according to nature, and distinguished by temperance and other virtues.

CHAPTER XXX

This objection also is cast in our teeth by Celsus: "From such signs and misinterpretations, and from proofs so mean, no one could prove him to be God, and the Son of God." Now it was his duty to enumerate the alleged misinterpretations, and to prove them to be such, and to show by reasoning the meanness of the evidence, in order that the Christian, if any of his objections should seem to be plausible, might be able to answer and confute his arguments. What he said, however, regarding Jesus, did indeed come to pass, because He was a mighty potentate, although Celsus refuses to see that it so happened, notwithstanding that the clearest evidence proves it true of Jesus. "For as the sun," he says, "which enlightens all other objects, first makes himself visible, so ought the Son of God to have done." We would say in reply, that so He did; for righteousness has arisen in His days, and there is abundance of peace, which took its commencement at His birth, God preparing the nations for His teaching, that they might be under one prince, the king of the Romans, and that it might not, owing to the want of union among the nations, caused by the existence of many kingdoms, be more difficult for the apostles of Jesus to accomplish the task enjoined upon them by their Master, when He said, "Go and teach all nations." Moreover it is certain that Jesus was born in the reign of Augustus, who, so to speak, fused together into one monarchy the many populations of the earth. Now the existence of many kingdoms would have been a hindrance to the spread of the doctrine of Jesus throughout the entire world; not only for the reasons mentioned, but also on account of the necessity of men everywhere engaging in war, and fighting on behalf of their native country, which was the case before the times of Augustus, and in periods still more remote, when necessity arose, as when the Peloponnesians and Athenians warred against each other, and other nations in like manner. How, then, was it possible for the Gospel doctrine of peace, which does not permit men to take vengeance even upon enemies, to prevail throughout the world, unless at the advent of Jesus a milder spirit had been everywhere introduced into the conduct of things?

CHAPTER XXXI

He next charges the Christians with being "guilty of sophistical reasoning, in saying that the Son of God is the Logos Himself." And he thinks that he strengthens the accusation, because "when we declare the Logos to be the Son of God, we do not present to view a pure and holy Logos, but a most degraded man, who was punished by scourging and crucifixion." Now, on this head we have briefly replied to the charges of Celsus in the preceding pages, where Christ was shown to be the first-born of all creation, who assumed a body and a human soul; and that God gave commandment respecting the creation of such mighty things in the world, and they were created; and that He who received the command was God the Logos. And seeing it is a Jew who makes these statements in the work of Celsus, it will not be out of place to quote the declaration, "He sent His word, and healed them, and delivered them from their destruction,"—a passage of which we spoke a little ago. Now, although I have conferred with many Jews who professed to be learned men, I never heard any one expressing his approval of the statement that the Logos is the Son of God, as Celsus declares they do, in putting into the mouth of the Jew such a declaration as this: "If your Logos is the Son of God, we also give our assent to the same."

CHAPTER XXXII

We have already shown that Jesus can be regarded neither as an arrogant man, nor a sorcerer; and therefore it is unnecessary to repeat our former arguments, lest, in replying to the tautologies of Celsus, we ourselves should be guilty of needless repetition. And now, in finding fault with our Lord's genealogy, there are certain points which occasion some difficulty even to Christians, and which, owing to the discrepancy between the genealogies, are advanced by some as arguments against their correctness, but which Celsus has not even mentioned. For Celsus, who is truly a braggart, and who professes to be acquainted with all matters relating to Christianity, does not know how to raise doubts in a skilful manner against the credibility of Scripture. But he asserts that the "framers of the genealogies, from a feeling of pride, made Jesus to be descended from the first man, and from the kings of the Jews." And he thinks that he makes a notable charge when he adds, that "the carpenters wife could not have been ignorant of the fact, had she been of such illustrious descent." But what has this to do with the question? Granted that she was not ignorant of her descent, how does that affect the result? Suppose that she *were* ignorant, how could her ignorance prove that she was not descended from the first man, or could not derive her origin from the Jewish kings? Does Celsus imagine that the poor must always be descended from ancestors who are poor, or that kings are always born of kings? But it appears folly to waste time upon such an argument as this, seeing it is well known that, even in our own days, some who are poorer than Mary are descended from ancestors of wealth and distinction, and that rulers of nations and kings have sprung from persons of no reputation.

CHAPTER XXXIII

"But," continues Celsus, "what great deeds did Jesus perform as being a God? Did he put his enemies to shame, or bring to a ridiculous conclusion what was designed against him?" Now to this question, although we are able to show the striking and miraculous character of the events which befell Him, yet from what other source can we furnish an answer than from the Gospel narratives, which state that "there was an earthquake, and that the rocks were split asunder, and the tombs opened, and the veil of the temple rent in twain from top to bottom, and that darkness prevailed in the day-time, the sun failing to give light?" But if Celsus believe the Gospel accounts when he thinks that he can find in them matter of charge against the Christians, and refuse to believe them when they establish the divinity of Jesus, our answer to him is: "Sir, either disbelieve all the Gospel narratives, and then no longer imagine that you can found charges upon them; or, in yielding your belief to their statements, look in admiration on the Logos of God, who became incarnate, and who desired to confer benefits upon the whole human race. And this feature evinces the nobility of the work of Jesus, that, down to the present time, those whom God wills are healed by His name. And with regard to the eclipse in the time of Tiberius Caesar, in whose reign Jesus appears to have been crucified, and the great earthquakes which then took place, Phlegon too, I think, has written in the thirteenth or fourteenth book of his Chronicles."

CHAPTER XXXIV

This Jew of Celsus, ridiculing Jesus, as he imagines, is described as being acquainted with the Bacchae of Euripides, in which Dionysus says:—

"The divinity himself will liberate me whenever I wish."

Now the Jews are not much acquainted with Greek literature; but suppose that there was a Jew so well versed in it (as to make such a quotation on his part appropriate), how (does it follow) that Jesus *could* not liberate Himself, because He did not do so? For let him believe from our own Scriptures that Peter obtained his freedom after having been bound in prison, an angel having loosed his chains; and that Paul, having been bound in the stocks along with Silas in Philippi of Macedonia, was liberated by divine power, when the gates of the prison were opened. But it is probable that Celsus treats these accounts with ridicule, or that he never read them; for he would probably say in reply, that there are certain sorcerers who are able by incantations to unloose chains and to open doors, so that he would liken the events related in our histories to the doings of sorcerers. "But," he continues, "no calamity happened even to him who condemned him, as there did to Pentheus, viz., madness or discerption." And yet he does not know that it was not so much Pilate that condemned Him (who knew that "for envy the Jews had delivered Him"), as the Jewish nation, which *has* been condemned by God, and rent in pieces, and dispersed over the whole earth, in a degree far beyond what happened to Pentheus. Moreover, why did he intentionally omit what is related of Pilate's wife, who beheld a vision, and who was so moved by it as to send a message to her husband, saying: "Have thou nothing to do with that just man; for I have suffered many things this day in a dream because of Him?"

And again, passing by in silence the proofs of the divinity of Jesus, Celsus endeavours to cast reproach upon Him from the narratives in the Gospel, referring to those who mocked Jesus, and put on Him the purple robe, and the crown of thorns, and placed the reed in His hand. From what source now, Celsus, did you derive these statements, save from the Gospel narratives? And did you, accordingly, see that they were fit matters for reproach; while they who recorded them did not think that you, and such as you, would turn them into ridicule; but that others would receive from them an example how to despise those who ridiculed and mocked Him on account of His religion, who appropriately laid down His life for its sake? Admire rather their love of truth, and that of the Being who bore these things voluntarily for the sake of men, and who endured them with all constancy and long-suffering. For it is not recorded that He uttered any lamentation, or that after His condemnation He either did or uttered anything unbecoming.

CHAPTER XXXV

But in answer to this objection, "If not before, yet why now, at least, does he not give some manifestation of his divinity, and free himself from this reproach, and take vengeance upon those who insult both him and his Father?" We have to reply, that it would be the same thing as if we were to say to those among the Greeks who accept the doctrine of providence, and who believe in portents, Why does God not punish those who insult the Divinity, and subvert the doctrine of providence? For as the Greeks would answer such objections, so would we, in the same, or a more effective manner. There was not only a portent from heaven—the eclipse of the sun—but also the other miracles, which show that the crucified One possessed something that was divine, and greater than was possessed by the majority of men.

CHAPTER XXXVI

Celsus next says: "What is the nature of the ichor in the body of the crucified Jesus? Is it 'such as flows in the bodies of the immortal gods?'" He puts this question in a spirit of mockery; but we shall show from the serious narratives of the Gospels, although Celsus may not like it, that it was no mythic and Homeric ichor which flowed from the body of Jesus, but that, after His death, "one of the soldiers with a spear pierced His side, and there came thereout blood and water. And he that saw it bare record, and his record is true, and he knoweth that he saith the truth." Now, in other dead bodies the blood congeals, and pure water does not flow forth; but the miraculous feature in the case of the dead body of Jesus was, that around the dead body blood and water flowed forth from the side. But if this Celsus, who, in order to find matter of accusation against Jesus and the Christians, extracts from the Gospel even passages which are incorrectly interpreted, but passes over in silence the evidences of the divinity of Jesus, would listen to divine portents, let him read the Gospel, and see that even the centurion, and they who with him kept watch over Jesus, on seeing the earthquake, and the events that occurred, were greatly afraid, saying, "This man was the Son of God."

CHAPTER XXXVII

After this, he who extracts from the Gospel narrative those statements on which he thinks he can found an accusation, makes the vinegar and the gall a subject of reproach to Jesus, saying that "he rushed with open mouth to drink of them, and could not endure his thirst as any ordinary man frequently endures it." Now this matter admits of an explanation of a peculiar and figurative kind; but on the present occasion, the statement that the prophets predicted this very incident may be accepted as the more common answer to the objection. For in the sixty-ninth Psalm there is written, with reference to Christ: "And they gave me gall for my meat, and in my thirst they gave me vinegar to drink." Now, let the Jews say who it is that the prophetic writing represents as uttering these words; and let them adduce from history one who received gall for his food, and to whom vinegar was given as drink. Would they venture to assert that the Christ whom they expect still to come might be placed in such circumstances? Then we would say, What prevents the prediction from having been already accomplished? For this very prediction was uttered many ages before, and is sufficient, along with the other prophetic utterances, to lead him who fairly examines the whole matter to the conclusion that Jesus is He who was prophesied of as Christ, and as the Son of God.

CHAPTER XXXVIII

The few next remarks: "You, O sincere believers, find fault with us, because we do not recognise this individual as God, nor agree with you that he endured these (sufferings) for the benefit of mankind, in order that we also might despise punishment." Now, in answer to this, we say that we blame the Jews, who have been brought up under the training of the law and the prophets (which foretell the coming of

Christ), because they neither refute the arguments which we lay before them to prove that He is the Messiah, adducing such refutation as a defence of their unbelief; nor yet, while not offering any refutation, do they believe in Him who was the subject of prophecy, and who clearly manifested through His disciples, even after the period of His appearance in the flesh, that He underwent these things for the benefit of mankind; having, as the object of His first advent, not to condemn men and their actions before He had instructed them, and pointed out to them their duty, nor to chastise the wicked and save the good, but to disseminate His doctrine in an extraordinary manner, and with the evidence of divine power, among the whole human race, as the prophets also have represented these things. And we blame them, moreover, because they did not believe in Him who gave evidence of the power that was in Him, but asserted that He cast out demons from the souls of men through Beelzebub the prince of the demons; and we blame them because they slander the philanthropic character of Him, who overlooked not only no city, but not even a single village in Judea, that He might everywhere announce the kingdom of God, accusing Him of leading the wandering life of a vagabond, and passing an anxious existence in a disgraceful body. But there is no disgrace in enduring such labours for the benefit of all those who may be able to understand Him.

CHAPTER XXXIX

And how can the following assertion of this Jew of Celsus appear anything else than a manifest falsehood, viz., that Jesus, "having gained over no one during his life, not even his own disciples, underwent these punishments and sufferings?" For from what other source sprang the envy which was aroused against Him by the Jewish high priests, and elders, and scribes, save from the fact that multitudes obeyed and followed Him, and were led into the deserts not only by the persuasive language of Him whose words were always appropriate to His hearers, but who also by His miracles made an impression on those who were not moved to belief by His words? And is it not a manifest falsehood to say that "he did not gain over even his own disciples," who exhibited, indeed, at that time some symptoms of human weakness arising from cowardly fear—for they had not yet been disciplined to the exhibition of full courage—but who by no means abandoned the judgments which they had formed regarding Him as the Christ? For Peter, after his denial, perceiving to what a depth of wickedness he had fallen, "went out and wept bitterly;" while the others, although stricken with dismay on account of what had happened to Jesus (for they still continued to admire Him), had, by His glorious appearance, their belief more firmly established than before that He was the Son of God.

CHAPTER XL

It is, moreover, in a very unphilosophical spirit that Celsus imagines our Lord's pre-eminence among men to consist, not in the preaching of salvation and in a pure morality, but in acting contrary to the character of that personality which He had taken upon Him, and in not dying, although He had assumed mortality; or, if dying, yet at least not such a death as might serve as a pattern to those who were to learn by that very act how to die for the sake of religion, and to comport themselves boldly through its help, before those who hold erroneous views on the subject of religion and irreligion, and who regard religious men as altogether irreligious, but imagine those to be most religious who err regarding God, and who apply to everything rather than to God the ineradicable idea of Him (which is implanted in the human mind), and especially when they eagerly rush to destroy those who have yielded themselves up with their whole soul (even unto death), to the clear evidence of one God who is over all things.

CHAPTER XLI

In the person of the Jew, Celsus continues to find fault with Jesus, alleging that "he did not show himself to be pure from all evil." Let Celsus state from what "evil" our Lord did not, show Himself to be pure. If he means that, He was not pure from what is properly termed "evil," let him clearly prove the existence of any wicked work in Him. But if he deems poverty and the cross to be evils, and conspiracy on the part of wicked men, then it is clear that he would say that evil had happened also to Socrates, who was unable to show himself pure from evils. And how great also the other band of poor men is among the Greeks, who have given themselves to philosophical pursuits, and have voluntarily accepted a life of poverty, is known to many among the Greeks from what is recorded of Democritus, who allowed his property to become pasture for sheep; and of Crates, who obtained his freedom by bestowing upon the Thebans the price received for the sale of his possessions. Nay, even Diogenes himself, from excessive poverty, came to live in a tub; and yet, in the opinion of no one possessed of moderate understanding, was Diogenes on that account considered to be in an evil (sinful) condition.

CHAPTER XLII

But further, since Celsus will have it that "Jesus was not irreproachable," let him instance any one of those who adhere to His doctrine, who has recorded anything that could truly furnish ground of reproach against Jesus; or if it be not from these that he derives his matter of accusation against Him, let him say from what quarter he has learned that which has induced him to say that He is not free from reproach. Jesus, however, performed all that He promised to do, and by which He conferred benefits upon his adherents. And we, continually seeing fulfilled all that was predicted by Him before it happened, viz., that this Gospel of His should be preached throughout the whole world, and that His disciples should go among all nations and announce His doctrine; and, moreover, that they should be brought before governors and kings on no other account than because of His teaching; we are lost in wonder at Him, and have our faith in Him daily confirmed. And I know not by what greater or more convincing proofs Celsus would have Him confirm His predictions; unless, indeed, as seems to be the case, not understanding that the Logos had become the man Jesus, he would have Him to be subject to no human weakness, nor to become an illustrious pattern to men of the manner in which they ought to bear the calamities of life, although these appear to Celsus to be most lamentable and disgraceful occurrences, seeing that he regards labour to be the greatest of evils, and pleasure the perfect good,—a view accepted by none of those philosophers who admit the doctrine of providence, and who allow that courage, and fortitude, and magnanimity are virtues. Jesus, therefore, by His sufferings cast no discredit upon the faith of which He was the object; but rather confirmed the same among those who would approve of manly courage, and among those who were taught by Him that what was truly and properly the happy life was not here below, but was to be found in that which was called, according to His own words, the "coming world;" whereas in what is called the "present world" life is a calamity, or at least the first and greatest struggle of the soul.

CHAPTER XLIII

Celsus next addresses to us the following remark: "You will not, I suppose, say of him, that, after failing to gain over those who were in this world, he went to Hades to gain over those who were there." But whether he like it or not, we assert that not only while Jesus was in the body did He win over not a few persons merely, but so great a number, that a conspiracy was formed against Him on account of the multitude of His followers; but also, that when He became a soul, without the covering of the body, He dwelt among those souls which were without bodily covering, converting such of them as were willing to Himself, or those whom He saw, for reasons known to Him alone, to be better adapted to such a course.

CHAPTER XLIV

Celsus in the next place says, with indescribable silliness: "If, after inventing defences which are absurd, and by which ye were ridiculously deluded, ye imagine that you really make a good defence, what prevents you from regarding those other individuals who have been condemned, and have died a miserable death, as greater and more divine messengers of heaven (than Jesus)?" Now, that manifestly and clearly there is no similarity between Jesus, who suffered what is described, and those who have died a wretched death on account of their sorcery, or whatever else be the charge against them, is patent to every one. For no one can point to any acts of a sorcerer which turned away souls from the practice of the many sins which prevail among men, and from the flood of wickedness (in the world). But since this Jew of Celsus compares Him to robbers, and says that "any similarly shameless fellow might be able to say regarding even a robber and murderer whom punishment had overtaken, that such an one was not a robber, but a god, because he predicted to his fellow-robbers that he would suffer such punishment as he actually did suffer," it might, in the first place, be answered, that it is not because He predicted that He would suffer such things that we entertain those opinions regarding Jesus which lead us to have confidence in Him, as one who has come down to us from God. And, in the second place, we assert that this very comparison has been somehow foretold in the Gospels; since God was numbered with the transgressors by wicked men, who desired rather a "murderer" (one who for sedition and murder had been cast into prison) to be released unto them, and Jesus to be crucified, and who crucified Him between two robbers. Jesus, indeed, is ever crucified with robbers among His genuine disciples and witnesses to the truth, and suffers the same condemnation which they do among men. And we say, that if those persons have any resemblance to robbers, who on account of their piety towards God suffer all kinds of injury and death, that they may keep it pure and unstained, according to the teaching of Jesus, then it is clear also that Jesus, the author of such teaching, is with good reason compared by Celsus to the captain of a band of robbers. But neither was He who died for the common good of mankind, nor they who suffered because of their religion, and alone of all men were persecuted because of what appeared to them the right way of honouring God, put to death in accordance with justice, nor was Jesus persecuted without the charge of impiety being incurred by His persecutors.

CHAPTER XLV

But observe the superficial nature of his argument respecting the former disciples of Jesus, in which he says: "In the next place, those who were his associates while alive, and who listened to his voice, and enjoyed his instructions as their teacher, on seeing him subjected to punishment and death, neither died with him, nor for him, nor were even induced to regard punishment with contempt, but denied even that they were his disciples, whereas now ye die along with him." And here he believes the sin which was committed by the disciples while they were yet beginners and imperfect, and which is recorded in the Gospels, to have been actually committed, in order that he may have matter of accusation against the Gospel; but their upright conduct after their transgression, when they behaved with courage before the Jews, and suffered countless cruelties at their hands, and at last suffered death for the doctrine of Jesus, he passes by in silence. For he would neither hear the words of Jesus, when He predicted to Peter, "When thou shalt be old, thou shalt stretch forth thy hands," etc., to which the Scripture adds, "This spake He, signifying by what death he should glorify God;" nor how James the brother of John—an apostle, the brother of an apostle—was slain with the sword by Herod for the doctrine of Christ; nor even the many instances of boldness displayed by Peter and the other apostles because of the Gospel, and "how they went forth from the presence of the Sanhedrim after being scourged, rejoicing that they were counted worthy to suffer shame for His name," and so surpassing many of the instances related by the Greeks of the fortitude and courage of their philosophers. From the very beginning, then, this was inculcated as a precept of Jesus among His hearers, which taught men to despise the life which is eagerly sought after by the multitude, but to be earnest in living the life which resembles that of God.

CHAPTER XLVI

But how can this Jew of Celsus escape the charge of falsehood, when he says that Jesus, "when on earth, gained over to himself only ten sailors and tax-gatherers of the most worthless character, and not even the whole of these?" Now it is certain that the Jews themselves would admit that He drew over not ten persons merely, nor a hundred, nor a thousand, but on one occasion five thousand at once, and on another four thousand; and that He attracted them to such a degree that they followed Him even into the deserts, which alone could contain the assembled multitude of those who believed in God through Jesus, and where He not only addressed to them discourses, but also manifested to them His works. And now, through his tautology, he compels us also to be tautological, since we are careful to guard against being supposed to pass over any of the charges advanced by him; and therefore, in reference to the matter before us following the order of his treatise as we have it, he says: "Is it not the height of absurdity to maintain, that if, while he himself was alive, he won over not a single person to his views, after his death any who wish are able to gain over such a multitude of individuals?" Whereas he ought to have said, in consistency with truth, that if, after His death, not simply those who will, but they who have the will and the power, can gain over so many proselytes, how much more consonant to reason is it, that while He was alive He should, through the greater power of His words and deeds, have won over to Himself manifold greater numbers of adherents?

CHAPTER XLVII

He represents, moreover, a statement of his own as if it were an answer to one of his questions, in which he asks: "By what train of argument were you led to regard him as the Son of God?" For he makes us answer that "we were won over to him, because we know that his punishment was undergone to bring about the destruction of the father of evil." Now we were won over to His doctrine by innumerable other considerations, of which we have stated only the smallest part in the preceding pages; but, if God permit, we shall continue to enumerate them, not only while dealing with the so-called *True Discourse* of Celsus, but also on many other occasions. And, as if we said that we consider Him to be the Son of God because He suffered punishment, he asks: "What then? have not many others, too, been punished, and that not less disgracefully?" And here Celsus acts like the most contemptible enemies of the Gospel, and like those who imagine that it follows as a consequence from our history of the crucified Jesus, that we should worship those who have undergone crucifixion!

CHAPTER XLVIII

Celsus, moreover, unable to resist the miracles which Jesus is recorded to have performed, has already on several occasions spoken of them slanderously as works of sorcery; and we also on several occasions have, to the best of our ability, replied to his statements. And now he represents us as saying that "we deemed Jesus to be the Son of God, because he healed the lame and the blind." And he adds: "Moreover, as you assert, he raised the dead." That He healed the lame and the blind, and that therefore we hold Him to be the Christ and the Son of God, is manifest to us from what is contained in the prophecies: "Then the eyes of the blind shall be opened, and the ears of the deaf shall hear; then shall the lame man leap as an hart." And that He also raised the dead, and that it is no fiction of those who composed the Gospels, is shown by this, that if it had been a fiction, *many* individuals would have been represented as having risen from the dead, and these, too, such as had been many years in their graves. But as it is no fiction, they are very easily counted of whom this is related to have happened; viz., the daughter of the ruler of the synagogue (of whom I know not why He said, "She is not dead, but sleepeth," stating regarding her something which does not apply to all who die); and the only son of the widow, on whom He took compassion and raised him up, making the bearers of the corpse to stand still; and the third instance, that of Lazarus, who had been four days in the grave. Now, regarding these cases we would say to all persons of candid mind, and especially to the Jew, that as there were many lepers in the days of Elisha the prophet, and none of them was healed save Naaman the Syrian, and many widows in the days of Elijah the prophet, to none of whom was Elijah sent save to Sarepta in Sidonia (for the widow there had been deemed worthy by a divine decree of the miracle which was wrought by the prophet in the matter of the bread); so also there were many dead in the days of Jesus, but those only rose from the grave whom the Logos knew to be fitted for a resurrection, in order that the works done by the Lord might not be merely symbols of certain things, but that by the very acts themselves He might gain over many to the marvellous doctrine of the Gospel. I would say, moreover, that, agreeably to the promise of Jesus, His disciples performed even greater works than these miracles of Jesus, which were perceptible only to the senses. For the eyes of those who are blind in soul are ever opened; and the ears of those who were deaf to virtuous words, listen readily to the doctrine of God, and of the blessed life with Him; and many, too, who were lame in the feet of the "inner man," as Scripture calls it, having now been healed by the word, do not simply leap, but leap as the hart, which is an animal hostile to serpents, and stronger than all the poison of vipers. And these lame who have been healed, receive from Jesus power to trample, with those feet in which they were formerly lame, upon the serpents and scorpions of wickedness, and generally upon all the power of the enemy; and though they tread upon it, they sustain no injury, for they also have become stronger than the poison of all evil and of demons.

CHAPTER XLIX

Jesus, accordingly, in turning away the minds of His disciples, not merely from giving heed to sorcerers in general, and those who profess in any other manner to work miracles—for His disciples did not need to be so warned—but from such as gave themselves out as the Christ of God, and who tried by certain apparent miracles to gain over to them the disciples of Jesus, said in a certain passage: "Then, if any man shall say unto you, Lo, here is Christ, or there; believe it not. For there shall arise false Christs, and false prophets, and shall show great signs and wonders; insomuch that, if it were possible, they shall deceive the very elect. Behold, I have told you before. Wherefore, if they shall say unto you, Behold, he is in the desert, go not forth; behold, he is in the secret chambers, believe it not. For as the lightning cometh out of the east, and shineth even to the west, so also shall the coming of the Son of man be." And in another passage: "Many will say unto Me in that day, Lord, Lord, have we not eaten and drunk in Thy name, and by Thy name have cast out demons, and done many wonderful works? And then will I say unto them, Depart from Me, because ye are workers of iniquity." But Celsus, wishing to assimilate the miracles of Jesus to the works of human sorcery, says in express terms as follows: "O light and truth! he distinctly declares, with his own voice, as ye yourselves have recorded, that there will come to you even others, employing miracles of a similar kind, who are wicked men, and sorcerers; and he calls him who makes use of such devices, one Satan. So that Jesus himself does not deny that these works at least are not at all divine, but are the acts of wicked men; and being compelled by the force of truth, he at the same time not only laid open the doings of others, but convicted himself of the same acts. Is it not, then, a miserable inference, to conclude from the same works that the one is God and the other sorcerers? Why ought the others, because of these acts, to be accounted wicked rather than this man, seeing they have him as their witness against himself? For he has himself acknowledged that these are not the works of a divine nature, but the inventions of certain deceivers, and of thoroughly wicked men." Observe, now, whether Celsus is not clearly convicted of slandering the Gospel by such statements, since what Jesus says regarding those who are to work signs and wonders is different from what this Jew of Celsus alleges it to be. For if Jesus had simply told His disciples to be on their guard against those who professed to work miracles, without declaring what they would give themselves out to be, then perhaps there would have been some ground for his suspicion. But since those against whom Jesus would have us to be on our guard give themselves out as the Christ—which is not a claim put forth by sorcerers—and since He says that even some who lead wicked lives will perform miracles in the name of Jesus, and expel demons out of men, sorcery in the case of these individuals, or any suspicion of such, is rather, if we may so speak, altogether banished, and the divinity of Christ established, as well as the divine mission of His disciples; seeing that it is possible that one who makes use of His name, and who is wrought upon by some power, in some way unknown, to make the pretence that he is the Christ, should seem to perform miracles like those of Jesus, while others through His name should do works resembling those of His genuine disciples.

Paul, moreover, in the second Epistle to the Thessalonians, shows in what manner there will one day be revealed "the man of sin, the son of perdition, who opposeth and exalteth himself above all that is called God, or that is worshipped; so that he sitteth in the temple of God, showing himself that he is God." And again he says to the Thessalonians: "And now ye know what withholdeth that he might be revealed in his time. For the mystery of iniquity doth already work: only he who now letteth will let, until he be taken out of the way: and then shall that Wicked be revealed, whom the Lord will consume with the spirit of His mouth, and shall destroy with the brightness of His coming: even him, whose cunning is after the working of Satan, with all power, and signs, and lying wonders, and with all deceivableness of unrighteousness in them that perish." And in assigning the reason why the man of sin is permitted to continue in existence, he says: "Because they received not the love of the truth, that they might be saved. And for this cause God shall send them strong delusion, that they should believe a lie; that they all might be damned who believed not the truth, but had pleasure in unrighteousness." Let any one now say whether any of the statements in the Gospel, or in the writings of the apostle, could give occasion for the suspicion that there is therein contained any prediction of sorcery. Any one, moreover, who likes may find the prophecy in Daniel respecting antichrist. But Celsus falsities the words of Jesus, since He did not say that others would come working similar miracles to Himself, but who are wicked men and sorcerers, although Celsus asserts that He uttered such words. For as the power of the Egyptian magicians was not similar to the divinely-bestowed grace of Moses, but the issue clearly proved that the acts of the former were the effect of magic, while those of Moses were wrought by divine power; so the proceedings of the antichrists, and of those who feign that they can work miracles as being the disciples of Christ, are said to be lying signs and wonders, prevailing with all deceivableness of unrighteousness among them that perish; whereas the works of Christ and His disciples had for their fruit, not deceit, but the salvation of human souls. And who would rationally maintain that an improved moral life, which daily lessened the number of a man's offences, could proceed from a system of deceit?

CHAPTER LI

Celsus, indeed, evinced a slight knowledge of Scripture when he made Jesus say, that it is "a certain Satan who contrives such devices;" although he begs the question when he asserts that "Jesus did not deny that these works have in them nothing of divinity, but proceed from wicked men," for he makes things which differ in kind to be the same. Now, as a wolf is not of the same species as a dog, although it may appear to have some resemblance in the figure of its body and in its voice, nor a common wood-pigeon the same as a dove, so there is no resemblance between what is done by the power of God and what is the effect of sorcery. And we might further say, in answer to the calumnies of Celsus, Are those to be regarded as miracles which are wrought through sorcery by wicked demons, but those not which are performed by a nature that is holy and divine? and does human life endure the worse, but never receive the better? Now it appears to me that we must lay it down as a general principle, that as, wherever anything that is evil would make itself to be of the same nature with the good, there must by all means be something that is good opposed to the evil; so also, in opposition to those things which are brought about by sorcery, there must also of necessity be some things in human life which are the result of divine power. And it follows from the same, that we must either annihilate both, and assert that neither exists, or, assuming the one, and particularly the evil, admit also the reality of the good. Now, if one were to lay it down that works are wrought by means of sorcery, but would not grant that there are also works which are the

382

product of divine power, he would seem to me to resemble him who should admit the existence of sophisms and plausible arguments, which have the appearance of establishing the truth, although really undermining it, while denying that truth had anywhere a home among men, or a dialectic which differed from sophistry. But if we once admit that it is consistent with the existence of magic and sorcery (which derive their power from evil demons, who are spell-bound by elaborate incantations, and become subject to sorcerers) that some works must be found among men which proceed from a power that is divine, why shall we not test those who profess to perform them by their lives and morals, and the consequences of their miracles, viz., whether they tend to the injury of men or to the reformation of conduct? What minister of evil demons, e.g., can do such things? and by means of what incantations and magic arts? And who, on the other hand, is it that, having his soul and his spirit, and I imagine also his body, in a pure and holy state, receives a divine spirit, and performs such works in order to benefit men, and to lead them to believe on the true God? But if we must once investigate (without being carried away by the miracles themselves) who it is that performs them by help of a good, and who by help of an evil power, so that we may neither slander all without discrimination, nor yet admire and accept all as divine, will it not be manifest, from what occurred in the times of Moses and Jesus, when entire nations were established in consequence of their miracles, that these men wrought by means of divine power what they are recorded to have performed? For wickedness and sorcery would not have led a whole nation to rise not only above idols and images erected by men, but also above all created things, and to ascend to the uncreated origin of the God of the universe.

CHAPTER LII

But since it is a Jew who makes these assertions in the treatise of Celsus, we would say to him: Pray, friend, why do you believe the works which are recorded in your writings as having been performed by God through the instrumentality of Moses to be really divine, and endeavour to refute those who slanderously assert that they were wrought by sorcery, like those of the Egyptian magicians; while, in imitation of your Egyptian opponents, you charge those which were done by Jesus, and which, you admit, were actually performed, with not being divine? For if the final result, and the founding of an entire nation by the miracles of Moses, manifestly demonstrate that it was God who brought these things to pass in the time of Moses the Hebrew lawgiver, why should not such rather be shown to be the case with Jesus, who accomplished far greater works than those of Moses? For the former took those of his own nation, the descendants of Abraham, who had observed the rite of circumcision transmitted by tradition, and who were careful observers of the Abrahamic usages, and led them out of Egypt, enacting for them those laws which you believe to be divine; whereas the latter ventured upon a greater undertaking, and superinduced upon the pre-existing constitution, and upon ancestral customs and modes of life agreeable to the existing laws, a constitution in conformity with the Gospel. And as it was necessary, in order that Moses should find credit not only among the elders, but the common people, that there should be performed those miracles which he is recorded to have performed, why should not Jesus also, in order that He may be believed on by those of the people who had learned to ask for signs and wonders, need to work such miracles as, on account of their greater grandeur and divinity (in comparison with those of Moses), were able to convert men from Jewish fables, and from the human traditions which prevailed among them, and make them admit that He who taught and did such things was greater than the prophets? For how was not He greater than the prophets, who was proclaimed by them to be the Christ, and the Saviour of the human race?

CHAPTER LIII

All the arguments, indeed, which this Jew of Celsus advances against those who believe on Jesus, may, by parity of reasoning, be urged as ground of accusation against Moses: so that there is no difference in asserting that the sorcery practised by Jesus and that by Moses were similar to each other,—both of them, so far as the language of this Jew of Celsus is concerned, being liable to the same charge; as, e.g., when this Jew says of Christ, "But, O light and truth! Jesus with his own voice expressly declares, as you yourselves have recorded, that there will appear among you others also, who will perform miracles like mine, but who are wicked men and sorcerers," some one, either Greek or Egyptian, or any other party who disbelieved the Jew, might say respecting Moses, "But, O light and truth! Moses with his own voice expressly declares, as ye also have recorded, that there will appear among you others also, who will perform miracles like mine, but who are wicked men and sorcerers. For it is written in your law, 'If there arise among you a prophet, or a dreamer of dreams, and giveth thee a sign or a wonder, and the sign or wonder come to pass whereof he spake unto thee, saying, Let us go after other gods which thou hast not known, and let us serve them; thou shalt not hearken to the words of that prophet, or dreamer of dreams,'" etc. Again, perverting the words of Jesus, he says, "And he terms him who devises such things, one Satan;" while one, applying this to Moses, might say, "And he terms him who devises such things, a prophet who dreams." And as this Jew asserts regarding Jesus, that "even he himself does not deny that these works have in them nothing of divinity, but are the acts of wicked men;" so any one who disbelieves the writings of Moses might say, quoting what has been already said, the same thing, viz., that, "even Moses does not deny that these works have in them nothing of divinity, but are the acts of wicked men." And he will do the same thing also with respect to this: "Being compelled by the force of truth, Moses at the same time both exposed the doings of others, and convicted himself of the same." And when the Jew says, "Is it not a wretched inference from the same acts, to conclude that the one is a God, and the others sorcerers?" one might object to him, on the ground of those words of Moses already quoted, "Is it not then a wretched inference from the same acts, to conclude that the one is a prophet and servant of God, and the others sorcerers?" But when, in addition to those comparisons which I have already mentioned, Celsus, dwelling upon the subject, adduces this also: "Why from these works should the others be accounted wicked, rather than this man, seeing they have him as a witness against himself?"—we, too, shall adduce the following, in addition to what has been already said: "Why, from those passages in which Moses forbids us to believe those who exhibit signs and wonders, ought we to consider such persons as wicked, rather than Moses, because he calumniates some of them in respect of their signs and wonders?" And urging more to the same effect, that he may appear to strengthen his attempt, he says: "He himself acknowledged that these were not the works of a divine nature, but were the inventions of certain deceivers, and of very wicked men." Who, then, is "himself?" You O Jew, say that it is Jesus; but he who accuses you as liable to the same charges, will transfer this "himself" to the person of Moses.

CHAPTER LIV

After this, forsooth, the Jew of Celsus, to keep up the character assigned to the Jew from the beginning, in his address to those of his countrymen who had become believers, says: "By what, then, were *you* induced (to become his followers)? Was it because he foretold that after his death he would rise again?" Now this question, like the others, can be retorted upon Moses. For we might say to the Jew: "By what, then, were you induced (to become the follower of Moses)? Was it because he put on record the following statement about his own death: 'And Moses, the servant of the LORD died there, in the land of Moab, according to the word of the LORD; and they buried him in Moab, near the house of Phogor: and no one knoweth his sepulchre until this day?'" For as the Jew casts discredit upon the statement, that "Jesus foretold that after His death He would rise again," another person might make a similar assertion about Moses, and would say in reply, that Moses also put on record (for the book of Deuteronomy is his composition) the statement, that "no one knoweth his sepulchre until this day," in order to magnify and enhance the importance of his place of burial, as being unknown to mankind.

CHAPTER LV

The Jew continues his address to those of his countrymen who are converts, as follows: "Come now, let us grant to you that the prediction was actually uttered. Yet how many others are there who practise such juggling tricks, in order to deceive their simple hearers, and who make gain by their deception?—as was the case, they say, with Zamolxis in Scythia, the slave of Pythagoras; and with Pythagoras himself in Italy; and with Rhampsinitus in Egypt (the latter of whom, they say, played at dice with Demeter in Hades, and returned to the upper world with a golden napkin which he had received from her as a gift); and also with Orpheus among the Odrysians, and Protesilaus in Thessaly, and Hercules at Cape Taenarus, and Theseus. But the question is, whether any one who was really dead ever rose with a veritable body. Or do you imagine the statements of others not only to be myths, but to have the appearance of such, while you have discovered a becoming and credible termination to your drama in the voice from the cross, when he breathed his last, and in the earthquake and the darkness? That while alive he was of no assistance to himself, but that when dead he rose again, and showed the marks of his punishment, and how his hands were pierced with nails: who beheld this? A half-frantic woman, as you state, and some other one, perhaps, of those who were engaged in the same system of delusion, who had either dreamed so, owing to a peculiar state of mind, or under the influence of a wandering imagination had formed to himself an appearance according to his own wishes, which has been the case with numberless individuals; or, which is most probable, one who desired to impress others with this portent, and by such a falsehood to furnish an occasion to impostors like himself."

Now, since it is a Jew who makes these statements, we shall conduct the defence of our Jesus as if we were replying to a Jew, still continuing the comparison derived from the accounts regarding Moses, and saying to him: "How many others are there who practise similar juggling tricks to those of Moses, in order to deceive their silly hearers, and who make gain by their deception?" Now this objection would be more appropriate in the mouth of one who did not believe in Moses (as we might quote the instances of Zamolxis and Pythagoras, who were engaged in such juggling tricks) than in that of a Jew, who is not very learned in the histories of the Greeks. An Egyptian, moreover, who did not believe the miracles of Moses, might credibly adduce the instance of Rhampsinitus, saying that it was far more credible that he had descended to Hades, and had played at dice with Demeter, and that after stealing from her a golden napkin he exhibited it as a sign of his having been in Hades, and of his having returned thence, than that Moses should have recorded that he entered into the darkness, where God was, and that he alone, above all others, drew near to God. For the following is his statement: "Moses alone shall come near the LORD; but the rest shall not come nigh." We, then, who are the disciples of Jesus, say to the Jew who urges these objections: "While assailing our belief in Jesus, defend yourself, and answer the Egyptian and the Greek objectors: what will you say to those charges which you brought against our Jesus, but which also might be brought against Moses first? And if you should make a vigorous effort to defend Moses, as indeed his history does admit of a clear and powerful defence, you will unconsciously, in your support of Moses, be an unwilling assistant in establishing the greater divinity of Jesus."

CHAPTER LVI

But since the Jew says that these histories of the alleged descent of heroes to Hades, and of their return thence, are juggling impositions, maintaining that these heroes disappeared for a certain time, and secretly withdrew themselves from the sight of all men, and gave themselves out afterwards as having returned from Hades,—for such is the meaning which his words seem to convey respecting the Odrysian Orpheus, and the Thessalian Protesilaus, and the Taenarian Hercules, and Theseus also,—let us endeavour to show that the account of Jesus being raised from the dead cannot possibly be compared to these. For each one of the heroes respectively mentioned might, had he wished, have secretly withdrawn himself from the sight of men, and returned again, if so determined, to those whom he had left; but seeing that Jesus was crucified before all the Jews, and His body slain in the presence of His nation, how can they bring themselves to say that He practised a similar deception with those heroes who are related to have gone down to Hades, and to have returned thence? But we say that the following consideration might be adduced, perhaps, as a defence of the public crucifixion of Jesus, especially in connection with the existence of those stories of heroes who are supposed to have been compelled to descend to Hades: that if we were to suppose Jesus to have died an obscure death, so that the fact of His decease was not patent to the whole nation of the Jews, and afterwards to have actually risen from the dead, there would, in such a case, have been ground for the same suspicion entertained regarding the heroes being also entertained regarding Himself. Probably, then, in addition to other causes for the crucifixion of Jesus, this also may have contributed to His dying a conspicuous death upon the cross, that no one might have it in his power to say that He voluntarily withdrew from the sight of men, and seemed only to die, without really doing so; but, appearing again, made a juggler's trick of the resurrection from the dead. But a clear and unmistakeable proof of the fact I hold to be the undertaking of His disciples, who devoted themselves to the teaching of a doctrine which was attended with danger to human life,—a doctrine which they would not have taught with such courage had they invented the resurrection of Jesus from the dead; and who also, at the same time, not only prepared others to despise death, but were themselves the first to manifest their disregard for its terrors.

CHAPTER LVII

But observe whether this Jew of Celsus does not talk very blindly, in saying that it is impossible for any one to rise from the dead with a veritable body, his language being: "But this is the question, whether any one who was really dead ever rose again with a veritable body?" Now a Jew would not have uttered these words, who believed what is recorded in the third and fourth books of Kings regarding little children, of whom the one was raised up by Elijah, and the other by Elisha. And on this account, too, I think it was that Jesus appeared to no other nation than the Jews, who had become accustomed to miraculous occurrences; so that, by comparing what they themselves believed with the works which were done by Him, and with what was related of Him, they might confess that He, in regard to whom greater things were done, and by whom mightier marvels were performed, was greater than all those who preceded Him.

CHAPTER LVIII

Further, after these Greek stories which the Jew adduced respecting those who were guilty of juggling practices, and who pretended to have risen from the dead, he says to those Jews who are converts to Christianity: "Do you imagine the statements of others not only to be myths, but to have the appearance of such, while you have discovered a becoming and credible termination to your drama in the voice from the cross, when he breathed his last?" We reply to the Jew: "What you adduce as myths, we regard also as such; but the statements of the Scriptures which are common to us both, in which not you only, but we also, take pride, we do not at all regard as myths. And therefore we accord our belief to those who have therein related that some rose from the dead, as not being guilty of imposition; and to Him especially there mentioned as having risen, who both predicted the event Himself, and was the subject of prediction by others. And His resurrection is more miraculous than that of the others in this respect, that they were raised by the prophets Elijah and Elisha, while He was raised by none of the prophets, but by His Father in heaven. And therefore His resurrection also produced greater results than theirs. For what great good has accrued to the world from the resurrection of the children through the instrumentality of Elijah and Elisha, such as has resulted from the preaching of the resurrection of Jesus, accepted as an article of belief, and as effected through the agency of divine power?"

CHAPTER LIX

He imagines also that both the earthquake and the darkness were an invention; but regarding these, we have in the preceding pages, made our defence, according to our ability, adducing the testimony of Phlegon, who relates that these events took place at the time when our Saviour suffered. And he goes on to say, that "Jesus, while alive, was of no assistance to himself, but that he arose after death, and exhibited the marks of his punishment, and showed how his hands had been pierced by nails." We ask him what he means by the expression, "was of no assistance to himself?" For if he means it to refer to want of virtue, we reply that He *was* of very great assistance. For He neither uttered nor committed anything that was improper, but was truly "led as a sheep to the slaughter, and was dumb as a lamb before the shearer;" and the Gospel testifies that He opened not His mouth. But if Celsus applies the expression to things indifferent and corporeal, (meaning that in such Jesus could render no help to Himself,) we say that we have proved from the Gospels that He went voluntarily to encounter His sufferings. Speaking next of the statements in the Gospels, that after His resurrection He showed the marks of His punishment, and how His hands had been pierced, he asks, "Who beheld this?" And discrediting the narrative of Mary Magdalene, who is related to have seen Him, he replies, "A half-frantic woman, as ye state." And because she is not the only one who is recorded to have seen the Saviour after His resurrection, but others also are mentioned, this Jew of Celsus calumniates these statements also in adding, "And some one else of those engaged in the same system of deception!"

CHAPTER LX

In the next place, as if this were possible, viz., that the image of a man who was dead could appear to another as if he were still living, he adopts this opinion as an Epicurean, and says, "That some one having so dreamed owing to a peculiar state of mind, or having, under the influence of a perverted imagination, formed such an appearance as he himself desired, reported that such had been seen; and this," he continues, "has been the case with numberless individuals." But even if this statement of his seems to have a considerable degree of force, it is nevertheless only fitted to confirm a necessary doctrine, that the soul of the dead exists in a separate state (from the body); and he who adopts such an opinion does not believe without good reason in the immortality, or at least continued existence, of the soul, as even Plato says in his treatise on the Soul that shadowy phantoms of persons already dead have appeared to some around their sepulchres. Now the phantoms which exist about the soul of the dead are produced by some substance, and this substance is in the soul, which exists apart in a body said to be of splendid appearance. But Celsus, unwilling to admit any such view, will have it that some dreamed a waking dream, and, under the influence of a perverted imagination, formed to themselves such an image as they desired. Now it is not irrational to believe that a dream may take place while one is asleep; but to suppose a waking vision in the case of those who are not altogether out of their senses, and under the influence of delirium or hypochondria, is incredible. And Celsus, seeing this, called the woman "half-mad,"—a statement which is not made by the history recording the fact, but from which he took occasion to charge the occurrences with being untrue.

CHAPTER LXI

Jesus accordingly, as Celsus imagines, exhibited after His death only the appearance of wounds received on the cross, and was not in reality so wounded as He is described to have been; whereas, according to the teaching of the Gospel—some portions of which Celsus arbitrarily accepts, in order to find ground of accusation, and other parts of which he rejects—Jesus called to Him one of His disciples who was sceptical, and who deemed the miracle an impossibility. That individual had, indeed, expressed his belief in the statement of the woman who said that she had seen Him, because he did not think it impossible that the soul of a dead man could be seen; but he did not yet consider the report to be true that He had been raised in a body, which was the antitype of the former. And therefore he did not merely say, "Unless I see, I will not believe;" but he added, "Unless I put my hand into the print of the nails, and lay my hands upon His side, I will not believe." These words were spoken by Thomas, who deemed it possible that the body of the soul might be seen by the eye of sense, resembling in all respects its former appearance,

"Both in size, and in beauty of eyes,
And in voice;"

and frequently, too,

"Having, also, such garments around the person (as when alive)."

Jesus accordingly, having called Thomas, said, "Reach hither thy finger, and behold My hands; and reach hither thy hand, and thrust it into My side: and be not faithless, but believing."

CHAPTER LXII

Now it followed from all the predictions which were uttered regarding Him—amongst which was this prediction of the resurrection—and, from all that was done by Him, and from all the events which befell Him, that this event should be marvellous above all others. For it had been said beforehand by the prophet in the person of Jesus: "My flesh shall rest in hope, and Thou wilt not leave my soul in Hades, and wilt not suffer Thine Holy One to see corruption." And truly, after His resurrection, He existed in a body intermediate, as it were, between the grossness of that which He had before His sufferings, and the appearance of a soul uncovered by such a body. And hence it was, that when His disciples were together, and Thomas with them, there "came Jesus, the doors being shut, and stood in the midst, and said, Peace be unto you. Then saith He to Thomas, Reach hither thy finger," etc. And in the Gospel of Luke also, while Simon and Cleopas were conversing with each other respecting all that had happened to them, Jesus "drew near, and went with them. And their eyes were holden, that they should not know Him. And He said unto them, What manner of communications are these that ye have one to another, as ye walk?" And when their eyes were opened, and they knew Him, then the Scripture says, in express words, "And He vanished out of their sight." And although Celsus may wish to place what is told of Jesus, and of those who saw Him after His resurrection, on the same level with imaginary appearances of a different kind, and those who have invented such, yet to those who institute a candid and intelligent examination, the events will appear only the more miraculous.

CHAPTER LXIII

After these points, Celsus proceeds to bring against the Gospel narrative a charge which is not to be lightly passed over, saying that "if Jesus desired to show that his power was really divine, he ought to have appeared to those who had ill-treated him, and to him who had condemned him, and to all men universally." For it appears to us also to be true, according to the Gospel account, that He was not seen after His resurrection in the same manner as He used formerly to show Himself—publicly, and to all men. But it is recorded in the Acts, that "being seen during forty days," He expounded to His disciples "the things pertaining to the kingdom of God." And in the Gospels it is not stated that He was always with them; but that on one occasion He appeared in their midst, after eight days, when the doors were shut, and on another in some similar fashion. And Paul also, in the concluding portions of the first Epistle to the Corinthians, in reference to His not having publicly appeared as He did in the period before He suffered, writes as follows: "For I delivered unto you first of all that which I also received, how that Christ died for our sins according to the Scriptures; and that He was seen of Cephas, then of the twelve: after that He was seen of above five hundred brethren at once, of whom the greater part remain unto the present time, but some are fallen asleep. After that He was seen of James, then of all the apostles. And last of all He was seen of me also, as of one born out of due time." I am of opinion now that the statements in this passage contain some great and wonderful mysteries, which are beyond the grasp not merely of the great multitude of ordinary believers, but even of those who are far advanced (in Christian knowledge), and that in them the reason would be explained why He did not show Himself, after His resurrection from the dead, in the same manner as before that event. And in a treatise of this nature, composed in answer to a work directed against the Christians and their faith, observe whether we are able to adduce a few rational arguments out of a greater number, and thus make an impression upon the hearers of this apology.

CHAPTER LXIV

Although Jesus was only a single individual, He was nevertheless more things than one, according to the different standpoint from which He might be regarded; nor was He seen in the same way by all who beheld Him. Now, that He was more things than one, according to the varying point of view, is clear from this statement, "I am the way, and the truth, and the life;" and from this, "I am the bread;" and this, "I am the door," and innumerable others. And that when seen He did not appear in like fashion to all those who saw Him, but according to their several ability to receive Him, will be clear to those who notice why, at the time when He was about to be transfigured on the high mountain, He did not admit all His apostles (to this sight), but only Peter, and James, and John, because they alone were capable of beholding His glory on that occasion, and of observing the glorified appearance of Moses and Elijah, and of listening to their conversation, and to the voice from the heavenly cloud. I am of opinion, too, that before He ascended the mountain where His disciples came to Him alone, and where He taught them the beatitudes, when He was somewhere in the lower part of the mountain, and when, as it became late, He healed those who were brought to Him, freeing them from all sickness and disease, He did not appear the same person to the sick, and to those who needed His healing aid, as to those who were able by reason of their strength to go up the mountain along with Him. Nay, even when He interpreted privately to His own disciples the parables which were delivered to the multitudes without, from whom the explanation was withheld, as they who heard them explained were endowed with higher organs of hearing than they who heard them without explanation, so was it altogether the same with the eyes of their soul, and, I think, also with those of their body. And the following statement shows that He had not always the same appearance, viz., that Judas, when about to betray Him, said to the multitudes who were setting out with him, as not being acquainted with Him, "Whomsoever I shall kiss, the same is He." And I think that the Saviour Himself indicates the same thing by the words: "I was daily with you, teaching in the temple, and ye laid no hold on Me." Entertaining, then, such exalted views regarding Jesus, not only with respect to the Deity within, and which was hidden from the view of the multitude, but with respect to the transfiguration of His body, which took place when and to whom He would, we say, that before Jesus had "put off the governments and powers," and while as yet He was not dead unto sin, all men were capable of seeing Him; but that, when He had "put off the governments and powers," and had no longer anything which was capable of being seen by the multitude, all who had formerly seen Him were not now able to behold Him. And therefore, sparing them, He did not show Himself to all after His resurrection from the dead.

CHAPTER LXV

And why do I say "to all?" For even with His own apostles and disciples He was not perpetually present, nor did He constantly show Himself to them, because they were not able without intermission to receive His divinity. For His deity was more resplendent after He had finished the economy (of salvation): and this Peter, surnamed Cephas, the first-fruits as it were of the apostles, was enabled to behold, and along with him the twelve (Matthias having been substituted in room of Judas); and after them He appeared to the five hundred brethren at once, and then to James, and subsequently to all the others besides the twelve apostles, perhaps to the seventy also, and lastly to Paul, as to one born out of due time, and who knew well how to say, "Unto me, who am less than the least of all saints, is this grace given;" and probably the expression "least of all" has the same meaning with "one born out of due time." For as no one could reasonably blame Jesus for not having admitted all His apostles to the high mountain, but only the three already mentioned, on the occasion of His transfiguration, when He was about to manifest the splendour which appeared in His garments, and the glory of Moses and Elias talking with Him, so none could reasonably object to the statements of the apostles, who introduce the appearance of Jesus after His resurrection as having been made not to all, but to those only whom He knew to have received eyes capable of seeing His resurrection. I think, moreover, that the following statement regarding Him has an apologetic value in reference to our subject, viz.: "For to this end Christ died, and rose again, that He might be Lord both of the dead and living." For observe, it is conveyed in these words, that Jesus died that He might be Lord of the dead; and that He rose again to be Lord not only of the dead, but also of the living. And the apostle understands, undoubtedly, by the dead over whom Christ is to be Lord, those who are so called in the first Epistle to the Corinthians, "For the trumpet shall sound, and the dead shall be raised incorruptible;" and by the living, those who are to be changed, and who are different from the dead who are to be raised. And respecting the living the words are these, "And we shall be changed;" an expression which follows immediately after the statement, "The dead shall be raised first." Moreover, in the first Epistle to the Thessalonians, describing the same change in different words, he says, that they who sleep are not the same as those who are alive; his language being, "I would not have you to be ignorant, brethren, concerning them who are asleep, that ye sorrow not, even as others which have no hope. For if we believe that Jesus died, and rose again, even so them also that sleep in Jesus will God bring with Him. For this we say unto you by the word of the Lord, that we who are alive and remain unto the coming of the Lord, shall not prevent them that are asleep." The explanation which appeared to us to be appropriate to this passage, we gave in the exegetical remarks which we have made on the first Epistle to the Thessalonians.

CHAPTER LXVI

And be not surprised if all the multitudes who have believed on Jesus do not behold His resurrection, when Paul, writing to the Corinthians, can say to them, as being incapable of receiving greater matters, "For I determined not to know anything among you, save Jesus Christ, and Him crucified;" which is the same as saying, "Hitherto ye were not able, neither yet now are ye able, for ye are still carnal." The Scripture, therefore, doing everything by appointment of God, has recorded of Jesus, that before His sufferings He appeared to all indifferently, but not always; while after His sufferings He no longer appeared to all in the same way, but with a certain discrimination which measured out to each his due. And as it is related that "God appeared to Abraham," or to one of the saints, and this "appearance" was not a thing of constant occurrence, but took place at intervals, and not to all, so understand that the Son of God appeared in the one case on the same principle that God appeared to the latter.

CHAPTER LXVII

To the best of our ability, therefore, as in a treatise of this nature, we have answered the objection, that "if Jesus had really wished to manifest his divine power, he ought to have shown himself to those who ill-treated him, and to the judge who condemned him, and to all without reservation." There was, however, no obligation on Him to appear either to the judge who condemned Him, or to those who ill-treated Him. For Jesus spared both the one and the other, that they might not be smitten with blindness, as the men of Sodom were when they conspired against the beauty of the angels entertained by Lot. And here is the account of the matter: "But the men put forth their hand, and pulled Lot into the house to them, and shut to the door. And they smote the men who were at the door of the house with blindness, both small and great; so that they wearied themselves to find the door." Jesus, accordingly, wished to show that His power was divine to each one who was capable of seeing it, and according to the measure of His capability. And I do not suppose that He guarded against being seen on any other ground than from a regard to the fitness of those who were incapable of seeing Him. And it is in vain for Celsus to add, "For he had no longer occasion to fear any man after his death, being, as you say, a God; nor was he sent into the world at all for the purpose of being hid." Yet He was sent into the world not only to become known, but also to be hid. For all that He was, was not known even to those to whom He was known, but a certain part of Him remained concealed even from them; and to some He was not known at all. And He opened the gates of light to those who were the sons of darkness and of night, and had devoted themselves to becoming the sons of light and of the day. For our Saviour Lord, like a good physician, came rather to us who were full of sins, than to those who were righteous.

CHAPTER LXVIII

But let us observe how this Jew of Celsus asserts that, "if this at least would have helped to manifest his divinity, he ought accordingly to have at once disappeared from the cross." Now this seems to me to be like the argument of those who oppose the doctrine of providence, and who arrange things differently from what they are, and allege that the world would be better if it were as they arrange it. Now, in those instances in which their arrangement is a possible one, they are proved to make the world, so far as depends upon them, worse by their arrangement than it actually is; while in those cases in which they do not portray things worse than they really are, they are shown to desire impossibilities; so that in either case they are deserving of ridicule. And here, accordingly, that there was no impossibility in His coming, as a being of diviner nature, in order to disappear when He chose, is clear from the very nature of the case; and is certain, moreover, from what is recorded of Him, in the judgment of those who do not adopt certain portions merely of the narrative that they may have ground for accusing Christianity, and who consider other portions to be fiction. For it is related in St. Luke's Gospel, that Jesus after His resurrection took bread, and blessed it, and breaking it, distributed it to Simon and Cleopas; and when they had received the bread, "their eyes were opened, and they knew Him, and He vanished out of their sight."

CHAPTER LXIX

But we wish to show that His instantaneous bodily disappearance from the cross was not better fitted to serve the purposes of the whole economy of salvation (than His remaining upon it was). For the mere letter and narrative of the events which happened to Jesus do not present the whole view of the truth. For each one of them can be shown, to those who have an intelligent apprehension of Scripture, to be a symbol of something else. Accordingly, as His crucifixion contains a truth, represented in the words, "I am crucified with Christ," and intimated also in these, "God forbid that I should glory, save in the cross of our Lord Jesus Christ, by whom the world is crucified to me, and I unto the world;" and as His death was necessary, because of the statement, "For in that He died, He died unto sin once," and this, "Being made conformable to His death," and this, "For if we be dead with Him, we shall also live with Him:" so also His burial has an application to those who have been made conformable to His death, who have been both crucified with Him, and have died with Him; as is declared by Paul, "For we were buried with Him by baptism, and have also risen with Him." These matters, however, which relate to His burial, and His sepulchre, and him who buried Him, we shall expound at greater length on a more suitable occasion, when it will be our professed purpose to treat of such things. But, for the present, it is sufficient to notice the clean linen in which the pure body of Jesus was to be enwrapped, and the new tomb which Joseph had hewn out of the rock, where "no one was yet lying," or, as John expresses it, "wherein was never man yet laid." And observe whether the harmony of the three evangelists here is not fitted to make an impression: for they have thought it right to describe the tomb as one that was "quarried or hewn out of the rock;" so that he who examines the words of the narrative may see something worthy of consideration, both in them and in the *newness* of the tomb,—a point mentioned by Matthew and John—and in the statement of Luke and John, that no one had ever been interred therein before. For it became Him, who was unlike other dead men (but who even in death manifested signs of life in the water and the blood), and who was, so to speak, a *new* dead man, to be laid in a new and clean tomb, in order that, as His birth was purer than any other (in consequence of His being born, not in the way of ordinary generation, but of a virgin), His burial also might have the purity symbolically indicated in His body being deposited in a sepulchre which was new, not built of stones gathered from various quarters, and having no natural unity, but quarried and hewed out of *one* rock, united together in all its parts. Regarding the explanation, however, of these points, and the method of ascending from the narratives themselves to the things which they symbolized, one might treat more profoundly, and in a manner more adapted to their divine character, on a more suitable occasion, in a work expressly devoted to such subjects. The literal narrative, however, one might thus explain, viz., that it was appropriate for Him who had resolved to endure suspension upon the cross, to maintain all the accompaniments of the character He had assumed, in order that He who as a man had been put to death, and who as a man had died, might also as a man be buried. But even if it had been related in the Gospels, according to the view of Celsus, that Jesus had immediately disappeared from the cross, he and other unbelievers would have found fault with the narrative, and would have brought against it some such objection as this: "Why, pray, did he disappear after he had been put upon the cross, and not disappear before he suffered?" If, then, after learning from the Gospels that He did not at once disappear from the cross, they imagine that they can find fault with the narrative, because it did not invent, as they consider it ought to have done, any such instantaneous disappearance, but gave a true account of the matter, is it not reasonable that they should accord their faith also to His resurrection, and should believe that He, according to His pleasure, on one occasion, when the doors were shut, stood in the midst of His disciples, and on another, after distributing bread to two of His acquaintances, immediately disappeared from view, after He had spoken to them certain words?

CHAPTER LXX

But how is it that this Jew of Celsus could say that Jesus concealed Himself? For his words regarding Him are these: "And who that is sent as a messenger ever conceals himself when he ought to make known his message?" Now, He did not conceal Himself, who said to those who sought to apprehend Him, "I was daily teaching openly in the temple, and ye laid no hold upon Me." But having once already answered this charge of Celsus, now again repeated, we shall content ourselves with what we have formerly said. We have answered, also, in the preceding pages, this objection, that "while he was in the body, and no one believed upon him, he preached to all without intermission; but when he might have produced a powerful belief in himself after rising from the dead, he showed himself secretly only to one woman, and to his own boon companions." Now it is not true that He showed Himself only to one woman; for it is stated in the Gospel according to Matthew, that "in the end of the Sabbath, as it began to dawn towards the first day of the week, came Mary Magdalene, and the other Mary, to see the sepulchre. And, behold, there had been a great earthquake: for the angel of the Lord had descended from heaven, and came and rolled back the stone." And, shortly after, Matthew adds: "And, behold, Jesus met *them*"—clearly meaning the afore-mentioned Marys—"saying, All hail. And they came and held Him by the feet, and worshipped Him." And we answered, too, the charge, that "while undergoing his punishment he was seen by all, but after his resurrection only by one," when we offered our defence of the fact that "He was not seen by all." And now we might say that His merely human attributes were visible to all men but those which were divine in their nature—I speak of the attributes not as related, but as distinct—were not capable of being received by all. But observe here the manifest contradiction into which Celsus falls. For having said, a little before, that Jesus had appeared secretly to one woman and His own boon companions, he immediately subjoins: "While undergoing his punishment he was seen by all men, but after his resurrection by one, whereas the opposite ought to have happened." And let us hear what he means by "ought to have happened." The being seen by all men while undergoing His punishment, but after His resurrection only by one individual, are opposites. Now, so far as his language conveys a meaning, he would have that to take place which is both impossible and absurd, viz., that while undergoing His punishment He should be seen only by one individual, but after His resurrection by all men! or else how will you explain his words, "The opposite ought to have happened?"

CHAPTER LXXI

Jesus taught us who it was that sent Him, in the words, "None knoweth the Father but the Son;" and in these, "No man hath seen God at any time; the only-begotten Son, who is in the bosom of the Father, He hath declared Him." He, treating of Deity, stated to His true disciples the doctrine regarding God; and we, discovering traces of such teaching in the Scripture narratives, take occasion from such to aid our theological conceptions, hearing it declared in one passage, that "God is light, and in Him there is no darkness at all;" and in another, "God is a Spirit, and they that worship Him must worship Him in spirit and in truth." But the purposes for which the Father sent Him are innumerable; and these any one may ascertain who chooses, partly from the prophets who prophesied of Him, and partly from the narratives of the evangelists. And not a few things also will he learn from the apostles, and especially from Paul. Moreover, those who are pious He leadeth to the light, and those who sin He will punish,—a circumstance which Celsus not observing, has represented Him "as one who will lead the pious to the light, and who will have mercy on others, whether they sin or repent."

CHAPTER LXXII

After the above statements, he continues: "If he wished to remain hid, why was there heard a voice from heaven proclaiming him to be the Son of God? And if he did not seek to remain concealed, why was he punished? or why did he die?" Now, by such questions he thinks to convict the histories of discrepancy, not observing that Jesus neither desired all things regarding Himself to be known to all whom He happened to meet, nor yet all things to be unknown. Accordingly, the voice from heaven which proclaimed Him to be the Son of God, in the words, "This is my beloved Son, in whom I am well pleased," is not stated to have been audible to the multitudes, as this Jew of Celsus supposed. The voice from the cloud on the high mountain, moreover, was heard only by those who had gone up with Him. For the divine voice is of such a nature, as to be heard only by those whom the speaker wishes to hear it. And I maintain, that the voice of God which is referred to, is neither air which has been struck, nor any concussion of the air, nor anything else which is mentioned in treatises on the voice; and therefore it is heard by a better and more divine organ of hearing than that of sense. And when the speaker will not have his voice to be heard by all, he that has the finer ear hears the voice of God, while he who has the ears of his soul deadened does not perceive that it is God who speaks. These things I have mentioned because of his asking, "Why was there heard a voice from heaven proclaiming him to be the Son of God?" while with respect to the query, "Why was he punished, if he wished to remain hid?" what has been stated at greater length in the preceding pages on the subject of His suffering may suffice.

CHAPTER LXXIII

The Jew proceeds, after this, to state as a consequence what does not follow from the premises; for it does *not* follow from "His having wished, by the punishments which He underwent, to teach us also to despise death," that after His resurrection He should openly summon all men to the light, and instruct them in the object of His coming. For He had formerly summoned all men to the light in the words, "Come unto Me, all ye that labour and are heavy laden, and I will give you rest." And the object of His coming had been explained at great length in His discourses on the beatitudes, and in the announcements which followed them, and in the parables, and in His conversations with the scribes and Pharisees. And the instruction afforded us by the Gospel of John, shows that the eloquence of Jesus consisted not in words, but in deeds; while it is manifest from the Gospel narratives that His speech was "with power," on which account also they marvelled at Him.

CHAPTER LXXIV

In addition to all this, the Jew further says: "All these statements are taken from your own books, in addition to which we need no other witness; for ye fall upon your own swords."

Now we have proved that many foolish assertions, opposed to the narratives of our Gospels, occur in the statements of the Jew, either with respect to Jesus or ourselves. And I do not think that he has shown that "we fall upon our own swords;" but he only so imagines. And when the Jew adds, in a general way, this to his former remarks: "O most high and heavenly one! what God, on appearing to men, is received with incredulity?" we must say to him, that according to the accounts in the law of Moses, God is related to have visited the Hebrews in a most public manner, not only in the signs and wonders performed in Egypt, and also in the passage of the Red Sea, and in the pillar of fire and cloud of light, but also when the Decalogue was announced to the whole people, and yet was received with incredulity by those who saw these things: for had they believed what they saw and heard, they would not have fashioned the calf, nor changed their own glory into the likeness of a grass-eating calf; nor would they have said to one another with reference to the calf, "These be thy gods, O Israel, who brought thee up out of the land of Egypt." And observe whether it is not entirely in keeping with the character of the same people, who formerly refused to believe such wonders and such appearances of divinity, throughout the whole period of wandering in the wilderness, as they are recorded in the law of the Jews to have done, to refuse to be convinced also, on occasion of the glorious advent of Jesus, by the mighty words which were spoken by Him with authority, and the marvels which He performed in the presence of all the people.

CHAPTER LXXV

I think what has been stated is enough to convince any one that the unbelief of the Jews with regard to Jesus was in keeping with what is related of this people from the beginning. For I would say in reply to this Jew of Celsus, when he asks, "What God that appeared among men is received with incredulity, and that, too, when appearing to those who expect him? or why, pray, is he not recognized by those who have been long looking for him?" what answer, friends, would you have us return to your questions? Which class of miracles, in your judgment, do you regard as the greater? Those which were wrought in Egypt and the wilderness, or those which we declare that Jesus performed among you? For if the former are in your opinion greater than the latter, does it not appear from this very fact to be in conformity with the character of those who disbelieved the greater to despise the less? And this is the opinion entertained with respect to our accounts of the miracles of Jesus. But if those related of Jesus are considered to be as great as those recorded of Moses, what strange thing has come to pass among a nation which has manifested incredulity with regard to the commencement of both dispensations? For the beginning of the legislation was in the time of Moses, in whose work are recorded the sins of the unbelievers and wicked among you, while the commencement of our legislation and second covenant is admitted to have been in the time of Jesus. And by your unbelief of Jesus ye show that ye are the sons of those who in the desert discredited the divine appearances; and thus what was spoken by our Saviour will be applicable also to you who believed not on Him: "Therefore ye bear witness that ye allow the deeds of your fathers." And there is fulfilled among you also the prophecy which said: "Your life shall hang in doubt before your eyes, and you will have no assurance of your life." For ye did not believe in the life which came to visit the human race.

CHAPTER LXXVI

Celsus, in adopting the character of a Jew, could not discover any objections to be urged against the Gospel which might not be retorted on him as liable to be brought also against the law and the prophets.

For he censures Jesus in such words as the following: "He makes use of threats, and reviles men on light grounds, when he says, 'Woe unto you,' and 'I tell you beforehand.' For by such expressions he manifestly acknowledges his inability to persuade; and this would not be the case with a God, or even a prudent man." Observe, now, whether these charges do not manifestly recoil upon the Jew. For in the writings of the law and the prophets God makes use of threats and revilings, when He employs language of not less severity than that found in the Gospel, such as the following expressions of Isaiah: "Woe unto them that join house to house, and lay field to field;" and, "Woe unto them that rise up early in the morning that they may follow strong drink;" and, "Woe unto them that draw their sins after them as with a long rope;" and, "Woe unto them that call evil good, and good evil;" and, "Woe unto those of you who are mighty to drink wine;" and innumerable other passages of the same kind. And does not the following resemble the threats of which he speaks: "Ah sinful nation, a people laden with iniquity, a seed of evildoers, children that are corrupters?" and so on, to which he subjoins such threats as are equal in severity to those which, he says, Jesus made use of. For is it not a threatening, and a great one, which declares, "Your country is desolate, your cities are burned with fire: your land, strangers devour it in your presence, and it is desolate, as overthrown by strangers?" And are there not revilings in Ezekiel directed against the people, when the Lord says to the prophet, "Thou dwellest in the midst of scorpions?" Were you serious, then, Celsus, in representing the Jew as saying of Jesus, that "he makes use of threats and revilings on slight grounds, when he employs the expressions, 'Woe unto you,' and 'I tell you beforehand?'" Do you not see that the charges which this Jew of yours brings against Jesus might be brought by him against God? For the God who speaks in the prophetic writings is manifestly liable to the same accusations, as Celsus regards them, of inability to persuade. I might, moreover, say to this Jew, who thinks that he makes a good charge against Jesus by such statements, that if he undertakes, in support of the scriptural account, to defend the numerous curses recorded in the books of Leviticus and Deuteronomy, we should make as good, or better, a defence of the revilings and threatenings which are regarded as having been spoken by Jesus. And as respects the law of Moses itself, we are in a position to make a better defence of it than the Jew is, because we have been taught by Jesus to have a more intelligent apprehension of the writings of the law. Nay, if the Jew perceive the meaning of the prophetic Scriptures, he will be able to show that it is for no light reason that God employs threatenings and revilings, when He says, "Woe unto you," and "I tell you beforehand." And how should God employ such expressions for the conversion of men, which Celsus thinks that even a prudent man would not have recourse to? But Christians, who know only one God—the same who spoke in the prophets and in the Lord (Jesus)—can prove the reasonableness of those threatenings and revilings, as Celsus considers and entitles them. And here a few remarks shall be addressed to this Celsus, who professes both to be a philosopher, and to be acquainted with all our system. How is it, friend, when Hermes, in Homer, says to Odysseus,

"Why, now, wretched man, do you come wandering alone over the mountain-tops?"

that you are satisfied with the answer, which explains that the Homeric Hermes addresses such language to Odysseus to remind him of his duty, because it is characteristic of the Sirens to flatter and to say pleasing things, around whom

"Is a huge heap of bones,"

and who say,

"Come hither, much lauded Odysseus, great glory of the Greeks;"

whereas, if our prophets and Jesus Himself, in order to turn their hearers from evil, make use of such expressions as "Woe unto you," and what you regard as revilings, there is no condescension in such language to the circumstances of the hearers, nor any application of such words to them as healing medicine? Unless, indeed, you would have God, or one who partakes of the divine nature, when conversing with men, to have regard to His own nature alone, and to what is worthy of Himself, but to have no regard to what is fitting to be brought before men who are under the dispensation and leading of His word, and with each one of whom He is to converse agreeably to his individual character. And is it not a ridiculous assertion regarding Jesus, to say that He was unable to persuade men, when you compare the state of matters not only among the Jews, who have many such instances recorded in the prophecies, but also among the Greeks, among whom all of those who have attained great reputation for their wisdom have been unable to persuade those who conspired against them, or to induce their judges or accusers to cease from evil, and to endeavour to attain to virtue by the way of philosophy?

CHAPTER LXXVII

After this the Jew remarks, manifestly in accordance with the Jewish belief: "We certainly hope that there will be a bodily resurrection, and that we shall enjoy an eternal life; and the example and archetype of this will be He who is sent to us, and who will show that nothing is impossible with God." We do not know, indeed, whether the Jew would say of the expected Christ, that He exhibits in Himself an example of the resurrection; but let it be supposed that he both thinks and says so. We shall give this answer, then, to him who has told us that he drew his information from our own writings: "Did you read those writings, friend, in which you think you discover matter of accusation against us, and not find there the resurrection of Jesus, and the declaration that He was the first-born from the dead? Or because you will not allow such things to have been recorded, were they not actually recorded?" But as the Jew still admits the resurrection of the body, I do not consider the present a suitable time to discuss the subject with one who both believes and says that there is a bodily resurrection, whether he has an articulate understanding of such a topic, and is able to plead well on its behalf, or not, but has only given his assent to it as being of a legendary character. Let the above, then, be our reply to this Jew of Celsus. And when he adds, "Where, then, is he, that we may see him and believe upon him?" we answer: Where is He now who spoke in the prophecies, and who wrought miracles, that we may see and believe that He is part of God? Are *you* to be allowed to meet the objection, that God does not perpetually show Himself to the Hebrew nation, while *we* are not to be permitted the same defence with regard to Jesus, who has both once risen Himself, and led His disciples to believe in His resurrection, and so thoroughly persuaded them of its truth, that they show to all men by their sufferings how they are able to laugh at all the troubles of life, beholding the life eternal and the resurrection clearly demonstrated to them both in word and deed?

CHAPTER LXXVIII

The Jew continues: "Did Jesus come into the world for this purpose, that we should not believe him?" To which we immediately answer, that He did not come with the object of producing incredulity among the Jews; but knowing beforehand that such would be the result, He foretold it, and made use of their unbelief for the calling of the Gentiles. For through their sin salvation came to the Gentiles, respecting whom the Christ who speaks in the prophecies says, "A people whom I did not know became subject to Me: they were obedient to the hearing of My ear;" and, "I was found of them who sought Me not; I became manifest to those who inquired not after Me." It is certain, moreover, that the Jews were punished even in this present life, after treating Jesus in the manner in which they did. And let the Jews assert what they will when we charge them with guilt, and say, "Is not the providence and goodness of God most wonderfully displayed in your punishment, and in your being deprived of Jerusalem, and of the sanctuary, and of your splendid worship?" For whatever they may say in reply with respect to the providence of God, we shall be able more effectually to answer it by remarking, that the providence of God was wonderfully manifested in using the transgression of that people for the purpose of calling into the kingdom of God, through Jesus Christ, those from among the Gentiles who were strangers to the covenant and aliens to the promises. And these things were foretold by the prophets, who said that, on account of the transgressions of the Hebrew nation, God would make choice, not of a nation, but of individuals chosen from all lands; and, having selected the foolish things of the world, would cause an ignorant nation to become acquainted with the divine teaching, the kingdom of God being taken from the one and given to the other. And out of a larger number it is sufficient on the present occasion to adduce the prediction from the song in Deuteronomy regarding the calling of the Gentiles, which is as follows, being spoken in the person of the Lord: "They have moved Me to jealousy with those who are not gods; they have provoked Me to anger with their idols: and I will move them to jealousy with those who are not a people; I will provoke them to anger with a foolish nation."

CHAPTER LXXIX

The conclusion of all these arguments regarding Jesus is thus stated by the Jew: "He was therefore a man, and of such a nature, as the truth itself proves, and reason demonstrates him to be." I do not know, however, whether a man who had the courage to spread throughout the entire world his doctrine of religious worship and teaching, could accomplish what he wished without the divine assistance, and could rise superior to all who withstood the progress of his doctrine—kings and rulers, and the Roman senate, and governors in all places, and the common people. And how could the nature of a man possessed of no inherent excellence convert so vast a multitude? For it would not be wonderful if it were only the wise who were so convened; but it is the most irrational of men, and those devoted to their passions, and who, by reason of their irrationality, change with the greater difficulty so as to adopt a more temperate course of life. And yet it is because Christ was the power of God and the wisdom of the Father that He accomplished, and still accomplishes, such results, although neither the Jews nor Greeks who disbelieve His word will so admit. And therefore we shall not cease to believe in God, according to the precepts of Jesus Christ, and to seek to convert those who are blind on the subject of religion, although it is they who are truly blind themselves that charge us with blindness: and they, whether Jews or Greeks, who lead astray those that follow them, accuse us of seducing men—a good seduction, truly!—that they may become temperate instead of dissolute, or at least may make advances to temperance; may become just instead of unjust, or at least may tend to become so; prudent instead of foolish, or be on the way to become such; and instead of cowardice, meanness, and timidity, may exhibit the virtues of fortitude and courage, especially displayed in the struggles undergone for the sake of their religion towards God, the Creator of all things. Jesus Christ therefore came announced beforehand, not by one prophet, but by all; and it was a proof of the ignorance of Celsus, to represent a Jew as saying that one prophet only had predicted the advent of Christ. But as this Jew of Celsus, after being thus introduced, asserting that these things were indeed in conformity with his own law, has somewhere here ended his discourse, with a mention of other matters not worthy of remembrance, I too shall here terminate this second book of my answer to his treatise. But if God permit, and the power of Christ abide in my soul, I shall endeavour in the third book to deal with the subsequent statements of Celsus.

BOOK III

CHAPTER I

IN the first book of our answer to the work of Celsus, who had boastfully entitled the treatise which he had composed against us *A True Discourse*, we have gone through, as you enjoined, my faithful Ambrosius, to the best of our ability, his preface, and the parts immediately following it, testing each one of his assertions as we went along, until we finished with the tirade of this Jew of his, feigned to have been delivered against Jesus. And in the second book we met, as we best could, all the charges contained in the invective of the said Jew, which were levelled at us who are believers in God through Christ; and now we enter upon this third division of our discourse, in which our object is to refute the allegations which he makes in his own person.

He gives it as his opinion, that "the controversy between Jews and Christians is a most foolish one," and asserts that "the discussions which we have with each other regarding Christ differ in no respect from what is called in the proverb, 'a fight about the shadow of an ass;'" and thinks that "there is nothing of importance in the investigations of the Jews and Christians: for both believe that it was predicted by the Divine Spirit that one was to come as a Saviour to the human race, but do not yet agree on the point whether the person predicted has actually come or not." For we Christians, indeed, have believed in Jesus, as He who came according to the predictions of the prophets. But the majority of the Jews are so far from believing in Him, that those of them who lived at the time of His coming conspired against Him; and those of the present day, approving of what the Jews of former times dared to do against Him, speak evil of Him, asserting that it was by means of sorcery that he passed himself off for Him who was predicted by the prophets as the One who was to come, and who was called, agreeably to the traditions of the Jews, the Christ.

CHAPTER II

But let Celsus, and those who assent to his charges, tell us whether it is at all like "an ass's shadow," that the Jewish prophets should have predicted the birth-place of Him who was to be the ruler of those who had lived righteous lives, and who are called the "heritage" of God; and that Emmanuel should be conceived by a virgin; and that such signs and wonders should be performed by Him who was the subject of prophecy; and that His word should have such speedy course, that the voice of His apostles should go forth into all the earth; and that He should undergo certain sufferings after His condemnation by the Jews; and that He should rise again from the dead. For was it by chance that the prophets made these announcements, with no persuasion of the truth in their minds, moving them not only to speak, but to deem their announcements worthy of being committed to writing? And did so great a nation as that of the Jews, who had long ago received a country of their own wherein to dwell, recognise certain men as prophets, and reject others as utterers of false predictions, without any conviction of the soundness of the distinction? And was there no motive which induced them to class with the books of Moses, which were held as sacred, the words of those persons who were afterwards deemed to be prophets? And can those who charge the Jews and Christians with folly, show us how the Jewish nation could have continued to subsist, had there existed among them no promise of the knowledge of future events? and how, while each of the surrounding nations believed, agreeably to their ancient institutions, that they received oracles and predictions from those whom they accounted gods, this people alone, who were taught to view with contempt all those who were considered gods by the heathen, as not being gods, but demons, according to the declaration of the prophets, "For all the gods of the nations are demons," had among them no one who professed to be a prophet, and who could restrain such as, from a desire to know the future, were ready to desert to the demons of other nations? Judge, then, whether it were not a necessity, that as the whole nation had been taught to despise the deities of other lands, they should have had an abundance of prophets, who made known events which were of far greater importance in themselves, and which surpassed the oracles of all other countries.

CHAPTER III

In the next place, miracles were performed in all countries, or at least in many of them, as Celsus himself admits, instancing the case of Aesculapius, who conferred benefits on many, and who foretold future events to entire cities, which were dedicated to him, such as Tricca, and Epidaurus, and Cos, and Pergamus; and along with Aesculapius he mentions Aristeas of Proconnesus, and a certain Clazomenian, and Cleomedes of Astypalaea. But among the Jews alone, who say they are dedicated to the God of all things, there was wrought no miracle or sign which might help to confirm their faith in the Creator of all things, and strengthen their hope of another and better life! But how can they imagine such a state of things? For they would immediately have gone over to the worship of those demons which gave oracles and performed cures, and deserted the God who was believed, as far as words went, to assist them, but who never manifested to them His visible presence. But if this result has not taken place, and if, on the contrary, they have suffered countless calamities rather than renounce Judaism and their law, and have been cruelly treated, at one time in Assyria, at another in Persia, and at another under Antiochus, is it not in keeping with the probabilities of the case for those to suppose who do not yield their belief to their miraculous histories and prophecies, that the events in question could not be inventions, but that a certain divine Spirit being in the holy souls of the prophets, as of men who underwent any labour for the cause of virtue, *did* move them to prophesy some things relating to their contemporaries, and others to their posterity, but chiefly regarding a certain personage who was to come as a Saviour to the human race?

CHAPTER IV

And if the above be the state of the case, how do Jews and Christians search after "the shadow of an ass," in seeking to ascertain from those prophecies which they believe in common, whether He who was foretold has come, or has not yet arrived, and is still an object of expectation? But even suppose it be granted to Celsus that it was not Jesus who was announced by the prophets, then, even on such a hypothesis, the investigation of the sense of the prophetic writings is no search after "the shadow of an ass," if He who was spoken of can be clearly pointed out, and it can be shown both what sort of person He was predicted to be, and what He was to do, and, if possible, when He was to arrive. But in the preceding pages we have already spoken on the point of Jesus being the individual who was foretold to be the Christ, quoting a few prophecies out of a larger number. Neither Jews nor Christians, then, are wrong in assuming that the prophets spoke under divine influence; but they are in error who form erroneous opinions respecting Him who was expected by the prophets to come, and whose person and character were made known in their "true discourses."

CHAPTER V

Immediately after these points, Celsus, imagining that the Jews are Egyptians by descent, and had abandoned Egypt, after revolting against the Egyptian state, and despising the customs of that people in matters of worship, says that "they suffered from the adherents of Jesus, who believed in Him as the Christ, the same treatment which they had inflicted upon the Egyptians; and that the cause which led to the new state of things in either instance was rebellion against the state." Now let us observe what Celsus has here done. The ancient Egyptians, after inflicting many cruelties upon the Hebrew race, who had settled in Egypt owing to a famine which had broken out in Judea, suffered, in consequence of their injustice to strangers and suppliants, that punishment which divine Providence had decreed was to fall on the whole nation for having combined against an entire people, who had been their guests, and who had done them no harm; and after being smitten by plagues from God, they allowed them, with difficulty, and after a brief period, to go wherever they liked, as being unjustly detained in slavery. Because, then, they were a selfish people, who honoured those who were in any degree related to them far more than they did strangers of better lives, there is not an accusation which they have omitted to bring against Moses and the Hebrews,—not altogether denying, indeed, the miracles and wonders done by him, but alleging that they were wrought by sorcery, and not by divine power. Moses, however, not as a magician, but as a devout man, and one devoted to the God of all things, and a partaker in the divine Spirit, both enacted laws for the Hebrews, according to the suggestions of the Divinity, and recorded events as they happened with perfect fidelity.

CHAPTER VI

Celsus, therefore, not investigating in a spirit of impartiality the facts, which are related by the Egyptians in one way, and by the Hebrews in another, but being bewitched, as it were, in favour of the former, accepted as true the statements of those who had oppressed the strangers, and declared that the Hebrews, who had been unjustly treated, had departed from Egypt after revolting against the Egyptians,—not observing how impossible it was for so great a multitude of rebellious Egyptians to become a nation, which, dating its origin from the said revolt, should change its language at the time of its rebellion, so that those who up to that time made use of the Egyptian tongue, should completely adopt, all at once, the language of the Hebrews! Let it be granted, however, according to his supposition, that on abandoning Egypt they did conceive a hatred also of their mother tongue, how did it happen that after so doing they did not rather adopt the Syrian or Phoenician language, instead of preferring the Hebrew, which is different from both? But reason seems to me to demonstrate that the statement is false, which makes those who were Egyptians by race to have revolted against Egyptians, and to have left the country, and to have proceeded to Palestine, and occupied the land now called Judea. For Hebrew was the language of their fathers before their descent into Egypt; and the Hebrew letters, employed by Moses in writing those five books which are deemed sacred by the Jews, were different from those of the Egyptians.

CHAPTER VII

In like manner, as the statement is false "that the Hebrews, being (originally) Egyptians, dated the commencement (of their political existence) from the time of their rebellion," so also is this, "that in the days of Jesus others who were Jews rebelled against the Jewish state, and became His followers;" for neither Celsus nor they who think with him are able to point out any act on the part of Christians which savours of rebellion. And yet, if a revolt had led to the formation of the Christian commonwealth, so that it derived its existence in this way from that of the Jews, who were permitted to take up arms in defence of the members of their families, and to slay their enemies, the Christian Lawgiver would not have altogether forbidden the putting of men to death; and yet He nowhere teaches that it is right for His own disciples to offer violence to any one, however wicked. For He did not deem it in keeping with such laws as His, which were derived from a divine source, to allow the killing of any individual whatever. Nor would the Christians, had they owed their origin to a rebellion, have adopted laws of so exceedingly mild a character as not to allow them, when it was their fate to be slain as sheep, on any occasion to resist their persecutors. And truly, if we look a little deeper into things, we may say regarding the exodus from Egypt, that it is a miracle if a whole nation *at once* adopted the language called Hebrew, as if it had been a gift from heaven, when one of their own prophets said, "As they went forth from Egypt, they heard a language which they did not understand."

CHAPTER VIII

In the following way, also, we may conclude that they who came out of Egypt with Moses were not Egyptians; for if they had been Egyptians, their *names* also would be Egyptian, because in every language the designations (of persons and things) are kindred to the language. But if it is certain, from the names being Hebrew, that the people were not Egyptians,—and the Scriptures are full of Hebrew names, and these bestowed, too, upon their children while they were in Egypt,—it is clear that the Egyptian account is false, which asserts that they were Egyptians, and went forth from Egypt with Moses. Now it is absolutely certain that, being descended, as the Mosaic history records, from Hebrew ancestors, they employed a language from which they also took the names which they conferred upon their children. But with regard to the Christians, because they were taught not to avenge themselves upon their enemies (and have thus observed laws of a mild and philanthropic character); and because they would not, although able, have made war even if they had received authority to do so,—they have obtained this reward from God, that He has always warred in their behalf, and on certain occasions has restrained those who rose up against them and desired to destroy them. For in order to remind others, that by seeing a *few* engaged in a struggle for their religion, they also might be better fitted to despise death, some, on special occasions, and these individuals who can be easily numbered, have endured death for the sake of Christianity,—God not permitting the whole nation to be exterminated, but desiring that it should continue, and that the whole world should be filled with this salutary and religious doctrine. And again, on the other hand, that those who were of weaker minds might recover their courage and rise superior to the thought of death, God interposed His providence on behalf of believers, dispersing by an act of His will alone all the conspiracies formed against them; so that neither kings, nor rulers, nor the populace, might be able to rage against them beyond a certain point. Such, then, is our answer to the assertions of Celsus, "that a revolt was the original commencement of the ancient Jewish state, and subsequently of Christianity."

CHAPTER IX

But since he is manifestly guilty of falsehood in the statements which follow, let us examine his assertion when he says, "If all men wished to become Christians, the latter would not desire such a result." Now that the above statement is false is clear from this, that Christians do not neglect, as far as in them lies, to take measures to disseminate their doctrine throughout the whole world. Some of them, accordingly, have made it their business to itinerate not only through cities, but even villages and country houses, that they might make converts to God. And no one would maintain that they did this for the sake of gain, when sometimes they would not accept even necessary sustenance; or if at any time they were pressed by a necessity of this sort, were contented with the mere supply of their wants, although many were willing to share (their abundance) with them, and to bestow help upon them far above their need. At the present day, indeed, when, owing to the multitude of Christian believers, not only rich men, but persons of rank, and delicate and high-born ladies, receive the teachers of Christianity, some perhaps will dare to say that it is for the sake of a little glory that certain individuals assume the office of Christian instructors. It is impossible, however, rationally to entertain such a suspicion with respect to Christianity in its beginnings, when the danger incurred, especially by its teachers, was great; while at the present day the discredit attaching to it among the rest of mankind is greater than any supposed honour enjoyed among those who hold the same belief, especially when such honour is not shared by all. It is false, then, from the very nature of the case, to say that "if all men wished to become Christians, the latter would not desire such a result."

CHAPTER X

But observe what he alleges as a proof of his statement: "Christians at first were few in number, and held the same opinions; but when they grew to be a great multitude, they were divided and separated, each wishing to have his own individual party: for this was their object from the beginning." That Christians at first were few in number, in comparison with the multitudes who subsequently became Christian, is undoubted; and yet, all things considered, they were not so very few. For what stirred up the envy of the Jews against Jesus, and aroused them to conspire against Him, was the great number of those who followed Him into the wilderness,—five thousand men on one occasion, and four thousand on another, having attended Him thither, without including the women and children. For such was the charm of Jesus' words, that not only were *men* willing to follow Him to the wilderness, but *women* also, forgetting the weakness of their sex and a regard for outward propriety in thus following their Teacher into desert places. Children, too, who are altogether unaffected by such emotions, either following their parents, or perhaps attracted also by His divinity, in order that it might be implanted within them, became His followers along with their parents. But let it be granted that Christians were few in number at the beginning, how does that help to prove that Christians would be unwilling to make all men believe the doctrine of the Gospel?

CHAPTER XI

He says, in addition, that "all the Christians were of one mind," not observing, even in this particular, that from the beginning there were differences of opinion among believers regarding the meaning of the books held to be divine. At all events, while the apostles were still preaching, and while eye-witnesses of (the works of) Jesus were still teaching His doctrine, there was no small discussion among the converts from Judaism regarding Gentile believers, on the point whether they ought to observe Jewish customs, or should reject the burden of clean and unclean meats, as not being obligatory on those who had abandoned their ancestral Gentile customs, and had become believers in Jesus. Nay, even in the Epistles of Paul, who was contemporary with those who had seen Jesus, certain particulars are found mentioned as having been the subject of dispute,—viz., respecting the resurrection, and whether it were already past, and the day of the Lord, whether it were nigh at hand or not. Nay, the very exhortation to "avoid profane and vain babblings, and oppositions of science falsely so called: which some professing, have erred concerning the faith," is enough to show that from the very beginning, when, as Celsus imagines, believers were few in number, there were certain doctrines interpreted in different ways.

CHAPTER XII

In the next place, since he reproaches us with the existence of heresies in Christianity as being a ground of accusation against it, saying that "when Christians had greatly increased in numbers, they were divided and split up into factions, each individual desiring to have his own party;" and further, that "being thus separated through their numbers, they confute one another, still having, so to speak, one *name* in common, if indeed they still retain it. And this is the only thing which they are yet ashamed to abandon, while other matters are determined in different ways by the various sects." In reply to which, we say that heresies of different kinds have never originated from any matter in which the principle involved was not important and beneficial to human life. For since the science of medicine is useful and necessary to the human race, and many are the points of dispute in it respecting the manner of curing bodies, there are found, for this reason, numerous heresies confessedly prevailing in the science of medicine among the Greeks, and also, I suppose, among those barbarous nations who profess to employ medicine. And, again, since philosophy makes a profession of the truth, and promises a knowledge of existing things with a view to the regulation of life, and endeavours to teach what is advantageous to our race, and since the investigation of these matters is attended with great differences of opinion, innumerable heresies have consequently sprung up in philosophy, some of which are more celebrated than others. Even Judaism itself afforded a pretext for the origination of heresies, in the different acceptation accorded to the writings of Moses and those of the prophets. So, then, seeing Christianity appeared an object of veneration to men, not to the more servile class alone, as Celsus supposes, but to many among the Greeks who were devoted to literary pursuits, there necessarily originated heresies,—not at all, however, as the result of faction and strife, but through the earnest desire of many literary men to become acquainted with the doctrines of Christianity. The consequence of which was, that, taking in different acceptations those discourses which were believed by all to be divine, there arose heresies, which received their names from those individuals who admired, indeed, the origin of Christianity, but who were led, in some way or other, by certain plausible reasons, to discordant views. And yet no one would act rationally in avoiding medicine because of its heresies; nor would he who aimed at that which is seemly entertain a hatred of philosophy, and adduce its many heresies as a pretext for his antipathy. And so neither are the sacred books of Moses and the prophets to be condemned on account of the heresies in Judaism.

CHAPTER XIII

Now, if these arguments hold good, why should we not defend, in the same way, the existence of heresies in Christianity? And respecting these, Paul appears to me to speak in a very striking manner when he says, "For there must be heresies among you, that they who are approved may be made manifest among you." For as that man is "approved" in medicine who, on account of his experience in various (medical) heresies, and his honest examination of the majority of them, has selected the preferable system,—and as the great proficient in philosophy is he who, after acquainting himself experimentally with the various views, has given in his adhesion to the best,—so I would say that the wisest Christian was he who had carefully studied the heresies both of Judaism and Christianity. Whereas he who finds fault with Christianity because of its heresies would find fault also with the teaching of Socrates, from whose school have issued many others of discordant views. Nay, the opinions of Plato might be chargeable with error, on account of Aristotle's having separated from his school, and founded a new one,—on which subject we have remarked in the preceding book. But it appears to me that Celsus has become acquainted with certain heresies which do not possess even the *name* of Jesus in common with us. Perhaps he had heard of the sects called Ophites and Cainites, or some others of a similar nature, which had departed in all points from the teaching of Jesus. And yet surely this furnishes no ground for a charge against the *Christian* doctrine.

CHAPTER XIV

After this he continues: "Their union is the more wonderful, the more it can be shown to be based on no substantial reason. And yet rebellion is a substantial reason, as well as the advantages which accrue from it, and the fear of external enemies. Such are the causes which give stability to their faith." To this we answer, that our union does thus rest upon a reason, or rather not upon a reason, but upon the divine working, so that its commencement was God's teaching men, in the prophetical writings, to expect the advent of Christ, who was to be the Saviour of mankind. For in so far as this point is not really refuted (although it may *seem* to be by unbelievers), in the same proportion is the doctrine commended as the doctrine of God, and Jesus shown to be the Son of God both before and after His incarnation. I maintain, moreover, that even after His incarnation, He is always found by those who possess the acutest spiritual vision to be most God-like, and to have really come down to us from God, and to have derived His origin or subsequent development not from human wisdom, but from the manifestation of God within Him, who by His manifold wisdom and miracles established Judaism first, and Christianity afterwards; and the assertion that rebellion, and the advantages attending it, were the originating causes of a doctrine which has converted and improved so many men was effectually refuted.

CHAPTER XV

But again, that it is not the fear of external enemies which strengthens our union, is plain from the fact that this cause, by God's will, has already, for a considerable time, ceased to exist. And it is probable that the secure existence, so far as regards the world, enjoyed by believers at present, will come to an end, since those who calumniate Christianity in every way are again attributing the present frequency of rebellion to the multitude of believers, and to their not being persecuted by the authorities as in old times. For we have learned from the Gospel neither to relax our efforts in days of peace, and to give ourselves up to repose, nor, when the world makes war upon us, to become cowards, and apostatize from the love of the God of all things which is in Jesus Christ. And we clearly manifest the illustrious nature of our origin, and do not (as Celsus imagines) conceal it, when we impress upon the minds of our first converts a contempt for idols, and images of all kinds, and, besides this, raise their thoughts from the worship of created things instead of God, and elevate them to the universal Creator; clearly showing Him to be the subject of prophecy, both from the predictions regarding Him—of which there are many—and from those traditions which have been carefully investigated by such as are able intelligently to understand the Gospels, and the declarations of the apostles.

CHAPTER XVI

"But what the legends are of every kind which we gather together, or the terrors which we invent," as Celsus without proof asserts, he who likes may show. I know not, indeed, what he means by "inventing terrors," unless it be our doctrine of God as Judge, and of the condemnation of men for their deeds, with the various proofs derived partly from Scripture, partly from probable reason. And yet—for truth is precious—Celsus says, at the close, "Forbid that either I, or these, or any other individual should ever reject the doctrine respecting the future punishment of the wicked and the reward of the good!" What terrors, then, if you except the doctrine of punishment, do we invent and impose upon mankind? And if he should reply that "we weave together erroneous opinions drawn from ancient sources, and trumpet them aloud, and sound them before men, as the priests of Cybele clash their cymbals in the ears of those who are being initiated in their mysteries;" we shall ask him in reply, "Erroneous opinions from what ancient sources?" For, whether he refers to Grecian accounts, which taught the existence of courts of justice under the earth, or Jewish, which, among other things, predicted the life that follows the present one; he will be unable to show that we who, striving to believe on grounds of reason, regulate our lives in conformity with such doctrines, have failed correctly to ascertain the truth.

CHAPTER XVII

He wishes, indeed, to compare the articles of our faith to those of the Egyptians; "among whom, as you approach their sacred edifices, are to be seen splendid enclosures, and groves, and large and beautiful gateways, and wonderful temples, and magnificent tents around them, and ceremonies of worship full of superstition and mystery; but when you have entered, and passed within, the object of worship is seen to be a cat, or an ape, or a crocodile, or a goat, or a dog!" Now, what is the resemblance between us and the splendours of Egyptian worship which are seen by those who draw near their temples? And where is the resemblance to those irrational animals which are worshipped within, after you pass through the splendid gateways? Are our prophecies, and the God of all things, and the injunctions against images, objects of reverence in the view of Celsus also, and Jesus Christ crucified, the analogue to the worship of the irrational animal? But if he should assert this—and I do not think that he will maintain anything else—we shall reply that we have spoken in the preceding pages at greater length in defence of those charges affecting Jesus, showing that what appeared to have happened to Him in the capacity of His human nature, was fraught with benefit to all men, and with salvation to the whole world.

CHAPTER XVIII

In the next place, referring to the statements of the Egyptians, who talk loftily about irrational animals, and who assert that they are a sort of symbols of God, or anything else which their prophets, so termed, are accustomed to call them, Celsus says that "an impression is produced in the minds of those who have learned these things; that they have not been initiated in vain;" while with regard to the truths which are taught in our writings to those who have made progress in the study of Christianity (through that which is called by Paul the gift consisting in the "word of wisdom" through the Spirit, and in the "word of knowledge" according to the Spirit), Celsus does not seem even to have formed an idea, judging not only from what he has already said, but from what he subsequently adds in his attack upon the Christian system, when he asserts that Christians "repel every wise man from the doctrine of their faith, and invite only the ignorant and the vulgar;" on which assertions we shall remark in due time, when we come to the proper place.

CHAPTER XIX

He says, indeed, that "we ridicule the Egyptians, although they present many by no means contemptible mysteries for our consideration, when they teach us that such rites are acts of worship offered to eternal ideas, and not, as the multitude think, to ephemeral animals; and that we are silly, because we introduce nothing nobler than the goats and dogs of the Egyptian worship in our narratives about Jesus." Now to this we reply, "Good sir, (suppose that) you are right in eulogizing the fact that the Egyptians present to view many by no means contemptible mysteries, and obscure explanations about the animals (worshipped) among them, you nevertheless do not act consistently in accusing us as if you believed that *we* had nothing to state which was worthy of consideration, but that all *our* doctrines were contemptible and of no account, seeing we unfold the narratives concerning Jesus according to the 'wisdom of the word' to those who are 'perfect' in Christianity. Regarding whom, as being competent to understand the wisdom that is in Christianity, Paul says: 'We speak wisdom among them that are perfect; yet not the wisdom of this world, nor of the princes of this world, who come to nought, but we speak the wisdom of God in a mystery, even the hidden wisdom, which God ordained before the world unto our glory; which none of the princes of this world knew.'"

CHAPTER XX

And we say to those who hold similar opinions to those of Celsus: "Paul then, we are to suppose, had before his mind the idea of no pre-eminent wisdom when he professed to speak wisdom among them that are perfect?" Now, as he spoke with his customary boldness when in making such a profession he said that *he* was possessed of no wisdom, we shall say in reply: first of all examine the Epistles of him who utters these words, and look carefully at the meaning of each expression in them—say, in those to the Ephesians, and Colossians, and Thessalonians, and Philippians, and Romans,—and show two things, both that you understand Paul's words, and that you can demonstrate any of them to be silly or foolish. For if any one give himself to their attentive perusal, I am well assured either that he will be amazed at the understanding of the man who can clothe great ideas in common language; or if he be not amazed, he will only exhibit himself in a ridiculous light, whether he simply state the meaning of the writer as if he had comprehended it, or try to controvert and confute what he only imagined that he understood!

CHAPTER XXI

And I have not yet spoken of the observance of all that is written in the Gospels, each one of which contains much doctrine difficult to be understood, not merely by the multitude, but even by certain of the more intelligent, including a very profound explanation of the parables which Jesus delivered to "those without," while reserving the exhibition of their full meaning for those who had passed beyond the stage of exoteric teaching, and who came to Him privately in the house. And when he comes to understand it, he will admire the reason why some are said to be "without," and others "in the house." And again, who would not be filled with astonishment that is able to comprehend the movements of Jesus; ascending at one time a mountain for the purpose of delivering certain discourses, or of performing certain miracles, or for His own transfiguration, and descending again to heal the sick and those who were unable to follow Him whither His disciples went? But it is not the appropriate time to describe at present the truly venerable and divine contents of the Gospels, or the mind of Christ—that is, the wisdom and the word—contained in the writings of Paul. But what we have said is sufficient by way of answer to the unphilosophic sneers of Celsus, in comparing the inner mysteries of the Church of God to the cats, and apes, and crocodiles, and goats, and dogs of Egypt.

CHAPTER XXII

But this low jester Celsus, omitting no species of mockery and ridicule which can be employed against us, mentions in his treatise the Dioscuri, and Hercules, and Aesculapius, and Dionysus, who are believed by the Greeks to have become gods after being men, and says that "we cannot bear to call such beings gods, because they were at first men, and yet they manifested many noble qualifies, which were displayed for the benefit of mankind, while we assert that Jesus was seen after His death by His own followers;" and he brings against us an additional charge, as if we said that "He was seen indeed, but was only a shadow!" Now to this we reply, that it was very artful of Celsus not here clearly to indicate that he did not regard these beings as gods, for he was afraid of the opinion of those who might peruse his treatise, and who might suppose him to be an atheist; whereas, if he had paid respect to what appeared to him to be the truth, he would not have *feigned* to regard them as gods. Now to either of the allegations we are ready with an answer. Let us, accordingly, to those who do *not* regard them as gods reply as follows: These beings, then, are not gods at all; but agreeably to the view of those who think that the soul of man perishes immediately (after death), the souls of these men also perished; or according to the opinion of those who say that the soul continues to subsist or is immortal, these men continue to exist or are immortal, and they are not gods but heroes,—or not even heroes, but simply souls. If, then, on the one hand, you suppose them *not* to exist, we shall have to prove the doctrine of the soul's immortality, which is to us a doctrine of pre-eminent importance; if, on the other hand, they *do* exist, we have *still* to prove the doctrine of immortality, not only by what the Greeks have so well said regarding it, but also in a manner agreeable to the teaching of Holy Scripture. And we shall demonstrate that it is impossible for those who were polytheists during their lives to obtain a better country and position after their departure from this world, by quoting the histories that are related of them, in which is recorded the great dissoluteness of Hercules, and his effeminate bondage with Omphale, together with the statements regarding Aesculapius, that their Zeus struck him dead by a thunderbolt. And of the Dioscuri, it will be said that they die often—

"At one time live on alternate days, and at another
Die, and obtain honour equally with the gods."

How, then, can they reasonably imagine that one of these is to be regarded as a god or a hero?

CHAPTER XXIII

But we, in proving the facts related of our Jesus from the prophetic Scriptures, and comparing afterwards His history with them, demonstrate that no dissoluteness on His part is recorded. For even they who conspired against Him, and who sought false witnesses to aid them, did not find even any plausible grounds for advancing a false charge against Him, so as to accuse Him of licentiousness; but His death was indeed the result of a conspiracy, and bore no resemblance to the death of Aesculapius by lightning. And what is there that is venerable in the madman Dionysus, and his female garments, that *he* should be worshipped as a god? And if they who would defend such beings betake themselves to allegorical interpretations, we must examine each individual instance, and ascertain whether it is well founded, and also in each particular case, whether those beings can have a real existence, and are deserving of respect and worship who were torn by the Titans, and cast down from their heavenly throne. Whereas our Jesus, who appeared to the members of His own troop—

for I will take the word that Celsus employs—did *really* appear, and Celsus makes a false accusation against the Gospel in saying that what appeared was a shadow. And let the statements of their histories and that of Jesus be carefully compared together. Will Celsus have the former to be true, but the latter, although recorded by eye-witnesses who showed by their acts that they clearly understood the nature of what they had seen, and who manifested their state of mind by what they cheerfully underwent for the sake of His Gospel, to be inventions? Now, who is there that, desiring to act always in conformity with right reason, would yield his assent at random to what is related of the one, but would rush to the history of Jesus, and without examination refuse to believe what is recorded of Him?

CHAPTER XXIV

And again, when it is said of Aesculapius that a great multitude both of Greeks and Barbarians acknowledge that they have frequently seen, and still see, no mere phantom, but Aesculapius himself, healing and doing good, and foretelling the future; Celsus requires us to believe this, and finds no fault with the believers in Jesus, when we express our belief in such stories, but when we give our assent to the disciples, and eye-witnesses of the miracles of Jesus, who clearly manifest the honesty of their convictions (because we see their guilelessness, as far as it is possible to see the conscience revealed in writing), we are called by him a set of "silly" individuals, although he cannot demonstrate that an incalculable number, as he asserts, of Greeks and Barbarians acknowledge the existence of Aesculapius; while we, if we deem this a matter of importance, can clearly show a countless multitude of Greeks and Barbarians who acknowledge the existence of Jesus. And some give evidence of their having received through this faith a marvellous power by the cures which they perform, revoking no other name over those who need their help than that of the God of all things, and of Jesus, along with a mention of His history. For by these means we too have seen many persons freed from grievous calamities, and from distractions of mind, and madness, and countless other ills, which could be cured neither by men nor devils.

CHAPTER XXV

Now, in order to grant that there did exist a healing spirit named Aesculapius, who used to cure the bodies of men, I would say to those who are astonished at such an occurrence, or at the prophetic knowledge of Apollo, that since the cure of bodies is a thing indifferent, and a matter within the reach not merely of the good, but also of the bad; and as the foreknowledge of the future is also a thing indifferent—for the possessor of foreknowledge does not necessarily manifest the possession of virtue—you must show that they who practise healing or who forefell the future are in no respect wicked, but exhibit a perfect pattern of virtue, and are not far from being regarded as gods. But they will *not* be able to show that they are virtuous who practise the art of healing, or who are gifted with foreknowledge, seeing many who are not fit to live are related to have been healed; and these, too, persons whom, as leading improper lives, no wise physician would wish to heal. And in the responses of the Pythian oracle also you may find some injunctions which are not in accordance with reason, two of which we will adduce on the present occasion; viz., when it gave commandment that Cleomedes—the boxer, I suppose—should be honoured with divine honours, seeing some great importance or other attaching to his pugilistic skill, but did not confer either upon Pythagoras or upon Socrates the honours which it awarded to pugilism; and also when it called Archilochus "the servant of the Muses"—a man who employed his poetic powers upon topics of the most wicked and licentious nature, and whose public character was dissolute and impure—and entitled him "pious," in respect of his being the servant of the Muses, who are deemed to be goddesses! Now I am inclined to think that no one would assert that he was a "pious" man who was not adorned with all moderation and virtue, or that a decorous man would utter such expressions as are contained in the unseemly iambics of Archilochus. And if nothing that is divine in itself is shown to belong either to the healing skill of Aesculapius or the prophetic power of Apollo, how could any one, even were I to grant that the facts are as alleged, reasonably worship them as pure divinities?—and especially when the prophetic spirit of Apollo, pure from any body of earth, secretly enters through the private parts the person of her who is called the priestess, as she is seated at the mouth of the Pythian cave! Whereas regarding Jesus and His power we have no such notion; for the body which was born of the Virgin was composed of human material, and capable of receiving human wounds and death.

CHAPTER XXVI

Let us see what Celsus says next, when he adduces from history marvellous occurrences, which in themselves seem to be incredible, but which are not discredited by him, so far at least as appears from his words. And, in the first place, regarding Aristeas of Proconnesus, of whom he speaks as follows: "Then, with respect to Aristeas of Proconnesus, who disappeared from among men in a manner so indicative of divine intervention, and who showed himself again in so unmistakeable a fashion, and on many subsequent occasions visited many parts of the world, and announced marvellous events, and whom Apollo enjoined the inhabitants of Metapontium to regard as a god, no one considers him to be a god." This account he appears to have taken from Pindar and Herodotus. It will be sufficient, however, at present to quote the statement of the latter writer from the fourth book of his histories, which is to the following effect: "Of what country Aristeas, who made these verses, was, has already been mentioned, and I shall now relate the account I heard of him in Proconnesus and Cyzicus. They say that Aristeas, who was inferior to none of the citizens by birth, entering into a fuller's shop in Proconnesus, died suddenly, and that the fuller, having closed his workshop, went to acquaint the relatives of the deceased. When the report had spread through the city that Aristeas was dead, a certain Cyzicenian, arriving from Artace, fell into a dispute with those who made the report, affirming that he had met and conversed with him on his way to Cyzicus, and he vehemently disputed the truth of the report; but the relations of the deceased went to the fuller's shop, taking with them what was necessary for the purpose of carrying the body away; but when the house was opened, Aristeas was not to be seen, either dead or alive. They say that afterwards, in the seventh year, he appeared in Proconnesus, composed those verses which by the Greeks are now called Arimaspian, and having composed them, disappeared a second time. Such is the story current in these cities. But these things I know happened to the Metapontines in Italy 340 years after the second disappearance of Aristeas, as I discovered by computation in Proconnesus and Metapontium. The Metapontines say that Aristeas himself, having appeared in their country, exhorted them to erect an altar to Apollo, and to place near it a statue bearing the name of Aristeas the Proconnesian; for he said that Apollo had visited their country only of all the Italians, and that he himself, who was now Aristeas, accompanied him; and that when he accompanied the god he was a crow; and after saying this he vanished. And the Metapontines say they sent to Delphi to inquire of the god what the apparition of the man meant; but the Pythian bade them obey the apparition, and if they obeyed it would conduce to their benefit. They accordingly, having received this answer, fulfilled the injunctions. And now, a statue bearing the name of Aristeas is placed near the image of Apollo, and around it laurels are planted: the image is placed in the public square.

Thus much concerning Aristeas."

CHAPTER XXVII

Now, in answer to this account of Aristeas, we have to say, that if Celsus had adduced it as history, without signifying his own assent to its truth, it is in a different way that we should have met his argument. But since he asserts that he "disappeared through the intervention of the divinity," and "showed himself again in an unmistakeable manner," and "visited many parts of the world," and "made marvellous announcements;" and, moreover, that there was "an oracle of Apollo, enjoining the Metapontines to treat Aristeas as a god," he gives the accounts relating to him as upon his own authority, and with his full assent. And (this being the case), we ask, How is it possible that, while supposing the marvels related by the disciples of Jesus regarding their Master to be wholly fictitious, and finding fault with those who believe them, you, O Celsus, do not regard these stories of yours to be either products of jugglery or inventions? And how, while charging others with an irrational belief in the marvels recorded of Jesus, can you show yourself justified in giving credence to such statement as the above, without producing some proof or evidence of the alleged occurrences having taken place? Or do Herodotus and Pindar appear to you to speak the truth, while they who have made it their concern to *die* for the doctrine of Jesus, and who have left to their successors writings so remarkable on the truths which they believed, entered for the sake of "fictions" (as you consider them), and "myths," and "juggleries," upon a struggle which entails a life of danger and a death of violence? Place yourself, then, as a neutral party, between what is related of Aristeas and what is recorded of Jesus, and see whether, from the result, and from the benefits which have accrued from the reformation of morals, and to the worship of the God who is over all things, it is not allowable to conclude that we must believe the events recorded of Jesus not to have happened without the divine intervention, but that this was not the case with the story of Aristeas the Proconnesian.

CHAPTER XXVIII

For with what purpose in view did Providence accomplish the marvels related of Aristeas? And to confer what benefit upon the human race did such remarkable events, as you regard them, take place? You cannot answer. But we, when we relate the events of the history of Jesus, have no ordinary defence to offer for their occurrence;—this, viz., that God desired to commend the doctrine of Jesus as a doctrine which was to save mankind, and which was based, indeed, upon the apostles as foundations of the rising edifice of Christianity, but which increased in magnitude also in the succeeding ages, in which not a few cures are wrought in the name of Jesus, and certain other manifestations of no small moment have taken place. Now what sort of person is Apollo, who enjoined the Metapontines to treat Aristeas as a god? And with what object does he do this? And what advantage was he procuring to the Metapontines from this divine worship, if they were to regard him as a god, who a little ago was a mortal? And yet the recommendations of Apollo (viewed by us as a demon who has obtained the honour of libation and sacrificial odours) regarding this Aristeas appear to you to be worthy of consideration; while those of the God of all things, and of His holy angels, made known beforehand through the prophets—not *after* the birth of Jesus, but *before* He appeared among men—do not stir you up to admiration, not merely of the prophets who received the Divine Spirit, but of Him also who was the object of their predictions, whose entrance into life was so clearly predicted many years beforehand by numerous prophets, that the whole Jewish people who were hanging in expectation of the coming of Him who was looked for, did, after the advent of Jesus, fall into a keen dispute with each other; and that a great multitude of them acknowledged Christ, and believed Him to be the object of prophecy, while others did not believe in Him, but, despising the meekness of those who, on account of the teaching of Jesus, were unwilling to cause even the most trifling sedition, dared to inflict on Jesus those cruelties which His disciples have so truthfully and candidly recorded, without secretly omitting from their marvellous history of Him what seems to the multitude to bring disgrace upon the doctrine of Christianity. But both Jesus Himself and His disciples desired that His followers should believe not merely in His Godhead and miracles, as if He had not also been a partaker of human nature, and had assumed the human flesh which "lusteth against the Spirit;" but they saw also that the power which had descended into human nature, and into the midst of human miseries, and which had assumed a human soul and body, contributed through faith, along with its divine elements, to the salvation of believers, when they see that from Him there began the union of the divine with the human nature, in order that the human, by communion with the divine, might rise to be divine, not in Jesus alone, but in all those who not only believe, but enter upon the life which Jesus taught, and which elevates to friendship with God and communion with Him every one who lives according to the precepts of Jesus.

CHAPTER XXIX

According to Celsus, then, Apollo wished the Metapontines to treat Aristeas as a god. But as the Metapontines considered the evidence in favour of Aristeas being a man—and probably not a virtuous one—to be stronger than the declaration of the oracle to the effect that he was a god or worthy of divine honours, they for that reason would not obey Apollo, and consequently no one regarded Aristeas as a god. But with respect to Jesus we would say that, as it was of advantage to the human race to accept him as the Son of God—God come in a human soul and body—and as this did not seem to be advantageous to the gluttonous appetites of the demons which love bodies, and to those who deem them to be gods on that account, the demons that are on earth (which are supposed to be gods by those who are not instructed in the nature of demons), and also their worshippers, were desirous to prevent the spread of the doctrine of Jesus; for they saw that the libations and odours in which they greedily delighted were being swept away by the prevalence of the instructions of Jesus. But the God who sent Jesus dissipated all the conspiracies of the demons, and made the Gospel of Jesus to prevail throughout the whole world for the conversion and reformation of men, and caused Churches to be everywhere established in opposition to those of superstitious and licentious and wicked men; for such is the character of the multitudes who constitute the citizens in the assemblies of the various cities. Whereas the Churches of God which are instructed by Christ, when carefully contrasted with the assemblies of the districts in which they are situated, are as beacons in the world; for who would not admit that even the inferior members of the Church, and those who in comparison with the better are less worthy, are nevertheless more excellent than many of those who belong to the assemblies in the different districts?

CHAPTER XXX

For the Church of God, e.g., which is at Athens, is a meek and stable body, as being one which desires to please God, who is over all things; whereas the assembly of the Athenians is given to sedition, and is not at all to be compared to the Church of God in that city. And you may say the same thing of the Church of God at Corinth, and of the assembly of the Corinthian people; and also of the Church of God at Alexandria, and of the assembly of the people of Alexandria. And if he who hears this be a candid man, and one who investigates things with a desire to ascertain the truth, he will be filled with admiration of Him who not only conceived the design, but also was able to secure in all places the establishment of Churches of God alongside of the assemblies of the people in each city. In like manner, also, in comparing the council of the Church of God with the council in any city, you would find that certain councillors of the Church are worthy to rule in the city of God, if there be any such city in the whole world; whereas the councillors in all other places exhibit in their characters no quality worthy of the conventional superiority which they appear to enjoy over their fellow-citizens. And so, too, you must compare *the ruler* of the *Church* in each city with the ruler of the *people* of the city, in order to observe that even amongst those councillors and rulers of the Church of God who come very far short of their duty, and who lead more indolent lives than others who are more energetic, it is nevertheless possible to discover a general superiority in what relates to the progress of virtue over the characters of the councillors and rulers in the various cities.

CHAPTER XXXI

Now if these things be so, why should it not be consistent with reason to hold with regard to Jesus, who was able to effect results so great, that there dwelt in *Him* no ordinary divinity? while this was not the case either with the Proconnesian Aristeas (although Apollo would have him regarded as a god), or with the other individuals enumerated by Celsus when he says, "No one regards Abaris the Hyperborean as a god, who was possessed of such power as to be borne along like an arrow from a bow." For with what object did the deity who bestowed upon this Hyperborean Abaris the power of being carried along like an arrow, confer upon him such a gift? Was it that the human race might be benefited thereby, or did he himself obtain any advantage from the possession of such a power?—always supposing it to be conceded that these statements are not wholly inventions, but that the thing actually happened through the co-operation of some demon. But if it be recorded that my Jesus was received up into glory, I perceive the divine arrangement in such an act, viz., because God, who brought this to pass, commends in this way the Teacher to those who witnessed it, in order that as men who are contending not for human doctrine, but for divine teaching, they may devote themselves as far as possible to the God who is over all, and may do all things in order to please Him, as those who are to receive in the divine judgment the reward of the good or evil which they have wrought in this life.

CHAPTER XXXII

But as Celsus next mentions the case of the Clazomenian, subjoining to the story about him this remark, "Do they not report that his soul frequently quitted his body, and flitted about in an incorporeal form? and yet men did not regard him as a god," we have to answer that probably certain wicked demons contrived that such statements should be committed to writing (for I do not believe that they contrived that such a thing should actually *take place*), in order that the predictions regarding Jesus, and the discourses uttered by Him, might either be evil spoken of, as inventions like these, or might excite no surprise, as not being more remarkable than other occurrences. But my Jesus said regarding His own soul (which was separated from the body, not by virtue of any human necessity, but by the miraculous power which was given Him also for this purpose): "No one taketh my life from Me, but I lay it down of Myself. I have power to lay it down, and I have power to take it again." For as He had power to lay it down, He laid it down when He said, "Father, why hast Thou forsaken Me? And when He had cried with a loud voice, He gave up the ghost," anticipating the public executioners of the crucified, who break the legs of the victims, and who do so in order that their punishment may not be further prolonged. And He "took His life," when He manifested Himself to His disciples, having in their presence foretold to the unbelieving Jews, "Destroy this temple, and in three days I will raise it up again," and "He spake this of the temple of His body;" the prophets, moreover, having predicted such a result in many other passages of their writings, and in this, "My flesh also shall rest in hope: for Thou wilt not leave my soul in hell, neither wilt Thou suffer Thine Holy One to see corruption."

CHAPTER XXXIII

Celsus, however, shows that he has read a good many Grecian histories, when he quotes further what is told of Cleomedes of Astypalaea, "who," he relates, "entered into an ark, and although shut up within it, was not found therein, but through some arrangement of the divinity, flew out, when certain persons had cut open the ark in order to apprehend him." Now this story, if an invention, as it appears to be, cannot be compared with what is related of Jesus, since in the lives of such men there is found no indication of their possessing the divinity which is ascribed to them; whereas the divinity of Jesus is established both by the existence of the Churches of the saved, and by the prophecies uttered concerning Him, and by the cures wrought in His name, and by the wisdom and knowledge which are in Him, and the deeper truths which are discovered by those who know how to ascend from a simple faith, and to investigate the meaning which lies in the divine Scriptures, agreeably to the injunctions of Jesus, who said, "Search the Scriptures," and to the wish of Paul, who taught that "we ought to know how to answer every man;" nay, also of him who said, "Be ready always to give an answer to every man that asketh of you a reason of the faith that is in you." If he wishes to have it conceded, however, that it is not a fiction, let him show with what object this supernatural power made him, through some arrangement of the divinity, flee from the ark. For if he will adduce any reason worthy of consideration, and point out any purpose worthy of God in conferring such a power on Cleomedes, we will decide on the answer which we ought to give; but if he fail to say anything convincing on the point, clearly because no reason *can* be discovered, then we shall either speak slightingly of the story to those who have not accepted it, and charge it with being false, or we shall say that some demoniac power, casting a glamour over the eyes, produced, in the case of the Astypalaean, a result like that which is produced by the performers of juggling tricks, while Celsus thinks that with respect to him he has spoken like an oracle, when he said that "by some divine arrangement he flew away from the ark."

CHAPTER XXXIV

I am, however, of opinion that these individuals are the only instances with which Celsus was acquainted. And yet, that he might appear voluntarily to pass by other similar cases, he says, "And one might name many others of the same kind." Let it be granted, then, that many such persons have existed who conferred no benefit upon the human race: what would each one of their acts be found to amount to in comparison with the work of Jesus, and the miracles related of Him, of which we have already spoken at considerable length? He next imagines that, "in worshipping him who," as *he* says, "was taken prisoner and put to death, we are acting like the Getae who worship Zamolxis, and the Cilicians who worship Mopsus, and the Acarnanians who pay divine honours to Amphilochus, and like the Thebans who do the same to Amphiaraus, and the Lebadians to Trophonius." Now in these instances we shall prove that he has compared us to the foregoing without good grounds. For these different tribes erected temples and statues to those individuals above enumerated, whereas we have refrained from offering to the Divinity honour by any such means (seeing they are adapted rather to demons, which are somehow fixed in a certain place which they prefer to any other, or which take up their dwelling, as it were, after being removed (from one place to another) by certain rites and incantations), and are lost in reverential wonder at Jesus, who has recalled our minds from all sensible things, as being not only corruptible, but destined to corruption, and elevated them to honour the God who is over all with prayers and a righteous life, which we offer to Him as being intermediate between the nature of the uncreated and that of all created things, and who bestows upon us the benefits which come from the Father, and who as High Priest conveys our prayers to the supreme God.

CHAPTER XXXV

But I should like, in answer to him who for some unknown reason advances such statements as the above, to make in a conversational way some such remarks as the following, which seem not inappropriate to him. Are then those persons whom you have mentioned nonentities, and is there no power in Lebadea connected with Trophonius, nor in Thebes with the temple of Amphiaraus, nor in Acarnania with Amphilochus, nor in Cilicia with Mopsus? Or is there in such persons some being, either a demon, or a hero, or even a god, working works which are beyond the reach of man? For if he answer that there is nothing either demoniacal or divine about these individuals more than others, then let him at once make known his own opinion, as being that of an Epicurean, and of one who does not hold the same views with the Greeks, and who neither recognises demons nor worships gods as do the Greeks; and let it be shown that it was to no purpose that he adduced the instances previously enumerated (as if he believed them to be true), together with those which he adds in the following pages. But if he will assert that the persons spoken of are either demons, or heroes, or even gods, let him notice that he will establish by what he has admitted a result which he does not desire, viz., that Jesus also was some such being; for which reason, too, he was able to demonstrate to not a few that He had come down from God to visit the human race. And if he once admit this, see whether he will not be forced to confess that He is mightier than those individuals with whom he classed Him, seeing none of the latter forbids the offering of honour to the others; while He, having confidence in Himself, because He is more powerful than all those others, forbids them to be received as divine because they are wicked demons, who have taken possession of places on earth,

432

through inability to rise to the purer and diviner region, whither the grossnesses of earth and its countless evils cannot reach.

CHAPTER XXXVI

But as he next introduces the case of the favourite of Adrian (I refer to the accounts regarding the youth Antinous, and the honours paid him by the inhabitants of the city of Antinous in Egypt), and imagines that the honour paid to him falls little short of that which we render to Jesus, let us show in what a spirit of hostility this statement is made. For what is there in common between a life lived among the favourites of Adrian, by one who did not abstain even from unnatural lusts, and that of the venerable Jesus, against whom even they who brought countless other charges, and who told so many falsehoods, were not able to allege that He manifested, even in the slightest degree, any tendency to what was licentious? Nay, further, if one were to investigate, in a spirit of truth and impartiality, the stories relating to Antinous, he would find that it was due to the magical arts and rites of the Egyptians that there was even the *appearance* of his performing anything (marvellous) in the city which bears his name, and that too only after his decease,—an effect which is said to have been produced in other temples by the Egyptians, and those who are skilled in the arts which they practise. For they set up in certain places demons claiming prophetic or healing power, and which frequently torture those who seem to have committed any mistake about ordinary kinds of food, or about touching the dead body of a man, that they may have the appearance of alarming the uneducated multitude. Of this nature is the being that is considered to be a god in Antinoopolis in Egypt, whose (reputed) virtues are the lying inventions of some who live by the gain derived therefrom; while others, deceived by the demon placed there, and others again convicted by a weak conscience, actually think that they are paying a divine penalty inflicted by Antinous. Of such a nature also are the mysteries which they perform, and the seeming predictions which they utter. Far different from such are those of Jesus. For it was no company of sorcerers, paying court to a king or ruler at his bidding, who seemed to have made him a god; but the Architect of the universe Himself, in keeping with the marvellously persuasive power of His words, commended Him as worthy of honour, not only to those men who were well disposed, but to demons also, and other unseen powers, which even at the present time show that they either fear the name of Jesus as that of a being of superior power, or reverentially accept Him as their legal ruler. For if the commendation had not been given Him by God, the demons would not have withdrawn from those whom they had assailed, in obedience to the mere mention of His name.

CHAPTER XXXVII

The Egyptians, then, having been taught to worship Antinous, will, if you compare him with Apollo or Zeus, endure such a comparison, Antinous being magnified in their estimation through being classed with these deities; for Celsus is clearly convicted of falsehood when he says, "that they will not endure his being compared with Apollo or Zeus." Whereas Christians (who have learned that their eternal life consists in knowing the only true God, who is over all, and Jesus Christ, whom He has sent; and who have learned also that all the gods of the heathen are greedy demons, which flit around sacrifices and blood, and other sacrificial accompaniments, in order to deceive those who have not taken refuge with the God who is over all, but that the divine and holy angels of God are of a different nature and will from all the demons on earth, and that they are known to those exceedingly few persons who have carefully and intelligently investigated these matters) will not endure a comparison to be made between them and Apollo or Zeus, or any being worshipped with odour and blood and sacrifices; some of them, so acting from their extreme simplicity, not being able to give a reason for their conduct, but sincerely observing the precepts which they have received; others, again, for reasons not to be lightly regarded, nay, even of a profound description, and (as a Greek would say) drawn from the inner nature of things; and amongst the latter of these God is a frequent subject of conversation, and those who are honoured by God, through His only-begotten Word, with participation in His divinity, and therefore also in His name. They speak much, too, both regarding the angels of God and those who are opposed to the truth, but have been deceived; and who, in consequence of being deceived, call them gods or angels of God, or good demons, or heroes who have become such by the transference into them of a good human soul. And such Christians will also show, that as in philosophy there are many who appear to be in possession of the truth, who have yet either deceived themselves by plausible arguments, or by rashly assenting to what was brought forward and discovered by others; so also, among those souls which exist apart from bodies, both angels and demons, there are some which have been induced by plausible reasons to declare themselves gods. And because it was impossible that the reasons of such things could be discovered by men with perfect exactness, it was deemed safe that no mortal should entrust himself to any being as to God, with the exception of Jesus Christ, who is, as it were, the Ruler over all things, and who both beheld these weighty secrets, and made them known to a few.

CHAPTER XXXVIII

The belief, then, in Antinous, or any other such person, whether among the Egyptians or the Greeks, is, so to speak, unfortunate; while the belief in Jesus would seem to be either a fortunate one, or the result of thorough investigation, having the appearance of the former to the multitude, and of the latter to exceedingly few. And when I speak of a certain belief being, as the multitude would call it, unfortunate, I in such a case refer the cause to God, who knows the reasons of the various fates allotted to each one who enters human life. The Greeks, moreover, will admit that even amongst those who are considered to be most largely endowed with wisdom, good fortune has had much to do, as in the choice of teachers of one kind rather than another, and in meeting with a better class of instructors (there being teachers who taught the most opposite doctrines), and in being brought up in better circumstances; for the bringing up of many has been amid surroundings of such a kind, that they were prevented from ever receiving any idea of better things, but constantly passed their life, from their earliest youth, either as the favourites of licentious men or of tyrants, or in some other wretched condition which forbade the soul to look upwards. And the causes of these varied fortunes, according to all probability, are to be found in the reasons of providence, though it is not easy for men to ascertain these; but I have said what I have done by way of digression from the main body of my subject, on account of the proverb, that "such is the power of faith, because it seizes that which first presents itself." For it was necessary, owing to the different methods of education, to speak of the differences of belief among men, some of whom are more, others less fortunate in their belief; and from this to proceed to show that what is termed good or bad fortune would appear to contribute even in the case of the most talented, to their appearing to be more fully endowed with reason and to give their assent on grounds of reason to the majority of human opinions. But enough on these points.

CHAPTER XXXIX

We must notice the remarks which Celsus next makes, when he says to us, that "faith, having taken possession of our minds, makes us yield the assent which we give to the doctrine of Jesus;" for of a truth it is faith which does produce such an assent. Observe, however, whether that faith does not of itself exhibit what is worthy of praise, seeing we entrust ourselves to the God who is over all, acknowledging our gratitude to Him who has led us to such a faith, and declaring that He could not have attempted or accomplished such a result without the divine assistance. And we have confidence also in the intentions of the writers of the Gospels, observing their piety and conscientiousness, manifested in their writings, which contain nothing that is spurious, or deceptive, or false, or cunning; for it is evident to us that souls unacquainted with those artifices which are taught by the cunning sophistry of the Greeks (which is characterized by great plausibility and acuteness), and by the kind of rhetoric in vogue in the courts of justice, would not have been able thus to invent occurrences which are fitted of themselves to conduct to faith, and to a life in keeping with faith. And I am of opinion that it was on this account that Jesus wished to employ such persons as teachers of His doctrines, viz., that there might be no ground for any suspicion of plausible sophistry, but that it might clearly appear to all who were capable of understanding, that the guileless purpose of the writers being, so to speak, marked with great simplicity, was deemed worthy of being accompanied by a diviner power, which accomplished far more than it seemed possible could be accomplished by a periphrasis of words, and a weaving of sentences, accompanied by all the distinctions of Grecian art.

CHAPTER XL

But observe whether the principles of our faith, harmonizing with the general ideas implanted in our minds at birth, do not produce a change upon those who listen candidly to its statements; for although a perverted view of things, with the aid of much instruction to the same effect, has been able to implant in the minds of the multitude the belief that images are gods, and that things made of gold, and silver, and ivory, and stone are deserving of worship, yet common sense forbids the supposition that God is at all a piece of corruptible matter, or is honoured when made to assume by men a form embodied in dead matter, fashioned according to some image or symbol of His appearance. And therefore we say at once of images that they are not gods, and of such creations (of art) that they are not to be compared with the Creator, but are small in contrast with the God who is over all, and who created, and upholds, and governs the universe. And the rational soul recognising, as it were, its relationship (to the divine), at once rejects what it for a time supposed to be gods, and resumes its natural love for its Creator; and because of its affection towards Him, receives Him also who first presented these truths to all nations through the disciples whom He had appointed, and whom He sent forth, furnished with divine power and authority, to proclaim the doctrine regarding God and His kingdom.

CHAPTER XLI

But since he has charged us, I know not how often already, "with regarding this Jesus, who was but a mortal body, as a God, and with supposing that we act piously in so doing," it is superfluous to say any more in answer to this, as a great deal has been said in the preceding pages. And yet let those who make this charge understand that He whom we regard and believe to have been from the beginning God, and the Son of God, is the very Logos, and the very Wisdom, and the very Truth; and with respect to His mortal body, and the human soul which it contained, we assert that not by their communion merely with Him, but by their unity and intermixture, they received the highest powers, and after participating in His divinity, were changed into God. And if any one should feel a difficulty at our saying this regarding His body, let him attend to what is said by the Greeks regarding matter, which, properly speaking, being without qualities, receives such as the Creator desires to invest it with, and which frequently divests itself of those which it formerly possessed, and assumes others of a different and higher kind. And if these opinions be correct, what is there wonderful in this, that the mortal quality of the body of Jesus, if the providence of God has so willed it, should have been changed into one that was ethereal and divine?

CHAPTER XLII

Celsus, then, does not speak as a good reasoner, when he compares the mortal flesh of Jesus to gold, and silver, and stone, asserting that the former is more liable to corruption than the latter. For, to speak correctly, that which is incorruptible is not more free from corruption than another thing which is incorruptible, nor that which is corruptible more liable to corruption than another corruptible thing. But, admitting that there are degrees of corruptibility, we can say in answer, that if it is possible for the matter which underlies all qualities to exchange some of them, how should it be impossible for the flesh of Jesus also to exchange qualities, and to become such as it was proper for a body to be which had its abode in the ether and the regions above it, and possessing no longer the infirmities belonging to the flesh, and those properties which Celsus terms "impurities," and in so terming them, speaks unlike a philosopher? For that which is properly impure, is so because of its wickedness. Now the nature of body is not impure; for in so far as it is bodily nature, it does not possess vice, which is the generative principle of impurity. But, as he had a suspicion of the answer which we would return, he says with respect to the change of the body of Jesus, "Well, after he has laid aside these qualities, he will be a God:" (and if so), why not rather Aesculapius, and Dionysus, and Hercules? To which we reply, "What great deed has Aesculapius, or Dionysus, or Hercules wrought?" And what individuals will they be able to point out as having been improved in character, and made better by their words and lives, so that they may make good their claim to be gods? For let us peruse the many narratives regarding them, and see whether they were free from licentiousness or injustice, or folly, or cowardice. And if nothing of that kind be found in them, the argument of Celsus might have force, which places the forenamed individuals upon an equality with Jesus. But if it is certain that, although some things are reported of them as reputable, they are recorded, nevertheless, to have done innumerable things which are contrary to right reason, how could you any longer say, with any show of reason, that these men, on putting aside their mortal body, became gods rather than Jesus?

CHAPTER XLIII

He next says of us, that "we ridicule those who worship Jupiter, because his tomb is pointed out in the island of Crete; and yet we worship him who rose from the tomb, although ignorant of the grounds on which the Cretans observe such a custom." Observe now that he thus undertakes the defence of the Cretans, and of Jupiter, and of his tomb, alluding obscurely to the allegorical notions, in conformity with which the myth regarding Jupiter is said to have been invented; while he assails us who acknowledge that our Jesus has been buried, indeed, but who maintain that He has also been *raised* from the tomb,— a statement which the Cretans have not yet made regarding Jupiter. But since he appears to admit that the tomb of Jupiter is in Crete, when he says that "we are ignorant of the grounds on which the Cretans observe such a custom," we reply that Callimachus the Cyrenian, who had read innumerable poetic compositions, and nearly the whole of Greek history, was not acquainted with any allegorical meaning which was contained in the stories about Jupiter and his tomb; and accordingly he accuses the Cretans in his hymn addressed to Jupiter, in the words:—

"The Cretans are always liars: for thy tomb, O king,
The Cretans have reared; and yet thou didst not die,
For thou ever livest."

Now he who said, "Thou didst not die, for thou ever livest," in denying that Jupiter's tomb was in Crete, records nevertheless that in Jupiter there was the beginning of death. But birth upon earth is the beginning of death. And his words run:—

"And Rhea bore thee among the Parrhasians;"—

whereas he ought to have seen, after denying that the birth of Jupiter took place in Crete because of his tomb, that it was quite congruous with his birth in Arcadia that he who was born should also die. And the following is the manner in which Callimachus speaks of these things: "O Jupiter, some say that thou wert born on the mountains of Ida, others in Arcadia. Which of them, O father, have lied? The Cretans are always liars," etc. Now it is Celsus who made us discuss these topics, by the unfair manner in which he deals with Jesus, in giving his assent to what is related about His death and burial, but regarding as an invention His resurrection from the dead, although this was not only foretold by innumerable prophets, but many proofs also were given of His having appeared after death.

CHAPTER XLIV

After these points Celsus quotes some objections against the doctrine of Jesus, made by a very few individuals who are considered Christians, not of the more intelligent, as he supposes, but of the more ignorant class, and asserts that "the following are the rules laid down by them. Let no one come to us who has been instructed, or who is wise or prudent (for such qualifications are deemed evil by us); but if there be any ignorant, or unintelligent, or uninstructed, or foolish persons, let them come with confidence. By which words, acknowledging that such individuals are worthy of their God, they manifestly show that they desire and are able to gain over only the silly, and the mean, and the stupid, with women and children." In reply to which, we say that, as if, while Jesus teaches continence, and says, "Whosoever looketh upon a woman to lust after her, hath already committed adultery with her in his heart," one were to behold a few of those who are deemed to be Christians living licentiously, he would most justly blame them for living contrary to the teaching of Jesus, but would act most unreasonably if he were to charge the Gospel with their censurable conduct; so, if he found nevertheless that the doctrine of the Christians invites men to wisdom, the blame then must remain with those who rest in their own ignorance, and who utter, not what Celsus relates (for although some of them are simple and ignorant, they do not speak so shamelessly as he alleges), but other things of much less serious import, which, however, serve to turn aside men from the practice of wisdom.

CHAPTER XLV

But that the object of Christianity is that we should become wise, can be proved not only from the ancient Jewish writings, which *we* also use, but especially from those which were composed after the time of Jesus, and which are believed among the Churches to be divine. Now, in the fiftieth Psalm, David is described as saying in his prayer to God these words: "The unseen and secret things of Thy wisdom Thou hast manifested to me." Solomon, too, because he asked for wisdom, received it; and if any one were to peruse the Psalms, he would find the book filled with many maxims of wisdom: and the evidences of his wisdom may be seen in his treatises, which contain a great amount of wisdom expressed in few words, and in which you will find many laudations of wisdom, and encouragements towards obtaining it. So wise, moreover, was Solomon, that "the queen of Sheba, having heard his name, and the name of the LORD, came to try him with difficult questions, and spake to him all things, whatsoever were in her heart; and Solomon answered her all her questions. There was no question omitted by the king which he did not answer her. And the queen of Sheba saw all the wisdom of Solomon, and the possessions which he had and there was no more spirit in her. And she said to the king, The report is true which I heard in mine own land regarding thee and thy wisdom; and I believed not them who told me, until I had come, and mine eyes have seen it. And, lo, they did not tell me the half. Thou hast added wisdom and possessions above all the report which I heard." It is recorded also of him, that "God gave Solomon wisdom and understanding exceeding much, and largeness of heart, even as the sand that is on the seashore. And the wisdom that was in Solomon greatly excelled the wisdom of all the ancients, and of all the wise men of Egypt; and he was wiser than all men, even than Gethan the Ezrahite, and Emad, and Chalcadi, and Aradab, the sons of Madi. And he was famous among all the nations round about. And Solomon spake three thousand proverbs, and his songs were five thousand. And he spake of trees, from the cedar that is in Lebanon even to the hyssop which springeth out of the wall; and also of fishes and of beasts. And all nations came to hear the wisdom of Solomon, and from all the kings of the earth who had heard of the fame of his wisdom."

And to such a degree does the Gospel desire that there should be wise men among believers, that for the sake of exercising the understanding of its hearers, it has spoken certain truths in enigmas, others in what are called "dark" sayings, others in parables, and others in problems. And one of the prophets—Hosea—says at the end of his prophecies: "Who is wise, and he will understand these things? or prudent, and he shall know them?" Daniel, moreover, and his fellow-captives, made such progress in the learning which the wise men around the king in Babylon cultivated, that they were shown to excel all of them in a tenfold degree. And in the book of Ezekiel it is said to the ruler of Tyre, who greatly prided himself on his wisdom, "Art thou wiser than Daniel? Every secret was not revealed to thee."

CHAPTER XLVI

And if you come to the books written after the time of Jesus, you will find that those multitudes of believers who hear the parables are, as it were, "without," and worthy only of exoteric doctrines, while the disciples learn in private the explanation of the parables. For, privately, to His own disciples did Jesus open up all things, esteeming above the multitudes those who desired to know His wisdom. And He promises to those who believe upon Him to send them wise men and scribes, saying, "Behold, I will send unto you wise men and scribes, and some of them they shall kill and crucify." And Paul also, in the catalogue of "charismata" bestowed by God, placed first "the word of wisdom," and second, as being inferior to it, "the word of knowledge," but third, and lower down, "faith." And because he regarded "the word" as higher than miraculous powers, he for that reason places "workings of miracles" and "gifts of healings" in a lower place than the gifts of the word. And in the Acts of the Apostles Stephen bears witness to the great learning of Moses, which he had obtained wholly from ancient writings not accessible to the multitude. For he says: "And Moses was learned in all the wisdom of the Egyptians." And therefore, with respect to his miracles, it was suspected that he wrought them perhaps, not in virtue of his professing to come from God, but by means of his Egyptian knowledge, in which he was well versed. For the king, entertaining such a suspicion, summoned the Egyptian magicians, and wise men, and enchanters, who were found to be of no avail as against the wisdom of Moses, which proved superior to all the wisdom of the Egyptians.

CHAPTER XLVII

But it is probable that what is written by Paul in the first Epistle to the Corinthians, as being addressed to Greeks who prided themselves greatly on their Grecian wisdom, has moved some to believe that it was not the object of the Gospel to win wise men. Now, let him who is of this opinion understand that the Gospel, as censuring wicked men, says of them that they are wise not in things which relate to the understanding, and which are unseen and eternal; but that in busying themselves about things of sense alone, and regarding these as all-important, they are wise men of the world: for as there are in existence a multitude of opinions, some of them espousing the cause of matter and bodies, and asserting that everything is corporeal which has a substantial existence, and that besides these nothing else exists, whether it be called invisible or incorporeal, it says also that these constitute the wisdom of the world, which perishes and fades away, and belongs only to this age, while those opinions which raise the soul from things here to the blessedness which is with God, and to His kingdom, and which teach men to despise all sensible and visible things as existing only for a season, and to hasten on to things invisible, and to have regard to those things which are not seen,—these, it says, constitute the wisdom of God. But Paul, as a lover of truth, says of certain wise men among the Greeks, when their statements are true, that "although they knew God, they glorified Him not as God, neither were thankful." And he bears witness that they knew God, and says, too, that this did not happen to them without divine permission, in these words: "For God showed it unto them;" dimly alluding, I think, to those who ascend from things of sense to those of the understanding, when he adds, "For the invisible things of God from the creation of the world are clearly seen, being understood by the things that are made, even His eternal power and Godhead; so that they are without excuse: because that, when they knew God, they glorified Him not as God, neither were thankful."

CHAPTER XLVIII

And perhaps also from the words, "For ye see your calling, brethren, how that not many wise men after the flesh, not many mighty, not many noble, are called: but God hath chosen the foolish things of the world to confound the wise; and the base things, and the things which are despised, hath God chosen, and things which are not, to bring to nought things that are, that no flesh may glory in His presence;" some have been led to suppose that no one who is instructed, or wise, or prudent, embraces the Gospel. Now, in answer to such an one, we would say that it has not been stated that "*no* wise man according to the flesh," but that "not *many* wise men according to the flesh," are called. It is manifest, further, that amongst the characteristic qualifications of those who are termed "bishops," Paul, in describing what kind of man the bishop ought to be, lays down as a qualification that he should also be a teacher, saying that he ought to be able to convince the gainsayers, that by the wisdom which is in him he may stop the mouths of foolish talkers and deceivers. And as he selects for the episcopate a man who has been once married rather than he who has twice entered the married state, and a man of blameless life rather than one who is liable to censure, and a sober man rather than one who is not such, and a prudent man rather than one who is not prudent, and a man whose behaviour is decorous rather than he who is open to the charge even of the slightest indecorum, so he desires that he who is to be chosen by preference for the office of a bishop should be apt to teach, and able to convince the gainsayers. How then can Celsus justly charge us with saying, "Let no one come to us who is 'instructed,' or 'wise,' or 'prudent?'" Nay, let him who wills come to us "instructed," and "wise," and "prudent;" and none the less, if any one be ignorant and unintelligent, and uninstructed and foolish, let him also come: for it is these whom the Gospel promises to cure, when they come, by rendering them all worthy of God.

CHAPTER XLIX

This statement also is untrue, that it is "only foolish and low individuals, and persons devoid of perception, and slaves, and women, and children, of whom the teachers of the divine word wish to make converts." Such indeed does the Gospel invite, in order to make them better; but it invites also others who are very different from these, since Christ is the Saviour of all men, and especially of them that believe, whether they be intelligent or simple; and "He is the propitiation with the Father for our sins; and not for ours only, but also for the sins of the whole world." After this it is superfluous for us to wish to offer a reply to such statements of Celsus as the following: "For why is it an evil to have been educated, and to have studied the best opinions, and to have both the reality and appearance of wisdom? What hindrance does this offer to the knowledge of God? Why should it not rather be an assistance, and a means by which one might be better able to arrive at the truth?" Truly it is no evil to have been educated, for education is the way to virtue; but to rank those amongst the number of the educated who hold erroneous opinions is what even the wise men among the Greeks would not do. On the other hand, who would not admit that to have studied the best opinions is a blessing? But what shall we call the best, save those which are true, and which incite men to virtue? Moreover, it is an excellent thing for a man to *be* wise, but not to *seem* so, as Celsus says. And it is no hindrance to the knowledge of God, but an assistance, to have been educated, and to have studied the best opinions, and to be wise. And it becomes us rather than Celsus to say this, especially if it be shown that he is an Epicurean.

CHAPTER L

But let us see what those statements of his are which follow next in these words: "Nay, we see, indeed, that even those individuals, who in the market-places perform the most disgraceful tricks, and who gather crowds around them, would never approach an assembly of wise men, nor dare to exhibit their arts among them; but wherever they see young men, and a mob of slaves, and a gathering of unintelligent persons, thither they thrust themselves in, and show themselves off." Observe, now, how he slanders us in these words, comparing us to those who in the market-places perform the most disreputable tricks, and gather crowds around them! What disreputable tricks, pray, do we perform? Or what is there in *our* conduct that resembles theirs, seeing that by means of readings, and explanations of the things read, we lead men to the worship of the God of the universe, and to the cognate virtues, and turn them away from contemning Deity, and from all things contrary to right reason? Philosophers verily would wish to collect together such hearers of their discourses as exhort men to virtue,—a practice which certain of the Cynics especially have followed, who converse publicly with those whom they happen to meet. Will they maintain, then, that these who do not gather together persons who are considered to have been educated, but who invite and assemble hearers from the public street, resemble those who in the market-places perform the most disreputable tricks, and gather crowds around them? Neither Celsus, however, nor any one who holds the same opinions, will blame those who, agreeably to what they regard as a feeling of philanthropy, address their arguments to the ignorant populace.

CHAPTER LI

And if they are not to be blamed for so doing, let us see whether Christians do not exhort multitudes to the practice of virtue in a greater and better degree than they. For the philosophers who converse in public do not pick and choose their hearers, but he who likes stands and listens. The Christians, however, having previously, so far as possible, tested the souls of those who wish to become their hearers, and having previously instructed them in private, when they appear (before entering the community) to have sufficiently evinced their desire towards a virtuous life, introduce them then, and not before, privately forming one class of those who are beginners, and are receiving admission, but who have not yet obtained the mark of complete purification; and another of those who have manifested to the best of their ability their intention to desire no other things than are approved by Christians; and among these there are certain persons appointed to make inquiries regarding the lives and behaviour of those who join them, in order that they may prevent those who commit acts of infamy from coming into their public assembly, while those of a different character they receive with their whole heart, in order that they may daily make them better. And this is their method of procedure, both with those who are sinners, and especially with those who lead dissolute lives, whom they exclude from their community, although, according to Celsus, they resemble those who in the market-places perform the most shameful tricks. Now the venerable school of the Pythagoreans used to erect a cenotaph to those who had apostatized from their system of philosophy, treating them as dead; but the Christians lament as dead those who have been vanquished by licentiousness or any other sin, because they are lost and dead to God, and as being risen from the dead (if they manifest a becoming change) they receive them afterwards, at some future time, after a greater interval than in the case of those who were admitted at first, but not placing in any office or post of rank in the Church of God those who, after professing the Gospel, lapsed and fell.

CHAPTER LII

Observe now with regard to the following statement of Celsus, "We see also those persons who in the market-places perform most disreputable tricks, and collect crowds around them," whether a manifest falsehood has not been uttered, and things compared which have no resemblance. He says that these individuals, to whom he compares us, who "perform the most disreputable tricks in the market-places and collect crowds, would never approach an assembly of wise men, nor dare to show off their tricks before them; but wherever they see young men, and a mob of slaves, and a gathering of foolish people, thither do they thrust themselves in and make a display." Now, in speaking thus he does nothing else than simply load us with abuse, like the women upon the public streets, whose object is to slander one another; for we do everything in our power to secure that our meetings should be composed of wise men, and those things among us which are especially excellent and divine we then venture to bring forward publicly in our discussions when we have an abundance of intelligent hearers, while we conceal and pass by in silence the truths of deeper import when we see that our audience is composed of simpler minds, which need such instruction as is figuratively termed "milk."

CHAPTER LIII

For the word is used by our Paul in writing to the Corinthians, who were Greeks, and not yet purified in their morals: "I have fed you with milk, not with meat; for hitherto ye were not able to bear it, neither yet now are ye able, for ye are yet carnal: for whereas there is among you envying and strife, are ye not carnal, and walk as men?" Now the same writer, knowing that there was a certain kind of nourishment better adapted for the soul, and that the food of those young persons who were admitted was compared to milk, continues: "And ye are become such as have need of milk, and not of strong meat. For every one that useth milk is unskilful in the word of righteousness; for he is a babe. But strong meat belongeth to them that are of full age, even those who by reason of use have their senses exercised to discern both good and evil." Would then those who believe these words to be well spoken, suppose that the noble doctrines of our faith would never be mentioned in an assembly of wise men, but that wherever (our instructors) see young men, and a mob of slaves, and a collection of foolish individuals, they bring publicly forward divine and venerable truths, and before such persons make a display of themselves in treating of them? But it is clear to him who examines the whole spirit of our writings, that Celsus is animated with a hatred against the human race resembling that of the ignorant populace, and gives utterance to these falsehoods without examination.

CHAPTER LIV

We acknowledge, however, although Celsus will not have it so, that we *do* desire to instruct all men in the word of God, so as to give to young men the exhortations which are appropriate to them, and to show to slaves how they may recover freedom of thought, and be ennobled by the word. And those amongst us who are the ambassadors of Christianity sufficiently declare that they are debtors to Greeks and Barbarians, to wise men and fools, (for they do not deny their obligation to cure the souls even of foolish persons,) in order that as far as possible they may lay aside their ignorance, and endeavour to obtain greater prudence, by listening also to the words of Solomon: "Oh, ye fools, be of an understanding heart," and "Who is the most simple among you, let him turn unto me;" and wisdom exhorts those who are devoid of understanding in the words, "Come, eat of my bread, and drink of the wine which I have mixed for you. Forsake folly that ye may live, and correct understanding in knowledge." This too would I say (seeing it bears on the point), in answer to the statement of Celsus: Do not philosophers invite young men to their lectures? and do they not encourage young men to exchange a wicked life for a better? and do they not desire slaves to learn philosophy? Must we find fault, then, with philosophers who have exhorted slaves to the practice of virtue? with Pythagoras for having so done with Zamolxis, Zeno with Perseus, and with those who recently encouraged Epictetus to the study of philosophy? Is it indeed permissible for you, O Greeks, to call youths and slaves and foolish persons to the study of philosophy, but if *we* do so, we do not act from philanthropic motives in wishing to heal every rational nature with the medicine of reason, and to bring them into fellowship with God, the Creator of all things? These remarks, then, may suffice in answer to what are slanders rather than accusations on the part of Celsus.

CHAPTER LV

But as Celsus delights to heap up calumnies against us, and, in addition to those which he has already uttered, has added others, let us examine these also, and see whether it be the Christians or Celsus who have reason to be ashamed of what is said. He asserts, "We see, indeed, in private houses workers in wool and leather, and fullers, and persons of the most uninstructed and rustic character, not venturing to utter a word in the presence of their elders and wiser masters; but when they get hold of the children privately, and certain women as ignorant as themselves, they pour forth wonderful statements, to the effect that they ought not to give heed to their father and to their teachers, but should obey them; that the former are foolish and stupid, and neither know nor can perform anything that is really good, being preoccupied with empty trifles; that *they* alone know how men ought to live, and that, if the children obey them, they will both be happy themselves, and will make their home happy also. And while thus speaking, if they see one of the instructors of youth approaching, or one of the more intelligent class, or even the father himself, the more timid among them become afraid, while the more forward incite the children to throw off the yoke, whispering that in the presence of father and teachers they neither will nor can explain to them any good thing, seeing they turn away with aversion from the silliness and stupidity of such persons as being altogether corrupt, and far advanced in wickedness, and such as would inflict punishment upon them; but that if they wish (to avail themselves of their aid) they must leave their father and their instructors, and go with the women and their playfellows to the women's apartments, or to the leather shop, or to the fuller's shop, that they may attain to perfection;—and by words like these they gain them over."

CHAPTER LVI

Observe now how by such statements he depreciates those amongst us who are teachers of the word, and who strive in every way to raise the soul to the Creator of all things, and who show that we ought to despise things "sensible," and "temporal," and "visible," and to do our utmost to reach communion with God, and the contemplation of things that are "intelligent," and "invisible," and a blessed life with God, and the friends of God; comparing them to "workers in wool in private houses, and to leather-cutters, and to fullers, and to the most rustic of mankind, who carefully incite young boys to wickedness, and women to forsake their fathers and teachers, and follow them." Now let Celsus point out from what wise parent, or from what teachers, we keep away children and women, and let him ascertain by comparison among those children and women who are adherents of our doctrine, whether any of the opinions which they formerly heard are better than ours, and in what manner we draw away children and women from noble and venerable studies, and incite them to worse things. But he will not be able to make good any such charge against us, seeing that, on the contrary, we turn away women from a dissolute life, and from being at variance with those with whom they live, from all mad desires after theatres and dancing, and from superstition; while we train to habits of self-restraint boys just reaching the age of puberty, and feeling a desire for sexual pleasures, pointing out to them not only the disgrace which attends those sins, but also the state to which the soul of the wicked is reduced through practices of that kind, and the judgments which it will suffer, and the punishments which will be inflicted.

CHAPTER LVII

But who are the teachers whom we call triflers and fools, whose defence is undertaken by Celsus, as of those who teach better things? (I know not,) unless he deem those to be good instructors of women, and no triflers, who invite them to superstition and to unchaste spectacles, and those, moreover, to be teachers not devoid of sense who lead and drag the young men to all those disorderly acts which we know are often committed by them. We indeed call away these also, as far as we can, from the dogmas of philosophy to our worship of God, by showing forth its excellence and purity. But as Celsus, by his statements, has declared that we do not do so, but that we call only the foolish, I would say to him, "If you had charged us with withdrawing from the study of philosophy those who were already preoccupied with it, you would not have spoken the truth, and yet your charge would have had an appearance of probability; but when you now say that we draw away our adherents from good teachers, show who are those other teachers save the teachers of philosophy, or those who have been appointed to give instruction in some useful branch of study."

He will be unable, however, to show any such; while we promise, openly and not in secret, that *they* will be happy who live according to the word of God, and who look to Him in all things, and who do everything, whatever it is, as if in the presence of God. Are these the instructions of workers in wool, and of leather-cutters, and fullers, and uneducated rustics? But such an assertion he cannot make good.

CHAPTER LVIII

But those who, in the opinion of Celsus, resemble the workers in wool in private houses, and the leather-cutters, and fullers, and uneducated rustics, will, he alleges, in the presence of father or teachers be unwilling to speak, or unable to explain to the boys anything that is good. In answer to which, we would say, What kind of father, my good sir, and what kind of teacher, do you mean? If you mean one who approves of virtue, and turns away from vice, and welcomes what is better, then know, that with the greatest boldness will we declare our opinions to the children, because we will be in good repute with such a judge. But if, in the presence of a father who has a hatred of virtue and goodness, we keep silence, and also before those who teach what is contrary to sound doctrine, do not blame us for so doing, since you will blame us without good reason. You, at all events, in a case where fathers deemed the mysteries of philosophy an idle and unprofitable occupation for their sons, and for young men in general, would not, in teaching philosophy, make known its secrets before worthless parents; but, desiring to keep apart those sons of wicked parents who had been turned towards the study of philosophy, you would observe the proper seasons, in order that the doctrines of philosophy might reach the minds of the young men. And we say the same regarding our teachers. For if we turn (our hearers) away from those instructors who teach obscene comedies and licentious iambics, and many other things which neither improve the speaker nor benefit the hearers (because the latter do not know how to listen to poetry in a philosophic frame of mind, nor the former how to say to each of the young men what tends to his profit), we are not, in following such a course, ashamed to confess what we do. But if you will show me teachers who train young men for philosophy, and who exercise them in it, I will not from such turn away young men, but will try to raise them, as those who have been previously exercised in the whole circle of learning and in philosophical subjects, to the venerable and lofty height of eloquence which lies hid from the multitude of Christians, where are discussed topics of the greatest importance, and where it is demonstrated and shown that they have been treated philosophically both by the prophets of God and the apostles of Jesus.

CHAPTER LIX

Immediately after this, Celsus, perceiving that he has slandered us with too great bitterness, as if by way of defence expresses himself as follows: "That I bring no heavier charge than what the truth compels me, any one may see from the following remarks. Those who invite to participation in other mysteries, make proclamation as follows: 'Every one who has clean hands, and a prudent tongue;' others again thus: 'He who is pure from all pollution, and whose soul is conscious of no evil, and who has lived well and justly.' Such is the proclamation made by those who promise purification from sins. But let us hear what kind of persons these Christians invite. Every one, they say, who is a sinner, who is devoid of understanding, who is a child, and, to speak generally, whoever is unfortunate, him will the kingdom of God receive. Do you not call him a sinner, then, who is unjust, and a thief, and a housebreaker, and a poisoner, and a committer of sacrilege, and a robber of the dead? What others would a man invite if he were issuing a proclamation for an assembly of robbers?" Now, in answer to such statements, we say that it is not the same thing to invite those who are *sick in soul* to be *cured*, and those who are *in health* to the *knowledge* and *study* of divine things. We, however, keeping both these things in view, at first invite all men to be healed, and exhort those who are sinners to come to the consideration of the doctrines which teach men not to sin, and those who are devoid of understanding to those which beget wisdom, and those who are children to rise in their thoughts to manhood, and those who are simply unfortunate to good fortune, or—which is the more appropriate term to use—to blessedness. And when those who have been turned towards virtue have made progress, and have shown that they have been purified by the word, and have led as far as they can a better life, then and not before do we invite them to participation in our mysteries. "For we speak wisdom among them that are perfect."

CHAPTER LX

And as we teach, moreover, that "wisdom will not enter into the soul of a base man, nor dwell in a body that is involved in sin," we say, Whoever has clean hands, and therefore lifts up holy hands to God, and by reason of being occupied with elevated and heavenly things, can say, "The lifting up of my hands is as the evening sacrifice," let him come to us; and whoever has a wise tongue through meditating on the law of the Lord day and night, and by "reason of habit has his senses exercised to discern between good and evil," let him have no reluctance in coming to the strong and rational sustenance which is adapted to those who are athletes in piety and every virtue. And since the grace of God is with all those who love with a pure affection the teacher of the doctrines of immortality, whoever is pure not only from all defilement, but from what are regarded as lesser transgressions, let him be boldly initiated in the mysteries of Jesus, which properly are made known only to the holy and the pure. The initiated of Celsus accordingly says, "Let him whose soul is conscious of no evil come." But he who acts as initiator, according to the precepts of Jesus, will say to those who have been purified in heart, "He whose soul has, for a long time, been conscious of no evil, and especially since he yielded himself to the healing of the word, let such an one hear the doctrines which were

451

spoken in private by Jesus to His genuine disciples." Therefore in the comparison which he institutes between the procedure of the initiators into the Grecian mysteries, and the teachers of the doctrine of Jesus, he does not know the difference between inviting the wicked to be healed, and initiating those already purified into the sacred mysteries!

CHAPTER LXI

Not to *participation in mysteries*, then, and to *fellowship in the wisdom hidden in a mystery*, which God ordained before the world to the glory of His saints, do we invite the *wicked* man, and the *thief*, and the *housebreaker*, and the *poisoner*, and the *committer of sacrilege*, and the *plunderer of the dead*, and all those others whom Celsus may enumerate in his exaggerating style, but such as these we invite to be *healed*. For there are in the divinity of the word some helps towards the cure of those who are sick, respecting which the word says, "They that be whole need not a physician, but they that are sick;" others, again, which to the pure in soul and body exhibit "the revelation of the mystery, which was kept secret since the world began, but now is made manifest by the Scriptures of the prophets," and "by the appearing of our Lord Jesus Christ," which "appearing" is manifested to each one of those who are perfect, and which enlightens the reason in the true knowledge of things. But as he exaggerates the charges against us, adding, after his list of those vile individuals whom he has mentioned, this remark, "What other persons would a robber summon to himself by proclamation?" we answer such a question by saying that a robber summons around him individuals of such a character, in order to make use of their villainy against the men whom they desire to slay and plunder. A Christian, on the other hand, even though he invite those whom the robber invites, invites them to a very different vocation, viz., to bind up these wounds by His word, and to apply to the soul, festering amid evils, the drugs obtained from the word, and which are analogous to the wine and oil, and plasters, and other healing appliances which belong to the art of medicine.

CHAPTER LXII

In the next place, throwing a slur upon the exhortations spoken and written to those who have led wicked lives, and which invite them to repentance and reformation of heart, he asserts that we say "that it was to sinners that God has been sent." Now this statement of his is much the same as if he were to find fault with certain persons for saying that on account of the sick who were living in a city, a physician had been sent them by a very benevolent monarch. God the Word was sent, indeed, as a physician to sinners, but as a teacher of divine mysteries to those who are already pure and who sin no more. But Celsus, unable to see this distinction,—for he had no desire to be animated with a love of truth,—remarks, "Why was he not sent to those who were without sin? What evil is it not to have committed sin?" To which we reply, that if by those "who were without sin" he means those who sin no more, then our Saviour Jesus was sent even to such, but not as a physician. While if by those "who were without sin" he means such as have never at any time sinned,—for he made no distinction in his statement,—we reply that it is impossible for a man thus to be without sin. And this we say, excepting, of course, the man understood to be in Christ Jesus, who "did no sin." It is with a malicious intent, indeed, that Celsus says of us that we assert that "God will receive the unrighteousness man if he humble himself on account of his wickedness, but that He will not receive the righteous man, although he look up to Him, (adorned) with virtue from the beginning." Now we assert that it is impossible for a man to look up to God (adorned) with virtue from the beginning. For wickedness must necessarily first exist in men. As Paul also says, "When the commandment came, sin revived, and I died." Moreover, we do not teach regarding the unrighteous man, that it is sufficient for him to humble himself on account of his wickedness in order to his being accepted by God, but that God will accept him if, after passing condemnation upon himself for his past conduct, he walk humbly on account of it, and in a becoming manner for the time to come.

CHAPTER LXIII

After this, not understanding how it has been said that "every one who exalted himself shall be abased;" nor (although taught even by Plato) that "the good and virtuous man walketh humbly and orderly;" and ignorant, moreover, that we give the injunction, "Humble yourselves, therefore, under the mighty hand of God, that He may exalt you in due time;" he says that "those persons who preside properly over a trial make those individuals who bewail before them their evil deeds to cease from their piteous wailings, lest their decisions should be determined rather by compassion than by a regard to truth; whereas God does not decide in accordance with truth, but in accordance with flattery." Now, what words of flattery and piteous wailing are contained in the Holy Scriptures when the sinner says in his prayers to God, "I have acknowledged my sin, and mine iniquity have I not hid. I said, I will confess my transgression to the Lord," etc., etc.? For is he able to show that a procedure of this kind is not adapted to the conversion of sinners, who humble themselves in their prayers under the hand of God? And, becoming confused by his efforts to accuse us, he contradicts himself; appearing at one time to know a man "without sin," and "a righteous man, who can look up to God (adorned) with virtue from the beginning;" and at another time accepting our statement that there is no man altogether righteous, or without sin; for, as if he admitted its truth, he remarks, "This is indeed apparently true, that somehow the human race is naturally inclined to sin." In the next place, as if all men were not invited by the word, he says, "All men, then, without distinction, ought to be invited, since all indeed are sinners." And yet, in the preceding pages, we have pointed out the words of Jesus: "Come unto Me, *all* ye that labour and are heavy laden, and I will give you rest." *All* men, therefore, labouring and being heavy laden on account of the nature of sin, are invited to the rest spoken of in the word of God, "for God sent His word, and healed them, and delivered them from their destructions."

CHAPTER LXIV

But since he says, in addition to this, "What is this preference of sinners over others?" and makes other remarks of a similar nature, we have to reply that absolutely a sinner is not preferred before one who is not a sinner; but that sometimes a sinner, who has become conscious of his own sin, and for that reason comes to repentance, being humbled on account of his sins, is preferred before one who is accounted a lesser sinner, but who does not consider himself one, but exalts himself on the ground of certain good qualities which he thinks he possesses, and is greatly elated on their account. And this is manifest to those who are willing to peruse the Gospels in a spirit of fairness, by the parable of the publican, who said, "Be merciful to me a sinner," and of the Pharisee who boasted with a certain wicked self-conceit in the words, "I thank Thee that I am not as other men are, extortioners, unjust, adulterers, or even as this publican." For Jesus subjoins to his narrative of them both the words: "This man went down to his house justified rather than the other: for every one that exalteth himself shall be abased; and he that humbleth himself shall be exalted." We utter no blasphemy, then, against God, neither are we guilty of falsehood, when we teach that every man, whoever he may be, is conscious of human infirmity in comparison with the greatness of God, and that we must ever ask from Him, who alone is able to supply our deficiencies, what is wanting to our (mortal) nature.

CHAPTER LXV

He imagines, however, that we utter these exhortations for the conversion of sinners, because we are able to gain over no one who is really good and righteous, and therefore open our gates to the most unholy and abandoned of men. But if any one will fairly observe our assemblies we can present a greater number of those who have been converted from not a very wicked life, than of those who have committed the most abominable sins. For naturally those who are conscious to themselves of better things, desire that those promises may be true which are declared by God regarding the reward of the righteous, and thus assent more readily to the statements (of Scripture) than those do who have led very wicked lives, and who are prevented by their very consciousness (of evil) from admitting that they will be punished by the Judge of all with such punishment as befits those who have sinned so greatly, and as would not be inflicted by the Judge of all contrary to right reason. Sometimes, also, when very abandoned men are willing to accept the doctrine of (future) punishment, on account of the hope which is based upon repentance, they are prevented from so doing by their habit of sinning, being constantly dipped, and, as it were, dyed in wickedness, and possessing no longer the power to turn from it easily to a proper life, and one regulated according to right reason. And although Celsus observes this, he nevertheless, I know not why, expresses himself in the following terms: "And yet, indeed, it is manifest to every one that no one by chastisement, much less by merciful treatment, could effect a complete change in those who are sinners both by nature and custom, for to change nature is an exceedingly difficult thing. But they who are without sin are partakers of a better life."

CHAPTER LXVI

Now here Celsus appears to me to have committed a great error, in refusing to those who are sinners by nature, and also by habit, the possibility of a complete transformation, alleging that they cannot be cured even by punishment. For it clearly appears that all men are inclined to sin by nature, and some not only by nature but by practice, while not all men are incapable of an entire transformation. For there are found in every philosophical sect, and in the word of God, persons who are related to have undergone so great a change that they may be proposed as a model of excellence of life. Among the names of the heroic age some mention Hercules and Ulysses, among those of later times, Socrates, and of those who have lived very recently, Musonius. Not only against us, then, did Celsus utter the calumny, when he said that "it was manifest to every one that those who were given to sin by nature and habit could not by any means—even by punishments—be completely changed for the better," but also against the noblest names in philosophy, who have not denied that the recovery of virtue was a possible thing for men. But although he did not express his meaning with exactness, we shall nevertheless, though giving his words a more favourable construction, convict him of unsound reasoning. For his words were: "Those who are inclined to sin by nature and habit, no one could completely reform even by chastisement;" and his words, as we understood them, we refuted to the best of our ability.

CHAPTER LXVII

It is probable, however, that he meant to convey some such meaning as this, that those who were both by nature and habit given to the commission of those sins which are committed by the most abandoned of men, could not be completely transformed even by punishment. And yet this is shown to be false from the history of certain philosophers. For who is there that would not rank among the most abandoned of men the individual who somehow submitted to yield himself to his master, when he placed him in a brothel, that he might allow himself to be polluted by any one who liked? And yet such a circumstance is related of Phaedo! And who will not agree that he who burst, accompanied with a flute-player and a party of revellers, his profligate associates, into the school of the venerable Xenocrates, to insult a man who was the admiration of his friends, was not one of the greatest miscreants among mankind? Yet, notwithstanding this, reason was powerful enough to effect their conversion, and to enable them to make such progress in philosophy, that the one was deemed worthy by Plato to recount the discourse of Socrates on immortality, and to record his firmness in prison, when he evinced his contempt of the hemlock, and with all fearlessness and tranquillity of mind treated of subjects so numerous and important, that it is difficult even for those to follow them who are giving their utmost attention, and who are disturbed by no distraction; while Polemon, on the other hand, who from a profligate became a man of most temperate life, was successor in the school of Xenocrates, so celebrated for his venerable character. Celsus then does not speak the truth when he says "that sinners by nature and habit cannot be completely reformed even by chastisement."

CHAPTER LXVIII

That philosophical discourses, however, distinguished by orderly arrangement and elegant expression, should produce such results in the case of those individuals just enumerated, and upon others who have led wicked lives, is not at all to be wondered at. But when we consider that those discourses, which Celsus terms "vulgar," are filled with power, as if they were spells, and see that they at once convert multitudes from a life of licentiousness to one of extreme regularity, and from a life of wickedness to a better, and from a state of cowardice or unmanliness to one of such high-toned courage as to lead men to despise even death through the piety which shows itself within them, why should we not justly admire the power which they contain? For the words of those who at the first assumed the office of (Christian) ambassadors, and who gave their labours to rear up the Churches of God,—nay, their preaching also,—were accompanied with a persuasive power, though not like that found among those who profess the philosophy of Plato, or of any other merely human philosopher, which possesses no other qualities than those of human nature. But the demonstration which followed the words of the apostles of Jesus was given from God, and was accredited by the Spirit and by power. And therefore *their* word ran swiftly and speedily, or rather the word of *God* through their instrumentality, transformed numbers of persons who had been sinners both by nature and habit, whom no one could have reformed by punishment, but who were changed by the word, which moulded and transformed them according to its pleasure.

CHAPTER LXIX

Celsus continues in his usual manner, asserting that "to change a nature entirely is exceedingly difficult." We, however, who know of only one nature in every rational soul, and who maintain that none has been created evil by the Author of all things, but that many have become wicked through education, and perverse example, and surrounding influences, so that wickedness has been naturalized in some individuals, are persuaded that for the word of God to change a nature in which evil has been naturalized is not only not impossible, but is even a work of no very great difficulty, if a man only believe that he must entrust himself to the God of all things, and do everything with a view to please Him with whom it cannot be that

"Both good and bad are in the same honour,
Or that the idle man and he who laboured much
Perish alike."

But even if it be exceedingly difficult to effect a change in some persons, the cause must be held to lie in their own will, which is reluctant to accept the belief that the God over all things is a just Judge of all the deeds done during life. For deliberate choice and practice avail much towards the accomplishment of things which appear to be very difficult, and, to speak hyperbolically, almost impossible. Has the nature of man, when desiring to walk along a rope extended in the air through the middle of the theatre, and to carry at the same time numerous and heavy weights, been able by practice and attention to accomplish such a feat; but when desiring to live in conformity with the practice of virtue, does it find it impossible to do so, although formerly it may have been exceedingly wicked? See whether he who holds such views does not bring a charge against the nature of the Creator of the rational animal rather than against the creature, if He has formed the nature of man with powers for the attainment of things of such difficulty, and of no utility whatever, but has rendered it incapable of securing its own blessedness. But these remarks may suffice as an answer to the assertion that "entirely to change a nature is exceedingly difficult." He alleges, in the next place, that "they who are without sin are partakers of a better life;" not making it clear what he means by "those who are without sin," whether those who are so from the beginning (of their lives), or those who become so by a transformation. Of those who were so from the beginning of their lives, there cannot possibly be any; while those who are so after a transformation (of heart) are found to be few in number, being those who have become so after giving in their allegiance to the saving word. And they were not such when they gave in their allegiance. For, apart from the aid of the word, and that too the word of perfection, it is impossible for a man to become free from sin.

CHAPTER LXX

In the next place, he objects to the statement, as if it were maintained by us, that "God will be able to do all things," not seeing even here how these words are meant, and what "the *all things*" are which are included in it, and how it is said that God "will be able." But on these matters it is not necessary now to speak; for although he might with a show of reason have opposed this proposition, he has not done so. Perhaps he did not understand the arguments which might be plausibly used against it, or if he did, he saw the answers that might be returned. Now in our judgment God can do everything which it is possible for Him to do without ceasing to be God, and good, and wise. But Celsus asserts—not comprehending the meaning of the expression "God can do all things"—"that He will not desire to do anything wicked," admitting that He has the *power*, but not the *will*, to commit evil. We, on the contrary, maintain that as that which by nature possesses the property of sweetening other things through its own inherent sweetness cannot produce bitterness contrary to its own peculiar nature, nor that whose nature it is to produce light through its being light can cause darkness; so neither is God able to commit wickedness, for the power of doing evil is contrary to His deity and its omnipotence. Whereas if any one among existing things is able to commit wickedness from being inclined to wickedness by nature, it does so from not having in its nature the ability not to do evil.

CHAPTER LXXI

He next assumes what is not granted by the more rational class of believers, but what perhaps is considered to be true by some who are devoid of intelligence,—viz., that "God, like those who are overcome with pity, being Himself overcome, alleviates the sufferings of the wicked through pity for their wailings, and casts off the good, who do nothing of that kind, which is the height of injustice." Now, in our judgment, God lightens the suffering of no wicked man who has not betaken himself to a virtuous life, and casts off no one who is already good, nor yet alleviates the suffering of any one who mourns, simply because he utters lamentation, or takes pity upon him, to use the word pity in its more common acceptation. But those who have passed severe condemnation upon themselves because of their sins, and who, as on that account, lament and bewail themselves as lost, so far as their previous conduct is concerned, and who have manifested a satisfactory change, are received by God on account of their repentance, as those who have undergone a transformation from a life of great wickedness. For virtue, taking up her abode in the souls of these persons, and expelling the wickedness which had previous possession of them, produces an oblivion of the past. And even although virtue do not effect an entrance, yet if a considerable progress take place in the soul, even that is sufficient, in the proportion that it is progressive, to drive out and destroy the flood of wickedness, so that it almost ceases to remain in the soul.

CHAPTER LXXII

In the next place, speaking as in the person of a teacher of our doctrine, he expresses himself as follows: "Wise men reject what we say, being led into error, and ensnared by their wisdom." In reply to which we say that, since wisdom is the knowledge of divine and human things and of their causes, or, as it is defined by the word of God, "the breath of the power of God, and a pure influence flowing from the glory of the Almighty; and the brightness of the everlasting light, and the unspotted mirror of the power of God, and the image of His goodness," no one who was really wise would reject what is said by a Christian acquainted with the principles of Christianity, or would be led into error, or ensnared by it. For true wisdom does not mislead, but ignorance does, while of existing things knowledge alone is permanent, and the truth which is derived from wisdom. But if, contrary to the definition of wisdom, you call any one whatever who dogmatizes with sophistical opinions wise, we answer that in conformity with what you call wisdom, such an one rejects the words of God, being misled and ensnared by plausible sophisms. And since, according to our doctrine, wisdom is not the knowledge of evil, but the knowledge of evil, so to speak, is in those who hold false opinions and who are deceived by them, I would therefore in such persons term it ignorance rather than wisdom.

CHAPTER LXXIII

After this he again slanders the ambassador of Christianity, and gives out regarding him that he relates "ridiculous things," although he does not show or clearly point out what are the things which he calls "ridiculous." And in his slanders he says that "no wise man believes the Gospel, being driven away by the multitudes who adhere to it." And in this he acts like one who should say that owing to the multitude of those ignorant persons who are brought into subjection to the laws, no wise man would yield obedience to Solon, for example, or to Lycurgus, or Zaleucus, or any other legislator, and especially if by wise man he means one who is wise (by living) in conformity with virtue. For, as with regard to these ignorant persons, the legislators, according to their ideas of utility, caused them to be surrounded with appropriate guidance and laws, so God, legislating through Jesus Christ for men in all parts of the world, brings to Himself even those who are not wise in the way in which it is possible for such persons to be brought to a better life. And God, well knowing this, as we have already shown in

460

the preceding pages, says in the books of Moses: "They have moved Me to jealousy with that which is not God; they have provoked Me to anger with their idols: and I will move them to jealousy with those which are not a people; I will provoke them to anger with a foolish nation." And Paul also, knowing this, said, "But God hath chosen the foolish things of the world to confound the wise," calling, in a general way, wise all who appear to have made advances in knowledge, but have fallen into an atheistic polytheism, since "professing themselves to be wise they became fools, and changed the glory of the incorruptible God into an image made like to corruptible man, and to birds, and four-footed beasts, and creeping things."

CHAPTER LXXIV

He accuses the Christian teacher, moreover of "seeking after the unintelligent." In answer we ask, Whom do you mean by the "unintelligent?" For, to speak accurately, every wicked man is "unintelligent." If then by "unintelligent" you mean the wicked, do you, in drawing men to philosophy, seek to gain the wicked or the virtuous? But it is impossible to gain the virtuous, because they have already given themselves to philosophy. The wicked, then, (you try to gain;) but if they are wicked, are they "unintelligent?" And many such you seek to win over to philosophy, and you therefore seek the "unintelligent." But if I seek after those who are thus termed "unintelligent," I act like a benevolent physician, who should seek after the sick in order to help and cure them. If, however, by "unintelligent" you mean persons who are not clever, but the inferior class of men intellectually, I shall answer that I endeavour to improve such also to the best of my ability, although I would not desire to build up the Christian community out of such materials. For I seek in preference those who are more clever and acute, because they are able to comprehend the meaning of the hard sayings, and of those passages in the law, and prophecies, and Gospels, which are expressed with obscurity, and which you have despised as not containing anything worthy of notice, because you have not ascertained the meaning which they contain, nor tried to enter into the aim of the writers.

CHAPTER LXXV

But as he afterwards says that "the teacher of Christianity acts like a person who promises to restore patients to bodily health, but who prevents them from consulting skilled physicians, by whom his ignorance would be exposed," we shall inquire in reply, "What are the physicians to whom you refer, from whom we turn away ignorant individuals? For you do not suppose that we exhort those to embrace the Gospel who are devoted to philosophy, so that you would regard the latter as the physicians from whom we keep away such as we invite to come to the word of God." He indeed will make no answer, because he cannot name the physicians; or else he will be obliged to betake himself to those of them who are ignorant, and who of their own accord servilely yield themselves to the worship of many gods, and to whatever other opinions are entertained by ignorant individuals. In either case, then, he will be shown to have employed to no purpose in his argument the illustration of "one who keeps others away from skilled physicians." But if, in order to preserve from the philosophy of Epicurus, and from such as are considered physicians after his system, those who are deceived by them, why should we not be acting most reasonably in keeping such away from a dangerous disease caused by the physicians of Celsus,—that, viz., which leads to the annihilation of providence, and the introduction of pleasure as a good? But let it be conceded that we do keep away those whom we encourage to become our disciples from other philosopher-physicians,—from the Peripatetics, for example, who deny the existence of providence and the relation of Deity to man,—why shall we not piously train and heal those who have been thus encouraged, persuading them to devote themselves to the God of all things, and free those who yield obedience to us from the great wounds inflicted by the words of such as are deemed to be philosophers? Nay, let it also be admitted that we turn away from physicians of the sect of the Stoics, who introduce a corruptible god, and assert that his essence consists of a body, which is capable of being changed and altered in all its parts, and who also maintain that all things will one day perish, and that God alone will be left; why shall we not even thus emancipate our subjects from evils, and bring them by pious arguments to devote themselves to the Creator, and to admire the Father of the Christian system, who has so arranged that instruction of the most benevolent kind, and fitted for the conversion of souls, should be distributed throughout the whole human race? Nay, if we should cure those who have fallen into the folly of believing in the transmigration of souls through the teaching of physicians, who will have it that the rational nature descends sometimes into all kinds of irrational animals, and sometimes into that state of being which is incapable of using the imagination, why should we not improve the souls of our subjects by means of a doctrine which does not teach that a state of insensibility or irrationalism is produced in the wicked instead of punishment, but which shows that the labours and chastisements inflicted upon the wicked by God are a kind of medicines leading to conversion? For those who are intelligent Christians, keeping this in view, deal with the simple-minded, as parents do with very young children. We do not betake ourselves then to young persons and silly rustics, saying to them, "Flee from physicians." Nor do we say, "See that none of you lay hold of knowledge;" nor do we assert that "knowledge is an evil;" nor are we mad enough to say that "knowledge causes men to lose their soundness of mind." We would not even say that any one ever perished through wisdom; and although we give instruction, we never say, "Give heed to me," but "Give heed to the God of all things, and to Jesus, the giver of instruction concerning Him." And none of us is so great a braggart as to say what Celsus put in the mouth of one of our teachers to his acquaintances, "I alone will save you." Observe here the lies which he utters against us! Moreover, we do *not* assert that "true physicians destroy those whom they promise to cure."

CHAPTER LXXVI

And he produces a second illustration to our disadvantage, saying that "our teacher acts like a drunken man, who, entering a company of drunkards, should accuse those who are sober of being drunk." But let him show, say from the writings of Paul, that the apostle of Jesus gave way to drunkenness, and that his words were not those of soberness; or from the writings of John, that his thoughts do not breathe a spirit of temperance and of freedom from the intoxication of evil. No one, then, who is of sound mind, and teaches the doctrines of Christianity, gets drunk with wine; but Celsus utters these calumnies against us in a spirit very unlike that of a philosopher. Moreover, let Celsus say who those "sober" persons are whom the ambassadors of Christianity accuse. For in our judgment all are intoxicated who address themselves to inanimate objects as to God. And why do I say "intoxicated?" "Insane" would be the more appropriate word for those who hasten to temples and worship images or animals as divinities. And they too are not less insane who think that images, fashioned by men of worthless and sometimes most wicked character, confer any honour upon genuine divinities.

CHAPTER LXXVII

He next likens our teacher to one suffering from ophthalmia, and his disciples to those suffering from the same disease, and says that "such an one amongst a company of those who are afflicted with ophthalmia, accuses those who are sharp-sighted of being blind." Who, then, would we ask, O Greeks, are they who in our judgment do not see, save those who are unable to look up from the exceeding greatness of the world and its contents, and from the beauty of created things, and to see that they ought to worship, and admire, and reverence Him alone who made these things, and that it is not befitting to treat with reverence anything contrived by man, and applied to the honour of God, whether it be without a reference to the Creator, or with one? For, to compare with that illimitable excellence, which surpasses all created being, things which ought not to be brought into comparison with it, is the act of those whose understanding is darkened. We do not then say that those who are sharp-sighted are suffering from ophthalmia or blindness; but we assert that those who, in ignorance of God, give themselves to temples and images, and so-called sacred seasons, are blinded in their minds, and especially when, in addition to their impiety, they live also in licentiousness, not even inquiring after any honourable work whatever, but doing everything that is of a disgraceful character.

CHAPTER LXXVIII

After having brought against us charges of so serious a kind, he wishes to make it appear that, although he has others to adduce, he passes them by in silence. His words are as follows: "These charges I have to bring against them, and others of a similar nature, not to enumerate them one by one, and I affirm that they are in error, and that they act insolently towards God, in order to lead on wicked men by empty hopes, and to persuade them to despise better things, saying that if they refrain from them it will be better for them." In answer to which, it might be said that from the power which shows itself in those who are converted to Christianity, it is not at all the "wicked" who are won over to the Gospel, as the more simple class of persons, and, as many would term them, the "unpolished." For such individuals, through fear of the punishments that are threatened, which arouses and exhorts them to refrain from those actions which are followed by punishments, strive to yield themselves up to the Christian religion, being influenced by the power of the word to such a degree, that through fear of what are called in the word "everlasting punishments," they despise all the tortures which are devised against them among men,—even death itself, with countless other evils,—which no wise man would say is the act of persons of wicked mind. How can temperance and sober-mindedness, or benevolence and liberality, be practised by a man of wicked mind? Nay, even the fear of God cannot be felt by such an one, with respect to which, because it is useful to the many, the Gospel encourages those who are not yet able to choose that which ought to be chosen for its own sake, to select it as the greatest blessing, and one above all promise; for this principle cannot be implanted in him who prefers to live in wickedness.

CHAPTER LXXIX

But if in these matters any one were to imagine that it is superstition rather than wickedness which appears in the multitude of those who believe the word, and should charge our doctrine with making men superstitious, we shall answer him by saying that, as a certain legislator replied to the question of one who asked him whether he had enacted for his citizens the best laws, that he had not given them absolutely the best, but the best which they were capable of receiving; so it might be said by the Father of the Christian doctrine, I have given the best laws and instruction for the improvement of morals of which the many were capable, not threatening sinners with imaginary labours and chastisements, but with such as are real, and necessary to be applied for the correction of those who offer resistance, although they do not at all understand the object of him who inflicts the punishment, nor the effect of the labours. For the doctrine of punishment is both attended with utility, and is agreeable to truth, and is stated in obscure terms with advantage. Moreover, as for the most part it is not the wicked whom the ambassadors of Christianity gain over, neither do we insult God. For we speak regarding Him both what is true, and what appears to be clear to the multitude, but not so clear to them as it is to those few who investigate the truths of the Gospel in a philosophical manner.

CHAPTER LXXX

Seeing, however, that Celsus alleges that "Christians are won over by us through vain hopes," we thus reply to him when he finds fault with our doctrine of the blessed life, and of communion with God: "As for you, good sir, they also are won over by vain hopes who have accepted the doctrine of Pythagoras and Plato regarding the soul, that it is its nature to ascend to the vault of heaven, and in the super-celestial space to behold the sights which are seen by the blessed spectators above. According to you, O Celsus, they also who have accepted the

465

doctrine of the duration of the soul (after death), and who lead a life through which they become heroes, and make their abodes with the gods, are won over by vain hopes. Probably also they who are persuaded that the soul comes (into the body) from without, and that it will be withdrawn from the power of death, would be said by Celsus to be won over by empty hopes. Let him then come forth to the contest, no longer concealing the sect to which he belongs, but confessing himself to be an Epicurean, and let him meet the arguments, which are not lightly advanced among Greeks and Barbarians, regarding the immortality of the soul, or its duration (after death), or the immortality of the thinking principle; and let him prove that these are words which deceive with empty hopes those who give their assent to them; but that the adherents of his philosophical system are pure from empty hopes, and that they indeed lead to hopes of good, or— what is more in keeping with his opinions—give birth to no hope at all, on account of the immediate and complete destruction of the soul (after death). Unless, perhaps, Celsus and the Epicureans will deny that it is a vain hope which they entertain regarding *their* end,—pleasure,— which, according to them, is the supreme good, and which consists in the permanent health of the body, and the hope regarding it which is entertained by Epicurus.

CHAPTER LXXXI

And do not suppose that it is not in keeping with the Christian religion for me to have accepted, against Celsus, the opinions of those philosophers who have treated of the immortality or after-duration of the soul; for, holding certain views in common with them, we shall more conveniently establish our position, that the future life of blessedness shall be for those only who have accepted the religion which is according to Jesus, and that devotion towards the Creator of all things which is pure and sincere, and unmingled with any created thing whatever. And let him who likes show what "better things" we persuade men to despise, and let him compare the blessed end with God in Christ,—that is, the word, and the wisdom, and all virtue;— which, according to our view, shall be bestowed, by the gift of God, on those who have lived a pure and blameless life, and who have felt a single and undivided love for the God of all things, with that end which is to follow according to the teaching of each philosophic sect, whether it be Greek or Barbarian, or according to the professions of religious mysteries; and let him prove that the end which is predicted by any of the others is superior to that which we promise, and consequently that

that is true, and ours not befitting the gift of God, nor those who have lived a good life; or let him prove that these words were not spoken by the divine Spirit, who filled the souls of the holy prophets. And let him who likes show that those words which are acknowledged among all men to be human, are superior to those which are proved to be divine, and uttered by inspiration. And what are the "better" things from which we teach those who receive them that it would be better to abstain? For if it be not arrogant so to speak, it is self-evident that nothing can be denied which is better than to entrust oneself to the God of all, and yield oneself up to the doctrine which raises us above all created things, and brings us, through the animate and living word— which is also living wisdom and the Son of God—to God who is over all. However, as the third book of our answers to the treatise of Celsus has extended to a sufficient length, we shall here bring our present remarks to a close, and in what is to follow shall meet what Celsus has subsequently written.

BOOK IV

CHAPTER I

HAVING, in the three preceding books, fully stated what occurred to us by way of answer to the treatise of Celsus, we now, reverend Ambrosius, with prayer to God through Christ, offer this fourth book as a reply to what follows. And we pray that words may be given us, as it is written in the book of Jeremiah that the Lord said to the prophet: "Behold, I have put My words in thy mouth as fire. See, I have set thee this day over the nations, and over the kingdoms, to root out and to pull down, and to destroy, and to throw down, and to build and to plant." For we need words now which will root out of every wounded soul the reproaches uttered against the truth by this treatise of Celsus, or which proceed from opinions like his. And we need also thoughts which will pull down all edifices based on false opinions, and especially the edifice raised by Celsus in his work which resembles the building of those who said, "Come, let us build us a city, and a tower whose top shall reach to heaven." Yea, we even require a wisdom which will throw down all high things that rise against the knowledge of God, and especially that height of arrogance which Celsus displays against us. And in the next place, as we must not stop with rooting out and pulling down the hindrances which have just been mentioned, but must, in room of what has been rooted out, plant the plants of "God's husbandry;" and in place of what has been pulled down, rear up the building of God, and the temple of His glory,—we must for that reason pray also to the Lord, who bestowed the gifts named in the book of Jeremiah, that He may grant even to us words adapted both for building up the (temple) of Christ, and for planting the spiritual law, and the prophetic words referring to the same. And above all is it necessary to show, as against the assertions of Celsus which follow those he has already made, that the prophecies regarding Christ are true predictions. For, arraying himself at the same time against both parties—against the Jews on the one hand, who deny that the advent of Christ has taken place, but who expect it as future, and against Christians on the other, who acknowledge that Jesus is the Christ spoken of in prophecy—he makes the following statement:—

CHAPTER II

"But that certain Christians and (all) Jews should maintain, the former that there *has* already descended, the latter that there *will* descend, upon the earth a certain God, or Son of a God, who will make the inhabitants of the earth righteous, is a most shameless assertion, and one the refutation of which does not need many words." Now here he appears to pronounce correctly regarding not "certain" of the Jews, but *all* of them, that they imagine that there is a certain (God) who will descend upon the earth; and with regard to Christians, that *certain of them* say that He has already come down. For he means those who prove from the Jewish Scriptures that the advent of Christ has already taken place, and he seems to know that there are certain heretical sects which deny that Christ Jesus was predicted by the prophets. In the preceding pages, however, we have already discussed, to the best of our ability, the question of Christ having been the subject of prophecy, and therefore, to avoid tautology, we do not repeat much that might be advanced upon this head. Observe, now, that if he had wished with a kind of apparent force to subvert faith in the prophetic writings, either with regard to the future or past advent of Christ, he ought to have set forth the prophecies themselves which we Christians and Jews quote in our discussions with each other. For in this way he would have appeared to turn aside those who are carried away by the plausible character of the prophetic statements, as he regards it, from assenting to their truth, and from believing, on account of these prophecies, that Jesus is the Christ; whereas now, being unable to answer the prophecies relating to Christ, or else not knowing at all what are the prophecies relating to Him, he brings forward no prophetic declaration, although there are countless numbers which refer to Christ; but he thinks that he prefers an accusation against the prophetic Scriptures, while he does not even state what he himself would call their "plausible character!" He is not, however, aware that it is not at all the Jews who say that Christ will descend as a God, or the Son of a God, as we have shown in the foregoing pages. And when he asserts that "he is said by us to have already come, but by the Jews that his advent as Messiah is still future," he appears by the very charge to censure our statement as one that is most shameless, and which needs no lengthened refutation.

CHAPTER III

And he continues: "What is the meaning of such a descent upon the part of God?" not observing that, according to our teaching, the meaning of the descent is pre-eminently to convert what are called in the Gospel the lost "sheep of the house of Israel;" and secondly, to take away from them, on account of their disobedience, what is called the "kingdom of God," and to give to other husbandmen than the ancient Jews, viz. to the Christians, who will render to God the fruits of His kingdom in due season (each action being a "fruit of the kingdom"). We shall therefore, out of a greater number, select a few remarks by way of answer to the question of Celsus, when he says, "What is the meaning of such a descent upon the part of God?" And Celsus here returns to himself an answer which would have been given neither by Jews nor by us, when he asks, "Was it in order to learn what goes on amongst men?" For not one of us asserts that it was in order to learn what goes on amongst men that Christ entered into this life. Immediately after, however, as if some would reply that it *was* "in order to learn what goes on among men," he makes this objection to his own statement: "Does he not know all things?" Then, as if we were to answer that He *does* know all things, he raises a new question, saying, "Then he does know, but does not make (men) better, nor is it possible for him by means of his divine power to make (men) better." Now all this on his part is silly talk; for God, by means of His word, which is continually passing from generation to generation into holy souls, and constituting them friends of God and prophets, *does* improve those who listen to His words; and by the coming of Christ He improves, through the doctrine of Christianity, not those who are unwilling, but those who have chosen the better life, and that which is pleasing to God. I do not know, moreover, what kind of improvement Celsus wished to take place when he raised the objection, asking, "Is it then not possible for him, by means of his divine power, to make (men) better, unless he send some one for that special purpose?" Would he then have the improvement to take place by God's filling the minds of men with new ideas, removing at once the (inherent) wickedness, and implanting virtue (in its stead)? Another person now would inquire whether this was not inconsistent or impossible in the very nature of things; we, however, would say, "Grant it to be so, and let it be possible." Where, then, is our free will? and what credit is there in assenting to the truth? or how is the rejection of what is false praiseworthy? But even if it were once granted that such a course was not only possible, but could be accomplished with propriety (by God), why would not one rather inquire (asking a question like that of Celsus) why it was not possible for God, by means of His divine power, to create men who needed no improvement, but who were of themselves virtuous and perfect, evil being altogether non-existent? These questions may perplex ignorant and foolish individuals, but not him who sees into the nature of things; for if you take away the spontaneity of virtue, you destroy its essence. But it would need an entire treatise to discuss these matters; and on this subject the Greeks have expressed themselves at great length in their works on providence. They truly would not say what Celsus has expressed in words, that "God knows (all things) indeed, but does not make (men) better, nor is able to do so by His divine power." We ourselves have spoken in many parts of our writings on these points to the best of our ability, and the Holy Scriptures have established the same to those who are able to understand them.

CHAPTER IV

The argument which Celsus employs against us and the Jews will be turned against himself thus: My good sir, does the God who is over all things know what takes place among men, or does He not know? Now if you admit the existence of a God and of providence, as your treatise indicates, He must of necessity know. And if He does know, why does He not make (men) better? Is it obligatory, then, on *us* to defend God's procedure in not making men better, although He knows their state, but not equally binding on *you*, who do not distinctly show by your treatise that you are an Epicurean, but pretend to recognise a providence, to explain why God, although knowing all that takes place among men, does not make them better, nor by divine power liberate all men from evil? We are not ashamed, however, to say that God is constantly sending (instructors) in order to make men better; for there are to be found amongst men reasons given by God which exhort them to enter on a better life. But there are many diversities amongst those who serve God, and they are few in number who are perfect and pure ambassadors of the truth, and who produce a complete reformation, as did Moses and the prophets. But above all these, great was the reformation effected by Jesus, who desired to heal not only those who lived in one corner of the world, but as far as in Him lay, men in every country, for He came as the Saviour of *all* men.

CHAPTER V

The illustrious Celsus, taking occasion I know not from what, next raises an additional objection against us, as if we asserted that "God Himself will come down to men." He imagines also that it follows from this, that "He has left His own abode;" for he does not know the power of God, and that "the Spirit of the Lord filleth the world, and that which upholdeth all things hath knowledge of the voice." Nor is he able to understand the words, "Do I not fill heaven and earth? saith the LORD." Nor does he see that, according to the doctrine of Christianity, we all "in Him live, and move, and have our being," as Paul also taught in his address to the Athenians; and therefore, although the God of the universe should through His own power descend with Jesus into the life of men, and although the Word which was in the beginning with God, which is also God Himself, should come to us, He does not give His place or vacate His own seat, so that one place should be empty of Him, and another which did not formerly contain Him be filled. But the power and divinity of God comes through him whom God chooses, and resides in him in whom it finds a place, not changing its situation, nor leaving its own place empty and filling another: for, in speaking of His quitting one place and occupying another, we do not mean such expressions to be taken *topically*; but we say that the soul of the bad man, and of him who is overwhelmed in wickedness, is abandoned by God, while we mean that the soul of him who wishes to live virtuously, or of him who is making progress (in a virtuous life), or who is already living conformably thereto, is filled with or becomes a partaker of the Divine Spirit. It is not necessary, then, for the descent of Christ, or for the coming of God to men, that He should abandon a greater seat, and that things on earth should be changed, as Celsus imagines when he says, "If you were to change a single one, even the least, of things on earth, all things would be overturned and disappear." And if we must speak of a change in any one by the appearing of the power of God, and by the entrance of the word among men, we shall not be reluctant to speak of changing from a wicked to a virtuous, from a dissolute to a temperate, and from a superstitious to a religious life, the person who has allowed the word of God to find entrance into his soul.

CHAPTER VI

But if you will have us to meet the most ridiculous among the charges of Celsus, listen to him when he says: "Now God, being unknown amongst men, and deeming himself on that account to have less than his due, would desire to make himself known, and to make trial both of those who believe upon him and of those who do not, like those of mankind who have recently come into the possession of riches, and who make a display of their wealth; and thus they testify to an excessive but very mortal ambition on the part of God." We answer, then, that God, not being known by wicked men, would desire to make Himself known, not because He thinks that He meets with less than His due, but because the knowledge of Him will free the possessor from unhappiness. Nay, not even with the desire to try those who do or who do not believe upon Him, does He, by His unspeakable and divine power, Himself take up His abode in certain individuals, or send His Christ; but He does this in order to liberate from all their wretchedness those who do believe upon Him, and who accept His divinity, and that those who do *not* believe may no longer have this as a ground of excuse, viz., that their unbelief is the consequence of their not having heard the word of instruction. What argument, then, proves that it follows from our views that God, according to our representations, is "like those of mankind who have recently come into the possession of riches, and who make a display of their wealth?" For God makes no display towards us, from a desire that we should understand and consider His pre-eminence; but desiring that the blessedness which results from His being known by us should be implanted in our souls, He brings it to pass through Christ, and His ever-indwelling word, that we come to an intimate fellowship with Him. No mortal ambition, then, does the Christian doctrine testify as existing on the part of God.

CHAPTER VII

I do not know how it is, that after the foolish remarks which he has made upon the subject which we have just been discussing, he should add the following, that "God does not desire to make himself known for his own sake, but because he wishes to bestow upon us the knowledge of himself for the sake of our salvation, in order that those who accept it may become virtuous and be saved, while those who do not accept may be shown to be wicked and be punished." And yet, after making such a statement, he raises a new objection, saying: "After so long a period of time, then, did God now bethink himself of making men live righteous lives, but neglect to do so before?" To which we answer, that there never was a time when God did not wish to make men live righteous lives; but He continually evinced His care for the improvement of the rational animal, by affording him occasions for the exercise of virtue. For in every generation the wisdom of God, passing into those souls which it ascertains to be holy, converts them into friends and prophets of God. And there may be found in the sacred book (the names of) those who in each generation were holy, and were recipients of the Divine Spirit, and who strove to convert their contemporaries so far as in their power.

CHAPTER VIII

And it is not matter of surprise that in certain generations there have existed prophets who, in the reception of divine influence, surpassed, by means of their stronger and more powerful (religious) life, other prophets who were their contemporaries, and others also who lived before and after them. And so it is not at all wonderful that there should also have been a time when something of surpassing excellence took up its abode among the human race, and which was distinguished above all that preceded or even that followed. But there is an element of profound mystery in the account of these things, and one which is incapable of being received by the popular understanding. And in order that these difficulties should be made to disappear, and that the objections raised against the advent of Christ should be answered—viz., that, "after so long a period of time, then, did God now bethink himself of making men live righteous lives, but neglect to do so before?"—it is necessary to touch upon the narrative of the divisions (of the nations), and to make it evident why it was, that "when the Most High divided the nations, when He separated the sons of Adam, He set the bounds of the nations according to the number of the angels of God, and the portion of the Lord was His people Jacob, Israel the cord of His inheritance;" and it will be necessary to state the reason why the birth of each man took place within each particular boundary, under him who obtained the boundary by lot, and how it rightly happened that "the portion of the Lord was His people Jacob, and Israel the cord of His inheritance," and why formerly the portion of the Lord was His people Jacob, and Israel the cord of His inheritance. But with respect to those who come after, it is said to the Saviour by the Father, "Ask of Me, and I will give Thee the heathen for Thine inheritance, and the uttermost parts of the earth for Thy possession." For there are certain connected and related reasons, bearing upon the different treatment of human souls, which are difficult to state and to investigate.

CHAPTER IX

There came, then, although Celsus may not wish to admit it, after the numerous prophets who were the reformers of that well-known Israel, the Christ, the Reformer of the whole world, who did not need to employ against men whips, and chains, and tortures, as was the case under the former economy. For when the sower went forth to sow, the doctrine sufficed to sow the word everywhere. But if there is a time coming which will necessarily circumscribe the duration of the world, by reason of its having had a beginning, and if there is to be an end to the world, and after the end a just judgment of all things, it will be incumbent on him who treats the declarations of the Gospels philosophically, to establish these doctrines by arguments of all kinds, not only derived directly from the sacred Scriptures, but also by inferences deducible from them; while the more numerous and simpler class of believers, and those who are unable to comprehend the many varied aspects of the divine wisdom, must entrust themselves to God, and to the Saviour of our race, and be contented with His "ipse dixit," instead of this or any other demonstration whatever.

CHAPTER X

In the next place, Celsus, as is his custom, having neither proved nor established anything, proceeds to say, as if we talked of God in a manner that was neither holy nor pious, that "it is perfectly manifest that they babble about God in a way that is neither holy nor reverential;" and he imagines that we do these things to excite the astonishment of the ignorant, and that we do not speak the truth regarding the necessity of punishments for those who have sinned. And accordingly he likens us to those who "in the Bacchic mysteries introduce phantoms and objects of terror." With respect to the mysteries of Bacchus, whether there is any trustworthy account of them, or none that is such, let the Greeks tell, and let Celsus and his boon-companions listen. But we defend our own procedure, when we say that our object is to reform the human race, either by the threats of punishments which we are persuaded are necessary for the whole world, and which perhaps are not without use to those who are to endure them; or by the promises made to those who have lived virtuous lives, and in which are contained the statements regarding the blessed termination which is to be found in the kingdom of God, reserved for those who are worthy of becoming His subjects.

CHAPTER XI

After this, being desirous to show that it is nothing either wonderful or new which we state regarding floods or conflagrations, but that, from misunderstanding the accounts of these things which are current among Greeks or barbarous nations, we have accorded our belief to our own Scriptures when treating of them, he writes as follows: "The belief has spread among them, from a misunderstanding of the accounts of these occurrences, that after lengthened cycles of time, and the returns and conjunctions of planets, conflagrations and floods are wont to happen, and because after the last flood, which took place in the time of Deucalion, the lapse of time, agreeably to the vicissitude of all things, requires a conflagration and this made them give utterance to the erroneous opinion that God will descend, bringing fire like a torturer." Now in answer to this we say, that I do not understand how Celsus, who has read a great deal, and who shows that he has perused many histories, had not his attention arrested by the antiquity of Moses, who is related by certain Greek historians to have lived about the time of Inachus the son of Phoroneus, and is acknowledged by the Egyptians to be a man of great antiquity, as well as by those who have studied the history of the Phoenicians. And any one who likes may peruse the two books of Flavius Josephus on the antiquities of the Jews, in order that he may see in what way Moses was more ancient than those who asserted that floods and conflagrations take place in the world after long intervals of time; which statement Celsus alleges the Jews and Christians to have misunderstood, and, not comprehending what was said about a conflagration, to have declared that "God will descend, bringing fire like a torturer."

CHAPTER XII

Whether, then, there are cycles of time, and floods, or conflagrations which occur periodically or not, and whether the Scripture is aware of this, not only in many passages, but especially where Solomon says, "What is the thing which hath been? Even that which shall be. And what is the thing which hath been done? Even that which shall be done," etc., etc., belongs not to the present occasion to discuss. For it is sufficient only to observe, that Moses and certain of the prophets, being men of very great antiquity, did not receive from others the statements relating to the (future) conflagration of the world; but, on the contrary (if we must attend to the matter of time), others rather misunderstanding them, and not inquiring accurately into their statements, invented the fiction of the same events recurring at certain intervals, and differing neither in their essential nor accidental qualities. But we do not refer either the deluge or the conflagration to cycles and planetary periods; but the cause of them we declare to be the extensive prevalence of wickedness, and its (consequent) removal by a deluge or a conflagration. And if the voices of the prophets say that God "comes down," who has said, "Do I not fill heaven and earth? saith the LORD," the term is used in a figurative sense. For God "comes down" from His own height and greatness when He arranges the affairs of men, and

476

especially those of the wicked. And as custom leads men to say that teachers "condescend" to children, and wise men to those youths who have just betaken themselves to philosophy, not by "descending" in a *bodily* manner; so, if God is said anywhere in the holy Scriptures to "come down," it is understood as spoken in conformity with the usage which so employs the word, and, in like manner also with the expression "go up."

CHAPTER XIII

But as it is in mockery that Celsus says we speak of "God coming down like a torturer bearing fire," and thus compels us unseasonably to investigate words of deeper meaning, we shall make a few remarks, sufficient to enable our hearers to form an idea of the defence which disposes of the ridicule of Celsus against us, and then we shall turn to what follows. The divine word says that our God is "a consuming fire," and that "He draws rivers of fire before Him;" nay, that He even entereth in as "a refiner's fire, and as a fuller's herb," to purify His own people. But when He is said to be a "consuming fire," we inquire what are the things which are appropriate to be consumed by God. And we assert that they are wickedness, and the works which result from it, and which, being figuratively called "wood, hay, stubble," God consumes as a fire. The wicked man, accordingly, is said to build up on the previously-laid foundation of reason, "wood, and hay, and stubble." If, then, any one can show that these words were differently understood by the writer, and can prove that the wicked man *literally* builds up "wood, or hay, or stubble," it is evident that the fire must be understood to be material, and an object of sense. But if, on the contrary, the works of the wicked man are spoken of *figuratively* under the names of "wood, or hay, or stubble," why does it not at once occur (to inquire) in what sense the word "fire" is to be taken, so that "wood" of such a kind should be consumed? for (the Scripture) says: "The fire will try each man's work of what sort it is. If any man's work abide which he hath built thereupon, he shall receive a reward. If any man's work be burned, he shall suffer loss." But what work can be spoken of in these words as being "burned," save all that results from wickedness? Therefore our God is a "consuming fire" in the sense in which we have taken the word; and thus He enters in as a "refiner's fire," to refine the rational nature, which has been filled with the lead of wickedness, and to free it from the other impure materials, which adulterate the natural gold or silver, so to speak, of the soul. And, in like manner, "rivers of fire" are said to be before God, who will thoroughly cleanse away the evil which is intermingled throughout the whole soul. But these remarks are sufficient in answer to the assertion, "that thus they were made to give expression to the erroneous opinion that God will come down bearing fire like a torturer."

CHAPTER XIV

But let us look at what Celsus next with great ostentation announces in the following fashion: "And again," he says, "let us resume the subject from the beginning, with a larger array of proofs. And I make no new statement, but say what has been long settled. God is good, and beautiful, and blessed, and that in the best and most beautiful degree. But if he come down among men, he must undergo a change, and a change from good to evil, from virtue to vice, from happiness to misery, and from best to worst. Who, then, would make choice of such a change? It is the nature of a mortal, indeed, to undergo change and remoulding, but of an immortal to remain the same and unaltered. God, then, could not admit of such a change." Now it appears to me that the fitting answer has been returned to these objections, when I have related what is called in Scripture the "condescension" of God to human affairs; for which purpose He did not need to undergo a transformation, as Celsus thinks we assert, nor a change from good to evil, nor from virtue to vice, nor from happiness to misery, nor from best to worst. For, continuing unchangeable in His essence, He condescends to human affairs by the economy of His providence. We show, accordingly, that the holy Scriptures represent God as unchangeable, both by such words as "Thou art the same," and" I change not;" whereas the gods of Epicurus, being composed of atoms, and, so far as their structure is concerned, capable of dissolution, endeavour to throw off the atoms which contain the elements of destruction. Nay, even the god of the Stoics, as being corporeal, at one time has his whole essence composed of the guiding principle when the conflagration (of the world) takes place; and at another, when a rearrangement of things occurs, he again becomes partly material. For even the Stoics were unable distinctly to comprehend the natural idea of God, as of a being altogether incorruptible and simple, and uncompounded and indivisible.

CHAPTER XV

And with respect to His having descended among men, He was "previously in the form of God;" and through benevolence, divested

Himself (of His glory), that He might be capable of being received by men. But He did not, I imagine, undergo any change from "good to evil," for "He did no *sin;*" nor from "virtue to vice," for "He knew no *sin.*" Nor did He pass from "happiness to misery," but He humbled Himself, and nevertheless was blessed, even when His humiliation was undergone in order to benefit our race. Nor was there any change in Him from "best to worst," for how can goodness and benevolence be of "the worst?" Is it befitting to say of the physician, who looks on dreadful sights and handles unsightly objects in order to cure the sufferers, that he passes from "good to evil," or from "virtue to vice," or from "happiness to misery?" And yet the physician, in looking on dreadful sights and handling unsightly objects, does not wholly escape the possibility of being involved in the same fate. But He who heals the wounds of our souls, through the word of God that is in Him, is Himself incapable of admitting any wickedness. But if the immortal God—the Word—by assuming a mortal body and a human soul, appears to Celsus to undergo a change and transformation, let him learn that the Word, still remaining essentially the Word, suffers none of those things which are suffered by the body or the soul; but, condescending occasionally to (the weakness of) him who is unable to look upon the splendours and brilliancy of Deity, He becomes as it were flesh, speaking with a literal voice, until he who has received Him in such a form is able, through being elevated in some slight degree by the teaching of the Word, to gaze upon what is, so to speak, His real and pre-eminent appearance.

CHAPTER XVI

For there are different appearances, as it were, of the Word, according as He shows Himself to each one of those who come to His doctrine; and this in a manner corresponding to the condition of him who is just becoming a disciple, or of him who has made a little progress, or of him who has advanced further, or of him who has already *nearly* attained to virtue, or who has even *already* attained it. And hence it is not the case, as Celsus and those like him would have it, that our God was transformed, and ascending the lofty mountain, showed that His real appearance was something different, and far more excellent than what those who remained below, and were unable to follow Him on high, beheld. For those below did not possess eyes capable of seeing the transformation of the Word into His glorious and more divine condition. But with difficulty were they able to receive Him as He was; so that it might be said of Him by those who were unable to behold His more excellent nature: "We saw Him, and He had no form nor comeliness; but His form was mean, and inferior to that of the sons of men." And let these remarks be an answer to the suppositions of Celsus, who does not understand the changes or transformations of Jesus, as related in the histories, nor His mortal and immortal nature.

CHAPTER XVII

But will not those narratives, especially when they are understood in their proper sense, appear far more worthy of respect than the story that Dionysus was deceived by the Titans, and expelled from the throne of Jupiter, and torn in pieces by them, and his remains being afterwards put together again, he returned as it were once more to life, and ascended to heaven? Or are the Greeks at liberty to refer such stories to the doctrine of the soul, and to interpret them figuratively, while the door of a consistent explanation, and one everywhere in accord and harmony with the writings of the Divine Spirit, who had His abode in pure souls, is closed against *us*? Celsus, then, is altogether ignorant of the purpose of our writings, and it is therefore upon his own acceptation of them that he casts discredit, and not upon their real meaning; whereas, if he had reflected on what is appropriate to a soul which is to enjoy an everlasting life, and on the opinion which we are to form of its essence and principles, he would not so have ridiculed the entrance of the immortal into a mortal body, which took place not according to the metempsychosis of Plato, but agreeably to another and higher view of things. And he would have observed one "descent," distinguished by its great benevolence, undertaken to convert (as the Scripture mystically terms them) the "lost sheep of the house of Israel," which had strayed down from the mountains, and to which the Shepherd is said in certain parables to have gone down, leaving on the mountains those "which had not strayed."

CHAPTER XVIII

But Celsus, lingering over matters which he does not understand, leads us to be guilty of tautology, as we do not wish even in appearance to leave any one of his objections unexamined. He proceeds, accordingly, as follows: "God either really changes himself, as these assert, into a mortal body, and the impossibility of that has been already declared; or else he does *not* undergo a change, but only causes the beholders to imagine so, and thus deceives them, and is guilty of falsehood. Now deceit and falsehood are nothing but evils, and would only be employed as a medicine, either in the case of sick and lunatic friends, with a view to their cure, or in that of enemies when one is taking measures to escape danger. But no sick man or lunatic is a friend of God, nor does God fear any one to such a degree as to shun danger by leading him into error." Now the answer to these statements might have respect partly to the nature of the Divine Word, who is God, and partly to the soul of Jesus. As respects the nature of the Word, in the same way as the quality of the food changes in the nurse into milk with reference to the nature of the child, or is arranged by the physician with a view to the good of his health in the case of a sick man or (is specially) prepared for a stronger man, because he possesses greater vigour, so does God appropriately change, in the case of each individual, the power of the Word to which belongs the natural property of nourishing the human soul. And to one is given, as the Scripture terms it, "the sincere milk of the word;" and to another, who is weaker, as it were, "herbs;" and to another who is full-grown, "strong meat." And the Word does not, I imagine, prove false to His own nature, in contributing nourishment to each one, according as he is capable of receiving Him. Nor does He mislead or prove false. But if one were to take the change as referring to the soul of Jesus after it had entered the body, we would inquire in what sense the term "change" is used. For if it be meant to apply to its essence, such a supposition is inadmissible, not only in relation to the soul of Jesus, but also to the rational soul of any other being. And if it be alleged that it suffers anything from the body when united with it, or from the place to which it has come, then what inconvenience can happen to the Word who, in great benevolence, brought down a Saviour to the human race?—seeing none of those who formerly professed to effect a cure could accomplish so much as that soul showed *it* could do, by what it performed, even by voluntarily descending to the level of human destinies for the benefit of our race. And the Divine Word, well knowing this, speaks to that effect in many passages of Scripture, although it is sufficient at present to quote one testimony of Paul to the following effect: "Let this mind be in you which was also in Christ Jesus; who, being in the form of God, thought it not robbery to be equal with God, but made Himself of no reputation, and took upon Him the form of a servant, and was made in the likeness of men; and being found in fashion as a man, He humbled Himself, and became obedient unto death, even the death of the cross. Wherefore God also hath highly exalted Him, and given Him a name which is above every name."

CHAPTER XIX

Others, then, may concede to Celsus that God does not undergo a change, but leads the spectators to imagine that He does; whereas we who are persuaded that the advent of Jesus among men was no mere appearance, but a real manifestation, are not affected by this charge of Celsus. We nevertheless will attempt a reply, because you assert, Celsus, do you not, that it is sometimes allowable to employ deceit and falsehood by way, as it were, of medicine? Where, then, is the absurdity, if such a saving result were to be accomplished, that some such events should have taken place? For certain words, when savouring of falsehood, produce upon such characters a corrective effect (like the similar declarations of physicians to their patients), rather than when spoken in the spirit of truth. This, however, must be our defence against other opponents. For there is no absurdity in Him who healed sick friends, healing the dear human race by means of such remedies as He would not employ preferentially, but only according to circumstances. The human race, moreover, when in a state of mental alienation, had to be cured by methods which the Word saw would aid in bringing back those so afflicted to a sound state of mind. But Celsus says also, that "one acts thus towards enemies when taking measures to escape danger. But God does not fear any one, so as to escape danger by leading into error those who conspire against him." Now it is altogether unnecessary and absurd to answer a charge which is advanced by no one against our Saviour. And we have already replied, when answering other charges, to the statement that "no one who is either in a state of sickness or mental alienation is a friend of God." For the answer is, that such arrangements have been made, not for the sake of those who, being already friends, afterwards fell sick or became afflicted with mental disease, but in order that those who were still enemies through sickness of the soul, and alienation of the natural reason, might become the friends of God. For it is distinctly stated that Jesus endured all things on behalf of sinners, that He might free them from sin, and convert them to righteousness.

CHAPTER XX

In the next place, as he represents the Jews accounting in a way peculiar to themselves for their belief that the advent of Christ among them is still in the future, and the Christians as maintaining in *their* way that the coming of the Son of God into the life of men has already taken place, let us, as far as we can, briefly consider these points. According to Celsus, the Jews say that "(human) life, being filled with all wickedness, needed one sent from God, that the wicked might be punished, and all things purified in a manner analogous to the first deluge which happened." And as the Christians are said to make statements additional to this, it is evident that he alleges that they admit these. Now, where is the absurdity in the coming of one who is, on account of the prevailing flood of wickedness, to purify the world, and to treat every one according to his deserts? For it is not in keeping with the character of God that the diffusion of wickedness should not cease, and all things be renewed. The Greeks, moreover, know of the earth's being purified at certain times by a deluge or a fire, as Plato, too, says somewhere to this effect: "And when the gods overwhelm the earth, purifying it with water, some of them on the mountains," etc., etc. Must it be said, then, that if the Greeks make such assertions, they are to be deemed worthy of respect and consideration, but that if we too maintain certain of these views, which are quoted with approval by the Greeks, they cease to be honourable? And yet they who care to attend to the connection and truth of all our records, will endeavour to establish not only the antiquity of the writers, but the venerable nature of their writings, and the consistency of their several parts.

CHAPTER XXI

But I do not understand how he can imagine the overturning of the tower (of Babel) to have happened with a similar object to that of the deluge, which effected a purification of the earth, according to the accounts both of Jews and Christians. For, in order that the narrative contained in Genesis respecting the tower may be held to convey no secret meaning, but, as Celsus supposes, may be taken as true to the letter, the event does not on such a view appear to have taken place for the purpose of purifying the earth; unless, indeed, he imagines that the so-called confusion of tongues is such a purificatory process. But on this point, he who has the opportunity will treat more seasonably when his object is to show not only what is the meaning of the narrative in its historical connection, but what metaphorical meaning may be deduced from it. Seeing that he imagines, however, that Moses, who wrote the account of the tower, and the confusion of tongues, has perverted the story of the sons of Aloeus, and referred it to the tower, we must remark that I do not think any one prior to the time of Homer has mentioned the sons of Aloeus, while I am persuaded that what is related about the tower has been recorded by Moses as being much

483

older not only than Homer, but even than the invention of letters among the Greeks. Who, then, are the perverters of each other's narratives? Whether do they who relate the story of the Aloadae pervert the history of the time, or he who wrote the account of the tower and the confusion of tongues the story of the Aloadae? Now to impartial hearers Moses appears to be more ancient than Homer. The destruction by fire, moreover, of Sodom and Gomorrah on account of their sins, related by Moses in Genesis, is compared by Celsus to the story of Phaethon,—all these statements of his resulting from one blunder, viz., his not attending to the (greater) antiquity of Moses. For they who relate the story of Phaethon seem to be younger even than Homer, who, again, is much younger than Moses. We do not deny, then, that the purificatory fire and the destruction of the world took place in order that evil might be swept away, and all things be renewed; for we assert that we have learned these things from the sacred books of the prophets. But since, as we have said in the preceding pages, the prophets, in uttering many predictions regarding future events, show that they have spoken the truth concerning many things that are past, and thus give evidence of the indwelling of the Divine Spirit, it is manifest that, with respect to things still future, we should repose faith in them, or rather in the Divine Spirit that is in them.

CHAPTER XXII

But, according to Celsus, "the Christians, making certain additional statements to those of the Jews, assert that the Son of God has been already sent on account of the sins of the Jews; and that the Jews having chastised Jesus, and given him gall to drink, have brought upon themselves the divine wrath." And any one who likes may convict this statement of falsehood, if it be not the case that the whole Jewish nation was overthrown within one single generation after Jesus had undergone these sufferings at their hands. For forty and two years, I think, after the date of the crucifixion of Jesus, did the destruction of Jerusalem take place. Now it has never been recorded, since the Jewish nation began to exist, that they have been expelled for so long a period from their venerable temple-worship and service, and enslaved by more powerful nations; for if at any time they appeared to be abandoned because of their sins, they were notwithstanding visited (by God), and returned to their own country, and recovered their possessions, and performed unhindered the observances of their law. One fact, then, which proves that Jesus was something divine and sacred, is this, that Jews should have suffered on His account now for a lengthened time calamities of such severity. And we say with confidence that they will never be restored to their former condition. For they committed a crime of the most unhallowed kind, in conspiring against the Saviour of the human race in that city where they offered up to God a worship containing the symbols of mighty mysteries. It accordingly behoved that city where Jesus underwent these sufferings to perish utterly, and the Jewish nation to be overthrown, and the invitation to happiness offered them by God to pass to others,—the Christians, I mean, to whom has come the doctrine of a pure and holy worship, and who have obtained new laws, in harmony with the established constitution in all countries; seeing those which were formerly imposed, as on a single nation which was ruled by princes of its own race and of similar manners, could not now be observed in all their entireness.

CHAPTER XXIII

In the next place, ridiculing after his usual style the race of Jews and Christians, he compares them all "to a flight of bats or to a swarm of ants issuing out of their nest, or to frogs holding council in a marsh, or to worms crawling together in the corner of a dunghill, and quarrelling with one another as to which of them were the greater sinners, and asserting that God shows and announces to us all things beforehand; and that, abandoning the whole world, and the regions of heaven, and this great earth, he becomes a citizen among us alone, and to us alone makes his intimations, and does not cease sending and inquiring, in what way we may be associated with him for ever." And in his fictitious representation, he compares us to "worms which assert that there is a God, and that immediately after him, we who are made by him are altogether like unto God, and that all things have been made subject to us,—earth, and water, and air, and stars,—and that all things exist for our sake, and are ordained to be subject to us." And, according to his representation, the worms—that is, we ourselves—say that "now, since certain amongst us commit sin, God will come or will send his Son to consume the wicked with fire, that the rest of us may have eternal life with him." And to all this he subjoins the remark, that "such wranglings would be more endurable amongst worms and frogs than betwixt Jews and Christians."

CHAPTER XXIV

In reply to these, we ask of those who accept such aspersions as are scattered against us, Do you regard all men as a collection of bats, or as frogs, or as worms, in consequence of the pre-eminence of God or do you not include the rest of mankind in this proposed comparison, but on account of their possession of reason, and of the established laws, treat *them* as men, while you hold cheap *Christians* and *Jews*, because their opinions are distasteful to you, and compare them to the animals above mentioned? And whatever answer you may return to our question, we shall reply by endeavouring to show that such assertions are most unbecoming, whether spoken of all men in general, or of us in particular. For, let it be supposed that you say justly that all men, as compared with God, are (rightly) likened to these worthless animals, since their littleness is not at all to be compared with the superiority of God, what then do you mean by littleness? Answer me, good sirs. If you refer to littleness of body, know that superiority and inferiority, if truth is to be judge, are not determined by a bodily standard. For, on such a view, vultures and elephants would be superior to us men; for they are larger, and stronger, and longer-lived than we. But no sensible person would maintain that these irrational creatures are superior to rational beings, merely on account of their bodies: for the possession of reason raises a rational being to a vast superiority over all irrational creatures. Even the race of virtuous and blessed beings would admit this, whether they are, as ye say, good demons, or, as we are accustomed to call them, the angels of God, or any other natures whatever superior to that of man, since the rational faculty within them has been made perfect, and endowed with all virtuous qualities.

CHAPTER XXV

But if you depreciate the littleness of man, not on account of his body, but of his soul, regarding it as inferior to that of other rational beings, and especially of those who are virtuous; and inferior, because evil dwells in it,—why should those among Christians who are wicked, and those among the Jews who lead sinful lives, be termed a collection of bats, or ants, or worms, or frogs, rather than those individuals among other nations who are guilty of wickedness?—seeing, in this respect, any individual whatever, especially if carried away by the tide of evil, is, in comparison with the rest of mankind, a bat, and worm, and frog, and ant. And although a man may be an orator like Demosthenes, yet, if stained with wickedness like his, and guilty of deeds proceeding, like his, from a wicked nature; or an Antiphon, who was also considered to be indeed an orator, yet who annihilated the doctrine of providence in his writings, which were entitled *Concerning Truth*, like that discourse of Celsus,—such individuals are notwithstanding worms, rolling in a corner of the dung-heap of stupidity and ignorance. Indeed, whatever be the nature of the rational faculty, it could not reasonably be compared to a worm, because it possesses capabilities of virtue. For these adumbrations towards virtue do not allow of those who possess the power of acquiring it, and who are incapable of wholly losing its seeds, to be likened to a worm. It appears, therefore, that neither can men in general be deemed worms in comparison with God. For reason, having its beginning in the reason of God, cannot allow of the rational animal being considered wholly alien from Deity. Nor can those among Christians and Jews who are wicked, and who, in truth, are neither Christians nor Jews, be compared, more than other wicked men, to worms rolling in a corner of a dunghill. And if the nature of reason will not permit of such comparisons, it is manifest that we must not calumniate human nature, which has been formed for virtue, even if it should sin through ignorance, nor liken it to animals of the kind described.

CHAPTER XXVI

But if it is on account of those opinions of the Christians and Jews which displease Celsus (and which he does not at all appear to understand) that they are to be regarded as worms and ants, and the rest of mankind as different, let us examine the acknowledged opinions of Christians and Jews, and compare them with those of the rest of mankind, and see whether it will not appear to those who have once admitted that certain men are worms and ants, that *they* are the worms and ants and frogs who have fallen away from sound views of God, and, under a vain appearance of piety, worship either irrational animals, or images, or other objects, the works of men's hands; whereas, from the beauty of such, they ought to admire the Maker of them, and worship Him: while those are indeed men, and more honourable than men (if there be anything that is so), who, in obedience to their reason, are able to ascend from stocks and stones, nay, even from what is reckoned the most precious of all matter—silver and gold; and who ascend up also from the beautiful things in the world to the Maker of all, and entrust themselves to Him who alone is able to satisfy all existing things, and to overlook the thoughts of all, and to hear the prayers of all; who send up their prayers to Him, and do all things as in the presence of Him who beholds everything, and who are careful, as in the presence of the Hearer of all things, to say nothing which might not with propriety be reported to God. Will not such piety as this— which can be overcome neither by labours, nor by the dangers of death, nor by logical plausibilities—be of no avail in preventing those who have obtained it from being any longer compared to worms, even if they had been so represented before their assumption of a piety so remarkable? Will they who subdue that fierce longing for sexual pleasures which has reduced the souls of many to a weak and feeble condition, and who subdue it because they are persuaded that they cannot otherwise have communion with God, unless they ascend to Him through the exercise of temperance, appear to you to be the brothers of worms, and relatives of ants, and to bear a likeness to frogs? What! is the brilliant quality of justice, which keeps inviolate the rights common to our neighbour, and our kindred, and which observes fairness, and benevolence, and goodness, of no avail in saving him who practises it from being termed a bird of the night? And are not they who wallow in dissoluteness, as do the majority of mankind, and they who associate promiscuously with common harlots, and who teach that such practices are not wholly contrary to propriety, worms who roll in mire?—especially when they are compared with those who have been taught not to take the "members of Christ," and the body inhabited by the Word, and make them the "members of a harlot;" and who have already learned that the body of the rational being, as consecrated to the God of all things, is the temple of the God whom they worship, becoming such from the pure conceptions which they entertain of the Creator, and who also, being careful not to corrupt the temple of God by unlawful pleasure; practise temperance as constituting piety towards God!

CHAPTER XXVII

And I have not yet spoken of the other evils which prevail amongst men, from which even those who have the appearance of philosophers are not speedily freed, for in philosophy there are many pretenders. Nor do I say anything on the point that many such evils are found to exist among those who are neither Jews nor Christians. Of a truth, such evil practices do not at all prevail among *Christians*, if you properly examine what constitutes a Christian. Or, if any persons of that kind should be discovered, they are at least not to be found among those who frequent the assemblies, and come to the public prayers, without their being excluded from them, unless it should happen, and that rarely, that some one individual of such a character escapes notice in the crowd. We, then, are not worms who assemble together; who take our stand against the Jews on those Scriptures which they believe to be divine, and who show that He who was spoken of in prophecy *has* come, and that *they* have been abandoned on account of the greatness of their sins, and that *we* who have accepted the Word have the highest hopes in God, both because of our faith in Him, and of His ability to receive us into His communion pure from all evil and wickedness of life. If a man, then, should call himself a Jew or a Christian, he would not say without qualification that God had made the whole world, and the vault of heaven for us in particular. But if a man is, as Jesus taught, pure in heart, and meek, and peaceful, and cheerfully submits to dangers for the sake of his religion, such an one might reasonably have confidence in God, and with a full apprehension of the word contained in the prophecies, might say this also: "All these things has God shown beforehand, and announced to us who believe."

CHAPTER XXVIII

But since he has represented those whom he regards as worms, viz., the Christians, as saying that "God, having abandoned the heavenly regions, and despising this great earth, takes up His abode amongst us alone, and to us alone makes His announcements, and ceases not His messages and inquiries as to how we may become His associates for ever," we have to answer that he attributes to us words which we never uttered, seeing we both read and know that God loves all existing things, and loathes nothing which He has made, for He would not have created anything in hatred. We have, moreover, read the declaration: "And Thou sparest all things, because they are Thine, O lover of souls. For Thine incorruptible Spirit is in all. And therefore those also who have fallen away for a little time Thou rebukest, and admonishest, reminding them of their sins." How can we assert that "God, leaving the regions of heaven, and the whole world, and despising this great earth, takes up His abode amongst us only," when we have found that all thoughtful persons must say in their prayers, that "the earth is full of the mercy of the LORD," and that "the mercy of the Lord is upon all flesh;" and that God, being good, "maketh His sun to arise upon the evil and the good, and sendeth His rain upon the just and the unjust;" and that He encourages us to a similar course of action, in order that we may become His sons, and teaches us to extend the benefits which we enjoy, so far as in our power, to all men? For He Himself is said to be the Saviour of all men, especially of them that believe; and His Christ to be the "propitiation for our sins, and not for ours only, but also for the sins of the whole world." And this, then, is our answer to the allegations of Celsus. Certain other statements, in keeping with the character of the Jews, might be made by some of that nation, but

489

certainly not by the Christians, who have been taught that "God commendeth His love towards us, in that, while we were yet sinners, Christ died for us;" and although "scarcely for a righteous man will one die, yet peradventure for a good man some would even dare to die." But now is Jesus declared to have come for the sake of sinners in all parts of the world (that they may forsake their sin, and entrust themselves to God), being called also, agreeably to an ancient custom of these Scriptures, the "Christ of God."

CHAPTER XXIX

But Celsus perhaps has misunderstood certain of those whom he has termed "worms," when they affirm that "God exists, and that *we* are next to Him." And he acts like those who would find fault with an entire sect of philosophers, on account of certain words uttered by some rash youth who, after a three days' attendance upon the lectures of a philosopher, should exalt himself above other people as inferior to himself, and devoid of philosophy. For we know that there are many creatures more honourable than man; and we have read that "God standeth in the congregation of gods," but of gods who are not worshipped by the nations, "for all the gods of the nations are idols." We have read also, that "God, standing in the congregation of the gods, judgeth among the gods." We know, moreover, that "though there be that are called gods, whether in heaven or in earth (as there be gods many and lords many), but to us there is one God, the Father, of whom are all things, and we in Him; and one Lord Jesus Christ, by whom are all things, and we by Him." And we know that in this way the angels are superior to men; so that men, when made perfect, become like the angels. "For in the resurrection they neither marry nor are given in marriage, but the righteous are as the angels in heaven," and also become "equal to the angels." We know, too, that in the arrangement of the universe there are certain beings termed "thrones," and others "dominions," and others "powers," and others "principalities;" and we see that we men, who are far inferior to these, may entertain the hope that by a virtuous life, and by acting in all things agreeably to reason, we may rise to a likeness with all these. And, lastly, because "it doth not yet appear what we shall be; but we know that when He shall appear, we shall be like God, and shall see Him as He is." And if any one were to maintain what is asserted by some (either by those who possess intelligence or who do not, but have misconceived sound reason), that "God exists, and we are next to Him," I would interpret the word "we," by using in its stead, "We who act according to reason," or rather, "We *virtuous*, who act according to reason." For, in our opinion, the same virtue belongs to *all* the blessed, so that the virtue of man and of God is identical. And therefore we are taught to become "perfect," as our Father in heaven is perfect. No good and virtuous man, then, is a "worm rolling in filth," nor is a pious man an "ant," nor a righteous man a "frog;" nor could one whose soul is enlightened with the bright light of truth be reasonably likened to a "bird of the night."

CHAPTER XXX

It appears to me that Celsus has also misunderstood this statement, "Let Us make man in Our image and likeness;" and has therefore represented the "worms" as saying that, being created by God, we altogether resemble Him. If, however, he had known the difference between man being created "in the image of God" and "after His likeness," and that God is recorded to have said, "Let Us make man after Our image and likeness," but that He made man "after the image" of God, but not then also "after His likeness," he would not have represented us as saying that "we are altogether like Him." Moreover, we do not assert that the stars are subject to us; since the resurrection which is called the "resurrection of the just," and which is understood by wise men, is compared to the sun, and moon, and stars, by him who said, "There is one glory of the sun, and another glory of the moon, and another glory of the stars; for one star differeth from another star in glory. So also is the resurrection of the dead." Daniel also prophesied long ago regarding these things. Celsus says further, that we assert that "all things have been arranged so as to be subject to us," having perhaps heard some of the intelligent among us speaking to that effect, and perhaps also not understanding the saying, that "he who is the greatest amongst us is the servant of all." And if the Greeks say, "Then sun and moon are the slaves of mortal men," they express approval of the statement, and give an explanation of its meaning; but since such a statement is either not made at all by us, or is expressed in a different way, Celsus here too falsely accuses us. Moreover, we who, according to Celsus, are "worms," are represented by him as saying that, "seeing some among us are guilty of sin, God will come to us, or will send His own Son, that He may consume the wicked, and that we other frogs may enjoy eternal life with Him." Observe how this venerable philosopher, like a low buffoon, turns into ridicule and mockery, and a subject of laughter, the announcement of a divine judgment, and of the punishment of the wicked, and of the reward of the righteous; and subjoins to all this the remark, that "such statements would be more endurable if made by worms and frogs than by Christians and Jews who quarrel with one another!" We shall not, however, imitate his example, nor say similar things regarding those philosophers who profess to know the nature of all things, and who discuss with each other the manner in which all things were created, and how the heaven and earth originated, and all things in them; and how the souls (of men), being either unbegotten, and not created by God, are yet governed by Him, and pass from one body to another; or being formed at the same time with the body, exist for ever or pass away. For instead of treating with respect and accepting the intention of those who have devoted themselves to the investigation of the truth, one might mockingly and revilingly say that such men were "worms," who did not measure themselves by their corner of their dung-heap in human life, and who accordingly gave forth their opinions on matters of such importance as if they understood them, and who strenuously assert that they have obtained a view of those things which cannot be seen without a higher inspiration and a diviner power. "For no man knoweth the things of a man, save the spirit of man which is in him: even so the things of God knoweth no man, but the Spirit of God." We are not, however, mad, nor do we compare such human wisdom (I use the word "wisdom" in the common acceptation), which busies itself not about the affairs of the multitude, but in the investigation of truth, to the wrigglings of worms or any other such creatures; but in the spirit of truth, we testify of certain Greek philosophers that they knew God, seeing "He manifested Himself to them," although "they glorified Him not as God, neither were thankful, but became vain in their imaginations; and professing themselves to be wise, they became foolish, and changed the glory of the incorruptible God into an image made like to corruptible man, and to birds, and four-footed beasts, and creeping things."

CHAPTER XXXI

After this, wishing to prove that there is no difference between Jews and Christians, and those animals previously enumerated by him, he asserts that the Jews were "fugitives from Egypt, who never performed anything worthy of note, and never were held in any reputation or account." Now, on the point of their not being fugitives, nor Egyptians, but Hebrews who settled in Egypt, we have spoken in the preceding pages. But if he thinks his statement, that "they were never held in any reputation or account," to be proved, because no remarkable event in their history is found recorded by the Greeks, we would answer, that if one will examine their polity from its first beginning, and the arrangement of their laws, he will find that they were men who represented upon earth the shadow of a heavenly life, and that amongst them God is recognised as nothing else, save He who is over all things, and that amongst them no maker of images was permitted to enjoy the rights of citizenship. For neither painter nor image-maker existed in their state, the law expelling all such from it; that there might be no pretext for the construction of images,—an art which attracts the attention of foolish men, and which drags down the eyes of the soul from God to earth. There was, accordingly, amongst them a law to the following effect: "Do not transgress the law, and make to yourselves a graven image, any likeness of male or female; either a likeness of any one of the creatures that are upon the earth, or a likeness of any winged fowl that flieth under the heaven, or a likeness of any creeping thing that creepeth upon the earth, or a likeness of any of the fishes which are in the waters under the earth." The law, indeed, wished them to have regard to the truth of each individual thing, and not to form representations of things contrary to reality, feigning the appearance merely of what was really male or really female, or the nature of animals, or of birds, or of creeping things, or of fishes. Venerable, too, and grand was this prohibition of theirs: "Lift not up thine eyes unto heaven, lest, when thou seest the sun, and the moon, and the stars, and all the host of heaven, thou shouldst be led astray to worship them, and serve them." And what a *regime* was that under which the whole nation was placed, and which rendered it impossible for any effeminate person to appear in public; and worthy of admiration, too, was the arrangement by which harlots were removed out of the state, those incentives to the passions of the youth! Their courts of justice also were composed of men of the strictest integrity, who, after having for a lengthened period set the example of an unstained life, were entrusted with the duty of presiding over the tribunals, and who, on account of the superhuman purity of their character, were said to be gods, in conformity with an ancient Jewish usage of speech. Here was the spectacle of a whole nation devoted to philosophy; and in order that there might be leisure to listen to their sacred laws, the days termed "Sabbath," and the other festivals which existed among them, were instituted. And why need I speak of the orders of their priests and sacrifices, which contain innumerable indications (of deeper truths) to those who wish to ascertain the signification of things?

CHAPTER XXXII

But since nothing belonging to human nature is permanent, this polity also must gradually be corrupted and changed. And Providence, having remodelled their venerable system where it needed to be changed, so as to adapt it to men of all countries, gave to believers of all nations, in place of the Jews, the venerable religion of Jesus, who, being adorned not only with understanding, but also with a share of divinity, and having overthrown the doctrine regarding earthly demons, who delight in frankincense, and blood, and in the exhalations of sacrificial odours, and who, like the fabled Titans or Giants, drag down men from thoughts of God; and having Himself disregarded their plots, directed chiefly against the better class of men, enacted laws which ensure happiness to those who live according to them, and who do not flatter the demons by means of sacrifices, but altogether despise them, through help of the word of God, which aids those who look upwards to Him. And as it was the will of God that the doctrine of Jesus should prevail amongst men, the demons could effect nothing, although straining every nerve to accomplish the destruction of Christians; for they stirred up both princes, and senates, and rulers in every place,—nay, even nations themselves, who did not perceive the irrational and wicked procedure of the demons,—against the word, and those who believed in it; yet, notwithstanding, the word of God, which is more powerful than all other things, even when meeting with opposition, deriving from the opposition, as it were, a means of increase, advanced onwards, and won many souls, such being the will of God. And we have offered these remarks by way of a necessary digression. For we wished to answer the assertion of Celsus concerning the Jews, that they were "fugitives from Egypt, and that these men, beloved by God, never accomplished anything worthy of note." And further, in answer to the statement that "they were never held in any reputation or account," we say, that living apart as a "chosen nation and a royal priesthood," and shunning intercourse with the many nations around them, in order that their morals might escape corruption, they enjoyed the protection of the divine power, neither coveting like the most of mankind the acquisition of other kingdoms, nor yet being abandoned so as to become, on account of their smallness, an easy object of attack to others, and thus be altogether destroyed; and this lasted so long as they were worthy of the divine protection. But when it became necessary for them, as a nation wholly given to sin, to be brought back by their sufferings to their God, they were abandoned (by Him), sometimes for a longer, sometimes for a shorter period, until in the time of the Romans, having committed the greatest of sins in putting Jesus to death, they were completely deserted.

CHAPTER XXXIII

Immediately after this, Celsus, assailing the contents of the first book of Moses, which is entitled "Genesis," asserts that "the Jews accordingly endeavoured to derive their origin from the first race of jugglers and deceivers, appealing to the testimony of dark and ambiguous words, whose meaning was veiled in obscurity, and which they misinterpreted to the unlearned and ignorant, and that, too, when such a point had never been called in question during the long preceding period." Now Celsus appears to me in these words to have expressed very obscurely the meaning which he intended to convey. It is probable, indeed, that his obscurity on this subject is intentional, inasmuch as he saw the strength of the argument which establishes the descent of the Jews from their ancestors; while again, on the other hand, he wished not to appear ignorant that the question regarding the Jews and their descent was one that could not be lightly disposed of. It is certain, however, that the Jews trace their genealogy back to the three fathers, Abraham, Isaac, and Jacob. And the names of these individuals possess such efficacy, when united with the name of God, that not only do those belonging to the nation employ in their prayers to God, and in the exorcising of demons, the words, "God of Abraham, and God of Isaac, and God of Jacob," but so also do almost all those who occupy themselves with incantations and magical rites. For there is found in treatises on magic in many countries such an invocation of God, and assumption of the divine name, as implies a familiar use of it by these men in their dealings with demons. These facts, then—adduced by Jews and Christians to prove the sacred character of Abraham, and Isaac, and Jacob, the fathers of the Jewish race—appear to me not to have been altogether unknown to Celsus, but not to have been distinctly set forth by him, because he was unable to answer the argument which might be founded on them.

CHAPTER XXXIV

For we inquire of all those who employ such invocations of God, saying: Tell us, friends, who was Abraham, and what sort of person was Isaac, and what power did Jacob possess, that the appellation "God," when joined with their name, could effect such wonders? And from whom have you learned, or can you learn, the facts relating to these individuals? And who has occupied himself with writing a history about them, either directly magnifying these men by ascribing to them mysterious powers, or hinting obscurely at their possession of certain

495

great and marvellous qualities, patent to those who are qualified to see them? And when, in answer to our inquiry, no one can show from what history—whether Greek or Barbarian—or, if not a history, yet at least from what mystical narrative, the accounts of these men are derived, we shall bring forward the book entitled "Genesis," which contains the acts of these men, and the divine oracles addressed to them, and will say, Does not the use by you of the names of these three ancestors of the race, establishing in the clearest manner that effects not to be lightly regarded are produced by the invocation of them, evidence the divinity of the men? And yet we know them from no other source than the sacred books of the Jews! Moreover, the phrases, "the God of Israel," and "the God of the Hebrews," and "the God who drowned in the Red Sea the king of Egypt and the Egyptians," are *formulae* frequently employed against demons and certain wicked powers. And we learn the history of the names and their interpretation from those Hebrews, who in their national literature and national tongue dwell with pride upon these things, and explain their meaning. How, then, should the Jews attempt to derive their origin from the first race of those whom Celsus supposed to be jugglers and deceivers, and shamelessly endeavour to trace themselves and their beginning back to these?—whose names, being Hebrew, are an evidence to the Hebrews, who have their sacred books written in the Hebrew language and letters, that their nation is akin to these men. For up to the present time, the Jewish names belonging to the Hebrew language were either taken from their writings, or generally from words the meaning of which was made known by the Hebrew language.

CHAPTER XXXV

And let any one who peruses the treatise of Celsus observe whether it does not convey some such insinuation as the above, when he says: "And they attempted to derive their origin from the first race of jugglers and deceivers, appealing to the testimony of dark and ambiguous words, whose meaning was veiled in obscurity." For these names are indeed obscure, and not within the comprehension and knowledge of many, though not in our opinion of doubtful meaning, even although assumed by those who are aliens to our religion; but as, according to Celsus, they do not convey any ambiguity, I am at a loss to know why he has rejected them. And yet, if he had wished honestly to overturn the genealogy which he deemed the Jews to have so shamelessly arrogated, in boasting of Abraham and his descendants (as their progenitors), he ought to have quoted *all* the passages bearing on the subject; and, in the first place, to have advocated his cause with such arguments as he thought likely to be convincing, and in the next to have bravely refuted, by means of what appeared to him to be the true meaning, and by arguments in its favour, the errors existing on the subject. But neither Celsus nor any one else will be able, by their discussions regarding the nature of names employed for miraculous purposes, to lay down the correct doctrine regarding them, and to demonstrate that those men were to be lightly esteemed whose names merely, not among their countrymen alone, but also amongst foreigners, could accomplish (such results). He ought to have shown, moreover, how we, in misinterpreting the passages in which these names are found, deceive our hearers, as he imagines, while he himself, who boasts that he is not ignorant or unintelligent, gives the true interpretation of them. And he hazarded the assertion, in speaking of those names, from which the Jews deduce their genealogies, that "never, during the long antecedent period, has there been any dispute about these names, but that at the present time the Jews dispute about them with certain others," whom he does not mention. Now, let him who chooses show who these are that dispute with the Jews, and who adduce even probable arguments to show that Jews and Christians do not decide correctly on the points relating to these names, but that there are others who have discussed these questions with the greatest learning and accuracy. But we are well assured that none can establish anything of the sort, it being manifest that these names are derived from the Hebrew language, which is found only among the Jews.

CHAPTER XXXVI

Celsus in the next place, producing from history other than that of the divine record, those passages which bear upon the claims to great antiquity put forth by many nations, as the Athenians, and Egyptians, and Arcadians, and Phrygians, who assert that certain individuals have existed among them who sprang from the earth, and who each adduce proofs of these assertions, says: "The Jews, then, leading a grovelling life in some corner of Palestine, and being a wholly uneducated people, who had not heard that these matters had been committed to verse long ago by Hesiod and innumerable other inspired men, wove together some most incredible and insipid stories, viz., that a certain man was formed by the hands of God, and had breathed into him the breath of life, and that a woman was taken from his side, and that God issued certain commands, and that a serpent opposed these, and gained a victory over the commandments of God; thus relating certain old wives' fables, and most impiously representing God as weak at the very beginning (of things), and unable to convince even a single human being whom He Himself had formed." By these instances, indeed, this deeply read and learned Celsus, who accuses Jews and Christians of ignorance and want of instruction, clearly evinces the accuracy of his knowledge of the chronology of the respective historians, whether Greek or Barbarian, since he imagines that Hesiod and the "innumerable" others, whom he styles "inspired" men, are older than Moses and his writings—that very Moses who is shown to be much older than the time of the Trojan war! It is not the Jews, then, who have composed incredible and insipid stories regarding the birth of man from the earth, but these "inspired" men of Celsus, Hesiod and his other "innumerable" companions, who, having neither learned nor heard of the far older and most venerable accounts existing in Palestine, have written such histories as their Theogonies, attributing, so far as in their power, "generation" to their deities, and innumerable other absurdities. And these are the writers whom Plato expels from his "State" as being corrupters of the youth,—Homer, viz., and those who have composed poems of a similar description! Now it is evident that Plato did not regard as "inspired" those men who had left behind them such works. But perhaps it was from a desire to cast reproach upon us, that this Epicurean Celsus, who is better able to judge than Plato (if it be the same Celsus who composed two other books against the Christians), called those individuals "inspired" whom he did not in reality regard as such.

CHAPTER XXXVII

He charges us, moreover, with introducing "a man formed by the *hands* of God," although the book of Genesis has made no mention of the "hands" of God, either when relating the creation or the "fashioning" of the man; while it is Job and David who have used the expression, "Thy hands have made me and fashioned me;" with reference to which it would need a lengthened discourse to point out the sense in which these words were understood by those who used them, both as regards the difference between "making" and "fashioning," and also the "hands" of God. For those who do not understand these and similar expressions in the sacred Scriptures, imagine that we attribute to the God who is over all things a form such as that of man; and according to their conceptions, it follows that we consider the body of God to be furnished with wings, since the Scriptures, literally understood, attribute such appendages to God. The

498

subject before us, however, does not require us to interpret these expressions; for, in our explanatory remarks upon the book of Genesis, these matters have been made, to the best of our ability, a special subject of investigation. Observe next the malignity of Celsus in what follows. For the Scripture, speaking of the "fashioning" of the man, says, "And breathed into his face the breath of life, and the man became a living soul." Whereon Celsus, wishing maliciously to ridicule the "inbreathing into his face of the breath of life," and not understanding the sense in which the expression was employed, states that "they composed a story that a man was fashioned by the hands of God, and was inflated by breath blown into him," in order that, taking the word "inflated" to be used in a similar way to the inflation of skins, he might ridicule the statement, "He breathed into his face the breath of life,"— terms which are used figuratively, and require to be explained in order to show that God communicated to man of His incorruptible Spirit; as it is said, "For Thine incorruptible Spirit is in all things."

CHAPTER XXXVIII

In the next place, as it is his object to slander our Scriptures, he ridicules the following statement: "And God caused a deep sleep to fall upon Adam, and he slept: and He took one of his ribs, and closed up the flesh instead thereof. And the rib, which He had taken from the man, made He a woman," and so on; without quoting the words, which would give the hearer the impression that they are spoken with a figurative meaning. He would not even have it appear that the words were used allegorically, although he says afterwards, that "the more modest among Jews and Christians are ashamed of these things, and endeavour to give them somehow an allegorical signification." Now we might say to him, Are the statements of your "inspired" Hesiod, which he makes regarding the woman in the form of a myth, to be explained allegorically, in the sense that she was given by Jove to men as an evil thing, and as a retribution for the theft of "the fire;" while that regarding the woman who was taken from the side of the man (after he had been buried in deep slumber), and was formed by God, appears to you to be related without any rational meaning and secret signification? But is it not uncandid, not to ridicule the former as myths, but to admire them as philosophical ideas in a mythical dress, and to treat with contempt the latter, as offending the understanding, and to declare that they are of no account? For if, because of the mere phraseology, we are to find fault with what is intended to have a secret meaning, see whether the following lines of Hesiod, a man, as you say," inspired," are not

499

better fitted to excite laughter:—

"'Son of Iapetus!' with wrathful heart
Spake the cloud-gatherer: 'Oh, unmatched in art!
Exultest thou in this the flame retrieved,
And dost thou triumph in the god deceived?
But thou, with the posterity of man,
Shalt rue the fraud whence mightier ills began;
I will send evil for thy stealthy fire,
While all embrace it, and their bane desire.'
The sire, who rules the earth, and sways the pole,
Had said, and laughter fill'd his secret soul.
He bade the artist-god his hest obey,
And mould with tempering waters ductile clay:
Infuse, as breathing life and form began,
The supple vigour, and the voice of man:
Her aspect fair as goddesses above,
A virgin's likeness, with the brows of love.
He bade Minerva teach the skill that dyes
The web with colours, as the shuttle flies;
He called the magic of Love's Queen to shed
A nameless grace around her courteous head;
Instil the wish that longs with restless aim,
And cares of dress that feed upon the frame:
Bade Hermes last implant the craft refined
Of artful manners, and a shameless mind.
He said; their king th' inferior powers obeyed:
The fictile likeness of a bashful maid
Rose from the temper'd earth, by Jove's behest,
Under the forming god; the zone and vest
Were clasp'd and folded by Minerva's hand:
The heaven-born graces, and persuasion bland
Deck'd her round limbs with chains of gold: the hours
Of loose locks twined her temples with spring flowers.
The whole attire Minerva's curious care
Form'd to her shape, and fitted to her air.
But in her breast the herald from above,
Full of the counsels of deep thundering Jove,
Wrought artful manners, wrought perfidious lies,
And speech that thrills the blood, and lulls the wise.
Her did th' interpreter of gods proclaim,
And named the woman with Pandora's name;
Since all the gods conferr'd their gifts, to charm,

For man's inventive race, this beauteous harm."

Moreover, what is said also about the casket is fitted of itself to excite laughter; for example:—

"Whilome on earth the sons of men abode
From ills apart, and labour's irksome load,
And sore diseases, bringing age to man;
Now the sad life of mortals is a span.
The woman's hands a mighty casket bear;
She lifts the lid; she scatters griefs in air:
Alone, beneath the vessel's rims detained,
Hope still within th' unbroken cell remained,
Nor fled abroad; so will'd cloud-gatherer Jove:
The woman's hand had dropp'd the lid above."

Now, to him who would give to these lines a grave allegorical meaning (whether any such meaning be contained in them or not), we would say: Are the Greeks alone at liberty to convey a philosophic meaning in a secret covering? or perhaps also the Egyptians, and those of the Barbarians who pride themselves upon their mysteries and the truth (which is concealed within them); while the Jews alone, with their lawgiver and historians, appear to you the most unintelligent of men? And is this the only nation which has not received a share of divine power, and which yet was so grandly instructed how to rise upwards to the uncreated nature of God, and to gaze on Him alone, and to expect from Him alone (the fulfilment of) their hopes?

CHAPTER XXXIX

But as Celsus makes a jest also of the serpent, as counteracting the injunctions given by God to the man, taking the narrative to be an old wife's fable, and has purposely neither mentioned the paradise of God, nor stated that God is said to have planted it in Eden towards the east, and that there afterwards sprang up from the earth every tree that was beautiful to the sight, and good for food, and the tree of life in the midst of the paradise, and the tree of the knowledge of good and evil, and the other statements which follow, which might of themselves lead a candid reader to see that all these things had not inappropriately an allegorical meaning, let us contrast with this the words of Socrates regarding Eros in the Symposium of Plato, and which are put in the mouth of Socrates as being more appropriate than what was said regarding him by all the others at the Symposium. The words of Plato are as follow: "When Aphrodite was born, the gods held a banquet, and there was present, along with the others, Porus the son of Metis. And after they had dined, Penia came to beg for something (seeing there was an entertainment), and she stood at the gate. Porus meantime, having become intoxicated with the nectar (for there was then no wine), went into the garden of Zeus, and, being heavy with liquor, lay down to sleep. Penia accordingly formed a secret plot, with a view of freeing herself from her condition of poverty, to get a child by Porus, and accordingly lay down beside him, and became pregnant with Eros. And on this account Eros has become the follower and attendant of Aphrodite, having been begotten on her birthday feast, and being at the same time by nature a lover of the beautiful, because Aphrodite too is beautiful. Seeing, then, that Eros is the son of Porus and Penia, the following is his condition. In the first place, he is always poor, and far from being delicate and beautiful, as most persons imagine; but is withered, and sunburnt, and unshod, and without a home, sleeping always upon the ground, and without a covering; lying in the open air beside gates, and on public roads; possessing the nature of his mother, and dwelling continually with indigence. But, on the other hand, in conformity with the character of his father, he is given to plotting against the beautiful and the good, being courageous, and hasty, and vehement; a keen hunter, perpetually devising contrivances; both much given to forethought, and also fertile in resources; acting like a philosopher throughout the whole of his life; a terrible sorcerer, and dealer in drugs, and a sophist as well; neither immortal by nature nor yet mortal, but on the same day, at one time he flourishes and lives when he has plenty, and again at another time dies, and once more is recalled to life through possessing the nature of his father. But the supplies furnished to him are always gradually disappearing, so that he is never at any time in want, nor yet rich; and, on the other hand, he occupies an intermediate position between wisdom and ignorance." Now, if those who read these words were to imitate the malignity of Celsus—which be it far from Christians to do!—they would ridicule the myth, and would turn this great Plato into a subject of jest; but if, on investigating in a philosophic spirit what is conveyed in the dress of a myth, they should be able to discover the meaning of Plato, (they will admire) the manner in which he was able to conceal, on account of the multitude, in the form of this myth, the great ideas which presented themselves to him, and to speak in a befitting manner to those who know how to ascertain from the myths the true meaning of him who wove them together. Now I have brought forward this myth occurring in the writings of Plato, because of the mention in it of the garden of Zeus, which appears to bear some resemblance to the paradise of God, and of the comparison between Penia and the serpent, and the plot against Porus by Penia, which may be compared with the plot of the serpent against the man. It is not very clear, indeed, whether Plato fell in with these stories by chance, or whether, as some think, meeting during his visit to Egypt with certain individuals who philosophized on the Jewish mysteries, and learning some things from them, he may have preserved a few of their ideas, and thrown others aside, being careful not to offend the Greeks by a complete adoption of all the points of the philosophy of the Jews, who were in bad repute with the multitude, on account of the foreign character of their laws and their peculiar polity. The present, however, is not the proper time for explaining either the myth of Plato, or the story of the serpent and the paradise of God, and all that is related to have taken place in it, as in our exposition of the book of Genesis we have especially occupied ourselves as we best could with these matters.

CHAPTER XL

But as he asserts that "the Mosaic narrative most impiously represents God as in a state of weakness from the very commencement (of things), and as unable to gain over (to obedience) even one single man whom He Himself had formed," we say in answer that the objection is much the same as if one were to find fault with the existence of evil, which God has not been able to prevent even in the case of a single individual, so that *one* man might be found from the very beginning of things who was born into the world untainted by sin. For as those whose business it is to defend the doctrine of providence do so by means of arguments which are not to be despised, so also the subjects of Adam and his son will be philosophically dealt with by those who are aware that in the Hebrew language Adam signifies man; and that in those parts of the narrative which appear to refer to Adam as an individual, Moses is discoursing upon the nature of man in general. For "in Adam" (as the Scripture says) "all die," and were condemned in the likeness of Adam's transgression, the word of God asserting this not so much of *one particular individual* as of the *whole human race*. For in the connected series of statements which appears to apply as to one particular individual, the curse pronounced upon Adam is regarded as common to all (the members of the race), and what was spoken with reference to the woman is spoken of *every* woman without exception. And the expulsion of the man and woman from paradise, and their being clothed with tunics of skins (which God, because of the transgression of men, made for those who had sinned), contain a certain secret and mystical doctrine (far transcending that of Plato) of the souls losing its wings, and being borne downwards to earth, until it can lay hold of some stable resting-place.

CHAPTER XLI

After this he continues as follows: "They speak, in the next place, of a deluge, and of a monstrous ark, having within it all things, and of a dove and a crow as messengers, falsifying and recklessly altering the story of Deucalion; not expecting, I suppose, that these things would come to light, but imagining that they were inventing stories merely for young children." Now in these remarks observe the hostility—so unbecoming a philosopher—displayed by this man towards this very ancient Jewish narrative. For, not being able to say anything against the history of the deluge, and not perceiving what he might have urged against the ark and its dimensions,—viz., that, according to the general opinion, which accepted the statements that it was three hundred cubits in length, and fifty in breadth, and thirty in height, it was impossible to maintain that it contained (all) the animals that were upon the earth, fourteen specimens of every clean and four of every unclean beast,— he merely termed it "monstrous, containing all things within it." Now wherein was its "monstrous" character, seeing it is related to have been a hundred years in building, and to have had the three hundred cubits of its length and the fifty of its breadth contracted, until the thirty cubits of its height terminated in a top one cubit long and one cubit broad? Why should we not rather admire a structure which resembled an extensive city, if its measurements be taken to mean what they are capable of meaning, so that it was nine myriads of cubits long in the base, and two thousand five hundred in breadth? And why should we not admire the design evinced in having it so compactly built, and rendered capable of sustaining a tempest which caused a deluge? For it was not daubed with pitch, or any material of that kind, but was securely coated with bitumen. And is it not a subject of admiration, that by the providential arrangement of God, the elements of all the races were brought into it, that the earth might receive again the seeds of all living things, while God made use of a most righteous man to be the progenitor of those who were to be born after the deluge?

CHAPTER XLII

In order to show that he had read the book of Genesis, Celsus rejects the story of the dove, although unable to adduce any reason which might prove it to be a fiction. In the next place, as his habit is, in order to put the narrative in a more ridiculous light, he converts the "raven" into a "crow," and imagines that Moses so wrote, having recklessly altered the accounts related of the Grecian Deucalion; unless perhaps he regards the narrative as not having proceeded from Moses, but from *several* individuals, as appears from his employing the *plural* number in the expressions, "falsifying and recklessly altering the story of Deucalion," as well as from the words, "For *they* did not expect, I suppose, that these things would come to light." But how should they, who gave their Scriptures to the *whole* nation, not expect that they would come to light, and who predicted, moreover, that this religion should be proclaimed to *all* nations? Jesus declared, "The kingdom of God shall be taken from you, and given to a nation bringing forth the fruits thereof;" and in uttering these words to the Jews, what other meaning did He intend to convey than this, viz., that He Himself should, through his divine power, bring forth into light the whole of the Jewish Scriptures, which contain the mysteries of the kingdom of God? If, then, they peruse the Theogonies of the Greeks, and the stories about the twelve gods, they impart to them an air of dignity, by investing them with an allegorical signification; but when they wish to throw contempt upon our biblical narratives, they assert that they are fables, clumsily invented for infant children!

CHAPTER XLIII

"Altogether absurd, and out of season," he continues, "is the (account of the) begetting of children," where, although he has mentioned no names, it is evident that he is referring to the history of Abraham and Sarah. Cavilling also at the "conspiracies of the brothers," he allies either to the story of Cain plotting against Abel, or, in addition, to that of Esau against Jacob; and (speaking) of "a father's sorrow," he probably refers to that of Isaac on account of the absence of Jacob, and perhaps also to that of Jacob because of Joseph having been sold into Egypt. And when relating the "crafty procedure of mothers," I suppose he means the conduct of Rebecca, who contrived that the blessing of Isaac should descend, not upon Esau, but upon Jacob. Now if we assert that in all these cases God interposed in a very marked degree, what absurdity do we commit, seeing we are persuaded that He never withdraws His providence from those who devote themselves to Him in an honourable and vigorous life? He ridicules, moreover, the acquisition of property made by Jacob while living with Laban, not understanding to what these words refer: "And those which had no spots were Laban's, and those which were spotted were Jacob's;" and he says that "God presented his sons with asses, and sheep, and camels," and did not see that "all these things happened unto them for ensamples, and were written for our sake, upon whom the ends of the world are come." The varying customs (prevailing among the different nations) becoming famous, are regulated by the word of God, being given as a possession to him who is figuratively termed Jacob. For those who become converts to Christ from among the heathen, are indicated by the history of Laban and Jacob.

CHAPTER XLIV

And erring widely from the meaning of Scripture, he says that "God gave wells also to the righteous." Now he did not observe that the righteous do not construct cisterns, but dig wells, seeking to discover the inherent ground and source of potable blessings, inasmuch as they receive in a figurative sense the commandment which enjoins, "Drink waters from your own vessels, and from your own wells of fresh water. Let not your water be poured out beyond your own fountain, but let it pass into your own streets. Let it belong to you alone, and let no alien partake with thee." Scripture frequently makes use of the histories of real events, in order to present to view more important truths, which are but obscurely intimated; and of this kind are the narratives relating to the "wells," and to the "marriages," and to the various acts of "sexual intercourse" recorded of righteous persons, respecting which, however, it will be more seasonable to offer an explanation in the exegetical writings referring to those very passages. But that wells were constructed by righteous men in the land of the Philistines, as related in the book of Genesis, is manifest from the wonderful wells which are shown at Ascalon, and which are deserving of mention on account of their structure, so foreign and peculiar compared with that of other wells. Moreover, that both young women and female servants are to be understood metaphorically, is not *our* doctrine merely, but one which we have received from the beginning from wise men, among whom a certain one said, when exhorting his hearers to investigate the figurative meaning: "Tell me, ye that read the law, do ye not hear the law? For it is written that Abraham had two sons; the one by a bond maid, the other by a free woman. But he who was of the bond woman was born after the flesh; but he of the free woman was by promise. Which things are an allegory: for these are the two covenants; the one from the Mount Sinai, which gendereth to bondage, which is Agar." And a little after, "But Jerusalem which is above is free, which is the mother of us all." And any one who will take up the Epistle to the Galatians may learn how the passages relating to the "marriages," and the intercourse with "the maid-servants," have been allegorized; the Scripture desiring us to imitate not the literal acts of those who did these things, but (as the apostles of Jesus are accustomed to call them) the spiritual.

CHAPTER XLV

And whereas Celsus ought to have recognised the love of truth displayed by the writers of sacred Scripture, who have not concealed even what is to their discredit, and thus been led to accept the other and more marvellous accounts as true, he has done the reverse, and has characterized the story of Lot and his daughters (without examining either its literal or its figurative meaning) as "worse than the crimes of Thyestes." The figurative signification of that passage of history it is not necessary at present to explain, nor what is meant by Sodom, and by the words of the angels to him who was escaping thence, when they said: "Look not behind thee, neither stay thou in all the surrounding district; escape to the mountain, lest thou be consumed;" nor what is intended by Lot and his wife, who became a pillar of salt because she turned back; nor by his daughters intoxicating their father, that they might become mothers by him. But let us in a few words soften down the repulsive features of the history. The nature of actions—good, bad, and indifferent—has been investigated by the Greeks; and the more successful of such investigators lay down the principle that intention alone gives to actions the character of good or bad, and that all things which are done without a purpose are, strictly speaking, indifferent; that when the intention is directed to a becoming end, it is praiseworthy; when the reverse, it is censurable. They have said, accordingly, in the section relating to "things indifferent," that, strictly speaking, for a man to have sexual intercourse with his daughters is a thing indifferent, although such a thing ought not to take place in established communities. And for the sake of hypothesis, in order to show that such an act belongs to the class of things indifferent, they have assumed the case of a wise man being left with an only daughter, the entire human race besides having perished; and they put the question whether the father can fitly have intercourse with his daughter, in order, agreeably to the supposition, to prevent the extermination of mankind. Is this to be accounted sound reasoning among the Greeks, and to be commended by the influential sect of the Stoics; but when young maidens, who had heard of the burning of the world, though without comprehending (its full meaning), saw fire devastating their city and country, and supposing that the only means left of rekindling the flame of human life lay in their father and themselves, should, on such a supposition, conceive the desire that the world should continue, shall their conduct be deemed worse than that of the wise man who, according to the hypothesis of the Stoics, acts becomingly in having intercourse with his daughter in the case already supposed, of all men having been destroyed? I am not unaware, however, that some have taken offence at the desire of Lot's daughters, and have regarded their conduct as very wicked; and have said that two accursed nations—Moab and Ammon—have sprung from that unhallowed intercourse. And yet truly sacred Scripture is nowhere found distinctly approving of their conduct as good, nor yet passing sentence upon it as blameworthy. Nevertheless, whatever be the real state of the case, it admits not only of a figurative meaning, but also of being defended on its own merits.

CHAPTER XLVI

Celsus, moreover, sneers at the "hatred" of Esau (to which, I suppose, he refers) against Jacob, although he was a man who, according to the Scriptures, is acknowledged to have been wicked; and not clearly stating the story of Simeon and Levi, who sallied out (on the Shechemites) on account of the insult offered to their sister, who had been violated by the son of the Shechemite king, he inveighs against their conduct. And passing on, he speaks of "brothers selling (one another)," alluding to the sons of Jacob; and of "a brother sold," Joseph to wit; and of "a father deceived," viz., Jacob, because he entertained no suspicion of his sons when they showed him Joseph's coat of many colours, but believed their statement, and mourned for his son, who was a slave in Egypt, as if he were dead. And observe in what a spirit of hatred and falsehood Celsus collects together the statements of the sacred history; so that wherever it appeared to him to contain a ground of accusation he produces the passage, but wherever there is any exhibition of virtue worthy of mention—as when Joseph would not gratify the lust of his mistress, refusing alike her allurements and her threats—he does not even mention the circumstance! He should see, indeed, that the conduct of Joseph was far superior to what is related of Bellerophon, since the former chose rather to be shut up in prison than do violence to his virtue. For although he might have offered a just defence against his accuser, he magnanimously remained silent, entrusting his cause to God.

CHAPTER XLVII

Celsus next, for form's sake, and with great want of precision, speaks of "the dreams of the chief butler and chief baker, and of Pharaoh, and of the explanation of them, in consequence of which Joseph was taken out of prison in order to be entrusted by Pharaoh with the second place in Egypt." What absurdity, then, did the history contain, looked at even in itself, that it should be adduced as matter of accusation by this Celsus, who gave the title of *True Discourse* to a treatise not containing doctrines, but full of charges against Jews and Christians? He adds: "He who had been sold behaved kindly to his brethren (who had sold him), when they were suffering from hunger, and had been sent with their asses to purchase (provisions);" although he has not related these occurrences (in his treatise). But he *does* mention the circumstance of Joseph making himself known to his brethren, although I know not with what view, or what absurdity he can point out in such an occurrence; since it is impossible for Momus himself, we might say, to find any reasonable fault with events which, apart from their figurative meaning, present so much that is attractive. He relates, further, that "Joseph, who had been sold as a slave, was restored to liberty, and went up with a solemn procession to his father's funeral," and thinks that the narrative furnishes matter of accusation against us, as he makes the following remark: "By whom (Joseph, namely) the illustrious and divine nation of the Jews, after growing up in Egypt to be a multitude of people, was commanded to sojourn somewhere beyond the limits of the kingdom, and to pasture their flocks in districts of no repute." Now the words, "that they were commanded to pasture their flocks in districts of no repute," are an addition, proceeding from his own feelings of hatred; for he has not shown that Goshen, the district of Egypt, is a place of no repute. The exodus of the people from Egypt he calls a flight, not at all remembering what is written in the book of Exodus regarding the departure of the Hebrews from the land of Egypt. We have enumerated these instances to show that what, literally considered, might appear to furnish ground of accusation, Celsus has not succeeded in proving to be either objectionable or foolish, having utterly failed to establish the evil character, as he regards it, of our Scriptures.

CHAPTER XLVIII

In the next place, as if he had devoted himself solely to the manifestation of his hatred and dislike of the Jewish and Christian doctrine, he says: "The more modest of Jewish and Christian writers give all these things an allegorical meaning;" and, "Because they are ashamed of these things, they take refuge in allegory." Now one might say to him, that if we must admit fables and fictions, whether written with a concealed meaning or with any other object, to be shameful narratives when taken in their literal acceptation, of what histories can this be said more truly than of the Grecian? In these histories, gods who are sons castrate the gods who are their fathers, and gods who are parents devour their own children, and a goddess-mother gives to the "father of gods and men" a stone to swallow instead of his own son, and a father has intercourse with his daughter, and a wife binds her own husband, having as her allies in the work the brother of the fettered god and his own daughter! But why should I enumerate these absurd stories of the Greeks regarding their gods, which are most shameful in themselves, even though invested with an allegorical meaning? (Take the instance) where Chrysippus of Soli, who is considered to be an ornament of the Stoic sect, on account of his numerous and learned treatises, explains a picture at Samos, in which Juno was represented as committing unspeakable abominations with Jupiter. This reverend philosopher says in his treatises, that matter receives the spermatic words of the god, and retains them within herself, in order to ornament the universe. For in the picture at Samos Juno represents matter, and Jupiter god. Now it is on account of these, and of countless other similar fables, that we would not even in word call the God of all things Jupiter, or the sun Apollo, or the moon Diana. But we offer to the Creator a worship which is pure, and speak with religious respect of His noble works of creation, not contaminating even in word the things of God; approving of the language of Plato in the *Philebus*, who would not admit that pleasure was a goddess, "so great is my reverence, Protarchus," he says, "for the very names of the gods." We verily entertain such reverence for the name of God, and for His noble works of creation, that we would not, even under pretext of an allegorical meaning, admit any fable which might do injury to the young.

CHAPTER XLIX

If Celsus had read the Scriptures in an impartial spirit, he would not have said that "our writings are incapable of admitting an allegorical meaning." For from the prophetic Scriptures, in which historical events are recorded (not from the historical), it is possible to be convinced that the historical portions also were written with an allegorical purpose, and were most skilfully adapted not only to the multitude of the simpler believers, but also to the few who are able or willing to investigate matters in an intelligent spirit. If, indeed, those writers at the present day who are deemed by Celsus the "more modest of the Jews and Christians" were the (first) allegorical interpreters of our Scriptures, he would have the appearance, perhaps, of making a plausible allegation. But since the very fathers and authors of the doctrines themselves give them an allegorical signification, what other inference can be drawn than that they were composed so as to be allegorically understood in their chief signification? And we shall adduce a few instances out of very many to show that Celsus brings an empty charge against the Scriptures, when he says "that they are incapable of admitting an allegorical meaning." Paul, the apostle of Jesus, says: "It is written in the law, Thou shalt not muzzle the mouth of the ox that treadeth out the corn. Doth God take care for oxen? or saith He it altogether for our sakes? For our sakes, no doubt, this is written, that he that plougheth should plough in hope, and he that thresheth in hope of partaking." And in another passage the same Paul says: "For it is written, For this cause shall a man leave his father and mother and shall be joined to his wife, and they two shall be one flesh. This is a great mystery; but I speak concerning Christ and the Church." And again, in another place: "We know that all our fathers were under the cloud, and all passed through the sea; and were all baptized unto Moses in the cloud, and in the sea." Then, explaining the history relating to the manna, and that referring to the miraculous issue of the water from the rock, he continues as follows: "And they did all eat the same spiritual meat, and did all drink the same spiritual drink. For they drank of that spiritual Rock that followed them, and that Rock was Christ." Asaph, moreover, who, in showing the histories in Exodus and Numbers to be full of difficulties and parables, begins in the following manner, as recorded in the book of Psalms, where he is about to make mention of these things: "Give ear, O my people, to my law: incline your ears to the words of my mouth. I will open my mouth in parables; I will utter dark sayings of old, which we have heard and known, and our fathers have told us."

CHAPTER L

Moreover, if the law of Moses had contained nothing which was to be understood as having a secret meaning, the prophet would not have said in his prayer to God, "Open Thou mine eyes, and I will behold wondrous things out of Thy law;" whereas he knew that there was a veil of ignorance lying upon the heart of those who read but do not understand the figurative meaning, which veil is taken away by the gift of God, when He hears him who has done all that he can, and who by reason of habit has his senses exercised to distinguish between good and evil, and who continually utters the prayer, "Open Thou mine eyes, and I will behold wondrous things out of Thy law." And who is there that, on reading of the dragon that lives in the Egyptian river, and of the fishes which lurk in his scales, or of the excrement of Pharaoh which fills the mountains of Egypt, is not led at once to inquire who he is that fills the Egyptian mountains with his stinking excrement, and what the Egyptian mountains are; and what the rivers in Egypt are, of which the aforesaid Pharaoh boastfully says, "The rivers are mine, and I have made them;" and who the dragon is, and the fishes in its scales,—and this so as to harmonize with the interpretation to be given of the rivers? But why establish at greater length what needs no demonstration? For to these things applies the saying: "Who is wise, and he shall understand these things? or who is prudent, and he shall know them?" Now I have gone at some length into the subject, because I wished to show the unsoundness of the assertion of Celsus, that "the more modest among the Jews and Christians endeavour somehow to give these stories an allegorical signification, although some of them do not admit of this, but on the contrary are exceedingly silly inventions." Much rather are the stories of the Greeks not only very silly, but very impious inventions. For our narratives keep expressly in view the multitude of simpler believers, which was not done by those who invented the Grecian fables. And therefore not without propriety does Plato expel from his state all fables and poems of such a nature as those of which we have been speaking.

CHAPTER LI

Celsus appears to me to have heard that there are treatises in existence which contain allegorical explanations of the law of Moses. These however, he could not have read; for if he had he would not have said: "The allegorical explanations, however, which have been devised are much more shameful and absurd than the fables themselves, inasmuch as they endeavour to unite with marvellous and altogether insensate folly things which cannot at all be made to harmonize." He seems to refer in these words to the works of Philo, or to those of still older writers, such as Aristobulus. But I conjecture that Celsus has not read their books, since it appears to me that in many passages they have so successfully hit the meaning (of the sacred writers), that even Grecian philosophers would have been captivated by their explanations; for in their writings we find not only a polished style, but exquisite thoughts and doctrines, and a rational use of what Celsus imagines to be fables in the sacred writings. I know, moreover, that Numenius the Pythagorean—a surpassingly excellent expounder of Plato, and who held a foremost place as a teacher of the doctrines of Pythagoras—in many of his works quotes from the writings of Moses and the prophets, and applies to the passages in question a not improbable allegorical meaning, as in his work called *Epops*, and in those which treat of "Numbers" and of "Place." And in the third book of his dissertation on *The Good*, he quotes also a narrative regarding Jesus—without, however, mentioning His name—and gives it an allegorical signification, whether successfully or the reverse I may state on another occasion. He relates also the account respecting Moses, and Jannes, and Jambres. But we are not elated on account of this instance, though we express our approval of Numenius, rather than of Celsus and other Greeks, because he was willing to investigate our histories from a desire to acquire knowledge, and was (duly) affected by them as narratives which were to be allegorically understood, and which did not belong to the category of foolish compositions.

CHAPTER LII

After this, selecting from all the treatises which contain allegorical explanations and interpretations, expressed in a language and style not to be despised, the least important, such as might contribute, indeed, to strengthen the faith of the multitude of simple believers, but were not adapted to impress those of more intelligent mind, he continues: "Of such a nature do I know the work to be, entitled *Controversy between one Papiscus and Jason*, which is fitted to excite pity and hatred instead of laughter. It is not my purpose, however, to confute the statements contained in such works; for their fallacy is manifest to all, especially if any one will have the patience to read the books themselves. Rather do I wish to show that Nature teaches this, that God made nothing that is mortal, but that His works, whatever they are, are immortal, and theirs mortal. And the soul is the work of God, while the nature of the body is different. And in this respect there is no difference between the body of a bat, or of a worm, or of a frog, and that of a man; for the matter is the same, and their corruptible part is alike." Nevertheless I could wish that every one who heard Celsus declaiming and asserting that the treatise entitled *Controversy between Jason and Papiscus regarding Christ* was fitted to excite not laughter, but hatred, could take the work into his hands, and patiently listen to its contents; that, finding in it nothing to excite hatred, he might condemn Celsus out of the book itself. For if it be impartially perused, it will be found that there is nothing to excite even laughter in a work in which a Christian is described as conversing with a Jew on the subject of the Jewish Scriptures, and proving that the predictions regarding Christ fitly apply to Jesus; although the other disputant maintains the discussion in no ignoble style, and in a manner not unbecoming the character of a Jew.

CHAPTER LIII

I do not know, indeed, how he could conjoin things that do not admit of union, and which cannot exist together at the same time in human nature, in saying, as he did, that "the above treatise deserved to be treated both with pity and hatred." For every one will admit that he who is the object of pity is not at the same moment an object of hatred, and that he who is the object of hatred is not at the same time a subject of pity. Celsus, moreover, says that it was not his purpose to refute such statements, because he thinks that their absurdity is evident to all, and that, even before offering any logical refutation, they will appear to be bad, and to merit both pity and hatred. But we invite him who peruses this reply of ours to the charges of Celsus to have patience, and to listen to our sacred writings themselves, and, as far as possible, to form an opinion from their *contents* of the purpose of the writers, and of their consciences and disposition of mind; for he will discover that they are men who strenuously contend for what they uphold, and that some of them show that the history which they narrate is one which they have both seen and experienced, which was miraculous, and worthy of being recorded for the advantage of their future hearers. Will any one indeed venture to say that it is not the source and fountain of all blessing (to men) to believe in the God of all things, and to perform all our actions with the view of pleasing Him in everything whatever, and not to entertain even a thought unpleasing to Him, seeing that not only our words and deeds, but our very thoughts, will be the subject of future judgment? And what other arguments would more effectually lead human nature to adopt a virtuous life, than the belief or opinion that the supreme God beholds all things, not only what is said and done, but even what is thought by us? And let any one who likes compare any other system which at the same time converts and ameliorates, not merely one or two individuals, but, as far as in it lies, countless numbers, that by the comparison of both methods he may form a correct idea of the arguments which dispose to a virtuous life.

CHAPTER LIV

But as in the words which I quoted from Celsus, which are a paraphrase from the *Timaeus*, certain expressions occur, such as, "God made nothing mortal, but immortal things alone, while mortal things are the works of others, and the soul is a work of God, but the nature of the body is different, and there is no difference between the body of a man and that of a bat, or of a worm, or of a frog; for the matter is the same, and their corruptible part alike,"—let us discuss these points for a little; and let us show that Celsus either does not disclose his Epicurean opinions, or, as might be said by one person, has exchanged them for better, or, as another might say, has nothing in common save the name, with Celsus, the Epicurean. For he ought, in giving expression to such opinions, and in proposing to contradict not only us, but the by no means obscure sect of philosophers who are the adherents of Zeno of Citium, to have proved that the bodies of animals are not the work of God, and that the great skill displayed in their construction did not proceed from the highest intelligence. And he ought also, with regard to the countless diversities of plants, which are regulated by an inherent, incomprehensible nature, and which have been created for the by no means despicable use of man in general, and of the animals which minister to man, whatever other reasons may be adduced for their existence, not only to have stated his opinion, but also to have shown us that it was no perfect intelligence which impressed these qualities upon the matter of plants. And when he had once represented (various) divinities as the creators of all the bodies, the soul alone being the work of God, why did not he, who separated these great acts of creation, and apportioned them among a plurality of creators, next demonstrate by some convincing reason the existence of these diversities among divinities, some of which construct the bodies of men, and others—those, say, of beasts of burden, and others—those of wild animals? And he who saw that some divinities were the creators of dragons, and of asps, and of basilisks, and others of each plant and herb according to its species, ought to have explained the causes of these diversities. For probably, had he given himself carefully to the investigation of each particular point, he would either have observed that it was one God who was the creator of all, and who made each thing with a certain object and for a certain reason; or if he had failed to observe this, he would have discovered the answer which he ought to return to those who assert that corruptibility is a thing indifferent in its nature; and that there was no absurdity in a world which consists of diverse materials, being formed by one architect, who constructed the different kinds of things so as to secure the good of the whole. Or, finally, he ought to have expressed no opinion at all on so important a doctrine, since he did not intend to prove what he professed to demonstrate; unless, indeed, he who censures others for professing a simple faith, would have us to believe his mere assertions, although he gave out that he would not merely assert, but would prove his assertions.

CHAPTER LV

But I maintain that, if he had the patience (to use his own expression) to listen to the writings of Moses and the prophets, he would have had his attention arrested by the circumstance that the expression "God made" is applied to heaven and earth, and to what is called the firmament, and also to the lights and stars; and after these, to the great fishes, and to every living thing among creeping animals which the waters brought forth after their kinds, and to every fowl of heaven after its kind; and after these, to the wild beasts of the earth after their kind, and the beasts after their kind, and to every creeping thing upon the earth after its kind; and last of all to man. The expression "made," however, is not applied to other things; but it is deemed sufficient to say regarding light, "And it was light;" and regarding the one gathering together of all the waters that are under the whole heaven, "It was so." And in like manner also, with regard to what grew upon the earth, where it is said, "The earth brought forth grass, and herb yielding seed after its kind and after its likeness, and the fruit-tree yielding fruit, whose seed is in itself, after its kind, upon the earth." He would have inquired, moreover, whether the recorded commands of God respecting the coming into existence of each part of the world were addressed to one thing or to several; and he would not lightly have charged with being unintelligible, and as having no secret meaning, the accounts related in these books, either by Moses, or, as *we* would say, by the Divine Spirit speaking in Moses, from whom also he derived the power of prophesying; since he "knew both the present, and the future, and the past," in a higher degree than those priests who are alleged by the poets to have possessed a knowledge of these things.

CHAPTER LVI

Moreover, since Celsus asserts that "the soul is the work of God, but that the nature of body is different; and that in this respect there is no difference between the body of a bat, or of a worm, or of a frog, and that of a man, for the matter is the same, and their corruptible part alike,"—we have to say in answer to this argument of his, that if, since the same matter underlies the body of a bat, or of a worm, or of a frog, or of a man, these bodies will differ in no respect from one another, it is evident then that these bodies also will differ in no respect from the sun, or the moon, or the stars, or the sky, or any other thing which is called by the Greeks a god, cognisable by the senses. For the same matter, underlying *all* bodies, is, properly speaking, without qualities and without form, and derives its qualities from some (other) source, I know not whence, since Celsus will have it that nothing corruptible can be the work of God. Now the corruptible part of everything whatever, being produced from the same underlying matter, must necessarily be the same, by Celsus' own showing; unless, indeed, finding himself here hard pressed, he should desert Plato, who makes the soul arise from a certain bowl, and take refuge with Aristotle and the Peripatetics, who maintain that the ether is *immaterial*, and consists of a fifth nature, separate from the other four elements, against which view both the Platonists and the Stoics have nobly protested. And we too, who are despised by Celsus, will contravene it, seeing we are required to explain and maintain the following statement of the prophet: The heavens shall perish, but Thou remainest: and they all shall wax old as a garment; and as a vesture shalt Thou fold them up, and they shall be changed: but Thou art the same." These remarks, however, are sufficient in reply to Celsus, when he asserts that "the soul is the work of God, but that the nature of body is different;" for from his argument it follows that there is no difference between the body of a bat, or of a worm, or of a frog, and that of a heavenly being.

CHAPTER LVII

See, then, whether we ought to yield to one who, holding such opinions, calumniates the Christians, and thus abandon a doctrine which explains the difference existing among bodies as due to the different qualities, internal and external, which are implanted in them. For we, too, know that there are "bodies celestial, and bodies terrestrial;" and that "the glory of the celestial is one, and the glory of the terrestrial another;" and that even the glory of the celestial bodies is not alike: for "one is the glory of the sun, and another the glory of the stars;" and among the stars themselves, "one star differeth from another star in glory." And therefore, as those who expect the resurrection of the dead, we assert that the qualities which are in bodies undergo change: since some bodies, which are sown in corruption, are raised in incorruption; and others, sown in dishonour, are raised in glory; and others, again, sown in weakness, are raised in power; and those which are sown natural bodies, are raised as spiritual. That the matter which underlies bodies is capable of receiving those qualities which the Creator pleases to bestow, is a point which all of us who accept the doctrine of providence firmly hold; so that, if God so willed, one quality is at the present time implanted in this portion of matter, and afterwards another of a different and better kind. But since there are, from the beginning of the world, laws established for the purpose of regulating the changes of bodies, and which will continue while the world lasts, I do not know whether, when a new and different order of things has succeeded after the destruction of the world, and what our Scriptures call the end (of the ages), it is not wonderful that at the present time a snake should be formed out of a dead man, growing, as the multitude affirm, out of the marrow of the back, and that a bee should spring from an ox, and a wasp from a horse, and a beetle from an ass, and, generally, worms from the most of bodies. Celsus, indeed, thinks that this can be shown to be the consequence of none of these bodies being the work of God, and that qualities (I know not whence it was so arranged that one should spring out of another) are not the work of a divine intelligence, producing the changes which occur in the qualities of matter.

CHAPTER LVIII

But we have something more to say to Celsus, when he declares that "the soul is the work of God, and that the nature of body is different," and puts forward such an opinion not only without proof, but even without clearly defining his meaning; for he did not make it evident whether he meant that every soul is the work of God, or only the rational soul. This, then, is what we have to say: If every soul is the work of God, it is manifest that those of the meanest irrational animals are God's work, so that the nature of all bodies is different from that of the soul. He appears, however, in what follows, where he says that "irrational animals are more beloved by God than we, and have a purer knowledge of divinity," to maintain that not only is the soul of man, but in a much greater degree that of irrational animals, the work of God; for this follows from their being said to be more beloved by God than we. Now if the rational soul alone be the work of God, then, in the first place, he did not clearly indicate that such was his opinion; and in the second place, this deduction follows from his indefinite language regarding the soul—viz., whether not every one, but only the rational, is the work of God—that neither is the nature of all bodies different (from the soul). But if the nature of all bodies be not different, although the body of each animal correspond to its soul, it is evident that the body of that animal whose soul was the work of God, would differ from the body of that animal in which dwells a soul which was not the work of God. And so the assertion will be false, that there is no difference between the body of a bat, or of a worm, or of a frog, and that of a man.

CHAPTER LIX

For it would, indeed, be absurd that certain stones and buildings should be regarded as more sacred or more profane than others, according as they were constructed for the honour of God, or for the reception of dishonourable and accursed persons; while bodies should not differ from bodies, according as they are inhabited by rational or irrational beings, and according as these rational beings are the most virtuous or most worthless of mankind. Such a principle of distinction, indeed, has led some to deify the bodies of distinguished men, as having received a virtuous soul, and to reject and treat with dishonour those of very wicked individuals. I do not maintain that such a principle has been always soundly exercised, but that it had its origin in a correct idea. Would a wise man, indeed, after the death of Anytus and Socrates, think of burying the bodies of both with like honours? And would he raise the same mound or tomb to the memory of both? These instances we have adduced because of the language of Celsus, that "none of these is the work of God" (where the words "of these" refer to the body of a man or to the snakes which come out of the body and to that of an ox, or of the bees which come from the body of an ox; and to that of a horse or of an ass, and to the wasps which come from a horse, and the beetles which proceed from an ass); for which reason we have been obliged to return to the consideration of his statement, that "the soul is the work of God, but that the nature of body is different."

CHAPTER LX

He next proceeds to say, that "a common nature pervades all the previously mentioned bodies, and one which goes and returns the same amid recurring changes." In answer to this it is evident from what has been already said that not only does a common nature pervade those bodies which have been previously enumerated, but the heavenly bodies as well. And if this is the case, it is clear also that, according to Celsus (although I do not know whether it is according to truth), it is one nature which goes and returns the same through all bodies amid recurring changes. It is evident also that this is the case in the opinion of those who hold that the world is to perish; while those also who hold the opposite view will endeavour to show, without the assumption of a fifth substance, that in their judgment too it is one nature "which goes and returns the same through all bodies amid recurring changes." And thus, even that which is perishable remains in order to undergo a change; for the matter which underlies (all things), while its properties perish, still abides, according to the opinion of those who hold it to be uncreated. If, however, it can be shown by any arguments not to be uncreated, but to have been created for certain purposes, it is clear that it will not have the same nature of permanency which it would possess on the hypothesis of being uncreated. But it is not our object at present, in answering the charges of Celsus, to discuss these questions of natural philosophy.

CHAPTER LXI

He maintains, moreover, that "no product of matter is immortal." Now, in answer to this it may be said, that if no product of matter is immortal, then either the whole world is immortal, and thus not a product of matter, or it is not immortal. If, accordingly, the world is immortal (which is agreeable to the view of those who say that the soul alone is the work of God, and was produced from a certain bowl), let Celsus show that the world was not produced from a matter devoid of qualities, remembering his own assertion that "no product of matter is immortal." If, however, the world is not immortal (seeing it is a product of matter), but mortal, does it also perish, or does it not? For if it perish, it will perish as being a work of God; and then, in the event of the *world* perishing, what will become of the *soul*, which is also a work of God? Let Celsus answer this! But if, perverting the notion of immortality, he will assert that, although *perishable*, it is immortal, because it does not *really* perish; that it is *capable* of dying, but does not *actually* die,—it is evident that, according to him, there will exist something which is at the same time mortal and immortal, by being capable of both conditions; and that which does not die will be mortal, and that which is not immortal by nature will be termed in a peculiar sense immortal, because it does not die! According to what distinction, then, in the meaning of words, will he maintain that no product of matter is immortal? And thus you see that the ideas contained in his writings,

520

when closely examined and tested, are proved *not* to be sound and incontrovertible. And after making these assertions he adds: "On this point these remarks are sufficient; and if any one is capable of hearing and examining further, he will come to know (the truth)." Let us, then, who in his opinion are unintelligent individuals, see what will result from our being able to listen to him for a little, and so continue our investigation.

CHAPTER LXII

After these matters, then, he thinks that he can make us acquainted in a few words with the questions regarding the nature of evil, which have been variously discussed in many important treatises, and which have received very opposite explanations. His words are: "There neither were formerly, nor are there now, nor will there be again, more or fewer evils in the world (than have always been). For the nature of all things is one and the same, and the generation of evils is always the same." He seems to have paraphrased these words from the discussions in the *Theaetetus*, where Plato makes Socrates say: "It is neither possible for evils to disappear from among men, nor for them to become established among the gods," and so on. But he appears to me not to have understood Plato correctly, although professing to include all truth in this one treatise, and giving to his own book against us the title of *A True Discourse*. For the language in the *Timaeus*, where it is said, "When the gods purify the earth with water," shows that the earth, when purified with water, contains less evil than it did before its purification. And this assertion, that there at one time were fewer evils in the world, is one which we make, in harmony with the opinion of Plato, because of the language in the *Theaetetus*, where he says that "evils cannot disappear from among men."

CHAPTER LXIII

I do not understand how Celsus, while admitting the existence of Providence, at least so far as appears from the language of this book, can say that there never existed (at any time) either more or fewer evils, but, as it were, a fixed number; thus annihilating the beautiful doctrine regarding the indefinite nature of evil, and asserting that evil, even in its own nature, is infinite. Now it appears to follow from the position, that there never have been, nor are now, nor ever will be, more or fewer evils in the world; that as, according to the view of those who hold the indestructibility of the world, the equipoise of the elements is maintained by a Providence (which does not permit one to gain the preponderance over the others, in order to prevent the destruction of the world), so a kind of Providence presides, as it were, over evils (the number of which is fixed), to prevent their being either increased or diminished! In other ways, too, are the arguments of Celsus concerning evil confuted, by those philosophers who have investigated the subjects of good and evil, and who have proved also from history that in former times it was without the city, and with their faces concealed by masks, that loose women hired themselves to those who wanted them; that subsequently, becoming more impudent, they laid aside their masks, though not being permitted by the laws to enter the cities, they (still) remained without them, until, as the dissoluteness of manners daily increased, they dared even to enter the cities. Such accounts are given by Chrysippus in the introduction to his work on *Good and Evil.* From this also it may be seen that evils both increase and decrease, viz., that those individuals who were called "Ambiguous" used formerly to present themselves openly to view, suffering and committing all shameful things, while subserving the passions of those who frequented their society; but recently they have been expelled by the authorities. And of countless evils which, owing to the spread of wickedness, have made their appearance in human life, we may say that formerly they did *not* exist. For the most ancient histories, which bring innumerable other accusations against sinful men, know nothing of the perpetrators of abominable crimes.

CHAPTER LXIV

And now, after these arguments, and others of a similar kind, how can Celsus escape appearing in a ridiculous light, when he imagines that there never has been in the past, nor will be in the future, a greater or less number of evils? For although the nature of all things is one and the same, it does not at all follow that the production of evils is a constant quantity. For although the nature of a certain individual is one and the same, yet his mind, and his reason, and his actions, are not always alike: there being a time when he had not yet attained to reason; and another, when, with the possession of reason, he had become stained with wickedness, and when this increased to a greater or less degree; and again, a time when he devoted himself to virtue, and made greater or less progress therein, attaining sometimes the very summit of perfection, through longer or shorter periods of contemplation. In like manner, we may make the same assertion in a higher degree of the nature of the universe, that although it is one and the same in kind, yet neither do exactly the same things, nor yet things that are similar, occur in it; for we neither have invariably productive nor unproductive seasons, nor yet periods of continuous rain or of drought. And so in the same way, with regard to virtuous souls, there are neither appointed periods of fertility nor of barrenness; and the same is the case with the greater or less spread of evil. And those who desire to investigate all things to the best of their ability, must keep in view this estimate of evils, that their amount is not always the same, owing to the working of a Providence which either preserves earthly things, or purges them by means of floods and conflagrations; and effects this, perhaps, not merely with reference to things on earth, but also to the whole universe of things which stands in need of purification, when the wickedness that is in it has become great.

CHAPTER LXV

After this Celsus continues: "It is not easy, indeed, for one who is not a philosopher to ascertain the origin of evils, though it is sufficient for the multitude to say that they do not proceed from God, but cleave to matter, and have their abode among mortal things; while the course of mortal things being the same from beginning to end, the same things must always, agreeably to the appointed cycles, recur in the past, present, and future." Celsus here observes that it is not easy for one who is not a philosopher to ascertain the origin of evils, as if it were an easy matter for a philosopher to gain this knowledge, while for one who is not a philosopher it was difficult, though still possible, for such an one, although with great labour, to attain it. Now, to this we say, that the origin of evils is a subject which is not easy even for a philosopher to master, and that perhaps it is impossible even for such to attain a clear understanding of it, unless it be revealed to them by divine inspiration, both what evils are, and how they originated, and how they shall be made to disappear. But although ignorance of God *is* an evil, and one of the greatest of these is not to know how God is to be served and worshipped, yet, as even Celsus would admit, there are undoubtedly some philosophers who have been ignorant of this, as is evident from the views of the different philosophical sects; whereas, according to our judgment, no one is capable of ascertaining the origin of evils who does not know that it is wicked to suppose that piety is preserved uninjured amid the laws that are established in different states, in conformity with the generally prevailing ideas of government. No one, moreover, who has not heard what is related of him who is called "devil," and of his "angels," and what he was before he became a devil, and *how* he became such, and what was the cause of the simultaneous apostasy of those who are termed his angels, will be able to ascertain the origin of evils. But he who would attain to this knowledge must learn more accurately the nature of demons, and know that they are not the work of God so far as respects their demoniacal nature, but only in so far as they are possessed of reason; and also what their origin was, so that they became beings of such a nature, that while converted into demons, the powers of their mind remain. And if there be any topic of human investigation which is difficult for our nature to grasp, certainly the origin of evils may be considered to be such.

CHAPTER LXVI

Celsus in the next place, as if he were able to tell certain secrets regarding the origin of evils, but chose rather to keep silence, and say only what was suitable to the multitude, continues as follows: "It is sufficient to say to the multitude regarding the origin of evils, that they do not proceed from God, but cleave to matter, and dwell among mortal things." It is true, certainly, that evils do not proceed from God; for according to Jeremiah, one of our prophets, it is certain that "out of the mouth of the Most High proceedeth not evil and good." But to maintain that matter, dwelling among mortal things, is the cause of evils, is in our opinion not true. For it is the mind of each individual which is the cause of the evil which arises in him, and this is evil (in the abstract); while the actions which proceed from it are wicked, and there is, to speak with accuracy, nothing else in our view that is evil. I am aware, however, that this topic requires very elaborate treatment, which (by the grace of God enlightening the mind) may be successfully attempted by him who is deemed by God worthy to attain the necessary knowledge on this subject.

CHAPTER LXVII

I do not understand how Celsus should deem it of advantage, in writing a treatise against us, to adopt an opinion which requires at least much plausible reasoning to make it appear, as far as he can do so, that "the course of *mortal* things is the same from beginning to end, and that the same things must always, according to the appointed cycles, recur in the past, present, and future." Now, if this be true, our free-will is annihilated. For if, in the revolution of mortal things, the same events must perpetually occur in the past, present, and future, according to the appointed cycles, it is clear that, of necessity, Socrates will always be a philosopher, and be condemned for introducing strange gods and for corrupting the youth. And Anytus and Melitus must always be his accusers, and the council of the Areopagus must ever condemn him to death by hemlock. And in the same way, according to the appointed cycles, Phalaris must always play the tyrant, and Alexander of Pherae commit the same acts of cruelty, and those condemned to the bull of Phalaris continually pour forth their wailings from it. But if these things be granted, I do not see how our free-will can be preserved, or how praise or blame can be administered with propriety. We may say further to Celsus, in answer to such a view, that "if the course of moral things be always the same from beginning to end, and if, according to the appointed cycles, the same events must always occur in the past, present, and future," then, according to the appointed cycles, Moses must again come forth from Egypt with the Jewish people, and Jesus again come to dwell in human life, and perform the same actions which (according to this view) he has done not once, but countless times, as the periods have revolved. Nay, Christians too will be the same in the appointed cycles; and Celsus will again write this treatise of his, which he has done innumerable times before.

CHAPTER LXVIII

Celsus, however, says that it is only "the course of mortal things which, according to the appointed cycles, must always be the same in the past, present, and future;" whereas the majority of the Stoics maintain that this is the case not only with the course of mortal, but also with that of immortal things, and of those whom they regard as gods. For after the conflagration of the world, which has taken place countless times in the past, and will happen countless times in the future, there has been, and will be, the same arrangement of all things from the beginning to the end. The Stoics, indeed, in endeavouring to parry, I don't know how, the objections raised to their views, allege that as cycle after cycle returns, all men will be altogether unchanged from those who lived in former cycles; so that Socrates will not live again, but one altogether like to Socrates, who will marry a wife exactly like Xanthippe, and will be accused by men exactly like Anytus and Melitus. I do not understand, however, how the world is to be always the same, and one individual not different from another, and yet the things in it not the same, though exactly alike. But the main argument in answer to the statements of Celsus and of the Stoics will be more appropriately investigated elsewhere, since on the present occasion it is not consistent with the purpose we have in view to expatiate on these points.

CHAPTER LXIX

He continues to say that "neither have visible things been given to man (by God), but each individual thing comes into existence and perishes for the sake of the safety of the whole passing agreeably to the change, which I have already mentioned, from one thing to another." It is unnecessary, however, to linger over the refutation of these statements, which have been already refuted to the best of my ability. And the following, too, has been answered, viz., that "there will neither be more nor less good and evil among mortals." This point also has been referred to, viz., that "God does not need to amend His work afresh." But it is not as a man who has imperfectly designed some piece of workmanship, and executed it unskilfully, that God administers correction to the world, in purifying it by a flood or by a conflagration, but in order to prevent the tide of evil from rising to a greater height; and, moreover, I am of opinion that it is at periods which are precisely determined beforehand that He sweeps wickedness away, so as to contribute to the good of the whole world. If, however, he should assert that, after the disappearance of evil, it again comes into existence, such questions will have to be examined in a special treatise. It is, then, always in order to repair what has become faulty that God desires to amend His work afresh. For although, in the creation of the world, all things had been arranged by Him in the most beautiful and stable manner, He nevertheless needed to exercise some healing power upon those who were labouring under the disease of wickedness, and upon a whole world, which was polluted as it were thereby. But nothing has been neglected by God, or will be neglected by Him; for He does at each particular juncture what it becomes Him to do in a perverted and changed world. And as a husbandman performs different acts of husbandry upon the soil and its productions, according to the varying seasons of the year, so God administers entire ages of time, as if they were, so to speak, so many individual years, performing during each one of them what is requisite with a reasonable regard to the care of the world; and this, as it is truly understood by God alone, so also is it accomplished by Him.

CHAPTER LXX

Celsus has made a statement regarding evils of the following nature, viz., that "although a thing may seem to you to be evil, it is by no means certain that it is so; for you do not know what is of advantage to yourself, or to another, or to the whole world." Now this assertion is made with a certain degree of caution; and it hints that the nature of evil is not wholly wicked, because that which may be considered so in individual cases, may contain something which is of advantage to the whole community. However, lest any one should mistake my words, and find a pretence of wrongdoing, as if his wickedness were profitable to the world, or at least *might* be so, we have to say, that although God, who preserves the free-will of each individual, may make use of the evil of the wicked for the administration of the world, so disposing them as to conduce to the benefit of the whole; yet, notwithstanding, such an individual is deserving of censure, and as such has been appointed for a use, which is a subject of loathing to each separate individual, although of advantage to the whole community. It is as if one were to say that in the case of a city, a man who had committed certain crimes, and on account of these had been condemned to serve in public works that were useful to the community, did something that was of advantage to the entire city, while he himself was engaged in an abominable task, in which no one possessed of moderate understanding would wish to be engaged. Paul also, the apostle of Jesus, teaches us that even the very wicked will contribute to the good of the whole, while in themselves they will be amongst the vile, but that the most virtuous men, too, will be of the greatest advantage to the world, and will therefore on that account occupy the noblest position. His words are: "But in a great house there are not only vessels of gold and silver, but also of wood and of earth; and some to honour, and some to dishonour. If a man therefore purge himself, he shall be a vessel unto honour, sanctified and meet for the Master's use, prepared unto every good work." These remarks I have thought it necessary to make in reply to the assertion, that "although a thing may seem to you to be evil, it is by no means certain that it is so, for you do not know what is of advantage either to yourself or to another," in order that no one may take occasion from what has been said on the subject to commit sin, on the pretext that he will thus be useful to the world.

CHAPTER LXXI

But as, in what follows, Celsus, not understanding that the language of Scripture regarding God is adapted to an anthropopathic point of view, ridicules those passages which speak of words of anger addressed to the ungodly, and of threatenings directed against sinners, we have to say that, as we ourselves, when talking with very young children, do not aim at exerting our own power of eloquence, but, adapting ourselves to the weakness of our charge, both say and do those things which may appear to us useful for the correction and improvement of the children as children, so the word of God appears to have dealt with the history, making the capacity of the hearers, and the benefit which they were to receive, the standard of the appropriateness of its announcements (regarding Him). And, generally, with regard to such a style of speaking about God, we find in the book of Deuteronomy the following: "The LORD thy God bare with your manners, as a man would bear with the manners of his son." It is, as it were, assuming the manners of a man in order to secure the advantage of men that the Scripture makes use of such expressions; for it would not have been suitable to the condition of the multitude, that what God had to say to them should be spoken by Him in a manner more befitting the majesty of His own person. And yet he who is anxious to attain a true understanding of holy Scripture, will discover the spiritual truths which are spoken by it to those who are called "spiritual," by comparing the meaning of what is addressed to those of weaker mind with what is announced to such as are of acuter understanding, both meanings being frequently found in the same passage by him who is capable of comprehending it.

CHAPTER LXXII

We speak, indeed, of the "wrath" of God. We do not, however, assert that it indicates any "passion" on His part, but that it is something which is assumed in order to discipline by stern means those sinners who have committed many and grievous sins. For that which is called God's "wrath," and "anger," is a means of discipline; and that such a view is agreeable to Scripture, is evident from what is said in the sixth Psalm, "O LORD, rebuke me not in Thine anger, neither chasten me in Thy hot displeasure;" and also in Jeremiah. "O LORD, correct me, but with judgment: not in Thine anger, lest Thou bring me to nothing." Any one, moreover, who reads in the second book of Kings of the "wrath" of God, inducing David to number the people, and finds from the first book of Chronicles that it was the devil who suggested this measure, will, on comparing together the two statements, easily see for what purpose the "wrath" is mentioned, of which "wrath," as the Apostle Paul declares, all men are children: "We were by nature children of wrath, even as others." Moreover, that "wrath" is no passion on the part of God, but that each one brings it upon himself by his sins, will be clear from the further statement of Paul: "Or despisest thou the riches of His goodness, and forbearance, and long-suffering, not knowing that the goodness of God leadeth thee to repentance? But after thy hardness and impenitent heart, treasurest up unto thyself wrath against the day of wrath, and revelation of the righteous judgment of God." How, then, can any one treasure up for himself "wrath" against a "day of wrath," if "wrath" be understood in the sense of "passion?" or how can the "passion of wrath" be a help to discipline? Besides, the Scripture, which tells us not to be angry at all, and which says in the thirty-seventh Psalm, "Cease from anger, and forsake wrath," and which commands us by the mouth of Paul to "put off all these, anger, wrath, malice, blasphemy, filthy communication," would not involve God in the same passion from which it would have us to be altogether free. It is manifest, further, that the language used regarding the wrath of God is to be understood *figuratively* from what is related of His "sleep," from which, as if awaking Him, the prophet says: "Awake, why sleepest Thou, Lord?" and again: "Then the Lord awaked as one out of sleep, and like a mighty man that shouteth by reason of wine." If, then, "sleep" must mean something else, and not what the first acceptation of the word conveys, why should not "wrath" also be understood in a similar way? The "threatenings," again, are intimations of the (punishments) which are to befall the wicked: for it is as if one were to call the words of a physician "threats," when he tells his patients, "I will have to use the knife, and apply cauteries, if you do not obey my prescriptions, and regulate your diet and mode of life in such a way as I direct you." It is no human passions, then, which we ascribe to God, nor impious opinions which we entertain of Him; nor do we err when we present the various narratives concerning Him, drawn from the Scriptures themselves, after careful comparison one with another. For those who are wise ambassadors of the "word" have no other object in view than to free as far as they can their hearers from weak opinions, and to endue them with intelligence.

CHAPTER LXXIII

And as a sequel to his non-understanding of the statements regarding the "wrath" of God, he continues: "Is it not ridiculous to suppose that, whereas a *man*, who became angry with the Jews, slew them all from the youth upwards, and burned their city (so powerless were they to resist him), the mighty *God*, as they say, being angry, and indignant, and uttering threats, should, (instead of punishing them) send His own *Son*, who endured the sufferings which He did?" If the Jews, then, after the treatment which they dared to inflict upon Jesus, perished with all their youth, and had their city consumed by fire, they suffered this punishment in consequence of no other wrath than that which they treasured up for themselves; for the judgment of God against them, which was determined by the divine appointment, is termed "wrath" agreeably to a traditional usage of the Hebrews. And what the Son of the mighty God suffered, He suffered voluntarily for the salvation of men, as has been stated to the best of my ability in the preceding pages. He then continues: "But that I may speak not of the Jews alone (for that is not my object), but of the whole of nature, as I promised, I will bring out more clearly what has been already stated." Now what modest man, on reading these words, and knowing the weakness of humanity, would not be indignant at the offensive nature of the promise to give an account of the "whole of nature," and at an arrogance like that which prompted him to inscribe upon his book the title which he ventured to give it (of a True Discourse)? But let us see what he has to say regarding the "whole of nature," and what he is to place "in a clearer light."

CHAPTER LXXIV

He next, in many words, blames us for asserting that God made all things for the sake of man. Because from the history of animals, and from the sagacity manifested by them, he would show that all things came into existence not more for the sake of man than of the irrational animals. And here he seems to me to speak in a similar manner to those who, through dislike of their enemies, accuse them of the same things for which their own friends are commended. For as, in the instance referred to, hatred blinds these persons from seeing that they are accusing their very dearest friends by the means through which they think they are slandering their enemies; so in the same way, Celsus also, becoming confused in his argument, does not see that he is bringing a charge against the philosophers of the Porch, who, not amiss, place man in the foremost rank, and rational nature in general before irrational animals, and who maintain that Providence created all things mainly on account of rational nature. Rational beings, then, as being the principal ones, occupy the place, as it were, of children in the womb, while irrational and soulless beings hold that of the envelope which is created along with the child. I think, too, that as in cities the superintendents of the goods and market discharge their duties for the sake of no other than human beings, while dogs and other irrational animals have the benefit of the superabundance; so Providence provides *in a special manner* for rational creatures; while this also follows, that irrational creatures likewise enjoy the benefit of what is done for the sake of man. And as he is in error who alleges that the superintendents of the markets make provision in no greater degree for men than for dogs, because dogs also get their share of the goods; so in a far greater degree are Celsus and they who think with him guilty of impiety towards the God who makes provision for rational beings, in asserting that His arrangements are made in no greater degree for the sustenance of human beings than for that of plants, and trees, and herbs, and thorns.

CHAPTER LXXV

For, in the first place, he is of opinion that "thunders, and lightnings, and rains are not the works of God,"—thus showing more clearly at last his Epicurean leanings; and in the second place, that "even if one were to grant that these were the works of God, they are brought into existence not more for the support of us who are human beings, than for that of plants, and trees, and herbs, and thorns,"—maintaining, like a true Epicurean, that these things are the product of chance, and not the work of Providence. For if these things are of no more use to us than to plants, and trees, and herbs, and thorns, it is evident either that they do not proceed from Providence at all, or from a providence which does not provide for us in a greater degree than for trees, and herbs, and thorns. Now, either of these suppositions is impious in itself, and it would be foolish to refute such statements by answering any one who brought against us the charge of impiety; for it is manifest to every one, from what has been said, who is the person guilty of impiety. In the next place, he adds: "Although you may say that these things, viz., plants, and trees, and herbs, and thorns, grow for the use of men, why will you maintain that they grow for the use of men rather than for that of the most savage of irrational animals?" Let Celsus then say distinctly that the great diversity among the products of the earth is not the work of Providence, but that a certain fortuitous concurrence of atoms gave birth to qualities so diverse, and that it was owing to chance that so many kinds of plants, and trees, and herbs resemble one another, and that no disposing reason gave existence to them, and that they do *not* derive their origin from an understanding that is beyond all admiration. We Christians, however, who are devoted to the worship of the only God, who created these things, feel grateful for them to Him who made them, because not only for us, but also (on our account) for the animals which are subject to us, He has prepared such a home, seeing "He causeth the grass to grow for the cattle, and herb for the service of man, that He may bring forth food out of the earth, and wine that maketh glad the heart of man, and oil to make his face to shine, and bread which strengtheneth man's heart." But that He should have provided food even for the most savage animals is not matter of surprise, for these very animals are said by some who have philosophized (upon the subject) to have been created for the purpose of affording exercise to the rational creature. And one of our own wise men says somewhere: "Do not say, What is this? or Wherefore is that? for all things have been made for their uses. And do not say, What is this? or Wherefore is that? for everything shall be sought out in its season."

CHAPTER LXXVI

After this, Celsus, desirous of maintaining that Providence created the products of the earth, not more on our account than on that of the most savage animals, thus proceeds: "We indeed by labour and suffering earn a scanty and toilsome subsistence, while all things are produced for them without their sowing and ploughing." He does not observe that God, wishing to exercise the human understanding in all countries (that it might not remain idle and unacquainted with the arts), created man a being full of wants, in order that by virtue of his very needy condition he might be compelled to be the inventor of arts, some of which minister to his subsistence, and others to his protection. For it was better that those who would not have sought out divine things, nor engaged in the study of philosophy, should be placed in a condition of want, in order that they might employ their understanding in the invention of the arts, than that they should altogether neglect the cultivation of their minds, because their condition was one of abundance. The want of the necessaries of human life led to the invention on the one hand of the art of husbandry, on the other to that of the cultivation of the vine; again, to the art of gardening, and the arts of carpentry and smithwork, by means of which were formed the tools required for the arts which minister to the support of life. The want of covering, again, introduced the art of weaving, which followed that of wool-carding and spinning; and again, that of house-building: and thus the intelligence of men ascended even to the art of architecture. The want of necessaries caused the products also of other places to be conveyed, by means of the arts of sailing and pilotage, to those who were without them; so that even on that account one might admire the Providence which made the rational being subject to want in a far higher degree than the irrational animals, and yet all with a view to his advantage. For the irrational animals have their food provided for them, because there is not in them even an impulse towards the invention of the arts. They have, besides, a natural covering; for they are provided either with hair, or wings, or scales, or shells. Let the above, then, be our answer to the assertions of Celsus, when he says that "we indeed by labour and suffering earn a scanty and toilsome subsistence, while all things are produced for them without their sowing and ploughing."

CHAPTER LXXVII

In the next place, forgetting that his object is to accuse both Jews and Christians, he quotes against himself an iambic verse of Euripides, which is opposed to his view, and, joining issue with the words, charges them with being an erroneous statement. His words are as follow: "But if you will quote the saying of Euripides, that

'The Sun and Night are to mortals slaves,'

why should they be so in a greater degree to us than to ants and flies? For the night is created for them in order that they may rest, and the day that they may see and resume their work." Now it is undoubted, that not only have certain of the Jews and Christians declared that the sun and the heavenly bodies are our servants; but he also has said this, who, according to some, is the philosopher of the stage, and who was a hearer of the lectures on the philosophy of nature delivered by Anaxagoras. But this man asserts that all things in the world are subject to all rational beings,—one rational nature being taken to represent all, on the principle of a part standing for the whole; which, again, clearly appears from the verse:—

"The Sun and Night are to mortals slaves."

Perhaps the tragic poet meant the day when he said the sun, inasmuch as it is the cause of the day,—teaching that those things which most need the day and night are the things which are under the moon, and other things in a less degree than those which are upon the earth. Day and night, then, are subject to mortals, being created for the sake of rational beings. And if ants and flies, which labour by day and rest by night, have, besides, the benefit of those things which were created for the sake of men, we must not say that day and night were brought into being for the sake of ants and flies, nor must we suppose that they were created for the sake of nothing, but, agreeably to the design of Providence, were formed for the sake of man.

CHAPTER LXXVIII

He next proceeds further to object against himself what is said on behalf of man, viz., that the irrational animals were created on his account, saying: "If one were to call us the lords of the animal creation because we hunt the other animals and live upon their flesh, we would say, Why were not we rather created on *their* account, since they hunt and devour us? Nay, *we* require nets and weapons, and the assistance of many persons, along with dogs, when engaged in the chase; while they are immediately and spontaneously provided by nature with weapons which easily bring us under their power." And here we may observe, that the gift of understanding has been bestowed upon us as a mighty aid, far superior to any weapon which wild beasts may seem to possess. We, indeed, who are far weaker in bodily strength than the beasts, and shorter in stature than some of them, yet by means of our understanding obtain the mastery, and capture the huge elephants. We subdue by our gentle treatment those animals whose nature it is to be tamed, while with those whose nature is different, or which do not appear likely to be of use to us when tamed, we take such precautionary measures, that when we desire it, we keep such wild beasts shut up; and when we need the flesh of their bodies for food, we slaughter them, as we do those beasts which are not of a savage nature. The Creator, then, has constituted all things the servants of the rational being and of his natural understanding. For some purposes we require dogs, say as guardians of our sheep-folds, or of our cattle-yards, or goat-pastures, or of our dwellings; and for other purposes we need oxen, as for agriculture; and for others, again, we make use of those which bear the yoke, or beasts of burden. And so it may be said that the race of lions, and bears, and leopards, and wild boars, and such like, has been given to us in order to call into exercise the elements of the manly character that exists within us.

CHAPTER LXXIX

In the next place, in answer to the human race, who perceive their own superiority, which far exceeds that of the irrational animals, he says: "With respect to your assertion, that God gave you the power to capture wild beasts, and to make your own use of them, we would say that, in all probability, before cities were built, and arts invented, and societies such as now exist were formed, and weapons and nets employed, men were generally caught and devoured by wild beasts, while wild beasts were very seldom captured by men." Now, in reference to this, observe that although men catch wild beasts, and wild beasts make prey of men, there is a great difference between the case of such as by means of their understanding obtain the mastery over those whose superiority consists in their savage and cruel nature, and that of those who do not make use of their understanding to secure their safety from injury by wild beasts. But when Celsus says, "before cities were built, and arts invented, and societies such as now exist were formed," he appears to have forgotten what he had before said, that "the world was uncreated and incorruptible, and that it was only the things on earth which underwent deluges and conflagrations, and that all these things did not happen at the same time." Now let it be granted that these admissions on his part are entirely in harmony with our views, though not at all with him and his statements made above; yet what does it all avail to prove that in the beginning men were mostly captured and devoured by wild beasts, while wild beasts were never caught by men? For, since the world was created in conformity with the will of Providence, and God presided over the universe of things, it was necessary that the elements of the human race should at the commencement of its existence be placed under some protection of the higher powers, so that there might be formed from the beginning a union of the divine nature with that of men. And the poet of Ascra, perceiving this, sings:—

"For common then were banquets, and common were seats,
Alike to immortal gods and mortal men."

CHAPTER LXXX

Those holy Scriptures, moreover, which bear the name of Moses, introduce the first men as hearing divine voices and oracles, and beholding sometimes the angels of God coming to visit them. For it was probable that in the beginning of the world's existence human nature would be assisted to a greater degree (than afterwards), until progress had been made towards the attainment of understanding and the other virtues, and the invention of the arts, and they should thus be able to maintain life of themselves, and no longer stand in need of superintendents, and of those to guide them who do so with a miraculous manifestation of the means which subserve the will of God. Now it follows from this, that it is false that "in the beginning men were captured and devoured by wild beasts, while wild beasts were very seldom caught by men." And from this, too, it is evident that the following statement of Celsus is untrue, that "in this way God rather subjected men to wild beasts." For God did not subject men to wild beasts, but gave wild beasts to be a prey to the understanding of man, and to the arts, which are directed against them, and which are the product of the understanding. For it was not without the help of God that men desired for themselves the means of protection against wild beasts, and of securing the mastery over them.

CHAPTER LXXXI

Our noble opponent, however, not observing how many philosophers there are who admit the existence of Providence, and who hold that Providence created all things for the sake of rational beings, overturns as far as he can those doctrines which are of use in showing the harmony that prevails in these matters between Christianity and philosophy; nor does he see how great is the injury done to religion from accepting the statement that before God there is no difference between a man and an ant or a bee, but proceeds to add, that "if men appear to be superior to irrational animals on this account, that they have built cities, and make use of a political constitution, and forms of government, and sovereignties, this is to say nothing to the purpose, for ants and bees do the same. Bees, indeed, have a sovereign, who has followers and attendants; and there occur among them wars and victories, and slaughterings of the vanquished, and cities and suburbs, and a succession of labours, and judgments passed upon the idle and the wicked; for the drones are driven away and punished." Now here he did not observe the difference that exists between what is done after reason and consideration, and what is the result of an irrational nature, and is purely mechanical. For the origin of these things is not explained by the existence of any rational principle in those who make them, because they do not possess any such principle; but the most ancient Being, who is also the Son of God, and the King of all things that exist, has created an irrational nature, which, as being irrational, acts as a help to those who are deemed worthy of reason. Cities, accordingly, were established among men, with many arts and well-arranged laws; while constitutions, and governments, and sovereignties among men are either such as are properly so termed, and which exemplify certain virtuous tendencies and workings, or they are those which are improperly so called, and which were devised, so far as could be done, in imitation of the former: for it was by contemplating these that the most successful legislators established the best constitutions, and governments, and sovereignties. None of these things, however, can be found among irrational animals, although Celsus may transfer rational names, and arrangements which belong to rational beings, as cities and constitutions, and rulers and sovereignties, even to ants and bees; in respect to which matters, however, ants and bees merit no approval, because they do not act from reflection. But we ought to admire the divine nature, which extended even to irrational animals the capacity, as it were, of imitating rational beings, perhaps with a view of putting rational beings to shame; so that by looking upon ants, for instance, they might become more industrious and more thrifty in the management of their goods; while, by considering the bees, they might place themselves in subjection to their Ruler, and take their respective parts in those constitutional duties which are of use in ensuring the safety of cities.

CHAPTER LXXXII

Perhaps also the so-called wars among the bees convey instruction as to the manner in which wars, if ever there arise a necessity for them, should be waged in a just and orderly way among men. But the bees have no cities or suburbs; while their hives and hexagonal cells, and succession of labours, are for the sake of men, who require honey for many purposes, both for cure of disordered bodies, and as a pure article of food. Nor ought we to compare the proceedings taken by the bees against the drones with the judgments and punishments inflicted on the idle and wicked in cities. But, as I formerly said, we ought on the one hand in these things to admire the divine nature, and on the other to express our admiration of man, who is capable of considering and admiring all things (as co-operating with Providence), and who executes not merely the works which are determined by the providence of God, but also those which are the consequences of his own foresight.

CHAPTER LXXXIII

After Celsus has finished speaking of the bees, in order to depreciate (as far as he can) the cities, and constitutions, and governments, and sovereignties not only of us Christians, but of all mankind, as well as the wars which men undertake on behalf of their native countries, he proceeds, by way of digression, to pass a eulogy upon the ants, in order that, while praising them, he may compare the measures which men take to secure their subsistence with those adopted by these insects, and so evince his contempt for the forethought which makes provision for winter, as being nothing higher than the irrational providence of the ants, as he regards it. Now might not some of the more simple-minded, and such as know not how to look into the nature of all things, be turned away (so far, at least, as Celsus could accomplish it) from helping those who are weighed down with the burdens (of life), and from sharing their toils, when he says of the ants, that "they help one another with their loads, when they see one of their number toiling under them?" For he who needs to be disciplined by the word, but who does not at all understand its voice, will say: "Since, then, there is no difference between us and the ants, even when we help those who are weary with bearing their heavy burdens, why should we continue to do so to no purpose?" And would not the ants, as being irrational creature, be greatly puffed up, and think highly of themselves, because their works were compared to those of men? while men, on the other hand, who by means of their reason are enabled to hear how their philanthropy towards others is contemned, would be injured, so far as could be effected by Celsus and his arguments: for he does not perceive that, while he wishes to turn away from Christianity those who read his treatise, he turns away also the sympathy of those who are not Christians from those who bear the heaviest burdens (of life). Whereas, had he been a philosopher, who was capable of perceiving the good which men may do each other, he ought, in addition to not removing along with Christianity the blessings which are found amongst men, to have lent his aid to co-operate (if he had it in his power) with those principles of excellence which are common to Christianity and the rest of mankind. Moreover, even if the ants set apart in a place by themselves those grains which sprout forth, that they may not swell into bud, but may continue throughout the year as their food, this is not to be deemed as evidence of the existence of *reason* among ants, but as the work of the universal mother, Nature, which adorned even irrational animals, so that even the most insignificant is not omitted, but bears traces of the reason implanted in it by nature. Unless, indeed, by these assertions Celsus means obscurely to intimate (for in many instances he would like to adopt Platonic ideas) that all souls are of the same species, and that there is no difference between that of a man and those of ants and bees, which is the act of one who would bring down the soul from the vault of heaven, and cause it to enter not only a human body, but that of an animal. Christians, however, will not yield their assent to such opinions: for they have been instructed before now that the human soul was created in the image of God; and they see that it is impossible for a nature fashioned in the divine image to have its (original) features altogether obliterated, and to assume others, formed after I know not what likeness of irrational animals.

CHAPTER LXXXIV

And since he asserts that, "when ants die, the survivors set apart a special place (for their interment), and that their ancestral sepulchres such a place is," we have to answer, that the greater the laudations which he heaps upon irrational animals, so much the more does he magnify (although against his will) the work of that reason which arranged all things in order, and points out the skill which exists among men, and which is capable of adorning by its reason even the gifts which are bestowed by nature on the irrational creation. But why do I say "irrational," since Celsus is of opinion that these animals, which, agreeably to the common ideas of all men, are termed irrational, are not really so? Nor does *he* regard the ants as devoid of reason, who professed to speak of "universal nature," and who boasted of his truthfulness in the inscription of his book. For, speaking of the ants conversing with one another, he uses the following language: "And when they meet one another they enter into conversation, for which reason they never mistake their way; consequently they possess a full endowment of reason, and some common ideas on certain general subjects, and a voice by which they express themselves regarding accidental things." Now conversation between one man and another is carried on by means of a voice, which gives expression to the meaning intended, and which also gives utterances concerning what are called "accidental things;" but to say that this was the case with ants would be a most ridiculous assertion.

CHAPTER LXXXV

He is not ashamed, moreover, to say, in addition to these statements (that the unseemly character of his opinions may be manifest to those who will live after him): "Come now, if one were to look down from heaven upon earth, in what respect would *our* actions appear to differ from those of ants and bees?" Now does he who, according to his own supposition, looks from heaven upon the proceedings of men and ants, look upon their bodies alone, and not rather have regard to the controlling reason which is called into action by reflection; while, on the other hand, the guiding principle of the latter is irrational, and set in motion irrationally by impulse and fancy, in conjunction with a certain natural apparatus? But it is absurd to suppose that he who looks from heaven upon earthly things would desire to look from such a distance upon the *bodies* of men and ants, and would not rather consider the nature of the guiding principles, and the source of impulses, whether that be rational or irrational. And if he once look upon the source of all impulses, it is manifest that he would behold also the difference which exists, and the superiority of man, not only over ants, but even over elephants. For he who looks from heaven will see among irrational creatures, however large their bodies, no other principle than, so to speak, irrationality; while amongst rational beings he will discover reason, the common possession of men, and of divine and heavenly beings, and perhaps of the Supreme God Himself, on account of which man is said to have been created in the image of God, for the image of the Supreme God is his reason.

CHAPTER LXXXVI

Immediately after this, as if doing his utmost to reduce the human race to a still lower position, and to bring them to the level of the irrational animals, and desiring to omit not a single circumstance related of the latter which manifests their greatness, he declares that "in certain individuals among the irrational creation there exists the power of sorcery;" so that even in this particular men cannot specially pride themselves, nor wish to arrogate a superiority over irrational creatures. And the following are his words: "If, however, men entertain lofty notions because of their possessing the power of sorcery, yet even in that respect are serpents and eagles their superiors in wisdom; for they are acquainted with many prophylactics against persons and diseases, and also with the virtues of certain stones which help to preserve their young. If men, however, fall in with these, they think that they have gained a wonderful possession." Now, in the first place, I know not why he should designate as sorcery the knowledge of natural prophylactics displayed by animals,—whether that knowledge be the result of experience, or of some natural power of apprehension; for the term "sorcery" has by usage been assigned to something else. Perhaps, indeed, he wishes quietly, as an Epicurean, to censure the entire use of such arts, as resting only on the professions of sorcerers. However, let it be granted him that men *do* pride themselves greatly upon the knowledge of such arts, whether they are sorcerers or not: how can serpents be in this respect wiser than men, when they make use of the well-known fennel to sharpen their power of vision and to produce rapidity of movement, having obtained this natural power not from the exercise of reflection, but from the constitution of their body, while men do not, like serpents, arrive at such knowledge merely by nature, but partly by experiment, partly by reason, and sometimes by reflection and knowledge? So, if eagles, too, in order to preserve their young in the nest, carry thither the eagle-stone when they have discovered it, how does it appear that they are wise, and more intelligent than men, who find out by the exercise of their reflective powers and of their understanding what has been bestowed by nature upon eagles as a gift?

CHAPTER LXXXVII

Let it be granted, however, that there are other prophylactics against poisons known to animals: what does that avail to prove that it is not nature, but reason, which leads to the discovery of such things among them? For if reason were the discoverer, this one thing (or, if you will, one or two more things) would not be (exclusive of all others) the sole discovery made by serpents, and some other thing the sole discovery of the eagle, and so on with the rest of the animals; but as many discoveries would have been made amongst them as among men. But now it is manifest from the determinate inclination of the nature of each animal towards certain kinds of help, that they possess neither wisdom nor reason, but a natural constitutional tendency implanted by the Logos towards such things in order to ensure the preservation of the animal. And, indeed, if I wished to join issue with Celsus in these matters, I might quote the words of Solomon from the book of Proverbs, which run thus: "There be four things which are little upon the earth, but these are wiser than the wise: The ants are a people not strong, yet they prepare their meat in the summer; the conies are but a feeble folk, yet make they their houses in the rocks; the locusts have no king, yet go they forth in order at one command; and the spotted lizard, though leaning upon its hands, and being easily captured, dwelleth in kings' fortresses." I do not quote these words, however, as taking them in their literal signification, but, agreeably to the title of the book (for it is inscribed "Proverbs"), I investigate them as containing a secret meaning. For it is the custom of these writers (of Scripture) to distribute into many classes those writings which express one sense when taken literally, but which convey a different signification as their hidden meaning; and one of these kinds of writing is "Proverbs." And for this reason, in our Gospels too, is our Saviour described as saying: "These things have I spoken to you in proverbs, but the time cometh when I shall no more speak unto you in proverbs." It is not, then, the *visible* ants which are "wiser even than the wise," but they who are indicated as such under the "proverbial" style of expression. And such must be our conclusion regarding the rest of the animal creation, although Celsus regards the books of the Jews and Christians as exceedingly simple and commonplace, and imagines that those who give them an allegorical interpretation do violence to the meaning of the writers. By what we have said, then, let it appear that Celsus calumniates us in vain, and let his assertions that serpents and eagles are wiser than men also receive their refutation.

CHAPTER LXXXVIII

And wishing to show at greater length that even the thoughts of God entertained by the human race are not superior to those of all other mortal creatures, but that certain of the irrational animals are capable of thinking about Him regarding whom opinions so discordant have existed among the most acute of mankind—Greeks and Barbarians—he continues: "If, because man has been able to grasp the idea of God, he is deemed superior to the other animals, let those who hold this opinion know that this capacity will be claimed by many of the other animals; and with good reason: for what would any one maintain to be more divine than the power of foreknowing and predicting future events? Men accordingly acquire the art from the other animals, and especially from birds. And those who listen to the indications furnished by them, become possessed of the gift of prophecy. If, then, birds, and the other prophetic animals, which are enabled by the gift of God to foreknow events, instruct us by means of signs, so much the nearer do they seem to be to the society of God, and to be endowed with greater wisdom, and to be more beloved by Him. The more intelligent of men, moreover, say that the animals hold meetings which are more sacred than our assemblies, and that they know what is said at these meetings, and show that in reality they possess this knowledge, when, having previously stated that the birds have declared their intention of departing to some particular place, and of doing this thing or the other, the truth of their assertions is established by the departure of the birds to the place in question, and by their doing what was foretold. And no race of animals appears to be more observant of oaths than the elephants are, or to show greater devotion to divine things; and this, I presume, solely because they have some knowledge of God." See here now how he at once lays hold of, and brings forward as acknowledged facts, questions which are the subject of dispute among those philosophers, not only among the Greeks, but also among the Barbarians, who have either discovered or learned from certain demons some things about birds of augury and other animals, by which certain prophetic intimations are said to be made to men. For, in the first place, it has been disputed whether there *is* an art of augury, and, in general, a method of divination by animals, or not. And, in the second place, they who admit that there is an art of divination by birds, are not agreed about the manner of the divination; since some maintain that it is from certain demons or gods of divination that the animals receive their impulses to action—the birds to flights and sounds of different kinds, and the other animals to movements of one sort or another. Others, again, believe that their souls are more divine in their nature, and fitted to operations of that kind, which is a most incredible supposition.

CHAPTER LXXXIX

Celsus, however, seeing he wished to prove by the foregoing statements that the irrational animals are more divine and intelligent than human beings, ought to have established at greater length the actual existence of such an art of divination, and in the next place have energetically undertaken its defence, and effectually refuted the arguments of those who would annihilate such arts of divination, and have overturned in a convincing manner also the arguments of those who say that it is from demons or from gods that animals receive the movements which lead them to divination, and to have proved in the next place that the soul of irrational animals is more divine than that of man. For, had he done so, and manifested a philosophical spirit in dealing with such things, we should to the best of our power have met his confident assertions, refuting in the first place the allegation that irrational animals are wiser than men, and showing the falsity of the statement that they have ideas of God more sacred than ours, and that they hold among themselves certain sacred assemblies. But now, on the contrary, *he* who accuses us because we believe in the Supreme God, requires us to believe that the souls of birds entertain ideas of God more divine and distinct than those of men. Yet if this is true, the birds have clearer ideas of God than Celsus himself; and it is not matter of surprise that it should be so with him, who so greatly depreciates human beings. Nay, so far as Celsus can make it appear, the birds possess grander and more divine ideas than, I do not say we Christians do, or than the Jews, who use the same Scriptures with ourselves, but even than are possessed by the theologians among the Greeks, for they were only human beings. According to Celsus, indeed, the tribe of birds that practise divination, forsooth, understand the nature of the Divine Being better than Pherecydes, and Pythagoras, and Socrates and Plato! We ought then to go to the birds as our teachers, in order that as, according to the view of Celsus, they instruct us by their power of divination in the knowledge of future events, so also they may free men from doubts regarding the Divine Being, by imparting to them the clear ideas which they have obtained respecting Him! It follows, accordingly, that Celsus, who regards birds as superior to men, ought to employ them as his instructors, and not one of the Greek philosophers.

CHAPTER XC

But we have a few remarks to make, out of a larger number, in answer to these statements of Celsus, that we may show the ingratitude towards his Maker which is involved in his holding these false opinions. For Celsus, although a man, and "being in honour," does not possess understanding, and therefore he did not compare himself with the birds and the other irrational animals, which he regards as capable of divining; but yielding to them the foremost place, he lowered himself, and as far as he could the whole human race with him (as entertaining lower and inferior views of God than the irrational animals), beneath the Egyptians, who worship irrational animals as divinities. Let the principal point of investigation, however, be this: whether there actually is or not an art of divination, by means of birds and other living things believed to have such power. For the arguments which tend to establish either view are not to be despised. On the one hand, it is pressed upon us not to admit such an art, lest the rational being should abandon the divine oracles, and betake himself to birds; and on the other, there is the energetic testimony of many, that numerous individuals have been saved from the greatest dangers by putting their trust in divination by birds. For the present, however, let it be granted that an art of divination does exist, in order that I may in this way show to those who are prejudiced on the subject, that if this be admitted, the superiority of man over irrational animals, even over those that are endowed with power of divination, is great, and beyond all reach of comparison with the latter. We have then to say, that if there was in them any divine nature capable of foretelling future events, and so rich (in that knowledge) as out of its superabundance to make them known to any man who wished to know them, it is manifest that they would know what concerned themselves far sooner (than what concerned others); and had they possessed this knowledge, they would have been upon their guard against flying to any particular place where men had planted snares and nets to catch them, or where archers took aim and shot at them in their flight. And especially, were eagles aware beforehand of the designs formed against their young, either by serpents crawling up to their nests and destroying them, or by men who take them for their amusement, or for any other useful purpose or service, they would not have placed their young in a spot where they were to be attacked; and, in general, not one of these animals would have been captured by men, because they were more divine and intelligent than they.

CHAPTER XCI

But besides, if birds of augury converse with one another, as Celsus maintains they do, the prophetic birds having a divine nature, and the other rational animals also ideas of the divinity and foreknowledge of future events; and if they had communicated this knowledge to others, the sparrow mentioned in Homer would not have built her nest in the spot where a serpent was to devour her and her young ones, nor would the serpent in the writings of the same poet have failed to take precautions against being captured by the eagle. For this wonderful poet says, in his poem regarding the former:—

"A mighty dragon shot, of dire portent;
From Jove himself the dreadful sign was sent.
Straight to the tree his sanguine spires he rolled,
And curled around in many a winding fold.
The topmost branch a mother-bird possessed;
Eight callow infants filled the mossy nest;
Herself the ninth: the serpent, as he hung,
Stretched his black jaws, and crashed the dying young;
While hovering near, with miserable moan,
The drooping mother wailed her children gone.
The mother last, as round the nest she flew,
Seized by the beating wing, the monster slew:
Nor long survived: to marble turned, he stands
A lasting prodigy on Aulis' sands.
Such was the will of Jove; and hence we dare
Trust in his omen, and support the war."

And regarding the second—the bird—the poet says:—

"Jove's bird on sounding pinions beat the skies;
A bleeding serpent of enormous size,
His talons twined; alive, and curling round,
He stung the bird, whose throat received the wound.
Mad with the smart, he drops the fatal prey,
In airy circles wings his painful way,
Floats on the winds, and rends the heaven with cries;
Amidst the host, the fallen serpent lies.
They, pale with terror, mark its spires unrolled,

And Jove's portent with beating hearts behold."

Did the eagle, then, possess the power of divination, and the serpent (since this animal also is made use of by the augurs) not? But as this distinction can be easily refuted, cannot the assertion that both were capable of divination be refuted also? For if the serpent had possessed this knowledge, would not he have been on his guard against suffering what he did from the eagle? And innumerable other instances of a similar character may be found, to show that animals do not possess a prophetic soul, but that, according to the poet and the majority of mankind, it is the "Olympian himself who sent him to the light." And it is with a symbolical meaning that Apollo employs the hawk as his messenger, for the hawk is called the "swift messenger of Apollo."

CHAPTER XCII

In my opinion, however, it is certain wicked demons, and, so to speak, of the race of Titans or Giants, who have been guilty of impiety towards the true God, and towards the angels in heaven, and who have fallen from it, and who haunt the denser parts of bodies, and frequent unclean places upon earth, and who, possessing some power of distinguishing future events, because they are without bodies of earthly material, engage in an employment of this kind, and desiring to lead the human race away from the true God, secretly enter the bodies of the more rapacious and savage and wicked of animals, and stir them up to do whatever they choose, and at whatever time they choose: either turning the fancies of these animals to make flights and movements of various kinds, in order that men may be caught by the divining power that is in the irrational animals, and neglect to seek after the God who contains all things; or to search after the pure worship of God, but allow their reasoning powers to grovel on the earth, and amongst birds and serpents, and even foxes and wolves. For it has been observed by those who are skilled in such matters, that the clearest prognostications are obtained from animals of this kind; because the demons cannot act so effectively in the milder sort of animals as they can in these, in consequence of the similarity between them in point of wickedness; and yet it is not wickedness, but something like wickedness, which exist in these animals.

CHAPTER XCIII

For which reason, whatever else there may be in the writings of

Moses which excites my wonder, I would say that the following is worthy of admiration, viz., that Moses, having observed the varying natures of animals, and having either learned from God what was peculiar to them, and to the demons which are kindred to each of the animals, or having himself ascertained these things by his own wisdom, has, in arranging the different kinds of animals, pronounced all those which are supposed by the Egyptians and the rest of mankind to possess the power of divination to be unclean, and, as a general rule, all that are not of that class to be clean. And amongst the unclean animals mentioned by Moses are the wolf, and fox, and serpent, and eagle, and hawk, and such like. And, generally speaking, you will find that not only in the law, but also in the prophets, these animals are employed as examples of all that is most wicked; and that a wolf or a fox is never mentioned for a good purpose. Each species of demon, consequently, would seem to possess a certain affinity with a certain species of animal. And as among men there are some who are stronger than others, and this not at all owing to their moral character, so, in the same way, some demons will be more powerful in things indifferent than others; and one class of them employs one kind of animal for the purpose of deluding men, in accordance with the will of him who is called in our Scriptures the "prince of this world," while others predict future events by means of another kind of animal. Observe, moreover, to what a pitch of wickedness the demons proceed, so that they even assume the bodies of weasels in order to reveal the future! And now, consider with yourself whether it is better to accept the belief that it is the Supreme God and His Son who stir up the birds and the other living creatures to divination, or that those who stir up these creatures, and not human beings (although they are present before them), are wicked, and, as they are called by our Scriptures, unclean demons.

CHAPTER XCIV

But if the soul of birds is to be esteemed divine because future events are predicted by them, why should we not rather maintain, that when omens are accepted by men, the souls of those are divine through which the omens are heard? Accordingly, among such would be ranked the female slave mentioned in Homer, who ground the corn, when she said regarding the suitors:—

"For the very last time, now, will they sup here."

This slave, then, was divine, while the great Ulysses, the friend of Homer's Pallas Athene, was *not* divine, but understanding the words

547

spoken by this "divine" grinder of corn as an omen, rejoiced, as the poet says:—

"The divine Ulysses rejoiced at the omen."

Observe, now, as the birds are possessed of a divine soul, and are capable of perceiving God, or, as Celsus says, the gods, it is clear that when we men also sneeze, we do so in consequence of a kind of divinity that is within us, and which imparts a prophetic power to our soul. For this belief is testified by many witnesses, and therefore the poet also says:—

"And while he prayed, he sneezed."

And Penelope, too, said:—

"Perceiv'st thou not that at every word my son did sneeze?"

CHAPTER XCV

The true God, however, neither employs irrational animals, nor any individuals whom chance may offer, to convey a knowledge of the future; but, on the contrary, the most pure and holy of human souls, whom He inspires and endows with prophetic power. And therefore, whatever else in the Mosaic writings may excite our wonder, the following must be considered as fitted to do so: "Ye shall not practise augury, nor observe the flight of birds;" and in another place: "For the nations whom the LORD thy God will destroy from before thy face, shall listen to omens and divinations; but as for thee, the LORD thy God has not suffered thee to do so." And he adds: "A prophet shall the LORD your God raise up unto you from among your brethren." On one occasion, moreover, God, wishing by means of an augur to turn away (His people) from the practice of divination, caused the spirit that was in the augur to speak as follows: "For there is no enchantment in Jacob, nor is there divination in Israel. In due time will it be declared to Jacob and Israel what the Lord will do." And now, we who knew these and similar sayings wish to observe this precept with the mystical meaning, viz., "Keep thy heart with all diligence," that nothing of a demoniacal nature may enter into our minds, or any spirit of our adversaries turn our imagination whither it chooses. But we pray that the light of the knowledge of the glory of God may shine in our hearts, and that the Spirit of God may dwell in our imaginations, and lead them to contemplate the things of God; for "as many as are led by the Spirit of God, they are the sons of God."

CHAPTER XCVI

We ought to take note, however, that the power of foreknowing the future is by no means a proof of divinity; for in itself it is a thing indifferent, and is found occurring amongst both good and bad. Physicians, at any rate, by means of their professional skill foreknow certain things, although their character may happen to be bad. And in the same way also pilots, although perhaps wicked men, are able to foretell the signs (of good or bad weather), and the approach of violent tempests of wind, and atmospheric changes, because they gather this knowledge from experience and observation, although I do not suppose that on that account any one would term them "gods" if their characters happened to be bad. The assertion, then, of Celsus is false, when he says: "What could be called more divine than the power of foreknowing and foretelling the future?" And so also is this, that "many of the animals claim to have ideas of God;" for none of the irrational animals possess any idea of God. And wholly false, too, is his assertion, that "the irrational animals are nearer the society of God (than men)," when even men who are still in a state of wickedness, however great their progress in knowledge, are far removed from that society. It is, then, those alone who are truly wise and sincerely religious who are nearer to God's society; such persons as were our prophets, and Moses, to the latter of whom, on account of his exceeding purity, the Scripture said: "Moses alone shall come near the Lord, but the rest shall not come nigh."

CHAPTER XCVII

How impious, indeed, is the assertion of this man, who charges us with impiety, that "not only are the irrational animals wiser than the human race, but that they are more beloved by God (than they)!" And who would not be repelled (by horror) from paying any attention to a man who declared that a serpent, and a fox, and a wolf, and an eagle, and a hawk, were more beloved by God than the human race? For it follows from his maintaining such a position, that if these animals be more beloved by God than human beings, it is manifest that they are dearer to God than Socrates, and Plato, and Pythagoras, and Pherecydes, and those theologians whose praises he had sung a little before. And one might address him with the prayer: "If these animals be dearer to God than men, may you be beloved of God along with them, and be made like to those whom you consider as dearer to Him than human beings!" And let no one suppose that such a prayer is meant as an imprecation; for who would not pray to resemble in all respects those whom he believes to be dearer to God than others, in order that he, like them, may enjoy the divine love? And as Celsus is desirous to show that the assemblies of the irrational animals are more sacred than ours, he ascribes the statement to that effect not to any ordinary individuals, but to persons of intelligence. Yet it is the virtuous alone who are truly wise, for no wicked man is so. He speaks, accordingly, in the following style: "Intelligent men say that these animals hold assemblies which are more sacred than ours, and that they know what is spoken at them, and actually prove that they are not without such knowledge, when they mention beforehand that the birds have announced their intention of departing to a particular place, or of doing this thing or that, and then show that they *have* departed to the place in question, and have done the particular thing which was foretold." Now, truly, no person of intelligence ever related such things; nor did any wise man ever say that the assemblies of the irrational animals were more sacred than those of men. But if, for the purpose of examining (the soundness of) his statements, we look to their consequences, it is evident that, in his opinion, the assemblies of the irrational animals are more sacred than those of the venerable Pherecydes, and Pythagoras, and Socrates, and Plato, and of philosophers in general; which assertion is not only incongruous in itself, but full of absurdity. In order that we may believe, however, that certain individuals *do* learn from the indistinct sound of birds that they are about to take their departure, and do this thing or that, and announce these things beforehand, we would say that this information is imparted to men by demons by means of signs, with the view of having men deceived by demons, and having their understanding dragged down from God and heaven to earth, and to places lower still.

CHAPTER XCVIII

I do not know, moreover, how Celsus could hear of the elephants' (fidelity to) oaths, and of their great devotedness to our God, and of the knowledge which they possess of Him. For I know many wonderful things which are related of the nature of this animal, and of its gentle disposition. But I am not aware that any one has spoken of its observance of oaths; unless indeed to its gentle disposition, and its observance of compacts, so to speak, when once concluded between it and man, he give the name of keeping its oath, which statement also in itself is false. For although rarely, yet sometimes it has been recorded that, after their apparent tameness, they have broken out against men in the most savage manner, and have committed murder, and have been on that account condemned to death, because no longer of any use. And seeing that after this, in order to establish (as he thinks he does) that the stork is more pious than any human being, he adduces the accounts which are narrated regarding that creature's display of filial affection in bringing food to its parents for their support, we have to say in reply, that this is done by the storks, not from a regard to what is proper, nor from reflection, but from a natural instinct; the nature which formed them being desirous to show an instance among the irrational animals which might put men to shame, in the matter of exhibiting their gratitude to their parents. And if Celsus had known how great the difference is between acting in this way from reason, and from an irrational natural impulse, he would not have said that storks are more pious than human beings. But further, Celsus, as still contending for the piety of the irrational creation, quotes the instance of the Arabian bird the phoenix, which after many years repairs to Egypt, and bears thither its parent, when dead and buried in a ball of myrrh, and deposits its body in the Temple of the Sun. Now this story is indeed recorded, and, if it be true, it is possible that it may occur in consequence of some provision of nature; divine providence freely displaying to human beings, by the differences which exist among living things, the variety of constitution which prevails in the world, and which extends even to birds, and in harmony with which He has brought into existence one creature, the only one of its kind, in order that by it men may be led to admire, not the creature, but Him who created it.

CHAPTER XCIX

In addition to all that he has already said, Celsus subjoins the following: "All things, accordingly, were not made for man, any more than they were made for lions, or eagles, or dolphins, but that this world, as being God's work, might be perfect and entire in all respects. For this reason all things have been adjusted, not with reference to each other, but with regard to their bearing upon the whole. And God takes care of the whole, and (His) providence will never forsake it; and it does not become worse; nor does God after a time bring it back to himself; nor is He angry on account of men any more than on account of apes or flies; nor does He threaten these beings, each one of which has received its appointed lot in its proper place." Let us then briefly reply to these statements. I think, indeed, that I have shown in the preceding pages that all things were created for man, and every rational being, and that it was chiefly for the sake of the rational creature that the creation took place. Celsus, indeed, may say that this was done not more for man than for lions, or the other creatures which he mentions; but we maintain that the Creator did not form these things for lions, or eagles, or dolphins, but all for the sake of the rational creature, and "in order that this world, as being God's work, might be perfect and complete in all things." For to this sentiment we must yield our assent as being well said. And God takes care, not, as Celsus supposes, merely of the *whole*, but beyond the whole, in a special degree of every rational being. Nor will Providence ever abandon the whole; for although it should become more wicked, owing to the sin of the rational being, which is a portion of the whole, He makes arrangements to purify it, and after a time to bring back the whole to Himself. Moreover, He is not angry with apes or flies; but on human beings, as those who have transgressed the laws of nature, He sends judgments and chastisements, and threatens them by the mouth of the prophets, and by the Saviour who came to visit the whole human race, that those who hear the threatenings may be converted by them, while those who neglect these calls to conversion may deservedly suffer those punishments which it becomes God, in conformity with that will of His which acts for the advantage of the whole, to inflict upon those who need such painful discipline and correction. But as our fourth book has now attained sufficient dimensions, we shall here terminate our discourse. And may God grant, through His Son, who is God the Word, and Wisdom, and Truth, and Righteousness, and everything else which the sacred Scriptures when speaking of God call Him, that we may make a good beginning of the fifth book, to the benefit of our readers, and may bring it to a successful conclusion, with the aid of His word abiding in our soul.

BOOK V

CHAPTER I

IT is not, my reverend Ambrosius, because we seek after many words—
a thing which is forbidden, and in the indulgence of which it is
impossible to avoid sin—that we now begin the fifth book of our reply
to the treatise of Celsus, but with the endeavour, so far as may be within
our power, to leave none of his statements without examination, and
especially those in which it might appear to some that he had skilfully
assailed us and the Jews. If it were possible, indeed, for me to enter
along with my words into the conscience of every one without
exception who peruses this work, and to extract each dart which
wounds him who is not completely protected with the "whole armour"
of God, and apply a rational medicine to cure the wound inflicted by
Celsus, which prevents those who listen to his words from remaining
"sound in the faith," I would do so. But since it is the work of God
alone, in conformity with His own Spirit, and along with that of Christ,
to take up His abode invisibly in those persons whom He judges worthy
of being visited; so, on the other hand, is *our* object to try, by means of
arguments and treatises, to confirm men in their faith, and to earn the
name of "workmen needing not to be ashamed, rightly dividing the
word of truth." And there is one thing above all which it appears to us
we ought to do, if we would discharge faithfully the task enjoined upon
us by you, and that is to overturn to the best of our ability the confident
assertions of Celsus. Let us then quote such assertions of his as follow
those which we have already refuted (the reader must decide whether
we have done so successfully or not), and let us reply to them. And may
God grant that we approach not our subject with our understanding
and reason empty and devoid of divine inspiration, that the faith of
those whom we wish to aid may not depend upon human wisdom, but
that, receiving the "mind" of Christ from His Father, who alone can
bestow it, and being strengthened by participating in the word of God,
we may pull down "every high thing that exalteth itself against the
knowledge of God," and the imagination of Celsus, who exalts himself
against us, and against Jesus, and also against Moses and the prophets,
in order that He who "gave the word to those who published it with
great power" may supply us also, and bestow upon us "great power,"
so that faith in the word and power of God may be implanted in the
minds of all who will peruse our work.

CHAPTER II

We have now, then, to refute that statement of his which runs as follows: "O Jews and Christians, no God or son of a God either came or will come down (to earth). But if you mean that certain angels did so, then what do you call them? Are they gods, or some other race of beings? Some other race of beings (doubtless), and in all probability demons." Now as Celsus here is guilty of repeating himself (for in the preceding pages such assertions have been frequently advanced by him), it is unnecessary to discuss the matter at greater length, seeing what we have already said upon this point may suffice. We shall mention, however, a few considerations out of a greater number, such as we deem in harmony with our former arguments, but which have not altogether the same bearing as they, and by which we shall show that in asserting generally that no God, or son of God, ever descended (among men), he overturns not only the opinions entertained by the majority of mankind regarding the manifestation of Deity, but also what was formerly admitted by himself. For if the general statement, that "no God or son of God has come down or will come down," be truly maintained by Celsus, it is manifest that we have here overthrown the belief in the existence of gods upon the earth who had descended from heaven either to predict the future to mankind or to heal them by means of divine responses; and neither the Pythian Apollo, nor Aesculapius, nor any other among those supposed to have done so, would be a god descended from heaven. He might, indeed, either be a god who had obtained as his lot (the obligation) to dwell on earth for ever, and be thus a fugitive, as it were, from the abode of the gods, or he might be one who had no power to share in the society of the gods in heaven; or else Apollo, and Aesculapius, and those others who are believed to perform acts on earth, would not be gods, but only certain demons, much inferior to those wise men among mankind, who on account of their virtue ascend to the vault of heaven.

CHAPTER III

But observe how, in his desire to subvert our opinions, he who never acknowledged himself throughout his whole treatise to be an Epicurean, is convicted of being a deserter to that sect. And now is the time for you, (reader), who peruse the works of Celsus, and give your assent to what has been advanced, either to overturn the belief in a God who visits the human race, and exercises a providence over each individual man, or to grant this, and prove the falsity of the assertions of Celsus. If you, then, wholly annihilate providence, you will falsify those assertions of his in which he grants the existence of "God and a providence," in order that you may maintain the truth of your own position; but if, on the other hand, you still admit the existence of providence, because you do not assent to the dictum of Celsus, that "neither has a God nor the son of a God come down nor is to come down to mankind," why not rather carefully ascertain from the statements made regarding Jesus, and the prophecies uttered concerning Him, who it is that we are to consider as having come down to the human race as God, and the Son of God?—whether that Jesus who said and ministered so much, or those who under pretence of oracles and divinations, do not reform the morals of their worshippers, but who have besides apostatized from the pure and holy worship and honour due to the Maker of all things, and who tear away the souls of those who give heed to them from the one only visible and true God, under a pretence of paying honour to a multitude of deities?

CHAPTER IV

But since he says, in the next place, as if the Jews or Christians had answered regarding those who come down to visit the human race, that they were angels: "But if ye say that they are angels, what do you call them?" he continues, "Are they gods, or some other race of beings?" and then again introduces us as if answering, "Some other race of beings, and probably demons,"—let us proceed to notice these remarks. For we indeed acknowledge that angels are "ministering spirits," and we say that "they are sent forth to minister for them who shall be heirs of salvation;" and that they ascend, bearing the supplications of men, to the purest of the heavenly places in the universe, or even to supercelestial regions purer still; and that they come down from these, conveying to each one, according to his deserts, something enjoined by God to be conferred by them upon those who are to be the recipients of His benefits. Having thus learned to call these beings "angels" from their employments, we find that because they are divine they are sometimes termed "god" in the sacred Scriptures, but not so that we are commanded to honour and worship in place of God those who minister to us, and bear to us His blessings. For every prayer, and supplication, and intercession, and thanksgiving, is to be sent up to the Supreme God through the High Priest, who is above all the angels, the living Word and God. And to the Word Himself shall we also pray and make intercessions, and offer thanksgivings and supplications to Him, if we have the capacity of distinguishing between the proper use and abuse of prayer.

CHAPTER V

For to invoke angels without having obtained a knowledge of their
nature greater than is possessed by men, would be contrary to reason.
But, conformably to our hypothesis, let this knowledge of them, which
is something wonderful and mysterious, be obtained. Then this
knowledge, making known to us their nature, and the offices to which
they are severally appointed, will not permit us to pray with confidence
to any other than to the Supreme God, who is sufficient for all things,
and that through our Saviour the Son of God, who is the Word, and
Wisdom, and Truth, and everything else which the writings of God's
prophets and the apostles of Jesus entitle Him. And it is enough to
secure that the holy angels of God be propitious to us, and that they
do all things on our behalf, that our disposition of mind towards God
should imitate as far as it is within the power of human nature the
example of these holy angels, who again follow the example of their
God; and that the conceptions which we entertain of His Son, the
Word, so far as attainable by us, should not be opposed to the clearer
conceptions of Him which the holy angels possess, but should daily
approach these in clearness and distinctness. But because Celsus has
not read our holy Scriptures, he gives himself an answer as if it came
from us, saying that we "assert that the angels who come down from
heaven to confer benefits on mankind are a different race from the
gods," and adds that "in all probability they would be called demons by
us:" not observing that the name "demons" is not a term of indifferent
meaning like that of "men," among whom some are good and some
bad, nor yet a term of excellence like that of "the gods," which is
applied not to wicked demons, or to statues, or to animals, but (by
those who know divine things) to what is truly divine and blessed;
whereas the term "demons" is always applied to those wicked powers,
freed from the encumbrance of a grosser body, who lead men astray,
and fill them with distractions and drag them down from God and
supercelestial thoughts to things here below.

CHAPTER VI

He next proceeds to make the following statement about the
Jews:—"The first point relating to the Jews which is fitted to excite
wonder, is that they should worship the heaven and the angels who
dwell therein, and yet pass by and neglect its most venerable and

powerful parts, as the sun, the moon, and the other heavenly bodies, both fixed stars and planets, as if it were possible that 'the whole' could be God, and yet its parts not divine; or (as if it were reasonable) to treat with the greatest respect those who are said to appear to such as are in darkness somewhere, blinded by some crooked sorcery, or dreaming dreams through the influence of shadowy spectres, while those who prophesy so clearly and strikingly to all men, by means of whom rain, and heat, and clouds, and thunder (to which they offer worship), and lightnings, and fruits, and all kinds of productiveness, are brought about,—by means of whom God is revealed to them,—the most prominent heralds among those beings that are above,—those that are truly heavenly angels,—are to be regarded as of no account!" In making these statements, Celsus appears to have fallen into confusion, and to have penned them from false ideas of things which he did not understand; for it is patent to all who investigate the practices of the Jews, and compare them with those of the Christians, that the Jews who follow the law, which, speaking in the person of God, says, "Thou shalt have no other gods before Me: thou shalt not make unto thee an image, nor a likeness of anything that is in heaven above, or that is in the earth beneath, or that is in the waters under the earth; thou shalt not bow down to them, nor serve them," worship nothing else than the Supreme God, who made the heavens, and all things besides. Now it is evident that those who live according to the law, and worship the *Maker* of heaven, will not worship the heaven at the same time with God. Moreover, no one who obeys the law of Moses will bow down to the angels who are in heaven; and, in like manner, as they do not bow down to sun, moon, and stars, the host of heaven, they refrain from doing obeisance to heaven and its angels, obeying the law which declares: "Lest thou lift up thine eyes to heaven, and when thou seest the sun, and the moon, and the stars, even all the host of heaven, shouldst be driven to worship them, and serve them, which the Lord thy God hath divided unto all nations."

CHAPTER VII

Having, moreover, assumed that the Jews consider the heaven to be God, he adds that this is absurd; finding fault with those who bow down to the heaven, but not also to the sun, and moon, and stars, saying that the Jews do this, as if it were possible that "the whole" should be God, and its several parts not divine. And he seems to call the heaven "a whole," and sun, moon, and stars its several parts. Now, certainly neither Jews nor Christians call the "heaven" God. Let it be granted, however, that, as he alleges, the heaven *is* called God by the Jews, and suppose that sun, moon, and stars *are* parts of "heaven,"— which is by no means true, for neither are the animals and plants upon the earth any portion of it,—how is it true, even according to the opinions of the Greeks, that if God be a whole, His parts also are divine? Certainly they say that the Cosmos taken as the whole is God, the Stoics calling it the First God, the followers of Plato the Second, and some of them the Third. According to these philosophers, then, seeing the whole Cosmos is God, its parts also are divine; so that not only are human beings divine, but the whole of the irrational creation, as being "*portions*" of the Cosmos; and besides these, the plants also are divine. And if the rivers, and mountains, and seas are portions of the Cosmos, then, since the whole Cosmos is God, are the rivers and seas also gods? But even this the Greeks will not assert. Those, however, who preside over rivers and seas (either demons or gods, as they call them), they would term gods. Now from this it follows that the general statement of Celsus, even according to the Greeks, who hold the doctrine of Providence, is false, that if any "whole" be a god, its parts necessarily are divine. But it follows from the doctrine of Celsus, that if the Cosmos be God, all that is in it is divine, being parts of the Cosmos. Now, according to this view, animals, as flies, and gnats, and worms, and every species of serpent, as well as of birds and fishes, will be divine,—an assertion which would not be made even by those who maintain that the Cosmos is God. But the Jews, who live according to the law of Moses, although they may not know how to receive the secret meaning of the law, which is conveyed in obscure language, will not maintain that either the heaven or the angels are God.

CHAPTER VIII

As we allege, however, that he has fallen into confusion in consequence of false notions which he has imbibed, come and let us point them out to the best of our ability, and show that although Celsus considers it to be a Jewish custom to bow down to the heaven and the angels in it, such a practice is not at all Jewish, but is in violation of Judaism, as it also is to do obeisance to sun, moon, and stars, as well as images. You will find at least in the book of Jeremiah the words of God censuring by the mouth of the prophet the Jewish people for doing obeisance to such objects, and for sacrificing to the queen of heaven, and to all the host of heaven. The writings of the Christians, moreover, show, in censuring the sins committed among the Jews, that when God abandoned that people on account of certain sins, these sins (of idol-worship) also were committed by them. For it is related in the Acts of the Apostles regarding the Jews, that "God turned, and gave them up to worship the host of heaven; as it is written in the book of the prophets, O ye house of Israel, have ye offered to Me slain beasts and sacrifices by the space of forty years in the wilderness? Yea, ye took up the tabernacle of Moloch, and the star of your god Remphan, figures which you made to worship them." And in the writings of Paul, who was carefully trained in Jewish customs, and converted afterwards to Christianity by a miraculous appearance of Jesus, the following words may be read in the Epistle to the Colossians: "Let no man beguile you of your reward in a voluntary humility and worshipping of angels, intruding into those things which he hath not seen, vainly puffed up by his fleshly mind; and not holding the Head, from which all the body by joint and bands having nourishment ministered, and knit together, increaseth with the increase of God." But Celsus, having neither read these verses, nor having learned their contents from any other source, has represented, I know not how, the Jews as not transgressing their law in bowing down to the heavens, and to the angels therein.

CHAPTER IX

And still continuing a little confused, and not taking care to see what was relevant to the matter, he expressed his opinion that the Jews were induced by the incantations employed in jugglery and sorcery (in consequence of which certain phantoms appear, in obedience to the spells employed by the magicians) to bow down to the angels in heaven, not observing that this was contrary to their law, which said to them who practised such observances: "Regard not them which have familiar spirits, neither seek after wizards, to be defiled by them: I am the Lord your God." He ought, therefore, either not to have at all attributed this practice to the Jews, seeing he has observed that they keep their law, and has called them "those who live according to their law;" or if he did attribute it, he ought to have shown that the Jews did this in violation of their code. But again, as they transgress their law who offer worship to those who are said to appear to them who are involved in darkness and blinded by sorcery, and who dream dreams, owing to obscure phantoms presenting themselves; so also do they transgress the law who offer sacrifice to sun, moon, and stars. And there is thus great inconsistency in the same individual saying that the Jews are careful to keep their law by not bowing down to sun, and moon, and stars, while they are not so careful to keep it in the matter of heaven and the angels.

CHAPTER X

And if it be necessary for us to offer a defence of our refusal to recognise as gods, equally with angels, and sun, and moon, and stars, those who are called by the Greeks "manifest and visible" divinities, we shall answer that the law of Moses knows that these latter have been apportioned by God among all the nations under the heaven, but not amongst those who were selected by God as His chosen people above all the nations of the earth. For it is written in the book of Deuteronomy: "And lest thou lift up thine eyes unto heaven, and when thou seest the sun, and the moon, and the stars, even all the host of heaven, shouldst be driven to worship them, and serve them, which the LORD thy God hath divided unto all nations unto the whole heaven. But the LORD hath taken us, and brought us forth out of the iron furnace, even out of Egypt, to be unto Him a people of inheritance, as ye are this day." The Hebrew people, then, being called by God a "chosen generation, and a royal priesthood, and a holy nation, and a purchased people," regarding whom it was foretold to Abraham by the voice of the Lord addressed to him, "Look now towards heaven, and tell the stars, if thou be able to number them: and He said unto him, So shall thy seed be;" and having thus a hope that they would become as the stars of heaven, were not likely to bow down to those objects which they were to resemble as a result of their understanding and observing the law of God. For it was said to them: "The Lord our God hath multiplied us; and, behold, ye are this day as the stars of heaven for multitude." In the book of Daniel, also, the following prophecies are found relating to those who are to share in the resurrection: "And at that time thy people shall be delivered, every one that has been written in the book. And many of them that sleep in the dust of the earth shall awake, some to everlasting life, and some to shame and everlasting contempt. And they that be wise shall shine as the brightness of the firmament, and (those) of the many righteous as the stars for ever and ever," etc. And hence Paul, too, when speaking of the resurrection, says: "And there are also celestial bodies, and bodies terrestrial: but the glory of the celestial is one, and the glory of the terrestrial is another. There is one glory of the sun, and another glory of the moon, and another glory of the stars; for one star differeth from another star in glory. So also is the resurrection of the dead." It was not therefore consonant to reason that those who had been taught sublimely to ascend above all created things, and to hope for the enjoyment of the most glorious rewards with God on account of their virtuous lives, and who had heard the words, "Ye are the light of the world," and, "Let your light so shine before men, that they, seeing your good works, may glorify your Father who is in heaven," and who possessed through practice this brilliant and unfading wisdom, or who had secured even the "very reflection of everlasting light," should be so impressed with the (mere) *visible* light of sun, and moon, and stars, that, on account of that sensible light of theirs, they should deem themselves (although possessed of so great a rational light of knowledge, and of the true light, and the light of the world, and the light of men) to be somehow inferior to them, and to bow down to them; seeing they ought to be worshipped, if they are to receive worship at all, not for the sake of the sensible light which is admired by the multitude, but because of the rational and true light, if indeed the stars in heaven are rational and virtuous beings, and have been illuminated with the light of knowledge by that wisdom which is the "reflection of everlasting light." For that sensible light of theirs is the work of the Creator of all things, while that rational light is derived perhaps from the principle of free-will within them.

CHAPTER XI

But even this rational light itself ought not to be worshipped by him who beholds and understands the true light, by sharing in which these also are enlightened; nor by him who beholds God, the Father of the true light,—of whom it has been said, "God is light, and in Him there is no darkness at all." Those, indeed, who worship sun, moon, and stars because their light is visible and celestial, would not bow down to a spark of fire or a lamp upon earth, because they see the incomparable superiority of those objects which are deemed worthy of homage to the light of sparks and lamps. So those who understand that God is light, and who have apprehended that the Son of God is "the true light which lighteth every man that cometh into the world," and who comprehend also how He says, "I am the light of the world," would not rationally offer worship to that which is, as it were, a spark in sun, moon, and stars, in comparison with God, who is light of the true light. Nor is it with a view to depreciate these great works of God's creative power, or to call them, after the fashion of Anaxagoras, "fiery masses," that we thus speak of sun, and moon, and stars; but because we perceive the inexpressible superiority of the divinity of God, and that of His only-begotten Son, which surpasses all other things. And being persuaded that the sun himself, and moon, and stars pray to the Supreme God through His only-begotten Son, we judge it improper to pray to those beings who themselves offer up prayers (to God), seeing even they themselves would prefer that we should send up our requests to the God to whom they pray, rather than send them downwards to themselves, or apportion our power of prayer between God and them. And here I may employ this illustration, as bearing upon this point: Our Lord and Saviour, hearing Himself on one occasion addressed as "Good Master," referring him who used it to His own Father, said, "Why callest thou Me good? There is none good but one, that is, God the Father." And since it was in accordance with sound reason that this should be said by the Son of His Father's love, as being the image of the goodness of God, why should not the sun say with greater reason to those that bow down to him, Why do you worship me? "for thou wilt worship the LORD thy God, and Him only shalt thou serve;" for it is He whom I and all who are with me serve and worship. And although one may not be so exalted (as the sun), nevertheless let such an one pray to the Word of God (who is able to heal him), and still more to His Father, who also to the righteous of former times "sent His word, and healed them, and delivered them from their destructions."

CHAPTER XII

God accordingly, in His kindness, condescends to mankind, not in any local sense, but through His providence; while the Son of God, not only (when on earth), but at *all* times, is with His own disciples, fulfilling the promise, "Lo, I am with you always, even to the end of the world." And if a branch cannot bear fruit except it abide in the vine, it is evident that the disciples also of the Word, who are the rational branches of the Word's true vine, cannot produce the fruits of virtue unless they abide in the true vine, the Christ of God, who is with us locally here below upon the earth, and who is with those who cleave to Him in all parts of the world, and is also in all places with those who do not know Him. Another is made manifest by that John who wrote the Gospel, when, speaking in the person of John the Baptist, he said, "There standeth one among you whom ye know not; He it is who cometh after me." And it is absurd, when He who fills heaven and earth, and who said, "Do I not fill heaven and earth? saith the LORD," is with us, and near us (for I believe Him when He says, "I am a God nigh at hand, and not afar off, saith the LORD") to seek to pray to sun or moon, or one of the stars, whose influence does not reach the whole of the world. But, to use the very words of Celsus, let it be granted that "the sun, moon, and stars *do* foretell rain, and heat, and clouds, and thunders," why, then, if they really do foretell such great things, ought we not rather to do homage to God, whose servant they are in uttering these predictions, and show reverence to *Him* rather than His *prophets?* Let them predict, then, the approach of lightnings, and fruits, and all manner of productions, and let all such things be under their administration; yet we shall not on that account worship those who themselves offer worship, as we do not worship even Moses, and those prophets who came from God after him, and who predicted better things than rain, and heat, and clouds, and thunders, and lightnings, and fruits, and all sorts of productions visible to the senses. Nay, even if sun, and moon, and stars were able to prophesy better things than rain, not even then shall we worship *them*, but the *Father* of the prophecies which are in them, and the *Word* of God, their minister. But grant that they are His heralds, and truly messengers of heaven, why, even then ought we not to worship the *God* whom they only proclaim and announce, rather than those who are the *heralds* and *messengers?*

CHAPTER XIII

Celsus, moreover, assumes that sun, and moon, and stars are regarded by us as of no account. Now, with regard to these, we acknowledge that they too are "waiting for the manifestation of the sons of God," being for the present subjected to the "vanity" of their material bodies, "by reason of Him who has subjected the same in hope." But if Celsus had read the innumerable other passages where we speak of sun, moon, and stars, and especially these,—"Praise Him, all ye stars, and thou, O light," and, "Praise Him, ye heaven of heavens,"—he would not have said of us that we regard such mighty beings, which "greatly praise" the Lord God, as of no account. Nor did Celsus know the passage: "For the earnest expectation of the creature waiteth for the manifestation of the sons of God. For the creature was made subject to vanity, not willingly, but by reason of Him who hath subjected the same in hope; because the creature itself also shall be delivered from the bondage of corruption into the glorious liberty of the children of God." And with these words let us terminate our defence against the charge of not worshipping sun, moon, and stars. And let us now bring forward those statements of his which follow, that we may, God willing, address to him in reply such arguments as shall be suggested by the light of truth.

CHAPTER XIV

The following, then, are his words: "It is folly on their part to suppose that when God, as if He were a cook, introduces the fire (which is to consume the world), all the rest of the human race will be burnt up, while they alone will remain, not only such of them as are then alive, but also those who are long since dead, which latter will arise from the earth clothed with the self-same flesh (as during life); for such a hope is simply one which might be cherished by worms. For what sort of human soul is that which would still long for a body that had been subject to corruption? Whence, also, this opinion of yours is not shared by some of the Christians, and they pronounce it to be exceedingly vile, and loathsome, and impossible; for what kind of body is that which, after being completely corrupted, can return to its original nature, and to that self-same first condition out of which it fell into dissolution? Being unable to return any answer, they betake themselves to a most absurd refuge, viz., that all things are possible to God. And yet God *cannot* do things that are disgraceful, nor does He wish to do things that are contrary to His nature; nor, if (in accordance with the wickedness of your own heart) you desired anything that was evil, would God accomplish it; nor must you believe at once that it will be done. For God does not rule the world in order to satisfy inordinate desires, or to allow disorder and confusion, but to govern a nature that is upright and just. For the *soul*, indeed, He might be able to provide an everlasting life; while dead *bodies*, on the contrary, are, as Heraclitus observes, more worthless than dung. God, however, neither can nor will declare, contrary to all reason, that the flesh, which is full of those things which it is not even honourable to mention, is to exist for ever. For He is the reason of all things that exist, and therefore can do nothing either contrary to reason or contrary to Himself."

CHAPTER XV

Observe, now, here at the very beginning, how, in ridiculing the doctrine of a conflagration of the world, held by certain of the Greeks who have treated the subject in a philosophic spirit not to be depreciated, he would make us, "representing God, as it were, as a cook, hold the belief in a general conflagration;" not perceiving that, as certain Greeks were of opinion (perhaps having received their information from the ancient nation of the Hebrews), it is a purificatory fire which is brought upon the world, and probably also on each one of those who stand in need of chastisement by the fire and healing at the same time, seeing it *burns* indeed, but does not *consume*, those who are without a material body, which needs to be consumed by that fire, and which burns and consumes those who by their actions, words, and thoughts have built up wood, or hay, or stubble, in that which is figuratively termed a "building." And the holy Scriptures say that the Lord will, like a refiner's fire and fullers' soap, visit each one of those who require purification, because of the intermingling in them of a flood of wicked matter proceeding from their evil nature; who need fire, I mean, to refine, as it were, (the dross of) those who are intermingled with copper, and tin, and lead. And he who likes may learn this from the prophet Ezekiel. But that we say that God brings fire upon the world, not like a cook, but like a God, who is the benefactor of them who stand in need of the discipline of fire, will be testified by the prophet Isaiah, in whose writings it is related that a sinful nation was thus addressed: "Because thou hast coals of fire, sit upon them: they shall be to thee a help." Now the Scripture is appropriately adapted to the multitudes of those who are to peruse it, because it speaks obscurely of things that are sad and gloomy, in order to terrify those who cannot by any other means be saved from the flood of their sins, although even then the attentive reader will clearly discover the end that is to be accomplished by these sad and painful punishments upon those who endure them. It is sufficient, however, for the present to quote the words of Isaiah: "For My name's sake will I show Mine anger, and My glory I will bring upon thee, that I may not destroy thee." We have thus been under the necessity of referring in obscure terms to questions not fitted to the capacity of simple believers, who require a simpler instruction in words, that we might not appear to leave unrefuted the accusation of Celsus, that "God introduces the fire (which is to destroy the world), as if He were a cook."

CHAPTER XVI

From what has been said, it will be manifest to intelligent hearers how we have to answer the following: "All the rest of the race will be completely burnt up, and they alone will remain." It is not to be wondered at, indeed, if such thoughts have been entertained by those amongst us who are called in Scripture the "foolish things" of the world, and "base things," and "things which are despised," and "things which are not," because "by the foolishness of preaching it pleased God to save them that believe on Him, after that, in the wisdom of God, the world by wisdom knew not God,"—because such individuals are unable to see distinctly the sense of each particular passage, or unwilling to devote the necessary leisure to the investigation of Scripture, notwithstanding the injunction of Jesus, "Search the Scriptures." The following, moreover, are his ideas regarding the fire which is to be brought upon the world by God, and the punishments which are to befall sinners. And perhaps, as it is appropriate to children that some things should be addressed to them in a manner befitting their infantile condition, to convert them, as being of very tender age, to a better course of life; so, to those whom the word terms "the foolish things of the world," and "the base," and "the despised," the just and obvious meaning of the passages relating to punishments is suitable, inasmuch as they cannot receive any other mode of conversion than that which is by fear and the presentation of punishment, and thus be saved from the many evils (which would befall them). The Scripture accordingly declares that only those who are unscathed by the fire and the punishments are to remain,—those, viz., whose opinions, and morals, and mind have been purified to the highest degree; while, on the other hand, those of a different nature—those, viz., who, according to their deserts, require the administration of punishment by fire—will be involved in these sufferings with a view to an end which it is suitable for God to bring upon those who have been created in His image, but who have lived in opposition to the will of that nature which is according to His image. And this is our answer to the statement, "All the rest of the race will be completely burnt up, but they alone are to remain."

CHAPTER XVII

Then, in the next place, having either himself misunderstood the sacred Scriptures, or those (interpreters) by whom they were not understood, he proceeds to assert that "it is said by us that there will remain at the time of the visitation which is to come upon the world by the fire of purification, not only those who are then alive, but also those who are long ago dead;" not observing that it is with a secret kind of wisdom that it was said by the apostle of Jesus: "We shall not all sleep, but we shall all be changed, in a moment, in the twinkling of an eye, at the last trump; for the trumpet shall sound, and the dead shall be raised incorruptible, and we shall be changed." Now he ought to have noticed what was the meaning of him who uttered these words, as being one who was by no means dead, who made a distinction between himself and those like him and the dead, and who said afterwards, "The dead shall be raised incorruptible," and "we shall be changed." And as a proof that such was the apostle's meaning in writing those words which I have quoted from the first Epistle to the Corinthians, I will quote also from the first to the Thessalonians, in which Paul, as one who is alive and awake, and different from those who are asleep, speaks as follows: "For this we say unto you by the word of the Lord, that we who are alive and remain unto the coming of the Lord, shall not prevent them who are asleep; for the Lord Himself shall descend from heaven with a shout, with the voice of the archangel, and with the trump of God." Then, again, after this, knowing that there were others dead in Christ besides himself and such as he, he subjoins the words, "The dead in Christ shall rise first; then we who are alive and remain shall be caught up together with them in the clouds, to meet the Lord in the air."

CHAPTER XVIII

But since he has ridiculed at great length the doctrine of the resurrection of the flesh, which has been preached in the Churches, and which is more clearly understood by the more intelligent believer; and as it is unnecessary again to quote his words, which have been already adduced, let us, with regard to the problem (as in an apologetic work directed against an alien from the faith, and for the sake of those who are still "children, tossed to and fro, and carried about with every wind of doctrine, by the sleight of men, and cunning craftiness, whereby they lie in wait to deceive"), state and establish to the best of our ability a few points expressly intended for our readers. Neither we, then, nor the holy Scriptures, assert that with the same bodies, without a change to a higher condition, "shall those who were long dead arise from the earth and live again;" for in so speaking, Celsus makes a false charge against us. For we may listen to many passages of Scripture treating of the resurrection in a manner worthy of God, although it may suffice for the present to quote the language of Paul from the first Epistle to the Corinthians, where he says: "But some man will say, How are the dead raised up? and with what body do they come? Thou fool, that which thou sowest is not quickened, except it die. And that which thou sowest, thou sowest not that body that shall be, but bare grain, it may chance of wheat, or of some other grain; but God giveth it a body as it hath pleased Him, and to every seed his own body." Now, observe how in these words he says that there is sown, "not that body that shall be;" but that of the body which is sown and cast naked into the earth (God giving to each seed its own body), there takes place as it were a resurrection: from the seed that was cast into the ground there arising a stalk, e.g., among such plants as the following, viz., the mustard plant, or of a larger tree, as in the olive, or one of the fruit-trees.

God, then, gives to each thing its own body as He pleases: as in the case of plants that are sown, so also in the case of those beings who are, as it were, sown in dying, and who in due time receive, out of what has been "sown," the body assigned by God to each one according to his deserts. And we may hear, moreover, the Scripture teaching us at great length the difference between that which is, as it were, "sown," and that which is, as it were, "raised" from it in these words: "It is sown in corruption, it is raised in incorruption; it is sown in dishonour, it is raised in glory; it is sown in weakness, it is raised in power; it is sown a natural body, it is raised a spiritual body." And let him who has the capacity understand the meaning of the words: "As is the earthy, such are they also that are earthy; and as is the heavenly, such are they also that are heavenly. And as we have borne the image of the earthy, we shall also bear the image of the heavenly." And although the apostle wished to conceal the secret meaning of the passage, which was not adapted to the simpler class of believers, and to the understanding of the common people, who are led by their faith to enter on a better course of life, he was nevertheless obliged afterwards to say (in order that we might not misapprehend his meaning), after "Let us bear the image of the heavenly," these words also: "Now this I say, brethren, that flesh and blood cannot inherit the kingdom of God; neither doth corruption inherit incorruption." Then, knowing that there was a secret and mystical meaning in the passage, as was becoming in one who was leaving, in his Epistles, to those who were to come after him words full of significance, he subjoins the following, "Behold, I show you a mystery;" which is his usual style in introducing matters of a profounder and more mystical nature, and such as are fittingly concealed from the multitude, as is written in the book of Tobit: "It is good to keep close the secret of a king, but honourable to reveal the works of God,"—in a way consistent with truth and God's glory, and so as to be to the advantage of the multitude. Our hope, then, is *not* "the hope of worms, nor does our soul long for a body that has seen corruption;" for although it may require a body, for the sake of moving from place to place, yet it understands—as having meditated on the wisdom (that is from above), agreeably to the declaration, "The mouth of the righteous will speak wisdom"—the difference between the "earthly house," in which is the tabernacle of the building that is to be dissolved, and that in which the righteous do groan, being burdened,— not wishing to "put off" the tabernacle, but to be "clothed therewith," that by being clothed upon, mortality might be swallowed up of life. For, in virtue of the whole nature of the body being corruptible, the corruptible tabernacle must put on incorruption; and its other part, being mortal, and becoming liable to the death which follows sin, must put on immortality, in order that, when the corruptible shall have put on incorruption, and the mortal immortality, then shall come to pass what was predicted of old by the prophets,—the annihilation of the "victory" of death (because it had conquered and subjected us to his sway), and of its "sting," with which it stings the imperfectly defended soul, and inflicts upon it the wounds which result from sin.

CHAPTER XX

But since our views regarding the resurrection have, as far as time would permit, been stated in part on the present occasion (for we have systematically examined the subject in greater detail in other parts of our writings); and as now we must by means of sound reasoning refute the fallacies of Celsus, who neither understands the meaning of our Scripture, nor has the capacity of judging that the meaning of our wise men is not to be determined by those individuals who make no profession of anything more than of a (simple) faith in the Christian system, let us show that men, not to be lightly esteemed on account of their reasoning powers and dialectic subtleties, have given expression to very absurd opinions. And if we must sneer at them as contemptible old wives' fables, it is at them rather than at our narrative that we must sneer. The disciples of the Porch assert, that after a period of years there will be a conflagration of the world, and after that an arrangement of things in which everything will be unchanged, as compared with the former arrangement of the world. Those of them, however, who evinced their respect for this doctrine have said that there will be a change, although exceedingly slight, at the end of the cycle, from what prevailed during the preceding. And these men maintain, that in the succeeding cycle the same things will occur, and Socrates will be again the son of Sophroniscus, and a native of Athens; and Phaenarete, being married to Sophroniscus, will again become his mother. And although they do not mention the word "resurrection," they show in reality that Socrates, who derived his origin from seed, will spring from that of Sophroniscus, and will be fashioned in the womb of Phaenarete; and being brought up at Athens, will practise the study of philosophy, as if his former philosophy had arisen again, and were to be in no respect different from what it was before. Anytus and Melitus, too, will arise again as accusers of Socrates, and the Council of Areopagus will condemn him to death! But what is more ridiculous still, is that Socrates will clothe himself with garments not at all different from those which he wore during the former cycle, and will live in the same unchanged state of poverty, and in the same unchanged city of Athens! And Phalaris will again play the tyrant, and his brazen bull will pour forth its bellowings from the voices of victims within, unchanged from those who were condemned in the former cycle! And Alexander of Pherae, too, will again act the tyrant with a cruelty unaltered from the former time, and will condemn to death the same "unchanged" individuals as before. But what need is there to go into detail upon the doctrine held by the Stoic philosophers on such things, and which escapes the ridicule of Celsus, and is perhaps even venerated by him, since he regards Zeno as a wiser man than Jesus?

CHAPTER XXI

The disciples of Pythagoras, too, and of Plato, although they appear to hold the incorruptibility of the world, yet fall into similar errors. For as the planets, after certain definite cycles, assume the same positions, and hold the same relations to one another, all things on earth will, they assert, be like what they were at the time when the same state of planetary relations existed in the world. From this view it necessarily follows, that when, after the lapse of a lengthened cycle, the planets come to occupy towards each other the same relations which they occupied in the time of Socrates, Socrates will again be born of the same parents, and suffer the same treatment, being accused by Anytus and Melitus, and condemned by the Council of Areopagus! The learned among the Egyptians, moreover, hold similar views, and yet they are treated with respect, and do not incur the ridicule of Celsus and such as he; while we, who maintain that all things are administered by God in proportion to the relation of the free-will of each individual, and are ever being brought into a better condition, so far as they admit of being so, and who know that the nature of our free-will admits of the occurrence of contingent events (for it is incapable of receiving the wholly unchangeable character of God), yet do not appear to say anything worthy of a testing examination.

CHAPTER XXII

Let no one, however, suspect that, in speaking as we do, we belong to those who are indeed called Christians, but who set aside the doctrine of the resurrection as it is taught in Scripture. For these persons cannot, so far as their principles apply, at all establish that the stalk or tree which springs up comes from the grain of wheat, or anything else (which was cast into the ground); whereas we, who believe that that which is "sown" is not "quickened" unless it die, and that there is sown not that body that shall be (for God gives it a body as it pleases Him, raising it in incorruption after it is sown in corruption; and after it is sown in dishonour, raising it in glory; and after it is sown in weakness, raising it in power; and after it is sown a natural body, raising it a spiritual),—we preserve both the doctrine of the Church of Christ and the grandeur of the divine promise, proving also the possibility of its accomplishment not by mere assertion, but by arguments; knowing that although heaven and earth, and the things that are in them, may pass away, yet His words regarding each individual thing, being, as parts of a whole, or species of a genus, the utterances of Him who was God the Word, who was in the beginning with God, shall by no means pass away. For we desire to listen to Him who said: "Heaven and earth shall pass away, but My words shall not pass away."

CHAPTER XXIII

We, therefore, do not maintain that the body which has undergone corruption resumes its original nature, any more than the grain of wheat which has decayed returns to its former condition. But we do maintain, that as above the grain of wheat there arises a stalk, so a certain power is implanted in the body, which is not destroyed, and from which the body is raised up in incorruption. The philosophers of the Porch, however, in consequence of the opinions which they hold regarding the unchangeableness of things after a certain cycle, assert that the body, after undergoing complete corruption, will return to its original condition, and will again assume that first nature from which it passed into a state of dissolution, establishing these points, as they think, by irresistible arguments. We, however, do not betake ourselves to a most absurd refuge, saying that with God *all* things are possible; for we know how to understand this word "all" as not referring either to things that are "non-existent" or that are inconceivable. But we maintain, at the same time, that God cannot do what is disgraceful, since then He would be capable of ceasing to be God; for if He do anything that is disgraceful, He is not God. Since, however, he lays it down as a principle, that "God does not desire what is contrary to nature," we have to make a distinction, and say that if any one asserts that wickedness is contrary to nature, while we maintain that "God does not desire what is contrary to nature,"—either what springs from wickedness or from an irrational principle,—yet, if such things happen according to the word and will of God, we must at once necessarily hold that they are not contrary to nature. Therefore things which are done by God, although they may be, or may *appear* to some to be incredible, are not contrary to nature. And if we must press the force of words, we would say that, in comparison with what is generally understood as "nature," there *are* certain things which are *beyond* its power, which God could at any time do; as, e.g., in raising man above the level of human nature, and causing him to pass into a better and more divine condition, and preserving him in the same, so long as he who is the object of His care shows by his actions that he desires (the continuance of His help).

CHAPTER XXIV

Moreover, as we have already said that for God to desire anything unbecoming Himself would be destructive of His existence as Deity, we will add that if man, agreeably to the wickedness of his nature, should desire anything that is abominable, God cannot grant it. And now it is from no spirit of contention that we answer the assertions of Celsus; but it is in the spirit of truth that we investigate them, as assenting to his view that "He is the God, not of inordinate desires, nor of error and disorder, but of a nature just and upright," because He is the source of all that is good. And that He is able to provide an eternal life for the soul we acknowledge; and that He possesses not only the "power," but the "will." In view, therefore, of these considerations, we are not at all distressed by the assertion of Heraclitus, adopted by Celsus, that "dead bodies are to be cast out as more worthless than dung;" and yet, with reference even to this, one might say that dung, indeed, ought to be cast out, while the dead bodies of men, on account of the soul by which they were inhabited, especially if it had been virtuous, ought not to be cast out. For, in harmony with those laws which are based upon the principles of equity, bodies are deemed worthy of sepulture, with the honours accorded on such occasions, that no insult, so far as can be helped, may be offered to the soul which dwelt within, by casting forth the body (after the soul has departed) like that of the animals. Let it not then be held, contrary to reason, that it is the will of God to declare that the grain of wheat is not immortal, but the stalk which springs from it, while the body which is sown in corruption is not, but that which is raised by Him in incorruption. But according to Celsus, God Himself is the reason of all things, while according to our view it is His Son, of whom we say in philosophic language, "In the beginning was the Word, and the Word was with God, and the Word was God;" while in our judgment also, God cannot do anything which is contrary to reason, or contrary to Himself.

CHAPTER XXV

Let us next notice the statements of Celsus, which follow the preceding, and which are as follow: "As the Jews, then, became a peculiar people, and enacted laws in keeping with the customs of their country, and maintain them up to the present time, and observe a mode of worship which, whatever be its nature, is yet derived from their fathers, they act in these respects like other men, because each nation retains its ancestral customs, whatever they are, if they happen to be established among them. And such an arrangement appears to be advantageous, not only because it has occurred to the mind of other nations to decide some things differently, but also because it is a duty to protect what has been established for the public advantage; and also because, in all probability, the various quarters of the earth were from the beginning allotted to different superintending spirits, and were thus distributed among certain governing powers, and in this manner the administration of the world is carried on. And whatever is done among each nation in this way would be rightly done, wherever it was agreeable to the wishes (of the superintending powers), while it would be an act of impiety to get rid of the institutions established from the beginning in the various places." By these words Celsus shows that the Jews, who were formerly Egyptians, subsequently became a "peculiar people," and enacted laws which they carefully preserve. And not to repeat his statements, which have been already before us, he says that it is advantageous to the Jews to observe their ancestral worship, as other nations carefully attend to theirs. And he further states a deeper reason why it is of advantage to the Jews to cultivate their ancestral customs, in hinting dimly that those to whom was allotted the office of superintending the country which was being legislated for, enacted the laws of each land in co-operation with its legislators. He appears, then, to indicate that both the country of the Jews, and the nation which inhabits it, are superintended by one or more beings, who, whether they were one or more, co-operated with Moses, and enacted the laws of the Jews.

CHAPTER XXVI

"We must," he says, "observe the laws, not only because it has occurred to the mind of others to decide some things differently, but because it is a duty to protect what has been enacted for the public advantage, and also because, in all probability, the various quarters of the earth were from the beginning allotted to different superintending spirits, and were distributed among certain governing powers, and in this manner the administration of the world is carried on." Thus Celsus, as if he had forgotten what he had said against the Jews, now includes them in the general eulogy which he passes upon all who observe their ancestral customs, remarking: "And whatever is done among each nation in this way, would be rightly done whenever agreeable to the wishes (of the superintendents)." And observe here, whether he does not openly, so far as he can, express a wish that the Jew should live in the observance of his own laws, and not depart from them, because he would commit an act of impiety if he apostatized; for his words are: "It would be an act of impiety to get rid of the institutions established from the beginning in the various places." Now I should like to ask him, and those who entertain his views, who it was that distributed the various quarters of the earth from the beginning among the different superintending spirits; and especially, who gave the country of the Jews, and the Jewish people themselves, to the one or more superintendents to whom it was allotted? Was it, as Celsus would say, Jupiter who assigned the Jewish people and their country to a certain spirit or spirits? And was it *his* wish, to whom they were thus assigned, to enact among them the laws which prevail, or was it *against* his will that it was done? You will observe that, whatever be his answer, he is in a strait. But if the various quarters of the earth were *not* allotted by some one being to the various superintending spirits, then each one at random, and without the superintendence of a higher power, divided the earth according to chance; and yet such a view is absurd, and destructive in no small degree of the providence of the God who presides over all things.

CHAPTER XXVII

Any one, indeed, who chooses, may relate how the various quarters of the earth, being distributed among certain governing powers, are administered by those who superintend them; but let him tell us also how what is done among each nation is done rightly when agreeable to the wishes of the superintendents. Let him, for example, tell us whether the laws of the Scythians, which permit the murder of parents, are right laws; or those of the Persians, which do not forbid the marriages of sons with their mothers, or of daughters with their own fathers. But what need is there for me to make selections from those who have been engaged in the business of enacting laws among the different nations, and to inquire how the laws are rightly enacted among each, according as they please the superintending powers? Let Celsus, however, tell us how it would be an act of impiety to get rid of those ancestral laws which permit the marriages of mothers and daughters; or which pronounce a man happy who puts an end to his life by hanging, or declare that they undergo entire purification who deliver themselves over to the fire, and who terminate their existence by fire; and how it is an act of impiety to do away with those laws which, for example, prevail in the Tauric Chersonese, regarding the offering up of strangers in sacrifice to Diana, or among certain of the Libyan tribes regarding the sacrifice of children to Saturn. Moreover, this inference follows from the dictum of Celsus, that it is an act of impiety on the part of the Jews to do away with those ancestral laws which forbid the worship of any other deity than the Creator of all things. And it will follow, according to his view, that piety is not divine by its own nature, but by a certain (external) arrangement and appointment. For it is an act of piety among certain tribes to worship a crocodile, and to eat what is an object of adoration among other tribes; while, again, with others it is a pious act to worship a calf, and among others, again, to regard the goat as a god. And, in this way, the same individual will be regarded as acting piously according to one set of laws, and impiously according to another; and this is the most absurd result that can be conceived!

CHAPTER XXVIII

It is probable, however, that to such remarks as the above, the answer returned would be, that he was pious who kept the laws of his *own* country, and not at all chargeable with impiety for the non-observance of those of *other* lands; and that, again, he who was deemed guilty of impiety among certain nations was not really so, when he worshipped his own gods, agreeably to his country's laws, although he made war against, and even feasted on, those who were regarded as divinities among those nations which possessed laws of an opposite kind. Now, observe here whether these statements do not exhibit the greatest confusion of mind regarding the nature of what is just, and holy, and religious; since there is no accurate definition laid down of these things, nor are they described as having a peculiar character of their own, and stamping as religious those who act according to their injunctions. If, then, religion, and piety, and righteousness belong to those things which are so only by comparison, so that the same act may be both pious and impious, according to different relations and different laws, see whether it will not follow that temperance also is a thing of comparison, and courage as well, and prudence, and the other virtues, than which nothing could be more absurd! What we have said, however, is sufficient for the more general and simple class of answers to the allegations of Celsus. But as we think it likely that some of those who are accustomed to deeper investigation will fall in with this treatise, let us venture to lay down some considerations of a profounder kind, conveying a mystical and secret view respecting the original distribution of the various quarters of the earth among different superintending spirits; and let us prove to the best of our ability, that our doctrine is free from the absurd consequences enumerated above.

CHAPTER XXIX

It appears to me, indeed, that Celsus has misunderstood some of the deeper reasons relating to the arrangement of terrestrial affairs, some of which are touched upon even in Grecian history, when certain of those who are considered to be gods are introduced as having contended with each other about the possession of Attica; while in the writings of the Greek poets also, some who are called gods are represented as acknowledging that certain places here are preferred by them before others. The history of barbarian nations, moreover, and especially that of Egypt, contains some such allusions to the division of the so-called Egyptian homes, when it states that Athena, who obtained Sais by lot, is the same who also has possession of Attica. And the learned among the Egyptians can enumerate innumerable instances of this kind, although I do not know whether they include the Jews and their country in this division. And now, so far as testimonies outside the word of God bearing on this point are concerned, enough have been adduced for the present. We say, moreover, that our prophet of God and His genuine servant Moses, in his song in the book of Deuteronomy, makes a statement regarding the portioning out of the earth in the following terms: "When the Most High divided the nations, when He dispersed the sons of Adam, He set the bounds of the people according to the number of the angels of God; and the portion was His people Jacob, and Israel the cord of His inheritance." And regarding the distribution of the nations, the same Moses, in his work entitled Genesis, thus expresses himself in the style of a historical narrative: "And the whole earth was of one language and of one speech; and it came to pass, as they journeyed from the east, that they found a plain in the land of Shinar, and they dwelt there." A little further on he continues: "And the LORD came down to see the city and the tower, which the children of men had built. And the LORD said, Behold, the people is one, and they have all one language; and this they have begun to do: and now nothing will be restrained from them which they have imagined to do. Go to, let Us go down, and there confound their language, that they may not understand one another's speech. And the LORD scattered them abroad from thence upon the face of all the earth: and they left off to build the city and the tower. Therefore is the name of it called Confusion; because the LORD did there confound the language of all the earth: and from thence did the LORD scatter them abroad upon the face of all the earth." In the treatise of Solomon, moreover, on "Wisdom," and on the events at the time of the confusion of languages, when the division of the earth took place, we find the following regarding Wisdom: "Moreover, the nations in their wicked conspiracy being confounded, she found out the righteous, and preserved him blameless unto God, and kept him strong in his tender compassion towards his son." But on these subjects much, and that of a mystical kind, might be said; in keeping with which is the following: "It is good to keep close the secret of a king,"—in order that the doctrine of the entrance of souls into bodies (not, however, that of the transmigration from one body into another) may not be thrown before the common understanding, nor what is holy given to the dogs, nor pearls be cast before swine. For such a procedure would be impious, being equivalent to a betrayal of the mysterious declarations of God's wisdom, of which it has been well said: "Into a malicious soul wisdom shall not enter, nor dwell in a body subject to sin." It is sufficient, however, to represent in the style of a historic narrative what is intended to convey a secret meaning in the garb of history, that those who have the capacity may work out for themselves all that relates to the subject. (The narrative, then, may be understood as follows.)

CHAPTER XXX

All the people upon the earth are to be regarded as having used one divine language, and so long as they lived harmoniously together were preserved in the use of this divine language, and they remained without moving from the east so long as they were imbued with the sentiments of the "light," and of the "reflection" of the eternal light. But when they departed from the east, and began to entertain sentiments alien to those of the east, they found a place in the land of Shinar (which, when interpreted, means "gnashing of teeth," by way of indicating symbolically that they had lost the means of their support), and in it they took up their abode. Then, desiring to gather together material things, and to join to heaven what had no natural affinity for it, that by means of material things they might conspire against such as were immaterial, they said, "Come, let us made bricks, and burn them with fire." Accordingly, when they had hardened and compacted these materials of clay and matter, and had shown their desire to make brick into stone, and clay into bitumen, and by these means to build a city and a tower, the head of which was, at least in their conception, to reach up to the heavens, after the manner of the "high things which exalt themselves against the knowledge of God," each one was handed over (in proportion to the greater or less departure from the east which had taken place among them, and in proportion to the extent in which bricks had been converted into stones, and clay into bitumen, and building carried on out of these materials) to angels of character more or less severe, and of a nature more or less stern, until they had paid the penalty of their daring deeds; and they were conducted by those angels, who imprinted on each his native language, to the different parts of the earth according to their deserts: some, for example, to a region of burning heat, others to a country which chastises its inhabitants by its cold; others, again, to a land exceedingly difficult of cultivation, others to one less so in degree; while a fifth were brought into a land filled with wild beasts, and a sixth to a country comparatively free of these.

CHAPTER XXXI

Now, in the next place, if any one has the capacity, let him understand that in what assumes the form of history, and which contains some things that are literally true, while yet it conveys a deeper meaning, those who preserved their original language continued, by reason of their not having migrated from the east, in possession of the east, and of their eastern language. And let him notice, that these alone became the portion of the Lord, and His people who were called Jacob, and Israel the cord of His inheritance; and these alone were governed by a ruler who did not receive those who were placed under him for the purpose of punishment, as was the case with the others. Let him also, who has the capacity to perceive as far as mortals may, observe that in the body politic of those who were assigned to the Lord as His pre-eminent portion, sins were committed, first of all, such as might be forgiven, and of such a nature as not to make the sinner worthy of entire desertion while subsequently they became more numerous though still of a nature to be pardoned. And while remarking that this state of matters continued for a considerable time, and that a remedy was always applied, and that after certain intervals these persons returned to their duty, let him notice that they were given over, in proportion to their transgressions, to those to whom had been assigned the other quarters of the earth; and that, after being at first slightly punished, and having made atonement, they returned, as if they had undergone discipline, to their proper habitations. Let him notice also that afterwards they were delivered over to rulers of a severer character—to Assyrians and Babylonians, as the Scriptures would call them. In the next place, notwithstanding that means of healing were being applied, let him observe that they were still multiplying their transgressions, and that they were on that account dispersed into other regions by the rulers of the nations that oppressed them. And their own ruler intentionally overlooked their oppression at the hands of the rulers of the other nations, in order that he also with good reason, as avenging himself, having obtained power to tear away from the other nations as many as he can, may do so, and enact for them laws, and point out a manner of life agreeably to which they ought to live, that so he may conduct them to the end to which those of the former people were conducted who did not commit sin.

CHAPTER XXXII

And by this means let those who have the capacity of comprehending truths so profound, learn that he to whom were allotted those who had not formerly sinned is far more powerful than the others, since he has been able to make a selection of individuals from the portion of the whole, and to separate them from those who received them for the purpose of punishment, and to bring them under the influence of laws, and of a mode of life which helps to produce an oblivion of their former transgressions. But, as we have previously observed, these remarks are to be understood as being made by us with a concealed meaning, by way of pointing out the mistakes of those who asserted that "the various quarters of the earth were from the beginning distributed among different superintending spirits, and being allotted among certain governing powers, were administered in this way;" from which statement Celsus took occasion to make the remarks referred to. But since those who wandered away from the east were delivered over, on account of their sins, to "a reprobate mind," and to "vile affections," and to "uncleanness through the lusts of their own hearts," in order that, being sated with sin, they might hate it, we shall refuse our assent to the assertion of Celsus, that "because of the superintending spirits distributed among the different parts of the earth, what is done among each nation is rightly done;" for our desire is to do what is not agreeable to these spirits. For we see that it is a religious act to do away with the customs originally established in the various places by means of laws of a better and more divine character, which were enacted by Jesus, as one possessed of the greatest power, who has rescued us "from the present evil world," and "from the princes of the world that come to nought;" and that it is a mark of irreligion not to throw ourselves at the feet of Him who has manifested Himself to be holier and more powerful than all other rulers, and to whom God said, as the prophets many generations before predicted: "Ask of Me, and I shall give Thee the heathen for Thine inheritance, and the uttermost parts of the earth for Thy possession." For He, too, has become the "expectation" of us who from among the heathen have believed upon Him, and upon His Father, who is God over all things.

CHAPTER XXXIII

The remarks which we have made not only answer the statements of Celsus regarding the superintending spirits, but anticipate in some measure what he afterwards brings forward, when he says: "Let the second party come forward; and I shall ask them whence they come, and whom they regard as the originator of their ancestral customs. They will reply, No one, because they spring from the same source as the Jews themselves, and derive their instruction and superintendence from no other quarter, and notwithstanding they have revolted from the Jews." Each one of us, then, is come "in the last days," when one Jesus has visited us, to the "visible mountain of the Lord," the Word that is above every word, and to the "house of God," which is "the Church of the living God, the pillar and ground of the truth." And we notice how it is built upon "the tops of the mountains," i.e., the predictions of all the prophets, which are its foundations. And this house is exalted above the hills, i.e., those individuals among men who make a profession of superior attainments in wisdom and truth; and all the nations come to it, and the "many nations" go forth, and say to one another, turning to the religion which in the last days has shone forth through Jesus Christ: "Come ye, and let us go up to the mountain of the LORD, to the house of the God of Jacob; and He will teach us of His ways, and we will walk in them." For the law came forth from the dwellers in Sion, and settled among us as a spiritual law. Moreover, the word of the LORD came forth from that very Jerusalem, that it might be disseminated through all places, and might judge in the midst of the heathen, selecting those whom it sees to be submissive, and rejecting the disobedient, who are many in number. And to those who inquire of us whence we come, or who is our founder, we reply that we are come, agreeably to the counsels of Jesus, to "cut down our hostile and insolent 'wordy' swords into ploughshares, and to convert into pruning-hooks the spears formerly employed in war." For we no longer take up "sword against nation," nor do we "learn war any more," having become children of peace, for the sake of Jesus, who is our leader, instead of those whom our fathers followed, among whom we were "strangers to the covenant," and having received a law, for which we give thanks to Him that rescued us from the error (of our ways), saying, "Our fathers honoured lying idols, and there is not among them one that causeth it to rain." Our Superintendent, then, and Teacher, having come forth from the Jews, regulates the whole world by the word of His teaching. And having made these remarks by way of anticipation, we have refuted as well as we could the untrue statements of Celsus, by subjoining the appropriate answer.

CHAPTER XXXIV

But, that we may not pass without notice what Celsus has said between these and the preceding paragraphs, let us quote his words: "We might adduce Herodotus as a witness on this point, for he expresses himself as follows: 'For the people of the cities Marea and Apis, who inhabit those parts of Egypt that are adjacent to Libya, and who look upon themselves as Libyans, and not as Egyptians, finding their sacrificial worship oppressive, and wishing not to be excluded from the use of cows' flesh, sent to the oracle of Jupiter Ammon, saying that there was no relationship between them and the Egyptians, that they dwelt outside the Delta, that there was no community of sentiment between them and the Egyptians, and that they wished to be allowed to partake of all kinds of food. But the god would not allow them to do as they desired, saying that that country was a part of Egypt, which was watered by the inundation of the Nile, and that those were Egyptians who dwell to the south of the city of Elephantine, and drink of the river Nile.' Such is the narrative of Herodotus. But," continues Celsus, "Ammon in divine things would not make a worse ambassador than the angels of the Jews, so that there is nothing wrong in each nation observing its established method of worship. Of a truth, we shall find very great differences prevailing among the nations, and yet each seems to deem its own by far the best. Those inhabitants of Ethiopia who dwell in Meroe worship Jupiter and Bacchus alone; the Arabians, Urania and Bacchus only; all the Egyptians, Osiris and Isis; the Saites, Minerva; while the Naucratites have recently classed Serapis among their deities, and the rest according to their respective laws. And some abstain from the flesh of sheep, and others from that of crocodiles; others, again, from that of cows, while they regard swine's flesh with loathing. The Scythians, indeed, regard it as a noble act to banquet upon human beings. Among the Indians, too, there are some who deem themselves discharging a holy duty in eating their fathers, and this is mentioned in a certain passage by Herodotus. For the sake of credibility, I shall again quote his very words, for he writes as follows: 'For if any one were to make this proposal to all men, viz., to bid him select out of all existing laws the best, each would choose, after examination, those of his own country. Men each consider their own laws much the best, and therefore it is not likely than any other than a madman would make these things a subject of ridicule. But that such are the conclusions of all men regarding the laws, may be determined by many other evidences, and especially by the following illustration. Darius, during his reign, having summoned before him those Greeks who happened to be present at the time, inquired of them for how much they would be willing to eat their deceased fathers? their answer was, that for no consideration would they do such a thing. After this, Darius summoned those Indians who are called Callatians, who are in the habit of eating their parents, and asked of them in the presence of these Greeks, who learned what passed through an interpreter, for what amount of money they would undertake to burn their deceased fathers with fire? on which they raised a loud shout, and bade the king say no more.' Such is the way, then, in which these matters are regarded. And Pindar appears to me to be right in saying that 'law' is the king of all things."

CHAPTER XXXV

The argument of Celsus appears to point by these illustrations to this conclusion: that it is "an obligation incumbent on all men to live according to their country's customs, in which case they will escape censure; whereas the Christians, who have abandoned their native usages, and who are not one nation like the Jews, are to be blamed for giving their adherence to the teaching of Jesus." Let him then tell us whether it is a becoming thing for philosophers, and those who have been taught not to yield to superstition, to abandon their country's customs, so as to eat of those articles of food which are prohibited in their respective cities? or whether this proceeding of theirs is opposed to what is becoming? For if, on account of their philosophy, and the instructions which they have received against superstition, they should eat, in disregard of their native laws, what was interdicted by their fathers, why should the Christians (since the Gospel requires *them* not to busy themselves about statues and images, or even about any of the created works of God but to ascend on high, and present the soul to the Creator); when acting in a similar manner to the philosophers, be censured for so doing? But if, for the sake of defending the thesis which he has proposed to himself, Celsus, or those who think with him, should say, that even one who had studied philosophy would keep his country's laws, then philosophers in Egypt, for example, would act most ridiculously in avoiding the eating of onions, in order to observe their country's laws, or certain parts of the body, as the head and shoulders, in order not to transgress the traditions of their fathers. And I do not speak of those Egyptians who shudder with fear at the discharge of wind from the body, because if any one of these were to become a philosopher, and still observe the laws of his country, he would be a ridiculous philosopher, acting very unphilosophically. In the same way, then, he who has been led by the Gospel to worship the God of all things, and, from regard to his country's laws, lingers here below among images and statues of men, and does not desire to ascend to the Creator, will resemble those who have indeed learned philosophy, but who are afraid of things which ought to inspire no terrors, and who regard it as an act of impiety to eat of those things which have been enumerated.

CHAPTER XXXVI

But what sort of being is this Ammon of Herodotus, whose words Celsus has quoted, as if by way of demonstrating how each one ought to keep his country's laws? For this Ammon would not allow the people of the cities of Marea and Apis, who inhabit the districts adjacent to Libya, to treat as a matter of indifference the use of cows' flesh, which is a thing not only indifferent in its own nature, but which does not prevent a man from being noble and virtuous. If Ammon, then, forbade the use of cows' flesh, because of the advantage which results from the use of the animal in the cultivation of the ground, and in addition to this, because it is by the female that the breed is increased, the account would possess more plausibility. But now he simply requires that those who drink of the Nile should observe the laws of the Egyptians regarding kine. And hereupon Celsus, taking occasion to pass a jest upon the employment of the angels among the Jews as the ambassadors of God, says that "Ammon did not make a worse ambassador of divine things than did the angels of the Jews," into the meaning of whose words and manifestations he instituted no investigation; otherwise he would have seen, that it is not for oxen that God is concerned, even where He may appear to legislate for them, or for irrational animals, but that what is written for the sake of men, under the appearance of relating to irrational animals, contains certain truths of nature. Celsus, moreover, says that no wrong is committed by any one who wishes to observe the religious worship sanctioned by the laws of his country; and it follows, according to his view, that the Scythians commit no wrong, when, in conformity with their country's laws, they eat human beings. And those Indians who eat their own fathers are considered, according to Celsus, to do a religious, or at least not a wicked act. He adduces, indeed, a statement of Herodotus which favours the principle that each one ought, from a sense of what is becoming, to obey his country's laws; and he appears to approve of the custom of those Indians called Callatians, who in the time of Darius devoured their parents, since, on Darius inquiring for how great a sum of money they would be willing to lay aside this usage, they raised a loud shout, and bade the king say no more.

CHAPTER XXXVII

As there are, then, generally two laws presented to us, the one being the law of nature, of which God would be the legislator, and the other being the written law of cities, it is a proper thing, when the written law is not opposed to that of God, for the citizens not to abandon it under pretext of foreign customs; but when the law of nature, that is, the law of God, commands what is opposed to the written law, observe whether reason will not tell us to bid a long farewell to the written code, and to the desire of its legislators, and to give ourselves up to the legislator God, and to choose a life agreeable to His word, although in doing so it may be necessary to encounter dangers, and countless labours, and even death and dishonour. For when there are some laws in harmony with the will of God, which are opposed to others which are in force in cities, and when it is impracticable to please God (and those who administer laws of the kind referred to), it would be absurd to contemn those acts by means of which we may please the Creator of all things, and to select those by which we shall become displeasing to God, though we may satisfy unholy laws, and those who love them. But since it is reasonable in other matters to prefer the law of nature, which is the law of God, before the written law, which has been enacted by men in a spirit of opposition to the law of God, why should we not do this still more in the case of those laws which relate to God? Neither shall we, like the Ethiopians who inhabit the parts about Meroe, worship, as is their pleasure, Jupiter and Bacchus only; nor shall we at all reverence Ethiopian gods in the Ethiopian manner; nor, like the Arabians, shall we regard Urania and Bacchus alone as divinities; nor in any degree at all deities in which the difference of sex has been a ground of distinction (as among the Arabians, who worship Urania as a female, and Bacchus as a male deity); nor shall we, like all the Egyptians, regard Osiris and Isis as gods; nor shall we enumerate Athena among these, as the Saites are pleased to do. And if to the ancient inhabitants of Naucratis it seemed good to worship other divinities, while their modern descendants have begun quite recently to pay reverence to Serapis, who never was a god at all, we shall not on that account assert that a new being who was not formerly a god, nor at all known to men, is a deity. For the Son of God, "the First-born of all creation," although He seemed recently to have become incarnate, is not by any means on that account recent. For the holy Scriptures know Him to be the most ancient of all the works of creation; for it was to Him that God said regarding the creation of man, "Let Us make man in Our image, after Our likeness."

CHAPTER XXXVIII

I wish, however, to show how Celsus asserts without any good reason, that each one reveres his domestic and native institutions. For he declares that "those Ethiopians who inhabit Meroe know only of two gods, Jupiter and Bacchus, and worship these alone; and that the Arabians also know only of two, viz., Bacchus, who is also an Ethiopian deity, and Urania, whose worship is confined to them." According to his account, neither do the Ethiopians worship Urania, nor the Arabians Jupiter. If, then, an Ethiopian were from any accident to fall into the hands of the Arabians, and were to be judged guilty of impiety because he did not worship Urania, and for this reason should incur the danger of death, would it be proper for the Ethiopian to die, or to act contrary to his country's laws, and do obeisance to Urania? Now, if it would be proper for him to act contrary to the laws of his country, he will do what is not right, so far as the language of Celsus is any standard; while, if he should be led away to death, let him show the reasonableness of selecting such a fate. I know not whether, if the Ethiopian doctrine taught men to philosophize on the immortality of the soul, and the honour which is paid to religion, they would reverence those as deities who are deemed to be such by the laws of the country. A similar illustration may be employed in the case of the Arabians, if from any accident they happened to visit the Ethiopians about Meroe. For, having been taught to worship Urania and Bacchus alone, they will not worship Jupiter along with the Ethiopians; and if, adjudged guilty of impiety, they should be led away to death, let Celsus tell us what it would be reasonable on their part to do. And with regard to the fables which relate to Osiris and Isis, it is superfluous and out of place at present to enumerate them. For although an allegorical meaning may be given to the fables, they will nevertheless teach us to offer divine worship to cold water, and to the earth, which is subject to men, and all the animal creation. For in this way, I presume, they refer Osiris to water, and Isis to earth; while with regard to Serapis the accounts are numerous and conflicting, to the effect that very recently he appeared in public, agreeably to certain juggling tricks performed at the desire of Ptolemy, who wished to show to the people of Alexandria as it were a visible god. And we have read in the writings of Numenius the Pythagorean regarding his formation, that he partakes of the essence of all the animals and plants that are under the control of nature, that he may appear to have been fashioned into a god, not by the makers of images alone, with the aid of profane mysteries, and juggling tricks employed to invoke demons, but also by magicians and sorcerers, and those demons who are bewitched by their incantations.

CHAPTER XXXIX

We must therefore inquire what may be fittingly eaten or not by the rational and gentle animal, which acts always in conformity with reason; and not worship at random, sheep, or goats, or kine; to abstain from which is an act of moderation, for much advantage is derived by men from these animals. Whereas, is it not the most foolish of all things to spare crocodiles, and to treat *them* as sacred to some fabulous divinity or other? For it is a mark of exceeding stupidity to spare those animals which do not spare us, and to bestow care on those which make a prey of human beings. But Celsus approves of those who, in keeping with the laws of their country, worship and tend crocodiles, and not a word does he say against them, while the Christians appear deserving of censure, who have been taught to loath evil, and to turn away from wicked works, and to reverence and honour virtue as being generated by God, and as being His Son. For we must not, on account of their feminine name and nature, regard wisdom and righteousness as females; for these things are in our view the Son of God, as His genuine disciple has shown, when he said of Him, "Who of God is made to us wisdom, and righteousness, and sanctification, and redemption." And although we may call Him a "second" God, let men know that by the term "second God" we mean nothing else than a virtue capable of including all other virtues, and a reason capable of containing all reason whatsoever which exists in all things, which have arisen naturally, directly, and for the general advantage, and which "reason," we say, dwelt in the soul of Jesus, and was united to Him in a degree far above all other souls, seeing He alone was enabled completely to receive the highest share in the absolute reason, and the absolute wisdom, and the absolute righteousness.

CHAPTER XL

But since, after Celsus had spoken to the above effect of the different kinds of laws, he adds the following remark, "Pindar appears to me to be correct in saying that law is king of all things," let us proceed to discuss this assertion. What law do you mean to say, good sir, is "king of all things?" If you mean those which exist in the various cities, then such an assertion is not true. For all men are not governed by the same law. You ought to have said that "laws are kings of all men," for in every nation some law is king of all. But if you mean that which is law in the proper sense, then it is this which is by nature "king of all things;" although there are some individuals who, having like robbers abandoned the law, deny its validity, and live lives of violence and injustice. We Christians, then, who have come to the knowledge of the law which is by nature "king of all things," and which is the same with the law of God, endeavour to regulate our lives by its prescriptions, having bidden a long farewell to those of an unholy kind.

CHAPTER XLI

Let us notice the charges which are next advanced by Celsus, in which there is exceedingly little that has reference to the Christians, as most of them refer to the Jews. His words are: "If, then, in these respects the Jews were carefully to preserve their own law, they are not to be blamed for so doing, but those persons rather who have forsaken their own usages, and adopted those of the Jews. And if they pride themselves on it, as being possessed of superior wisdom, and keep aloof from intercourse with others, as not being equally pure with themselves, they have already heard that their doctrine concerning heaven is not peculiar to them, but, to pass by all others, is one which has long ago been received by the Persians, as Herodotus somewhere mentions. 'For they have a custom,' he says, 'of going up to the tops of the mountains, and of offering sacrifices to Jupiter, giving the name of Jupiter to the whole circle of the heavens.' And I think," continues Celsus, "that it makes no difference whether you call the highest being Zeus, or Zen, or Adonai, or Sabaoth, or Ammoun like the Egyptians, or Pappaeus like the Scythians. Nor would they be deemed at all holier than others in this respect, that they observe the rite of circumcision, for this was done by the Egyptians and Colchians before them; nor because they abstain from swine's flesh, for the Egyptians practised abstinence not only from it, but from the flesh of goats, and sheep, and oxen, and fishes as well; while Pythagoras and his disciples do not eat beans, nor anything that contains life. It is not probable, however, that they enjoy God's favour, or are loved by Him differently from others, or that angels were sent from heaven to them alone, as if they had had allotted to them 'some region of the blessed,' for we see both themselves and the country of which they were deemed worthy. Let this band, then, take its departure, after paying the penalty of its vaunting, not having a knowledge of the great God, but being led away and deceived by the artifices of Moses, having become his pupil to no good end."

CHAPTER XLII

It is evident that, by the preceding remarks, Celsus charges the Jews with falsely giving themselves out as the chosen portion of the Supreme God above all other nations. And he accuses them of boasting, because they gave out that they knew the great God, although they did not really know Him, but were led away by the artifices of Moses, and were deceived by him, and became his disciples to no good end. Now we have in the preceding pages already spoken in part of the venerable and distinguished polity of the Jews, when it existed amongst them as a symbol of the city of God, and of His temple, and of the sacrificial worship offered in it and at the altar of sacrifice. But if any one were to turn his attention to the meaning of the legislator, and to the constitution which he established, and were to examine the various points relating to him, and compare them with the present method of worship among other nations, there are none which he would admire to a greater degree; because, so far as can be accomplished among mortals, everything that was not of advantage to the human race was withheld from them, and only those things which are useful bestowed. And for this reason they had neither gymnastic contests, nor scenic representations, nor horse-races; nor were there among them women who sold their beauty to any one who wished to have sexual intercourse without offspring, and to cast contempt upon the nature of human generation. And what an advantage was it to be taught from their tender years to ascend above all visible nature, and to hold the belief that God was not fixed anywhere within its limits, but to look for Him on high, and beyond the sphere of all bodily substance! And how great was the advantage which they enjoyed in being instructed almost from their birth, and as soon as they could speak, in the immortality of the soul, and in the existence of courts of justice under the earth, and in the rewards provided for those who have lived righteous lives! These truths, indeed, were proclaimed in the veil of fable to children, and to those whose views of things were childish; while to those who were already occupied in investigating the truth, and desirous of making progress therein, these fables, so to speak, were transfigured into the truths which were concealed within them. And I consider that it was in a manner worthy of their name as the "portion of God" that they despised all kinds of divination, as that which bewitches men to no purpose, and which proceeds rather from wicked demons than from anything of a better nature; and sought the knowledge of future events in the souls of those who, owing to their high degree of purity, received the spirit of the Supreme God.

CHAPTER XLIII

But what need is there to point out how agreeable to sound reason, and unattended with injury either to master or slave, was the law that one of the same faith should not be allowed to continue in slavery more than six years? The Jews, then, cannot be said to preserve their own law in the same points with the other nations. For it would be censurable in them, and would involve a charge of insensibility to the superiority of their law, if they were to believe that they had been legislated for in the same way as the other nations among the heathen. And although Celsus will not admit it, the Jews nevertheless are possessed of a wisdom superior not only to that of the multitude, but also of those who have the appearance of philosophers; because those who engage in philosophical pursuits, after the utterance of the most venerable philosophical sentiments, fall away into the worship of idols and demons, whereas the very lowest Jew directs his look to the Supreme God alone; and they do well, indeed, so far as this point is concerned, to pride themselves thereon, and to keep aloof from the society of others as accursed and impious. And would that they had not sinned, and transgressed the law, and slain the prophets in former times, and in these latter days conspired against Jesus, that we might be in possession of a pattern of a heavenly city which even Plato would have sought to describe; although I doubt whether he could have accomplished as much as was done by Moses and those who followed him, who nourished a "chosen generation," and "a holy nation," dedicated to God, with words free from all superstition.

CHAPTER XLIV

But as Celsus would compare the venerable customs of the Jews with the laws of certain nations, let us proceed to look at them. He is of opinion, accordingly, that there is no difference between the doctrine regarding "heaven" and that regarding "God;" and he says that "the Persians, like the Jews, offer sacrifices to Jupiter upon the tops of the mountains,"—not observing that, as the Jews were acquainted with one God, so they had only one holy house of prayer, and one altar of whole burnt-offerings, and one censer for incense, and one high priest of God. The Jews, then, had nothing in common with the Persians, who ascend the summits of their mountains, which are many in number, and offer up sacrifices which have nothing in common with those which are regulated by the Mosaic code,—in conformity to which the Jewish priests "served unto the example and shadow of heavenly things," explaining enigmatically the object of the law regarding the sacrifices, and the things of which these sacrifices were the symbols. The Persians therefore may call the "whole circle of heaven" Jupiter; but we maintain that "the heaven" is neither Jupiter nor God, as we indeed know that certain beings of a class inferior to God have ascended above the heavens and all visible nature: and in this sense we understand the words, "Praise God, ye heaven of heavens, and ye waters that be above the heavens: let them praise the name of the Lord."

CHAPTER XLV

As Celsus, however, is of opinion that it matters nothing whether the highest being be called Jupiter, or Zen, or Adonai, or Sabaoth, or Ammoun (as the Egyptians term him), or Pappaeus (as the Scythians entitle him), let us discuss the point for a little, reminding the reader at the same time of what has been said above upon this question, when the language of Celsus led us to consider the subject. And now we maintain that the nature of names is not, as Aristotle supposes, an enactment of those who impose them. For the languages which are prevalent among men do not derive their origin from men, as is evident to those who are able to ascertain the nature of the charms which are appropriated by the inventors of the languages differently, according to the various tongues, and to the varying pronunciations of the names, on which we have spoken briefly in the preceding pages, remarking that when those names which in a certain language were possessed of a natural power were translated into another, they were no longer able to accomplish what they did before when uttered in their native tongues. And the same peculiarity is found to apply to men; for if we were to translate the name of one who was called from his birth by a certain appellation in the Greek language into the Egyptian or Roman, or any other tongue, we could not make him do or suffer the same things which he would have done or suffered under the appellation first bestowed upon him. Nay, even if we translated into the Greek language the name of an individual who had been originally invoked in the Roman tongue, we could not produce the result which the incantation professed itself capable of accomplishing had it preserved the name first conferred upon him. And if these statements are true when spoken of the names of *men*, what are we to think of those which are transferred, for any cause whatever, to the *Deity*? For example, something is transferred from the name Abraham when translated into Greek, and something is signified by that of Isaac, and also by that of Jacob; and accordingly, if any one, either in an invocation or in swearing an oath, were to use the expression, "the God of Abraham," and "the God of Isaac," and "the God of Jacob," he would produce certain effects, either owing to the nature of these names or to their powers, since even demons are vanquished and become submissive to him who pronounces these names; whereas if we say, "the god of the chosen father of the echo, and the god of laughter, and the god of him who strikes with the heel," the mention of the name is attended with no result, as is the case with other names possessed of no power. And in the same way, if we translate the word "Israel" into Greek or any other language, we shall produce no result; but if we retain it as it is, and join it to those expressions to which such as are skilled in these matters think it ought to be united, there would then follow some result from the pronunciation of the word which would accord with the professions of those who employ such invocations. And we may say the same also of the pronunciation of "Sabaoth," a word which is frequently employed in incantations; for if we translate the term into "Lord of hosts," or "Lord of armies," or "Almighty" (different acceptation of it having been proposed by the interpreters), we shall accomplish nothing; whereas if we retain the original pronunciation, we shall, as those who are skilled in such matters maintain, produce some effect. And the same observation holds good of Adonai. If, then, neither "Sabaoth" nor "Adonai," when rendered into what appears to be their meaning in the Greek tongue, can accomplish anything, how much less would be the result among those who regard it as a matter of indifference whether the highest being be called Jupiter, or Zen, or Adonai, or Sabaoth!

CHAPTER XLVI

It was for these and similar mysterious reasons, with which Moses and the prophets were acquainted, that they forbade the name of other gods to be pronounced by him who bethought himself of praying to the one Supreme God alone, or to be remembered by a heart which had been taught to be pure from all foolish thoughts and words. And for these reasons we should prefer to endure all manner of suffering rather than acknowledge Jupiter to be God. For we do not consider Jupiter and Sabaoth to be the same, nor Jupiter to be at all divine, but that some demon, unfriendly to men and to the true God, rejoices under this title. And although the Egyptians were to hold Ammon before us under threat of death, we would rather die than address him as God, it being a name used in all probability in certain Egyptian incantations in which this demon is invoked. And although the Scythians may call Pappaeus the supreme God, yet we will not yield our assent to this; granting, indeed, that there *is* a Supreme Deity, although we do not give the name Pappaeus to Him as His proper title, but regard it as one which is agreeable to the demon to whom was allotted the desert of Scythia, with its people and its language. He, however, who gives God His title in the Scythian tongue, or in the Egyptian or in any language in which he has been brought up, will not be guilty of sin.

CHAPTER XLVII

Now the reason why circumcision is practised among the Jews is not the same as that which explains its existence among the Egyptians and Colchians, and therefore it is not to be considered the same circumcision. And as he who sacrifices does not sacrifice to the same god, although he appears to perform the rite of sacrifice in a similar manner, and he who offers up prayer does not pray to the same divinity, although he asks the same things in his supplication; so, in the same way, if one performs the rite of circumcision, it by no means follows that it is not a different act from the circumcision performed upon another. For the purpose, and the law, and the wish of him who performs the rite, place the act in a different category. But that the whole subject may be still better understood, we have to remark that the term for "righteousness" is the same among all the Greeks; but righteousness is shown to be one thing according to the view of Epicurus; and another according to the Stoics, who deny the threefold division of the soul; and a different thing again according to the followers of Plato, who hold that righteousness is the proper business of the parts of the soul. And so also the "courage" of Epicures is one thing, who would undergo some labours in order to escape from a greater number; and a different thing that of the philosopher of the Porch, who would choose all virtue for its own sake; and a different thing still that of Plato, who maintains that virtue itself is the act of the irascible part of the soul, and who assigns to it a place about the breast. And so circumcision will be a different thing according to the varying opinions of those who undergo it. But on such a subject it is unnecessary to speak on this occasion in a treatise like the present; for whoever desires to see what led us to the subject, can read what we have said upon it in the Epistle of Paul to the Romans.

CHAPTER XLVIII

Although the Jews, then, pride themselves on circumcision, they will separate it not only from that of the Colchians and Egyptians, but also from that of the Arabian Ishmaelites; and yet the latter was derived from their ancestor Abraham, the father of Ishmael, who underwent the rite of circumcision along with his father. The Jews say that the circumcision performed on the eighth day is the principal circumcision, and that which is performed according to circumstances is different; and probably it was performed on account of the hostility of some angel towards the Jewish nation, who had the power to injure such of them as were not circumcised, but was powerless against those who had undergone the rite. This may be said to appear from what is written in the book of Exodus, where the angel before the circumcision of Eliezer was able to work against Moses, but could do nothing after his son was circumcised. And when Zipporah had learned this, she took a pebble and circumcised her child, and is recorded, according to the reading of the common copies, to have said, "The blood of my child's circumcision is stayed," but according to the Hebrew text, "A bloody husband art thou to me." For she had known the story about a certain angel having power before the shedding of the blood, but who became powerless through the blood of circumcision. For which reason the words were addressed to Moses, "A bloody husband art thou to me."

But these things, which appear rather of a curious nature, and not level to the comprehension of the multitude, I have ventured to treat at such length; and now I shall only add, as becomes a Christian, one thing more, and shall then pass on to what follows. For this angel might have had power, I think, over those of the people who were not circumcised, and generally over all who worshipped only the Creator; and this power lasted so long as Jesus had not assumed a human body. But when He had done this, and had undergone the rite of circumcision in His own person, all the power of the angel over those who practise the same worship, but are not circumcised, was abolished; for Jesus reduced it to nought by (the power of) His unspeakable divinity. And therefore His disciples are forbidden to circumcise themselves, and are reminded (by the apostle): "If ye be circumcised, Christ shall profit you nothing."

CHAPTER XLIX

But neither do the Jews pride themselves upon abstaining from swine's flesh, as if it were some great thing; but upon their having ascertained the nature of clean and unclean animals, and the cause of the distinction, and of swine being classed among the unclean. And these distinctions were signs of certain things until the advent of Jesus; after whose coming it was said to His disciple, who did not yet comprehend the doctrine concerning these matters, but who said, "Nothing that is common or unclean hath entered into my mouth," "What God hath cleansed, call not thou common." It therefore in no way affects either the Jews or us that the Egyptian priests abstain not only from the flesh of swine, but also from that of goats, and sheep, and oxen, and fish. But since it is not that "which entereth into the mouth that defiles a man," and since "meat does not commend us to God," we do not set great store on refraining from eating, nor yet are we induced to eat from a gluttonous appetite. And therefore, so far as we are concerned, the followers of Pythagoras, who abstain from all things that contain life may do as they please; only observe the different reason for abstaining from things that have life on the part of the Pythagoreans and our ascetics. For the former abstain on account of the fable about the transmigration of souls, as the poet says:—

"And some one, lifting up his beloved son,
Will slay him after prayer; O how foolish he!"

We, however, when we do abstain, do so because "we keep under our body, and bring it into subjection," and desire "to mortify our members that are upon the earth, fornication, uncleanness, inordinate affection, evil concupiscence;" and we use every effort to "mortify the deeds of the flesh."

CHAPTER L

Celsus, still expressing his opinion regarding the Jews, says: "It is not probable that they are in great favour with God, or are regarded by Him with more affection than others, or that angels are sent by Him to them alone, as if to them had been allotted some region of the blessed. For we may see both the people themselves, and the country of which they were deemed worthy." We shall refute this, by remarking that it is evident that this nation *was* in great favour with God, from the fact that the God who presides over all things was called the God of the Hebrews, even by those who were aliens to our faith. And because they were in favour with God, they were not abandoned by Him; but although few in number, they continued to enjoy the protection of the divine power, so that in the reign of Alexander of Macedon they sustained no injury from him, although they refused, on account of certain covenants and oaths, to take up arms against Darius. They say that on that occasion the Jewish high priest, clothed in his sacred robe, received obeisance from Alexander, who declared that he had beheld an individual arrayed in this fashion, who announced to him in his sleep that he was to be the subjugator of the whole of Asia. Accordingly, we Christians maintain that "it was the fortune of that people in a remarkable degree to enjoy God's favour, and to be loved by Him in a way different from others;" but that this economy of things and this divine favour were transferred to us, after Jesus had conveyed the power which had been manifested among the Jews to those who had become converts to Him from among the heathen. And for this reason, although the Romans desired to perpetrate many atrocities against the Christians, in order to ensure their extermination, they were unsuccessful; for there was a divine hand which fought on their behalf, and whose desire it was that the word of God should spread from one corner of the land of Judea throughout the whole human race.

CHAPTER LI

But seeing that we have answered to the best of our ability the charges brought by Celsus against the Jews and their doctrine, let us proceed to consider what follows, and to prove that it is no empty boast on our part when we make a profession of knowing the great God, and that we have not been led away by any juggling tricks of Moses (as

Celsus imagines), or even of our own Saviour Jesus; but that for a good end we listen to the God who speaks in Moses, and have accepted Jesus, whom he testifies to be God, as the Son of God, in hope of receiving the best rewards if we regulate our lives according to His word. And we shall willingly pass over what we have already stated by way of anticipation on the points, "whence we came and who is our leader, and what law proceeded from Him." And if Celsus would maintain that there is no difference between us and the Egyptians, who worship the goat, or the ram, or the crocodile, or the ox, or the river-horse, or the dog-faced baboon, or the cat, he can ascertain if it be so, and so may any other who thinks alike on the subject. We, however, have to the best of our ability defended ourselves at great length in the preceding pages on the subject of the honour which we render to our Jesus, pointing out that we have found the better part; and that in showing that the truth which is contained in the teaching of Jesus Christ is pure and unmixed with error, we are not commending ourselves, but our Teacher, to whom testimony was borne through many witnesses by the Supreme God and the prophetic writings among the Jews, and by the very clearness of the case itself, for it is demonstrated that He could not have accomplished such mighty works without the divine help.

CHAPTER LII

But the statement of Celsus which we wish to examine at present is the following: "Let us then pass over the refutations which might be adduced against the claims of their teacher, and let him be regarded as really an angel. But is he the first and only one who came (to men), or were there others before him? If they should say that he is the only one, they would be convicted of telling lies against themselves. For they assert that on many occasions others came, and sixty or seventy of them together, and that these became wicked, and were cast under the earth and punished with chains, and that from this source originate the warm springs, which are their tears; and, moreover, that there came an angel to the tomb of this said being—according to some, indeed, one, but according to others, two—who answered the women that he had arisen. For the Son of God could not himself, as it seems, open the tomb, but needed the help of another to roll away the stone. And again, on account of the pregnancy of Mary, there came an angel to the carpenter, and once more another angel, in order that they might take up the young Child and flee away (into Egypt). But what need is there to particularize everything, or to count up the number of angels said to have been sent to Moses, and others amongst them? If, then, others were sent, it is manifest that he also came from the same God. But he may be supposed to have the appearance of announcing something of greater importance (than those who preceded him), as if the Jews had been committing sin, or corrupting their religion, or doing deeds of impiety; for these things are obscurely hinted at."

CHAPTER LIII

The preceding remarks might suffice as an answer to the charges of Celsus, so far as regards those points in which our Saviour Jesus Christ is made the subject of special investigation. But that we may avoid the appearance of intentionally passing over any portion of his work, as if we were unable to meet him, let us, even at the risk of being tautological (since we are challenged to this by Celsus), endeavour as far as we can with all due brevity to continue our discourse, since perhaps something either more precise or more novel may occur to us upon the several topics. He says, indeed, that "he has omitted the refutations which have been adduced against the claims which Christians advance on behalf of their teacher," although he has not omitted anything which he was able to bring forward, as is manifest from his previous language, but makes this statement only as an empty rhetorical device. That we are not refuted, however, on the subject of our great Saviour, although the accuser may *appear* to refute us, will be manifest to those who peruse in a spirit of truth-loving investigation all that is predicted and recorded of Him. And, in the next place, since he considers that he makes a concession in saying of the Saviour, "Let him appear to be really an angel," we reply that we do not accept of such a concession from Celsus; but we look to the work of Him who came to visit the whole human race in His word and teaching, as each one of His adherents was capable of receiving Him. And this was the work of one who, as the prophecy regarding Him said, was not simply an angel, but the "Angel of the great counsel:" for He announced to men the great counsel of the God and Father of all things regarding them, (saying) of those who yield themselves up to a life of pure religion, that they ascend by means of their great deeds to God; but of those who do not adhere to Him, that they place themselves at a distance from God, and journey on to destruction through their unbelief of Him. He then continues: "If even the angel came to men, is he the first and only one who came, or did others come on former occasions?" And he thinks he can meet either of these dilemmas at great length, although there is not a single real Christian who asserts that Christ was the only being that visited the human race. For, as Celsus says, "If they should say the only one," there are others who appeared to different individuals.

CHAPTER LIV

In the next place, he proceeds to answer himself as he thinks fit in the following terms: "And so he is not the only one who is recorded to have visited the human race, as even those who, under pretext of teaching in the name of Jesus, have apostatized from the Creator as an inferior being, and have given in their adherence to one who is a superior God and father of him who visited (the world), assert that before him certain beings came from the Creator to visit the human race." Now, as it is in the spirit of truth that we investigate all that relates to the subject, we shall remark that it is asserted by Apelles, the celebrated disciple of Marcion, who became the founder of a certain sect, and who treated the writings of the Jews as fabulous, that Jesus is the only one that came to visit the human race. Even against him, then, who maintained that Jesus was the only one that came from God to men, it would be in vain for Celsus to quote the statements regarding the descent of other angels, seeing Apelles discredits, as we have already mentioned, the miraculous narratives of the Jewish Scriptures; and much more will he decline to admit what Celsus has adduced, from not understanding the contents of the book of Enoch. No one, then, convicts us of falsehood, or of making contradictory assertions, as if we maintained both that our Saviour was the only being that ever came to men, and yet that many others came on different occasions. And in a most confused manner, moreover, does he adduce, when examining the subject of the visits of angels to men, what he has derived, without seeing its meaning, from the contents of the book of Enoch; for he does not appear to have read the passages in question, nor to have been aware that the books which bear the name Enoch do not at all circulate in the Churches as divine, although it is from this source that he might be supposed to have obtained the statement, that "sixty or seventy angels descended at the same time, who fell into a state of wickedness."

CHAPTER LV

But, that we may grant to him in a spirit of candour what he has not discovered in the contents of the book of Genesis, that "the sons of God, seeing the daughters of men, that they were fair, took to them wives of all whom they chose," we shall nevertheless even on this point persuade those who are capable of understanding the meaning of the prophet, that even before us there was one who referred this narrative to the doctrine regarding souls, which became possessed with a desire for the corporeal life of men, and this in metaphorical language, he said, was termed "daughters of men." But whatever may be the meaning of the "sons of God desiring to possess the daughters of men," it will not at all contribute to prove that Jesus was not the only one who visited mankind as an angel, and who manifestly became the Saviour and benefactor of all those who depart from the flood of wickedness. Then, mixing up and confusing whatever he had at any time heard, or had anywhere found written—whether held to be of divine origin among Christians or not—he adds: "The sixty or seventy who descended together were cast under the earth, and were punished with chains." And he quotes (as from the book of Enoch, but without naming it) the following: "And hence it is that the tears of these angels are warm springs,"—a thing neither mentioned nor heard of in the Churches of God! For no one was ever so foolish as to materialize into human tears those which were shed by the angels who had come down from heaven. And if it were right to pass a jest upon what is advanced against us in a serious spirit by Celsus, we might observe that no one would ever have said that hot springs, the greater part of which are fresh water, were the tears of the angels, since tears are saltish in their nature, unless indeed the angels, in the opinion of Celsus, shed tears which are fresh.

CHAPTER LVI

Proceeding immediately after to mix up and compare with one another things that are dissimilar, and incapable of being united, he subjoins to his statement regarding the sixty or seventy angels who came down from heaven, and who, according to him, shed fountains of warm water for tears, the following: "It is related also that there came to the tomb of Jesus himself, according to some, two angels, according to others, one;" having failed to notice, I think, that Matthew and Mark speak of one, and Luke and John of two, which statements are not contradictory. For they who mention "one," say that it was he who rolled away the stone from the sepulchre; while they who mention "two," refer to those who appeared in shining raiment to the women that repaired to the sepulchre, or who were seen within sitting in white garments. Each of these occurrences might now be demonstrated to have actually taken place, and to be indicative of a figurative meaning existing in these "phenomena," (and intelligible) to those who were prepared to behold the resurrection of the Word. Such a task, however, does not belong to our present purpose, but rather to an exposition of the Gospel.

CHAPTER LVII

Now, that miraculous appearances have sometimes been witnessed by human beings, is related by the Greeks; and not only by those of them who might be suspected of composing fabulous narratives, but also by those who have given every evidence of being genuine philosophers, and of having related with perfect truth what had happened to them. Accounts of this kind we have read in the writings of Chrysippus of Soli, and also some things of the same kind relating to Pythagoras; as well as in some of the more recent writers who lived a very short time ago, as in the treatise of Plutarch of Chaeronea "on the Soul," and in the second book of the work of Numenius the Pythagorean on the "Incorruptibility of the Soul." Now, when such accounts are related by the Greeks, and especially by the philosophers among them, they are not to be received with mockery and ridicule, nor to be regarded as fictions and fables; but when those who are devoted to the God of all things, and who endure all kinds of injury, even to death itself, rather than allow a falsehood to escape their lips regarding God, announce the appearances of angels which they have themselves witnessed, they are to be deemed unworthy of belief, and their words are not to be regarded as true! Now it is opposed to sound reason to judge in this way whether individuals are speaking truth or falsehood. For those who act honestly, only after a long and careful examination into the details of a subject, slowly and cautiously express their opinion of the veracity or falsehood of this or that person with regard to the marvels which they may relate; since it is the case that neither do all men show themselves worthy of belief, nor do all make it distinctly evident that they are relating to men only fictions and fables. Moreover, regarding the resurrection of Jesus from the dead, we have this remark to make, that it is not at all wonderful if, on such an occasion, either one or two angels should have appeared to announce that Jesus had risen from the dead, and to provide for the safety of those who believed in such an event to the advantage of their souls. Nor does it appear to me at all unreasonable, that those who believe in the resurrection of Jesus, and who manifest, as a fruit of their faith not to be lightly esteemed, their possession of a virtuous life, and their withdrawal from the flood of evils, should not be unattended by angels who lend their help in accomplishing their conversion to God.

CHAPTER LVIII

But Celsus challenges the account also that an angel rolled away the stone from the sepulchre where the body of Jesus lay, acting like a lad at school, who should bring a charge against any one by help of a string of commonplaces. And, as if he had discovered some clever objection to the narrative, he remarks: "The Son of God, then, it appears, could not open his tomb, but required the aid of another to roll away the stone." Now, not to overdo the discussion of this matter, or to have the appearance of unreasonably introducing philosophical remarks, by explaining the figurative meaning at present, I shall simply say of the narrative alone, that it does appear in itself a more respectful proceeding, that the servant and inferior should have rolled away the stone, than that such an act should have been performed by Him whose resurrection was to be for the advantage of mankind. I do not speak of the desire of those who conspired against the Word, and who wished to put Him to death, and to show to all men that He *was* dead and non-existent, that His tomb should not be opened, in order that no one might behold the Word alive after their conspiracy; but the "Angel of God" who came into the world for the salvation of men, with the help of another angel, proved more powerful than the conspirators, and rolled away the weighty stone, that those who deemed the Word to be dead might be convinced that He is not with the "departed," but is alive, and precedes those who are willing to follow Him, that He may manifest to them those truths which come after those which He formerly showed them at the time of their first entrance (into the school of Christianity), when they were as yet incapable of receiving deeper instruction. In the next place, I do not understand what advantage he thinks will accrue to his purpose when he ridicules the account of "the angel's visit to Joseph regarding the pregnancy of Mary;" and again, that of the angel to warn the parents "to take up the new-born Child, whose life was in danger, and to flee with it into Egypt." Concerning these matters, however, we have in the preceding pages answered his statements. But what does Celsus mean by saying, that "according to the Scriptures, angels are recorded to have been sent to Moses, and others as well?" For it appears to me to contribute nothing to his purpose, and especially because none of them made any effort to accomplish, as far as in his power, the conversion of the human race from their sins. Let it be granted, however, that other angels were sent from God, but that he came to announce something of greater importance (than any others who preceded him); and when the Jews had fallen into sin, and corrupted their religion, and had done unholy deeds, transferred the kingdom of God to other husbandmen, who in all the Churches take special care of themselves, and use every endeavour by means of a holy life, and by a doctrine conformable thereto, to win over to the God of all things those who would rush away from the teaching of Jesus.

CHAPTER LIX

Celsus then continues: "The Jews accordingly, and these (clearly meaning the Christians), have the same God;" and as if advancing a proposition which would not be conceded, he proceeds to make the following assertion: "It is certain, indeed, that the members of the great Church admit this, and adopt as true the accounts regarding the creation of the world which are current among the Jews, viz., concerning the six days and the seventh;" on which day, as the Scripture says, God "ceased" from His works, retiring into the contemplation of Himself, but on which, as Celsus says (who does not abide by the letter of the history, and who does not understand its meaning), God "rested,"—a term which is not found in the record. With respect, however, to the creation of the world, and the "rest which is reserved after it for the people of God," the subject is extensive, and mystical, and profound, and difficult of explanation. In the next place, as it appears to me, from a desire to fill up his book, and to give it an appearance of importance, he recklessly adds certain statements, such as the following, relating to the first man, of whom he says: "We give the same account as do the Jews, and deduce the same genealogy from him as they do." However, as regards "the conspiracies of brothers against one another," we know of none such, save that Cain conspired against Abel, and Esau against Jacob; but not Abel against Cain, nor Jacob against Esau: for if this had been the case, Celsus would have been correct in saying that we give the same accounts as do the Jews of "the conspiracies of brothers against one another." Let it be granted, however, that we speak of the same descent into Egypt as they, and of their return thence, which was not a "flight," as Celsus considers it to have been, what does that avail towards founding an accusation against us or against the Jews? Here, indeed, he thought to cast ridicule upon us, when, in speaking of the Hebrew people, he termed their exodus a "flight;" but when it was his business to investigate the account of the punishments inflicted by God upon Egypt, that topic he purposely passed by in silence.

CHAPTER LX

If, however, it be necessary to express ourselves with precision in our answer to Celsus, who thinks that we hold the same opinions on the matters in question as do the Jews, we would say that we both agree that the books (of Scripture) were written by the Spirit of God, but that we do *not* agree about the meaning of their contents; for we do not regulate our lives like the Jews, because we are of opinion that the literal acceptation of the laws is not that which conveys the meaning of the legislation. And we maintain, that "when Moses is read, the veil is upon their heart," because the meaning of the law of Moses has been concealed from those who have not welcomed the way which is by Jesus Christ. But we know that if one turn to the Lord (for "the Lord is that Spirit"), the veil being taken away, "he beholds, as in a mirror with unveiled face, the glory of the Lord" in those thoughts which are concealed in their literal expression, and to his own glory becomes a participator of the divine glory; the term "face" being used figuratively for the "understanding," as one would call it without a figure, in which is the face of the "inner man," filled with light and glory, flowing from the true comprehension of the contents of the law.

CHAPTER LXI

After the above remarks he proceeds as follows: "Let no one suppose that I am ignorant that some of them will concede that their God is the same as that of the Jews, while others will maintain that he is a different one, to whom the latter is in opposition, and that it was from the former that the Son came." Now, if he imagine that the existence of numerous heresies among the Christians is a ground of accusation against Christianity, why, in a similar way, should it not be a ground of accusation against philosophy, that the various sects of philosophers differ from each other, not on small and indifferent points, but upon those of the highest importance? Nay, medicine also ought to be a subject of attack, on account of its many conflicting schools. Let it be admitted, then, that there are amongst us some who deny that our God is the same as that of the Jews: nevertheless, on that account those are not to be blamed who prove from the same Scriptures that one and the same Deity is the God of the Jews and of the Gentiles alike, as Paul, too, distinctly says, who was a convert from Judaism to Christianity, "I thank my God, whom I serve from my forefathers with a pure conscience." And let it be admitted also, that there is a third class who call certain persons "carnal," and others "spiritual,"—I think he here means the followers of Valentinus,—yet what does this avail against us, who belong to the Church, and who make it an accusation against such as hold that certain natures are saved, and that others perish in consequence of their natural constitution? And let it be admitted further, that there are some who give themselves out as Gnostics, in the same way as those Epicureans who call themselves philosophers: yet neither will they who annihilate the doctrine of providence be deemed true philosophers, nor those true Christians who introduce monstrous inventions, which are disapproved of by those who are the disciples of Jesus. Let it be admitted, moreover, that there are some who accept Jesus, and who boast on that account of being Christians, and yet would regulate their lives, like the Jewish multitude, in accordance with the Jewish law,— and these are the twofold sect of Ebionites, who either acknowledge with us that Jesus was born of a virgin, or deny this, and maintain that He was begotten like other human beings,—what does that avail by way of charge against such as belong to the Church, and whom Celsus has styled "those of the multitude?" He adds, also, that certain of the Christians are believers in the Sibyl, having probably misunderstood some who blamed such as believed in the existence of a prophetic Sibyl, and termed those who held this belief Sibyllists.

CHAPTER LXII

He next pours down upon us a heap of names, saying that he knows of the existence of certain Simonians who worship Helene, or Helenus, as their teacher, and are called Helenians. But it has escaped the notice of Celsus that the Simonians do not at all acknowledge Jesus to be the Son of God, but term Simon the "power" of God, regarding whom they relate certain marvellous stories, saying that he imagined that if he could become possessed of similar powers to those with which be believed Jesus to be endowed, he too would become as powerful among men as Jesus was amongst the multitude. But neither Celsus nor Simon could comprehend how Jesus, like a good husbandman of the word of God, was able to sow the greater part of Greece, and of barbarian lands, with His doctrine, and to fill these countries with words which transform the soul from all that is evil, and bring it back to the Creator of all things. Celsus knows, moreover, certain Marcellians, so called from Marcellina, and Harpocratians from Salome, and others who derive their name from Mariamme, and others again from Martha. We, however, who from a love of learning examine to the utmost of our ability not only the contents of Scripture, and the differences to which they give rise, but have also, from love to the truth, investigated as far as we could the opinions of philosophers, have never at any time met with these sects. He makes mention also of the Marcionites, whose leader was Marcion.

CHAPTER LXIII

In the next place, that he may have the appearance of knowing still more than he has yet mentioned, he says, agreeably to his usual custom, that "there are others who have wickedly invented some being as their teacher and demon, and who wallow about in a great darkness, more unholy and accursed than that of the companions of the Egyptian Antinous." And he seems to me, indeed, in touching on these matters, to say with a certain degree of truth, that there are certain others who have wickedly invented another demon, and who have found him to be their lord, as they wallow about in the great darkness of their ignorance. With respect, however, to Antinous, who is compared with our Jesus, we shall not repeat what we have already said in the preceding pages. "Moreover," he continues, "these persons utter against one another dreadful blasphemies, saying all manner of things shameful to be spoken; nor will they yield in the slightest point for the sake of harmony, hating each other with a perfect hatred." Now, in answer to this, we have already said that in philosophy and medicine sects are to be found warring against sects. We, however, who are followers of the word of Jesus, and have exercised ourselves in thinking, and saying, and doing what is in harmony with His words, "when reviled, bless; being persecuted, we suffer it; being defamed, we entreat;" and we would *not* utter "all manner of things shameful to be spoken" against those who have adopted different opinions from ours, but, if possible, use every exertion to raise them to a better condition through adherence to the Creator alone, and lead them to perform every act as those who will (one day) be judged. And if those who hold different opinions will not be convinced, we observe the injunction laid down for the treatment of such: "A man that is a heretic, after the first and second admonition, reject, knowing that he that is such is subverted, and sinneth, being condemned of himself." Moreover, we who know the maxim, "Blessed are the peacemakers," and this also, "Blessed are the meek," would not regard with hatred the corrupters of Christianity, nor term those who had fallen into error Circes and flattering deceivers.

CHAPTER LXIV

Celsus appears to me to have misunderstood the statement of the apostle, which declares that "in the latter times some shall depart from the faith, giving heed to seducing spirits and doctrines of devils; speaking lies in hypocrisy, having their conscience seared with a hot iron; forbidding to marry, and commanding to abstain from meats, which God hath created to be received with thanksgiving of them who believe;" and to have misunderstood also those who employed these declarations of the apostle against such as had corrupted the doctrines of Christianity. And it is owing to this cause that Celsus has said that "certain among the Christians are called 'cauterized in the ears;'" and also that some are termed "enigmas,"—a term which we have never met. The expression "stumbling-block" is, indeed, of frequent occurrence in these writings,—an appellation which we are accustomed to apply to those who turn away simple persons, and those who are easily deceived, from sound doctrine. But neither we, nor, I imagine, any other, whether Christian or heretic, know of any who are styled Sirens, who betray and deceive, and stop their ears, and change into swine those whom they delude. And yet this man, who affects to know everything, uses such language as the following: "You may hear," he says, "all those who differ so widely, and who assail each other in their disputes with the most shameless language, uttering the words, 'The world is crucified to me, and I unto the world.'" And this is the only phrase which, it appears, Celsus could remember out of Paul's writings; and yet why should we not also employ innumerable other quotations from the Scriptures, such as, "For though we do walk in the flesh, we do not war after the flesh; (for the weapons of our warfare are not carnal, but mighty through God to the pulling down of strongholds,) casting down imaginations, and every high thing that exalteth itself against the knowledge of God?"

CHAPTER LXV

But since he asserts that "you may hear all those who differ so widely saying, 'The world is crucified to me, and I unto the world,'" we shall show the falsity of such a statement. For there are certain heretical sects which do not receive the Epistles of the Apostle Paul, as the two sects of Ebionites, and those who are termed Encratites. Those, then, who do not regard the apostle as a holy and wise man, will not adopt his language, and say, "The world is crucified to me, and I unto the world." And consequently in this point, too, Celsus is guilty of falsehood. He continues, moreover, to linger over the accusations which he brings against the diversity of sects which exist, but does not appear to me to be accurate in the language which he employs, nor to have carefully observed or understood how it is that those Christians who have made progress in their studies say that they are possessed of greater knowledge than the Jews; and also, whether they acknowledge the same Scriptures, but interpret them differently, or whether they do not recognise these books as divine. For we find both of these views prevailing among the sects. He then continues: "Although they have no foundation for the doctrine, let us examine the system itself; and, in the first place, let us mention the corruptions which they have made through ignorance and misunderstanding, when in the discussion of elementary principles they express their opinions in the most absurd manner on things which they do not understand, such as the following." And then, to certain expressions which are continually in the mouths of the believers in Christianity, he opposes certain others from the writings of the philosophers, with the object of making it appear that the noble sentiments which Celsus supposes to be used by Christians have been expressed in better and clearer language by the philosophers, in order that he might drag away to the study of philosophy those who are caught by opinions which at once evidence their noble and religious character. We shall, however, here terminate the fifth book, and begin the sixth with what follows.

BOOK VI

CHAPTER I

IN beginning this our sixth book, we desire, my reverend Ambrosius, to answer in it those accusations which Celsus brings against the *Christians*, not, as might be supposed, those objections which he has adduced from *writers on philosophy*. For he has quoted a considerable number of passages, chiefly from Plato, and has placed alongside of these such declarations of holy Scripture as are fitted to impress even the intelligent mind; subjoining the assertion that "these things are stated much better among the Greeks (than in the Scriptures), and in a manner which is free from all exaggerations and promises on the part of God, or the Son of God." Now we maintain, that if it is the object of the ambassadors of the truth to confer benefits upon the greatest possible number, and, so far as they can, to win over to its side, through their love to men, every one without exception—intelligent as well as simple—not Greeks only, but also Barbarians (and great, indeed, is the humanity which should succeed in converting the rustic and the ignorant), it is manifest that they must adopt a style of address fitted to do good to all, and to gain over to them men of every sort. Those, on the other hand, who turn away from the ignorant as being mere slaves, and unable to understand the flowing periods of a polished and logical discourse, and so devote their attention solely to such as have been brought up amongst literary pursuits, confine their views of the public good within very strait and narrow limits.

CHAPTER II

I have made these remarks in reply to the charges which Celsus and others bring against the simplicity of the language of Scripture, which appears to be thrown into the shade by the splendour of polished discourse. For our prophets, and Jesus Himself, and His apostles, were careful to adopt a style of address which should not merely convey the truth, but which should be fitted to gain over the multitude, until each one, attracted and led onwards, should ascend as far as he could towards the comprehension of those mysteries which are contained in these apparently simple words. For, if I may venture to say so, few have been benefited (if they have indeed been benefited at all) by the beautiful and polished style of Plato, and those who have written like him; while, on the contrary, many have received advantage from those who wrote and taught in a simple and practical manner, and with a view to the wants of the multitude. It is easy, indeed, to observe that Plato is found only in the hands of those who profess to be literary men; while Epictetus is admired by persons of ordinary capacity, who have a desire to be benefited, and who perceive the improvement which may be derived from his writings. Now we make these remarks, not to disparage Plato (for the great world of men has found even him useful), but to point out the aim of those who said: "And my speech and my preaching was not with enticing words of man's wisdom, but in demonstration of the Spirit and of power, that our faith should not stand in the wisdom of men, but in the power of God." For the word of God declares that the preaching (although in itself true and most worthy of belief) is not sufficient to reach the human heart, unless a certain power be imparted to the speaker from God, and a grace appear upon his words; and it is only by the divine agency that this takes place in those who speak effectually. The prophet says in the sixty-seventh Psalm, that "the Lord will give a word with great power to them who preach." If, then, it should be granted with respect to certain points, that the same doctrines are found among the Greeks as in our own Scriptures, yet they do not possess the same power of attracting and disposing the souls of men to follow them. And therefore the disciples of Jesus, men ignorant so far as regards Grecian philosophy, yet traversed many countries of the world, impressing, agreeably to the desire of the Logos, each one of their hearers according to his deserts, so that they received a moral amelioration in proportion to the inclination of their will to accept of that which is good.

CHAPTER III

Let the ancient sages, then, make known their sayings to those who are capable of understanding them. Suppose that Plato, for example, the son of Ariston, in one of his Epistles, is discoursing about the "chief good," and that he says, "The chief good can by no means be described in words, but is produced by long habit, and bursts forth suddenly as a light in the soul, as from a fire which had leapt forth." We, then, on hearing these words, admit that they are well said, for it is God who revealed to men these as well as all other noble expressions. And for this reason it is that we maintain that those who have entertained correct ideas regarding God, but who have not offered to Him a worship in harmony with the truth, are liable to the punishments which fall on sinners. For respecting such Paul says in express words: "The wrath of God is revealed from heaven against all ungodliness and unrighteousness of men, who hold the truth in unrighteousness; because that which may be known of God is manifest in them; for God hath showed it unto them. For the invisible things of Him from the creation of the world are clearly seen, being understood by the things that are made, even His eternal power and Godhead; so that they are without excuse: because that, when they knew God, they glorified Him not as God, neither were thankful; but became vain in their imaginations, and their foolish heart was darkened. Professing themselves to be wise, they became fools, and changed the glory of the incorruptible God into an image made like to corruptible man, and to birds, and four-footed beasts, and creeping things." The truth, then, is verily held (in unrighteousness), as our Scriptures testify, by those who are of opinion that "the chief good cannot be described in words," but who assert that, "after long custom and familiar usage, a light becomes suddenly kindled in the soul, as if by a fire springing forth, and that it now supports itself alone."

CHAPTER IV

Notwithstanding, those who have written in this manner regarding the "chief good" will go down to the Piraeus and offer prayer to Artemis, as if she were God, and will look (with approval) upon the solemn assembly held by ignorant men; and after giving utterance to philosophical remarks of such profundity regarding the soul, and describing its passage (to a happier world) after a virtuous life, they pass from those great topics which God has revealed to them, and adopt mean and trifling thoughts, and offer a cock to Aesculapius! And although they had been enabled to form representations both of the "invisible things" of God and of the "archetypal forms" of things from the creation of the world, and from (the contemplation of) sensible things, from which they ascend to those objects which are comprehended by the understanding alone,—and although they had no mean glimpses of His "eternal power and Godhead," they nevertheless became "foolish in their imaginations," and their "foolish heart" was involved in darkness and ignorance as to the (true) worship of God. Moreover, we may see those who greatly pride themselves upon their wisdom and theology worshipping the image of a corruptible man, *in honour*, they say, of Him, and sometimes even descending, with the Egyptians, to the worship of birds, and four-footed beasts, and creeping things! And although some may appear to have risen above such practices, nevertheless they will be found to have changed the truth of God into a lie, and to worship and serve the "creature more than the Creator." As the wise and learned among the Greeks, then, commit errors in the service which they render to God, God "chose the foolish things of the world to confound the wise; and base things of the world, and things that are weak, and things which are despised, and things which are nought, to bring to nought things that are;" and this, truly, "that no flesh should glory in the presence of God." *Our* wise men, however,—Moses, the most ancient of them all, and the prophets who followed him,—knowing that the chief good could by no means be described in words, were the first who wrote that, as God manifests Himself to the deserving, and to those who are qualified to behold Him, He appeared to Abraham, or to Isaac, or to Jacob. But who He was that appeared, and of what form, and in what manner, and like to which of mortal beings, they have left to be investigated by those who are able to show that they resemble those persons to whom God showed Himself: for He was seen not by their bodily eyes, but by the pure heart. For, according to the declaration of our Jesus, "Blessed are the pure in heart, for they shall see God."

CHAPTER V

But that a light is suddenly kindled in the soul, as by a fire leaping forth, is a fact known long ago to our Scriptures; as when the prophet said, "Light ye for yourselves the light of knowledge." John also, who lived after him, said, "That which was in the Logos was life, and the life was the light of men;" which "true light lighteneth every man that cometh into the world" (i.e., the true world, which is perceived by the understanding), and maketh him a light of the world:" For this light shone in our hearts, to give the light of the glorious Gospel of God in the face of Christ Jesus." And therefore that very ancient prophet, who prophesied many generations before the reign of Cyrus (for he was older than he by more than fourteen generations), expressed himself in these words: "The Lord is my light and my salvation: whom shall I fear?" and, "Thy law is a lamp unto my feet, and a light unto my path;" and again, "The light of Thy countenance, O Lord, was manifested towards us;" and, "In Thy light we shall see light." And the Logos, exhorting us to come to this light, says, in the prophecies of Isaiah: "Enlighten thyself, enlighten thyself, O Jerusalem; for thy light is come, and the glory of the LORD is risen upon thee." The same prophet also, when predicting the advent of Jesus, who was to turn away men from the worship of idols, and of images, and of demons, says, "To those that sat in the land and shadow of death, upon them hath the light arisen;" and again, "The people that sat in darkness saw a great light."

Observe now the difference between the fine phrases of Plato respecting the "chief good," and the declarations of our prophets regarding the "light" of the blessed; and notice that the truth as it is contained in Plato concerning this subject did not at all help his readers to attain to a pure worship of God, nor even himself, who could philosophize so grandly about the "chief good," whereas the simple language of the holy Scriptures has led to their honest readers being filled with a divine spirit; and this light is nourished within them by the oil, which in a certain parable is said to have preserved the light of the torches of the five wise virgins.

CHAPTER VI

Seeing, however, that Celsus quotes from an epistle of Plato another statement to the following effect, viz.: "If it appeared to me that these matters could be adequately explained to the multitude in writing and in oral address, what nobler pursuit in life could have been followed by me, than to commit to writing what was to prove of such advantage to human beings, and to lead the nature of all men onwards to the light?"—let us then consider this point briefly, viz., whether or not Plato were acquainted with any doctrines more profound than are contained in his writings, or more divine than those which he has left behind him, leaving it to each one to investigate the subject according to his ability, while we demonstrate that our prophets did know of greater things than any in the Scriptures, but which they did not commit to writing. Ezekiel, e.g., received a roll, written within and without, in which were contained "lamentations," and "songs," and "denunciations;" but at the command of the Logos he swallowed the book, in order that its contents might not be written, and so made known to unworthy persons. John also is recorded to have seen and done a similar thing. Nay, Paul even heard "unspeakable words, which it is not lawful for a man to utter." And it is related of Jesus, who was greater than all these, that He conversed with His disciples in private, and especially in their sacred retreats, concerning the Gospel of God; but the words which He uttered have not been preserved, because it appeared to the evangelists that they could not be adequately conveyed to the multitude in writing or in speech. And if it were not tiresome to repeat the truth regarding these illustrious individuals, I would say that they saw better than Plato (by means of the intelligence which they received by the grace of God), what things were to be committed to *writing*, and how this was to be done, and what was by no means to be written to the multitude, and what was to be expressed in *words*, and what was not to be so conveyed. And once more, John, in teaching us the difference between what ought to be committed to writing and what not, declares that he heard seven thunders instructing him on certain matters, and forbidding him to commit their words to writing.

CHAPTER VII

There might also be found in the writings of Moses and of the prophets, who are older not only than Plato, but even than Homer and the invention of letters among the Greeks, passages worthy of the grace of God bestowed upon them, and filled with great thoughts, to which they gave utterance, but not because they understood Plato imperfectly, as Celsus imagines. For how was it possible that they should have heard one who was not yet born? And if any one should apply the words of Celsus to the apostles of Jesus, who were younger than Plato, say whether it is not on the very face of it an incredible assertion, that Paul the tentmaker, and Peter the fisherman, and John who left his father's nets, should, through misunderstanding the language of Plato in his Epistles, have expressed themselves as they have done regarding God? But as Celsus now, after having often required of us immediate assent (to his views), as if he were babbling forth something new in addition to what he has already advanced, only repeats himself, what we have said in reply may suffice. Seeing, however, he produces another quotation from Plato, in which he asserts that the employment of the method of question and answer sheds light on the thoughts of those who philosophize like him, let us show from the holy Scriptures that the word of God also encourages us to the practice of dialectics: Solomon, e.g., declaring in one passage, that "instruction unquestioned goes astray;" and Jesus the son of Sirach, who has left us the treatise called "Wisdom," declaring in another, that "the knowledge of the unwise is as words that will not stand investigation." Our methods of discussion, however, are rather of a gentle kind; for we have learned that he who presides over the preaching of the word ought to be able to confute gainsayers. But if some continue indolent, and do not train themselves so as to attend to the reading of the word, and "to search the Scriptures," and, agreeably to the command of Jesus, to investigate the *meaning* of the sacred writings, and to ask of God concerning them, and to keep "knocking" at what may be closed within them, the Scripture is not on that account to be regarded as devoid of wisdom.

CHAPTER VIII

In the next place, after other Platonic declarations, which demonstrate that "the good" can be known by few, he adds: "Since the multitude, being puffed up with a contempt for others, which is far from right, and being filled with vain and lofty hopes, assert that, because they have come to the knowledge of some venerable doctrines, certain things are true." "Yet although Plato predicted these things, he nevertheless does not talk marvels, nor shut the mouth of those who wish to ask him for information on the subject of his promises; nor does he command them to come at once and believe that a God of a particular kind exists, and that he has a son of a particular nature, who descended (to earth) and conversed with me." Now, in answer to this we have to say, that with regard to Plato, it is Aristander, I think, who has related that he was not the son of Ariston, but of a phantom, which approached Amphictione in the guise of Apollo. And there are several other of the followers of Plato who, in their lives of their master, have made the same statement. What are we to say, moreover, about Pythagoras, who relates the greatest possible amount of wonders, and who, in a general assembly of the Greeks, showed his ivory thigh, and asserted that he recognised the shield which he wore when he was Euphorbus, and who is said to have appeared on one day in two different cities! He, moreover, who will declare that what is related of Plato and Socrates belongs to the marvellous, will quote the story of the swan which was recommended to Socrates while he was asleep, and of the master saying when he met the young man, "This, then, was the swan!" Nay, the third eye which Plato saw that he himself possessed, he will refer to the category of prodigies. But occasion for slanderous accusations will never be wanting to those who are ill-disposed, and who wish to speak evil of what has happened to such as are raised above the multitude. Such persons will deride as a fiction even the demon of Socrates. We do not, then, relate marvels when we narrate the history of Jesus, nor have His genuine disciples recorded any such stories of Him; whereas this Celsus, who professes universal knowledge, and who quotes many of the sayings of Plato, is, I think, intentionally silent on the discourse concerning the Son of God which is related in Plato's Epistle to Hermeas and Coriscus. Plato's words are as follows: "And calling to witness the God of all things—the ruler both of things present and things to come, father and lord both of the ruler and cause—whom, if we are philosophers indeed, we shall all clearly know, so far as it is possible for happy human beings to attain such knowledge."

CHAPTER IX

Celsus quotes another saying of Plato to the following effect: "It has occurred to me to speak once more upon these subjects at greater length, as perhaps I might express myself about them more clearly than I have already done for there is a certain 'real' cause, which proves a hindrance in the way of him who has ventured, even to a slight extent, to write on such topics; and as this has been frequently mentioned by me on former occasions, it appears to me that it ought to be stated now. In each of existing things, which are necessarily employed in the acquisition of knowledge, there are three elements; knowledge itself is the fourth; and that ought to be laid down as the fifth which is both capable of being known and is true. Of these, one is 'name;' the second is 'word;' the third, 'image;' the fourth, 'knowledge.'" Now, according to this division, John is introduced before Jesus as the voice of one crying in the wilderness, so as to correspond with the "name" of Plato; and the second after John, who is pointed out by him, is Jesus, with whom agrees the statement, "The Word became flesh;" and that corresponds to the "word" of Plato. Plato terms the third "image;" but we, who apply the expression "image" to something different, would say with greater precision, that the mark of the wounds which is made in the soul by the word is the Christ which is in each one of us and this mark is impressed by Christ the Word. And whether Christ, the wisdom which is in those of us who are perfect, correspond to the "fourth" element—knowledge—will become known to him who has the capacity to ascertain it.

CHAPTER X

He next continues: "You see how Plato, although maintaining that (the chief good) cannot be described in words, yet, to avoid the appearance of retreating to an irrefutable position, subjoins a reason in explanation of this difficulty, as even 'nothing' might perhaps be explained in words." But as Celsus adduces this to prove that we ought not to yield a simple assent, but to furnish a reason for our belief, we shall quote also the words of Paul, where he says, in censuring the hasty believer, "unless ye have believed inconsiderately." Now, through his practice of repeating himself, Celsus, so far as he can, forces us to be guilty of tautology, reiterating, after the boastful language which has been quoted, that "Plato is not guilty of boasting and falsehood, giving out that he has made some new discovery, or that he has come down from heaven to announce it, but acknowledges whence these statements are derived." Now, if one wished to reply to Celsus, one might say in answer to such assertions, that even Plato is guilty of boasting, when in the *Timaeus* he puts the following language in the month of Zeus: "Gods of gods, whose creator and father I am," and so on. And if any one will defend such language on account of the meaning which is conveyed under the name of Zeus, thus speaking in the dialogue of Plato, why should not he who investigates the meaning of the words of the Son of God, or those of the Creator in the prophets, express a profounder meaning than any conveyed by the words of Zeus in the *Timaeus*? For the characteristic of divinity is the announcement of future events, predicted not by human power, but shown by the result to be due to a divine spirit in him who made the announcement. Accordingly, we do not say to each of our hearers, "Believe, first of all, that He whom I introduce to thee is the Son of God;" but we put the Gospel before each one, as his character and disposition may fit him to receive it, inasmuch as we have learned to know "how we ought to answer every man." And there are some who are capable of receiving nothing more than an exhortation to believe, and to these we address that alone; while we approach others, again, as far as possible, in the way of demonstration, by means of question and answer. Nor do we at all say, as Celsus scoffingly alleges, "Believe that he whom I introduce to thee is the Son of God, although he was shamefully bound, and disgracefully punished, and very recently was most contumeliously treated before the eyes of all men;" neither do we add, "Believe it even the more (on that account)." For it is our endeavour to state, on each individual point, arguments more numerous even than we have brought forward in the preceding pages.

CHAPTER XI

After this Celsus continues: "If these (meaning the Christians) bring forward this person, and others, again, a different individual (as the Christ), while the common and ready cry of all parties is, 'Believe, if thou wilt be saved, or else begone,' what shall those do who are in earnest about their salvation? Shall they cast the dice, in order to divine whither they may betake themselves, and whom they shall join?" Now we shall answer this objection in the following manner, as the clearness of the case impels us to do. If it had been recorded that several individuals had appeared in human life as sons of God in the manner in which Jesus did, and if each of them had drawn a party of adherents to his side, so that, on account of the similarity of the profession (in the case of each individual) that he was the Son of God, he to whom

616

his followers bore testimony to that effect was an object of dispute, there would have been ground for his saying, "If these bring forward this person, and others a different individual, while the common and ready cry of all parties is, 'Believe, if thou wilt be saved, or else begone,'" and so on; whereas it has been proclaimed to the entire world that Jesus Christ is the only Son of God who visited the human race: for those who, like Celsus, have supposed that (the acts of Jesus) were a series of prodigies, and who for that reason wished to perform acts of the same kind, that they, too, might gain a similar mastery over the minds of men, were convicted of being utter nonentities. Such were Simon, the Magus of Samaria, and Dositheus, who was a native of the same place; since the former gave out that he was the power of God that is called great, and the latter that he was the Son of God. Now Simonians are found nowhere throughout the world; and yet, in order to gain over to himself many followers, Simon freed his disciples from the danger of death, which the Christians were taught to prefer, by teaching them to regard idolatry as a matter of indifference. But even at the beginning of their existence the followers of Simon were not exposed to persecution. For that wicked demon who was conspiring against the doctrine of Jesus, was well aware that none of his own maxims would be weakened by the teaching of Simon. The Dositheans, again, even in former times, did not rise to any eminence, and now they are completely extinguished, so that it is said their whole number does not amount to thirty. Judas of Galilee also, as Luke relates in the Acts of the Apostles, wished to call himself some great personage, as did Theudas before him; but as their doctrine was not of God, they were destroyed, and all who obeyed them were immediately dispersed. We do not, then, "cast the dice in order to divine whither we shall betake ourselves, and whom we shall join," as if there were many claimants able to draw us after them by the profession of their having come down from God to visit the human race. On these points, however, we have said enough.

CHAPTER XII

Accordingly, let us pass on to another charge made by Celsus, who is not even acquainted with the words (of our sacred books), but who, from misunderstanding them, has said that "we declare the wisdom that is among men to be foolishness with God;" Paul having said that "the wisdom of the *world* is foolishness with God." Celsus says that "the reason of this has been stated long ago." And the reason he imagines to be, "our desire to win over by means of this saying the ignorant and foolish alone." But, as he himself has intimated, he has said the same thing before; and we, to the best of our ability, replied to it. Notwithstanding this, however, he wished to show that this statement was an invention of ours, and borrowed from the Grecian sages, who declare that human wisdom is of one kind, and divine of another. And he quotes the words of Heraclitus, where he says in one passage, that "man's method of action is not regulated by fixed principles, but that of God is;" and in another, that "a foolish man listens to a demon, as a boy does to a man." He quotes, moreover, the following from the *Apology of Socrates*, of which Plato was the author: "For I, O men of Athens, have obtained this name by no other means than by my wisdom. And of what sort is this wisdom? Such, probably, as is human; for in that respect I venture to think that I am in reality wise." Such are the passages adduced by Celsus. But I shall subjoin also the following from Plato's letter to Hermeas, and Erastus, and Coriscus: "To Erastus and Coriscus I say, although I am an old man, that, in addition to this noble knowledge of 'forms' (which they possess), they need a wisdom, with regard to the class of wicked and unjust persons, which may serve as a protective and repelling force against them. For they are inexperienced, in consequence of having passed a large portion of their lives with us, who are moderate individuals, and not wicked. I have accordingly said that they need these things, in order that they may not be compelled to neglect the true wisdom, and to apply themselves in a greater degree than is proper to that which is necessary and human."

CHAPTER XIII

According to the foregoing, then, the one kind of wisdom is human, and the other divine. Now the "human" wisdom is that which is termed by us the wisdom of the "world," which is "foolishness with God;" whereas the "divine"—being different from the "human," because it is "divine"—comes, through the grace of God who bestows it, to those who have evinced their capacity for receiving it, and especially to those who, from knowing the difference between either kind of wisdom, say, in their prayers to God, "Even if one among the sons of men be perfect, while the wisdom is wanting that comes from Thee, he shall be accounted as nothing." We maintain, indeed, that "human" wisdom is an exercise for the soul, but that "divine" wisdom is the "end," being also termed the "strong" meat of the soul by him who has said that "strong meat belongeth to them that are perfect, even those who by reason of use have their senses exercised to discern both good and evil." This opinion, moreover, is truly an ancient one, its antiquity not being referred back, as Celsus thinks, merely to Heraclitus and Plato. For before these individuals lived, the prophets distinguished between the two kinds of wisdom. It is sufficient for the present to quote from the words of David what he says regarding the man who is wise, according to divine wisdom, that "he will not see corruption when he beholds wise men dying." Divine wisdom, accordingly, being different from faith, is the "first" of the so-called "charismata" of God; and the "second" after it—in the estimation of those who know how to distinguish such things accurately—is what is called "knowledge;" and the "third"—seeing that even the more simple class of men who adhere to the service of God, so far as they can, must be saved—is faith. And therefore Paul says: "To one is given by the Spirit the word of wisdom; to another the word of knowledge by the same Spirit; to another faith by the same Spirit." And therefore it is no ordinary individuals whom you will find to have participated in the "divine" wisdom, but the more excellent and distinguished among those who have given in their adherence to Christianity; for it is not "to the most ignorant, or servile, or most uninstructed of mankind," that one would discourse upon the topics relating to the divine wisdom.

CHAPTER XIV

In designating others by the epithets of "uninstructed, and servile, and ignorant," Celsus, I suppose, means those who are not acquainted with his laws, nor trained in the branches of Greek learning; while we, on the other hand, deem those to be "uninstructed" who are not ashamed to address (supplications) to inanimate objects, and to call upon those for health that have no strength, and to ask the dead for life, and to entreat the helpless for assistance. And although some may say that these objects are not gods, but only imitations and symbols of real divinities, nevertheless these very individuals, in imagining that the hands of low mechanics can frame imitations of divinity, are "uninstructed, and servile, and ignorant;" for we assert that the lowest among us have been set free from this ignorance and want of knowledge, while the most intelligent can understand and grasp the divine hope. We do *not* maintain, however, that it is impossible for one who has not been trained in earthly wisdom to receive the "divine," but we *do* acknowledge that all human wisdom is "folly" in comparison with the "divine." In the next place, instead of endeavouring to adduce reasons, as he ought, for his assertions, he terms us "sorcerers," and asserts that "we flee away with headlong speed from the more polished class of persons, because they are not suitable subjects for our impositions, while we seek to decoy those who are more rustic." Now he did not observe that from the very beginning our wise men were trained in the external branches of learning: Moses, e.g., in all the wisdom of the Egyptians; Daniel, and Ananias, and Azariah, and Mishael, in all Assyrian learning, so that they were found to surpass in tenfold degree all the wise men of that country. At the present time, moreover, the Churches have, in proportion to the multitudes (of ordinary believers), a few "wise" men, who have come over to them from that wisdom which is said by us to be "according to the flesh;" and they have also some who have advanced from it to that wisdom which is "divine."

CHAPTER XV

Celsus, in the next place, as one who has heard the subject of humility greatly talked about, but who has not been at the pains to understand it, would wish to speak evil of that humility which is practised among us, and imagines that it is borrowed from some words of Plato imperfectly understood, where he expresses himself in the *Laws* as follows: "Now God, according to the ancient account, having in Himself both the beginning and end and middle of all existing things, proceeds according to nature, and marches straight on. He is constantly followed by justice, which is the avenger of all breaches of the divine law: he who is about to become happy follows her closely in humility, and becomingly adorned." He did not observe, however, that in writers much older than Plato the following words occur in a prayer: "Lord, my heart is not haughty, nor mine eyes lofty, neither do I walk in great matters, nor in things too wonderful for me; if I had not been humble," etc. Now these words show that he who is of humble mind does not by any means humble himself in an unseemly or inauspicious manner, falling down upon his knees, or casting himself headlong on the ground, putting on the dress of the miserable, or sprinkling himself with dust. But he who is of humble mind in the sense of the prophet, while "walking in great and wonderful things," which are above his capacity—viz., those doctrines that are truly great, and those thoughts that are wonderful—"humbles himself under the mighty hand of God." If there are some, however, who through their stupidity have not clearly understood the doctrine of humiliation, and act as they do, it is not our doctrine which is to be blamed; but we must extend our forgiveness to the stupidity of those who aim at higher things, and owing to their fatuity of mind fail to attain them. He who is "humble and becomingly adorned," is so in a greater degree than Plato's "humble and becomingly adorned" individual: for he is becomingly adorned, on the one hand, because "he walks in things great and wonderful," which are beyond his capacity; and humble, on the other hand, because, while being in the midst of such, he yet voluntarily humbles himself, not under any one at random, but under "the mighty hand of God," through Jesus Christ, the teacher of such instruction, "who did not deem equality with God a thing to be eagerly clung to, but made Himself of no reputation, and took on Him the form of a servant, and being found in fashion as a man, humbled Himself, and became obedient unto death, even the death of the cross." And so great is this doctrine of humiliation, that it has no ordinary individual as its teacher; but our great Saviour Himself says: "Learn of Me, for I am meek and lowly of heart, and ye shall find rest for your souls."

CHAPTER XVI

In the next place, with regard to the declaration of Jesus against rich men, when He said, "It is easier for a camel to go through the eye of a needle, than for a rich man to enter into the kingdom of God," Celsus alleges that this saying manifestly proceeded from Plato, and that Jesus perverted the words of the philosopher, which were, that "it was impossible to be distinguished for goodness, and at the same time for riches." Now who is there that is capable of giving even moderate attention to affairs—not merely among the believers on Jesus, but among the rest of mankind—that would not laugh at Celsus, on hearing that Jesus, who was born and brought up among the Jews, and was supposed to be the son of Joseph the carpenter, and who had not studied literature—not merely that of the Greeks, but not even that of the Hebrews—as the truth-loving Scriptures testify regarding Him, had read Plato, and being pleased with the opinion he expressed regarding rich men, to the effect that "it was impossible to be distinguished for goodness and riches at the same time," had perverted this, and changed it into, "It is easier for a camel to go through the eye of a needle, than for a rich man to enter into the kingdom of God!" Now, if Celsus had not perused the Gospels in a spirit of hatred and dislike, but had been imbued with a love of truth, he would have turned his attention to the point why a camel—that one of animals which, as regards its physical structure, is crooked—was chosen as an object of comparison with a rich man, and what signification the "narrow eye of a needle" had for him who saw that "strait and narrow was the way that leadeth unto life;" and to this point also, that this animal. according to the law, is described as "unclean," having one element of acceptability, viz. that it ruminates, but one of condemnation, viz., that it does not divide the hoof. He would have inquired, moreover, how often the camel was adduced as an object of comparison in the sacred Scriptures, and in reference to what objects, that he might thus ascertain the meaning of the Logos concerning the rich men. Nor would he have left without examination the fact that "the poor" are termed "blessed" by Jesus, while "the rich" are designated as "miserable;" and whether these words refer to the rich and poor who are visible to the senses, or whether there is any kind of poverty known to the Logos which is to be deemed "altogether blessed," and any rich man who is to be wholly condemned. For even a common individual would not thus indiscriminately have praised the poor, many of whom lead most wicked lives. But on this point we have said enough.

CHAPTER XVII

Since Celsus, moreover, from a desire to depreciate the accounts which our Scriptures give of the kingdom of God, has quoted none of them, as if they were unworthy of being recorded by him (or perhaps because he was unacquainted with them), while, on the other hand, he quotes the sayings of Plato, both from his *Epistles* and the *Phaedrus*, as if these were divinely inspired, but our Scriptures were not, let us set forth a few points, for the sake of comparison with these plausible declarations of Plato, which did not however, dispose the philosopher to worship in a manner worthy of him the Maker of all things. For he ought not to have adulterated or polluted this worship with what we call "idolatry," but what the many would describe by the term "superstition." Now, according to a Hebrew figure of speech, it is said of God in the eighteenth Psalm, that "He made darkness His secret place," to signify that those notions which should be worthily entertained of God are invisible and unknowable, because God conceals Himself in darkness, as it were, from those who cannot endure the splendours of His knowledge, or are incapable of looking at them, partly owing to the pollution of their understanding, which is clothed with the body of mortal lowliness, and partly owing to its feebler power of comprehending God. And in order that it may appear that the knowledge of God has rarely been vouchsafed to men, and has been found in very few individuals, Moses is related to have entered into the darkness where God was. And again, with regard to Moses it is said: "Moses alone shall come near the LORD, but the rest shall not come nigh." And again, that the prophet may show the depth of the doctrines which relate to God, and which is unattainable by those who do not possess the "Spirit which searcheth all things, even the deep things of God," he added: "The abyss like a garment is His covering." Nay, our Lord and Saviour, the Logos of God, manifesting that the greatness of the knowledge of the Father is appropriately comprehended and known pre-eminently by Him alone, and in the second place by those whose minds are enlightened by the Logos Himself and God, declares: "No man knoweth the Son, but the Father; neither knoweth any man the Father but the Son, and he to whomsoever the Son will reveal Him." For no one can worthily know the "uncreated" and first-born of all created nature like the Father who begat Him, nor any one the Father like the living Logos, and His Wisdom and Truth. By sharing in Him who takes away from the Father what is called "darkness," which He "made His secret place," and "the abyss," which is called His "covering," and in this way unveiling the Father, every one knows the Father who is capable of knowing Him.

CHAPTER XVIII

I thought it right to quote these few instances from a much larger number of passages, in which our sacred writers express their ideas regarding God, in order to show that, to those who have eyes to behold the venerable character of Scripture, the sacred writings of the prophets contain things more worthy of reverence than those sayings of Plato which Celsus admires. Now the declaration of Plato, quoted by Celsus, runs as follows: "All things are around the King of all, and all things exist for his sake, and he is the cause of all good things. With things of the second rank he is second, and with those of the third rank he is third. The human soul, accordingly, is eager to learn what these things are, looking to such things as are kindred to itself, none of which is perfect. But as regards the King and those things which I mentioned, there is nothing which resembles them." I might have mentioned, moreover, what is said of those beings which are called seraphim by the Hebrews, and described in Isaiah, who cover the face and feet of God, and of those called cherubim, whom Ezekiel has described, and the postures of these, and of the manner in which God is said to be borne upon the cherubim. But since they are mentioned in a very mysterious manner, on account of the unworthy and the indecent, who are unable to enter into the great thoughts and venerable nature of theology, I have not deemed it becoming to discourse of them in this treatise.

CHAPTER XIX

Celsus in the next place alleges, that "certain Christians, having misunderstood the words of Plato, loudly boast of a 'super-celestial' God, thus ascending beyond the heaven of the Jews." By these words, indeed, he does not make it clear whether they also ascend beyond the *God* of the Jews, or only beyond the heaven by which they swear. It is not our purpose at present, however, to speak of those who acknowledge another god than the one worshipped by the Jews, but to defend ourselves, and to show that it was impossible for the prophets of the Jews, whose writings are reckoned among ours, to have borrowed anything from Plato, because they were older than he. They did not then borrow from him the declaration, that "all things are around the King of all, and that all exist on account of him;" for we have learned that nobler thoughts than these have been uttered by the prophets, by Jesus Himself and His disciples, who have clearly indicated the meaning of the spirit that was in them, which was none other than the spirit of Christ. Nor was the philosopher the first to present to view the "super-celestial" place; for David long ago brought to view the profundity and multitude of the thoughts concerning God entertained by those who have ascended above visible things, when he said in the book of Psalms: "Praise God, ye heaven of heavens and ye waters that be above the heavens, let them praise the name of the LORD." I do not, indeed, deny that Plato learned from certain Hebrews the words quoted from the *Phaedrus*, or even, as some have recorded, that he quoted them from a perusal of our prophetic writings, when he said: "No poet here below has ever sung of the super-celestial place, or ever will sing in a becoming manner," and so on. And in the same passage is the following: "For the essence, which is both colourless and formless, and which cannot be touched, which really exists, is the pilot of the soul, and is beheld by the understanding alone; and around it the genus of true knowledge holds this place." Our Paul, moreover, educated by these words, and longing after things "supra-mundane" and "super-celestial," and doing his utmost for their sake to attain them, says in the second Epistle to the Corinthians: "For our light affliction, which is but for a moment, worketh for us a far more exceeding and eternal weight of glory; while we look not at the things which are seen, but at the things which are not seen: for the things which are seen are temporal; but the things which are unseen are eternal."

CHAPTER XX

Now, to those who are capable of understanding him, the apostle manifestly presents to view "things which are the objects of perception," calling them "things seen;" while he terms "unseen," things which are the object of the understanding, and cognisable by it alone. He knows, also, that things "seen" and visible are "temporal," but that things cognisable by the mind, and "not seen," are "eternal;" and desiring to remain in the contemplation of these, and being assisted by his earnest longing for them, he deemed all affliction as "light" and as "nothing," and during the season of afflictions and troubles was not at all bowed down by them, but by his contemplation of (divine) things deemed every calamity a light thing, seeing we also have "a great High Priest," who by the greatness of His power and understanding "has passed through the heavens, even Jesus the Son of God," who has promised to all that have truly learned divine things, and have lived lives in harmony with them, to go before them to the things that are supramundane; for His words are: "That where I go, ye may be also." And therefore we hope, after the troubles and struggles which we suffer here, to reach the highest heavens, and receiving, agreeably to the teaching of Jesus, the fountains of water that spring up unto eternal life, and being filled with the rivers of knowledge, shall be united with those waters that are said to be above the heavens, and which praise His name. And as many of us as praise Him shall not be carried about by the revolution of the heaven, but shall be ever engaged in the contemplation of the invisible things of God, which are no longer understood by us through the things which He hath made from the creation of the world, but seeing, as it was expressed by the true disciple of Jesus in these words, "then face to face;" and in these, "When that which is perfect is come, then that which is in part will be done away."

CHAPTER XXI

The Scriptures which are current in the Churches of God do not speak of "seven" heavens, or of any definite number at all, but they do appear to teach the existence of "heavens," whether that means the "spheres" of those bodies which the Greeks call "planets," or something more mysterious. Celsus, too, agreeably to the opinion of Plato, asserts that souls can make their way to and from the earth through the planets; while Moses, our most ancient prophet, says that a divine vision was presented to the view of our prophet Jacob,—a ladder stretching to heaven, and the angels of God ascending and descending upon it, and the Lord supported upon its top,—obscurely pointing, by this matter of the ladder, either to the same truths which Plato had in view, or to something greater than these. On this subject Philo has composed a treatise which deserves the thoughtful and intelligent investigation of all lovers of truth.

CHAPTER XXII

After this, Celsus, desiring to exhibit his learning in his treatise against us, quotes also certain Persian mysteries, where he says: "These things are obscurely hinted at in the accounts of the Persians, and especially in the mysteries of Mithras, which are celebrated amongst them. For in the latter there is a representation of the two heavenly revolutions,—of the movement, viz., of the fixed stars, and of that which take place among the planets, and of the passage of the soul through these. The representation is of the following nature: There is a ladder with lofty gates, and on the top of it an eighth gate. The first gate consists of lead, the second of tin, the third of copper, the fourth of iron, the fifth of a mixture of metals, the sixth of silver, and the seventh of gold. The first gate they assign to Saturn, indicating by the 'lead' the slowness of this star; the second to Venus, comparing her to the splendour and softness of tin; the third to Jupiter, being firm and solid; the fourth to Mercury, for both Mercury and iron are fit to endure all things, and are money-making and laborious; the fifth to Mars, because, being composed of a mixture of metals, it is varied and unequal; the sixth, of silver, to the Moon; the seventh, of gold, to the Sun,—thus imitating the different colours of the two latter." He next proceeds to examine the reason of the stars being arranged in this order, which is symbolized by the names of the rest of matter. Musical reasons, moreover, are added or quoted by the Persian theology; and to these, again, he strives to add a second explanation, connected also with musical considerations. But it seems to me, that to quote the language of Celsus upon these matters would be absurd, and similar to what he himself has done, when, in his accusations against Christians and Jews, he quoted, most inappropriately, not only the words of Plato; but, dissatisfied even with these, he adduced in addition the mysteries of the Persian Mithras, and the explanation of them. Now, whatever be the case with regard to these,—whether the Persians and those who conduct the mysteries of Mithras give false or true accounts regarding them,—why did he select these for quotation, rather than some of the other mysteries, with the explanation of them? For the mysteries of Mithras do not appear to be more famous among the Greeks than those of Eleusis, or than those in Aegina, where individuals are initiated in the rites of Hecate. But if he must introduce barbarian mysteries with their explanation, why not rather those of the Egyptians, which are highly regarded by many, or those of the Cappadocians regarding the Comanian Diana, or those of the Thracians, or even those of the Romans themselves, who initiate the noblest members of their senate? But if he deemed it inappropriate to institute a comparison with any of these, because they furnished no aid in the way of accusing Jews or Christians, why did it not also appear to him inappropriate to adduce the instance of the mysteries of Mithras?

CHAPTER XXIII

If one wished to obtain means for a profounder contemplation of the entrance of souls into divine things, not from the statements of that very insignificant sect from which he quoted, but from books—partly those of the Jews, which are read in their synagogues, and adopted by Christians, and partly from those of Christians alone—let him peruse, at the end of Ezekiel's prophecies, the visions beheld by the prophet, in which gates of different kinds are enumerated, which obscurely refer to the different modes in which divine souls enter into a better world; and let him peruse also, from the Apocalypse of John, what is related of the city of God, the heavenly Jerusalem, and of its foundations and gates. And if he is capable of finding out also the road, which is indicated by symbols, of those who will march on to divine things, let him read the book of Moses entitled Numbers, and let him seek the help of one who is capable of initiating him into the meaning of the narratives concerning the encampments of the children of Israel; viz., of what sort those were which were arranged towards the east, as was the case with the first; and what those towards the south-west and south; and what towards the sea; and what the last were, which were stationed towards the north. For he will see that there is in the respective places a meaning not to be lightly treated, nor, as Celsus imagines, such as calls only for silly and servile listeners: but he will distinguish in the encampments certain things relating to the numbers that are enumerated, and which are specially adapted to each tribe, of which the present does not appear to us to be the proper time to speak. Let Celsus know, moreover, as well as those who read his book, that in no part of the genuine and divinely accredited Scriptures are "seven" heavens mentioned; neither do our prophets, nor the apostles of Jesus, nor the Son of God Himself, repeat anything which they borrowed from the Persians or the Cabiri.

CHAPTER XXIV

After the instance borrowed from the Mithraic mysteries, Celsus declares that he who would investigate the Christian mysteries, along with the aforesaid Persian, will, on comparing the two together, and on unveiling the rites of the Christians, see in this way the difference between them. Now, wherever he was able to give the names of the various sects, he was nothing loth to quote those with which he thought himself acquainted; but when he ought most of all to have done this, if they were really known to him, and to have informed us which was the sect that makes use of the diagram he has drawn, he has not done so. It seems to me, however, that it is from some statements of a very insignificant sect called Ophites, which he has misunderstood, that, in my opinion, he has partly borrowed what he says about the diagram. Now, as we have always been animated by a love of learning, we have fallen in with this diagram, and we have found in it the representations of men who, as Paul says, "creep into houses, and lead captive silly women laden with sins, led away with divers lusts; ever learning, and never able to come to the knowledge of the truth." The diagram was, however, so destitute of all credibility, that neither these easily deceived women, nor the most rustic class of men, nor those who were ready to be led away by any plausible pretender whatever, ever gave their assent to the diagram. Nor, indeed, have we ever met any individual, although we have visited many parts of the earth, and have sought out all those who anywhere made profession of knowledge, that placed any faith in this diagram.

CHAPTER XXV

In this diagram were described ten circles, distinct from each other, but united by one circle, which was said to be the soul of all things, and was called "Leviathan." This Leviathan, the Jewish Scriptures say, whatever they mean by the expression, was created by God for a plaything; for we find in the Psalms: "In wisdom hast Thou made all things: the earth is full of Thy creatures; so is this great and wide sea. There go the ships; small animals with great; there is this dragon, which Thou hast formed to play therein." Instead of the word "dragon," the term "leviathan" is in the Hebrew. This impious diagram, then, said of this leviathan, which is so clearly depreciated by the Psalmist, that it was the soul which had travelled through all things! We observed, also, in the diagram, the being named "Behemoth," placed as it were under the lowest circle. The inventor of this accursed diagram had inscribed this leviathan at its circumference and centre, thus placing its name in two separate places. Moreover, Celsus says that the diagram was "divided by a thick black line, and this line he asserted was called Gehenna, which is Tartarus." Now as we found that Gehenna was mentioned in the Gospel as a place of punishment, we searched to see whether it is mentioned anywhere in the ancient Scriptures, and especially because the Jews too use the word. And we ascertained that where the valley of the son of Ennom was named in Scripture in the Hebrew, instead of "valley," with fundamentally the same meaning, it was termed both the valley of Ennom and also Geenna. And continuing our researches, we find that what was termed "Geenna," or "the valley of Ennom," was included in the lot of the tribe of Benjamin, in which Jerusalem also was situated. And seeking to ascertain what might be the inference from the heavenly Jerusalem belonging to the lot of Benjamin and the valley of Ennom, we find a certain confirmation of what is said regarding the place of punishment, intended for the purification of such souls as are to be purified by torments, agreeably to the saying: "The Lord cometh like a refiner's fire, and like fullers' soap: and He shall sit as a refiner and purifier of silver and of gold."

CHAPTER XXVI

It is in the precincts of Jerusalem, then, that punishments will be inflicted upon those who undergo the process of purification, who have received into the substance of their soul the elements of wickedness, which in a certain place is figuratively termed "lead," and on that account iniquity is represented in Zechariah as sitting upon a "talent of lead." But the remarks which might be made on this topic are neither to be made to all, nor to be uttered on the present occasion; for it is not unattended with danger to commit to writing the explanation of such subjects, seeing the multitude need no further instruction than that which relates to the punishment of sinners; while to ascend beyond this is not expedient, for the sake of those who are with difficulty restrained, even by fear of eternal punishment, from plunging into any degree of wickedness, and into the flood of evils which result from sin. The doctrine of Geenna, then, is unknown both to the diagram and to Celsus: for had it been otherwise, the framers of the former would not have boasted of their pictures of animals and diagrams, as if the truth were represented by these; nor would Celsus, in his treatise against the Christians, have introduced among the charges directed against them statements which they never uttered instead of what was spoken by some who perhaps are no longer in existence, but have altogether disappeared, or been reduced to a very few individuals, and these easily counted. And as it does not beseem those who profess the doctrines of Plato to offer a defence of Epicurus and his impious opinions, so neither is it for us to defend the diagram, or to refute the accusations brought against it by Celsus. We may therefore allow his charges on these points to pass as superfluous and useless, for we would censure more severely than Celsus any who should be carried away by such opinions.

CHAPTER XXVII

After the matter of the diagram, he brings forward certain monstrous statements, in the form of question and answer, regarding what is called by ecclesiastical writers the "seal," statements which did not arise from imperfect information; such as that "he who impresses the seal is called father, and he who is sealed is called young man and son;" and who answers, "I have been anointed with white ointment from the tree of life,"—things which we never heard to have occurred even among the heretics. In the next place, he determines even the number mentioned by those who deliver over the seal, as that "of *seven* angels, who attach themselves to both sides of the soul of the dying body; the one party being named angels of light, the others 'archontics;'" and he asserts that the "ruler of those named 'archontics' is termed the 'accursed' god." Then, laying hold of the expression, he assails, not without reason, those who venture to use such language; and on that account we entertain a similar feeling of indignation with those who censure such individuals, if indeed there exist any who call the God of the Jews—who sends rain and thunder, and who is the Creator of this world, and the God of Moses, and of the cosmogony which he records—an "accursed" divinity. Celsus, however, appears to have had in view in employing these expressions, not a *rational* object, but one of a most irrational kind, arising out of his hatred towards us, which is so unlike a philosopher. For his aim was, that those who are unacquainted with our customs should, on perusing his treatise, at once assail us as if we called the noble Creator of this world an "accursed divinity." He appears to me, indeed, to have acted like those Jews who, when Christianity began to be first preached, scattered abroad false reports of the Gospel, such as that "Christians offered up an infant in sacrifice, and partook of its flesh;" and again, "that the professors of Christianity, wishing to do the 'works of darkness,' used to extinguish the lights (in their meetings), and each one to have sexual intercourse with any woman whom he chanced to meet." These calumnies have long exercised, although unreasonably, an influence over the minds of very many, leading those who are aliens to the Gospel to believe that Christians are men of such a character; and even at the present day they mislead some, and prevent them from entering even into the simple intercourse of conversation with those who are Christians.

CHAPTER XXVIII

With some such object as this in view does Celsus seem to have been actuated, when he alleged that Christians term the Creator an "accursed divinity;" in order that he who believes these charges of his against us, should, if possible, arise and exterminate the Christians as the most impious of mankind. Confusing, moreover, things that are distinct, he states also the reason why the God of the Mosaic cosmogony is termed "accursed," asserting that "such is his character, and worthy of execration in the opinion of those who so regard him, inasmuch as he pronounced a curse upon the serpent, who introduced the first human beings to the knowledge of good and evil." Now he ought to have known that those who have espoused the cause of the serpent, because he gave good advice to the first human beings, and who go far beyond the Titans and Giants of fable, and are on this account called Ophites, are so far from being Christians, that they bring accusations against Jesus to as great a degree as Celsus himself; and they do not admit any one into their assembly until he has uttered maledictions against Jesus. See, then, how irrational is the procedure of Celsus, who, in his discourse against the Christians, represents as such those who will not even listen to the *name* of Jesus, or omit even that He was a wise man, or a person of virtuous character! What, then, could evince greater folly or madness, not only on the part of those who wish to derive their name from the serpent as the author of good, but also on the part of Celsus, who thinks that the accusations with which the Ophites are charged, are chargeable also against the Christians! Long ago, indeed, that Greek philosopher who preferred a state of poverty, and who exhibited the pattern of a happy life, showing that he was not excluded from happiness although he was possessed of nothing, termed himself a Cynic; while these impious wretches, as not being human beings, whose enemy the serpent is, but as being serpents, pride themselves upon being called Ophites from the serpent, which is an animal most hostile to and greatly dreaded by man, and boast of one Euphrates as the introducer of these unhallowed opinions.

CHAPTER XXIX

In the next place, as if it were the Christians whom he was calumniating, he continues his accusations against those who termed the God of Moses and of his law an "accursed" divinity; and imagining that it is the Christians who so speak, he expresses himself thus: "What could be more foolish or insane than such senseless wisdom? For what blunder has the Jewish lawgiver committed? and why do you accept, by means, as you say, of a certain allegorical and typical method of interpretation, the cosmogony which he gives, and the law of the Jews, while it is with unwillingness, O most impious man, that you give praise to the Creator of the world, who promised to give them all things; who promised to multiply their race to the ends of the earth, and to raise them up from the dead with the same flesh and blood, and who gave inspiration to their prophets; and, again, you slander Him! When you feel the force of such considerations, indeed, you acknowledge that you worship the same God; but when your teacher Jesus and the Jewish Moses give contradictory decisions, you seek another God, instead of Him, and the Father!" Now, by such statements, this illustrious philosopher Celsus distinctly slanders the Christians, asserting that, when the Jews press them hard, they acknowledge the same God as they do; but that when Jesus legislates differently from Moses, they seek another god instead of Him. Now, whether we are conversing with the Jews, or are alone with ourselves, we know of only one and the same God, whom the Jews also worshipped of old time, and still profess to worship as God, and we are guilty of no impiety towards Him. We do *not* assert, however, that God will raise men from the dead with the same flesh and blood, as has been shown in the preceding pages; for we do not maintain that the natural body, which is sown in corruption, and in dishonour, and in weakness, will rise again such as it was sown. On such subjects, however, we have spoken at adequate length in the foregoing pages.

CHAPTER XXX

He next returns to the subject of the Seven ruling Demons, whose names are not found among Christians, but who, I think, are accepted by the Ophites. We found, indeed, that in the diagram, which on their account we procured a sight of, the same order was laid down as that which Celsus has given. Celsus says that "the goat was shaped like a lion," not mentioning the name given him by those who are truly the most impious of individuals; whereas *we* discovered that He who is honoured in holy Scripture as the angel of the Creator is called by this accursed diagram Michael the Lion-like. Again, Celsus says that the "second in order is a bull;" whereas the diagram which we possessed made him to be Suriel, the bull-like. Further, Celsus termed the third "an amphibious sort of animal, and one that hissed frightfully;" while the diagram described the third as Raphael, the serpent-like. Moreover, Celsus asserted that the "fourth had the form of an eagle;" the diagram representing him as Gabriel, the eagle-like. Again, the "fifth," according to Celsus, "had the countenance of a bear;" and this, according to the diagram, was Thauthabaoth, the bear-like. Celsus continues his account, that the "sixth was described as having the face of a dog;" and him the diagram called Erataoth. The "seventh," he adds, "had the countenance of an ass, and was named Thaphabaoth or Onoel;" whereas we discovered that in the diagram he is called Onoel, or Thartharaoth, being somewhat asinine in appearance. We have thought it proper to be exact in stating these matters, that we might not appear to be ignorant of those things which Celsus professed to know, but that we Christians, knowing them better than he, may demonstrate that these are not the words of Christians, but of those who are altogether alienated from salvation, and who neither acknowledge Jesus as Saviour, nor God, nor Teacher, nor Son of God.

CHAPTER XXXI

Moreover, if any one would wish to become acquainted with the artifices of those sorcerers, through which they desire to lead men away by their teaching (as if they possessed the knowledge of certain secret rites), but are not at all successful in so doing, let him listen to the instruction which they receive after passing through what is termed the "fence of wickedness,"—gates which are subjected to the world of ruling spirits. (The following, then, is the manner in which they proceed): "I salute the one-formed king, the bond of blindness, complete oblivion, the first power, preserved by the spirit of providence and by wisdom, from whom I am sent forth pure, being already part of the light of the son and of the father: grace be with me; yea, O father, let it be with me." They say also that the beginnings of the Ogdoad are derived from this. In the next place, they are taught to say as follows, while passing through what they call Ialdabaoth: "Thou, O first and seventh, who art born to command with confidence, thou, O Ialdabaoth, who art the rational ruler of a pure mind, and a perfect work to son and father, bearing the symbol of life in the character of a type, and opening to the world the gate which thou didst close against thy kingdom, I pass again in freedom through thy realm. Let grace be with me; yea, O father, let it be with me." They say, moreover, that the star Phaenon is in sympathy with the lion-like ruler. They next imagine that he who has passed through Ialdabaoth and arrived at Iao ought thus to speak: "Thou, O second Iao, who shinest by night, who art the ruler of the secret mysteries of son and father, first prince of death, and portion of the innocent, bearing now mine own beard as symbol, I am ready to pass through thy realm, having strengthened him who is born of thee by the living word. Grace be with me; father, let it be with me." They next come to Sabaoth, to whom they think the following should be addressed: "O governor of the fifth realm, powerful Sabaoth, defender of the law of thy creatures, who are liberated by thy grace through the help of a more powerful Pentad, admit me, seeing the faultless symbol of their art, preserved by the stamp of an image, a body liberated by a Pentad. Let grace be with me, O father, let grace be with me." And after Sabaoth they come to Astaphaeus, to whom they believe the following prayer should be offered: "O Astaphaeus, ruler of the third gate, overseer of the first principle of water, look upon me as one of thine initiated, admit me who am purified with the spirit of a virgin, thou who seest the essence of the world. Let grace be with me, O father, let grace be with me." After him comes Aloaeus, who is to be thus addressed: "O Aloaeus, governor of the second gate, let me pass, seeing I bring to thee the symbol of thy mother, a grace which is hidden by the powers of the realms. Let grace be with me, O father, let it be with me." And last of all they name Horaeus, and think that the following prayer ought to be offered to him: "Thou who didst fearlessly overleap the rampart of fire, O Horaeus, who didst obtain the government of the first gate, let me pass, seeing thou beholdest the symbol of thine own power, sculptured on the figure of the tree of life, and formed after this image, in the likeness of innocence. Let grace be with me, O father, let grace be with me."

CHAPTER XXXII

The supposed great learning of Celsus, which is composed, however, rather of curious trifles and silly talk than anything else, has made us touch upon these topics, from a wish to show to every one who peruses his treatise and our reply, that we have no lack of information on those subjects, from which he takes occasion to calumniate the Christians, who neither are acquainted with, nor concern themselves about, such matters. For we, too, desired both to learn and set forth these things, in order that sorcerers might not, under pretext of knowing more than we, delude those who are easily carried away by the glitter of names. And I could have given many more illustrations to show that we are acquainted with the opinions of these deluders, and that we disown them, as being alien to ours, and impious, and not in harmony with the doctrines of true Christians, of which we are ready to make confession even to the death. It must be noticed, too, that those who have drawn up this array of fictions, have, from neither understanding magic, nor discriminating the meaning of holy Scripture, thrown everything into confusion; seeing that they have borrowed from magic the names of Ialdabaoth, and Astaphaeus, and Horaeus, and from the Hebrew Scriptures him who is termed in Hebrew Iao or Jah, and Sabaoth, and Adonaeus, and Eloaeus. Now the names taken from the Scriptures are names of one and the same God; which, not being understood by the enemies of God, as even themselves acknowledge, led to their imagining that Iao was a different God, and Sabaoth another, and Adonaeus, whom the Scriptures term Adonai, a third besides, and that Eloaeus, whom the prophets name in Hebrew Eloi, was also different

CHAPTER XXXIII

Celsus next relates other fables, to the effect that "certain persons return to the shapes of the archontics, so that some are called lions, others bulls, others dragons, or eagles, or bears, or dogs." We found also in the diagram which we possessed, and which Celsus called the "square pattern," the statements made by these unhappy beings concerning the gates of Paradise. The flaming sword was depicted as the diameter of a flaming circle, and as if mounting guard over the tree of knowledge and of life. Celsus, however, either would not or could not repeat the harangues which, according to the fables of these impious individuals, are represented as spoken at each of the gates by those who pass through them; but this we have done in order to show to Celsus and those who read his treatise, that we know the depth of these unhallowed mysteries, and that they are far removed from the worship which Christians offer up to God.

CHAPTER XXXIV

After finishing the foregoing, and those analogous matters which we ourselves have added, Celsus continues as follows: "They continue to heap together one thing after another,—discourses of prophets, and circles upon circles, and effluents from an earthly church, and from circumcision; and a power flowing from one Prunicos, a virgin and a living soul; and a heaven slain in order to live, and an earth slaughtered by the sword, and many put to death that they may live, and death ceasing in the world, when the sin of the world is dead; and, again, a narrow way, and gates that open spontaneously. And in all their writings (is mention made) of the tree of life, and a resurrection of the flesh by means of the 'tree,' because, I imagine, their teacher was nailed to a cross, and was a carpenter by craft; so that if he had chanced to have been cast from a precipice, or thrust into a pit, or suffocated by hanging, or had been a leather-cutter, or stone-cutter, or worker in iron, there would have been (invented) a precipice of life beyond the heavens, or a pit of resurrection, or a cord of immortality, or a blessed stone, or an iron of love, or a sacred leather! Now what old woman would not be ashamed to utter such things in a whisper, even when making stories to lull an infant to sleep?" In using such language as this, Celsus appears to me to confuse together matters which he has imperfectly heard. For it seems likely that, even supposing that he had heard a few words traceable to some existing heresy, he did not clearly understand the meaning intended to be conveyed; but heaping the words together, he wished to show before those who knew nothing either of our opinions or of those of the heretics, that he was acquainted with all the doctrines of the Christians. And this is evident also from the foregoing words.

CHAPTER XXXV

It is our practice, indeed, to make use of the words of the prophets, who demonstrate that Jesus is the Christ predicted by them, and who show from the prophetic writings the events in the Gospels regarding Jesus have been fulfilled. But when Celsus speaks of "circles upon circles," (he perhaps borrowed the expression) from the aforementioned heresy, which includes in one circle (which they call the soul of all things, and Leviathan) the seven circles of archontic demons, or perhaps it arises from misunderstanding the preacher, when he says: "The wind goeth in a circle of circles, and returneth again upon its circles." The expression, too, "effluents of an earthly church and of circumcision," was probably taken from the fact that the church on earth was called by some an effluent from a heavenly church and a better world; and that the circumcision described in the law was a symbol of the circumcision performed there, in a certain place set apart for purification. The adherents of Valentinus, moreover, in keeping with their system of error, give the name of Prunicos to a certain kind of wisdom, of which they would have the woman afflicted with the twelve years' issue of blood to be the symbol; so that Celsus, who confuses together all sorts of opinions—Greek, Barbarian, and Heretical—having heard of her, asserted that it was a power flowing forth from one Prunicos, a virgin. The "living soul," again, is perhaps mysteriously referred by some of the followers of Valentinus to the being whom they term the psychic creator of the world; or perhaps, in contradistinction to a "dead" soul, the "living" soul is termed by some, not inelegantly, the soul of "him who is saved." I know nothing, however, of a "heaven which is said to be slain," or of an "earth slaughtered by the sword," or of many persons slain in order that they might live; for it is not unlikely that these were coined by Celsus out of his own brain.

CHAPTER XXXVI

We would say, moreover, that death ceases in the world when the sin of the world dies, referring the saying to the mystical words of the apostle, which run as follows: "When He shall have put all enemies under His feet, then the last enemy that shall be destroyed is death." And also: "When this corruptible shall have put on incorruption, then shall be brought to pass the saying that is written, Death is swallowed up in victory." The "strait descent," again, may perhaps be referred by those who hold the doctrine of transmigration of souls to that view of things. And it is not incredible that the gates which are said to open spontaneously are referred obscurely by some to the words, "Open to me the gates of righteousness, that I may go into them, and praise the LORD; this gate of the LORD, into it the righteous shall enter;" and again, to what is said in the ninth psalm, "Thou that liftest me up from the gates of death, that I may show forth all Thy praise in the gates of the daughter of Zion." The Scripture further gives the name of "gates of death" to those sins which lead to destruction, as it terms, on the contrary, good actions the "gates of Zion." So also "the gates of righteousness," which is an equivalent expression to "the gates of virtue," and these are ready to be opened to him who follows after virtuous pursuits. The subject of the "tree of life" will be more appropriately explained when we interpret the statements in the book of Genesis regarding the paradise planted by God. Celsus, moreover, has often mocked at the subject of a resurrection,—a doctrine which he did not comprehend; and on the present occasion, not satisfied with what he has formerly said, he adds, "And there is said to be a

637

resurrection of the flesh by means of the tree;" not understanding, I think, the symbolical expression, that "through the tree came death, and through the tree comes life," because death was in Adam, and life in Christ. He next scoffs at the "tree," assailing it on two grounds, and saying, "For this reason is the tree introduced, either because our teacher was nailed to a cross, or because he was a carpenter by trade;" not observing that the tree of life is mentioned in the Mosaic writings, and being blind also to this, that in none of the Gospels current in the Churches is Jesus Himself ever described as being a carpenter.

CHAPTER XXXVII

Celsus, moreover, thinks that we have invented this "tree of life" to give an allegorical meaning to the cross; and in consequence of his error upon this point, he adds: "If he had happened to be cast down a precipice, or shoved into a pit, or suffocated by hanging, there would have been invented a precipice of life far beyond the heavens, or a pit of resurrection, or a cord of immortality." And again: "If the 'tree of life' were an invention, because he—Jesus—(is reported) to have been a carpenter, it would follow that if he had been a leather-cutter, something would have been said about holy leather; or had he been a stone-cutter, about a blessed stone; or if a worker in iron, about an iron of love." Now, who does not see at once the paltry nature of his charge, in thus calumniating men whom he professed to convert on the ground of their being deceived? And after these remarks, he goes on to speak in a way quite in harmony with the tone of those who have invented the fictions of lion-like, and ass-headed, and serpent-like ruling angels, and other similar absurdities, but which does not affect those who belong to the Church. Of a truth, even a drunken old woman would be ashamed to chaunt or whisper to an infant, in order to lull him to sleep, any such fables as those have done who invented the beings with asses' heads, and the harangues, so to speak, which are delivered at each of the gates. But Celsus is not acquainted with the doctrines of the members of the Church, which very few have been able to comprehend, even of those who have devoted all their lives, in conformity with the command of Jesus, to the searching of the Scriptures, and have laboured to investigate the meaning of the sacred books, to a greater degree than Greek philosophers in their efforts to attain a so-called wisdom.

CHAPTER XXXVIII

Our noble (friend), moreover, not satisfied with the objections which he has drawn from the diagram, desires, in order to strengthen his accusations against us, who have nothing in common with it, to introduce certain other charges, which he adduces from the same (heretics), but yet as if they were from a different source. His words are: "And that is not the least of their marvels, for there are between the upper circles—those that are above the heavens—certain inscriptions of which they give the interpretation, and among others two words especially, 'a greater and a less,' which they refer to Father and Son." Now, in the diagram referred to, we found the greater and the lesser circle, upon the diameter of which was inscribed "Father and Son;" and between the greater circle (in which the lesser was contained) and another composed of two circles,—the outer one of which was yellow, and the inner blue,—a barrier inscribed in the shape of a hatchet. And above it, a short circle, close to the greater of the two former, having the inscription "Love;" and lower down, one touching the same circle, with the word "Life." And on the second circle, which was intertwined with and included two other circles, another figure, like a rhomboid, (entitled) "The foresight of wisdom." And within their point of common section was "The nature of wisdom." And above their point of common section was a circle, on which was inscribed "Knowledge;" and lower down another, on which was the inscription, "Understanding." We have introduced these matters into our reply to Celsus, to show to our readers that we know better than he, and not by mere report, those things, even although we also disapprove of them. Moreover, if those who pride themselves upon such matters profess also a kind of magic and sorcery,—which, in their opinion, is the summit of wisdom,—we, on the other hand, make no affirmation about it, seeing we never have discovered anything of the kind. Let Celsus, however, who has been already often convicted of false witness and irrational accusations, see whether he is not guilty of falsehood in these also, or whether he has not extracted and introduced into his treatise, statements taken from the writings of those who are foreigners and strangers to our Christian faith.

CHAPTER XXXIX

In the next place, speaking of those who employ the arts of magic and sorcery, and who invoke the barbarous names of demons, he remarks that such persons act like those who, in reference to the same things, perform marvels before those who are ignorant that the names of demons among the Greeks are different from what they are among the Scythians. He then quotes a passage from Herodotus, stating that "Apollo is called Gongosyrus by the Scythians; Poseidon, Thagimasada; Aphrodite, Argimpasan; Hestia, Tabiti." Now, he who has the capacity can inquire whether in these matters Celsus and Herodotus are not both wrong; for the Scythians do not understand the same thing as the Greeks, in what relates to those beings which are deemed to be gods. For how is it credible that Apollo should be called Gongosyrus by the Scythians? I do not suppose that Gongosyrus, when transferred into the Greek language, yields the same etymology as Apollo; or that Apollo, in the dialect of the Scythians, has the signification of Gongosyrus. Nor has any such assertion hitherto been made regarding the other names, for the Greeks took occasion from different circumstances and etymologies to give to those who are by them deemed gods the names which they bear; and the Scythians, again, from another set of circumstances; and the same also was the case with the Persians, or Indians, or Ethiopians, or Libyans, or with those who delight to bestow names (from fancy), and who do not abide by the just and pure idea of the Creator of all things. Enough, however, has been said by us in the preceding pages, where we wished to demonstrate that Sabaoth and Zeus were not the same deity, and where also we made some remarks, derived from the holy Scriptures, regarding the different dialects. We willingly, then, pass by these points, on which Celsus would make us repeat ourselves. In the next place, again, mixing up together matters which belong to magic and sorcery, and referring them perhaps to no one,—because of the non-existence of any who practise magic under pretence of a worship of this character,—and yet, perhaps, having in view some who *do* employ such practices in the presence of the simple (that they may have the appearance of acting by divine power), he adds: "What need to number up all those who have taught methods of purification, or expiatory hymns, or spells for averting evil, or (the making of) images, or resemblances of demons, or the various sorts of antidotes against poison (to be found) in clothes, or in numbers, or stones, or plants, or roots, or generally in all kinds of things?" In respect to these matters, reason does not require us to offer any defence, since we are not liable in the slightest degree to suspicions of such a nature.

CHAPTER XL

After these things, Celsus appears to me to act like those who, in their intense hatred of the Christians, maintain, in the presence of those who are utterly ignorant of the Christian faith, that they have actually ascertained that Christians devour the flesh of infants, and give themselves without restraint to sexual intercourse with their women. Now, as these statements have been condemned as falsehoods invented against the Christians, and this admission made by the multitude and those altogether aliens to our faith; so would the following statements of Celsus be found to be calumnies invented against the Christians, where he says that "he has seen in the hands of certain presbyters belonging to our faith barbarous books, containing the names and marvellous doings of demons;" asserting further, that "these presbyters of our faith professed to do no good, but all that was calculated to injure human beings." Would, indeed, that all that is said by Celsus against the Christians was of such a nature as to be refuted by the multitude, who have ascertained by experience that such things are untrue, seeing that most of them have lived as neighbours with the Christians, and have not even heard of the existence of any such alleged practices!

CHAPTER XLI

In the next place, as if he had forgotten that it was his object to write against the Christians, he says that, "having become acquainted with one Dionysius, an Egyptian musician, the latter told him, with respect to magic arts, that it was only over the uneducated and men of corrupt morals that they had any power, while on philosophers they were unable to produce any effect, because they were careful to observe a healthy manner of life." If, now, it had been our purpose to treat of magic, we could have added a few remarks in addition to what we have already said on this topic; but since it is only the more important matters which we have to notice in answer to Celsus, we shall say of magic, that any one who chooses to inquire whether philosophers were ever led captive by it or not, can read what has been written by Moiragenes regarding the memoirs of the magician and philosopher Apollonius of Tyana, in which this individual, who is not a Christian, but a philosopher, asserts that some philosophers of no mean note were won over by the magic power possessed by Apollonius, and resorted to him as a sorcerer; and among these, I think, he especially mentioned Euphrates and a certain Epicurean. Now *we*, on the other hand, affirm, and have learned by experience, that they who worship the God of all things in conformity with the Christianity which comes by Jesus, and who live according to His Gospel, using night and day, continuously and becomingly, the prescribed prayers, are not carried away either by magic or demons. For verily "the angel of the LORD encamps round about them that fear Him, and delivereth them" from all evil; and the angels of the little ones in the Church, who are appointed to watch over them, are said always to behold the face of their Father who is in heaven, whatever be the meaning of "face" or of "behold."

CHAPTER XLII

After these matters, Celsus brings the following charges against us from another quarter: "Certain most impious errors," he says, "are committed by them, due to their extreme ignorance, in which they have wandered away from the meaning of the divine enigmas, creating an adversary to God, the devil, and naming him in the Hebrew tongue, Satan. Now, of a truth, such statements are altogether of mortal invention, and not even proper to be repeated, viz., that the mighty God, in His desire to confer good upon men, has yet one counterworking Him, and is helpless. The Son of God, it follows, is vanquished by the devil; and being punished by him, teaches us also to despise the punishments which he inflicts, telling us beforehand that Satan, after appearing to men as He Himself had done, will exhibit great and marvellous works, claiming for himself the glory of God, but that those who wish to keep him at a distance ought to pay no attention to these works of Satan, but to place their faith in Him alone. Such statements are manifestly the words of a deluder, planning and manoeuvring against those who are opposed to his views, and who rank themselves against them." In the next place, desiring to point out the "enigmas," our mistakes regarding which lead to the introduction of our views concerning Satan, he continues: "The ancients allude obscurely to a certain war among the gods, Heraclitus speaking thus of it: 'If one must say that there is a general war and discord, and that all things are done and administered in strife.' Pherecydes, again, who is much older than Heraclitus, relates a myth of one army drawn up in hostile array against another, and names Kronos as the leader of the one, and Ophioneus of the other, and recounts their challenges and struggles, and mentions that agreements were entered into between them, to the end that whichever party should fall into the ocean should be held as vanquished, while those who had expelled and conquered them should have possession of heaven. The mysteries relating to the Titans and Giants also had some such (symbolical) meaning, as well as the Egyptian mysteries of Typhon, and Horus, and Osiris." After having made such statements, and not having got over the difficulty as to the way in which these accounts contain a higher view of things, while our accounts are erroneous copies of them, he continues his abuse of us, remarking that "these are not like the stories which are related of a devil, or demon, or, as he remarks with more truth, of a man who is an impostor, who wishes to establish an opposite doctrine." And in the same way he understands Homer, as if he referred obscurely to matters similar to those mentioned by Heraclitus, and Pherecydes, and the originators of the mysteries about the Titans and Giants, in those words which Hephaestus addresses to Hera as follows:—

"Once in your cause I felt his matchless might,
Hurled headlong downward from the ethereal height."

And in those of Zeus to Hera:—

"Hast thou forgot, when, bound and fix'd on high,
From the vast concave of the spangled sky,
I hung thee trembling in a golden chain,
And all the raging gods opposed in vain?
Headlong I hurled them from the Olympian hall,
Stunn'd in the whirl, and breathless with the fall."

Interpreting, moreover, the words of Homer, he adds: "The words of Zeus addressed to Hera are the words of God addressed to matter; and the words addressed to matter obscurely signify that the matter which at the beginning was in a state of discord (with God), was taken by Him, and bound together and arranged under laws, which may be analogically compared to chains; and that by way of chastising the demons who create disorder in it, he hurls them down headlong to this lower world." These words of Homer, he alleges, were so understood by Pherecydes, when he said that beneath that region is the region of Tartarus, which is guarded by the Harpies and Tempest, daughters of Boreas, and to which Zeus banishes any one of the gods who becomes disorderly. With the same ideas also are closely connected the *peplos* of Athena, which is beheld by all in the procession of the *Panathenaea*. For it is manifest from this, he continues, that a motherless and unsullied demon has the mastery over the daring of the Giants. While accepting, moreover, the fictions of the Greeks, he continues to heap against us such accusations as the following, viz., that "the Son of God is punished by the devil, and teaches us that we also, when punished by him, ought to endure it. Now these statements are altogether ridiculous. For it is the devil, I think, who ought rather to be punished, and those human beings who are calumniated by him ought not to be threatened with chastisement."

643

CHAPTER XLIII

Mark now, whether he who charges us with having committed errors of the most impious kind, and with having wandered away from the (true meaning) of the divine enigmas, is not himself clearly in error, from not observing that in the writings of Moses, which are much older not merely than Heraclitus and Pherecydes, but even than Homer, mention is made of this wicked one, and of his having fallen from heaven. For the serpent—from whom the Ophioneus spoken of by Pherecydes is derived—having become the cause of man's expulsion from the divine Paradise, obscurely shadows forth something similar, having deceived the woman by a promise of divinity and of greater blessings; and her example is said to have been followed also by the man. And, further, who else could the destroying angel mentioned in the Exodus of Moses be, than he who was the author of destruction to them that obeyed him, and did not withstand his wicked deeds, nor struggle against them? Moreover (the goat), which in the book of Leviticus is sent away (into the wilderness), and which in the Hebrew language is named Azazel, was none other than this; and it was necessary to send it away into the desert, and to treat it as an expiatory sacrifice, because on it the lot fell. For all who belong to the "worse" part, on account of their wickedness, being opposed to those who are God's heritage, are deserted by God. Nay, with respect to the sons of Belial in the book of Judges, whose sons are they said to be, save his, on account of their wickedness? And besides all these instances, in the book of Job, which is older even than Moses himself, the devil is distinctly described as presenting himself before God, and asking for power against Job, that he might involve him in trials of the most painful kind; the first of which consisted in the loss of all his goods and of his children, and the second in afflicting the whole body of Job with the so-called disease of elephantiasis. I pass by what might be quoted from the Gospels regarding the devil who tempted the Saviour, that I may not appear to quote in reply to Celsus from more recent writings on this question. In the last (chapter) also of Job, in which the Lord utters to Job amid tempest and clouds what is recorded in the book which bears his name, there are not a few things referring to the serpent. I have not yet mentioned the passages in Ezekiel, where he speaks, as it were, of Pharaoh, or Nebuchadnezzar, or the prince of Tyre; or those in Isaiah, where lament is made for the king of Babylon, from which not a little might be learned concerning evil, as to the nature of its origin and generation, and as to how it derived its existence from some who had lost their wings, and who had followed him who was the first to lose his own.

CHAPTER XLIV

For it is impossible that the good which is the result of accident, or of communication, should be like that good which comes by nature; and yet the former will never be lost by him who, so to speak, partakes of the "living" bread with a view to his own preservation. But if it should fail any one, it must be through his own fault, in being slothful to partake of this "living bread" and "genuine drink," by means of which the wings, nourished and watered, are fitted for their purpose, even according to the saying of Solomon, the wisest of men, concerning the truly rich man, that "he made to himself wings like an eagle, and returns to the house of his patron." For it became God, who knows how to turn to proper account even those who in their wickedness have apostatized from Him, to place wickedness of this sort in some part of the universe, and to appoint a training-school of virtue, wherein those must exercise themselves who would desire to recover in a "lawful manner" the possession (which they had lost); in order that being tested, like gold in the fire, by the wickedness of these, and having exerted themselves to the utmost to prevent anything base injuring their rational nature, they may appear deserving of an ascent to divine things, and may be elevated by the Word to the blessedness which is above all things, and so to speak, to the very summit of goodness. Now he who in the Hebrew language is named Satan, and by some Satanas— as being more in conformity with the genius of the Greek language— signifies, when translated into Greek, "adversary." But every one who prefers vice and a vicious life, is (because acting in a manner contrary to virtue) Satanas, that is, an "adversary" to the Son of God, who is righteousness, and truth, and wisdom. With more propriety, however, is *he* called "adversary," who was the first among those that were living a peaceful and happy life to lose his wings, and to fall from blessedness; he who, according to Ezekiel, walked faultlessly in all his ways, "until iniquity was found in him," and who being the "seal of resemblance" and the "crown of beauty" in the paradise of God, being filled as it were with good things, fell into destruction, in accordance with the word which said to him in a mystic sense: "Thou hast fallen into destruction, and shalt not abide for ever." We have ventured somewhat rashly to make these few remarks, although in so doing we have added nothing of importance to this treatise. If any one, however, who has leisure for the examination of the sacred writings, should collect together from all sources and form into one body of doctrine what is recorded concerning the origin of evil, and the manner of its dissolution, he would see that the views of Moses and the prophets regarding Satan had not been even dreamed of either by Celsus or any one of those whose soul had been dragged down, and torn away from God, and from right views of Him, and from His word, by this wicked demon.

CHAPTER XLV

But since Celsus rejects the statements concerning Antichrist, as it is termed, having neither read what is said of him in the book of Daniel nor in the writings of Paul, nor what the Saviour in the Gospels has predicted about his coming, we must make a few remarks upon this subject also; because, "as faces do not resemble faces," so also neither do men's "hearts" resemble one another. It is certain, then, that there will be diversities amongst the hearts of men,—those which are inclined to virtue not being all modelled and shaped towards it in the same or like degree; while others, through neglect of virtue, rush to the opposite extreme. And amongst the latter are some in whom evil is deeply engrained, and others in whom it is less deeply rooted. Where is the absurdity, then, in holding that there exist among men, so to speak, two extremes,—the one of virtue, and the other of its opposite; so that the perfection of virtue dwells in the man who realizes the ideal given in Jesus, from whom there flowed to the human race so great a conversion, and healing, and amelioration, while the opposite extreme is in the man who embodies the notion of him that is named Antichrist? For God, comprehending all things by means of His foreknowledge, and foreseeing what consequences would result from both of these, wished to make these known to mankind by His prophets, that those who understand their words might be familiarized with the good, and be on their guard against its opposite. It was proper, moreover, that the one of these extremes, and the best of the two, should be styled the Son of God, on account of His pre-eminence; and the other, who is diametrically opposite, be termed the son of the wicked demon, and of Satan, and of the devil. And, in the next place, since evil is specially characterized by its diffusion, and attains its greatest height when it simulates the appearance of the good, for that reason are signs, and marvels, and lying miracles found to accompany evil, through the co-operation of its father the devil. For, far surpassing the help which these demons give to jugglers (who deceive men for the basest of purposes), is the aid which the devil himself affords in order to deceive the human race. Paul, indeed, speaks of him who is called Antichrist, describing, though with a certain reserve, both the manner, and time, and cause of his coming to the human race. And notice whether his language on this subject is not most becoming, and undeserving of being treated with even the slightest degree of ridicule.

CHAPTER XLVI

It is thus that the apostle expresses himself: "We beseech you, brethren, by the coming of our Lord Jesus Christ, and by our gathering together unto Him, that ye be not soon shaken in mind, or be troubled, neither by word, nor by spirit, nor by letter as from us, as that the day of the Lord is at hand. Let no man deceive you by any means: for *that day shall not come*, except there come a falling away first, and that man of sin be revealed, the son of perdition; who opposeth and exalteth himself above all that is called God, or that is worshipped; so that he sitteth in the temple of God, showing himself that he is God. Remember ye not, that, when I was yet with you, I told you these things? And now ye know what withholdeth, that he might be revealed in his time. For the mystery of iniquity doth already work: only he who now letteth *will let*, until he be taken out of the way. And then shall that Wicked be revealed, whom the Lord shall consume with the spirit of His mouth, and shall destroy with the brightness of His coming: *even him*, whose coming is after the working of Satan, with all power, and signs, and lying wonders, and with all deceivableness of unrighteousness in them that perish; because they received not the love of the truth, that they might be saved. And for this cause God shall send them strong delusion, that they should believe a lie; that they all might be damned who believed not the truth, but had pleasure in unrighteousness." To explain each particular here referred to does not belong to our present purpose. The prophecy also regarding Antichrist is stated in the book of Daniel, and is fitted to make an intelligent and candid reader admire the words as truly divine and prophetic; for in them are mentioned the things relating to the coming kingdom, beginning with the times of Daniel, and continuing to the destruction of the world. And any one who chooses may read it. Observe, however, whether the prophecy regarding Antichrist be not as follows: "And at the latter time of their kingdom, when their sins are coming to the full, there shall arise a king, bold in countenance, and understanding riddles. And his power shall be great, and he shall destroy wonderfully, and prosper, and practise; and shall destroy mighty men, and the holy people. And the yoke of his chain shall prosper: there is craft in his hand, and he shall magnify himself in his heart, and by craft shall destroy many; and he shall stand up for the destruction of many, and shall crush them as eggs in his hand." What is stated by Paul in the words quoted from him, where he says, "so that he sitteth in the temple of God, showing himself that he is God," is in Daniel referred to in the following fashion: "And on the temple shall be the abomination of desolations, and at the end of the time an end shall be put to the desolation." So many, out of a greater number of passages, have I thought it right to adduce, that the hearer may understand in some slight degree the meaning of holy Scripture, when it gives us information concerning the devil and Antichrist; and being satisfied with what we have quoted for this purpose, let us look at another of the charges of Celsus, and reply to it as we best may.

CHAPTER XLVII

Celsus, after what has been said, goes on as follows: "I can tell how the very thing occurred, viz., that they should call him 'Son of God.' Men of ancient times termed this world, as being born of God, both his child and his son. Both the one and other 'Son of God,' then, greatly resembled each other." He is therefore of opinion that we employed the expression "Son of God," having perverted what is said of the world, as being born of God, and being His "Son," and "a God." For he was unable so to consider the times of Moses and the prophets, as to see that the Jewish prophets predicted generally that there was a "Son of God" long before the Greeks and those men of ancient time of whom Celsus speaks. Nay, he would not even quote the passage in the letters of Plato, to which we referred in the preceding pages, concerning Him who so beautifully arranged this world, as being the Son of God; lest he too should be compelled by Plato, whom he often mentions with respect, to admit that the architect of this world *is* the Son of God, and that His Father is the first God and Sovereign Ruler over all things. Nor is it at all wonderful if we maintain that the soul of Jesus is made one with so great a Son of God through the highest union with Him, being no longer in a state of separation from Him. For the sacred language of holy Scripture knows of other things also, which, although "dual" in their own nature, are considered to be, and really are, "one" in respect to one another. It is said of husband and wife, "They are no longer twain, but one flesh;" and of the perfect man, and of him who is joined to the true Lord, Word, and Wisdom, and Truth, that "he who is joined to the Lord is one spirit." And if he who "is joined to the Lord is one spirit," who has been joined to the Lord, the

Very Word, and Wisdom, and Truth, and Righteousness, in a more intimate union, or even in a manner at all approaching to it than the soul of Jesus? And if this be so, then the soul of Jesus and God the Word—the first-born of every creature—are no longer two, (but one).

CHAPTER XLVIII

In the next place, when the philosophers of the Porch, who assert that the virtue of God and man is the same, maintain that the God who is over all things is not happier than *their* wise man, but that the happiness of both is equal, Celsus neither ridicules nor scoffs at their opinion. If, however, holy Scripture says that the perfect man is joined to and made one with the Very Word by means of virtue, so that we infer that the soul of Jesus is not separated from the first-born of all creation, he laughs at Jesus being called "Son of God," not observing what is said of Him with a secret and mystical signification in the holy Scriptures. But that we may win over to the reception of our views those who are willing to accept the inferences which flow from our doctrines, and to be benefited thereby, we say that the holy Scriptures declare the body of Christ, animated by the Son of God, to be the whole Church of God, and the members of this body—considered as a whole—to consist of those who are believers; since, as a soul vivifies and moves the body, which of itself has not the natural power of motion like a living being, so the Word, arousing and moving the whole body, the Church, to befitting action, awakens, moreover, each individual member belonging to the Church, so that they do nothing apart from the Word. Since all this, then, follows by a train of reasoning not to be depreciated, where is the difficulty in maintaining that, as the *soul* of Jesus is joined in a perfect and inconceivable manner with the very Word, so the person of Jesus, generally speaking, is not separated from the only-begotten and first-born of all creation, and is not a different being from Him? But enough here on this subject.

CHAPTER XLIX

Let us notice now what follows, where, expressing in a single word his opinion regarding the Mosaic cosmogony, without offering, however, a single argument in its support, he finds fault with it, saying: "Moreover, their cosmogony is extremely silly." Now, if he had produced some credible proofs of its silly character, we should have endeavoured to answer them; but it does not appear to me reasonable that I should be called upon to demonstrate, in answer to his mere *assertion*, that it is *not* "silly." If any one, however, wishes to see the reasons which led us to accept the Mosaic account, and the arguments by which it may be defended, he may read what we have written upon Genesis, from the beginning of the book up to the passage, "And this is the book of the generation of men," where we have tried to show from the holy Scriptures themselves what the "heaven" was which was created in the beginning; and what the "earth," and the "invisible part of the earth," and that which was "without form;" and what the "deep" was, and the "darkness" that was upon it; and what the "water" was, and the "Spirit of God" which was "borne over it;" and what the "light" which was created, and what the "firmament," as distinct from the "heaven" which was created in the beginning; and so on with the other subjects that follow. Celsus has also expressed his opinion that the narrative of the creation of man is "exceedingly silly," without stating any proofs, or endeavouring to answer our arguments; for he had no evidence, in my judgment, which was fitted to overthrow the statement that "man has been made in the image of God." He does not even understand the meaning of the "Paradise" that was planted by God, and of the life which man first led in it; and of that which resulted from accident, when man was cast forth on account of his sin, and was settled opposite the Paradise of delight. Now, as he asserts that these are silly statements, let him turn his attention not merely to each one of them (in general), but to this in particular, "He placed the cherubim, and the flaming sword, which turned every way, to keep the way of the tree of life," and say whether Moses wrote these words with no serious object in view, but in the spirit of the writers of the old Comedy, who have sportively related that "Proetus slew Bellerophon," and that "Pegasus came from Arcadia." Now their object was to create laughter in composing such stories; whereas it is incredible that he who left behind him laws for a whole nation, regarding which he wished to persuade his subjects that they were given by God, should have written words so little to the purpose, and have said without any meaning, "He placed the cherubim, and the flaming sword, which turned every way, to keep the way of the tree of life," or made any other statement regarding the creation of man, which is the subject of philosophic investigation by the Hebrew sages.

CHAPTER L

In the next place, Celsus, after heaping together, simply as mere assertions, the varying opinions of some of the ancients regarding the world, and the origin of man, alleges that "Moses and the prophets, who have left to us our books, not knowing at all what the nature of the world is, and of man, have woven together a web of sheer nonsense." If he had shown, now, *how* it appeared to him that the holy Scriptures contained "sheer nonsense," we should have tried to demolish the arguments which appeared to him to establish their nonsensical character; but on the present occasion, following his own example, we also sportively give it as our opinion that Celsus, knowing nothing at all the nature of the meaning and language of the prophets, composed a work which contained "sheer nonsense," and boastfully gave it the title of a "true discourse." And since he makes the statements about the "days of creation" ground of accusation,—as if he understood them clearly and correctly, some of which elapsed *before* the creation of light and heaven, and sun, and moon, and stars, and some of them *after* the creation of these,—we shall only make this observation, that Moses must then have forgotten that he had said a little before, "that in six days the creation of the world had been finished," and that in consequence of this act of forgetfulness he subjoins to these words the following: "This is the book of the creation of man, in the day when God made the heaven and the earth!" But it is not in the least credible, that after what he had said respecting the six days, Moses should immediately add, without a special meaning, the words, "in the day that God made the heavens and the earth;" and if any one thinks that these words may be referred to the statement, "In the beginning God made the heaven and the earth," let him observe that before the words, "Let there be light, and there was light," and these, "God called the light day," it has been stated that "in the beginning God made the heaven and the earth."

CHAPTER LI

On the present occasion, however, it is not our object to enter into an explanation of the subject of intelligent and sensible beings, nor of the manner in which the different kinds of days were allotted to both sorts, nor to investigate the details which belong to the subject, for we should need whole treatises for the exposition of the Mosaic cosmogony; and that work we had already performed, to the best of our ability, a considerable time before the commencement of this answer to Celsus, when we discussed with such measure of capacity as we then possessed the question of the Mosaic cosmogony of the six days. We must keep in mind, however, that the Word promises to the righteous through the mouth of Isaiah, that days will come when not the sun, but the LORD Himself, will be to them an everlasting light, and

God will be their glory. And it is from misunderstanding, I think, some pestilent heresy which gave an erroneous interpretation to the words, "Let there be light," as if they were the expression of a *wish* merely on the part of the Creator, that Celsus made the remark: "The Creator did not borrow light from above, like those persons who kindle their lamps at those of their neighbours." Misunderstanding, moreover, another impious heresy, he has said: "If, indeed, there did exist an accursed god opposed to the great God, who did this contrary to his approval, why did he lend him the light?" So far are we from offering a defence of such puerilities, that we desire, on the contrary, distinctly to arraign the statements of these heretics as erroneous, and to undertake to refute, not those of their opinions with which we are *unacquainted*, as Celsus does, but those of which we have attained an accurate knowledge, derived in part from the statements of their own adherents, and partly from a careful perusal of their writings.

CHAPTER LII

Celsus proceeds as follows: "With regard to the origin of the world and its destruction, whether it is to be regarded as uncreated and indestructible, or as created indeed, but not destructible, or the reverse, I at present say nothing." For this reason we too say nothing on these points, as the work in hand does not require it. Nor do we allege that the Spirit of the universal God mingled itself in things here below as in things alien to itself, as might appear from the expression, "The Spirit of God moved upon the water;" nor do we assert that certain wicked devices directed against His Spirit, as if by a different creator from the great God, and which were tolerated by the Supreme Divinity, needed to be completely frustrated. And, accordingly, I have nothing further to say to those who utter such absurdities; nor to Celsus, who does not refute them with ability. For he ought either *not* to have mentioned such matters at all, or else, in keeping with that character for philanthropy which he assumes, have carefully set them forth, and then endeavoured to rebut these impious assertions. Nor have we ever heard that the great God, after giving his spirit to the creator, demands it back again. Proceeding next foolishly to assail these impious assertions, he asks: "What god gives anything with the intention of demanding it back? For it is the mark of a needy person to demand back (what he has given), whereas God stands in need of nothing." To this he adds, as if saying something clever against certain parties: "Why, when he lent (his spirit), was he ignorant that he was lending it to an evil being?" He asks, further: "Why does he pass without notice a wicked creator who was counter-working his purposes?"

CHAPTER LIII

In the next place, mixing up together various heresies, and not observing that some statements are the utterances of one heretical sect, and others of a different one, he brings forward the objections which we raised against Marcion. And, probably, having heard them from some paltry and ignorant individuals, he assails the very arguments which combat them, but not in a way that shows much intelligence. Quoting then our arguments against Marcion, and not observing that it is *against* Marcion that he is speaking, he asks: "Why does he send secretly, and destroy the works which he has created? Why does he secretly employ force, and persuasion, and deceit? Why does he allure those who, as ye assert, have been condemned or accused by him, and carry them away like a slave-dealer? Why does he teach them to steal away from their Lord? Why to flee from their father? Why does he claim them for himself against the father's will? Why does he profess to be the father of strange children?" To these questions he subjoins the following remark, as if by way of expressing his surprise: "Venerable, indeed, is the god who desires to be the father of those sinners who are condemned by another (god), and of the needy, and, as themselves say, of the very offscourings (of men), and who is unable to capture and punish his messenger, who escaped from him!" After this, as if addressing us who acknowledge that this world is not the work of a different and strange god, he continues in the following strain: "If these are his works, how is it that God created evil? And how is it that he cannot persuade and admonish (men)? And how is it that he repents on account of the ingratitude and wickedness of men? He finds fault, moreover, with his own handwork, and hates, and threatens, and destroys his own offspring? Whither can he transport them out of this world, which he himself has made?" Now it does not appear to me that by these remarks he makes clear what "evil" is; and although there have been among the Greeks many sects who differ as to the nature of good and evil, he hastily concludes, as if it were a consequence of our maintaining that this world also is a work of the universal God, that in *our* judgment *God* is the author of evil. Let it be, however, regarding evil as it may—whether created by God or not—it nevertheless follows only as a *result* when you compare the principal design. And I am greatly surprised if the inference regarding God's authorship of evil, which he thinks follows from our maintaining that this world also is the work of the universal God, does not follow too from his *own* statements. For one might say to Celsus: "If these are His works, how is it that God created evil? and how is it that He cannot persuade and admonish men?" It is indeed the greatest error in reasoning to accuse those who are of different opinions of holding unsound doctrines, when the accuser himself is much more liable to the same charge with regard to his own.

CHAPTER LIV

Let us see, then, briefly what holy Scripture has to say regarding good and evil, and what answer we are to return to the questions, "How is it that God created evil?" and, "How is He incapable of persuading and admonishing men?" Now, according to holy Scripture, properly speaking, virtues and virtuous actions are good, as, properly speaking, the reverse of these are evil. We shall be satisfied with quoting on the present occasion some verses from the thirty-fourth Psalm, to the following effect: "They that seek the LORD shall not want any good thing. Come, ye children, hearken unto me; I will teach you the fear of the LORD. What man is he that desireth life, and loveth many days, that he may see good? Keep thy tongue from evil, and thy lips from speaking guile. Depart from evil, and do good." Now, the injunctions to "depart from evil, and to do good," do not refer either to *corporeal* evils or *corporeal* blessings, as they are termed by some, nor to external things at all, but to blessings and evils of a *spiritual* kind; since he who departs from such evils, and performs such virtuous actions, will, as one who desires the true life, come to the enjoyment of it; and as one loving to see "good days," in which the word of righteousness will be the Sun, he will see them, God taking him away from this "present evil world," and from those evil days concerning which Paul said: "Redeeming the time, because the days are evil."

CHAPTER LV

Passages, indeed, might be found where corporeal and external (benefits) are improperly called "good,"—those things, viz., which contribute to the natural life, while those which do the reverse are termed "evil." It is in this sense that Job says to his wife: "If we have received good at the hand of the Lord, shall we not also receive evil?" Since, then, there is found in the sacred Scriptures, in a certain passage, this statement put into the mouth of God, "I make peace, and create evil;" and again another, where it is said of Him that "evil came down from the LORD to the gate of Jerusalem, the noise of chariots and horsemen,"—passages which have disturbed many readers of Scripture, who are unable to see what Scripture means by "good" and "evil,"—it is probable that Celsus, being perplexed thereby, gave utterance to the question, "How is it that God created evil?" or, perhaps, having heard some one discussing the matters relating to it in an ignorant manner, he made this statement which we have noticed. We, on the other hand, maintain that "evil," or "wickedness," and the actions which proceed from it, were *not* created by God. For if God created that which is *really* evil, how was it possible that the proclamation regarding (the last) judgment should be confidently announced, which informs us that the wicked are to be punished for their evil deeds in proportion to the amount of their wickedness, while those who have lived a virtuous life, or performed virtuous actions, will be in the enjoyment of blessedness, and will receive rewards from God? I am well aware that those who would daringly assert that these evils were created by God will quote certain expressions of Scripture (in their support), because we are not able to show one consistent series of passages; for although Scripture (generally) blames the wicked and approves of the righteous, it nevertheless contains some statements which, although comparatively few in number, seem to disturb the minds of ignorant readers of holy Scripture. I have not, however, deemed it appropriate to my present treatise to quote on the present occasion those discordant statements, which are many in number, and their explanations, which would require a long array of proofs. Evils, then, if those be meant which are *properly* so called, were not created by God; but some, although *few* in comparison with the order of the *whole* world, *have* resulted from His principal works, as there follow from the chief works of the carpenter such things as spiral shavings and sawdust, or as architects might appear to be the cause of the rubbish which lies around their buildings in the form of the filth which drops from the stones and the plaster.

CHAPTER LVI

If we speak, however, of what are called "corporeal" and "external" evils,—which are improperly so termed,—then it may be granted that there *are* occasions when some of these have been called into existence by God, in order that by their means the conversion of certain individuals might be effected. And what absurdity would follow from such a course? For as, if we should hear those sufferings improperly termed "evils" which are inflicted by fathers, and instructors, and pedagogues upon those who are under their care, or upon patients who are operated upon or cauterized by the surgeons in order to effect a cure, we were to say that a father was ill-treating his son, or pedagogues and instructors their pupils, or physicians their patients, no blame would be laid upon the operators or chastisers; so, in the same way, if God is said to bring upon men such evils for the conversion and cure of those who need this discipline, there would be no absurdity in the view, nor would "evils come down from the LORD upon the gates of Jerusalem,"—which evils consist of the punishments inflicted upon the Israelites by their enemies with a view to their conversion; nor would one visit "with a rod the transgressions of those who forsake the law of the Lord, and their iniquities with stripes;" nor could it be said, "Thou hast coals of fire to set upon them; they shall be to thee a help." In the same way also we explain the expressions, "I, who make peace, and create evil;" for He calls into existence "corporeal" or "external" evils, while purifying and training those who would not be disciplined by the word and sound doctrine. This, then, is our answer to the question, "How is it that God created evil?"

CHAPTER LVII

With respect to the question, "How is he incapable of persuading and admonishing men?" it has been already stated that, if such an objection were really a ground of charge, then the objection of Celsus might be brought against those who accept the doctrine of providence. Any one might answer the charge that God is incapable of admonishing men; for He conveys His admonitions throughout the whole of Scripture, and by means of those persons who, through God's gracious appointment, are the instructors of His hearers. Unless, indeed, some peculiar meaning be understood to attach to the word "admonish," as if it signified both to penetrate into the mind of the person admonished, and to make him hear the words of his instructor, which is contrary to the usual meaning of the word. To the objection, "How is he incapable of persuading?"—which also might be brought against all who believe in providence,—we have to make the following remarks. Since the expression "to be persuaded" belongs to those words which are termed, so to speak, "reciprocal" (compare the phrase "to shave a man," when he makes an effort to submit himself to the barber), there is for this reason needed not merely the effort of him who persuades, but also the submission, so to speak, which is to be yielded to the persuader, or the acceptance of what is said by him. And therefore it must not be said that it is because God is *incapable* of persuading men that they are not persuaded, but because they will not accept the faithful words of God. And if one were to apply this expression to men who are the "artificers of persuasion," he would not be wrong; for it is possible for a man who has thoroughly learned the principles of rhetoric, and who employs them properly, to do his utmost to persuade, and yet appear to fail, because he cannot overcome the will of him who ought to yield to his persuasive arts. Moreover, that persuasion does not come from God, although persuasive words may be uttered by him, is distinctly taught by Paul, when he says: "This persuasion cometh not of him that calleth you." Such also is the view indicated by these words: "If ye be willing and obedient, ye shall eat the good of the land; but if ye refuse and rebel, a sword shall devour you." For that one may (really) desire what is addressed to him by one who admonishes, and may become deserving of those promises of God which he hears, it is necessary to secure the will of the hearer, and his inclination to what is addressed to him. And therefore it appears to me, that in the book of Deuteronomy the following words are uttered with peculiar emphasis: "And now, O Israel, what doth the LORD thy God require of thee, but to fear the LORD thy God, and to walk in all His ways, and to love Him, and to keep His commandments?"

CHAPTER LVIII

There is next to be answered the following query: "And how is it that he repents when men become ungrateful and wicked; and finds fault with his own handwork, and hates, and threatens, and destroys his own offspring?" Now Celsus here calumniates and falsities what is written in the book of Genesis to the following effect: "And the LORD God, seeing that the wickedness of men upon the earth was increasing, and that every one in his heart carefully meditated to do evil continually, was grieved He had made man upon the earth. And God meditated in His heart, and said, I will destroy man, whom I have made, from the face of the earth, both man and beast, and creeping thing, and fowl of the air, because I am grieved that I made them;" quoting words which are not written in Scripture, as if they conveyed the meaning of what was actually written. For there is no mention in these words of the repentance of God, nor of His blaming and hating His own handwork. And if there is the appearance of God threatening the catastrophe of the deluge, and thus destroying His own children in it, we have to answer that, as the soul of man is immortal, the supposed threatening has for its object the conversion of the hearers, while the destruction of men by the flood is a purification of the earth, as certain among the Greek philosophers of no mean repute have indicated by the expression: "When the gods purify the earth." And with respect to the transference to God of those anthropopathic phrases, some remarks have been already made by us in the preceding pages.

CHAPTER LIX

Celsus, in the next place, suspecting, or perhaps seeing clearly enough, the answer which might be returned by those who defend the destruction of men by the deluge, continues: "But if he does not destroy his own offspring, whither does he convey them out of this world which he himself created?" To this we reply, that God by no means removes out of the whole world, consisting of heaven and earth, those who suffered death by the deluge, but removes them from a life in the flesh, and, having set them free from their bodies, liberates them at the same time from an existence upon earth, which in many parts of Scripture it is usual to call the "world." In the Gospel according to John especially, we may frequently find the regions of earth termed "world," as in the passage, "He was the true Light, which lighteneth every man that cometh into the 'world;'" as also in this, "In the world ye shall have tribulation; but be of good cheer, I have overcome the world." If, then, we understand by "removing out of the world" a transference from "regions on earth," there is nothing absurd in the expression. If, on the contrary, the system of things which consists of heaven and earth be termed "world," then those who perished in the deluge are by no means removed out of the so-called "world." And yet, indeed, if we have regard to the words, "Looking not at the things which are seen, but at the things which are not seen;" and also to these, "For the invisible things of Him from the creation of the world are clearly seen, being understood by the things that are made,"—we might say that he who dwells amid the "invisible" things, and what are called generally "things not seen," *is* gone out of the world, the Word having removed him hence, and transported him to the heavenly regions, in order to behold all beautiful things.

CHAPTER LX

But after this investigation of his assertions, as if his object were to swell his book by many words, he repeats, in different language, the same charges which we have examined a little ago, saying: "By far the most silly thing is the distribution of the creation of the world over certain days, *before days existed*: for, as the heaven was not yet created, nor the foundation of the earth yet laid, nor the sun yet revolving, how could there be *days*?" Now, what difference is there between these words and the following: "Moreover, taking and looking at these things from the beginning, would it not be absurd in the first and greatest God to issue the command, Let this (first thing) come into existence, and this second thing, and this (third); and after accomplishing so much on the first day, to do so much more again on the second, and third, and fourth, and fifth, and sixth?" We answered to the best of our ability this objection to God's "commanding this first, second, and third thing to be created," when we quoted the words, "He said, and it was done; He commanded, and all things stood fast;" remarking that the immediate Creator, and, as it were, very Maker of the world was the Word, the Son of God; while the Father of the Word, by commanding His own Son—the Word—to create the world, is *primarily* Creator. And with regard to the creation of the light upon the first day, and of the firmament upon the second, and of the gathering together of the waters that are under the heaven into their several reservoirs on the third (the earth thus causing to sprout forth those (fruits) which are under the control of nature alone), and of the (great) lights and stars upon the fourth, and of aquatic animals upon the fifth, and of land animals and man upon the sixth, we have treated to the best of our ability in our notes upon Genesis, as well as in the foregoing pages, when we found fault with those who, taking the words in their *apparent* signification, said that the time of six days was occupied in the creation of the world, and quoted the words: "These are the generations of the heavens and of the earth when they were created, in the day that the LORD God made the earth and the heavens."

CHAPTER LXI

Again, not understanding the meaning of the words, "And God ended on the sixth day His works which He had made, and ceased on the seventh day from all His works which He had made: and God blessed the seventh day, and hallowed it, because on it He had ceased from all His works which He had begun to make;" and imagining the expression, "He *ceased* on the seventh day," to be the same as this, "He *rested* on the seventh day," he makes the remark: "After this, indeed, he is weary, like a very bad workman, who stands in need of rest to refresh himself!" For he knows nothing of the day of the Sabbath and rest of God, which follows the completion of the world's creation, and which lasts during the duration of the world, and in which all those will keep festival with God who have done all *their* works in *their* six days, and who, because they have omitted none of their duties, will ascend to the contemplation (of celestial things), and to the assembly of righteous and blessed beings. In the next place, as if either the Scriptures made such a statement, or as if we ourselves so spoke of God as having rested from fatigue, he continues: "It is not in keeping with the fitness of things that the first God should feel fatigue, or work with His hands, or give forth commands." Celsus says, that "it is not in keeping with the fitness of things that the first God should feel fatigue. Now we would say that neither does God the Word feel fatigue, nor any of those beings who belong to a better and diviner order of things, because the sensation of fatigue is peculiar to those who are in the body. You can examine whether this is true of those who possess a body of any kind, or of those who have an *earthly* body, or one a little better than this. But "neither is it consistent with the fitness of things that the first God should work with His own hands." If you understand the words "work with His own hands" *literally*, then neither are they applicable to the *second* God, nor to any other being partaking of divinity. But suppose that they are spoken in an improper and figurative sense, so that we may translate the following expressions, "And the firmament showeth forth His handywork," and "the heavens are the work of Thy hands," and any other similar phrases, in a figurative manner, so far as respects the "hands" and "limbs" of Deity, where is the absurdity in the words, "God thus working with His own hands?" And as there is no absurdity in God thus working, so neither is there in His issuing "commands;" so that what is done at His bidding should be beautiful and praiseworthy, because it was God who commanded it to be performed.

CHAPTER LXII

Celsus, again, having perhaps misunderstood the words, "For the mouth of the Lord hath spoken it," or perhaps because some ignorant individuals had rashly ventured upon the explanation of such things, and not understanding, moreover, on what principles parts called after the names of the bodily members are assigned to the attributes of God, asserts: "He has neither mouth nor voice." Truly, indeed, God can have no voice, if the voice is a concussion of the air, or a stroke on the air, or a species of air, or any other definition which may be given to the voice by those who are skilled in such matters; but what is called the "voice of God" is said to be *seen* as "God's voice" by the people in the passage, "And all the people saw the voice of God;" the word "saw" being taken, agreeably to the custom of Scripture, in a spiritual sense. Moreover, he alleges that "God possesses nothing else of which *we* have any knowledge;" but of what things *we* have knowledge he gives no indication. If he means "limbs," we agree with him, understanding the things "of which we have knowledge" to be those called corporeal, and pretty generally so termed. But if we are to understand the words "of which *we* have knowledge" in a universal sense, then there are many things of which we have knowledge, (and which may be attributed to God); for He possesses virtue, and blessedness, and divinity. If we, however, put a higher meaning upon the words, "of which *we* have knowledge," since all that we know is less than God, there is no absurdity in our also admitting that God possesses none of those things "of which *we* have knowledge." For the attributes which belong to God are far superior to all things with which not merely the nature of man is acquainted, but even that of those who have risen far above it. And if he had read the writings of the prophets, David on the one hand saying, "But Thou art the same," and Malachi on the other, "I am (the LORD), and change not," he would have observed that none of us assert that there is any change in God, either in act or thought. For abiding the same, He administers mutable things according to their nature, and His word elects to undertake their administration.

CHAPTER LXIII

Celsus, not observing the difference between "after the image of God" and "God's image," next asserts that the "first-born of every creature" is the image of God,—the very word and truth, and also the very wisdom, being the image of His goodness, while man has been created *after* the image of God; moreover, that every man whose head is Christ is the image and glory of God;—and further, not observing to which of the characteristics of humanity the expression "after the image of God" belongs, and that it consists in a nature which never had nor longer has "the old man with his deeds," being called "after the image of Him who created it," from its not possessing these qualities,—he maintains: "Neither did He make man His image; for God is not such an one, nor like any other species of (visible) being." Is it possible to suppose that the element which is "after the image of God" should exist in the inferior part—I mean the body—of a compound being like man, because Celsus has explained that to be made after the image of God? For if that which is "after the image of God" be in the body only, the better part, the soul, has been deprived of that which is "after His image," and this (distinction) exists in the corruptible body,—an assertion which is made by none of us. But if that which is "after the image of God" be in *both together*, then God must necessarily be a compound being, and consist, as it were, of soul and body, in order that the element which is "after God's image," the better part, may be in the soul; while the inferior part, and that which "is according to the body," may be in the body,—an assertion, again, which is made by none of us. It remains, therefore, that that which is "after the image of God" must be understood to be in our "inner man," which is also renewed, and whose nature it is to be "after the image of Him who created it," when a man becomes "perfect," as "our Father in heaven is perfect," and hears the command, "Be ye holy, for I the LORD your God am holy," and learning the precept, "Be ye followers of God," receives into his virtuous soul the traits of God's image. The body, moreover, of him who possesses such a soul is a temple of God; and in the soul God dwells, because it has been made after His image.

CHAPTER LXIV

Celsus, again, brings together a number of statements, which he gives as admissions on our part, but which no intelligent Christian would allow. For not one of us asserts that "God partakes of form or colour." Nor does He even partake of "motion," because He stands firm, and His nature is permanent, and He invites the righteous man also to do the same, saying: "But as for thee, stand thou here by Me." And if certain expressions indicate a kind of motion, as it were, on His part, such as this, "They heard the voice of the LORD God *walking* in the garden in the cool of the day," we must understand them in this way, that it is by sinners that God is understood as moving, or as we understand the "sleep" of God, which is taken in a figurative sense, or His "anger," or any other similar attribute. But "God does not partake even of substance." For He is partaken of (by others) rather than that Himself partakes of them, and He is partaken of by those who have the Spirit of God. Our Saviour, also, does not partake of righteousness; but being Himself "righteousness," He is partaken of *by* the righteous. A discussion about "substance" would be protracted and difficult, and especially if it were a question whether that which is permanent and immaterial be "substance" properly so called, so that it would be found that God is *beyond* "substance," communicating of His "substance," by means of office and power, to those to whom He communicates Himself by His Word, as He does to the Word Himself; or even if He is "substance," yet He is said be in His nature "invisible," in these words respecting our Saviour, who is said to be "the image of the *invisible* God," while from the term "invisible" it is indicated that He is "immaterial." It is also a question for investigation, whether the "only-begotten" and "first-born of every creature" is to be called "substance of substances," and "idea of ideas," and the "principle of all things," while above all there is His Father and God.

CHAPTER LXV

Celsus proceeds to say of God that "of Him are all things," abandoning (in so speaking), I know not how, all his principles; while our Paul declares, that "of Him, and through Him, and to Him are all things," showing that He is the beginning of the substance of all things by the words "of Him," and the bond of their subsistence by the expression "through Him," and their final end by the terms "to Him." Of a truth, God is of nothing. But when Celsus adds, that "He is not to be reached by word," I make a distinction, and say that if he means the word that is in us—whether the word conceived in the mind, or the word that is uttered—I, too, admit that God is not to be reached by word. If, however, we attend to the passage, "In the beginning was the Word, and the Word was with God, and the Word was God," we are of opinion that God is to be reached by *this* Word, and is comprehended not by Him only, but by any one whatever to whom He may reveal the Father; and thus we shall prove the falsity of the assertion of Celsus, when he says, "Neither is God to be reached by word." The statement, moreover, that "He cannot be expressed by name," requires to be taken with a distinction. If he means, indeed, that there is no word or sign that can represent the attributes of God, the statement is true, since there are many qualities which cannot be indicated by words. Who, for example, could describe in words the difference betwixt the quality of sweetness in a palm and that in a fig? And who could distinguish and set forth in words the peculiar qualities of each individual thing? It is no wonder, then, if in this way God cannot be described by name. But if you take the phrase to mean that it is possible to represent by words something of God's attributes, in order to lead the hearer by the hand, as it were, and so enable him to comprehend something of God, so far as attainable by human nature, then there is no absurdity in saying that "He *can* be described by name." And we make a similar distinction with regard to the expression, "for He has undergone no suffering that can be conveyed by words." It *is* true that the Deity is beyond all suffering. And so much on this point.

CHAPTER LXVI

Let us look also at his next statement, in which he introduces, as it were, a certain person, who, after hearing what has been said, expresses himself in the following manner, "How, then, shall I know God? and how shall I learn the way that leads to Him? And how will you show Him to me? Because now, indeed, you throw darkness before my eyes, and I see nothing distinctly." He then answers, as it were, the individual who is thus perplexed, and thinks that he assigns the reason why darkness has been poured upon the eyes of him who uttered the foregoing words, when he asserts that "those whom one would lead forth out of darkness into the brightness of light, being unable to withstand its splendours, have their power of vision affected and injured, and so imagine that they are smitten with blindness." In answer to this, we would say that all those indeed sit in darkness, and are rooted in it, who fix their gaze upon the evil handiwork of painters, and moulders and sculptors, and who will not look upwards, and ascend in thought from all visible and sensible things, to the Creator of all things, who is light; while, on the other hand, every one is in light who has followed the radiance of the Word, who has shown in consequence of what ignorance, and impiety, and want of knowledge of divine things these objects were worshipped instead of God, and who has conducted the soul of him who desires to be saved towards the uncreated God, who is over all. For "the people that sat in darkness—the Gentiles— saw a great light, and to them who sat in the region and shadow of death light is sprung up,"—the God Jesus. No Christian, then, would give Celsus, or any accuser of the divine Word, the answer, "How shall I know God?" for each one of them knows God according to his capacity. And no one asks, "How shall I learn the way which leads to Him?" because he has heard Him who says, "I am the way, and the truth, and the life," and has tasted, in the course of the journey, the happiness which results from it. And not a single Christian would say to Celsus, "How will you show me God?"

CHAPTER LXVII

The remark, indeed, was true which Celsus made, that any one, on hearing his words, would answer, seeing that his words *are* words of darkness, "You pour darkness before my eyes." Celsus verily, and those like him, do desire to pour darkness before our eyes: we, however, by means of the light of the Word, disperse the darkness of their impious opinions. The Christian, indeed, could retort on Celsus, who says nothing that is distinct or true, "I see nothing that is distinct among all *your* statements." It is not, therefore, "out of darkness" into "the brightness of light" that Celsus leads us forth: he wishes, on the contrary, to transport us from light into darkness, making the darkness light and the light darkness, and exposing himself to the woe well described by the prophet Isaiah in the following manner: "Woe unto them that put darkness for light, and light for darkness." But we, the eyes of whose soul have been opened by the Word, and who see the difference between light and darkness, prefer by all means to take our stand "in the light," and will have nothing to do with darkness at all. The true light, moreover, being endued with life, knows to whom his full splendours are to be manifested, and to whom his light; for he does not display his brilliancy on account of the still existing weakness in the eyes of the recipient. And if we must speak at all of "sight being affected and injured," what other eyes shall we say are in this condition, than his who is involved in ignorance of God, and who is prevented by his passions from seeing the truth? Christians, however, by no means consider that they are blinded by the words of Celsus, or any other who is opposed to the worship of God. But let those who perceive that they are blinded by following multitudes who are in error, and tribes of those who keep festivals to demons, draw near to the Word, who can bestow the gift of sight, in order that, like those poor and blind who had thrown themselves down by the wayside, and who were healed by Jesus because they said to Him, "Son of David, have mercy upon me," they too may receive mercy and recover their eyesight, fresh and beautiful, as the Word of God can create it.

CHAPTER LXVIII

Accordingly, if Celsus were to ask us how we think we know God, and how we shall be saved by Him, we would answer that the Word of God, which entered into those who seek Him, or who accept Him when He appears, is able to make known and to reveal the Father, who was not seen (by any one) before the appearance of the Word. And who else is able to save and conduct the soul of man to the God of all things, save God the Word, who, "being in the beginning with God," became flesh for the sake of those who had cleaved to the flesh, and had become as flesh, that He might be received by those who could not behold Him, inasmuch as He was the Word, and was with God, and was God? And discoursing in human form, and announcing Himself as flesh, He calls to Himself those who are flesh, that He may in the first place cause them to be transformed according to the Word that was made flesh, and afterwards may lead them upwards to behold Him as He was before He became flesh; so that they, receiving the benefit, and ascending from their great introduction to Him, which was according to the flesh, say, "Even if we have known Christ after the flesh, yet henceforth know we Him no more." Therefore He became flesh, and having become flesh, "He tabernacled among us," not dwelling without us; and after tabernacling and dwelling *within* us, He did not continue in the form in which He first presented Himself, but caused us to ascend to the lofty mountain of His word, and showed us His own glorious form, and the splendour of His garments; and not His own form alone, but that also of the spiritual law, which is Moses, seen in glory along with Jesus. He showed to us, moreover, all prophecy, which did not perish even after His incarnation, but was received up into heaven, and whose symbol was Elijah. And he who beheld these things could say, "We beheld His glory, the glory as of the only-begotten of the Father, full of grace and truth." Celsus, then, has exhibited considerable ignorance in the imaginary answer to his question which he puts into our mouth, "How we think we can know God? and how we know we shall be saved by Him?" for our answer is what we have just stated.

CHAPTER LXIX

Celsus, however, asserts that the answer which we give is based upon a probable conjecture, admitting that he describes our answer in the following terms: "Since God is great and difficult to see, He put His own Spirit into a body that resembled ours, and sent it down to us, that we might be enabled to hear Him and become acquainted with Him." But the God and Father of all things is not the only being that is great in our judgment; for He has imparted (a share) of Himself and His greatness to His Only-begotten and First-born of every creature, in order that He, being the image of the invisible God, might preserve, even in His greatness, the image of the Father. For it was not possible that there could exist a well-proportioned, so to speak, and beautiful image of the invisible God, which did not at the same time preserve the image of His greatness. God, moreover, is in our judgment invisible, because He is not a body, while He *can* be seen by those who see with the heart, that is, the understanding; not indeed with any kind of heart, but with one which is pure. For it is inconsistent with the fitness of things that a polluted heart should look upon God; for that must be itself pure which would worthily behold that which is pure. Let it be granted, indeed, that God is "difficult to see," yet He is not the only being who is so; for His Only-begotten also is "difficult to see." For God the Word is "difficult to see," and so also is His wisdom, by which God created all things. For who is capable of seeing the wisdom which is displayed in each individual part of the whole system of things, and by which God created every individual thing? It was not, then, because God was "difficult to see" that He sent God His Son to be an object "easy to be seen." And because Celsus does not understand this, he has represented us as saying, "Because God was difficult to see, He put His own Spirit in a body resembling ours, and sent it down to us, that we might be enabled to hear Him and become acquainted with Him." Now, as we have stated, the Son also is "difficult to see," because He is God the Word, through whom all things were made, and who "tabernacled amongst us."

CHAPTER LXX

If Celsus, indeed, had understood our teaching regarding the Spirit of God, and had known that "as many as are led by the Spirit of God, these are the sons of God," he would not have returned to himself the answer which he represents as coming from us, that "God put His own Spirit into a body, and sent it down to us;" for God is perpetually bestowing of His own Spirit to those who are capable of receiving it, although it is not by way of division and separation that He dwells in (the hearts of) the deserving. Nor is the Spirit, in our opinion, a "body," any more than fire is a "body," which God is said to be in the passage, "Our God is a consuming fire." For all these are figurative expressions, employed to denote the nature of "intelligent beings" by means of familiar and corporeal terms. In the same way, too, if sins are called "wood, and straw, and stubble," we shall not maintain that sins are corporeal; and if blessings are termed "gold, and silver, and precious stones," we shall not maintain that blessings are "corporeal;" so also, if God be said to be a fire that consumes wood, and straw, and stubble, and all substance of sin, we shall not understand Him to be a "body," so neither do we understand Him to be a body if He should be called "fire." In this way, if God be called "spirit," we do not mean that He is a "body." For it is the custom of Scripture to give to "intelligent beings" the names of "spirits" and "spiritual things," by way of distinction from those which are the objects of "sense;" as when Paul says, "But our sufficiency is of God; who hath also made us able ministers of the New Testament; not of the letter, but of the spirit; for the letter killeth, but the spirit giveth life," where by the "letter" he means that "exposition of Scripture which is apparent to the senses," while by the "spirit" that which is the object of the "understanding." It is the same, too, with the expression, "God is a Spirit." And because the prescriptions of the law were obeyed both by Samaritans and Jews in a corporeal and literal manner, our Saviour said to the Samaritan woman, "The hour is coming, when neither in Jerusalem, nor in this mountain, shall ye worship the Father. God is a Spirit; and they that worship Him must worship Him in spirit and in truth." And by these words He taught men that God must be worshipped not in the flesh, and with fleshly sacrifices, but in the spirit. And He will be understood to be a Spirit in proportion as the worship rendered to Him is rendered in spirit, and with understanding. It is not, however, with images that we are to worship the Father, but "in truth," which "came by Jesus Christ," after the giving of the law by Moses. For when we turn to the Lord (and the Lord is a Spirit), He takes away the veil which lies upon the heart when Moses is read.

CHAPTER LXXI

Celsus accordingly, as not understanding the doctrine relating to the Spirit of God ("for the natural man receiveth not the things of the Spirit of God, for they are foolishness unto him; neither can he know them, because they are spiritually discerned"), weaves together (such a web) as pleases himself, imagining that we, in calling God a Spirit, differ in no respect in this particular from the Stoics among the Greeks, who maintain that "God is a Spirit, diffused through all things, and containing all things within Himself." Now the superintendence and providence of God does extend through all things, but not in the way that spirit does, according to the Stoics. Providence indeed contains all things that are its objects, and comprehends them all, but not as a containing body includes its contents, because they also are "body," but as a *divine* power does it comprehend what it contains. According to the philosophers of the Porch, indeed, who assert that principles are "corporeal," and who on that account make all things perishable, and who venture even to make the God of all things capable of perishing, the very Word of God, who descends even to the lowest of mankind, would be—did it not appear to them to be too gross an incongruity—nothing else than a "corporeal" spirit; whereas, in our opinion,—who endeavour to demonstrate that the rational soul is superior to all "corporeal" nature, and that it is an invisible substance, and incorporeal,—God the Word, by whom all things were made, who came, in order that all things might be made by the Word, not to men only, but to what are deemed the very lowest of things, under the dominion of nature alone, would be no body. The Stoics, then, may consign all things to destruction by fire; we, however, know of no incorporeal substance that is destructible by fire, nor (do we believe) that the soul of man, or the substance of "angels," or of "thrones," or dominions," or "principalities," or "powers," can be dissolved by fire.

CHAPTER LXXII

It is therefore in vain that Celsus asserts, as one who knows not the nature of the Spirit of God, that "as the Son of God, who existed in a human body, is a Spirit, this very Son of God would not be immortal." He next becomes confused in his statements, as if there were some of us who did not admit that God is a Spirit, but maintain that only with regard to His Son, and he thinks that he can answer us by saying that there "is no kind of spirit which lasts for ever." This is much the same as if, when we term God a "consuming fire," he were to say that there "is no kind of fire which lasts for ever;" not observing the sense in which we say that our God is a fire, and what the things are which He consumes, viz., sins, and wickedness. For it becomes a God of goodness, after each individual has shown, by his efforts, what kind of combatant he has been, to consume vice by the fire of His chastisements. He proceeds, in the next place, to assume what we do not maintain, that "God must necessarily have given up the ghost;" from which also it follows that Jesus could not have risen again with His body. For God would not have received back the spirit which He had surrendered after it had been stained by contact with the body. It is foolish, however, for us to answer statements as ours which were never made by us.

CHAPTER LXXIII

He proceeds to repeat himself, and after saying a great deal which he had said before, and ridiculing the birth of God from a virgin,—to which we have already replied as we best could,—he adds the following: "If God had wished to send down His Spirit from Himself, what need was there to breathe it into the womb of a woman? For as one who knew already how to form men, He could also have fashioned a body for this person, without casting His own Spirit into so much pollution; and in this way He would not have been received with incredulity, if He had derived His existence immediately from above." He had made these remarks, because he knows not the pure and virgin birth, unaccompanied by any corruption, of that body which was to minister to the salvation of men. For, quoting the sayings of the Stoics, and affecting not to know the doctrine about "things indifferent," he thinks that the divine nature was cast amid pollution, and was stained either by being in the body of a woman, until a body was formed

669

around it, or by assuming a body. And in this he acts like those who imagine that the sun's rays are polluted by dung and by foul-smelling bodies, and do not remain pure amid such things. If, however, according to the view of Celsus, the body of Jesus had been fashioned without generation, those who beheld the body would at once have believed that it had not been formed by generation; and yet an object, when seen, does not at the same time indicate the nature of that from which it has derived its origin. For example, suppose that there were some honey (placed before one) which had not been manufactured by bees, no one could tell from the taste or sight that it was not their workmanship, because the honey which comes from bees does not make known its origin by the senses, but experience alone can tell that it does not proceed from them. In the same way, too, experience teaches that wine comes from the vine, for taste does not enable us to distinguish (the wine) which comes from the vine. In the same manner, therefore, the visible body does not make known the manner of its existence. And you will be induced to accept this view, by (regarding) the heavenly bodies, whose existence and splendour we perceive as we gaze at them; and yet, I presume, their appearance does not suggest to us whether they are created or uncreated; and accordingly different opinions have existed on these points. And yet those who say that they are created are not agreed as to the manner of their creation, for their appearance does not suggest it, although the force of reason may have discovered that they are created, and how their creation was effected.

CHAPTER LXXIV

After this he returns to the subject of Marcion's opinions (having already spoken frequently of them), and states some of them correctly, while others he has misunderstood; these, however, it is not necessary for us to answer or refute. Again, after this he brings forward the various arguments that may be urged on Marcion's behalf, and also against him, enumerating what the opinions are which exonerate him from the charges, and what expose him to them; and when he desires to support the statement which declares that Jesus has been the subject of prophecy,—in order to found a charge against Marcion and his followers,—he distinctly asks, "How could he, who was punished in such a manner, be shown to be God's Son, unless these things had been predicted of him?" He next proceeds to jest, and, as his custom is, to pour ridicule upon the subject, introducing "two sons of God, one the son of the Creator, and the other the son of Marcion's God; and he portrays their single combats, saying that the Theomachies of the

Fathers are like the battles between quails; or that the Fathers, becoming useless through age, and falling into their dotage do not meddle at all with one another, but leave their sons to fight it out." The remark which he made formerly we will turn against himself: "What old woman would not be ashamed to lull a child to sleep with such stories as he has inserted in the work which he entitles *A True Discourse*? For when he ought seriously to apply himself to argument, he leaves serious argument aside, and betakes himself to jesting and buffoonery, imagining that he is writing mimes or scoffing verses; not observing that such a method of procedure defeats his purpose, which is to make us abandon Christianity and give in our adherence to his opinions, which, perhaps, had they been stated with some degree of gravity, would have appeared more likely to convince, whereas since he continues to ridicule, and scoff, and play the buffoon, we answer that it is because he has no argument of weight (for such he neither had, nor could understand) that he has betaken himself to such drivelling."

CHAPTER LXXV

To the preceding remarks he adds the following: "Since a divine Spirit inhabited the body (of Jesus), it must certainly have been different from that of other beings, in respect of grandeur, or beauty, or strength, or voice, or impressiveness, or persuasiveness. For it is impossible that He, to whom was imparted some divine quality beyond other beings, should not differ from others; whereas this person did not differ in any respect from another, but was, as they report, little, and ill-favoured, and ignoble." Now it is evident by these words, that when Celsus wishes to bring a charge against Jesus, he adduces the sacred writings, as one who believed them to be writings apparently fitted to afford a handle for a charge against Him; but wherever, in the same writings, statements would appear to be made opposed to those charges which are adduced, he pretends not even to know them! There are, indeed, admitted to be recorded some statements respecting the body of Jesus having been "ill-favoured;" not, however, "ignoble," as has been stated, nor is there any certain evidence that he was "little." The language of Isaiah runs as follows, who prophesied regarding Him that He would come and visit the multitude, not in comeliness of form, nor in any surpassing beauty: "LORD, who hath believed our report, and to whom was the arm of the LORD revealed? He made announcement before Him, as a child, as a root in a thirsty ground. He has no form nor glory, and we beheld Him, and He had no form nor beauty; but His form was without honour, and inferior to that of the sons of men." These passages, then, Celsus listened to, because he thought they were of use to him in bringing a charge against Jesus; but he paid no attention to the words of the forty-fifth Psalm, and why it is then said, "Gird Thy sword upon Thy thigh, O most mighty, with Thy comeliness and beauty; and continue, and prosper, and reign."

CHAPTER LXXVI

Let it be supposed, however, that he had not read the prophecy, or that he *had* read it, but had been drawn away by those who misinterpreted it as not being spoken of Jesus Christ. What has he to say of the Gospel, in the narratives of which Jesus ascended up into a high mountain, and was transfigured before the disciples, and was seen in glory, when both Moses and Elias, "being seen in glory, spake of the decease which He was about to accomplish at Jerusalem?" or when the prophet says, "We beheld Him, and He had no form nor beauty," etc.? and Celsus accepts this prophecy as referring to Jesus, being blinded in so accepting it, and not seeing that it is a great proof that the Jesus who appeared to be "without form" was the Son of God, that His very appearance should have been made the subject of prophecy many years before His birth. But if another prophet speak of His comeliness and beauty, he will no longer accept the prophecy as referring to Christ! And if it were to be clearly ascertained from the Gospels that "He had no form nor beauty, but that His appearance was without honour, and inferior to that of the sons of men," it might be said that it was not with reference to the prophetic writings, but to the Gospels, that Celsus made his remarks. But now, as neither the Gospels nor the apostolic writings indicate that "He had no form nor beauty," it is evident that we must accept the declaration of the prophets as true of Christ, and this will prevent the charge against Jesus from being advanced.

CHAPTER LXXVII

But again, how did he who said, "Since a divine Spirit inhabited the body (of Jesus), it must certainly have been different from that of other beings in respect of grandeur, or voice, or strength, or impressiveness, or persuasiveness," not observe the changing relation of His body according to the capacity of the spectators (and therefore its corresponding utility), inasmuch as it appeared to each one of such a nature as it was requisite for him to behold it? Moreover it is not a subject of wonder that the matter, which is by nature susceptible of being altered and changed, and of being transformed into anything which the Creator chooses, and is capable of receiving all the qualities which the Artificer desires, should at one time possess a quality, agreeably to which it is said, "He had no form nor beauty," and at another, one so glorious, and majestic, and marvellous, that the spectators of such surpassing loveliness—three disciples who had ascended (the mount) with Jesus—should fall upon their faces. He will say, however, that these are inventions, and in no respect different from myths, as are also the other marvels related of Jesus; which objection we have answered at greater length in what has gone before. But there is also something mystical in this doctrine, which announces that the varying appearances of Jesus are to be referred to the nature of the divine Word, who does not show Himself in the same manner to the multitude as He does to those who are capable of following Him to the high mountain which we have mentioned; for to those who still remain below, and are not yet prepared to ascend, the Word "has neither form nor beauty," because to such persons His form is "without honour," and inferior to the words given forth by men, which are figuratively termed "sons of men." For we might say that the words of philosophers—who are "sons of men"—appear far more beautiful than the Word of God, who is proclaimed to the multitude, and who also exhibits (what is called) the "foolishness of preaching," and on account of this apparent "foolishness of preaching" those who look at this alone say, "We saw Him; but He had no form nor beauty." To those, indeed, who have received power to follow Him, in order that they may attend Him even when He ascends to the "lofty mount," He *has* a diviner appearance, which they behold, if there happens to be (among them) a Peter, who has received within himself the edifice of the Church based upon the Word, and who has gained such a habit (of goodness) that none of the gates of Hades will prevail against him, having been exalted by the Word from the gates of death, that he may "publish the praises of God in the gates of the daughter of Sion," and any others who have derived their birth from impressive preaching, and who are not at all inferior to "sons of thunder." But how can Celsus and the enemies of the divine Word, and those who have not examined the doctrines of Christianity in the spirit of truth, know the meaning of the different appearances of Jesus? And I refer also to the different stages of His life, and to any actions performed by Him before His sufferings, and after His resurrection from the dead.

CHAPTER LXXVIII

Celsus next makes certain observations of the following nature:

"Again, if God, like Jupiter in the comedy, should, on awaking from a lengthened slumber, desire to rescue the human race from evil, why did He send this Spirit of which you speak into one corner (of the earth)? He ought to have breathed it alike into many bodies, and have sent them out into all the world. Now the comic poet, to cause laughter in the theatre, wrote that Jupiter, after awakening, despatched Mercury to the Athenians and Lacedaemonians; but do not you think that you have made the Son of God more ridiculous in sending Him to the Jews?" Observe in such language as this the irreverent character of Celsus, who, unlike a philosopher, takes the writer of a comedy, whose business is to cause laughter, and compares our God, the Creator of all things, to the being who, as represented in the play, on awaking, despatches Mercury (on an errand)! We stated, indeed, in what precedes, that it was not as if awakening from a lengthened slumber that God sent Jesus to the human race, who has now, for good reasons, fulfilled the economy of His incarnation, but who has always conferred benefits upon the human race. For no noble deed has ever been performed amongst men, where the divine Word did not visit the souls of those who were capable, although for a little time, of admitting such operations of the divine Word. Moreover, the advent of Jesus apparently to one corner (of the earth) was founded on good reasons, since it was necessary that He who was the subject of prophecy should make His appearance among those who had become acquainted with the doctrine of one God, and who perused the writings of His prophets, and who had come to know the announcement of Christ, and that He should come to them at a time when the Word was about to be diffused from one corner over the whole world.

CHAPTER LXXIX

And therefore there was no need that there should everywhere exist many bodies, and many spirits like Jesus, in order that the whole world of men might be enlightened by the Word of God. For the one Word was enough, having arisen as the "Sun of righteousness," to send forth from Judea His coming rays into the soul of all who were willing to receive Him. But if any one desires to see many bodies filled with a divine Spirit, similar to the one Christ, ministering to the salvation of men everywhere, let him take note of those who teach the Gospel of Jesus in all lands in soundness of doctrine and uprightness of life, and who are themselves termed "christs" by the holy Scriptures, in the passage, "Touch not Mine anointed, and do not My prophets any harm." For as we have heard that Antichrist cometh, and yet have learned that there are many antichrists in the world, in the same way, knowing that Christ has come, we see that, owing to Him, there are many christs in the world, who, like Him, have loved righteousness and hated iniquity, and therefore God, the God of Christ, anointed them also with the "oil of gladness." But inasmuch as He loved righteousness and hated iniquity above those who were His partners, He also obtained the first-fruits of His anointing, and, if we must so term it, the entire unction of the oil of gladness; while they who were His partners shared also in His unction, in proportion to their individual capacity. Therefore, since Christ is the Head of the Church, so that Christ and the Church form one body, the ointment descended from the head to the beard of Aaron,—the symbols of the perfect man,—and this ointment in its descent reached to the very skirt of his garment. This is my answer to the irreverent language of Celsus when he says, "He ought to have breathed (His Spirit) alike into many bodies, and have sent it forth into all the world." The comic poet, indeed, to cause laughter, has represented Jupiter asleep and awaking from slumber, and despatching Mercury to the Greeks; but the Word, knowing that the nature of God is unaffected by sleep, may teach us that God administers in due season, and as right reason demands, the affairs of the world. It is not, however, a matter of surprise that, owing to the greatness and incomprehensibility of the divine judgments, ignorant persons should make mistakes, and Celsus among them. There is therefore nothing ridiculous in the Son of God having been sent to the Jews, amongst whom the prophets had appeared, in order that, making a commencement among them in a bodily shape, He might arise with might and power upon a world of souls, which no longer desired to remain deserted by God.

CHAPTER LXXX

After this, it seemed proper to Celsus to term the Chaldeans a most divinely-inspired nation from the very earliest times, from whom the delusive system of astrology has spread abroad among men. Nay, he ranks the Magi also in the same category, from whom the art of magic derived its name and has been transmitted to other nations, to the corruption and destruction of those who employ it. In the preceding part of this work, (we mentioned) that, in the opinion even of Celsus, the Egyptians also were guilty of error, because they had indeed solemn enclosures around what they considered their temples, while within them there was nothing save apes, or crocodiles, or goats, or asps, or some other animal; but on the present occasion it pleases him to speak of the Egyptian people too as most divinely inspired, and that, too, from the earliest times,—perhaps because they made war upon the Jews from an early date. The Persians, moreover, who marry their own mothers, and have intercourse with their own daughters, are, in the opinion of Celsus, an inspired race; nay, even the Indians are so, some of whom, in the preceding, he mentioned as eaters of human flesh. To the Jews, however, especially those of ancient times, who employ none of these practices, he did not merely refuse the name of inspired, but declared that they would immediately perish. And this prediction he uttered respecting them, as being doubtless endued with prophetic power, not observing that the whole history of the Jews, and their ancient and venerable polity, were administered by God; and that it is by their fall that salvation has come to the Gentiles, and that "their fall is the riches of the world, and the diminishing of them the riches of the Gentiles," until the fulness of the Gentiles come, that after that the whole of Israel, whom Celsus does not know, may be saved.

CHAPTER LXXXI

I do not understand, however, how he should say of God, that although "knowing all things, He was not aware of this, that He was sending His Son amongst wicked men, who were both to be guilty of sin, and to inflict punishment upon Him." Certainly he appears, in the present instance, to have forgotten that all the sufferings which Jesus was to undergo were foreseen by the Spirit of God, and foretold by His prophets; from which it does not follow that "God did not know that He was sending His Son amongst wicked and sinful men, who were also to inflict punishment upon Him." He immediately adds, however, that "our defence on this point is that all these things were predicted." But as our sixth book has now attained sufficient dimensions, we shall stop here, and begin, God willing, the argument of the seventh, in which we shall consider the reasons which he thinks furnish an answer to our statement, that everything regarding Jesus was foretold by the prophets; and as these are numerous, and require to be answered at length, we wished neither to cut the subject short, in consequence of the size of the present book, nor, in order to avoid doing so, to swell this sixth book beyond its proper proportions.

BOOK VII

CHAPTER I

IN the six former books we have endeavoured, reverend brother Ambrosius, according to our ability to meet the charges brought by Celsus against the Christians, and have as far as possible passed over nothing without first subjecting it to a full and close examination. And now, while we enter upon the seventh book, we call upon God through Jesus Christ, whom Celsus accuses, that He who is the truth of God would shed light into our hearts and scatter the darkness of error, in accordance with that saying of the prophet which we now offer as our prayer, "Destroy them by Thy truth." For it is evidently the words and reasonings opposed to the truth that God destroys by His truth; so that when these are destroyed, all who are delivered from deception may go on with the prophet to say, "I will freely sacrifice unto Thee," and may offer to the Most High a reasonable and smokeless sacrifice.

CHAPTER II

Celsus now sets himself to combat the views of those who say that the Jewish prophets foretold events which happened in the life of Christ Jesus. At the outset let us refer to a notion he has, that those who assume the existence of another God besides the God of the Jews have no ground on which to answer his objections; while we who recognise the same God rely for our defence on the prophecies which were delivered concerning Jesus Christ. His words are: "Let us see how they can raise a defence. To those who admit another God, no defence is possible; and they who recognise the same God will always fall back upon the same reason, 'This and that must have happened.' And why? 'Because it had been predicted long before.'" To this we answer, that the arguments recently raised by Celsus against Jesus and Christians were so utterly feeble, that they might easily be overthrown even by those who are impious enough to bring in another God. Indeed, were it not dangerous to give to the weak any excuse for embracing false notions, we could furnish the answer ourselves, and show Celsus how unfounded is his opinion, that those who admit another God are not in a position to meet his arguments. However, let us for the present confine ourselves to a defence of the prophets, in continuation of what we have said on the subject before.

CHAPTER III

Celsus goes on to say of us: "They set no value on the oracles of the Pythian priestess, of the priests of Dodona, of Clarus, of Branchidae, of Jupiter Ammon, and of a multitude of others; although under their guidance we may say that colonies were sent forth, and the whole world peopled. But those sayings which were uttered or not uttered in Judea, after the manner of that country, as indeed they are still delivered among the people of Phoenicia and Palestine—these they look upon as marvellous sayings, and unchangeably true." In regard to the oracles here enumerated, we reply that it would be possible for us to gather from the writings of Aristotle and the Peripatetic school not a few things to overthrow the authority of the Pythian and the other oracles. From Epicurus also, and his followers, we could quote passages to show that even among the Greeks themselves there were some who utterly discredited the oracles which were recognised and admired throughout the whole of Greece. But let it be granted that the responses delivered by the Pythian and other oracles were not the utterances of false men who pretended to a divine inspiration; and let us see if, after all, we cannot convince any sincere inquirers that there is no necessity to attribute these oracular responses to any divinities, but that, on the other hand, they may be traced to wicked demons—to spirits which are at enmity with the human race, and which in this way wish to hinder the soul from rising upwards, from following the path of virtue, and from returning to God in sincere piety. It is said of the Pythian priestess, whose oracle seems to have been the most celebrated, that when she sat down at the mouth of the Castalian cave, the prophetic Spirit of Apollo entered her private parts; and when she was filled with it, she gave utterance to responses which are regarded with awe as divine truths. Judge by this whether that spirit does not show its profane and impure nature, by choosing to enter the soul of the prophetess not through the more becoming medium of the bodily pores which are both open and invisible, but by means of what no modest man would ever see or speak of. And this occurs not once or twice, which would be more permissible, but as often as she was believed to receive inspiration from Apollo. Moreover, it is not the part of a divine spirit to drive the prophetess into such a state of ecstasy and madness that she loses control of herself. For he who is under the influence of the Divine Spirit ought to be the first to receive the beneficial effects; and these ought not to be first enjoyed by the persons who consult the oracle about the concerns of natural or civil life, or for purposes of temporal gain or interest; and, moreover, that should be the time of clearest perception, when a person is in close intercourse with the Deity.

CHAPTER IV

Accordingly, we can show from an examination of the sacred Scriptures, that the Jewish prophets, who were enlightened as far as was necessary for their prophetic work by the Spirit of God, were the first to enjoy the benefit of the inspiration; and by the contact—if I may so say—of the Holy Spirit they became clearer in mind, and their souls were filled with a brighter light. And the body no longer served as a hindrance to a virtuous life; for to that which we call "the lust of the flesh" it was deadened. For we are persuaded that the Divine Spirit "mortifies the deeds of the body," and destroys that enmity against God which the carnal passions serve to excite. If, then, the Pythian priestess is beside herself when she prophesies, what spirit must that be which fills her mind and clouds her judgment with darkness, unless it be of the same order with those demons which many Christians cast out of persons possessed with them? And this, we may observe, they do without the use of any curious arts of magic, or incantations, but merely by prayer and simple adjurations which the plainest person can use. Because for the most part it is unlettered persons who perform this work; thus making manifest the grace which is in the word of Christ, and the despicable weakness of demons, which, in order to be overcome and driven out of the bodies and souls of men, do not require the power and wisdom of those who are mighty in argument, and most learned in matters of faith.

CHAPTER V

Moreover, if it is believed not only among Christians and Jews, but also by many others among the Greeks and Barbarians, that the human soul lives and subsists after its separation from the body; and if reason supports the idea that pure souls which are not weighed down with sin as with a weight of lead ascend on high to the region of purer and more ethereal bodies, leaving here below their grosser bodies along with their impurities; whereas souls that are polluted and dragged down to the earth by their sins, so that they are unable even to breathe upwards, wander hither and thither, at some times about sepulchres, where they appear as the apparitions of shadowy spirits, at others among other objects on the ground;—if this is so, what are we to think of those spirits that are attached for entire ages, as I may say, to particular dwellings and places, whether by a sort of magical force or by their own natural wickedness? Are we not compelled by reason to set down as evil such spirits as employ the power of prophesying—a power in itself neither good nor bad—for the purpose of deceiving men, and thus turn them away from God, and from the purity of His service? It is moreover evident that this is their character, when we add that they delight in the blood of victims, and in the smoke odour of sacrifices, and that they feed their bodies on these, and that they take pleasure in such haunts as these, as though they sought in them the sustenance of their lives; in this resembling those depraved men who despise the purity of a life apart from the senses, and who have no inclination except for the pleasures of the body, and for that earthly and bodily life in which these pleasures are found. If the Delphian Apollo were a god, as the Greeks suppose, would he not rather have chosen as his prophet some wise man? or if such an one was not to be found, then one who was endeavouring to become wise? How came he not to prefer a man to a woman for the utterance of his prophesies? And if he preferred the latter sex, as though he could only find pleasure in the breast of a woman, why did he not choose among women a virgin to interpret his will?

CHAPTER VI

But no; the Pythian, so much admired among the Greeks, judged no wise man, nay, no man at all, worthy of the divine possession, as they call it. And among women he did not choose a virgin, or one recommended by her wisdom, or by her attainments in philosophy; but he selects a common woman. Perhaps the better class of men were too good to become the subjects of the inspiration. Besides, if he were a god, he should have employed his prophetic power as a bait, so to speak, with which he might draw men to a change of life, and to the practice of virtue. But history nowhere makes mention of anything of the kind. For if the oracle did call Socrates the wisest of all men, it takes from the value of that eulogy by what is said in regard to Euripides and Sophocles. The words are:—

"Sophocles is wise, and Euripides is wiser,
But wiser than all men is Socrates."

As, then, he gives the designation "wise" to the tragic poets, it is not on account of his philosophy that he holds up Socrates to veneration, or because of his love of truth and virtue. It is poor praise of Socrates to say that he prefers him to men who for a paltry reward compete upon the stage, and who by their representations excite the spectators at one time to tears and grief, and at another to unseemly laughter (for such is the intention of the satyric drama). And perhaps it was not so much in regard to his philosophy that he called Socrates the wisest of all men, as on account of the victims which he sacrificed to him and the other demons. For it seems that the demons pay more regard in distributing their favours to the sacrifices which are offered them than to deeds of virtue. Accordingly, Homer, the best of the poets, who describes what usually took place, when, wishing to show us what most influenced the demons to grant an answer to the wishes of their votaries, introduces Chryses, who, for a few garlands and the thighs of bulls and goats, obtained an answer to his prayers for his daughter Chryseis, so that the Greeks were driven by a pestilence to restore her back to him. And I remember reading in the book of a certain Pythagorean, when writing on the hidden meanings in that poet, that the prayer of Chryses to Apollo, and the plague which Apollo afterwards sent upon the Greeks, are proofs that Homer knew of certain evil demons who delight in the smoke of sacrifices, and who, to reward those who offer them, grant in answer to their prayers the destruction of others. "He," that is, Jupiter, "who rules over wintry Dodona, where his prophets have ever unwashed feet, and sleep upon the ground," has rejected the male sex, and, as Celsus observes, employs the women of Dodona for the prophetic office. Granting that there are oracles similar to these, as that at Clarus, another in Branchidae, another in the temple of Jupiter Ammon, or anywhere else; yet how shall it be proved that these are gods, and not demons?

CHAPTER VII

In regard to the prophets among the Jews, some of them were wise men before they became divinely inspired prophets, while others became wise by the illumination which their minds received when divinely inspired. They were selected by Divine Providence to receive the Divine Spirit, and to be the depositaries of His holy oracles, on the ground of their leading a life of almost unapproachable excellence, intrepid, noble, unmoved by danger or death. For reason teaches that such ought to be the character of the prophets of the Most High, in comparison with which the firmness of Antisthenes, Crates, and Diogenes will seem but as child's play. It was therefore for their firm adherence to truth, and their faithfulness in the reproof of the wicked, that "they were stoned; they were sawn asunder, were tempted, were slain with the sword; they wandered about in sheepskins and goatskins; being destitute, afflicted, tormented; they wandered in deserts and in mountains, and in dens and caves of the earth, of whom the world was not worthy:" for they looked always to God and to His blessings, which, being invisible, and not to be perceived by the senses, are eternal. We have the history of the life of each of the prophets; but it will be enough at present to direct attention to the life of Moses, whose prophecies are contained in the law; to that of Jeremiah, as it is given in the book which bears his name; to that of Isaiah, who with unexampled austerity walked naked and barefooted for the space of three years. Read and consider the severe life of those children, Daniel and his companions, how they abstained from flesh, and lived on water and pulse. Or if you will go back to more remote times, think of the life of Noah, who prophesied; and of Isaac, who gave his son a prophetic blessing; or of Jacob, who addressed each of his twelve sons, beginning with "Come, that I may tell you what shall befall you in the last days." These, and a multitude of others, prophesying on behalf of God, foretold events relating to Jesus Christ. We therefore for this reason set at nought the oracles of the Pythian priestess, or those delivered at Dodona, at Clarus, at Branchidae, at the temple of Jupiter Ammon, or by a multitude of other so-called prophets; whilst we regard with reverent awe the Jewish prophets: for we see that the noble, earnest, and devout lives of these men were worthy of the inspiration of the Divine Spirit, whose wonderful effects were widely different from the divination of demons.

CHAPTER VIII

I do not know what led Celsus, when saying, "But what things were spoken or not spoken in the land of Judea, according to the custom of the country," to use the words "or not spoken," as though implying that he was incredulous, and that he suspected that those things which were written were never spoken. In fact, he is unacquainted with these times; and he does not know that those prophets who foretold the coming of Christ, predicted a multitude of other events many years beforehand. He adds, with the view of casting a slight upon the ancient prophets, that "they prophesied in the same way as we find them still doing among the inhabitants of Phoenicia and Palestine." But he does not tell us whether he refers to persons who are of different principles from those of the Jews and Christians, or to persons whose prophecies are of the same character as those of the Jewish prophets. However it be, his statement is false, taken in either way. For never have any of those who have not embraced our faith done any thing approaching to what was done by the ancient prophets; and in more recent times, since the coming of Christ, no prophets have arisen among the Jews, who have confessedly been abandoned by the Holy Spirit on account of their impiety towards God, and towards Him of whom their prophets spoke. Moreover, the Holy Spirit gave signs of His presence at the beginning of Christ's ministry, and after His ascension He gave still more; but since that time these signs have diminished, although there are still traces of His presence in a few who have had their souls purified by the Gospel, and their actions regulated by its influence. "For the holy Spirit of discipline will flee deceit, and remove from thoughts that are without understanding."

CHAPTER IX

But as Celsus promises to give an account of the manner in which prophecies are delivered in Phoenicia and Palestine, speaking as though it were a matter with which he had a full and personal acquaintance, let us see what he has to say on the subject. First he lays it down that there are several kinds of prophecies, but he does not specify what they are; indeed, he could not do so, and the statement is a piece of pure ostentation. However, let us see what he considers the most perfect kind of prophecy among these nations. "There are many," he says, "who, although of no name, with the greatest facility and on the slightest occasion, whether within or without temples, assume the motions and gestures of inspired persons; while others do it in cities or among armies, for the purpose of attracting attention and exciting surprise. These are accustomed to say, each for himself, 'I am God; I am the Son of God; or, I am the Divine Spirit; I have come because the world is perishing, and you, O men, are perishing for your iniquities. But I wish to save you, and you shall see me returning again with heavenly power. Blessed is he who now does me homage. On all the rest I will send down eternal fire, both on cities and on countries. And those who know not the punishments which await them shall repent and grieve in vain; while those who are faithful to me I will preserve eternally.'" Then he goes on to say: "To these promises are added strange, fanatical, and quite unintelligible words, of which no rational person can find the meaning: for so dark are they, as to have no meaning at all; but they give occasion to every fool or impostor to apply them to suit his own purposes."

CHAPTER X

But if he were dealing honestly in his accusations, he ought to have given the exact terms of the prophecies, whether those in which the speaker is introduced as claiming to be God Almighty, or those in which the Son of God speaks, or finally those under the name of the Holy Spirit. For thus he might have endeavoured to overthrow these assertions, and have shown that there was no divine inspiration in those words which urged men to forsake their sins, which condemned the past and foretold the future. For the prophecies were recorded and preserved by men living at the time, that those who came after might read and admire them as the oracles of God, and that they might profit not only by the warnings and admonitions, but also by the predictions, which, being shown by events to have proceeded from the Spirit of God, bind men to the practice of piety as set forth in the law and the prophets. The prophets have therefore, as God commanded them, declared with all plainness those things which it was desirable that the hearers should understand at once for the regulation of their conduct; while in regard to deeper and more mysterious subjects, which lay beyond the reach of the common understanding, they set them forth in the form of enigmas and allegories, or of what are called dark sayings, parables, or similitudes. And this plan they have followed, that those who are ready to shun no labour and spare no pains in their endeavours after truth and virtue might search into their meaning, and having found it, might apply it as reason requires. But Celsus, ever vigorous in his denunciations, as though he were angry at his inability to understand the language of the prophets, scoffs at them thus: "To these grand promises are added strange, fanatical, and quite unintelligible words, of which no rational person can find the meaning; for so dark are they as to have no meaning at all; but they give occasion to every fool or impostor to apply them so as to suit his own purposes." This statement of Celsus seems ingeniously designed to dissuade readers from attempting any inquiry or careful search into their meaning. And in this he is not unlike certain persons, who said to a man whom a prophet had visited to announce future events, "Wherefore came this mad fellow to thee?"

CHAPTER XI

I am convinced, indeed, that much better arguments could be adduced than any I have been able to bring forward, to show the falsehood of these allegations of Celsus, and to set forth the divine inspiration of the prophecies; but we have according to our ability, in our commentaries on Isaiah, Ezekiel, and some of the twelve minor prophets, explained literally and in detail what he calls "those fanatical and utterly unintelligible passages." And if God give us grace in the time that He appoints for us, to advance in the knowledge of His word, we shall continue our investigation into the parts which remain, or into such at least as we are able to make plain. And other persons of intelligence who wish to study Scripture may also find out its meaning for themselves; for although there are many places in which the meaning is not obvious, yet there are none where, as Celsus affirms, "there is no sense at all." Neither is it true that "any fool or impostor can explain the passages so as to make them suit his own purposes." For it belongs only to those who are wise in the truth of Christ (and to all them it does belong) to unfold the connection and meaning of even the obscure parts of prophecy, "comparing spiritual things with spiritual," and interpreting each passage according to the usage of Scripture writers. And Celsus is not to be believed when he says that he has heard such men prophesy; for no prophets bearing any resemblance to the ancient prophets have appeared in the time of Celsus. If there had been any, those who heard and admired them would have followed the example of the ancients, and have recorded the prophecies in writing. And it seems quite clear that Celsus is speaking falsely, when he says that "those prophets whom he had heard, on being pressed by him, confessed their true motives, and acknowledged that the ambiguous words they used really meant nothing." He ought to have given the names of those whom he says he had heard, if he had any to give, so that those who were competent to judge might decide whether his allegations were true or false.

CHAPTER XII

He thinks, besides, that those who support the cause of Christ by a reference to the writings of the prophets can give no proper answer in regard to statements in them which attribute to God that which is wicked, shameful, or impure; and assuming that no answer can be given, he proceeds to draw a whole train of inferences, none of which can be allowed. But he ought to know that those who wish to live according to the teaching of sacred Scripture understand the saying, "The knowledge of the unwise is as talk without sense," and have learnt "to be ready always to give an answer to every one that asketh us a reason for the hope that is in us." And they are not satisfied with affirming that such and such things have been predicted; but they endeavour to remove any apparent inconsistencies, and to show that, so far from there being anything evil, shameful, or impure in these predictions, everything is worthy of being received by those who understand the sacred Scriptures. But Celsus ought to have adduced from the prophets examples of what he thought bad, or shameful, or impure, if he saw any such passages; for then his argument would have had much more force, and would have furthered his purpose much better. He gives no instances, however, but contents himself with loudly asserting the false charge that these things are to be found in Scripture. There is no reason, then, for us to defend ourselves against groundless charges, which are but empty sounds, or to take the trouble of showing that in the writings of the prophets there is nothing evil, shameful, impure, or abominable.

CHAPTER XIII

And there is no truth in the statement of Celsus, that "God does the most shameless deeds, or suffers the most shameless sufferings," or that "He favours the commission of evil;" for whatever he may say, no such things have ever been foretold. He ought to have cited from the prophets the passages in which God is represented as favouring evil, or as doing and enduring the most shameless deeds, and not to have sought without foundation to prejudice the minds of his readers. The prophets, indeed, foretold what Christ should suffer, and set forth the reason why He should suffer. God therefore also knew what Christ would suffer; but where has he learnt that those things which the Christ of God should suffer were most base and dishonourable? He goes on to explain what those most shameful and degrading things were which Christ suffered, in these words: "For what better was it for God to eat the flesh of sheep, or to drink vinegar and gall, than to feed on filth?" But God, according to us, did not eat the flesh of sheep; and while it may seem that Jesus ate, He did so only as possessing a body. But in regard to the vinegar and gall mentioned in the prophecy, "They gave me also gall for my meat; and in my thirst they gave me vinegar to drink," we have already referred to this point; and as Celsus compels us to recur to it again, we would only say further, that those who resist the word of truth do ever offer to Christ the Son of God the gall of their own wickedness, and the vinegar of their evil inclinations; but though He tastes of it, yet He will not drink it.

CHAPTER XIV

In the next place, wishing to shake the faith of those who believe in Jesus on the ground of the prophecies which were delivered in regard to Him, Celsus says: "But pray, if the prophets foretold that the great

God—not to put it more harshly—would become a slave, or become sick or die; would there be therefore any necessity that God should die, or suffer sickness, or become a slave, simply because such things had been foretold? Must he die in order to prove his divinity? But the prophets never would utter predictions so wicked and impious. We need not therefore inquire whether a thing has been predicted or not, but whether the thing is honourable in itself, and worthy of God. In that which is evil and base, although it seemed that all men in the world had foretold it in a fit of madness, we must not believe. How then can the pious mind admit that those things which are said to have happened to him, could have happened to one who is God?" From this it is plain that Celsus feels the argument from prophecy to be very effective for convincing those to whom Christ is preached; but he seems to endeavour to overthrow it by an opposite probability, namely, "that the question is not whether the prophets uttered these predictions or not." But if he wished to reason justly and without evasion, he ought rather to have said, "We must show that these things were never predicted, or that those things which were predicted of Christ have never been fulfilled in him," and in that way he would have established the position which he holds. In that way it would have been made plain what those prophecies are which we apply to Jesus, and how Celsus could justify himself in asserting that that application was false. And we should thus have seen whether he fairly disproved all that we bring from the prophets in behalf of Jesus, or whether he himself is convicted of a shameless endeavour to resist the plainest truths by violent assertions.

CHAPTER XV

After assuming that some things were foretold which are impossible in themselves, and inconsistent with the character of God, he says: "If these things were predicted of the Most High God, are we bound to believe them of God simply because they were predicted?" And thus he thinks he proves, that although the prophets may have foretold truly such things of the Son of God, yet it is impossible for us to believe in those prophecies declaring that He would do or suffer such things. To this our answer is that the supposition is absurd, for it combines two lines of reasoning which are opposed to each other, and therefore mutually destructive. This may be shown as follows. The one argument is: "If any true prophets of the Most High say that God will become a slave, or suffer sickness, or die, these things will come to God; for it is impossible that the prophets of the great God should utter lies." The other is: "If even true prophets of the Most High God say that these same things shall come to pass, seeing that these things foretold are by the nature of things impossible, the prophecies are not true, and therefore those things which have been foretold will not happen to God." When, then, we find two processes of reasoning in both of which the major premiss is the same, leading to two contradictory conclusions, we use the form of argument called "the theorem of two propositions," to prove that the major premiss is false, which in the case before us is this, "that the prophets have foretold that the great God should become a slave, suffer sickness, or die." We conclude, then, that the prophets never foretold such things; and the argument is formally expressed as follows: 1*st*, Of two things, if the first is true, the second is true; 2*d*, if the first is true, the second is not true, therefore the first is not true. The concrete example which the Stoics give to illustrate this form of argument is the following: 1*st*, If you know that you are dead, you are dead; 2*d*, if you know that you are dead, you are not dead. And the conclusion is—"you do not know that you are dead." These propositions are worked out as follows: If you know that you are dead, that which you know is certain; therefore you are dead. Again, if you know that you are dead, your death is an object of knowledge; but as the dead know nothing, your knowing this proves that you are not dead. Accordingly, by joining the two arguments together, you arrive at the conclusion—"you do not know that you are dead." Now the hypothesis of Celsus which we have given above is much of the same kind.

CHAPTER XVI

But besides, the prophecies which he introduces into his argument are very different from what the prophets actually foretold of Jesus Christ. For the prophecies do not foretell that God will be crucified, when they say of Him who should suffer, "We beheld Him, and He had no form or comeliness; but His form was dishonoured and marred more than the sons of men; He was a man of sorrows, and acquainted with grief." Observe, then, how distinctly they say that it was a man who should endure these human sufferings. And Jesus Himself, who knew perfectly that one who was to die must be a man, said to His accusers: "But now ye seek to kill Me, a man that hath spoken unto you the truth which I heard of God." And if in that man as He appeared among men there was something divine, namely the only-begotten Son of God, the first-born of all creation, one who said of Himself, "I am the truth," "I am the life," "I am the door," "I am the way," "I am the living bread which came down from heaven," of this Being and His nature we must judge and reason in a way quite different from that in which we judge of the man who was seen in Jesus Christ. Accordingly, you will find no Christian, however simple he may be, and however little versed in critical studies, who would say that He who died was "the truth," "the life," "the way," "the living bread which came down from heaven," "the resurrection;" for it was He who appeared to us in the form of the man Jesus, who taught us, saying, "I am the resurrection." There is no one amongst us, I say, so extravagant as to affirm "the Life died," "the Resurrection died." The supposition of Celsus would have some foundation if we were to say that it had been foretold by the prophets that death would befall God the Word, the Truth, the Life, the Resurrection, or any other name which is assumed by the Son of God.

CHAPTER XVII

In one point alone is Celsus correct in his statements on this subject. It is that in which he says: "The prophets would not foretell this, because it involves that which is wicked and impious,"—namely, that the great God should become a slave or suffer death. But that which is predicted by the prophets is worthy of God, that He who is the brightness and express image of the divine nature should come into the world with the holy human soul which was to animate the body of Jesus, to sow the seed of His word, which might bring all who received and cherished it into union with the Most High God, and which would lead to perfect blessedness all those who felt within them the power of God the Word, who was to be in the body and soul of a man. He was to be in it indeed, but not in such a way as to confine therein all the rays of His glory; and we are not to suppose that the light of Him who is God the Word is shed forth in no other way than in this. If, then, we consider Jesus in relation to the divinity that was in Him, the things which He did in this capacity present nothing to offend our ideas of God, nothing but what is holy; and if we consider Him as man, distinguished beyond all other men by an intimate communion with the Eternal Word, with absolute Wisdom, He suffered as one who was wise and perfect, whatever it behoved Him to suffer who did all for the good of the human race, yea, even for the good of all intelligent beings. And there is nothing absurd in a man having died, and in His death being not only an example of death endured for the sake of piety, but also the first blow in the conflict which is to overthrow the power of that evil spirit the devil, who had obtained dominion over the whole world. For we have signs and pledges of the destruction of his empire, in those who through the coming of Christ are everywhere escaping from the power of demons, and who, after their deliverance from this bondage in which they were held, consecrate themselves to God, and earnestly devote themselves day by day to advancement in a life of piety.

CHAPTER XVIII

Celsus adds: "Will they not besides make this reflection? If the prophets of the God of the Jews foretold that he who should come into the world would be the Son of this same God, how could he command them through Moses to gather wealth, to extend their dominion, to fill the earth, to put their enemies of every age to the sword, and to destroy them utterly, which indeed he himself did—as Moses says—threatening them, moreover, that if they did not obey his commands, he would treat them as his avowed enemies; whilst, on the other hand, his Son, the man of Nazareth, promulgated laws quite opposed to these, declaring that no one can come to the Father who loves power, or riches, or glory; that men ought not to be more careful in providing food than the ravens; that they were to be less concerned about their raiment than the lilies; that to him who has given them one blow, they should offer to receive another? Whether is it Moses or Jesus who teaches falsely? Did the Father, when he sent Jesus, forget the commands which he had given to Moses? Or did he change his mind, condemn his own laws, and send forth a messenger with counter instructions?" Celsus, with all his boasts of universal knowledge, has here fallen into the most vulgar of errors, in supposing that in the law and the prophets there is not a meaning deeper than that afforded by a literal rendering of the words. He does not see how manifestly incredible it is that worldly riches should be promised to those who lead upright lives, when it is a matter of common observation that the best of men have lived in extreme poverty. Indeed, the prophets themselves, who for the purity of their lives received the Divine Spirit, "wandered about in sheepskins and goatskins; being destitute, afflicted, tormented: they wandered in deserts, and in mountains, and in dens and caves of the earth." For, as the Psalmist, says, "many are the afflictions of the righteous." If Celsus had read the writings of Moses, he would, I daresay, have supposed that when it is said to him who kept the law, "Thou shalt lend unto many nations, and thou thyself shalt not borrow," the promise is made to the just man, that his temporal riches should be so abundant, that he would be able to lend not only to the Jews, not only to two or three nations, but "to many nations." What, then, must have been the wealth which the just man received according to the law for his righteousness, if he could lend to many nations? And must we not suppose also, in accordance with this interpretation, that the just man would never borrow anything? For it is written, "and thou shalt thyself borrow nothing." Did then that nation remain for so long a period attached to the religion which was taught by Moses, whilst, according to the supposition of Celsus, they saw themselves so grievously deceived by that lawgiver? For nowhere is it said of any one that he was so rich as to lend to many nations. It is not to be believed that they would have fought so zealously in defence of a law whose promises had proved glaringly false, if they understood them in the sense which Celsus gives to them. And if any one should say that the sins which are recorded to have been committed by the people are a proof that they despised the law, doubtless from the feeling that they had been deceived by it, we may reply that we have only to read the history of the times in order to find it shown that the whole people, after having done that which was evil in the sight of the Lord, returned afterwards to their duty, and to the religion prescribed by the law.

CHAPTER XIX

Now if these words in the law, "Thou shalt have dominion over many nations, and no one shall rule over thee," were simply a promise to them of dominion, and if they contain no deeper meaning than this, then it is certain that the people would have had still stronger grounds for despising the promises of the law. Celsus brings forward another passage, although he changes the terms of it, where it is said that the whole earth shall be filled with the Hebrew race; which indeed, according to the testimony of history, did actually happen after the coming of Christ, although rather as a result of God's anger, if I may so say, than of His blessing. As to the promise made to the Jews that they should slay their enemies, it may be answered that any one who examines carefully into the meaning of this passage will find himself unable to interpret it literally. It is sufficient at present to refer to the manner in which in the Psalms the just man is represented as saying, among other things, "Every morning will I destroy the wicked of the land; that I may cut off all workers of iniquity from the city of Jehovah." Judge, then, from the words and spirit of the speaker, whether it is conceivable that, after having in the preceding part of the Psalm, as any one may read for himself, uttered the noblest thoughts and purposes, he should in the sequel, according to the literal rendering of his words, say that in the morning, and at no other period of the day, he would destroy all sinners from the earth, and leave none of them alive, and that he would slay every one in Jerusalem who did iniquity. And there are many similar expressions to be found in the law, as this, for example: "We left not anything alive."

CHAPTER XX

Celsus adds, that it was foretold to the Jews, that if they did not obey the law, they would be treated in the same way as they treated their enemies; and then he quotes from the teaching of Christ some precepts which he considers contrary to those of the law, and uses that as an argument against us. But before proceeding to this point, we must speak of that which precedes. We hold, then, that the law has a twofold sense,—the one literal, the other spiritual,—as has been shown by some before us. Of the first or literal sense it is said, not by us, but by God, speaking in one of the prophets, that "the statutes are not good, and the judgments not good;" whereas, taken in a spiritual sense, the same prophet makes God say that "His statutes are good, and His judgments good." Yet evidently the prophet is not saying things which are contradictory of each other. Paul in like manner says, that "the letter killeth, and the spirit giveth life," meaning by "the letter" the literal sense, and by "the spirit" the spiritual sense of Scripture. We may therefore find in Paul, as well as in the prophet, apparent contradictions. Indeed, if Ezekiel says in one place, "I gave them commandments which were not good, and judgments whereby they should not live," and in another, "I gave them good commandments and judgments, which if a man shall do, he shall live by them," Paul in like manner, when he wishes to disparage the law taken literally, says, "If the ministration of death, written and engraven in stones, was glorious, so that the children of Israel could not stedfastly behold the face of Moses for the glory of his countenance, which glory was to be done away; how shall not the ministration of the Spirit be rather glorious?" But when in another place he wishes to praise and recommend the law, he calls it "spiritual," and says, "We know that the law is spiritual;" and, "Wherefore the law is holy, and the commandment holy, and just, and good."

CHAPTER XXI

When, then, the letter of the law promises riches to the just, Celsus may follow the letter which killeth, and understand it of worldly riches, which blind men; but we say that it refers to those riches which enlighten the eyes, and which enrich a man "in all utterance and in all knowledge." And in this sense we "charge them that are rich in this world, that they be not high-minded, nor trust in uncertain riches, but in the living God, who giveth us richly all things to enjoy; that they do good, that they be rich in good works, ready to distribute, willing to communicate." For, as Solomon says, "riches" are the true good, which "are the ransom of the life of a man;" but the poverty which is the opposite of these riches is destructive, for by it "the poor cannot bear rebuke." And what has been said of riches applies to dominion, in regard to which it is said, "The just man shall chase a thousand, and two put ten thousand to flight." Now if riches are to be taken in the sense we have just explained, consider if it is not according to God's promise that he who is rich in all utterance, in all knowledge, in all wisdom, in all good works, may not out of these treasures of utterance, of wisdom, and of knowledge, lend to many nations. It was thus that Paul lent to all the nations that he visited, "carrying the Gospel of Christ from Jerusalem, and round about unto Illyricum." And as the divine knowledge was given to him by revelation, and his mind was illumined by the Divine Word, he himself therefore needed to borrow from no one, and required not the ministry to any man to teach him the word of truth. Thus, as it had been written, "Thou shalt have dominion over many nations, and they shall not have dominion over thee," he ruled over the Gentiles whom he brought under the teaching of Jesus Christ; and he never "gave place by subjection to men, no, not for an hour," as being himself mightier than they. And thus also he "filled the earth."

CHAPTER XXII

If I must now explain how the just man "slays his enemies," and prevails everywhere, it is to be observed that, when he says, "Every morning will I destroy the wicked of the land, that I may cut off all workers of iniquity from the city of Jehovah," by "the land" he means the flesh whose lusts are at enmity with God; and by "the city of Jehovah" he designates his own soul, in which was the temple of God, containing the true idea and conception of God, which makes it to be admired by all who look upon it. As soon, then, as the rays of the Sun of righteousness shine into his soul, feeling strengthened and invigorated by their influence, he sets himself to destroy all the lusts of the flesh, which are called "the wicked of the land," and drives out of that city of the Lord which is in his soul all thoughts which work iniquity, and all suggestions which are opposed to the truth. And in this way also the just give up to destruction all their enemies, which are their vices, so that they do not spare even the children, that is, the early beginnings and promptings of evil. In this sense also we understand the language of the 137th Psalm: "O daughter of Babylon, who art to be destroyed; happy shall he be that rewardeth thee as thou hast served us: happy shall he be that taketh and dasheth thy little ones against the stones." For "the little ones" of Babylon (which signifies confusion) are those troublesome sinful thoughts which arise in the soul and he who subdues them by striking, as it were, their heads against the firm and solid strength of reason and truth, is the man who "dasheth the little ones against the stones;" and he is therefore truly blessed. God may therefore have commanded men to destroy all their vices utterly, even at their birth, without having enjoined anything contrary to the teaching of Christ; and He may Himself have destroyed before the eyes of those who were "Jews inwardly" all the offspring of evil as His enemies. And, in like manner, those who disobey the law and word of God may well be compared to His enemies led astray by sin; and they may well be said to suffer the same fate as they deserve who have proved traitors to the truth of God.

CHAPTER XXIII

From what has been said, it is clear then that Jesus, "the man of Nazareth," did not promulgate laws opposed to those just considered in regard to riches, when He said, "It is hard for the rich man to enter into the kingdom of God;" whether we take the word "rich" in its simplest sense, as referring to the man whose mind is distracted by his wealth, and, as it were, entangled with thorns, so that he brings forth no spiritual fruit; or whether it is the man who is rich in the sense of abounding in false notions, of whom it is written in the Proverbs, "Better is the poor man who is just, than the rich man who is false." Perhaps it is the following passages which have led Celsus to suppose that Jesus forbids ambition to His disciples: "Whoever of you will be the chiefest, shall be servant of all;" "The princes of the Gentiles exercise dominion over them," and "they that exercise authority upon them are called benefactors." But there is nothing here inconsistent with the promise, "Thou shalt rule over many nations, and they shall not rule over thee," especially after the explanation which we have given of these words. Celsus next throws in an expression in regard to wisdom, as though he thought that, according to the teaching of Christ, no wise man could come to the Father. But we would ask in what sense he speaks of a wise man. For if he means one who is wise in "the wisdom of this world," as it is called, "which is foolishness with God," then we would agree with him in saying that access to the Father is denied to one who is wise in that sense. But if by wisdom any one means Christ, who is "the power and wisdom of God," far from such a wise man being refused access to the Father, we hold that he who is adorned by the Holy Spirit with that gift which is called "the word of wisdom," far excels all those who have not received the same grace.

CHAPTER XXIV

The pursuit of human glory, we maintain, is forbidden not only by the teaching of Jesus, but also by the Old Testament. Accordingly we find one of the prophets, when imprecating upon himself certain punishments for the commission of certain sins, includes among the punishments this one of earthly glory. He says, "O Lord my God, if I have done this; if there be iniquity in my hands; if I have rewarded evil unto him that was at peace with me; (yea, rather, I have delivered him that without cause is mine enemy;) let the enemy persecute my soul, and take it; yea, let him tread down my life upon the earth, and *set my glory up on high.*" And these precepts of our Lord, "Take no thought what ye shall eat, or what ye shall drink. Behold the fowls of the air, or behold the ravens: for they sow not, neither do they reap; yet your heavenly Father feedeth them. How much better are ye than they! And why take ye thought for raiment? Consider the lilies of the field;"— these precepts, and those which follow, are not inconsistent with the promised blessings of the law, which teaches that the just "shall eat their bread to the full;" nor with that saying of Solomon, "The righteous eateth to the satisfying of his soul, but the belly of the wicked shall want." For we must consider the food promised in the law as the food of the soul, which is to satisfy not both parts of man's nature, but the soul only. And the words of the Gospel, although probably containing a deeper meaning, may yet be taken in their more simple and obvious sense, as teaching us not to be disturbed with anxieties about our food and clothing, but, while living in plainness, and desiring only what is needful, to put our trust in the providence of God.

CHAPTER XXV

Celsus then extracts from the Gospel the precept, "To him who strikes thee once, thou shalt offer thyself to be struck again," although without giving any passage from the Old Testament which he considers opposed to it. On the one hand, we know that "it was said to them in old time, An eye for an eye, and a tooth for a tooth;" and on the other, we have read, "I say unto you, Whoever shall smite thee on the one cheek, turn to him the other also." But as there is reason to believe that Celsus produces the objections which he has heard from those who wish to make a difference between the God of the Gospel and the God of the law, we must say in reply, that this precept, "Whosoever shall strike thee on the one cheek, turn to him the other," is not unknown in the older Scriptures. For thus, in the Lamentations of Jeremiah, it is said, "It is good for a man that he bear the yoke in his youth: he sitteth alone, and keepeth silence, because he hath borne it upon him. He giveth his cheek to him that smiteth him; he is filled full with reproach." There is no discrepancy, then, between the God of the Gospel and the God of the law, even when we take literally the precept regarding the blow on the face. So, then, we infer that neither "Jesus nor Moses has taught falsely." The Father in sending Jesus did not "forget the commands which He had given to Moses:" He did not "change His mind, condemn His own laws, and send by His messenger counter instructions."

CHAPTER XXVI

However, if we must refer briefly to the difference between the constitution which was given to the Jews of old by Moses, and that which the Christians, under the direction of Christ's teaching, wish now to establish, we would observe that it must be impossible for the legislation of Moses, taken literally, to harmonize with the calling of the Gentiles, and with their subjection to the Roman government; and on the other hand, it would be impossible for the Jews to preserve their civil economy unchanged, supposing that they should embrace the Gospel. For Christians could not slay their enemies, or condemn to be burned or stoned, as Moses commands, those who had broken the law, and were therefore condemned as deserving of these punishments; since the Jews themselves, however desirous of carrying out their law, are not able to inflict these punishments. But in the case of the ancient Jews, who had a land and a form of government of their own, to take from them the right of making war upon their enemies, of fighting for their country, of putting to death or otherwise punishing adulterers, murderers, or others who were guilty of similar crimes, would be to subject them to sudden and utter destruction whenever the enemy fell upon them; for their very laws would in that case restrain them, and prevent them from resisting the enemy. And that same providence which of old gave the law, and has now given the Gospel of Jesus Christ, not wishing the Jewish state to continue longer, has destroyed their city and their temple: it has abolished the worship which was offered to God in that temple by the sacrifice of victims, and other ceremonies which He had prescribed. And as it has destroyed these things, not wishing that they should longer continue, in like manner it has extended day by day the Christian religion, so that it is now preached everywhere with boldness, and that in spite of the numerous obstacles which oppose the spread of Christ's teaching in the world. But since it was the purpose of God that the nations should receive the benefits of Christ's teaching, all the devices of men against Christians have been brought to nought; for the more that kings, and rulers, and peoples have persecuted them everywhere, the more have they increased in number and grown in strength.

CHAPTER XXVII

After this Celsus relates at length opinions which he ascribes to us, but which we do not hold, regarding the Divine Being, to the effect that "he is corporeal in his nature, and possesses a body like a man." As he undertakes to refute opinions which are none of ours, it would be needless to give either the opinions themselves or their refutation. Indeed, if we did hold those views of God which he ascribes to us, and which he opposes, we would be bound to quote his words, to adduce our own arguments, and to refute his. But if he brings forward opinions which he has either heard from no one, or if it be assumed that he has heard them, it must have been from those who are very simple and ignorant of the meaning of Scripture, then we need not undertake so superfluous a task as that of refuting them. For the Scriptures plainly speak of God as of a being without body. Hence it is said, "No man hath seen God at any time;" and the First-born of all creation is called "the image of the invisible God," which is the same as if it were said that He is incorporeal. However, we have already said something on the nature of God while examining into the meaning of the words, "God is a Spirit, and they who worship Him must worship Him in spirit and in truth."

CHAPTER XXVIII

After thus misrepresenting our views of the nature of God, Celsus goes on to ask of us "where we hope to go after death;" and he makes our answer to be, "to another land better than this." On this he comments as follows: "The divine men of a former age have spoken of a happy life reserved for the souls of the blessed. Some designated it 'the isles of the blest,' and others the 'Elysian plain,' so called because they were there to be delivered from their present evils. Thus Homer says: 'But the gods shall send thee to the Elysian plain, on the borders of the earth, where they lead a most quiet life.' Plato also, who believed in the immortality of the soul, distinctly gives the name 'land' to the place where it is sent. 'The extent of it,' says he, 'is immense, and we only occupy a small portion of it, from the Phasis to the Pillars of Hercules, where we dwell along the shores of the sea, as grasshoppers and frogs beside a marsh. But there are many other places inhabited in like manner by other men. For there are in different parts of the earth cavities, varying in form and in magnitude, into which run water, and clouds, and air. But that land which is pure lies in the pure region of heaven.'" Celsus therefore supposes that what we say of a land which is much better and more excellent than this, has been borrowed from certain ancient writers whom he styles "divine," and chiefly from Plato, who in his *Phaedon* discourses on the pure land lying in a pure heaven. But he does not see that Moses, who is much older than the Greek literature, introduces God as promising to those who lived according to His law the holy land, which is "a good land and a large, a land flowing with milk and honey;" which promise is not to be understood to refer, as some suppose, to that part of the earth which we call Judea; for it, however good it may be, still forms part of the earth, which was originally cursed for the transgression of Adam. For these words, "Cursed shall the ground be for what thou hast done; with grief, that is, with labour, shalt thou eat of the fruit of it all the days of thy life," were spoken of the whole earth, the fruit of which every man who died in Adam eats with sorrow or labour all the days of his life. And as all the earth has been cursed, it brings forth thorns and briers all the days of the life of those who in Adam were driven out of paradise; and in the sweat of his face every man eats bread until he returns to the ground from which he was taken. For the full exposition of all that is contained in this passage much might be said; but we have confined ourselves to these few words at present, which are intended to remove the idea, that what is said of the good land promised by God to the righteous, refers to the land of Judea.

CHAPTER XXIX

If, then, the whole earth has been cursed in the deeds of Adam and of those who died in him, it is plain that all parts of the earth share in the curse, and among others the land of Judea; so that the words, "a good land and a large, a land flowing with milk and honey, cannot apply to it, although we may say of it, that both Judea and Jerusalem were the shadow and figure of that pure land, goodly and large, in the pure region of heaven, in which is the heavenly Jerusalem. And it is in reference to this Jerusalem that the apostle spoke, as one who, "being risen with Christ, and seeking those things which are above," had found a truth which formed no part of the Jewish mythology. "Ye are come," says he, "unto Mount Sion, and unto the city of the living God, the heavenly Jerusalem, and to an innumerable company of angels." And in order to be assured that our explanation of "the good and large land" of Moses is not contrary to the intention of the Divine Spirit, we have only to read in all the prophets what they say of those who, after having left Jerusalem, and wandered astray from it, should afterwards return and be settled in the place which is called the habitation and city of God, as in the words, "His dwelling is in the holy place;" and, "Great is the Lord, and greatly to be praised in the city of our God, in the mountain of His holiness, beautiful for situation, the joy of the whole earth." It is enough at present to quote the words of the thirty-seventh Psalm, which speaks thus of the land of the righteous, "Those that wait upon the LORD they shall inherit the earth;" and a little after, "But the meek shall inherit the earth, and shall delight themselves in the abundance of peace;" and again, "Those who bless Him shall inherit the earth;" and, "The righteous shall inherit the land, and dwell therein for ever." And consider whether it is not evident to intelligent readers that the following words from this same Psalm refer to the pure land in the pure heaven: "Wait on the LORD, and keep His way; and He shall exalt thee to inherit the land."

CHAPTER XXX

It seems to me also that the fancy of Plato, that those stones which we call precious stones derive their lustre from a reflection, as it were, of the stones in that better land, is taken from the words of Isaiah in describing the city of God, "I will make thy battlements of jasper, thy stones shall be crystal, and thy borders of precious stones;" and, "I will lay thy foundations with sapphires." Those who hold in greatest reverence the teaching of Plato, explain this myth of his as an allegory. And the prophecies from which, as we conjecture, Plato has borrowed, will be explained by those who, leading a godly life like that of the prophets, devote all their time to the study of the sacred Scriptures, to those who are qualified to learn by purity of life, and their desire to advance in divine knowledge. For our part, our purpose has been simply to say that what we affirm of that sacred land has not been taken from Plato or any of the Greeks, but that they rather—living as they did not only after Moses, who was the oldest, but even after most of the prophets—borrowed from them, and in so doing either misunderstood their obscure intimations on such subjects, or else endeavoured, in their allusions to the better land, to imitate those portions of Scripture which had fallen into their hands. Haggai expressly makes a distinction between the earth and the dry land, meaning by the latter the land in which we live. He says: "Yet once, and I will shake the heavens, and the earth, and the dry land, and the sea."

CHAPTER XXXI

Referring to the passage in the *Phaedon* of Plato, Celsus says: "It is not easy for every one to understand the meaning of Plato's words, when he says that on account of our weakness and slowness we are unable to reach the highest region of the air; but that if our nature were capable of so sublime a contemplation, we would then be able to understand that that is the true heaven, and that the true light." As Celsus has deferred to another opportunity the explanation of Plato's idea, we also think that it does not fall within our purpose at present to enter into any full description of that holy and good land, and of the city of God which is in it; but reserve the consideration of it for our Commentary on the Prophets, having already in part, according to our power, treated of the city of God in our remarks on the forty-sixth and forty-eighth Psalms. The writings of Moses and the prophets—the most ancient of all books—teach us that all things here on earth which are in common use among men, have other things corresponding to them in name which are alone real. Thus, for instance, there is the true light, and another heaven beyond the firmament, and a Sun of righteousness other than the sun we see. In a word, to distinguish those things from the objects of sense, which have no true reality, they say of God that "His works are truth;" thus making a distinction between the works of God and the works of God's hands, which latter are of an inferior sort. Accordingly, God in Isaiah complains of men, that "they regard not the works of the LORD, nor consider the operation of His hands." But enough on this point.

CHAPTER XXXII

Celsus next assails the doctrine of the resurrection, which is a high and difficult doctrine, and one which more than others requires a high and advanced degree of wisdom to set forth how worthy it is of God; and how sublime a truth it is which teaches us that there is a seminal principle lodged in that which Scripture speaks of as the "tabernacle" of the soul, in which the righteous "do groan, being burdened, not for that they would be unclothed, but clothed upon." Celsus ridicules this doctrine because he does not understand it, and because he has learnt it from ignorant persons, who were unable to support it on any reasonable grounds. It will be profitable, therefore, that in addition to what we have said above, we should make this one remark. Our teaching on the subject of the resurrection is not, as Celsus imagines, derived from anything that we have heard on the doctrine of metempsychosis; but we know that the soul, which is immaterial and invisible in its nature, exists in no material place, without having a body suited to the nature of that place. Accordingly, it at one time puts off one body which was necessary before, but which is no longer adequate in its changed state, and it exchanges it for a second; and at another time it assumes another in addition to the former, which is needed as a better covering, suited to the purer ethereal regions of heaven. When it comes into the world at birth, it casts off the integuments which it needed in the womb; and before doing this, it puts on another body suited for its life upon earth. Then, again, as there is "a tabernacle" and "an earthly house" which is in some sort necessary for this tabernacle, Scripture teaches us that "the earthly house of this tabernacle shall be dissolved," but that the tabernacle shall "be clothed upon with a house not made with hands, eternal in the heavens." The men of God say also that "the corruptible shall put on incorruption," which is a different thing from "the incorruptible;" and "the mortal shall put on immortality," which is different from "the immortal." Indeed, what "wisdom" is to "the wise," and "justice" to "the just," and "peace" to "the peaceable," the same relation does "incorruption" hold to "the incorruptible," and "immortality" to "the immortal." Behold, then, to what a prospect Scripture encourages us to look, when it speaks to us of being clothed with incorruption and immortality, which are, as it were, vestments which will not suffer those who are covered with them to come to corruption or death. Thus far I have taken the liberty of referring to this subject, in answer to one who assails the doctrine of the resurrection without understanding it, and who, simply because he knew nothing about it, made it the object of contempt and ridicule.

CHAPTER XXXIII

As Celsus supposes that we uphold the doctrine of the resurrection in order that we may see and know God, he thus follows out his notions on the subject: "After they have been utterly refuted and vanquished, they still, as if regardless of all objections, come back again to the same question, 'How then shall we see and know God? how shall we go to Him?'" Let any, however, who are disposed to hear us observe, that if we have need of a body for other purposes, as for occupying a material locality to which this body must be adapted, and if on that account the "tabernacle" is clothed in the way we have shown, we have no need of a body in order to know God. For that which sees God is not the eye of the body; it is the mind which is made in the image of the Creator, and which God has in His providence rendered capable of that knowledge. To see God belongs to the pure heart, out of which no longer proceed "evil thoughts, murders, adulteries, fornications, thefts, false witness, blasphemies, the evil eye," or any other evil thing. Wherefore it is said, "Blessed are the pure in heart, for they shall see God." But as the strength of our will is not sufficient to procure the perfectly pure heart, and as we need that God should create it, he therefore who prays as he ought, offers this petition to God, "Create in me a clean heart, O God."

CHAPTER XXXIV

And we do not ask the question, "How shall we go to God?" as though we thought that God existed in some place. God is of too excellent a nature for any place: He holds all things in His power, and is Himself not confined by anything whatever. The precept, therefore, "Thou shalt walk after the LORD thy God," does not command a bodily approach to God; neither does the prophet refer to physical nearness to God, when he says in his prayer, "My soul followeth hard after Thee." Celsus therefore misrepresents us, when he says that we expect to see God with our bodily eyes, to hear Him with our ears, and to touch Him sensibly with our hands. We know that the holy Scriptures make mention of eyes, of ears, and of hands, which have nothing but the name in common with the bodily organs; and what is more wonderful, they speak of a diviner sense, which is very different from the senses as commonly spoken of. For when the prophet says, "Open Thou mine eyes, that I may behold wondrous things out of thy law," or, "the commandment of the Lord is pure, enlightening the eyes," or, "Lighten mine eyes, lest I sleep the sleep of death," no one is so foolish as to suppose that the eyes of the body behold the wonders of the divine law, or that the law of the Lord gives light to the bodily eyes, or that the sleep of death falls on the eyes of the body. When our Saviour says, "He that hath ears to hear, let him hear," any one will understand that the ears spoken of are of a diviner kind. When it is said that the word of the Lord was "in the hand" of Jeremiah or of some other prophet; or when the expression is used, "the law by the hand of Moses," or, "I sought the Lord with my hands, and was not deceived,"—no one is so foolish as not to see that the word "hands" is taken figuratively, as when John says, "Our hands have handled the Word of life." And if you wish further to learn from the sacred writings that there is a diviner sense than the senses of the body, you have only to hear what Solomon says, "Thou shalt find a divine sense."

CHAPTER XXXV

Seeking God, then, in this way, we have no need to visit the oracles of Trophonius, of Amphiaraus, and of Mopsus, to which Celsus would send us, assuring us that we would there "see the gods in human form, appearing to us with all distinctness, and without illusion." For we know that these are demons, feeding on the blood, and smoke, and odour of victims, and shut up by their base desires in prisons, which the Greeks call temples of the gods, but which we know are only the dwellings of deceitful demons. To this Celsus maliciously adds, in regard to these gods which, according to him, are in human form, "they do not show themselves for once, or at intervals, like him who has deceived men, but they are ever open to intercourse with those who desire it." From this remark, it would seem that Celsus supposes that the appearance of Christ to His disciples after His resurrection was like that of a spectre flitting before their eyes; whereas these gods, as he calls them, in human shape always present themselves to those who desire it. But how is it possible that a phantom which, as he describes it, flew past to deceive the beholders, could produce such effects after it had passed away, and could so turn the hearts of men as to lead them to regulate their actions according to the will of God, as in view of being hereafter judged by Him? And how could a phantom drive away demons, and show other indisputable evidences of power, and that not in any one place, like these so-called gods in human form, but making its divine power felt through the whole world, in drawing and congregating together all who are found disposed to lead a good and noble life?

CHAPTER XXXVI

After these remarks of Celsus, which we have endeavoured to answer as we could, he goes on to say, speaking of us: "Again they will ask, 'How can we know God, unless by the perception of the senses?

for how otherwise than through the senses are we able to gain any knowledge?'" To this he replies: "This is not the language of a man; it comes not from the soul, but from the flesh. Let them hearken to us, if such a spiritless and carnal race are able to do so: if, instead of exercising the senses, you look upwards with the soul; if, turning away the eye of the body, you open the eye of the mind, thus and thus only will you be able to see God. And if you seek one to be your guide along this way, you must shun all deceivers and jugglers, who will introduce you to phantoms. Otherwise you will be acting the most ridiculous part, if, whilst you pronounce imprecations upon those others that are recognised as gods, treating them as idols, you yet do homage to a more wretched idol than any of these, which indeed is not even an idol or a phantom, but a dead man, and you seek a father like to him." The first remark which we have to make on this passage is in regard to his use of personification, by which he makes us defend in this way the doctrine of the resurrection. This figure of speech is properly employed when the character and sentiments of the person introduced are faithfully preserved; but it is an abuse of the figure when these do not agree with the character and opinions of the speaker. Thus we should justly condemn a man who put into the mouths of barbarians, slaves, or uneducated people the language of philosophy; because we know that the philosophy belonged to the author, and not to such persons, who could not know anything of philosophy. And in like manner we should condemn a man for introducing persons who are represented as wise and well versed in divine knowledge, and should make them give expression to language which could only come out of the mouths of those who are ignorant or under the influence of vulgar passions. Hence Homer is admired, among other things, for preserving a consistency of character in his heroes, as in Nestor, Ulysses, Diomede, Agamemnon, Telemachus, Penelope, and the rest. Euripides, on the contrary, was assailed in the comedies of Aristophanes as a frivolous talker, often putting into the mouth of a barbarian woman, a wretched slave, the wise maxims which he had learned from Anaxagoras or some other philosophers.

CHAPTER XXXVII

Now if this is a true account of what constitutes the right and the wrong use of personification, have we not grounds for holding Celsus up to ridicule for thus ascribing to Christians words which they never uttered? For if those whom he represents as speaking are the unlearned, how is it possible that such persons could distinguish between "sense"

704

and "reason," between "objects of sense" and "objects of the reason?" To argue in this way, they would require to have studied under the Stoics, who deny all intellectual existences, and maintain that all that we apprehend is apprehended through the senses, and that all knowledge comes through the senses. But if, on the other hand, he puts these words into the mouth of philosophers who search carefully into the meaning of Christian doctrines, the statements in question do not agree with their character and principles. For no one who has learnt that God is invisible, and that certain of His works are invisible, that is to say, apprehended by the reason, can say, as if to justify his faith in a resurrection, "How can they know God, except by the perception of the senses?" or, "How otherwise than through the senses can they gain any knowledge?" For it is not in any secret writings, perused only by a few wise men, but in such as are most widely diffused and most commonly known among the people, that these words are written: "The invisible things of God from the creation of the world are clearly seen, being understood by the things that are made." From whence it is to be inferred, that though men who live upon the earth have to begin with the use of the senses upon sensible objects, in order to go on from them to a knowledge of the nature of things intellectual, yet their knowledge must not stop short with the objects of sense. And thus, while Christians would not say that it is impossible to have a knowledge of intellectual objects without the senses, but rather that the senses supply the first means of obtaining knowledge, they might well ask the question, "Who can gain any knowledge without the senses?" without deserving the abuse of Celsus, when he adds, "This is not the language of a man; it comes not from the soul, but from the flesh."

CHAPTER XXXVIII

Since we hold that the great God is in essence simple, invisible, and incorporeal, Himself pure intelligence, or something transcending intelligence and existence, we can never say that God is apprehended by any other means than through the intelligence which is formed in His image, though now, in the words of Paul, "we see in a glass obscurely, but then face to face." And if we use the expression "face to face," let no one pervert its meaning; but let it be explained by this passage, "Beholding with open face the glory of the Lord, we are changed into the same image, from glory to glory," which shows that we do not use the word in this connection to mean the visible face, but take it figuratively, in the same way as we have shown that the eyes, the ears, and the other parts of the body are employed. And it is certain that a man—I mean a soul using a body, otherwise called "the inner man," or simply "the soul"—would answer, not as Celsus makes us answer, but as the man of God himself teaches. It is certain also that a Christian will not make use of "the language of the flesh," having learnt as he has "to mortify the deeds of the body" by the spirit, and "to bear about in his body the dying of Jesus;" and "mortify your members which are on the earth," and with a true knowledge of these words, "My spirit shall not always strive with man, for that he also is flesh," and again, "They that are in the flesh cannot please God," he strives in every way to live no longer according to the flesh, but only according to the Spirit.

CHAPTER XXXIX

Now let us hear what it is that he invites us to learn, that we may ascertain from him how we are to know God, although he thinks that his words are beyond the capacity of all Christians. "Let them hear," says he, "if they are able to do so." We have then to consider what the philosopher wishes us to hear from him. But instead of instructing us as he ought, he abuses us; and while he should have shown his goodwill to those whom he addresses at the outset of his discourse, he stigmatizes as "a cowardly race" men who would rather die than abjure Christianity even by a word, and who are ready to suffer every form of torture, or any kind of death. He also applies to us that epithet "carnal" or "flesh-indulging," "although," as we are wont to say, "we have known Christ after the flesh, yet now henceforth we know Him no more," and although we are so ready to lay down our lives for the cause of religion, that no philosopher could lay aside his robes more readily. He then addresses to us these words: "If, instead of exercising your senses, you look upwards with the soul; if, turning away the eye of the body, you open the eye of the mind, thus and thus only you will be able to see God." He is not aware that this reference to the two eyes, the eye of the body and the eye of the mind, which he has borrowed from the Greeks, was in use among our own writers; for Moses, in his account of the creation of the world, introduces man before his transgression as both seeing and not seeing: seeing, when it is said of the woman, "The woman saw that the tree was good for food, and that it was pleasant to the eyes, and a tree to be desired to make one wise;" and again not seeing, as when he introduces the serpent saying to the woman, as if she and her husband had been blind, "God knows that on the day that ye eat thereof your eyes shall be opened;" and also when it is said, "They did eat, and the eyes of both of them were opened."

The eyes of sense were then opened, which they had done well to keep shut, that they might not be distracted, and hindered from seeing with the eyes of the mind; and it was those eyes of the mind which in consequence of sin, as I imagine, were then closed, with which they had up to that time enjoyed the delight of beholding God and His paradise. This twofold kind of vision in us was familiar to our Saviour, who says, "For judgment I am come into this world, that they which see not, might see, and that they which see might be made blind,"—meaning, by the eyes that see not, the eyes of the mind, which are enlightened by His teaching; and the eyes which see are the eyes of sense, which His words do render blind, in order that the soul may look without distraction upon proper objects. All true Christians therefore have the eye of the mind sharpened, and the eye of sense closed; so that each one, according to the degree in which his better eye is quickened, and the eye of sense darkened, sees and knows the Supreme God, and His Son, who is the Word, Wisdom, and so forth.

CHAPTER XL

Next to the remarks of Celsus on which we have already commented, come others which he addresses to all Christians, but which, if applicable to any, ought to be addressed to persons whose doctrines differ entirely from those taught by Jesus. For it is the Ophians who, as we have before shown, have utterly renounced Jesus, and perhaps some others of similar opinions who are "the impostors and jugglers, leading men away to idols and phantoms;" and it is they who with miserable pains learn off the names of the heavenly doorkeepers. These words are therefore quite inappropriate as addressed to Christians: "If you seek one to be your guide along this way, you must shun all deceivers and jugglers, who will introduce you to phantoms." And, as though quite unaware that these impostors entirely agree with him, and are not behind him in speaking ill of Jesus and His religion, he thus continues, confounding us with them: "otherwise you will be acting the most ridiculous part, if, whilst you pronounce imprecations upon those other recognised gods, treating them as idols, you yet do homage to a more wretched idol than any of these, which indeed is not even an idol or a phantom, but a dead man, and you seek a father like to himself." That he is ignorant of the wide difference between our opinions and those of the inventors of these fables, and that he imagines the charges which he makes against them applicable to us, is evident from the following passage: "For the sake of such a monstrous delusion, and in support of those wonderful advisers, and those wonderful words which you address to the lion, to the amphibious creature, to the creature in the form of an ass, and to others, for the sake of those divine doorkeepers whose names you commit to memory with such pains, in such a cause as this you suffer cruel tortures, and perish at the stake." Surely, then, he is unaware that none of those who regard beings in the form of an ass, a lion, or an amphibious animal, as the doorkeepers or guides on the way to heaven, ever expose themselves to death in defence of that which they think the truth. That excess of zeal, if it may be so called, which leads us for the sake of religion to submit to every kind of death, and to perish at the stake, is ascribed by Celsus to those who endure no such sufferings; and he reproaches us who suffer crucifixion for our faith, with believing in fabulous creatures—in the lion, the amphibious animal, and other such monsters. If we reject all these fables, it is not out of deference to Celsus, for we have never at any time held any such fancies; but it is in accordance with the teaching of Jesus that we oppose all such notions, and will not allow to Michael, or to any others that have been referred to, a form and figure of that sort.

CHAPTER XLI

But let us consider who those persons are whose guidance Celsus would have us to follow, so that we may not be in want of guides who are recommended both by their antiquity and sanctity. He refers us to divinely inspired poets, as he calls them, to wise men and philosophers, without mentioning their names; so that, after promising to point out those who should guide us, he simply hands us over in a general way to divinely inspired poets, wise men, and philosophers. If he had specified their names in particular, we should have felt ourselves bound to show him that he wished to give us as guides men who were blinded to the truth, and who must therefore lead us into error; or that if not wholly blinded, yet they are in error in many matters of belief. But whether Orpheus, Parmenides, Empedocles, or even Homer himself, and Hesiod, are the persons whom he means by "inspired poets," let any one show how those who follow their guidance walk in a better way, or lead a more excellent life, than those who, being taught in the school of Jesus Christ, have rejected all images and statues, and even all Jewish superstition, that they may look upward through the Word of God to the one God, who is the Father of the Word. Who, then, are those wise men and philosophers from whom Celsus would have us to learn so many divine truths, and for whom we are to give up Moses the servant of God, the prophets of the Creator of the world, who have spoken so many things by a truly divine inspiration, and even Him who has given light and taught the way of piety to the whole human race, so that no one can reproach Him if he remains without a share in the knowledge of His mysteries? Such, indeed, was the abounding love which He had for men, that He gave to the more learned a theology capable of raising the soul far above all earthly things; while with no less consideration He comes down to the weaker capacities of ignorant men, of simple women, of slaves, and, in short, of all those who from Jesus alone could have received that help for the better regulation of their lives which is supplied by his instructions in regard to the Divine Being, adapted to their wants and capacities.

CHAPTER XLII

Celsus next refers us to Plato as to a more effective teacher of theological truth, and quotes the following passage from the *Timaeus*: "It is a hard matter to find out the Maker and Father of this universe; and after having found Him, it is impossible to make Him known to all." To which he himself adds this remark: "You perceive, then, how divine men seek after the way of truth, and how well Plato knew that it was impossible for all men to walk in it. But as wise men have found it for the express purpose of being able to convey to us some notion of Him who is the first, the unspeakable Being,—a notion, namely; which may represent Him to us through the medium of other objects,—they endeavour either by synthesis, which is the combining of various qualities, or by analysis, which is the separation and setting aside of some qualities, or finally by analogy;—in these ways, I say, they endeavour to set before us that which it is impossible to express in words. I should therefore be surprised if you could follow in that course, since you are so completely wedded to the flesh as to be incapable of seeing ought but what is impure." These words of Plato are noble and admirable; but see if Scripture does not give us an example of a regard for mankind still greater in God the Word, who was "in the beginning with God," and "who was made flesh," in order that He might reveal to all men truths which, according to Plato, it would be impossible to make known to all men, even after he had found them himself. Plato may say that "it is a hard thing to find out the Creator and Father of this universe;" by which language he implies that it is not wholly beyond the power of human nature to attain to such a knowledge as is either worthy of God, or if not, is far beyond that which is commonly attained (although if it were true that Plato or any other of the Greeks had found God, they would never have given homage and worship, or ascribed the name of God, to any other than to Him: they would have abandoned all others, and would not have associated with this great God objects which can have nothing in common with Him). For ourselves, we maintain that human nature is in no way able to seek after God, or to attain a clear knowledge of Him without the help of Him whom it seeks. He makes Himself known to those who, after doing all that their powers will allow, confess that they need help from Him, who discovers Himself to those whom He approves, in so far as it is possible for man and the soul still dwelling in the body to know God.

CHAPTER XLIII

Observe that when Plato says, that "after having found out the Creator and Father of the universe, it is impossible to make Him known to all men," he does not speak of Him as unspeakable, and as incapable of being expressed in words. On the contrary, he implies that He may be spoken of, and that there are a few to whom He may be made known. But Celsus, as if forgetting the language which he had just quoted from Plato, immediately gives God the name of "the unspeakable." He says: "since the wise men have found out this way, in order to be able to give us some idea of the First of Beings, who is unspeakable." For ourselves, we hold that not God alone is unspeakable, but other things also which are inferior to Him. Such are the things which Paul labours to express when he says, "I heard unspeakable words, which it is not lawful for a man to utter," where the word "heard" is used in the sense of "understood;" as in the passage, "He who hath ears to hear, let him hear." We also hold that it is a hard matter to see the Creator and Father of the universe; but it is possible to see Him in the way thus referred to, "Blessed are the pure in heart, for they shall see God;" and not only so, but also in the sense of the words of Him "who is the image of the invisible God;" "He who hath seen Me hath seen the Father who sent Me." No sensible person could suppose that these last words were spoken in reference to His bodily presence, which was open to the view of all; otherwise all those who said, "Crucify him, crucify him," and Pilate, who had power over the humanity of Jesus, were among those who saw God the Father, which is absurd. Moreover, that these words, "He that hath seen Me, hath seen the Father who sent Me," are not to be taken in their grosser sense, is plain from the answer which He gave to Philip, "Have I been so long time with you, and yet dost thou not know Me, Philip?" after Philip had asked, "Show us the Father, and it sufficeth us." He, then, who perceives how these words, "The Word was made flesh," are to be understood of the only-begotten Son of God, the first-born of all creation, will also understand how, in seeing the image of the invisible God, we see "the Creator and Father of the universe."

CHAPTER XLIV

Celsus supposes that we may arrive at a knowledge of God either by combining or separating certain things after the methods which mathematicians call synthesis and analysis, or again by analogy, which is employed by them also, and that in this way we may as it were gain admission to the chief good. But when the Word of God says, "No man knoweth the Father but the Son, and he to whomsoever the Son will reveal Him," He declares that no one can know God but by the help of divine grace coming from above, with a certain divine inspiration. Indeed, it is reasonable to suppose that the knowledge of God is beyond the reach of human nature, and hence the many errors into which men have fallen in their views of God. It is, then, through the goodness and love of God to mankind, and by a marvellous exercise of divine grace to those whom He saw in His foreknowledge, and knew that they would walk worthy of Him who had made Himself known to them, and that they would never swerve from a faithful attachment to His service, although they were condemned to death or held up to ridicule by those who, in ignorance of what true religion is, give that name to what deserves to be called anything rather than religion. God doubtless saw the pride and arrogance of those who, with contempt for all others, boast of their knowledge of God, and of their profound acquaintance with divine things obtained from philosophy, but who still, not less even than the most ignorant, run after their images, and temples, and famous mysteries; and seeing this, He "has chosen the foolish things of this world"—the simplest of Christians, who lead, however, a life of greater moderation and purity than many philosophers—"to confound the wise," who are not ashamed to address inanimate things as gods or images of the gods. For what reasonable man can refrain from smiling when he sees that one who has learned from philosophy such profound and noble sentiments about God or the gods, turns straightway to images and offers to them his prayers, or imagines that by gazing upon these material things he can ascend from the visible symbol to that which is spiritual and immaterial. But a Christian, even of the common people, is assured that every place forms part of the universe, and that the whole universe is God's temple. In whatever part of the world he is, he prays; but he rises above the universe, "shutting the eyes of sense, and raising upwards the eyes of the soul." And he stops not at the vault of heaven; but passing in thought beyond the heavens, under the guidance of the Spirit of God, and having thus as it were gone beyond the visible universe, he offers prayers to God. But he prays for no trivial blessings, for he has learnt from Jesus to seek for nothing small or mean, that is, sensible objects, but to ask only for what is great and truly divine; and these things God grants to us, to lead us to that blessedness which is found only with Him through His Son, the Word, who is God.

CHAPTER XLV

But let us see further what the things are which he proposes to teach us, if indeed we can comprehend them, since he speaks of us as being "utterly wedded to the flesh;" although if we live well, and in accordance with the teaching of Jesus, we hear this said of us: "Ye are not in the flesh, but in the Spirit, if the Spirit of God dwelleth in you." He says also that we look upon nothing that is pure, although our endeavour is to keep even our thoughts free from all defilement of sin, and although in prayer we say, "Create in me a clean heart, O God, and renew a right spirit within me," so that we may behold Him with that "pure heart" to which alone is granted the privilege of seeing Him. This, then, is what he proposes for our instruction: "Things are either *intelligible*, which we call substance—being; or *visible*, which we call *becoming*: with the former is truth; from the latter arises error. Truth is the object of knowledge; truth and error form opinion. Intelligible objects are known by the reason, visible objects by the eyes; the action of the reason is called intelligent perception, that of the eyes vision. As, then, among visible things the sun is neither the eye nor vision, but that which enables the eye to see, and renders vision possible, and in consequence of it visible things are seen, all sensible things exist and itself is rendered visible; so among things intelligible, that which is neither reason, nor intelligent perception, nor knowledge, is yet the cause which enables the reason to know, which renders intelligent perception possible; and in consequence of it knowledge arises, all things intelligible, truth itself and substance have their existence; and itself, which is above all these things, becomes in some ineffable way intelligible. These things are offered to the consideration of the intelligent; and if even you can understand any of them, it is well. And if you think that a Divine Spirit has descended from God to announce divine things to men, it is doubtless this same Spirit that reveals these truths, and it was under the same influence that men of old made known many important truths. But if you cannot comprehend these things, then keep silence; do not expose your own ignorance, and do not accuse of blindness those who see, or of lameness those who run, while you yourselves are utterly lamed and mutilated in mind, and lead a merely animal life—the life of the body, which is the dead part of our nature."

CHAPTER XLVI

We are careful not to oppose fair arguments even if they proceed from those who are not of our faith; we strive not to be captious, or to seek to overthrow any sound reasonings. But here we have to reply to those who slander the character of persons wishing to do their best in the service of God, who accepts the faith which the meanest place in Him, as well as the more refined and intelligent piety of the learned; seeing that both alike address to the Creator of the world their prayers and thanksgivings through the High Priest who has set before men the nature of pure religion. We say, then, that those who are stigmatized as "lamed and mutilated in spirit," as "living only for the sake of the body which is dead," are persons whose endeavour it is to say with sincerity: "For though we live in the flesh, we do not war according to the flesh; for the weapons of our warfare are not fleshly, but mighty through God." It is for those who throw out such vile accusations against men who desire to be God's servants, to beware lest, by the calumnies which they cast upon others who strive to live well, they "lame" their own souls, and "mutilate" the inner man, by severing from it that justice and moderation of mind which the Creator has planted in the nature of all His rational creatures. As for those, however, who, along with other lessons given by the Divine Word, have learned and practised this, "when reviled to bless, when persecuted to endure, when defamed to entreat," they may be said to be walking in spirit in the ways of uprightness, to be purifying and setting in order the whole soul. They distinguish—and to them the distinction is not one of words merely—between "substance," or that which is, and that which is "becoming;" between things apprehended by reason, and things apprehended by sense; and they connect truth with the one, and avoid the errors arising out of the other; looking, as they have been taught, not at the things "becoming" or phenomenal, which are seen, and therefore temporary, but at better things than these, whether we call them "substance," or "spiritual" things, as being apprehended by reason, or "invisible," because they lie out of the reach of the senses. The disciples of Jesus regard these phenomenal things only that they may use them as steps to ascend to the knowledge of the things of reason. For "the invisible things of God," that is, the objects of the reason, "from the creation of the world are clearly seen" by the reason, "being understood by the things that are made." And when they have risen from the created things of this world to the invisible things of God, they do not stay there; but after they have sufficiently exercised their minds upon these, and have understood their nature, they ascend to "the eternal power of God," in a word, to His divinity. For they know that God, in His love to men, has "manifested" His truth, and "that which is known of Him," not only to those who devote themselves to His service, but also to some who are far removed from the purity of worship and service which He requires; and that some of those who by the providence of God had attained a knowledge of these truths, were yet doing things unworthy of that knowledge, and "holding the truth in unrighteousness," and who are unable to find any excuse before God after the knowledge of such great truths which He has given them.

CHAPTER XLVII

For Scripture testifies, in regard to those who have a knowledge of those things of which Celsus speaks, and who profess a philosophy founded on these principles, that they, "when they knew God, glorified Him not as God, neither were thankful, but became vain in their imaginations;" and notwithstanding the bright light of knowledge with which God had enlightened them, "their foolish heart" was carried away, and became "darkened." Thus we may see how those who accounted themselves wise gave proofs of great folly, when, after such grand arguments delivered in the schools on God and on things apprehended by the reason, they "changed the glory of the incorruptible God into an image made like to corruptible man, and to birds, and four-footed beasts, and creeping things." As, then, they lived in a way unworthy of the knowledge which they had received from God, His providence leaving them to themselves, they were given "up to uncleanness, through the lusts of their own hearts to dishonour their own bodies," in shamelessness and licentiousness, because they "changed the truth of God into a lie, and worshipped and served the creature more than the Creator."

CHAPTER XLVIII

But those who are despised for their ignorance, and set down as fools and abject slaves, no sooner commit themselves to God's guidance by accepting the teaching of Jesus, than, so far from defiling themselves by licentious indulgence or the gratification of shameless passion, they in many cases, like perfect priests, for whom such pleasures have no charm, keep themselves in act and in thought in a state of virgin purity. The Athenians have one hierophant, who, not having confidence in his power to restrain his passions within the limits he prescribed for himself, determined to check them at their seat by the application of hemlock; and thus he was accounted pure, and fit for the celebration of religious worship among the Athenians. But among Christians may be found men who have no need of hemlock to fit them for the pure service of God, and for whom the Word in place of hemlock is able to drive all evil desires from their thoughts, so that they may present their prayers to the Divine Being. And attached to the other so-called gods are a select number of virgins, who are guarded by men, or it may be not guarded (for that is not the point in question at present), and who are supposed to live in purity for the honour of the god they serve. But among Christians, those who maintain a perpetual virginity do so for no human honours, for no fee or reward, from no motive of vainglory; but "as they choose to retain God in their knowledge," they are preserved by God in a spirit well-pleasing to Him, and in the discharge of every duty, being filled with all righteousness and goodness.

CHAPTER XLIX

What I have now said, then, is offered not for the purpose of cavilling with any right opinions or sound doctrines held even by Greeks, but with the desire of showing that the same things, and indeed much better and diviner things than these, have been said by those divine men, the prophets of God and the apostles of Jesus. These truths are fully investigated by all who wish to attain a perfect knowledge of Christianity, and who know that "the mouth of the righteous speaketh wisdom, and his tongue talketh of judgment; the law of his God is in his heart." But even in regard to those who, either from deficiency or knowledge or want of inclination, or from not having Jesus to lead them to a rational view of religion, have not gone into these deep questions, we find that they believe in the Most High God, and in His Only-begotten Son, the Word and God, and that they often exhibit in their character a high degree of gravity, of purity, and integrity; while those who call themselves wise have despised these virtues, and have wallowed in the filth of sodomy, in lawless lust, "men with men working that which is unseemly."

CHAPTER L

Celsus has not explained how error accompanies the "becoming," or product of generation; nor has he expressed himself with sufficient clearness to enable us to compare his ideas with ours, and to pass judgment on them. But the prophets, who have given some wise suggestions on the subject of things produced by generation, tell us that a sacrifice for sin was offered even for new-born infants, as not being free from sin. They say, "I was shapen in iniquity, and in sin did my mother conceive me;" also, "They are estranged from the womb;" which is followed by the singular expression, "They go astray as soon as they are born, speaking lies." Besides, our wise men have such a contempt for all sensible objects, that sometimes they speak of all material things as vanity: thus, "For the creature was made subject to vanity, not willingly, but by reason of him that subjected the same in hope;" at other times as vanity of vanities, "Vanity of vanities, saith the Preacher, all is vanity." Who has given so severe an estimate of the life of the human soul here on earth, as he who says: "Verily every man at his best estate is altogether vanity?" He does not hesitate at all as to the difference between the present life of the soul and that which it is to lead hereafter. He does not say, "Who knows if to die is not to live, and if to live is not death" But he boldly proclaims the truth, and says, "Our soul is bowed down to the dust;" and, "Thou hast brought me into the dust of death;" and similarly, "Who will deliver me from the body of this death?" also, "Who will change the body of our humiliation." It is a prophet also who says, "Thou hast brought us down in a place of affliction;" meaning by the "place of affliction" this earthly region, to which Adam, that is to say, man, came after he was driven out of paradise for sin. Observe also how well the different life of the soul here and hereafter has been recognised by him who says, "Now we see in a glass, obscurely, but then face to face;" and, "Whilst we are in our home in the body, we are away from our home in the Lord;" wherefore "we are well content to go from our home in the body, and to come to our home with the Lord."

CHAPTER LI

But what need is there to quote any more passages against Celsus, in order to prove that his words contain nothing which was not said long before among themselves, since that has been sufficiently established by what we have said? It seems that what follows has some reference to this: "If you think that a Divine Spirit has descended from God to announce divine things to men, it is doubtless this same Spirit that reveals these truths; and it was under the same influence that men of old made known many important truths." But he does not know how great is the difference between those things and the clear and certain teaching of those who say to us, "Thine incorruptible spirit is in all things, wherefore God chasteneth them by little and little that offend;" and of those who, among their other instructions, teach us that words, "Receive ye the Holy Ghost," refer to a degree of spiritual influence higher than that in the passage, "Ye shall be baptized with the Holy Ghost not many days hence." But it is a difficult matter, even after much careful consideration, to perceive the difference between those who have received a knowledge of the truth and a notion of God at different intervals and for short periods of time, and those who are more fully inspired by God, who have constant communion with Him, and are always led by His Spirit. Had Celsus set himself to understand this, he would not have reproached as with ignorance, or forbidden us to characterize as "blind" those who believe that religion shows itself in such products of man's mechanical art as images. For every one who sees with the eyes of his soul serves the Divine Being in no other way than in that which leads him ever to have regard to the Creator of all, to address his prayers to Him alone, and to do all things as in the sight of God, who sees us altogether, even to our thoughts. Our earnest desire then is both to see for ourselves, and to be leaders of the blind, to bring them to the Word of God, that He may take away from their minds the blindness of ignorance. And if our actions are worthy of Him who taught His disciples, "Ye are the light of the world," and of the Word, who says, "The light shineth in darkness," then we shall be light to those who are in darkness; we shall give wisdom to those who are without it, and we shall instruct the ignorant.

CHAPTER LII

And let not Celsus be angry if we describe as lame and mutilated in soul those who run to the temples as to places having a real sacredness and who cannot see that no mere mechanical work of man can be truly sacred. Those whose piety is grounded on the teaching of Jesus also run until they come to the end of their course, when they can say in all truth and confidence: "I have fought a good fight, I have finished my course, I have kept the faith; henceforth there is laid up for me a crown of righteousness." And each of us runs "not as uncertain," and he so fights with evil "not as one beating the air," but as against those who are subject to "the prince of the power of the air, the spirit that now worketh in the children of disobedience." Celsus may indeed say of us that we "live with the body which is a dead thing;" but we have learnt, "If ye live after the flesh, ye shall die; but if ye by the Spirit do mortify the deeds of the body, ye shall live;" and, "If we live in the Spirit, let us also walk in the Spirit." Would that we might convince him by our actions that he did us wrong, when he said that we "live with the body which is dead!"

CHAPTER LIII

After these remarks of Celsus, which we have done our best to refute, he goes on to address us thus: "Seeing you are so eager for some novelty, how much better it would have been if you had chosen as the object of your zealous homage some one of those who died a glorious death, and whose divinity might have received the support of some myth to perpetuate his memory! Why, if you were not satisfied with Hercules or Aesculapius, and other heroes of antiquity, you had Orpheus, who was confessedly a divinely inspired man, who died a violent death. But perhaps some others have taken him up before you. You may then take Anaxarchus, who, when cast into a mortar, and beaten most barbarously, showed a noble contempt for his suffering, and said, 'Beat, beat the shell of Anaxarchus, for himself you do not beat,'—a speech surely of a spirit truly divine. But others were before you in following his interpretation of the laws of nature. Might you not, then, take Epictetus, who, when his master was twisting his leg, said, smiling and. unmoved, 'You will break my leg;' and when it was broken, he added, 'Did I not tell you that you would break it?' What saying equal to these did your god utter under suffering? If you had said even of the Sibyl, whose authority some of you acknowledge, that she was a child of God, you would have said something more reasonable. But you have had the presumption to include in her writings many impious things, and set up as a god one who ended a most infamous life by a most miserable death. How much more suitable than he would have been Jonah in the whale's belly, or Daniel delivered from the wild beasts, or any of a still more portentous kind!"

CHAPTER LIV

But since he sends us to Hercules, let him repeat to us any of his sayings, and let him justify his shameful subjection to Omphale. Let him show that divine honours should be paid to one who, like a highway robber, carries off a farmer's ox by force, and afterwards devours it, amusing himself meanwhile with the curses of the owner; in memory of which even to this day sacrifices offered to the demon of Hercules are accompanied with curses. Again he proposes Aesculapius to us, as if to oblige us to repeat what we have said already; but we forbear. In regard to Orpheus, what does he admire in him to make him assert that, by common consent, he was regarded as a divinely inspired man, and lived a noble life? I am greatly deceived if it is not the desire which Celsus has to oppose us and put down Jesus that leads him to sound forth the praises of Orpheus; and whether, when he made himself acquainted with his impious fables about the gods, he did not cast them aside as deserving, even more than the poems of Homer, to be excluded from a well-ordered state. For, indeed, Orpheus says much worse things than Homer of those whom they call gods. Noble, indeed, it was in Anaxarchus to say to Aristocreon, tyrant of Cyprus, "Beat on, beat the shell of Anaxarchus," but it is the one admirable incident in the life of Anaxarchus known to the Greeks; and although, on the strength of that, some like Celsus might deservedly honour the man for his courage, yet to look up to Anaxarchus as a god is not consistent with reason. He also directs us to Epictetus, whose firmness is justly admired, although his saying when his leg was broken by his master is not to be compared with the marvellous acts and words of Jesus which Celsus refuses to believe; and these words were accompanied by such a divine power, that even to this day they convert not only some of the more ignorant and simple, but many also of the most enlightened of men.

CHAPTER LV

When, to his enumeration of those to whom he would send us, he adds, "What saying equal to these did your god utter under sufferings?" we would reply, that the silence of Jesus under scourgings, and amidst all His sufferings, spoke more for His firmness and submission than all that was said by the Greeks when beset by calamity. Perhaps Celsus may believe what was recorded with all sincerity by trustworthy men, who, while giving a truthful account of all the wonders performed by Jesus, specify among these the silence which He preserved when subjected to scourgings; showing the same singular meekness under the insults which were heaped upon Him, when they put upon Him the purple robe, and set the crown of thorns upon His head, and when they put in His hand a reed in place of a sceptre: no unworthy or angry word escaped Him against those who subjected Him to such outrages. Since, then, He received the scourgings with silent firmness, and bore with meekness all the insults of those who outraged Him, it cannot be said, as is said by some, that it was in cowardly weakness that He uttered the words: "Father, if it be possible, let this cup pass from Me: nevertheless, not as I will, but as Thou wilt." The prayer which seems to be contained in these words for the removal of what He calls "the cup" bears a sense which we have elsewhere examined and set forth at large. But taking it in its more obvious sense, consider if it be not a prayer offered to God with all piety. For no man naturally regards anything which may befall him as necessary and inevitable; though he may submit to what is not inevitable, if occasion requires. Besides, these words, "nevertheless, not as I will, but as Thou wilt," are not the language of one who yielded to necessity, but of one who was contented with what was befalling Him, and who submitted with reverence to the arrangements of Providence.

CHAPTER LVI

Celsus then adds, for what reason I know not, that instead of calling Jesus the Son of God, we had better have given that honour to the Sibyl, in whose books he maintains we have interpolated many impious statements, though he does not mention what those interpolations are. He might have proved his assertion by producing some older copies which are free from the interpolations which he attributes to us; but he does not do so even to justify his statement that these passages are of an impious character. Moreover, he again speaks of the life of Jesus as "a most infamous life," as he has done before, not once or twice, but many times, although he does not stay to specify any of the actions of His life which he thinks most infamous. He seems to think that he may in this way make assertions without proving them, and rail against one of whom he knows nothing. Had he set himself to show what sort of infamy he found in the actions of Jesus, we should have repelled the several charges brought against Him. Jesus did indeed meet with a most sad death; but the same might be said of Socrates, and of Anaxarchus, whom he had just mentioned, and a multitude of others. If the death of Jesus was a miserable one, was not that of the others so too? And if their death was not miserable, can it be said that the death of Jesus was? You see from this, then, that the object of Celsus is to vilify the character of Jesus; and I can only suppose that he is driven to it by some spirit akin to those whose power has been broken and vanquished by Jesus, and which now finds itself deprived of the smoke and blood on which it lived, whilst deceiving those who sought for God here upon earth in images, instead of looking up to the true God, the Governor of all things.

CHAPTER LVII

After this, as though his object was to swell the size of his book, he advises us "to choose Jonah rather than Jesus as our God;" thus setting Jonah, who preached repentance to the single city of Nineveh, before Jesus, who has preached repentance to the whole world, and with much greater results. He would have us to regard as God a man who, by a strange miracle, passed three days and three nights in the whale's belly; and he is unwilling that He who submitted to death for the sake of men, He to whom God bore testimony through the prophets, and who has done great things in heaven and earth, should receive on that ground honour second only to that which is given to the Most High God. Moreover, Jonah was swallowed by the whale for refusing to preach as God had commanded him; while Jesus suffered death for men after He had given the instructions which God wished Him to give. Still further, he adds that Daniel rescued from the lions is more worthy of our adoration than Jesus, who subdued the fierceness of every opposing power, and gave to us "authority to tread on serpents and scorpions, and over all the power of the enemy." Finally, having no other names to offer us, he adds, "and others of a still more monstrous kind," thus casting a slight upon both Jonah and Daniel, for the spirit which is in Celsus cannot speak well of the righteous.

CHAPTER LVIII

Let us now consider what follows. "They have also," says he, "a precept to this effect, that we ought not to avenge ourselves on one who injures us, or, as he expresses it, 'Whosoever shall strike thee on the one cheek, turn to him the other also.' This is an ancient saying, which had been admirably expressed long before, and which they have only reported in a coarser way. For Plato introduces Socrates conversing with Crito as follows: 'Must we never do injustice to any?' 'Certainly not.' 'And since we must never do injustice, must we not return injustice for an injustice that has been done to us, as most people think?' 'It seems to me that we should not.' 'But tell me, Crito, may we do evil to any one or not?' 'Certainly not, O Socrates.' 'Well, is it just, as is commonly said, for one who has suffered wrong to do wrong in return, or is it unjust?' 'It is unjust. Yes; for to do harm to a man is the same as to do him injustice.' 'You speak truly. We must then not do injustice in return for injustice, nor must we do evil to any one, whatever evil we may have suffered from him.' Thus Plato speaks; and he adds, 'Consider, then, whether you are at one with me, and whether, starting from this principle, we may not come to the conclusion that it is never right to do injustice, even in return for an injustice which has been received; or whether, on the other hand, you differ from me, and do not admit the principle from which we started. That has always been my opinion, and is so still.' Such are the sentiments of Plato, and indeed they were held by divine men before his time. But let this suffice as one example of the way in which this and other truths have been borrowed and corrupted. Any one who wishes can easily by searching find more of them."

CHAPTER LIX

When Celsus here or elsewhere finds himself unable to dispute the truth of what we say, but avers that the same things were said by the Greeks, our answer is, that if the doctrine be sound, and the effect of it good, whether it was made known to the Greeks by Plato or any of the wise men of Greece, or whether it was delivered to the Jews by Moses or any of the prophets, or whether it was given to the Christians in the recorded teaching of Jesus Christ, or in the instructions of His apostles, that does not affect the value of the truth communicated. It is no objection to the principles of Jews or Christians, that the same things were also said by the Greeks, especially if it be proved that the writings of the Jews are older than those of the Greeks. And further, we are not to imagine that a truth adorned with the graces of Grecian speech is necessarily better than the same when expressed in the more humble and unpretending language used by Jews and Christians, although indeed the language of the Jews, in which the prophets wrote the books which have come down to us, has a grace of expression peculiar to the genius of the Hebrew tongue. And even if we were required to show that the same doctrines have been better expressed among the Jewish prophets or in Christian writings, however paradoxical it may seem, we are prepared to prove this by an illustration taken from different kinds of food, and from the different modes of preparing them. Suppose that a kind of food which is wholesome and nutritious has been prepared and seasoned in such a way as to be fit, not for the simple tastes of peasants and poor labourers, but for those only who are rich and dainty in their tastes. Suppose, again, that that same food is prepared not to suit the tastes of the more delicate, but for the peasants, the poor labourers, and the common people generally, in short, so that myriads of persons might eat of it. Now if, according to the supposition, the food prepared in the one way promotes the health of those only who are styled the better classes, while none of the others could taste it, whereas when prepared in the other way it promoted the health of great multitudes of men, which shall we esteem as most contributing to the public welfare,—those who prepare food for persons of mark, or those who prepare it for the multitudes?— taking for granted that in both cases the food is equally wholesome and nourishing; while it is evident that the welfare of mankind and the common good are promoted better by that physician who attends to the health of the many, than by one who confines his attention to a few.

CHAPTER LX

Now, after understanding this illustration, we have to apply it to the qualities of spiritual food with which the rational part of man is nourished. See, then, if Plato and the wise men among the Greeks, in the beautiful things they say, are not like those physicians who confine their attentions to what are called the better classes of society, and despise the multitude; whereas the prophets among the Jews, and the disciples of Jesus, who despise mere elegances of style, and what is called in Scripture "the wisdom of men," "the wisdom according to the flesh," which delights in what is obscure, resemble those who study to provide the most wholesome food for the largest number of persons. For this purpose they adapt their language and style to the capacities of the common people, and avoid whatever would seem foreign to them, lest by the introduction of strange forms of expression they should produce a distaste for their teaching. Indeed, if the true use of spiritual food, to keep up the figure, is to produce in him who partakes of it the virtues of patience and gentleness, must that discourse not be better prepared when it produces patience and gentleness in multitudes, or makes them grow in these virtues, than that which confines its effects to a select few, supposing that it does really make them gentle and patient? If a Greek wished by wholesome instruction to benefit people who understood only Egyptian or Syriac, the first thing that he would do would be to learn their language; and he would rather pass for a Barbarian among the Greeks, by speaking as the Egyptians or Syrians, in order to be useful to them, than always remain Greek, and be without the means of helping them. In the same way the divine nature, having the purpose of instructing not only those who are reputed to be learned in the literature of Greece, but also the rest of mankind, accommodated itself to the capacities of the simple multitudes whom it addressed. It seeks to win the attention of the more ignorant by the use of language which is familiar to them, so that they may easily be induced, after their first introduction, to strive after an acquaintance with the deeper truths which lie hidden in Scripture. For even the ordinary reader of Scripture may see that it contains many things which are too deep to be apprehended at first; but these are understood by such as devote themselves to a careful study of the divine word, and they become plain to them in proportion to the pains and zeal which they expend upon its investigation.

CHAPTER LXI

From these remarks it is evident, that when Jesus said "coarsely," as Celsus terms it, "To him who shall strike thee on the one cheek, turn the other also; and if any man be minded to sue thee at the law, and take away thy coat, let him have thy cloak also," He expressed Himself in such a way as to make the precept have more practical effect than the words of Plato in the *Crito*; for the latter is so far from being intelligible to ordinary persons, that even those have a difficulty in understanding him, who have been brought up in the schools of learning, and have been initiated into the famous philosophy of Greece. It may also be observed, that the precept enjoining patience under injuries is in no way corrupted or degraded by the plain and simple language which our Lord employs, but that in this, as in other cases, it is a mere calumny against our religion which he utters when he says: "But let this suffice as one example of the way in which this and other truths have been borrowed and corrupted. Any one who wishes can easily by searching find more of them."

CHAPTER LXII

Let us now see what follows. "Let us pass on," says he, "to another point. They cannot tolerate temples, altars, or images. In this they are like the Scythians, the nomadic tribes of Libya, the Seres who worship no god, and some other of the most barbarous and impious nations in the world. That the Persians hold the same notions is shown by Herodotus in these words: 'I know that among the Persians it is considered unlawful to erect images, altars, or temples; but they charge those with folly who do so, because, as I conjecture, they do not, like the Greeks, suppose the gods to be of the nature of men.' Heraclitus also says in one place: 'Persons who address prayers to these images act like those who speak to the walls, without knowing who the gods or the heroes are.' And what wiser lesson have they to teach us than Heraclitus? He certainly plainly enough implies that it is a foolish thing for a man to offer prayers to images, whilst he knows not who the gods and heroes are. This is the opinion of Heraclitus; but as for them, they go further, and despise without exception all images. If they merely mean that the stone, wood, brass, or gold which has been wrought by this or that workman cannot be a god, they are ridiculous with their wisdom. For who, unless he be utterly childish in his simplicity, can take these for gods, and not for offerings consecrated to the service of the gods, or images representing them? But if we are not to regard these as representing the Divine Being, seeing that God has a different form, as the Persians concur with them in saying, then let them take care that they do not contradict themselves; for they say that God made man His own image, and that He gave him a form like to Himself. However, they will admit that these images, whether they are like or not, are made and dedicated to the honour of certain beings. But they will hold that the beings to whom they are dedicated are not gods, but demons, and that a worshipper of God ought not to worship demons."

CHAPTER LXIII

To this our answer is, that if the Scythians, the nomadic tribes of Libya, the Seres, who according to Celsus have no god, if those other most barbarous and impious nations in the world, and if the Persians even cannot bear the sight of temples, altars, and images, it does not follow because we cannot suffer them any more than they, that the grounds on which we object to them are the same as theirs. We must inquire into the principles on which the objection to temples and images is founded, in order that we may approve of those who object on sound principles, and condemn those whose principles are false. For one and the same thing may be done for different reasons. For example, the philosophers who follow Zeno of Citium abstain from committing adultery, the followers of Epicurus do so too, as well as others again who do so on no philosophical principles; but observe what different reasons determine the conduct of these different classes. The first consider the interests of society, and hold it to be forbidden by nature that a man who is a reasonable being should corrupt a woman whom the laws have already given to another, and should thus break up the household of another man. The Epicureans do not reason in this way; but if they abstain from adultery, it is because, regarding pleasure as the chief end of man, they perceive that one who gives himself up to adultery, encounters for the sake of this one pleasure a multitude of obstacles to pleasure, such as imprisonment, exile, and death itself. They often, indeed, run considerable risk at the outset, while watching for the departure from the house of the master and those in his interest. So that, supposing it possible for a man to commit adultery, and escape the knowledge of the husband, of his servants, and of others whose esteem he would forfeit, then the Epicurean would yield to the commission of the crime for the sake of pleasure. The man of no philosophical system, again, who abstains from adultery when the opportunity comes to him, does so generally from dread of the law and its penalties, and not for the sake of enjoying a greater number of other pleasures. You see, then, that an act which passes for being one and the same—namely, abstinence from adultery—is not the same, but differs in different men according to the motives which actuate it: one man refraining for sound reasons, another for such bad and impious ones as those of the Epicurean, and the common person of whom we have spoken.

CHAPTER LXIV

As, then, this act of self-restraint, which in appearance is one and the same, is found in fact to be different in different persons, according to the principles and motives which lead to it; so in the same way with those who cannot allow in the worship of the Divine Being altars, or temples, or images. The Scythians, the Nomadic Libyans, the godless Seres, and the Persians, agree in this with the Christians and Jews, but they are actuated by very different principles. For none of these former abhor altars and images on the ground that they are afraid of degrading the worship of God, and reducing it to the worship of material things wrought by the hands of men. Neither do they object to them from a belief that the demons choose certain forms and places, whether because they are detained there by virtue of certain charms, or because for some other possible reason they have selected these haunts, where they may pursue their criminal pleasures, in partaking of the smoke of sacrificial victims. But Christians and Jews have regard to this command, "Thou shalt fear the LORD thy God, and serve Him alone;" and this other, "Thou shalt have no other gods before Me: thou shalt not make unto thee any graven image, or any likeness of anything that is in heaven above, or that is in the earth beneath, or that is in the water under the earth: thou shalt not bow down thyself to them, nor serve them;" and again, "Thou shalt worship the LORD thy God, and Him only shalt thou serve." It is in consideration of these and many other such commands, that they not only avoid temples, altars, and images, but are ready to suffer death when it is necessary, rather than debase by any such impiety the conception which they have of the Most High God.

CHAPTER LXV

In regard to the Persians, we have already said that though they do not build temples, yet they worship the sun and the other works of God. This is forbidden to us, for we have been taught not to worship the creature instead of the Creator, but to know that "the creation shall be delivered from the bondage of corruption into the liberty of the glory of the children of God;" and "the earnest expectation of the creation is waiting for the revelation of the sons of God;" and "the creation was made subject to vanity, not willingly, but by reason of him who made it subject, in hope." We believe, therefore, that things "under the bondage of corruption," and "subject to vanity," which remain in this condition "in hope" of a better state, ought not in our worship to hold the place of God, the all-sufficient, and of His Son, the First-born of all creation. Let this suffice, in addition to what we have already said of the Persians, who abhor altars and images, but who serve the creature instead of the Creator. As to the passage quoted by Celsus from Heraclitus, the purport of which he represents as being, "that it is childish folly for one to offer prayers to images, whilst he knows not who the gods and heroes are," we may reply that it is easy to know that God and the Only-begotten Son of God, and those whom God has honoured with the title of God, and who partake of His divine nature, are very different from all the gods of the nations which are demons; but it is not possible at the same time to know God and to address prayers to images.

CHAPTER LXVI

And the charge of folly applies not only to those who offer prayers to images, but also to such as pretend to do so in compliance with the example of the multitude: and to this class belong the Peripatetic philosophers and the followers of Epicurus and Democritus. For there is no falsehood or pretence in the soul which is possessed with true piety towards God. Another reason also why we abstain from doing honour to images, is that we may give no support to the notion that the images are gods. It is on this ground that we condemn Celsus, and all others who, while admitting that they are not gods, yet, with the reputation of being wise men, render to them what passes for homage.

In this way they lead into sin the multitude who follow their example, and who worship these images not simply out of deference to custom, but from a belief into which they have fallen that they are true gods, and that those are not to be listened to who hold that the objects of their worship are not true gods. Celsus, indeed, says that "they do not take them for gods, but only as offerings dedicated to the gods." But he does not prove that they are not rather dedicated to men than, as he says, to the honour of the gods themselves; for it is clear that they are the offerings of men who were in error in their views of the Divine Being. Moreover, we do not imagine that these images are representations of God, for they cannot represent a being who is invisible and incorporeal. But as Celsus supposes that we fall into a contradiction, whilst on the one hand we say that God has not a human form, and on the other we profess to believe that God made man the image of Himself, and created man the image of God; our answer is the same as has been given already, that we hold the resemblance to God to be preserved in the reasonable soul, which is formed to virtue, although Celsus, who does not see the difference between "being the image of God," and "being created after the image of God," pretends that we said, "God made man His own image, and gave him a form like to His own." But this also has been examined before.

CHAPTER LXVII

His next remark upon the Christians is: "They will admit that these images, whether they are like or not, are made and dedicated to the honour of certain beings; but they will hold that the beings to whom they are dedicated are not gods, but demons, and that a worshipper of God ought not to worship demons." If he had been acquainted with the nature of demons, and with their several operations, whether led on to them by the conjurations of those who are skilled in the art, or urged on by their own inclination to act according to their power and inclination; if, I say, he had thoroughly understood this subject, which is both wide in extent and difficult for human comprehension, he would not have condemned us for saying that those who worship the Supreme Being should not serve demons. For ourselves, so far are we from wishing to serve demons, that by the use of prayers and other means which we learn from Scripture, we drive them out of the souls of men, out of places where they have established themselves, and even sometimes from the bodies of animals; for even these creatures often suffer from injuries inflicted upon them by demons.

CHAPTER LXVIII

After all that we have already said concerning Jesus, it would be a useless repetition for us to answer these words of Celsus: "It is easy to convict them of worshipping not a god, not even demons, but a dead person." Leaving, then, this objection for the reason assigned, let us pass on to what follows: "In the first place, I would ask why we are not to serve demons? Is it not true that all things are ordered according to God's will, and that His providence governs all things? Is not everything which happens in the universe, whether it be the work of God, of angels, of other demons, or of heroes, regulated by the law of the Most High God? Have these not had assigned them various departments of which they were severally deemed worthy? Is it not just, therefore, that he who worships God should serve those also to whom God has assigned such power? Yet it is impossible, he says, for a man to serve many masters." Observe here again how he settles at once a number of questions which require considerable research, and a profound acquaintance with what is most mysterious in the government of the universe. For we must inquire into the meaning of the statement, that "all things are ordered according to God's will," and ascertain whether sins are or are not included among the things which God orders. For if God's government extends to sins not only in men, but also in demons and in any other spiritual beings who are capable of sin, it is for those who speak in this manner to see how inconvenient is the expression that "all things are ordered by the will of God." For it follows from it that all sins and all their consequences are ordered by the will of God, which is a different thing from saying that they come to pass with God's permission. For if we take the word "ordered" in its proper signification, and say that "all the results of sin were ordered," then it is evident that all things are ordered according to God's will, and that all, therefore, who do evil do not offend against His government. And the same distinction holds in regard to "providence." When we say that "the providence of God regulates all things," we utter a great truth if we attribute to that providence nothing but what is just and right. But if we ascribe to the providence of God all things whatsoever, however unjust they may be, then it is no longer true that the providence of God regulates all things, unless we refer directly to God's providence things which flow as results from His arrangements. Celsus maintains also, that "whatever happens in the universe, whether it be the work of God, of angels, of other demons, or of heroes, is regulated by the law of the Most High God." But this also is incorrect; for we cannot say that transgressors follow the law of God when they transgress; and Scripture declares that it is not only wicked men who are transgressors, but also wicked demons and wicked angels.

CHAPTER LXIX

And it is not we alone who speak of wicked demons, but almost all who acknowledge the existence of demons. Thus, then, it is not true that all observe the law of the Most High; for all who fall away from the divine law, whether through heedlessness, or through depravity and vice, or through ignorance of what is right, all such do not keep the law of God, but, to use a new phrase which we find in Scripture, "the law of sin." I say, then, that in the opinion of most of those who believe in the existence of demons, some of them are wicked; and these, instead of keeping the law of God, offend against it. But, according to our belief, it is true of all demons, that they were not demons originally, but they became so in departing from the true way; so that the name "demons" is given to those beings who have fallen away from God. Accordingly, those who worship God must not serve demons. We may also learn the true nature of demons if we consider the practice of those who call upon them by charms to prevent certain things, or for many other purposes. For this is the method they adopt, in order by means of incantations and magical arts to invoke the demons, and induce them to further their wishes. Wherefore, the worship of all demons would be inconsistent in us who worship the Supreme God; and the service of demons is the service of so-called gods, for "all the gods of the heathen are demons." The same thing also appears from the fact that the dedication of the most famous of the so-called sacred places, whether temples or statues, was accompanied by curious magical incantations, which were performed by those who zealously served the demons with magical arts. Hence we are determined to avoid the worship of demons even as we would avoid death; and we hold that the worship, which is supposed among the Greeks to be rendered to gods at the altars, and images, and temples, is in reality offered to demons.

CHAPTER LXX

His next remark was, "Have not these inferior powers had assigned to them by God different departments, according as each was deemed worthy?" But this is a question which requires a very profound knowledge. For we must determine whether the Word of God, who governs all things, has appointed wicked demons for certain employments, in the same way as in states exccutioners are appointed, and other officers with cruel but needful duties to discharge; or whether as among robbers, who infest desert places, it is customary for them to choose out of their number one who may be their leader,—so the demons, who are scattered as it were in troops in different parts of the earth, have chosen for themselves a chief under whose command they may plunder and pillage the souls of men. To explain this fully, and to justify the conduct of the Christians in refusing homage to any object except the Most High God, and the First-born of all creation, who is His Word and God, we must quote this from Scripture, "All that ever came before Me are thieves and robbers: but the sheep did not hear them;" and again, "The thief cometh not, but for to steal, and to kill, and to destroy;" and other similar passages, as, "Behold, I have given you authority to tread on serpents and scorpions, and over all the power of the enemy: and nothing shall by any means hurt you;" and again, "Thou shalt tread upon the lion and adder: the young lion and the dragon shalt thou trample under feet." But of these things Celsus knew nothing, or he would not have made use of language like this: "Is not everything which happens in the universe, whether it be the work of God, of angels, of other demons, or of heroes, regulated by the law of the Most High God? Have these not had assigned to them various departments of which they were severally deemed worthy? Is it not just, therefore, that he who serves God should serve those also to whom God has assigned such power?" To which he adds, "It is impossible, they say, for a man to serve many masters." This last point we must postpone to the next book; for this, which is the seventh book which we have written in answer to the treatise of Celsus, is already of sufficient length.

BOOK VIII

CHAPTER I

HAVING completed seven books, I now propose to begin the eighth. And may God and His Only-begotten Son the Word be with us, to enable us effectively to refute the falsehoods which Celsus has published under the delusive title of *A True Discourse*, and at the same time to unfold the truths of Christianity with such fulness as our purpose requires. And as Paul said, "We are ambassadors for Christ, as though God did beseech you by us," so would we in the same spirit and language earnestly desire to be ambassadors for Christ to men, even as the Word of God beseeches them to the love of Himself, seeking to win over to righteousness, truth, and the other virtues, those who, until they receive the doctrines of Jesus Christ, live in darkness about God and in ignorance of their Creator. Again, then, I would say, may God bestow upon us His pure and true Word, even "the Lord strong and mighty in battle" against sin. We must now proceed to state the next objection of Celsus, and afterwards to answer it.

CHAPTER II

In a passage previously quoted Celsus asks us why we do not worship demons, and to his remarks on demons we gave such an answer as seemed to us in accordance with the divine word. After having put this question for the purpose of leading us to the worship of demons, he represents us as answering that it is impossible to serve many masters. "This," he goes on to say, "is the language of sedition, and is only used by those who separate themselves and stand aloof from all human society. Those who speak in this way ascribe," as he supposes, "their own feelings and passions to God. It does hold true among men, that he who is in the service of one master cannot well serve another, because the service which he renders to the one interferes with that which he owes to the other; and no one, therefore, who has already engaged himself to the service of one, must accept that of another. And, in like manner, it is impossible to serve at the same time heroes or demons of different natures. But in regard to God, who is subject to no suffering or loss, it is," he thinks, "absurd to be on our guard against serving more gods, as though we had to do with demi-gods, or other spirits of that sort." He says also, "He who serves many gods does that which is pleasing to the Most High, because he honours

732

that which belongs to Him." And he adds, "It is indeed wrong to give honour to any to whom God has not given honour." "Wherefore," he says, "in honouring and worshipping all belonging to God, we will not displease Him to whom they all belong."

CHAPTER III

Before proceeding to the next point, it may be well for us to see whether we do not accept with approval the saying, "No man can serve two masters," with the addition, "for either he will hate the one, and love the other; or else he will hold to the one, and despise the other," and further, "Ye cannot serve God and mammon." The defence of this passage will lead us to a deeper and more searching inquiry into the meaning and application of the words "gods" and "lords." Divine Scripture teaches us that there is "a great LORD above all gods." And by this name "gods" we are not to understand the objects of heathen worship (for we know that "all the gods of the heathen are demons"), but the gods mentioned by the prophets as forming an assembly, whom God "judges," and to each of whom He assigns his proper work. For "God standeth in the assembly of the gods: He judgeth among the gods." For "God is Lord of gods," who by His Son "hath called the earth from the rising of the sun unto the going down thereof." We are also commanded to "give thanks to the God of gods." Moreover, we are taught that "God is not the God of the dead, but of the living." Nor are these the only passages to this effect; but there are very many others.

CHAPTER IV

The sacred Scriptures teach us to think, in like manner, of the Lord of lords. For they say in one place, "Give thanks to the God of gods, for His mercy endureth for ever. Give thanks to the Lord of lords, for His mercy endureth for ever;" and in another, "God is King of kings, and Lord of lords." For Scripture distinguishes between those gods which are such only in name and those which are truly gods, whether they are called by that name or not; and the same is true in regard to the use of the word "lords." To this effect Paul says, "For though there be that are called gods, whether in heaven or in earth, as there are gods many, and lords many." But as the God of gods calls whom He pleases through Jesus to his inheritance, "from the east and from the west," and the Christ of God thus shows His superiority to all rulers by entering into their several provinces, and summoning men out of them to be subject to Himself, Paul therefore, with this in view, goes on to say, "But to us there is but one God, the Father, of whom are all things, and one Lord Jesus Christ, by whom are all things, and we by Him;" adding, as if with a deep sense of the marvellous and mysterious nature of the doctrine, "Howbeit there is not in every man that knowledge." When he says, "To us there is but one God, the Father, of whom are all things; and one Lord Jesus Christ, by whom are all things," by "us" he means himself and all those who have risen up to the supreme God of gods and to the supreme Lord of lords. Now he has risen to the supreme God who gives Him an entire and undivided worship through His Son—the word and wisdom of God made manifest in Jesus. For it is the Son alone who leads to God those who are striving, by the purity of their thoughts, words, and deeds, to come near to God the Creator of the universe. I think, therefore, that the prince of this world, who "transforms himself into an angel of light," was referring to this and such like statements in the words, "Him follows a host of gods and demons, arranged in eleven bands." Speaking of himself and the philosophers, he says, "We are of the party of Jupiter; others belong to other demons."

CHAPTER V

Whilst there are thus many gods and lords, whereof some are such in reality, and others are such only in name, we strive to rise not only above those whom the nations of the earth worship as gods, but also beyond those spoken of as gods in Scripture, of whom they are wholly ignorant who are strangers to the covenants of God given by Moses and by our Saviour Jesus, and who have no part in the promises which He has made to us through them. That man rises above all demon-worship who does nothing that is pleasing to demons; and he rises to a blessedness beyond that of those whom Paul calls "gods," if he is enabled, like them, or in any way he may, "to look not at the things which are seen, but at the things which are unseen." And he who considers that "the earnest expectation of the creature waiteth for the manifestation of the sons of God, not willingly, but by reason of him who subjected the same in hope," whilst he praises the creature, and sees how "it shall be freed altogether from the bondage of corruption, and restored to the glorious liberty of the children of God,"—such a one cannot be induced to combine with the service of God the service of any other, or to serve two masters. There is therefore nothing seditious or factious in the language of those who hold these views, and who refuse to serve more masters than one. To them Jesus Christ is an all-sufficient Lord, who Himself instructs them, in order that when fully instructed He may form them into a kingdom worthy of God, and present them to God the Father. But indeed they do in a sense separate themselves and stand aloof from those who are aliens from the commonwealth of God and strangers to His covenants, in order that they may live as citizens of heaven, "coming to the living God, and to the city of God, the heavenly Jerusalem, and to an innumerable company of angels, to the general assembly and Church of the first-born, which are written in heaven."

CHAPTER VI

But when we refuse to serve any other than God through His word and wisdom, we do so, not as though we would thereby be doing any harm or injury to God, in the same way as injury would be done to a man by his servant entering into the service of another, but we fear that we ourselves should suffer harm by depriving ourselves of our portion in God, through which we live in the participation of the divine blessedness, and are imbued with that excellent spirit of adoption which in the sons of the heavenly Father cries, not with words, but with deep effect in the inmost heart, "Abba, Father." The Lacedaemonian ambassadors, when brought before the king of Persia, refused to prostrate themselves before him, when the attendants endeavoured to compel them to do so, out of respect for that which alone had authority and lordship over them, namely, the law of Lycurgus. But they who have a much greater and diviner embassy in "being ambassadors for Christ" should not worship any ruler among Persians, or Greeks or Egyptians, or of any nation whatever, even although their officers and ministers, demons and angels of the devil, should seek to compel them to do so, and should urge them to set at nought a law which is mightier than all the laws upon earth. For the Lord of those who are "ambassadors for Christ" is Christ Himself, whose ambassadors they are, and who is "the Word, who was in the beginning, was with God, and was God."

CHAPTER VII

But when Celsus speaks of heroes and demons, he starts a deeper question than he is aware of. For after the statement which he made in regard to service among men, that "the first master is injured when any of his servants wishes at the same time to serve another," he adds, that "the same holds true of heroes, and other demons of that kind." Now we must inquire of him what nature he thinks those heroes and demons possess of whom he affirms that he who serves one hero may not serve another, and he who serves one demon may not serve another, as though the former hero or demon would be injured in the same way as men are injured when they who serve them first afterwards give themselves to the service of others. Let him also state what loss he supposes those heroes or demons will suffer. For he will be driven either to plunge into endless absurdities, and first repeat, then retract his previous statements; or else to abandon his frivolous conjectures, and confess that he understands nothing of the nature of heroes and demons. And in regard to his statement, that men suffer injury when the servant of one man enters the service of a second master, the question arises: "What is the nature of the injury which is done to the former master by a servant who, while serving him, wishes at the same time to serve another?"

CHAPTER VIII

For if he answers, as one who is unlearned and ignorant of philosophy, that the injury sustained is one which regards things that are outside of us, it will be plainly manifest that he knows nothing of that famous saying of Socrates, "Anytus and Melitus may kill me, but they cannot injure me; for it is impossible that the better should ever be injured by the worse." But if by injury he means a wicked impulse or an evil habit, it is plain that no injury of this kind would befall the wise, by one man serving two wise men in different places. If this sense does not suit his purpose, it is evident that his endeavours are vain to weaken the authority of the passage, "No man can serve two masters;" for these words can be perfectly true only when they refer to the service which we render to the Most High through His Son, who leadeth us to God. And we will not serve God as though He stood in need of our service, or as though He would be made unhappy if we ceased to serve Him; but we do it because we are ourselves benefited by the service of God, and because we are freed from griefs and troubles by serving the Most High God through His only-begotten Son, the Word and Wisdom.

CHAPTER IX

And observe the recklessness of that expression, "For if thou worship any other of the things in the universe," as though he would have us believe that we are led by our service of God to the worship of any other things which belong to God, without any injury to ourselves.

But, as if feeling his error, he corrects the words, "If thou worship any other of the things in the universe," by adding, "We may honour none, however, except those to whom that right has been given by God." And we would put to Celsus this question in regard to those who are honoured as gods, as demons, or as heroes: "Now, sir, can you prove that the right to be honoured has been given to these by God, and that it has not arisen from the ignorance and folly of men who in their wanderings have fallen away from Him to whom alone worship and service are properly due? You said a little ago, O Celsus, that Antinous, the favourite of Adrian, is honoured; but surely you will not say that the right to be worshipped as a god was given to him by the God of the universe? And so of the others, we ask proof that the right to be worshipped was given to them by the Most High God." But if the same question is put to us in regard to the worship of Jesus, we will show that the right to be honoured was given to Him by God, "that all may honour the Son, even as they honour the Father." For all the prophecies which preceded His birth were preparations for His worship. And the wonders which He wrought—through no magical art, as Celsus supposes, but by a divine power, which was foretold by the prophets—have served as a testimony from God in behalf of the worship of Christ. He who honours the Son, who is the Word and Reason, acts in nowise contrary to reason, and gains for himself great good; he who honours Him, who is the Truth, becomes better by honouring truth: and this we may say of honouring wisdom, righteousness, and all the other names by which the sacred Scriptures are wont to designate the Son of God.

CHAPTER X

But that the honour which we pay to the Son of God, as well as that which we render to God the Father, consists of an upright course of life, is plainly taught us by the passage, "Thou that makest thy boast of the law, through breaking the law dishonourest thou God?" and also, "Of how much sorer punishment, suppose ye, shall he be thought worthy, who hath trodden under foot the Son of God, and hath counted the blood of the covenant, wherewith he was sanctified, an unholy thing, and hath done despite unto the Spirit of grace?" For if he who transgresses the law dishonours God by his transgression, and he who treads under foot the word treads under foot the Son of God, it is evident that he who keeps the law honours God, and that the worshipper of God is he whose life is regulated by the principles and precepts of the divine word. Had Celsus known who they are who are

God's people, and that they alone are wise,—and who they are who are strangers to God, and that these are all the wicked who have no desire to give themselves to virtue, he would have considered before he gave expression to the words, "How can he who honours any of those whom God acknowledges as His own be displeasing to God, to whom they all belong?"

CHAPTER XI

He adds, "And indeed he who, when speaking of God, asserts that there is only one who may be called Lord, speaks impiously, for he divides the kingdom of God, and raises a sedition therein, implying that there are separate factions in the divine kingdom, and that there exists one who is His enemy." He might speak after this fashion, if he could prove by conclusive arguments that those who are worshipped as gods by the heathens are truly gods, and not merely evil spirits, which are supposed to haunt statues and temples and altars. But we desire not only to understand the nature of that divine kingdom of which we are continually speaking and writing, but also ourselves to be of those who are under the rule of God alone, so that the kingdom of God may be ours. Celsus, however, who teaches us to worship many gods, ought in consistency not to speak of "the kingdom of God," but of "the kingdom of the gods." There are therefore no factions in the kingdom of God, nor is there any god who is an adversary to Him, although there are some who, like the Giants and Titans, in their wickedness wish to contend with God in company with Celsus, and those who declare war against Him who has by innumerable proofs established the claims of Jesus, and against Him who, as the Word, did, for the salvation of our race, show Himself before all the world in such a form as each was able to receive Him.

CHAPTER XII

In what follows, some may imagine that he says something plausible against us. "If," says he, "these people worshipped one God alone, and no other, they would perhaps have some valid argument against the worship of others. But they pay excessive reverence to one who has but lately appeared among men, and they think it no offence against God if they worship also His servant." To this we reply, that if Celsus had known that saying, "I and My Father are one," and the words used in prayer by the Son of God, "As Thou and I are one," he would not have supposed that we worship any other besides Him who is the

738

Supreme God. "For," says He, "My Father is in Me, and I in Him." And if any should from these words be afraid of our going over to the side of those who deny that the Father and the Son are two persons, let him weigh that passage, "And the multitude of them that believed were of one heart and of one soul," that he may understand the meaning of the saying, "I and My Father are one." We worship one God, the Father and the Son, therefore, as we have explained; and our argument against the worship of other gods still continues valid. And we do not "reverence beyond measure one who has but lately appeared," as though He did not exist before; for we believe Himself when He says, "Before Abraham was, I am." Again He says, "I am the truth;" and surely none of us is so simple as to suppose that truth did not exist before the time when Christ appeared. We worship, therefore, the Father of truth, and the Son, who is the truth; and these, while they are two, considered as persons or subsistences, are one in unity of thought, in harmony and in identity of will. So entirely are they one, that he who has seen the Son, "who is the brightness of God's glory, and the express image of His person," has seen in Him who is the image of God, God Himself.

CHAPTER XIII

He further supposes, that "because we join along with the worship of God the worship of His Son, it follows that, in our view, not only God, but also the servants of God, are to be worshipped." If he had meant this to apply to those who are truly the servants of God, after His only-begotten Son,—to Gabriel and Michael, and the other angels and archangels, and if he had said of these that they ought to be worshipped,—if also he had clearly defined the meaning of the word "worship," and the duties of the worshippers,—we might perhaps have brought forward such thoughts as have occurred to us on so important a subject. But as he reckons among the servants of God the demons which are worshipped by the heathen, he cannot induce us, on the plea of consistency, to worship such as are declared by the word to be servants of the evil one, the prince of this world, who leads astray from God as many as he can. We decline, therefore, altogether to worship and serve those whom other men worship, for the reason that they are not servants of God. For if we had been taught to regard them as servants of the Most High, we would not have called them demons. Accordingly, we worship with all our power the one God, and His only Son, the Word and the Image of God, by prayers and supplications; and we offer our petitions to the God of the universe through His only-begotten Son. To the Son we first present them, and beseech Him, as "the propitiation for our sins," and our High Priest, to offer our desires, and sacrifices, and prayers, to the Most High. Our faith, therefore, is directed to God through His Son, who strengthens it in us; and Celsus can never show that the Son of God is the cause of any sedition or disloyalty in the kingdom of God. We honour the Father when we admire His Son, the Word, and Wisdom, and Truth, and Righteousness, and all that He who is the Son of so great a Father is said in Scripture to be. So much on this point.

CHAPTER XIV

Again Celsus proceeds: "If you should tell them that Jesus is not the Son of God, but that God is the Father of all, and that He alone ought to be truly worshipped, they would not consent to discontinue their worship of him who is their leader in the sedition. And they call him Son of God, not out of any extreme reverence for God, but from an extreme desire to extol Jesus Christ." We, however, have learned who the Son of God is, and know that He is "the brightness of His glory, and the express image of His person," and "the breath of the power of God, and a pure influence flowing from the glory of the Almighty;" moreover, "the brightness of the everlasting light, the unspotted mirror of the power of God, and the image of His goodness." We know, therefore, that He is the Son of God, and that God is His father. And there is nothing extravagant or unbecoming the character of God in the doctrine that He should have begotten such an only Son; and no one will persuade us that such a one is not a Son of the unbegotten God and Father. If Celsus has heard something of certain persons holding that the Son of God is not the Son of the Creator of the universe, that is a matter which lies between him and the supporters of such an opinion. Jesus is, then, not the leader of any seditious movement, but the promoter of peace. For He said to His disciples, "Peace I leave with you, My peace I give unto you;" and as He knew that it would be men of the world, and not men of God, who would wage war against us, he added, "Not as the world giveth peace, do I give peace unto you." And even although we are oppressed in the world, we have confidence in Him who said, "In the world ye shall have tribulation; but be of good cheer, I have overcome the world." And it is He whom we call Son of God—Son of that God, namely, whom, to quote the words of Celsus, "we most highly reverence;" and He is the Son who has been most highly exalted by the Father. Grant that there may be some individuals among the multitudes of believers who are not in entire agreement with us, and who incautiously assert that the Saviour is the Most High God; however, we do not hold with them, but rather believe Him when He says, "The Father who sent Me is greater than I." We would not therefore make Him whom we call Father inferior—as Celsus accuses us of doing—to the Son of God.

CHAPTER XV

Celsus goes on to say: "That I may give a true representation of their faith, I will use their own words, as given in what is called *A Heavenly Dialogue*: 'If the Son is mightier than God, and the Son of man is Lord over Him, who else than the Son can be Lord over that God who is the ruler over all things? How comes it, that while so many go about the well, no one goes down into it? Why art thou afraid when thou hast gone so far on the way? Answer: Thou art mistaken, for I lack neither courage nor weapons.' Is it not evident, then, that their views are precisely such as I have described them to be? They suppose that another God, who is above the heavens, is the Father of him whom with one accord they honour, that they may honour this Son of man alone, whom they exalt under the form and name of the great God, and whom they assert to be stronger than God, who rules the world, and that he rules over Him. And hence that maxim of theirs, 'It is impossible to serve two masters,' is maintained for the purpose of keeping up the party who are on the side of this Lord." Here, again, Celsus quotes opinions from some most obscure sect of heretics, and ascribes them to all Christians. I call it "a most obscure sect;" for although we have often contended with heretics, yet we are unable to discover from what set of opinions he has taken this passage, if indeed he has quoted it from any author, and has not rather concocted it himself, or added it as an inference of his own. For we who say that the visible world is under the government to Him who created all things, do thereby declare that the Son is not mightier than the Father, but inferior to Him. And this belief we ground on the saying of Jesus Himself, "The Father who sent Me is greater than I." And none of us is so insane as to affirm that the Son of man is Lord over God. But when we regard the Saviour as God the Word, and Wisdom, and Righteousness, and Truth, we certainly do say that He has dominion over all things which have been subjected to Him in this capacity, but not that His dominion extends over the God and Father who is Ruler over all. Besides, as the Word rules over none against their will, there are still wicked beings—not only men, but also angels, and all demons—over whom we say that in a sense He does not rule, since they do not yield Him a willing obedience; but, in another sense of the word, He rules even over them, in the same way as we say that man rules over the irrational animals,—not by persuasion, but as one who tames and subdues lions and beasts of burden. Nevertheless, he leaves no means untried to persuade even those who are still disobedient to submit to His authority. So far as we are concerned, therefore, we deny the truth of that which Celsus quotes as one of our sayings, "Who else than He can be Lord over Him who is God over all?"

CHAPTER XVI

The remaining part of the extract given by Celsus seems to have been taken from some other form of heresy, and the whole jumbled together in strange confusion: "How is it, that while so many go about the well, no one goes down into it? Why dost thou shrink with fear when thou hast gone so far on the way? Answer: Thou art mistaken, for I lack neither courage nor weapons." We who belong to the Church which takes its name from Christ, assert that none of these statements are true. For he seems to have made them simply that they might harmonize with what he had said before; but they have no reference to us. For it is a principle with us, not to worship any god whom we merely "suppose" to exist, but Him alone who is the Creator of this universe, and of all things besides which are unseen by the eye of sense. These remarks of Celsus may apply to those who go on another road and tread other paths from us,—men who deny the Creator, and make to themselves another god under a new form, having nothing but the name of God, whom they esteem higher than the Creator; and with these may be joined any that there may be who say that the Son is greater than the God who rules all things. In reference to the precept that we ought not to serve two masters, we have already shown what appears to us the principle contained in it, when we proved that no sedition or disloyalty could be charged against the followers of Jesus their Lord, who confess that they reject every other lord, and serve Him alone who is the Son and Word of God.

CHAPTER XVII

Celsus then proceeds to say that "we shrink from raising altars, statues, and temples; and this," he thinks, "has been agreed upon among us as the badge or distinctive mark of a secret and forbidden society." He does not perceive that we regard the spirit of every good man as an altar from which arises an incense which is truly and spiritually sweet-smelling, namely, the prayers ascending from a pure conscience. Therefore it is said by John in the Revelation, "The odours are the prayers of saints;" and by the Psalmist, "Let my prayer come up before Thee as incense." And the statues and gifts which are fit offerings to God are the work of no common mechanics, but are wrought and fashioned in us by the Word of God, to wit, the virtues in which we imitate "the First-born of all creation," who has set us an example of justice, of temperance, of courage, of wisdom, of piety, and of the other virtues. In all those, then, who plant and cultivate within their souls, according to the divine word, temperance, justice, wisdom, piety, and other virtues, these excellences are their statues they raise, in which we are persuaded that it is becoming for us to honour the model and prototype of all statues: "the image of the invisible God," God the Only-begotten. And again, they who "put off the old man with his deeds, and put on the new man, which is renewed in knowledge after the image of Him that hath created him," in taking upon them the image of Him who hath created them, do raise within themselves a statue like to what the Most High God Himself desires. And as among statuaries there are some who are marvellously perfect in their art, as for example Pheidias and Polycleitus, and among painters, Zeuxis and Apelles, whilst others make inferior statues, and others, again, are inferior to the second-rate artists,—so that, taking all together, there is a wide difference in the execution of statues and pictures,—in the same way there are some who form images of the Most High in a better manner and with a more perfect skill; so that there is no comparison even between the Olympian Jupiter of Pheidias and the man who has been fashioned according to the image of God the Creator. But by far the most excellent of all these throughout the whole creation is that image in our Saviour who said, "My Father is in Me."

CHAPTER XVIII

And every one who imitates Him according to his ability, does by this very endeavour raise a statue according to the image of the Creator, for in the contemplation of God with a pure heart they become imitators of Him. And, in general, we see that all Christians strive to raise altars and statues as we have described them and these not of a lifeless and senseless kind and not to receive greedy spirits intent upon lifeless things, but to be filled with the Spirit of God who dwells in the images of virtue of which we have spoken, and takes His abode in the soul which is conformed to the image of the Creator. Thus the Spirit of Christ dwells in those who bear, so to say, a resemblance in form and feature to Himself. And the Word of God, wishing to set this clearly before us, represents God as promising to the righteous, "I will dwell in them, and walk among them; and I will be their God, and they shall be My people." And the Saviour says, "If any man hear My words, and do them, I and My Father will come to him, and make Our abode with him." Let any one, therefore, who chooses compare the altars which I have described with those spoken of by Celsus, and the images in the souls of those who worship the Most High God with the statues of Pheidias, Polycleitus, and such like, and he will clearly perceive, that while the latter are lifeless things, and subject to the ravages of time, the former abide in the immortal spirit as long as the reasonable soul wishes to preserve them.

CHAPTER XIX

And if, further, temples are to be compared with temples, that we may prove to those who accept the opinions of Celsus that we do not object to the erection of temples suited to the images and altars of which we have spoken, but that we do refuse to build lifeless temples to the Giver of all life, let any one who chooses learn how we are taught, that our bodies are the temple of God, and that if any one by lust or sin defiles the temple of God, he will himself be destroyed, as acting impiously towards the true temple. Of all the temples spoken of in this sense, the best and most excellent was the pure and holy body of our Saviour Jesus Christ. When He knew that wicked men might aim at the destruction of the temple of God in Him, but that their purposes of destruction would not prevail against the divine power which had built that temple, He says to them, "Destroy this temple, and in three days I will raise it again. . . . This He said of the temple of His body." And in other parts of holy Scripture where it speaks of the mystery of the resurrection to those whose ears are divinely opened, it says that the temple which has been destroyed shall be built up again of living and most precious stones, thereby giving us to understand that each of those who are led by the word of God to strive together in the duties of piety, will be a precious stone in the one great temple of God. Accordingly, Peter says, "Ye also, as lively stones, are built up a spiritual house, an holy priesthood, to offer up spiritual sacrifices, acceptable to God by Jesus Christ;" and Paul also says, "Being built upon the foundation of the apostles and prophets, Jesus Christ our Lord being the chief cornerstone." And there is a similar hidden allusion in this passage in Isaiah, which is addressed to Jerusalem: "Behold, I will lay thy stones with carbuncles, and lay thy foundations with sapphires. And

I will make thy battlements of jasper, and thy gates of crystal, and all thy borders of pleasant stones. And all thy children shall be taught of the LORD; and great shall be the peace of thy children. In righteousness shalt thou be established."

CHAPTER XX

There are, then, among the righteous some who are carbuncles, others sapphires, others jaspers, and others crystals, and thus there is among the righteous every kind of choice and precious stone. As to the spiritual meaning of the different stones,—what is their nature, and to what kind of soul the name of each precious stone especially applies,— we cannot at present stay to examine. We have only felt it necessary to show thus briefly what we understand by temples, and what the one Temple of God built of precious stones truly means. For as if in some cities a dispute should arise as to which had the finest temples, those who thought their own were the best would do their utmost to show the excellence of their own temples and the inferiority of the others,— in like manner, when they reproach us for not deeming it necessary to worship the Divine Being by raising lifeless temples, we set before them our temples, and show to such at least as are not blind and senseless, like their senseless gods, that there is no comparison between our statues and the statues of the heathen, nor between our altars, with what we may call the incense ascending from them, and the heathen altars, with the fat and blood of the victims; nor, finally, between the temples of senseless gods, admired by senseless men, who have no divine faculty for perceiving God, and the temples, statues, and altars which are worthy of God. It is not therefore true that we object to building altars, statues, and temples, because we have agreed to make this the badge of a secret and forbidden society; but we do so, because we have learnt from Jesus Christ the true way of serving God, and we shrink from whatever, under a pretence of piety, leads to utter impiety those who abandon the way marked out for us by Jesus Christ. For it is He who alone is the way of piety, as He truly said, "I am the way, the truth, the life."

CHAPTER XXI

Let us see what Celsus further says of God, and how he urges us to the use of those things which are properly called idol offerings, or, still better, offerings to demons, although, in his ignorance of what true sanctity is, and what sacrifices are well-pleasing to God, he call them "holy sacrifices." His words are, "God is the God of all alike; He is good, He stands in need of nothing, and He is without jealousy. What, then, is there to hinder those who are most devoted to His service from taking part in public feasts. I cannot see the connection which he fancies between God's being good, and independent, and free from jealousy, and His devoted servants taking part in public feasts. I confess, indeed, that from the fact that God is good, and without want of anything, and free from jealousy, it would follow as a consequence that we might take part in public feasts, if it were proved that the public feasts had nothing wrong in them, and were grounded upon true views of the character of God, so that they resulted naturally from a devout service of God. If, however, the so-called public festivals can in no way be shown to accord with the service of God, but may on the contrary be proved to have been devised by men when occasion offered to commemorate some human events, or to set forth certain qualities of water or earth, or the fruits of the earth,—in that case, it is clear that those who wish to offer an enlightened worship to the Divine Being will act according to sound reason, and not take part in the public feasts. For "to keep a feast," as one of the wise men of Greece has well said, "is nothing else than to do one's duty;" and that man truly celebrates a feast who does his duty and prays always, offering up continually bloodless sacrifices in prayer to God. That therefore seems to me a most noble saying of Paul, "Ye observe days, and months, and times, and years. I am afraid of you, lest I have bestowed upon you labour in vain."

CHAPTER XXII

If it be objected to us on this subject that we ourselves are accustomed to observe certain days, as for example the Lord's day, the Preparation, the Passover, or Pentecost, I have to answer, that to the perfect Christian, who is ever in his thoughts, words, and deeds serving his natural Lord, God the Word, all his days are the Lord's, and he is always keeping the Lord's day. He also who is unceasingly preparing himself for the true life, and abstaining from the pleasures of this life which lead astray so many,—who is not indulging the lust of the flesh, but "keeping under his body, and bringing it into subjection,"—such a one is always keeping Preparation-day. Again, he who considers that "Christ our Passover was sacrificed for us," and that it is his duty to keep the feast by eating of the flesh of the Word, never ceases to keep the paschal feast; for the *pascha* means a "passover," and he is ever striving in all his thoughts, words, and deeds, to pass over from the things of this life to God, and is hastening towards the city of God. And, finally, he who can truly say, "We are risen with Christ," and "He hath exalted us, and made us to sit with Him in heavenly places in Christ," is always living in the season of Pentecost; and most of all, when going up to the upper chamber, like the apostles of Jesus, he gives himself to supplication and prayer, that he may become worthy of receiving "the mighty wind rushing from heaven," which is powerful to destroy sin and its fruits among men, and worthy of having some share of the tongue of fire which God sends.

CHAPTER XXIII

But the majority of those who are accounted believers are not of this advanced class; but from being either unable or unwilling to keep every day in this manner, they require some sensible memorials to prevent spiritual things from passing altogether away from their minds. It is to this practice of setting apart some days distinct from others, that Paul seems to me to refer in the expression, "part of the feast;" and by these words he indicates that a life in accordance with the divine word consists not "in a part of the feast," but in one entire and never ceasing festival. Again, compare the festivals, observed among us as these have been described above, with the public feasts of Celsus and the heathen, and say if the former are not much more sacred observances than those feasts in which the lust of the flesh runs riot, and leads to drunkenness and debauchery. It would be too long for us at present to show why we are required by the law of God to keep its festivals by eating "the bread of affliction," or "unleavened with bitter herbs," or why it says, "Humble your souls," and such like. For it is impossible for man, who is a compound being, in which "the flesh lusteth against the Spirit, and the Spirit against the flesh," to keep the feast with his whole nature; for either he keeps the feast with his spirit and afflicts the body, which through the lust of the flesh is unfit to keep it along with the spirit, or else he keeps it with the body, and the spirit is unable to share in it. But we have for the present said enough on the subject of feasts.

CHAPTER XXIV

Let us now see on what grounds Celsus urges us to make use of the idol offerings and the public sacrifices in the public feasts. His words are, "If these idols are nothing, what harm will there be in taking part in the feast? On the other hand, if they are demons, it is certain that they too are God's creatures, and that we must believe in them, sacrifice to them according to the laws, and pray to them that they may be propitious." In reference to this statement, it would be profitable for us to take up and clearly explain the whole passage of the first Epistle to the Corinthians, in which Paul treats of offerings to idols. The apostle draws from the fact that "an idol is nothing in the world," the consequence that it is injurious to use things offered to idols; and he shows to those who have ears to hear on such subjects, that he who partakes of things offered to idols is worse than a murderer, for he destroys his own brethren, for whom Christ died. And further, he maintains that the sacrifices are made to demons; and from that he proceeds to show that those who join the table of demons become associated with the demons; and he concludes that a man cannot both be a partaker of the table of the Lord and of the table of demons. But since it would require a whole treatise to set forth fully all that is contained on this subject in the Epistle to the Corinthians, we shall content ourselves with this brief statement of the argument; for it will be evident to any one who carefully considers what has been said, that even if idols are nothing, nevertheless it is an awful thing to join in idol festivals. And even supposing that there are such beings as demons to whom the sacrifices are offered, it has been clearly shown that we are forbidden to take part in these festivals, when we know the difference between the table of the Lord and the table of demons. And knowing this, we endeavour as much as we can to be always partakers of the Lord's table, and beware to the utmost of joining at any time the table of demons.

CHAPTER XXV

Celsus says that "the demons belong to God, and are therefore to be believed, to be sacrificed to according to laws, and to be prayed to that they may be propitious." Those who are disposed to learn, must know that the word of God nowhere says of evil things that they belong to God, for it judges them unworthy of such a Lord. Accordingly, it is not all men who bear the name of "men of God," but only those who are worthy of God,—such as Moses and Elias, and any others who are so called, or such as resemble those who are so called in Scripture. In the same way, all angels are not said to be angels of God, but only those that are blessed: those that have fallen away into sin are called "angels of the devil," just as bad men are called "men of sin," "sons of perdition," or "sons of iniquity." Since, then, among men some are good and others bad, and the former are said to be God's and the latter the devil's, so among angels some are angels of God, and others angels

748

of the devil. But among demons there is no such distinction, for all are said to be wicked. We do not therefore hesitate to say that Celsus is false when he says, "If they are demons, it is evident that they must also belong to God." He must either show that this distinction of good and bad among angels and men has no foundation, or else that a similar distinction may be shown to hold among demons. If that is impossible, it is plain that demons do not belong to God; for their prince is not God, but, as holy Scripture says, "Beelzebub."

CHAPTER XXVI

And we are not to believe in demons, although Celsus urges us to do so; but if we are to obey God, we must die, or endure anything, sooner than obey demons. In the same way, we are not to propitiate demons; for it is impossible to propitiate beings that are wicked and that seek the injury of men. Besides, what are the laws in accordance with which Celsus would have us propitiate the demons? For if he means laws enacted in states, he must show that they are in agreement with the divine laws. But if that cannot be done, as the laws of many states are quite inconsistent with each other, these laws, therefore, must of necessity either be no laws at all in the proper sense of the word, or else the enactments of wicked men; and these we must not obey, for "we must obey God rather than men." Away, then, with this counsel, which Celsus gives us, to offer prayer to demons: it is not to be listened to for a moment; for our duty is to pray to the Most High God alone, and to the Only-begotten, the First-born of the whole creation, and to ask Him as our High Priest to present the prayers which ascend to Him from us, to His God and our God, to His Father and the Father of those who direct their lives according to His word. And as we would have no desire to enjoy the favour of those men who wish us to follow their wicked lives, and who give us their favour only on condition that we choose nothing opposed to their wishes, because their favour would make us enemies of God, who cannot be pleased with those who have such men for their friends,—in the same way those who are acquainted with the nature, the purposes, and the wickedness of demons, can never wish to obtain their favour.

CHAPTER XXVII

And Christians have nothing to fear, even if demons should not be well-disposed to them; for they are protected by the Supreme God, who is well pleased with their piety, and who sets His divine angels to watch over those who are worthy of such guardianship, so that they can suffer nothing from demons. He who by his piety possesses the favour of the Most High, who has accepted the guidance of Jesus, the "Angel of the great counsel," being well contented with the favour of God through Christ Jesus, may say with confidence that he has nothing to suffer from the whole host of demons. "The LORD is my light and my salvation; whom shall I fear? The LORD is the strength of my life; of whom shall I be afraid? Though an host should encamp against me, my heart shall not fear." So much, then, in reply to those statements of Celsus: "If they are demons, they too evidently belong to God, and they are to be believed, to be sacrificed to according to the laws, and prayers are to be offered to them that they may be propitious."

CHAPTER XXVIII

We shall now proceed to the next statement of Celsus, and examine it with care: "If in obedience to the traditions of their fathers they abstain from such victims, they must also abstain from all animal food, in accordance with the opinions of Pythagoras, who thus showed his respect for the soul and its bodily organs. But if, as they say, they abstain that they may not eat along with demons, I admire their wisdom, in having at length discovered, that whenever they eat they eat with demons, although they only refuse to do so when they are looking upon a slain victim; for when they eat bread, or drink wine, or taste fruits, do they not receive these things, as well as the water they drink and the air they breathe, from certain demons, to whom have been assigned these different provinces of nature?" Here I would observe that I cannot see how those whom he speaks of as abstaining from certain victims, in accordance with the traditions of their fathers, are consequently bound to abstain from the flesh of all animals. We do not indeed deny that the divine word does seem to command something similar to this, when to raise us to a higher and purer life it says, "It is good neither to eat flesh, nor to drink wine, nor anything whereby thy brother stumbleth, or is offended, or is made weak;" and again, "Destroy not him with thy meat, for whom Christ died;" and again, "If meat make my brother to offend, I will eat no flesh while the world standeth, lest I make my brother to offend."

CHAPTER XXIX

But it is to be observed that the Jews, who claim for themselves a correct understanding of the law of Moses, carefully restrict their food to such things as are accounted clean, and abstain from those that are unclean. They also do not use in their food the blood of an animal nor the flesh of an animal torn by wild beasts, and some other things which it would take too long for us at present to detail. But Jesus, wishing to lead all men by His teaching to the pure worship and service of God, and anxious not to throw any hindrance in the way of many who might be benefited by Christianity, through the imposition of a burdensome code of rules in regard to food, has laid it down, that "not that which goeth into the mouth defileth a man, but that which cometh out of the mouth; for whatsoever entereth in at the mouth goeth into the belly, and is cast out into the draught. But those things which proceed out of the mouth are evil thoughts when spoken, murders, adulteries, fornications, thefts, false witness, blasphemies." Paul also says, "Meat commendeth us not to God: for neither, if we eat, are we the better; neither, if we eat not, are we the worse." Wherefore, as there is some obscurity about this matter, without some explanation is given, it seemed good to the apostles of Jesus and the elders assembled together at Antioch, and also, as they themselves say, to the Holy Spirit, to write a letter to the Gentile believers, forbidding them to partake of those things from which alone they say it is necessary to abstain, namely, "things offered to idols, things strangled, and blood."

CHAPTER XXX

For that which is offered to idols is sacrificed to demons, and a man of God must not join the table of demons. As to things strangled, we are forbidden by Scripture to partake of them, because the blood is still in them; and blood, especially the odour arising from blood, is said to be the food of demons. Perhaps, then, if we were to eat of strangled animals, we might have such spirits feeding along with us. And the reason which forbids the use of strangled animals for food is also applicable to the use of blood. And it may not be amiss, as bearing on this point, to recall a beautiful saying in the writings of Sextus, which is known to most Christians: "The eating of animals," says he, "is a matter of indifference; but to abstain from them is more agreeable to reason." It is not, therefore, simply an account of some traditions of our fathers that we refrain from eating victims offered to those called gods or heroes or demons, but for other reasons, some of which I have here mentioned. It is not to be supposed, however, that we are to abstain from the flesh of animals in the same way as we are bound to abstain from all race and wickedness: we are indeed to abstain not only from the flesh of animals, but from all other kinds of food, if we cannot partake of them without incurring evil, and the consequences of evil. For we are to avoid eating for gluttony, or for the mere gratification of the appetite, without regard to the health and sustenance of the body. We do not believe that souls pass from one body to another, and that they may descend so low as to enter the bodies of the brutes. If we abstain at times from eating the flesh of animals, it is evidently, therefore, not for the same reason as Pythagoras; for it is the reasonable soul alone that we honour, and we commit its bodily organs with due honours to the grave. For it is not right that the dwelling-place of the rational soul should be cast aside anywhere without honour, like the carcases of brute beasts; and so much the more when we believe that the respect paid to the body redounds to the honour of the person who received from God a soul which has nobly employed the organs of the body in which it resided. In regard to the question, "How are the dead raised up, and with what body do they come?" we have already answered it briefly, as our purpose required.

CHAPTER XXXI

Celsus afterwards states what is adduced by Jews and Christians alike in defence of abstinence from idol sacrifices, namely, that it is wrong for those who have dedicated themselves to the Most High God to eat with demons. What he brings forward against this view, we have already seen. In our opinion, a man can only be said to eat and drink with demons when he eats the flesh of what are called sacred victims, and when he drinks the wine poured out to the honour of the demons. But Celsus thinks that we cannot eat bread or drink wine in any way whatever, or taste fruits, or even take a draught of water, without eating and drinking with demons. He adds also, that the air which we breathe is received from demons, and that not an animal can breathe without receiving the air from the demons who are set over the air. If any one wishes to defend this statement of Celsus, let him show that it is not the divine angels of god, but demons, the whole race of whom are bad, that have been appointed to communicate all those blessings which have been mentioned. We indeed also maintain with regard not only to the fruits of the earth, but to every flowing stream and every breath of air that the ground brings forth those things which are said to grow up naturally,—that the water springs in fountains, and refreshes the earth with running streams,—that the air is kept pure, and supports the life of those who breathe it, only in consequence of the agency and control of certain beings whom we may call invisible husbandmen and guardians; but we deny that those invisible agents are demons. And if we might speak boldly, we would say that if demons have any share at all in these things, to them belong famine, blasting of the vine and fruit trees, pestilence among men and beasts: all these are the proper occupations of demons, who in the capacity of public executioners receive power at certain times to carry out the divine judgments, for the restoration of those who have plunged headlong into wickedness, or for the trial and discipline of the souls of the wise. For those who through all their afflictions preserve their piety pure and unimpaired, show their true character to all spectators, whether visible or invisible, who behold them; while those who are otherwise minded, yet conceal their wickedness, when they have their true character exposed by misfortunes, become manifest to themselves as well as to those whom we may also call spectators.

CHAPTER XXXII

The Psalmist bears witness that divine justice employs certain evil angels to inflict calamities upon men: "He cast upon them the fierceness of His anger, wrath, and indignation, and trouble, sent by evil angels." Whether demons ever go beyond this when they are suffered to do what they are ever ready, though through the restraint put upon them they are not always able to do, is a question to be solved by that man who can conceive, in so far as human nature will allow, how it accords with the divine justice, that such multitudes of human souls are separated from the body while walking in the paths which lead to certain death. "For the judgments of God are so great," that a soul which is still clothed with a mortal body cannot comprehend them; "and they cannot be expressed: therefore by unnurtured souls" they are not in any measure to be understood. And hence, too, rash spirits, by their ignorance in these matters, and by recklessly setting themselves against the Divine Being, multiply impious objections against providence. It is not from demons, then, that men receive any of those things which meet the necessities of life, and least of all ourselves, who have been taught to make a proper use of these things. And they who partake of corn and wine, and the fruits of trees, of water and of air, do not feed with demons, but rather do they feast with divine angels, who are appointed for this purpose, and who are as it were invited to the table of the pious man, who hearkens to the precept of the word, which says, "Whether ye eat or drink, or whatever ye do, do all to the glory of God." And again, in another place it is written, "Do all things in the name of God." When, therefore, we eat and drink and breathe to the glory of God, and act in all things according to what is right, we feast with no demons, but with divine angels: "For every creature is good, and nothing to be refused, if it be received with thanksgiving: for it is sanctified by the word of God and prayer." But it could not be good, and it could not be sanctified, if these things were, as Celsus supposes, entrusted to the charge of demons.

CHAPTER XXXIII

From this it is evident that we have already met the next statement of Celsus, which is as follows: "We must either not live, and indeed not come into this life at all, or we must do so on condition that we give thanks and first-fruits and prayers to demons, who have been set over the things of this world: and that we must do as long as we live, that they may prove good and kind." We must surely live, and we must live according to the word of God, as far as we are enabled to do so. And we are thus enabled to live, when, "whether we eat or drink, we do all to the glory of God;" and we are not to refuse to enjoy those things which have been created for our use, but must receive them with thanksgiving to the Creator. And it is under these conditions, and not such as have been imagined by Celsus, that we have been brought into life by God; and we are not placed under demons, but we are under the government of the Most High God, through Him who hath brought us to God—Jesus Christ. It is not according to the law of God that any demon has had a share in worldly affairs, but it was by their own lawlessness that they perhaps sought out for themselves places destitute of the knowledge of God and of the divine life, or places where there are many enemies of God. Perhaps also, as being fit to rule over and punish them, they have been set by the Word, who governs all things, to rule over those who subjected themselves to evil and not to God. For this reason, then, let Celsus, as one who knows not God, give thank-offerings to demons. But we give thanks to the Creator of all, and, along with thanksgiving and prayer for the blessings we have received, we also eat the bread presented to us; and this bread becomes by prayer a sacred body, which sanctifies those who sincerely partake of it.

CHAPTER XXXIV

Celsus would also have us to offer first-fruits to demons. But we would offer them to Him who said, "Let the earth bring forth grass, the herb yielding seed, and the fruit tree yielding fruit after his kind, whose seed is in itself upon the earth." And to Him to whom we offer first-fruits we also send up our prayers, "having a great high priest, that is passed into the heavens, Jesus the Son of God," and "we hold fast this profession" as long as we live; for we find God and His only-begotten Son, manifested to us in Jesus, to be gracious and kind to us. And if we would wish to have besides a great number of beings who shall ever prove friendly to us, we are taught that "thousand thousands stood before Him, and ten thousand times ten thousand ministered unto Him." And these, regarding all as their relations and friends who imitate their piety towards God, and in prayer call upon Him with sincerity, work along with them for their salvation, appear unto them, deem it their office and duty to attend to them, and as if by common agreement they visit with all manner of kindness and deliverance those who pray to God, to whom they themselves also pray: "For they are all ministering spirits, sent forth to minister for those who shall be heirs of salvation." Let the learned Greeks say that the human soul at its birth is placed under the charge of demons: Jesus has taught us not to despise even the little ones in His Church, saying, "Their angels do always behold the face of My Father which is in heaven." And the prophet says, "The angel of the Lord encampeth round about them that fear Him, and delivereth them." We do not, then, deny that there are many demons upon earth, but we maintain that they exist and exercise power among the wicked, as a punishment of their wickedness. But they have no power over those who "have put on the whole armour of God," who have received strength to "withstand the wiles of the devil," and who are ever engaged in contests with them, knowing that "we wrestle not against flesh and blood, but against principalities, against powers, against the rulers of the darkness of this world, against spiritual wickedness in high places."

CHAPTER XXXV

Now let us consider another saying of Celsus, which is as follows: "The satrap of a Persian or Roman monarch, or ruler or general or governor, yea, even those who fill lower offices of trust or service in the state, would be able to do great injury to those who despised them; and will the satraps and ministers of earth and air be insulted with impunity?" Observe now how he introduces servants of the Most High—rulers, generals, governors, and those filling lower offices of trust and service—as, after the manner of men, inflicting injury upon those who insult them. For he does not consider that a wise man would not wish to do harm to any, but would strive to the utmost of his power to change and amend them; unless, indeed, it be that those whom

Celsus makes servants and rulers appointed by the Most High are behind Lycurgus, the lawgiver of the Lacedaemonians, or Zeno of Citium. For when Lycurgus had had his eye put out by a man, he got the offender into his power; but instead of taking revenge upon him, he ceased not to use all his arts of persuasion until he induced him to become a philosopher. And Zeno, on the occasion of some one saying, "Let me perish rather than not have my revenge on thee," answered him, "But rather let me perish if I do not make a friend of thee." And I am not yet speaking of those whose characters have been formed by the teaching of Jesus, and who have heard the words, "Love your enemies, and pray for them which despitefully use you, that ye may be the children of your Father which is in heaven; for He maketh His sun to rise on the evil and on the good, and sendeth rain on the just and on the unjust." And in the prophetical writings the righteous man says, "O LORD my God, if I have done this; if there be iniquity in my hands; if I have returned evil to those who have done evil to me, let me fall helpless under mine enemies: let my enemy persecute my soul, and take it; yea, let him tread down my life upon the earth."

CHAPTER XXXVI

But the angels, who are the true rulers and generals and ministers of God, do not, as Celsus supposes, "injure those who offend them;" and if certain demons, whom Celsus had in mind, do inflict evils, they show that they are wicked, and that they have received no office of the kind from God. And they even do injury to those who are under them, and who have acknowledged them as their masters; and accordingly, as it would seem that those who break through the regulations which prevail in any country in regard to matters of food, suffer for it if they are under the demons of that place, while those who are not under them, and have not submitted to their power, are free from all harm, and bid defiance to such spirits; although if, in ignorance of certain things, they have come under the power of other demons, they may suffer punishment from them. But the Christian—the true Christian, I mean—who has submitted to God alone and His Word, will suffer nothing from demons, for He is mightier than demons. And the Christian will suffer nothing, for "the angel of the Lord will encamp about them that fear Him, and will deliver them," and his "angel," who "always beholds the face of his Father in heaven," offers up his prayers through the one High Priest to the God of all, and also joins his own prayers with those of the man who is committed to his keeping. Let not, then, Celsus try to scare us with threats of mischief from demons, for we despise them. And the demons, when despised, can do no harm to those who are under the protection of Him who can alone help all who deserve His aid; and He does no less than set His own angels over His devout servants, so that none of the hostile angels, nor even he who is called "the prince of this world," can effect anything against those who have given themselves to God.

CHAPTER XXXVII

In the next place, Celsus forgets that he is addressing Christians, who pray to God alone through Jesus; and mixing up other notions with theirs, he absurdly attributes them all to Christians. "If," says he, "they who are addressed are called upon by barbarous names, they will have power, but no longer will they have any if they are addressed in Greek or Latin." Let him, then, state plainly whom we call upon for help by barbarous names. Any one will be convinced that this is a false charge which Celsus brings against us, when he considers that Christians in prayer do not even use the precise names which divine Scripture applies to God; but the Greeks use Greek names, the Romans Latin names, and every one prays and sings praises to God as he best can, in his mother tongue. For the Lord of all the languages of the earth hears those who pray to Him in each different tongue, hearing, if I may so say, but one voice, expressing itself in different dialects. For the Most High is not as one of those who select one language, Barbarian or Greek, knowing nothing of any other, and caring nothing for those who speak in other tongues.

CHAPTER XXXVIII

He next represents Christians as saying what he never heard from any Christian; or if he did, it must have been from one of the most ignorant and lawless of the people. "Behold," they are made to say, "I go up to a statue of Jupiter or Apollo, or some other god: I revile it, and beat it, yet it takes no vengeance on me." He is not aware that among the prohibitions of the divine law is this, "Thou shalt not revile the gods," and this is intended to prevent the formation of the habit of reviling any one whatever; for we have been taught, "Bless, and curse not," and it is said that "revilers shall not inherit the kingdom of God." And who amongst us is so foolish as to speak in the way Celsus describes, and to fail to see that such contemptuous language can be of no avail for removing prevailing notions about the gods? For it is matter of observation that there are men who utterly deny the existence of a God or of an overruling providence, and who by their impious and destructive teaching have founded sects among those who are called philosophers, and yet neither they themselves, nor those who have embraced their opinions, have suffered any of those things which mankind generally account evils: they are both strong in body and rich in possessions. And yet if we ask what loss they have sustained, we shall find that they have suffered the most certain injury. For what greater injury can befall a man than that he should be unable amidst the order of the world to see Him who has made it? and what sorer affliction can come to any one than that blindness of mind which prevents him from seeing the Creator and Father of every soul?

CHAPTER XXXIX

After putting such words into our mouth, and maliciously charging Christians with sentiments which they never held, he then proceeds to give to this supposed expression of Christian feeling an answer, which is indeed more a mockery than an answer, when he says, "Do you not see, good sir, that even your own demon is not only reviled, but banished from every land and sea, and you yourself, who are as it were an image dedicated to him, are bound and led to punishment, and fastened to the stake, whilst your demon—or, as you call him, 'the Son of God'—takes no vengeance on the evil-doer?" This answer would be admissible if we employed such language as he ascribes to us; although even then he would have no right to call the Son of God a demon. For as we hold that all demons are evil, He who turns so many men to God is in our view no demon, but God the Word, and the Son of God. And I know not how Celsus has so far forgotten himself as to call Jesus Christ a demon, when he nowhere alludes to the existence of any evil demons. And finally, as to the punishments threatened against the ungodly, these will come upon them after they have refused all remedies, and have been, as we may say, visited with an incurable malady of sinfulness.

CHAPTER XL

Such is our doctrine of punishment; and the inculcation of this doctrine turns many from their sins. But let us see, on the other hand, what is the response given on this subject by the priest of Jupiter or Apollo of whom Celsus speaks. It is this: "The mills of the gods grind slowly." Another describes punishment as reaching "to children's children, and to those who came after them." How much better are those words of Scripture: "The fathers shall not be put to death for the children, nor the children for the fathers. Every man shall be put to death for his own sin." And again, "Every man that eateth the sour grape, his teeth shall be set on edge." And, "The son shall not bear the iniquity of the father, neither shall the father bear the iniquity of the son: the righteousness of the righteous shall be upon him, and the wickedness of the wicked shall be upon him." If any shall say that the response, "To children's children, and to those who come after them," corresponds with that passage, "Who visits the iniquity of the fathers upon the children unto the third and fourth generation of them that hate Me," let him learn from Ezekiel that this language is not to be taken literally; for he reproves those who say, "Our fathers have eaten sour grapes, and the children's teeth are set on edge," and then he adds, "As I live, saith the Lord, every one shall die for his own sin." As to the proper meaning of the figurative language about sins being visited unto the third and fourth generation, we cannot at present stay to explain.

CHAPTER XLI

He then goes on to rail against us after the manner of old wives. "You," says he, "mock and revile the statues of our gods; but if you had reviled Bacchus or Hercules in person, you would not perhaps have done so with impunity. But those who crucified your God when present among men, suffered nothing for it, either at the time or during the whole of their lives. And what new thing has there happened since then to make us believe that he was not an impostor, but the Son of God? And forsooth, he who sent his Son with certain instructions for mankind, allowed him to be thus cruelly treated, and his instructions to perish with him, without ever during all this long time showing the slightest concern. What father was ever so inhuman? Perhaps, indeed, you may say that he suffered so much, because it was his wish to bear what came to him. But it is open to those whom you maliciously revile, to adopt the same language, and say that they wish to be reviled, and therefore they bear it with patience; for it is best to deal equally with both sides,—although these (gods) severely punish the scorner, so that he must either flee and hide himself, or be taken and perish." Now to these statements I would answer that we revile no one, for we believe that "revilers will not inherit the kingdom of God." And we read, "Bless them that curse you; bless, and curse not;" also, "Being reviled, we bless." And even although the abuse which we pour upon another may seem to have some excuse in the wrong which we have received from him, yet such abuse is not allowed by the word of God. And how much more ought we to abstain from reviling others, when we consider what a great folly it is! And it is equally foolish to apply abusive language to stone or gold or silver, turned into what is supposed to be the form of God by those who have no knowledge of God. Accordingly, we throw ridicule not upon lifeless images, but upon those only who worship them. Moreover, if certain demons reside in certain images, and one of them passes for Bacchus, another for Hercules, we do not vilify them: for, on the one hand, it would be useless; and, on the other, it does not become one who is meek, and peaceful, and gentle in spirit, and who has learnt that no one among men or demons is to be reviled, however wicked he may be.

CHAPTER XLII

There is an inconsistency into which, strangely enough, Celsus has fallen unawares. Those demons or gods whom he extolled a little before, he now shows to be in fact the vilest of creatures, punishing more for their own revenge than for the improvement of those who revile them. His words are, "If you had reviled Bacchus or Hercules when present in person, you would not have escaped with impunity." How any one can hear without being present in person, I leave any one who will to explain; as also those other questions, "Why he is sometimes present, and sometimes absent?" and, "What is the business which takes demons away from place to place?" Again, when he says, "Those who crucified your God himself, suffered no harm for doing so," he supposes that it is the body of Jesus extended on the cross and slain, and not His divine nature, that we call God; and that it was as God that Jesus was crucified and slain. As we have already dwelt at length on the sufferings which Jesus suffered as a man, we shall purposely say no more here, that we may not repeat what we have said already. But when he goes on to say that "those who inflicted death upon Jesus suffered nothing afterwards through so long a time," we must inform him, as well as all who are disposed to learn the truth, that the city in which the Jewish people called for the crucifixion of Jesus with shouts of "Crucify him, crucify him," preferring to have the robber set free, who had been cast into prison for sedition and murder, and Jesus, who had been delivered through envy, to be crucified,—that this city not long afterwards was attacked, and, after a long siege, was utterly overthrown and laid waste; for God judged the inhabitants of that place unworthy of living together the life of citizens. And yet, though it may seem an incredible thing to say, God spared this people in delivering them to their enemies; for He saw that they were incurably averse to any amendment, and were daily sinking deeper and deeper into evil. And all this befell them, because the blood of Jesus was shed at their instigation and on their land; and the land was no longer able to bear those who were guilty of so fearful a crime against Jesus.

CHAPTER XLIII

Some new thing, then, has come to pass since the time that Jesus suffered,—that, I mean, which has happened to the city, to the whole nation, and in the sudden and general rise of a Christian community. And that, too, is a new thing, that those who were strangers to the covenants of God, with no part in His promises, and far from the truth, have by a divine power been enabled to embrace the truth. These things were not the work of an impostor, but were the work of God, who sent His Word, Jesus Christ, to make known His purposes. The sufferings and death which Jesus endured with such fortitude and meekness, show the cruelty and injustice of those who inflicted them, but they did not destroy the announcement of the purposes of God; indeed, if we may so say, they served rather to make them known. For Jesus Himself taught us this when He said, "Except a grain of wheat fall into the ground and die, it abideth by itself alone: but if it die, it bringeth forth much fruit." Jesus, then, who is this grain of wheat, died, and brought forth much fruit. And the Father is ever looking forward for the results of the death of the grain of wheat, both those which are arising now, and those which shall arise hereafter. The Father of Jesus is therefore a tender and loving Father, though "He spared not His own Son, but delivered Him up" as His lamb "for us all," that so "the Lamb of God," by dying for all men, might "take away the sin of the world." It was not by compulsion, therefore, but willingly, that He bore the reproaches of those who reviled Him. Then Celsus, returning to those who apply abusive language to images, says: "Of those whom you load with insults, you may in like manner say that they voluntarily submit to such treatment, and therefore they bear insults with patience; for it is best to deal equally with both sides. Yet these severely punish the scorner, so that he must either flee and hide himself, or be taken and perish." It is not, then, because Christians cast insults upon demons that they incur their revenge, but because they drive them away out of the images, and from the bodies and souls of men. And here, although Celsus perceives it not, he has on this subject spoken something like the truth; for it is true that the souls of those who condemn Christians, and betray them, and rejoice in persecuting them, are filled with wicked demons.

CHAPTER XLIV

But when the souls of those who die for the Christian faith depart from the body with great glory, they destroy the power of the demons, and frustrate their designs against men. Wherefore I imagine, that as the demons have learnt from experience that they are defeated and overpowered by the martyrs for the truth, they are afraid to have recourse again to violence. And thus, until they forget the defeats they have sustained, it is probable that the world will be at peace with the Christians. But when they recover their power, and, with eyes blinded by sin, wish again to take their revenge on Christians, and persecute them, then again they will be defeated, and then again the souls of the godly, who lay down their lives for the cause of godliness, shall utterly destroy the army of the wicked one. And as the demons perceive that those who meet death victoriously for the sake of religion destroy their authority, while those who give way under their sufferings, and deny the faith, come under their power, I imagine that at times they feel a deep interest in Christians when on their trial, and keenly strive to gain them over to their side, feeling as they do that their confession is torture to them, and their denial is a relief and encouragement to them. And traces of the same feeling may be seen in the demeanour of the judges; for they are greatly distressed at seeing those who bear outrage and torture with patience, but are greatly elated when a Christian gives way under it. Yet it is from no feeling of humanity that this arises. They see well, that, while "the tongues" of those who are overpowered by the tortures "may take the oath, the mind has not sworn." And this may serve as an answer to the remark of Celsus: "But they severely punish one who reviles them, so that he must either flee and hide himself, or be taken and perish." If a Christian ever flees away, it is not from fear, but in obedience to the command of his Master, that so he may preserve himself, and employ his strength for the benefit of others.

CHAPTER XLV

Let us see what Celsus next goes on to say. It is as follows: "What need is there to collect all the oracular responses, which have been delivered with a divine voice by priests and priestesses, as well as by others, whether men or women, who were under a divine influence?— all the wonderful things that have been heard issuing from the inner sanctuary?—all the revelations that have been made to those who consulted the sacrificial victims?—and all the knowledge that has been conveyed to men by other signs and prodigies? To some the gods have appeared in visible forms. The world is full of such instances. How many cities have been built in obedience to commands received from oracles; how often, in the same way, delivered from disease and famine! Or again, how many cities, from disregard or forgetfulness of these oracles, have perished miserably! How many colonies have been established and made to flourish by following their orders! How many princes and private persons have, from this cause, had prosperity or adversity! How many who mourned over their childlessness, have obtained the blessing they asked for! How many have turned away from themselves the anger of demons! How many who were maimed in their limbs, have had them restored! And again, how many have met with summary punishment for showing want of reverence to the temples— some being instantly seized with madness, others openly confessing their crimes, others having put an end to their lives, and others having become the victims of incurable maladies! Yea, some have been slain by a terrible voice issuing from the inner sanctuary." I know not how it comes that Celsus brings forward these as undoubted facts, whilst at the same time he treats as mere fables the wonders which are recorded and handed down to us as having happened among the Jews, or as having been performed by Jesus and His disciples. For why may not our accounts be true, and those of Celsus fables and fictions? At least, these latter were not believed by the followers of Democritus, Epicurus, and Aristotle, although perhaps these Grecian sects would have been convinced by the evidence in support of our miracles, if Moses or any of the prophets who wrought these wonders, or Jesus Christ Himself, had come in their way.

CHAPTER XLVI

It is related of the priestess of Apollo, that she at times allowed herself to be influenced in her answers by bribes; but our prophets were admired for their plain truthfulness, not only by their contemporaries, but also by those who lived in later times. For through the commands pronounced by the prophets cities were founded, men were cured, and plagues were stayed. Indeed, the whole Jewish race went out as a colony from Egypt to Palestine, in accordance with the divine oracles. They also, when they followed the commands of God, were prosperous; when they departed from them, they suffered reverses. What need is there to quote all the princes and private persons in Scripture history who fared well or ill according as they obeyed or despised the words of the prophets? If we refer to those who were unhappy because they were childless, but who, after offering prayers to the Creator of all, became fathers and mothers, let any one read the accounts of Abraham and Sarah, to whom at an advanced age was born Isaac, the father of the whole Jewish nation: and there are other instances of the same thing. Let him also read the account of Hezekiah, who not only recovered from his sickness, according to the prediction of Isaiah, but was also bold enough to say, "Afterwards I shall beget children, who shall declare Thy righteousness." And in the fourth book of Kings we read that the prophet Elisha made known to a woman who had received him hospitably, that by the grace of God she should have a son; and through the prayers of Elisha she became a mother. The maimed were cured by Jesus in great numbers. And the books of the Maccabees relate what punishments were inflicted upon those who dared to profane the Jewish service in the temple at Jerusalem.

CHAPTER XLVII

But the Greeks will say that these accounts are fabulous, although two whole nations are witnesses to their truth. But why may we not consider the accounts of the Greeks as fabulous rather than those? Perhaps some one, however, wishing not to appear blindly to accept his own statements and reject those of others, would conclude, after a close examination of the matter, that the wonders mentioned by the Greeks were performed by certain demons; those among the Jews by prophets or by angels, or by God through the means of angels; and those recorded by Christians by Jesus Himself, or by His power working in His apostles. Let us, then, compare all these accounts together; let us examine into the aim and purpose of those who performed them; and let us inquire what effect was produced upon the persons on whose account these acts of kindness were performed, whether beneficial or hurtful, or neither the one nor the other. The ancient Jewish people, before they sinned against God, and were for their great wickedness cast off by Him, must evidently have been a people of great wisdom. But Christians, who have in so wonderful a manner formed themselves into a community, appear at first to have been more induced by miracles than by exhortations to forsake the institutions of their fathers, and to adopt others which were quite strange to them. And indeed, if we were to reason from what is probable as to the first formation of the Christian society, we should say that it is incredible that the apostles of Jesus Christ, who were unlettered men of humble life, could have been emboldened to preach Christian truth to men by anything else than the power which was conferred upon them, and the grace which accompanied their words and rendered them effective; and those who heard them would not have renounced the old-established usages of their fathers, and been induced to adopt notions so different from those in which they had been brought up, unless they had been moved by some extraordinary power, and by the force of miraculous events.

CHAPTER XLVIII

In the next place, Celsus, after referring to the enthusiasm with which men will contend unto death rather than abjure Christianity, adds strangely enough some remarks, in which he wishes to show that our doctrines are similar to those delivered by the priests at the celebration of the heathen mysteries. He says, "Just as you, good sir, believe in eternal punishments, so also do the priests who interpret and initiate into the sacred mysteries. The same punishments with which you threaten others, they threaten you. Now it is worthy of examination, which of the two is more firmly established as true; for both parties contend with equal assurance that the truth is on their side. But if we require proofs, the priests of the heathen gods produce many that are clear and convincing, partly from wonders performed by demons, and partly from the answers given by oracles, and various other modes of divination." He would, then, have us believe that we and the interpreters of the mysteries equally teach the doctrine of eternal punishment, and that it is a matter for inquiry on which side of the two the truth lies. Now I should say that the truth lies with those who are able to induce their hearers to live as men who are convinced of the truth of what they have heard. But Jews and Christians have been thus affected by the doctrines they hold about what we speak of as the world to come, and the rewards of the righteous, and the punishments of the wicked. Let Celsus then, or any one who will, show us who have been moved in this way in regard to eternal punishments by the teaching of heathen priests and mystagogues. For surely the purpose of him who brought to light this doctrine was not only to reason upon the subject of punishments, and to strike men with terror of them, but to induce those who heard the truth to strive with all their might against those sins which are the causes of punishment. And those who study the prophecies with care, and are not content with a cursory perusal of the predictions contained in them, will find them such as to convince the intelligent and sincere reader that the Spirit of God was in those men, and that with their writings there is nothing in all the works of demons, responses of oracles, or sayings of soothsayers, for one moment to be compared.

CHAPTER XLIX

Let us see in what terms Celsus next addresses us: "Besides, is it not most absurd and inconsistent in you, on the one hand, to make so much of the body as you do—to expect that the same body will rise again, as though it were the best and most precious part of us; and yet, on the other, to expose it to such tortures as though it were worthless? But men who hold such notions, and are so attached to the body, are not worthy of being reasoned with; for in this and in other respects they show themselves to be gross, impure, and bent upon revolting without any reason from the common belief. But I shall direct my discourse to those who hope for the enjoyment of eternal life with God by means of the soul or mind, whether they choose to call it a spiritual substance, an intelligent spirit, holy and blessed, or a living soul, or the heavenly and indestructible offspring of a divine and incorporeal nature, or by whatever name they designate the spiritual nature of man. And they are rightly persuaded that those who live well shall be blessed, and the unrighteous shall all suffer everlasting punishments. And from this doctrine neither they nor any other should ever swerve." Now, as he has often already reproached us for our opinions on the resurrection, and as we have on these occasions defended our opinions in what seemed to us a reasonable way, we do not intend, at each repetition of the one objection, to go into a repetition of our defence. Celsus makes an unfounded charge against us when he ascribes to us the opinion that "there is nothing in our complex nature better or more precious than the body;" for we hold that far beyond all bodies is the soul, and especially the reasonable soul; for it is the soul, and not the body, which bears the likeness of the Creator. For, according to us, God is not corporeal, unless we fall into the absurd errors of the followers of Zeno and Chrysippus.

CHAPTER L

But since he reproaches us with too great an anxiety about the body, let him know that when that feeling is a wrong one we do not share in it, and when it is indifferent we only long for that which God has promised to the righteous. But Celsus considers that we are inconsistent with ourselves when we count the body worthy of honour from God, and therefore hope for its resurrection, and yet at the same time expose it to tortures as though it were not worthy of honour. But surely it is not without honour for the body to suffer for the sake of godliness, and to choose afflictions on account of virtue: the dishonourable thing would be for it to waste its powers in vicious indulgence. For the divine word says: "What is an honourable seed? The seed of man. What is a dishonourable seed? The seed of man." Moreover, Celsus thinks that he ought not to reason with those who hope for the good of the body, as they are unreasonably intent upon an object which can never satisfy their expectations. He also calls them gross and impure men, bent upon creating needless dissensions. But surely he ought, as one of superior humanity, to assist even the rude and depraved. For society does not exclude from its pale the coarse and uncultivated, as it does the irrational animals, but our Creator made us on the same common level with all mankind. It is not an undignified thing, therefore, to reason even with the coarse and unrefined, and to try to bring them as far as possible to a higher state of refinement—to bring the impure to the highest practicable degree of purity—to bring the unreasoning multitude to reason, and the diseased in mind to spiritual health.

CHAPTER LI

In the next place, he expresses his approval of those who "hope that eternal life shall be enjoyed with God by the soul or mind, or, as it is variously called, the spiritual nature, the reasonable soul, intelligent, holy, and blessed;" and he allows the soundness of the doctrine, "that those who had a good life shall be happy, and the unrighteous shall suffer eternal punishments." And yet I wonder at what follows, more than at anything that Celsus has ever said; for he adds, "And from this doctrine let not them or any one ever swerve." For certainly in writing against Christians, the very essence of whose faith is God, and the promises made by Christ to the righteous, and His warnings of punishment awaiting the wicked, he must see that, if a Christian were brought to renounce Christianity by his arguments against it, it is beyond doubt that, along with his Christian faith, he would cast off the very doctrine from which he says that no Christian and no man should ever swerve. But I think Celsus has been far surpassed in consideration for his fellow-men by Chrysippus in his treatise, *On the Subjugation of the Passions*. For when he sought to apply remedies to the affections and passions which oppress and distract the human spirit, after employing such arguments as seemed to himself to be strong, he did not shrink from using in the second and third place others which he did not himself approve of. "For," says he, "if it were held by any one that there are three kinds of good, we must seek to regulate the passions in accordance with that supposition; and we must not too curiously inquire into the opinions held by a person at the time that he is under the influence of passion, lest, if we delay too long for the purpose of overthrowing the opinions by which the mind is possessed, the opportunity for curing the passion may pass away." And he adds, "Thus, supposing that pleasure were the highest good, or that he was of that opinion whose mind was under the dominion of passion, we should not the less give him help, and show that, even on the principle that pleasure is the highest and final good of man, all passion is disallowed." And Celsus, in like manner, after having embraced the doctrine, "that the righteous shall be blessed, and the wicked shall suffer eternal punishments," should have followed out his subject; and, after having advanced what seemed to him the chief argument, he should have proceeded to prove and enforce by further reasons the truth that the unjust shall surely suffer eternal punishment, and those who lead a good life shall be blessed.

CHAPTER LII

For we who have been persuaded by many, yea by innumerable, arguments to lead a Christian life, are especially anxious to bring all men as far as possible to receive the whole system of Christian truth; but when we meet with persons who are prejudiced by the calumnies thrown out against Christians, and who, from a notion that Christians are an impious people, will not listen to any who offer to instruct them in the principles of the divine word, then, on the common principles of humanity, we endeavour to the best of our ability to convince them of the doctrine of the punishment of the wicked, and to induce even those who are unwilling to become Christians to accept that truth. And we are thus anxious to persuade them of the rewards of right living, when we see that many things which we teach about a healthy moral life are also taught by the enemies of our faith. For you will find that they have not entirely lost the common notions of right and wrong, of good and evil. Let all men, therefore, when they look upon the universe, observe the constant revolution of the unerring stars, the converse motion of the planets, the constitution of the atmosphere, and its adaptation to the necessities of the animals, and especially of man, with all the innumerable contrivances for the well-being of mankind; and then, after thus considering the order of the universe, let them beware of doing ought which is displeasing to the Creator of this universe, of the soul and its intelligent principle; and let them rest assured that punishment shall be inflicted on the wicked, and rewards shall be bestowed upon the righteous, by Him who deals with every one as he deserves, and who will proportion His rewards to the good that each has done, and to the account of himself that he is able to give. And let all men know that the good shall be advanced to a higher state, and that the wicked shall be delivered over to sufferings and torments, in punishment of their licentiousness and depravity, their cowardice, timidity, and all their follies.

CHAPTER LIII

Having said so much on this subject, let us proceed to another statement of Celsus: "Since men are born united to a body, whether to suit the order of the universe, or that they may in that way suffer the punishment of sin; or because the soul is oppressed by certain passions until it is purged from these at the appointed period of time,—for, according to Empedocles, all mankind must be banished from the abodes of the blessed for 30,000 periods of time,—we must therefore believe that they are entrusted to certain beings as keepers of this prison-house." You will observe that Celsus, in these remarks, speaks of such weighty matters in the language of doubtful human conjecture. He adds also various opinions as to the origin of man, and shows considerable reluctance to set down any of these opinions as false. When he had once come to the conclusion neither indiscriminately to accept nor recklessly to reject the opinions held by the ancients, would it not have been in accordance with that same rule of judging, if, when he found himself not disposed to believe the doctrines taught by the Jewish prophets and by Jesus, at any rate to have held them as matters open to inquiry? And should he not have considered whether it is very probable that a people who faithfully served the Most High God, and who ofttimes encountered numberless dangers, and even death, rather than sacrifice the honour of God, and what they believed to be the revelations of His will, should have been wholly overlooked by God? Should it not rather be thought probable that people who despised the efforts of human art to represent the Divine Being, but strove rather to rise in thought to the knowledge of the Most High, should have been favoured with some revelation from Himself? Besides, he ought to have considered that the common Father and Creator of all, who sees and hears all things, and who duly esteems the intention of every man who seeks Him and desires to serve Him, will grant unto these also some of the benefits of His rule, and will give them an enlargement of that knowledge of Himself which He has once bestowed upon them.

If this had been remembered by Celsus and the others who hate Moses and the Jewish prophets, and Jesus, and His faithful disciples, who endured so much for the sake of His word, they would not thus have reviled Moses, and the prophets, and Jesus, and His apostles; and they would not have singled out for their contempt the Jews beyond all the nations of the earth, and said they were worse even than the Egyptians,—a people who, either from superstition or some other form of delusion, went as far as they could in degrading the Divine Being to the level of brute beasts. And we invite inquiry, not as though we wished to lead any to doubt regarding the truths of Christianity, but in order to show that it would be better for those who in every way revile the doctrines of Christianity, at any rate to suspend their judgment, and not so rashly to state about Jesus and His apostles such things as they do not know, and as they cannot prove, either by what the Stoics call "apprehensive perception," or by any other methods used by different sects of philosophers as criteria of truth.

CHAPTER LIV

When Celsus adds, "We must therefore believe that men are entrusted to certain beings who are the keepers of this prison-house," our answer is, that the souls of those who are called by Jeremiah "prisoners of the earth," when eager in the pursuit of virtue, are even in this life delivered from the bondage of evil; for Jesus declared this, as was foretold long before His advent by the prophet Isaiah, when he said that "the prisoners would go forth, and they that were in darkness would show themselves." And Jesus Himself, as Isaiah also foretold of Him, arose as "a light to them that sat in darkness and in the shadow of death," so that we may therefore say, "Let us break their bands asunder, and cast their cords from us." If Celsus, and those who like him are opposed to us, had been able to sound the depths of the Gospel narratives, they would not have counselled us to put our confidence in those beings whom they call "the keepers of the prison-house." It is written in the Gospel that a woman was bowed together, and could in no wise lift up herself. And when Jesus beheld her, and perceived from what cause she was bowed together, he said, "Ought not this daughter of Abraham, whom Satan has bound, lo, these eighteen years, to be loosed from this bond on the Sabbath day?" And how many others are still bowed down and bound by Satan, who hinders them from looking up at all, and who would have us to look down also! And no one can raise them up, except the Word, that came by Jesus Christ, and that aforetime inspired the prophets. And Jesus came to release those who were under the dominion of the devil; and, speaking of him, He said with that depth of meaning which characterized His words, "Now is the prince of this world judged." We are, then, indulging in no baseless calumnies against demons, but are condemning their agency upon earth as destructive to mankind, and show that, under cover of oracles and bodily cures, and such other means, they are seeking to separate from God the soul which has descended to this "body of humiliation;" and those who feel this humiliation exclaim, "O wretched man that I am! who shall deliver me from the body of this death?" It is not in vain, therefore, that we expose our bodies to be beaten and tortured; for surely it is not in vain for a man to submit to such sufferings, if by that means he may avoid bestowing the name of gods on those earthly spirits that unite with their worshippers to bring him to destruction. Indeed, we think it both reasonable in itself and well-pleasing to God, to suffer pain for the sake of virtue, to undergo torture for the sake of piety, and even to suffer death for the sake of holiness; for "precious in the sight of God is the death of His saints;" and we maintain that to overcome the love of life is to enjoy a great good. But when Celsus compares us to notorious criminals, who justly suffer punishment for their crimes, and does not shrink from placing so laudable a purpose as that which we set before us upon the same level with the obstinacy of criminals, he makes himself the brother and companion of those who accounted Jesus among criminals, fulfilling the Scripture, which saith, "He was numbered with transgressors."

CHAPTER LV

Celsus goes on to say: "They must make their choice between two alternatives. If they refuse to render due service to the gods, and to respect those who are set over this service, let them not come to manhood, or marry wives, or have children, or indeed take any share in the affairs of life; but let them depart hence with all speed, and leave no posterity behind them, that such a race may become extinct from the face of the earth. Or, on the other hand, if they will take wives, and bring up children, and taste of the fruits of the earth, and partake of all the blessings of life, and bear its appointed sorrows (for nature herself hath allotted sorrows to all men; for sorrows must exist, and earth is the only place for them), then must they discharge the duties of life until they are released from its bonds, and render due honour to those beings who control the affairs of this life, if they would not show themselves ungrateful to them. For it would be unjust in them, after receiving the good things which they dispense, to pay them no tribute in return." To this we reply, that there appears to us to be no good reason for our leaving this world, except when piety and virtue require it; as when, for example, those who are set as judges, and think that they have power over our lives, place before us the alternative either to live in violation of the commands of Jesus, or to die if we continue obedient to them. But God has allowed us to marry, because all are not fit for the higher, that is, the perfectly pure life; and God would have us to bring up all our children, and not to destroy any of the offspring given us by His providence. And this does not conflict with our purpose not to obey the demons that are on the earth; for, "being armed with the whole armour of God, we stand" as athletes of piety against the race of demons that plot against us.

CHAPTER LVI

Although, therefore, Celsus would, in his own words, "drive us with all haste out of life," so that "such a race may become extinct from the earth;" yet we, along with those who worship the Creator, will live according to the laws of God, never consenting to obey the laws of sin. We will marry if we wish, and bring up the children given to us in marriage; and if need be, we will not only partake of the blessings of life, but bear its appointed sorrows as a trial to our souls. For in this way is divine Scripture accustomed to speak of human afflictions, by which, as gold is tried in the fire, so the spirit of man is tried, and is found to be worthy either of condemnation or of praise. For those things which Celsus calls evils we are therefore prepared, and are ready to say, "Try me, O LORD, and prove me; purge my reins and my heart." For "no one will be crowned," unless here upon earth, with this body of humiliation, "he strive lawfully." Further, we do not pay honours supposed to be due to those whom Celsus speaks of as being set over the affairs of the world. For we worship the Lord our God, and Him only do we serve, and desire to be followers of Christ, who, when the devil said to Him, "All these things will I give thee if thou wilt fall down and worship me," answered him by the words, "Thou shalt worship the LORD thy God, and Him only shalt thou serve." Wherefore we do not render the honour supposed to be due to those who, according to Celsus, are set over the affairs of this world; for "no man can serve two masters," and we "cannot serve God and mammon," whether this name be applied to one or more. Moreover, if any one "by transgressing the law dishonours the lawgiver," it seems clear to us that if the two laws, the law of God and the law of mammon, are completely opposed to each other, it is better for us by transgressing the law of mammon to dishonour mammon, that we may honour God by keeping His law, than by transgressing the law of God to dishonour God, that by obeying the law of mammon we may honour mammon.

CHAPTER LVII

Celsus supposes that men "discharge the duties of life until they are loosened from its bonds," when, in accordance with commonly received customs, they offer sacrifices to each of the gods recognised in the state; and he fails to perceive the true duty which is fulfilled by an earnest piety. For we say that he truly discharges the duties of life who is ever mindful who is his Creator, and what things are agreeable to Him, and who acts in all things so that he may please God. Again, Celsus wishes us to be thankful to these demons, imagining that we owe them thank-offerings. But we, while recognising the duty of thankfulness, maintain that we show no ingratitude by refusing to give thanks to beings who do us no good, but who rather set themselves against us when we neither sacrifice to them nor worship them. We are much more concerned lest we should be ungrateful to God, who has loaded us with His benefits, whose workmanship we are, who cares for us in whatever condition we may be, and who has given us hopes of things beyond this present life. And we have a symbol of gratitude to God in the bread which we call the Eucharist. Besides, as we have shown before, the demons have not the control of those things which have been created for our use; we commit no wrong, therefore, when we partake of created things, and yet refuse to offer sacrifices to beings who have no concern with them. Moreover, as we know that it is not demons, but angels, who have been set over the fruits of the earth, and over the birth of animals, it is the latter that we praise and bless, as having been appointed by God over the things needful for our race; yet even to them we will not give the honour which is due to God. For this would not be pleasing to God, nor would it be any pleasure to the angels themselves to whom these things have been committed. Indeed, they are much more pleased if we refrain from offering sacrifices to them than if we offer them; for they have no desire for the sacrificial odours which rise from the earth.

CHAPTER LVIII

Celsus goes on to say: "Let any one inquire of the Egyptians, and he will find that everything, even to the most insignificant, is committed to the care of a certain demon. The body of man is divided into thirty-six parts, and as many demons of the air are appointed to the care of it, each having charge of a different part, although others make the number much larger. All these demons have in the language of that country distinct names; as Chnoumen, Chnachoumen, Cnat, Sicat, Biou, Erou, Erebiou, Ramanor, Reianoor, and other such Egyptian names. Moreover, they call upon them, and are cured of diseases of particular parts of the body. What, then, is there to prevent a man from giving honour to these or to others, if he would rather be in health than be sick, rather have prosperity than adversity, and be freed as much as possible from all plagues and troubles?" In this way, Celsus seeks to degrade our souls to the worship of demons, under the assumption that they have possession of our bodies, and that each one has power over a separate member. And he wishes us on this ground to put confidence in these demons of which he speaks, and to serve them, in order that we may be in health rather than be sick, have prosperity rather than adversity, and may as far as possible escape all plagues and troubles. The honour of the Most High God, which cannot be divided or shared with another, is so lightly esteemed by him, that he cannot believe in the ability of God, if called upon and highly honoured, to give to those who serve Him a power by which they may be defended from the assaults directed by demons against the righteous. For he has never beheld the efficacy of those words, "in the name of Jesus," when uttered by the truly faithful, to deliver not a few from demons and demoniacal possessions and other plagues.

CHAPTER LIX

Probably those who embrace the views of Celsus will smile at us when we say, "At the name of Jesus every knee shall bow, of things in heaven, of things on earth, and of things under the earth, and every tongue" is brought to "confess that Jesus Christ is Lord, to the glory of God the Father." But although they may ridicule such a statement, yet they will receive much more convincing arguments in support of it than Celsus brings in behalf of Chnoumen, Chnachoumen, Cnat, Sicat, and the rest of the Egyptian catalogue, whom he mentions as being called upon, and as healing the diseases of different parts of the human body. And observe how, while seeking to turn us away from our faith in the God of all through Jesus Christ, he exhorts us for the welfare of our bodies to faith in six-and-thirty barbarous demons, whom the Egyptian magi alone call upon in some unknown way, and promise us in return great benefits. According to Celsus, then, it would be better for us now to give ourselves up to magic and sorcery than to embrace Christianity, and to put our faith in an innumerable multitude of demons than in the almighty, living, self-revealing God, who has manifested Himself by Him who by His great power has spread the true principles of holiness among all men throughout the world; yea, I may add without exaggeration, He has given this knowledge to all beings everywhere possessed of reason, and needing deliverance from the plague and corruption of sin.

CHAPTER LX

Celsus, however, suspecting that the tendency of such teaching as he here gives is to lead to magic, and dreading that harm may arise from these statements, adds: "Care, however, must be taken lest any one, by familiarizing his mind with these matters, should become too much engrossed with them, and lest, through an excessive regard for the body, he should have his mind turned away from higher things, and allow them to pass into oblivion. For perhaps we ought not to despise the opinion of those wise men who say that most of the earth-demons are taken up with carnal indulgence, blood, odours, sweet sounds, and other such sensual things; and therefore they are unable to do more than heal the body, or foretell the fortunes of men and cities, and do other such things as relate to this mortal life." If there is, then, such a dangerous tendency in this direction, as even the enemy of the truth of God confesses, how much better is it to avoid all danger of giving ourselves too much up to the power of such demons, and of becoming turned aside from higher things, and suffering them to pass into oblivion through an excessive attention to the body; by entrusting ourselves to the Supreme God through Jesus Christ, who has given us such instruction, and asking of Him all help, and the guardianship of holy and good angels, to defend us from the earth-spirits intent on lust, and blood, and sacrificial odours, and strange sounds, and other sensual things! For even, by the confession of Celsus, they can do nothing more than cure the body. But, indeed, I would say that it is not clear that these demons, however much they are reverenced, can even cure the body. But in seeking recovery from disease, a man must either follow the more ordinary and simple method, and have recourse to medical art; or if he would go beyond the common methods adopted by men, he must rise to the higher and better way of seeking the blessing of Him who is God over all, through piety and prayers.

CHAPTER LXI

For consider with yourself which disposition of mind will be more acceptable to the Most High, whose power is supreme and universal, and who directs all for the welfare of mankind in body, and in mind, and in outward things,—whether that of the man who gives himself up to God in all things, or that of the man who is curiously inquisitive about the names of demons, their powers and agency, the incantations, the herbs proper to them, and the stones with the inscriptions graven on them, corresponding symbolically or otherwise to their traditional shapes? It is plain even to the least intelligent, that the disposition of the man who is simpleminded and not given to curious inquiries, but in all things devoted to the divine will, will be most pleasing to God, and to all those who are like God; but that of the man who, for the sake of bodily health, of bodily enjoyment, and outward prosperity, busies himself about the names of demons, and inquires by what incantations he shall appease them, will be condemned by God as bad and impious, and more agreeable to the nature of demons than of men, and will be given over to be torn and otherwise tormented by demons. For it is probable that they, as being wicked creatures, and, as Celsus confesses, addicted to blood, sacrificial odours, sweet sounds, and such like, will not keep their most solemn promises to those who supply them with these things. For if others invoke their aid against the persons who have already called upon them, and purchase their favour with a larger supply of blood, and odours, and such offerings as they require, they will take part against those who yesterday sacrificed and presented pleasant offerings to them.

CHAPTER LXII

In a former passage, Celsus had spoken at length on the subject of oracles, and had referred us to their answers as being the voice of the gods; but now he makes amends, and confesses that "those who foretell the fortunes of men and cities, and concern themselves about mortal affairs, are earth-spirits, who are given up to fleshly lust, blood, odours, sweet sounds, and other such things, and who are unable to rise above these sensual objects." Perhaps, when we opposed the theological teaching of Celsus in regard to oracles, and the honour done to those called gods, some one might suspect us of impiety when we alleged that these were stratagems of demoniacal powers, to draw men away to carnal indulgence. But any who entertained this suspicion against us, may now believe that the statements put forth by Christians were well-founded, when they see the above passage from the writings of one who is a professed adversary of Christianity, but who now at length writes as one who has been overcome by the spirit of truth. Although, therefore, Celsus says that "we must offer sacrifices to them, in so far as they are profitable to us, for to offer them indiscriminately is not allowed by reason," yet we are not to offer sacrifices to demons addicted to blood and odours; nor is the Divine Being to be profaned in our minds, by being brought down to the level of wicked demons. If Celsus had carefully weighed the meaning of the word "profitable," and had considered that the truest profit lies in virtue and in virtuous action, he would not have applied the phrase "as far as it is profitable" to the service of such demons, as he has acknowledged them to be. If, then, health of body and success in life were to come to us on condition of our serving such demons, we should prefer sickness and misfortune accompanied with the consciousness of our being truly devoted to the will of God. For this is preferable to being mortally diseased in mind, and wretched through being separate and outcasts from God, though healthy in body and abounding in earthly prosperity. And we would rather go for help to one who seeks nothing whatever but the well-being of men and of all rational creatures, than to those who delight in blood and sacrificial odours.

CHAPTER LXIII

After having said so much of the demons, and of their fondness for blood and the odour of sacrifices, Celsus adds, as though wishing to retract the charge he had made: "The more just opinion is, that demons desire nothing and need nothing, but that they take pleasure in those who discharge towards them offices of piety." If Celsus believed this to be true, he should have said so, instead of making his previous statements. But, indeed, human nature is never utterly forsaken by God and His only-begotten Son, the Truth. Wherefore even Celsus spoke the truth when he made the demons take pleasure in the blood and smoke of victims; although, by the force of his own evil nature, he falls back into his errors, and compares demons with men who rigorously discharge every duty, even to those who show no gratitude; while to those who are grateful they abound in acts of kindness. Here Celsus appears to me to get into confusion. At one time his judgment is darkened by the influence of demons, and at another he recovers from their deluding power, and gets some glimpses of the truth. For again he adds: "We must never in any way lose our hold of God, whether by day or by night, whether in public or in secret, whether in word or in deed, but in whatever we do, or abstain from doing." That is, as I understand it, whatever we do in public, in all our actions, in all our words, "let the soul be constantly fixed upon God." And yet again, as though, after struggling in argument against the insane inspirations of demons, he were completely overcome by them, he adds: "If this is the case, what harm is there in gaining the favour of the rulers of the earth, whether of a nature different from ours, or human princes and kings? For these have gained their dignity through the instrumentality of demons." In a former part, Celsus did his utmost to debase our souls to the worship of demons; and now he wishes us to seek the favour of kings and princes, of whom, as the world and all history are full of them, I do not consider it necessary to quote examples.

CHAPTER LXIV

There is therefore One whose favour we should seek, and to whom we ought to pray that He would be gracious to us—the Most High God, whose favour is gained by piety and the practice of every virtue. And if he would have us to seek the favour of others after the Most High God, let him consider that, as the motion of the shadow follows that of the body which casts it, so in like manner it follows, that when we have the favour of God, we have also the good-will of all angels and spirits who are friends of God. For they know who are worthy of the divine approval, and they are not only well disposed to them, but they co-operate with them in their endeavours to please God: they seek His favour on their behalf; with their prayers they join their own prayers and intercessions for them. We may indeed boldly say, that men who aspire after better things have, when they pray to God, tens of thousands of sacred powers upon their side. These, even when not asked, pray with them, they bring succour to our mortal race, and if I may so say, take up arms alongside of it: for they see demons warring and fighting most keenly against the salvation of those who devote themselves to God, and despise the hostility of demons; they see them savage in their hatred of the man who refuses to serve them with the blood and fumes of sacrifices, but rather strives in every way, by word and deed, to be in peace and union with the Most High through Jesus, who put to flight multitudes of demons when He went about "healing," and delivering "all who were oppressed by the devil."

CHAPTER LXV

Moreover, we are to despise ingratiating ourselves with kings or any other men, not only if their favour is to be won by murders, licentiousness, or deeds of cruelty, but even if it involves impiety towards God, or any servile expressions of flattery and obsequiousness, which things are unworthy of brave and high-principled men, who aim at joining with their other virtues that highest of virtues, patience and fortitude. But whilst we do nothing which is contrary to the law and word of God, we are not so mad as to stir up against us the wrath of kings and princes, which will bring upon us sufferings and tortures, or even death. For we read: "Let every soul be subject unto the higher powers. For there is no power but of God: the powers that be are ordained of God. Whosoever therefore resisteth the power, resisteth the ordinance of God." These words we have in our exposition of the Epistle to the Romans, to the best of our ability, explained at length, and with various applications; but for the present we have taken them in their more obvious and generally received acceptation, to meet the saying of Celsus, that "it is not without the power of demons that kings have been raised to their regal dignity." Here much might be said on the constitution of kings and rulers, for the subject is a wide one, embracing such rulers as reign cruelly and tyrannically, and such as make the kingly office the means of indulging in luxury and sinful pleasures. We shall therefore, for the present, pass over the full consideration of this subject. We will, however, never swear by "the fortune of the king," nor by ought else that is considered equivalent to God. For if the word "fortune" is nothing but an expression for the uncertain course of events, as some say, although they seem not to be agreed, we do not swear by that as God which has no existence, as though it did really exist and was able to do something, lest we should bind ourselves by an oath to things which have no existence. If, on the other hand (as is thought by others, who say that to swear by the fortune of the king of the Romans is to swear by his demon), what is called the fortune of the king is in the power of demons, then in that case we must die sooner than swear by a wicked and treacherous demon, that ofttimes sins along with the man of whom it gains possession, and sins even more than he.

CHAPTER LXVI

Then Celsus, following the example of those who are under the influence of demons—at one time recovering, at another relapsing, as though he were again becoming sensible—says: "If, however, any worshipper of God should be ordered to do anything impious, or to say anything base, such a command should in no wise be regarded; but we must encounter all kinds of torment, or submit to any kind of death, rather than say or even think anything unworthy of God." Again, however, from ignorance of our principles, and in entire confusion of thought, he says: "But if any one commands you to celebrate the sun, or to sing a joyful triumphal song in praise of Minerva, you will by celebrating their praises seem to render the higher praise to God; for piety, in extending to all things, becomes more perfect." To this our answer is, that we do not wait for any command to celebrate the praises of the sun; for we have been taught to speak well not only of those creatures that are obedient to the will of God, but even of our enemies. We therefore praise the sun as the glorious workmanship of God, which obeys His laws and hearkens to the call, "Praise the Lord, sun and moon," and with all your powers show forth the praises of the Father and Creator of all. Minerva, however, whom Celsus classes with the sun, is the subject of various Grecian myths, whether these contain any hidden meaning or not. They say that Minerva sprang fully armed from the brain of Jupiter; that when she was pursued by Vulcan, she fled from him to preserve her honour; and that from the seed which fell to the ground in the heat of Vulcan's passion, there grew a child whom Minerva brought up and called Erichthonius,

"That owed his nurture to the blue-eyed maid,
But from the teeming furrow took his birth,
The mighty offspring of the foodful earth."

It is therefore evident, that if we admit Minerva the daughter of Jupiter, we must also admit many fables and fictions which can be allowed by no one who discards fables and seeks after truth.

CHAPTER LXVII

And to regard these myths in a figurative sense, and consider Minerva as representing prudence, let any one show what were the actual facts of her history, upon which this allegory is based. For, supposing honour was given to Minerva as having been a woman of ancient times, by those who instituted mysteries and ceremonies for their followers, and who wished her name to be celebrated as that of a goddess, much more are we forbidden to pay divine honours to Minerva, if we are not permitted to worship so glorious an object as the sun, although we may celebrate its glory. Celsus, indeed, says that "we seem to do the greater honour to the great God when we sing hymns in honour of the sun and Minerva;" but we know it to be the opposite of that. For we sing hymns to the Most High alone, and His

Only-begotten, who is the Word and God; and we praise God and His Only-begotten, as do also the sun, the moon, the stars, and all the host of heaven. For these all form a divine chorus, and unite with the just among men in celebrating the praises of the Most High God and His Only-begotten. We have already said that we must not swear by a human king, or by what is called "the fortune of the king." It is therefore unnecessary for us again to refute these statements: "If you are commanded to swear by a human king, there is nothing wrong in that. For to him has been given whatever there is upon earth; and whatever you receive in this life, you receive from him." We deny, however, that all things which are on the earth have been given to the king, or that whatever we receive in this life we receive from him. For whatever we receive rightly and honourably we receive from God, and by His providence, as ripe fruits, and "corn which strengtheneth man's heart, and the pleasant vine, and wine which rejoiceth the heart of man." And moreover, the fruit of the olive-tree, to make his face to shine, we have from the providence of God.

CHAPTER LXVIII

Celsus goes on to say: "We must not disobey the ancient writer, who said long ago,

'Let one be king, whom the son of crafty Saturn appointed;'"

and adds: "If you set aside this maxim, you will deservedly suffer for it at the hands of the king. For if all were to do the same as you, there would be nothing to prevent his being left in utter solitude and desertion, and the affairs of the earth would fall into the hands of the wildest and most lawless barbarians; and then there would no longer remain among men any of the glory of your religion or of the true wisdom." If, then, "there shall be one lord, one king," he must be, not the man "whom the son of crafty Saturn appointed," but the man to whom He gave the power, who "removeth kings and setteth up kings," and who "raiseth up the useful man in time of need upon earth." For kings are not appointed by that son of Saturn, who, according to Grecian fable, hurled his father from his throne, and sent him down to Tartarus (whatever interpretation may be given to this allegory), but by God, who governs all things, and who wisely arranges whatever belongs to the appointment of kings. We therefore do set aside the maxim contained in the line,

"Whom the son of crafty Saturn appointed;"

for we know that no god or father of a god ever devises anything crooked or crafty. But we are far from setting aside the notion of a providence, and of things happening directly or indirectly through the agency of providence. And the king will not "inflict deserved punishment" upon us, if we say that not the son of crafty Saturn gave him his kingdom, but He who "removeth and setteth up kings." And would that all were to follow my example in rejecting the maxim of Homer, maintaining the divine origin of the kingdom, and observing the precept to honour the king! In these circumstances the king will not "be left in utter solitude and desertion," neither will "the affairs of the world fall into the hands of the most impious and wild barbarians." For if, in the words of Celsus, "they do as I do," then it is evident that even the barbarians, when they yield obedience to the word of God, will become most obedient to the law, and most humane; and every form of worship will be destroyed except the religion of Christ, which will alone prevail. And indeed it will one day triumph, as its principles take possession of the minds of men more and more every day.

CHAPTER LXIX

Celsus, then, as if not observing that he was saying anything inconsistent with the words he had just used, "if all were to do the same as you," adds: "You surely do not say that if the Romans were, in compliance with your wish, to neglect their customary duties to gods and men, and were to worship the Most High, or whatever you please to call him, that he will come down and fight for them, so that they shall need no other help than his. For this same God, as yourselves say, promised of old this and much more to those who served him, and see in what way he has helped them and you! They, in place of being masters of the whole world, are left with not so much as a patch of ground or a home; and as for you, if any of you transgresses even in secret, he is sought out and punished with death." As the question started is, "What would happen if the Romans were persuaded to adopt the principles of the Christians, to despise the duties paid to the recognised gods and to men, and to worship the Most High?" this is my answer to the question. We say that "if two" of us "shall agree on earth as touching anything that they shall ask, it shall be done for them of the Father" of the just, "which is in heaven;" for God rejoices in the agreement of rational beings, and turns away from discord. And what are we to expect, if not only a very few agree, as at present, but the whole of the empire of Rome? For they will pray to the Word, who of old said to the Hebrews, when they were pursued by the Egyptians,

"The Lord shall fight for you, and ye shall hold your peace;" and if they all unite in prayer with one accord, they will be able to put to flight far more enemies than those who were discomfited by the prayer of Moses when he cried to the Lord, and of those who prayed with him. Now, if what God promised to those who keep His law has not come to pass, the reason of its nonfulfilment is not to be ascribed to the unfaithfulness of God. But He had made the fulfilment of His promises to depend on certain conditions,—namely, that they should observe and live according to His law; and if the Jews have not a plot of ground nor a habitation left to them, although they had received these conditional promises, the entire blame is to be laid upon their crimes, and especially upon their guilt in the treatment of Jesus.

CHAPTER LXX

But if all the Romans, according to the supposition of Celsus, embrace the Christian faith, they will, when they pray, overcome their enemies; or rather, they will not war at all, being guarded by that divine power which promised to save five entire cities for the sake of fifty just persons. For men of God are assuredly the salt of the earth: they preserve the order of the world; and society is held together as long as the salt is uncorrupted: for "if the salt have lost its savour, it is neither fit for the land nor for the dunghill; but it shall be cast out, and trodden under foot of men. He that hath ears, let him hear" the meaning of these words. When God gives to the tempter permission to persecute us, then we suffer persecution; and when God wishes us to be free from suffering, even in the midst of a world that hates us, we enjoy a wonderful peace, trusting in the protection of Him who said, "Be of good cheer, I have overcome the world." And truly He has overcome the world. Wherefore the world prevails only so long as it is the pleasure of Him who received from the Father power to overcome the world; and from His victory we take courage. Should He even wish us again to contend and struggle for our religion, let the enemy come against us, and we will say to them, "I can do all things, through Christ Jesus our Lord, which strengtheneth me." For of "two sparrows which are sold for a farthing," as the Scripture says, "not one of them falls on the ground without our Father in heaven." And so completely does the Divine Providence embrace all things, that not even the hairs of our head fail to be numbered by Him.

CHAPTER LXXI

Celsus again, as is usual with him, gets confused, and attributes to us things which none of us have ever written. His words are: "Surely it is intolerable for you to say, that if our present rulers, on embracing your opinions, are taken by the enemy, you will still be able to persuade those who rule after them; and after these have been taken you will persuade their successors and so on, until at length, when all who have yielded to your persuasion have been taken, some prudent ruler shall arise, with a foresight of what is impending, and he will destroy you all utterly before he himself perishes." There is no need of any answer to these allegations: for none of us says of our present rulers, that if they embrace our opinions, and are taken by the enemy, we shall be able to persuade their successors; and when these are taken, those who come after them, and so on in succession. But on what does he ground the assertion, that when a succession of those who have yielded to our persuasion have been taken because they did not drive back the enemy, some prudent ruler shall arise, with a foresight of what is impending, who shall utterly destroy us? But here he seems to me to delight in inventing and uttering the wildest nonsense.

CHAPTER LXXII

Afterwards he says: "If it were possible," implying at the same time that he thought it most desirable, "that all the inhabitants of Asia, Europe, and Libya, Greeks and Barbarians, all to the uttermost ends of the earth, were to come under one law;" but judging this quite impossible, he adds, "Any one who thinks this possible, knows nothing." It would require careful consideration and lengthened argument to prove that it is not only possible, but that it will surely come to pass, that all who are endowed with reason shall come under one law. However, if we must refer to this subject, it will be with great brevity. The Stoics, indeed, hold that, when the strongest of the elements prevails, all things shall be turned into fire. But our belief is, that the Word shall prevail over the entire rational creation, and change every soul into His own perfection; in which state every one, by the mere exercise of his power, will choose what he desires, and obtain what he chooses. For although, in the diseases and wounds of the body, there are some which no medical skill can cure, yet we hold that in the mind there is no evil so strong that it may not be overcome by the Supreme Word and God. For stronger than all the evils in the soul is the Word, and the healing power that dwells in Him; and this healing

He applies, according to the will of God, to every man. The consummation of all things is the destruction of evil, although as to the question whether it shall be so destroyed that it can never anywhere arise again, it is beyond our present purpose to say. Many things are said obscurely in the prophecies on the total destruction of evil, and the restoration to righteousness of every soul; but it will be enough for our present purpose to quote the following passage from Zephaniah: "Prepare and rise early; all the gleanings of their vineyards are destroyed. Therefore wait ye upon Me, saith the LORD, on the day that I rise up for a testimony; for My determination is to gather the nations, that I may assemble the kings, to pour upon them Mine indignation, even all My fierce anger: for all the earth shall be devoured with the fire of My jealousy. For then will I turn to the people a pure language, that they may all call upon the name of the Lord, to serve Him with one consent. From beyond the rivers of Ethiopia My suppliants, even the daughter of My dispersed, shall bring My offering. In that day shalt thou not be ashamed for all thy doings, wherein thou hast transgressed against Me: for then I will take away out of the midst of thee them that rejoice in thy pride; and thou shalt no more be haughty because of My holy mountain. I will also leave in the midst of thee an afflicted and poor people, and they shall trust in the name of the Lord. The remnant of Israel shall not do iniquity, nor speak lies; neither shall a deceitful tongue be found in their mouth: for they shall feed and lie down, and none shall make them afraid." I leave it to those who are able, after a careful study of the whole subject, to unfold the meaning of this prophecy, and especially to inquire into the signification of the words, "When the whole earth is destroyed, there will be turned upon the peoples a language according to their race," as things were before the confusion of tongues. Let them also carefully consider the promise, that all shall call upon the name of the Lord, and serve Him with one consent; also that all contemptuous reproach shall be taken away, and there shall be no longer any injustice, or vain speech, or a deceitful tongue. And thus much it seemed needful for me to say briefly, and without entering into elaborate details, in answer to the remark of Celsus, that he considered any agreement between the inhabitants of Asia, Europe, and Libya, as well Greeks as Barbarians, was impossible. And perhaps such a result would indeed be impossible to those who are still in the body, but not to those who are released from it.

CHAPTER LXXIII

In the next place, Celsus urges us "to help the king with all our might, and to labour with him in the maintenance of justice, to fight for him; and if he requires it, to fight under him, or lead an army along with him." To this our answer is, that we do, when occasion requires, give help to kings, and that, so to say, a divine help, "putting on the whole armour of God." And this we do in obedience to the injunction of the apostle, "I exhort, therefore, that first of all, supplications, prayers, intercessions, and giving of thanks, be made for all men; for kings, and for all that are in authority;" and the more any one excels in piety, the more effective help does he render to kings, even more than is given by soldiers, who go forth to fight and slay as many of the enemy as they can. And to those enemies of our faith who require us to bear arms for the commonwealth, and to slay men, we can reply: "Do not those who are priests at certain shrines, and those who attend on certain gods, as you account them, keep their hands free from blood, that they may with hands unstained and free from human blood offer the appointed sacrifices to your gods; and even when war is upon you, you never enlist the priests in the army. If that, then, is a laudable custom, how much more so, that while others are engaged in battle, these too should engage as the priests and ministers of God, keeping their hands pure, and wrestling in prayers to God on behalf of those who are fighting in a righteous cause, and for the king who reigns righteously, that whatever is opposed to those who act righteously may be destroyed!" And as we by our prayers vanquish all demons who stir up war, and lead to the violation of oaths, and disturb the peace, we in this way are much more helpful to the kings than those who go into the field to fight for them. And we do take our part in public affairs, when along with righteous prayers we join self-denying exercises and meditations, which teach us to despise pleasures, and not to be led away by them. And none fight better for the king than we do. We do not indeed fight under him, although he require it; but we fight on his behalf, forming a special army—an army of piety—by offering our prayers to God.

CHAPTER LXXIV

And if Celsus would have us to lead armies in defence of our country, let him know that we do this too, and that not for the purpose of being seen by men, or of vainglory. For "in secret," and in our own hearts, there are prayers which ascend as from priests in behalf of our fellow-citizens. And Christians are benefactors of their country more than others. For they train up citizens, and inculcate piety to the Supreme Being; and they promote those whose lives in the smallest cities have been good and worthy, to a divine and heavenly city, to whom it may be said, "Thou hast been faithful in the smallest city, come into a great one," where "God standeth in the assembly of the gods, and judgeth the gods in the midst;" and He reckons thee among them, if thou no more "die as a man, or fall as one of the princes."

CHAPTER LXXV

Celsus also urges us to "take office in the government of the country, if that is required for the maintenance of the laws and the support of religion." But we recognise in each state the existence of another national organization, founded by the Word of God, and we exhort those who are mighty in word and of blameless life to rule over Churches. Those who are ambitious of ruling we reject; but we constrain those who, through excess of modesty, are not easily induced to take a public charge in the Church of God. And those who rule over us well are under the constraining influence of the great King, whom we believe to be the Son of God, God the Word. And if those who govern in the Church, and are called rulers of the divine nation—that is, the Church—rule well, they rule in accordance with the divine commands, and never suffer themselves to be led astray by worldly policy. And it is not for the purpose of escaping public duties that Christians decline public offices, but that they may reserve themselves for a diviner and more necessary service in the Church of God—for the salvation of men. And this service is at once necessary and right. They take charge of all—of those that are within, that they may day by day lead better lives, and of those that are without, that they may come to abound in holy words and in deeds of piety; and that, while thus worshipping God truly, and training up as many as they can in the same way, they may be filled with the word of God and the law of God, and thus be united with the Supreme God through His Son the Word, Wisdom, Truth, and Righteousness, who unites to God all who are resolved to conform their lives in all things to the law of God.

CHAPTER LXXVI

You have here, reverend Ambrosius, the conclusion of what we have been enabled to accomplish by the power given to us in obedience to your command. In eight books we have embraced all that we considered it proper to say in reply to that book of Celsus which he entitles *A True Discourse*. And now it remains for the readers of his discourse and of my reply to judge which of the two breathes most of the Spirit of the true God, of piety towards Him, and of that truth which leads men by sound doctrines to the noblest life. You must know, however, that Celsus had promised another treatise as a sequel to this one, in which he engaged to supply practical rules of living to those who felt disposed to embrace his opinions. If, then, he has not fulfilled his promise of writing a second book, we may well be contented with these eight books which we have written in answer to his discourse. But if he has begun and finished that second book, pray obtain it and send it to us, that we may answer it as the Father of truth may give us ability, and either overthrow the false teaching that may be in it, or, laying aside all jealousy, we may testify our approval of whatever truth it may contain.

GLORY BE TO THEE, OUR GOD; GLORY BE TO THEE.

Made in the USA
Las Vegas, NV
23 April 2024